THE POLITICAL ECONOMY OF THE WORLD TRADING SYSTEM

Second Edition

The Political Economy of the World Trading System

The WTO and Beyond

Second Edition

BERNARD M. HOEKMAN
MICHEL M. KOSTECKI

OXFORD

UNIVERSITY PRESS

OXFORD

UNIVERSITY PRESS

Great Clarendon Street, Oxford OX2 6DP

Oxford University Press is a department of the University of Oxford.
It furthers the University's objective of excellence in research, scholarship,
and education by publishing worldwide in

Oxford New York

Auckland Bangkok Buenos Aires Cape Town Chennai
Dar es Salaam Delhi Hong Kong Istanbul Karachi Kolkata
Kuala Lumpur Madrid Melbourne Mexico City Mumbai Nairobi
São Paulo Shanghai Taipei Tokyo Toronto

Oxford is a registered trade mark of Oxford University Press
in the UK and in certain other countries

Published in the United States
by Oxford University Press Inc., New York

British Library Cataloguing in Publication Data

Data available

Library of Congress Cataloging in Publication Data
Hoekman, Bernard M., 1959–
the political economy of the world trading system : the WTO and beyond /
Bernard M. Hoekman and Michel M. Kostecki
p. cm.
Includes bibliographical references and index.
1. International economic relations. 2. General Agreement on Tariffs and Trade
(Organization) 3. World Trade Organization. 4. International trade. 5. Tariff.
I. Kostecki M. M. II. title.
HF1359 .H64 2001 382—dc21 00-068686
ISBN 0-19-829434-4
ISBN 0-19-829431-X (Pbk.)

3 5 7 9 10 8 6 4

Printed in Great Britain
on acid-free paper by
T.J. International Ltd., Padstow, Cornwall

To Adriaan, Alexandre, Isabelle, and Thomas

PREFACE

Starting as an obscure trade agreement, unknown to most citizens of participating countries, by the early 1990s the General Agreement on Tariffs and Trade (GATT) had become a prominent institution. The Uruguay Round of multilateral trade negotiations, held under its auspices during 1986–93, played an important role in raising its public profile, catapulting it into the limelight for the first time in its history. The Uruguay Round led to the creation of the World Trade Organization (WTO), and expanded the coverage of the multilateral trading system to include trade in services and intellectual property rights.

At the time the first edition of this book was being written (1993–4), no readily accessible, yet comprehensive, introduction to the economics and politics of the trading system existed. The GATT was a rather reclusive institution. Information about its operation was not easy to obtain. Many documents were confidential, with distribution restricted to government officials. This situation changed dramatically subsequent to the establishment of the WTO and the concurrent emergence of the Internet. A plethora of WTO documents and reports can now be downloaded freely from the WTO home page (www.wto.org). Greatly expanded coverage of the institution in the press—both print and online—also makes it much easier than in the past to remain up-to-date with respect to WTO-related events. At the same time, interest in the WTO has increased. The WTO is repeatedly at the center of highly visible and public disputes on issues that go beyond trade and concern large groups of people. Examples are disputes between the US and the European Union (EU) on the use of hormones in beef, and disputes between the US and other WTO members regarding the extra-territorial application of US laws. Some argue strongly that the institution needs to expand its mandate and develop clear rules of the game in these areas, others argue equally vehemently that it needs to be scaled back.

As in the first edition, the bulk of the material in this book is devoted to systemic and conceptual questions relating to the functioning of the trading system. What matters in this connection is not only an understanding of the rules, but also the political and economic forces that sculpted them, and the incentives for countries to abide by them. Governments are not necessarily the social welfare-maximizing entities found in introductory economics textbooks, but develop policy subject to the pressures of a variety of interest groups. A political economy approach helps to understand how the WTO functions, why the GATT was very successful in reducing tariffs, and why it has proven much more difficult to expand the reach of multilateral disciplines to domestic policies that have an impact on trade.

This second edition is almost a complete rewrite. It updates all data and references to the rapidly expanding literature, including relevant Internet web sites. All chapters have been revised extensively, and a number are new. A significant amount of new material on the operation of the WTO has been added. This includes discussions of the dispute settlement mechanism, the outcome of sectoral negotiations undertaken since the conclusion of the Uruguay Round in 1994, the experience with the process of accession, participation by developing countries, the role and interests of nongovernmental organizations in the trading system, concerns regarding the governance and legitimacy of the WTO, and the need for multilateral rules on investment and competition. More boxes and examples have been incorporated into the text to relate the operation of the trading system to the real-world economic interests that underpin and are affected by it. A new annex has been added providing a succinct introduction to basic economic concepts and tools that are helpful in understanding the effects of trade policy instruments and key WTO disciplines.

To enhance the readability of the book we have kept footnotes to a minimum and avoided the use of endnotes altogether. This implies that readers will not find detailed references to WTO cases and documents. Information on all WTO dispute settlement cases discussed in this book can readily be found on the home page of the WTO and in the specialized works cited at the end of each chapter. There is an immense legal literature on WTO issues and cases—one objective we had in writing this book was to complement the many legal articles and books by focusing more on the policy, economic and development-related aspects of the trading system.

We owe a substantial intellectual debt to those who have written on various aspects of the multilateral trade regime, to many members of the WTO secretariat, both past and present, as well as to numerous trade negotiators, government officials and scholars. Some of the material used in this book draws on joint work and interactions with numerous colleagues and friends, including Kym Anderson, J. Michael Finger, Joseph Francois, Peter Holmes, Michael Leidy, Patrick Low, Aaditya Mattoo, Petros C. Mavroidis, Patrick Messerlin, Carlos Primo Braga, Jayanta Roy, Kamal Saggi, Maurice Schiff and L. Alan Winters.

We are indebted to Petros C. Mavroidis for reading and commenting on drafts of both the first and second editions of this book, to Mark Koulen for identifying sins of commission and omission in the penultimate draft of the manuscript, to Maarten de Groot, Maria Kasilag, and Francis Ng for pulling together data and preparing the figures, and to Lili Tabada for helping to put together the Index.

We are also grateful to Marco Bronckers, Rashad Cassim, Bill Davey, Alan Deardorff, Ishac Diwan, Alice Enders, Philip English, Simon Evenett, Mike Finger, Gary Horlick, Henrik Horn, Bob Hudec, Serafino Marchese, Will Martin, Keith Maskus, Aaditya Mattoo, Patrick Messerlin, Costas Michalopoulos, Marcelo Olarreaga, Pier Carlo Padoan, David Palmeter, Carmen Pont-Viera, Garry Pursell, Frieder Roessler, André Sapir, Richard Snape, T.N. Srinivasan, Bob Stern, David Tarr, Diana Tussie, John Whalley, John Wilson, Alan Winters, Jamel Zarrouk and B.K. Zutshi for helpful comments, discussions and suggestions along the way. Last but not least, we are indebted to Maria Kasilag for her invaluable assistance in preparing the camera-ready copy of the manuscript and finalizing the index, to Yvette Fischer, Rebecca Martin, and Ana Rivas for helping bring the project to fruition and to the University of Neuchatel for financial support. None of the above is responsible for the views expressed in this volume or any inaccuracies. That responsibility is ours alone.

B.M.H.
M.M.K.

CONTENTS

PART III: THE MULTILATERAL TRADE AGREEMENTS

PART IV: HOLES AND LOOPHOLES

PART V: CHALLENGES FOR THE TRADING SYSTEM

LIST OF FIGURES

LIST OF TABLES

LIST OF BOXES

LIST OF ABBREVIATIONS

ACP	African, Caribbean and Pacific (Lomé convention)
ACWL	Advisory Centre on WTO Law
AD	antidumping
AMS	aggregate measure of support
APEC	Asian-Pacific Economic Cooperation
ASEAN	Association of South-East Asian Nations
ATC	Agreement on Textiles and Clothing (WTO)
Benelux	Belgium, Netherlands and Luxembourg
BIT	Bilateral Investment Treaty
BOP	balance of payments
BTN	Brussels Tariff Nomenclature
CAP	Common Agricultural Policy (EU)
CCC	Customs Cooperation Council
CCCN	Customs Cooperation Council Nomenclature
CEEC	Central and Eastern European country
CGE	computable general equilibrium (model)
c.i.f.	cost, insurance and freight
CMEA	Council of Mutual Economic Assistance
CRTA	Committee on Regional Trade Agreements (WTO)
CTE	Committee on Trade and the Environment (WTO)
CTH	change in tariff heading
COMECON	see: CMEA
CVD	countervailing duty
DSB	Dispute Settlement Body (WTO)
DSP	dispute settlement procedures (WTO)
DSU	Dispute Settlement Understanding (WTO)
ECE	Economic Commission for Europe (UN)
ECOSOC	Economic and Social Council (UN)
ECJ	European Court of Justice (EU)
EDI	electronic data interchange
EEC	European Economic Community
EFTA	European Free Trade Association
ECSC	European Coal and Steel Community
EU	European Union
FAO	Food and Agricultural Organization (United Nations)
FDI	foreign direct investment
f.o.b.	free on board
FSC	foreign sales corporation (US)

FTA	free trade area
FTAA	Free Trade Area of the Americas
GATS	General Agreement on Trade in Services
GATT	General Agreement on Tariffs and Trade
GMO	genetically modified organism
GPA	Agreement on Government Procurement
GDP	gross domestic product
GSP	Generalized System of Preferences
GTAP	Global Trade and Analysis Project
HS	Harmonized Commodity Description and Coding System
ICC	International Chamber of Commerce
ICTSD	International Centre for Trade and Sustainable Development
IECC	International Express Carriers Conference
IFIA	International Federation of Inspection Agencies
ILO	International Labor Office
IMF	International Monetary Fund
INR	initial negotiating right
IPRs	intellectual property rights
ITA	Information Technology Agreement (WTO)
ITC	International Trade Centre (UNCTAD and WTO)
ITO	International Trade Organization
ISO	International Organization for Standardization
LDC	least-developed country
MAI	Multilateral Agreement on Investment
MEA	Multilateral Environmental Agreement
MENA	Middle East and North Africa
MFA	Multifibre Arrangement
MFN	most-favored-nation
MRA	mutual recognition agreement
MTN	multilateral trade negotiation
NGO	nongovernmental organization
NTB	nontariff barrier
NTM	nontariff measure
NAFTA	North American Free Trade Agreement
NATO	North Atlantic Treaty Organization
OAU	Organization for African Unity
OECD	Organization for Economic Cooperation and Development
OMA	orderly marketing arrangement
OTC	Organization for Trade Cooperation
PPM	Production and processing method
PSI	preshipment inspection

QR	quantitative restriction
R&D	research and development
RCA	revealed comparative advantage
RIA	regional integration agreement
ROO	rules of origin
SADC	Southern African Development Community
SCM	subsidies and countervailing measures
SPS	sanitary and phytosanitary
S&D	special and differential treatment
SDR	Special Drawing Right
SGS	Société Générale de Surveillance
SITC	Standard International Trade Classification
STE	state-trading enterprise
TABD	Trans-Atlantic Business Dialogue
TBT	technical barrier to trade
TMB	Textiles Monitoring Body (WTO)
TPRB	Trade Policies Review Body (WTO)
TPRM	Trade Policies Review Mechanism (WTO)
TRIM	trade-related investment measure
TRIPs	trade-related intellectual property rights
TRQ	tariff rate quota
TRS	technical regulations and standards
UK	United Kingdom
UN	United Nations
UNCITRAL	United Nations Committee on International Trade Law
UNCTAD	United Nations Conference on Trade and Development
UNDP	United Nations Development Programme
USSR	Union of Soviet Socialist Republics
USTR	United States Trade Representative
VER	voluntary export restraint
VIE	voluntary import expansion
WCO	World Customs Organization
WHO	World Health Organization
WIPO	World Intellectual Property Organization
WTO	World Trade Organization
WWF	Worldwide Fund for Nature

Introduction

Established in 1995, the World Trade Organization (WTO) administers the trade agreements negotiated by its members, in particular the General Agreement on Tariffs and Trade (GATT), the General Agreement on Trade in Services (GATS), and the Agreement on Trade-related Intellectual Property Rights (TRIPs). Total world trade in goods, services, and intellectual property stood at US$6.8 trillion (thousand billion) in 1999, of which services and intellectual property accounted for some US$1.4 trillion. The WTO's rules and principles establish a framework in which this exchange takes place. The disciplines and rules are negotiated among members through periodic rounds of multilateral negotiations and ad hoc or permanent interaction in various WTO fora.

The WTO builds upon the organizational structure that had developed under GATT auspices as of the early 1990s. Since its creation in 1947, the GATT progressively developed into a system of great complexity. Initially largely limited to a tariff agreement, over time, as average tariff levels fell, the GATT increasingly came to focus on nontariff trade policies and domestic policies with an impact on trade. Its success was reflected in a steady expansion in the number of contracting parties. By the end of the Uruguay Round (1994), 128 countries had joined the GATT. Since the entry into force of the WTO, another twelve countries have acceded, bringing the total to 141 as of December 2000. Suggestions made during the Uruguay Round negotiations that 'GATT is dead' sit oddly with these signs of popularity.

The underlying philosophy of the WTO is that open markets, nondiscrimination and global competition in international trade are conducive to the national welfare of all countries. A rationale for the organization is that political constraints prevent governments from adopting more efficient trade policies, and that through the reciprocal exchange of liberalization commitments these political constraints can be overcome. The WTO differs in a number of important respects from the old GATT. These differences have potentially important implications for the functioning of the trading system, in particular for developing and transition economies. The GATT was a rather flexible institution. Bargaining and deal-making lay at its core, with significant opportunities for countries to 'opt out' of specific disciplines. This is much less the case under the WTO. The rules apply to all members, who are subject to binding dispute settlement procedures. This is attractive to groups seeking to introduce multilateral disciplines on a variety of subjects—ranging from the environment and labor standards to competition and investment policies to defenders of animal rights. But it is a source of concern to groups who perceive the (proposed) multilateral rules to be inappropriate or worry that the adoption of specific rules may affect detrimentally the ability of governments to regulate domestic activities and deal with market failures.

The WTO attracted a significant amount of attention, much of it critical, during its first five years of operation. Public opposition to the WTO is to some extent a reflection of the increasing speed at which global integration is occurring. Over the past two decades the volume of international trade has doubled and the crossborder flow of foreign direct investment has grown 10 times faster than world production (WTO, 1999). These trends coincided with more liberal trade policies and acceleration of deregulation and market-oriented reforms. Only one employee in 10 is currently working in countries that are largely separated from the world market, compared to two-thirds some two decades ago (Dicken, 1998). Multinational corporations have assumed a much greater role in the world economy. In 2000, about 75 million people were employed by foreign affiliates of multinational companies, of which about one fifth were located in developing countries (Hirst and Thompson, 1999). These developments have been beneficial from an economic point of view, but they have also given rise to fears of a loss of national sovereignty and concerns about the ability of countries to handle exogenous shocks. The financial crises that erupted in the late 1990s in East Asia and Russia, and the contagion effects experienced by Latin American and East European countries are a case in point.

A number of ministerial meetings of the WTO were accompanied by violence and demonstrations by groups spanning the nongovernmental organization (NGO) community and labor unions seeking to limit or to expand the reach of multilateral disciplines. Contradictory demands by these groups pose a great challenge for WTO members. High-profile street protests during the Seattle WTO ministerial helped scuttle efforts to launch the so-called 'millennium round'. The mass media reports surrounding that poorly prepared conference could have a lasting impact on public perceptions of the WTO. The public relations challenge was illustrated in a 1999 Swiss TV program where a small boy is scared to go to sleep because 'there is a WTO under my bed'. Such a scene would have been unimaginable a decade earlier. Although opposition to the GATT and the Uruguay Round was quite intense at times—giving rise to posters representing the institution as a 'GATTzilla' (referring to the cartoon monster Godzilla)—it never reached the point where a TV producer could feel comfortable assuming it impacted on the fears of children.

Although efforts to liberalize trade have always been opposed—sometimes very vocally—by domestic groups who stand to lose from greater competition (farmers in high-income countries are a good example), the terms of the debate surrounding the WTO now extend well beyond the traditional trade liberalization agenda. Understanding how the WTO works, its strengths and weaknesses, and what might be done to make the institution a more effective tool of multilateral cooperation is vital. Many of the WTO's critics have serious misconceptions about the organization, while many of those who are seeking to expand the WTO's mandate appear to be ignorant of basic principles of good economics and political economy. At the same time, some of the criticism reflects deeply held beliefs and concerns. Many of the issues cannot (or should not) be dealt with by the WTO and claims of sins of commission or omission are therefore often inappropriate. But some issues can and should be laid at the door of the WTO. There are governance, legitimacy, and transparency problems that must be addressed. The public relations problems the WTO confronted in the late 1990s were partially of its own making. In early 2000, the Internet home page of Public Citizen's Global Trade Watch—which opposes the WTO—prominently misquoted Renato Ruggiero, the WTO Director-General during 1996–9, as having stated that 'We are writing the constitution of a single global economy'.[1] Although an inaccurate attribution, speeches emanating from the WTO leadership did suggest the organization was a major facilitator of globalization. Such strong claims—which overstated what the WTO does, can and should do—served to needlessly mobilize opposition to the organization.

Our goal in this book is to provide a succinct description of the multilateral trading system's principles, rules and procedures, as well as a political economy-based discussion of how it functions. It is not a negotiating history—who did what and when—although the results of negotiations and ministerial meetings are discussed at some length. Being an introduction, this book cannot be more than a starting point. Guides to further reading are provided at the end of every chapter. Readers interested in pursuing specific issues are invited to consult the listed works, the bibliography, which includes works that may not be cited in the text, and the web sites of the major think tanks and international organizations that maintain active research programs in international economics.[2]

---

[1] In the speech concerned, Mr. Ruggiero cited the law professor John H. Jackson. The relevant passage stated that 'John Jackson has described the multilateral trade system as a "constitution for the world economy"' (see WTO Press/91, downloadable from www.wto.org).

[2] Useful sites with downloadable documents and links to many other sites include Harvard University's global trade negotiations home page (www.cid.harvard.edu/cidtrade), the World Bank (www.worldbank.org/trade), the International Centre for Trade and Sustainable Development, (www.ictsd.org), and the Institute for International Economics (www.iie.com).

The book has five parts. Part I presents a brief historical overview of the evolution of the trading system and introduces the basic functions of the trade regimeand the challenges that confront it (chapter 1). Part II turns to the WTO. Chapter 2 describes the organizational structure of the WTO, its scope and functions. WTO dispute settlement and enforcement provisions are discussed in chapter 3. Chapter 4 analyzes the role of the WTO as a forum for negotiations. Special attention is given to the concept of reciprocity, this being a central element of multilateral trade negotiations (MTNs). Part III discusses the three multilateral agreements. Chapter 5 describes the GATT rules on tariffs, quotas, subsidies, customs procedures, and product standards, and discusses the political economy rationale underlying them. Chapter 6 turns to the major sector-specific agreements that have been negotiated under GATT auspices, in particular agriculture and textiles and clothing. Both are sectors that have a long history of protectionism in many countries, and much remains to be done to lower barriers to trade to levels that approach the average prevailing in other sectors. Chapters 7 and 8 discuss trade in services and the GATS, and the agreement on TRIPs, respectively.

In Part IV, we describe and assess the major 'holes and loopholes' in the WTO. The various mechanisms allowing for the reimposition of trade barriers are discussed in chapter 9, which summarizes the rules on—and the economics of—the use of instruments of contingent protection. These have been very important in dealing with domestic political pressures and allowing the pursuit of noneconomic objectives. In practice they have often been abused, to the detriment of both national and global welfare. Chapter 10 deals with one of the most important exceptions to the most-favored-nation rule allowed by the WTO: regional integration agreements (RIAs). Almost all WTO members are participants in one or more RIA, raising serious questions about the relevance of the WTO's nondiscrimination principle. Chapter 11 discusses the provisions of the WTO allowing for the negotiation of so-called plurilateral agreements, which apply only to those members that sign them. The most important of these is currently the Agreement on Government Procurement.

Part V looks to the future. Chapter 12 discusses the evolving role of developing countries and economies in transition in the multilateral trading system, and the concerns that these countries have regarding its operation. Chapter 13 discusses a number of the issues that are likely to be on the negotiating agenda for some time to come, including competition (antitrust) policy, labor standards, trade facilitation, investment and environmental policies. Chapter 14 turns to the issue of governance of the trading system, the role of NGOs and the importance of ensuring domestic transparency of trade and investment policies. Chapter 15 concludes with some final remarks on the future of the WTO and the challenge of international cooperation in the trade area.

Annex 1 provides a listing of WTO members. Annex 2 summarizes the economics of major trade policy instruments and many of the issues discussed in the book. It covers tariffs, quotas, subsidies, externalities and market failure, price discrimination (dumping), trade preferences and discrimination, and rent seeking. Although the discussion in the volume is deliberately nontechnical, we hope inclusion of this material will assist students of international relations, economics and business, as well as the interested reader, to better understand the economic effects of alternative policy instruments.

PART I
THE GLOBAL TRADING SYSTEM

1
The Trading System in Perspective

Although economic theory suggests that countries should pursue liberal trade policies and exchange goods and services on the basis of their comparative advantage, in practice most nations actively intervene in international trade. Since 1947, the GATT has been the major focal point for industrialized country governments seeking to lower trade barriers. In the process, an ever more complex network of rights and obligations regulating international trade relations emerged. Progress towards liberalization of trade was fitful at times, often involving two steps forward and one step back. None the less, recurring MTNs and the positive demonstration effects of the success of outward-oriented development strategies aimed at integration into the world economy resulted in a steady decline in the average level of protection in most countries. The principles and disciplines of the GATT helped governments to liberalize trade and to resist pressures for protection. This in turn helped foster ever-greater integration of the global economy through trade.

1.1. TRADE AND GLOBAL INTEGRATION

At the beginning of the new century, the value of global trade in goods and services exceeded US$7 trillion (thousand billion). At US$6 trillion, trade in goods accounted for the lion's share of global flows, followed by trade in commercial services, which reached the US$1 trillion mark in 1992, and had grown to US$1.5 trillion in 1999 (WTO, 2000). Data on trade in knowledge, as measured by payments of royalties for use of trademarks, patents, and so forth, is incomplete, but has been estimated to account for at least US$75 billion (Karsenty, 2000).

Global trade flows are dominated by exchanges within and between the three major regions of the global economy (the so-called triad): Europe, North America, and East Asia. Trade flows involving other parts of the globe are relatively small, accounting for some 15 percent of world trade (Figure 1.1). Intra-EU and intra-North America trade accounts for 52 percent of industrial trade (shaded area, Figure 1.1). All 48 least-developed countries together accounted for only 0.5 percent of world trade, reflecting the small size of their economies and very low per capita incomes. Their share has actually fallen over time—it stood at 1.7 percent in 1970. South Asia and Sub-Saharan Africa each represent just over one percent of world trade.

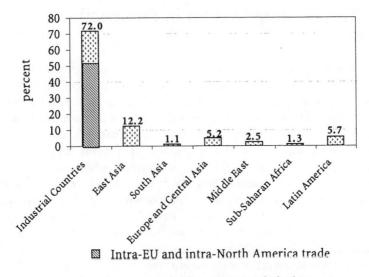

Source: Computed from UN Comtrade database.
FIG. 1.1 Regional shares in world trade, 1998

Although the trade shares and trade-output ratios of many of the poorest countries has fallen, in the last thirty years many developing countries have expanded their share of world trade. Developing countries have also shifted increasingly to becoming producers and traders of manufactures. The share of manufactures in total exports of developing countries reached 70 percent in the 1990s and is projected to rise to 80 percent in 2005. Some 40 percent of all developing country exports are destined for other developing countries (Figure 1.2).

Trade to GDP or openness ratios have also expanded rapidly for most developing countries (Figure 1.3), driven by unilateral (autonomous) economic reforms—including liberalization of trade—that were pursued during the 1980s and 1990s. These reforms were often supported by the international financial organizations, in particular the World Bank and the IMF. As discussed later in this book, the GATT played at best a marginal role in this process. Until the conclusion of the Uruguay Round, its impact was largely restricted to inducing OECD countries to reduce trade barriers.

Commodity shares of merchandise exports from developing countries

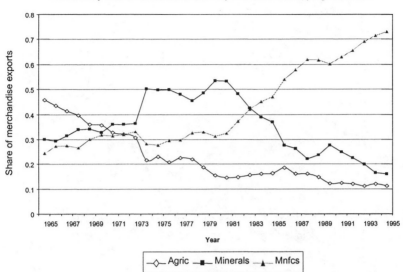

Share of developing country merchandise exports to other developing countries

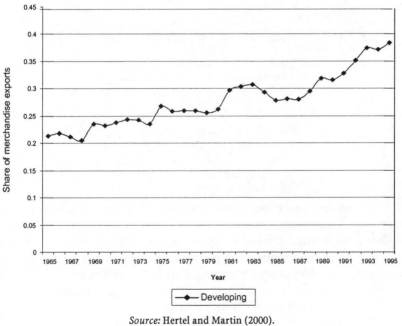

Source: Hertel and Martin (2000).

FIG. 1.2   Developing countries in manufactures

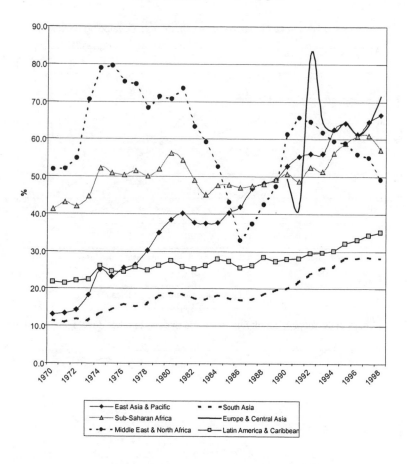

Source: World Bank SIMA database.
FIG. 1.3   Trade openness, 1970–97

A substantial proportion of global trade in manufactures, especially between OECD countries, comprises intra-industry trade—the exchange of
similar, differentiated products. Intra-industry trade ratios are frequently
above 0.6 for OECD countries, and have risen to similar levels for dynamic
developing and transition economies. This is one reflection of the process
of globalization, which increasingly involves the fragmentation of production of a good across many different countries.

In 1997, intra-industry trade ratios for Israel, Brazil, Korea, Chinese Taipei and the Czech Republic stood at 0.66, 0.54, 0.61, 0.60, and 0.68, respectively.[1] Much of this trade involves trade in semi-finished goods and components that are processed further after importation and re-exported subsequently. Global outsourcing practices have resulted in increasing fragmentation or splintering of the production process. So-called global production networks have expanded rapidly, in part driven by rapid growth in FDI flows (Figure 1.4). Of the US$6 trillion trade in goods, some 40 percent is intra-firm,

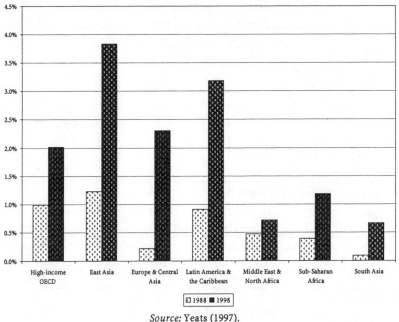

Source: Yeats (1997).

FIG. 1.4   Shares of FDI in GDP by region

involving exchanges between affiliated firms. An estimated 30 percent of global trade in manufactures comprises components (Yeats 1997). The rapid increase in the share of trade in manufactures that consists of components and parts is one striking illustration of the process of globalization of production.

---

[1] Calculated at the 3-digit SITC level, using the UN Comtrade database and the Grubel-Lloyd definition of intra-industry trade (1- $\Sigma |Xi - Mi| / \Sigma (Xi + Mi)$ where X and M are exports and imports of commodity i. This index ranges between 0 (no intra-industry trade) and 1 (all trade is intra-industry).

The factor content of trade has also changed significantly. Just a decade ago, many developing country exports were predominantly natural resource and unskilled-labor intensive. In East Asia and Latin America, in particular, the importance of technology and human capital inputs increased rapidly, whereas South Asia began to exploit its endowments of unskilled labor and shift away from natural resource intensive products (commodities) (Table 1.1). The outlier, as is the case for most indicators, is Sub-Saharan Africa.

TABLE 1.1 *Factor intensity of exports, 1988 and 1998*

	Natural Resource		Unskilled Labor		Technology		Human Capital	
	1988	1998	1988	1998	1988	1998	1988	1998
Industrial Countries	22.5	17.9	9.8	9.7	39.4	45.2	28.3	27.1
Developing Countries								
East Asia	27.2	16.8	30.5	24.0	23.8	42.6	18.5	16.6
South Asia	50.2	15.9	35.9	81.2	7.9	2.2	6.1	0.6
Latin America	67.0	42.4	5.8	9.3	13.4	25.4	13.8	22.9
Sub-Saharan Africa	78.3	79.0	6.0	5.9	6.6	7.7	9.1	7.4
E. Europe & C. Asia	38.0	37.6	23.9	18.4	20.2	21.3	17.8	22.7
M. East & N. Africa	80.3	65.6	3.7	8.0	13.1	22.0	2.9	4.3

Source: UN Comtrade and The World Bank.

TABLE 1.2 *The Relative Importance of Imports of Parts and Components*

Regional and Product Group (SITC)	Share of Parts and Components In Product Group Imports (%)	
	1985	1996
East Asia		
General Industrial Machinery (74)	8.7	13.3
Office Machinery (75)	32.5	47.2
Telecommunications (76)	43.0	71.8
Electric Machinery (77)	33.3	25.2
Road Vehicles (78)	25.1	35.6
Other Transport Machinery (79)	8.4	19.3
East Asia (All Products)	19.5	25.1
OECD Europe (All Products)	21.5	23.4
North America (All Products)	23.5	22.9

Note: Totals include listed product groups and Power Generating Equipment (71), Special Industry Machinery (72) Metal Working Machinery (73) and Misc. Manufactures.
Source: Ng and Yeats (1999).

In many respects the East Asian countries took the lead in pursuing trade-driven development strategies. For example, Ng and Yeats (1999) find that

East Asian global exports of components grew at an annual rate of 15 percent during 1984–96, more than four percentage points above the growth rate for all goods, accounting for 25 percent of all exports in 1996 (Table 1.2). Moreover, exports of components to other East Asian markets grew even faster (about 20.9 percent). As a result, the share of all parts and components exports destined for regional markets almost doubled from 25 to 46 percent. (Box 1.1). This illustrates another phenomenon—the increasing pace of regionalization of the world economy. Although potentially incompatible with the process of globalization of production, it reinforces the process if driven by economic forces and regional economies maintain an open policy stance towards trade with the rest of the world.

Box 1.1. Changes in Global Production Sharing

The geographic fragmentation of manufacturing processes has long been a major and evolving process. One of its earlier forms involved the production of primary commodities in developing (and some developed) countries, shipment of these goods to (largely) industrial nations for further processing, and then the re-exportation (in part) of the processed product back to the primary commodity producer or third countries. As an example, tin ores might be mined in Thailand or Malaysia, shipped to Japan for refinement and further manufacture and re-export. In part, these production sharing trade flows were based on comparative advantage, but factors such as escalation of industrial country trade barriers contributed to this exchange pattern.

The magnitude of such traditional production sharing trade has been eclipsed by international exchange of manufactured parts and components. A comparison of the value of East Asian trade in traditional inputs—agricultural raw materials, ores, minerals and nonferrous metals and unprocessed foodstuffs like cocoa and coffee beans—with manufactured components reveals that in 1984, Asian imports of traditional inputs were more than double those of manufactured components. By 1996, component imports were US$67 billion higher. At 20.4 percent, the average annual growth rate for components over this period was about two and one half times greater than that for traditional products. A similar pattern is observed for Asian exports (see Box Table).

Trade Flow and Product	Value (US$bn)		Growth (%)
	1984	1996	1984–96
East Asian Imports			
Traditional Production Inputs	39.2	98.9	8.0
Manufactured Components	17.9	165.6	20.4
East Asian Exports			
Traditional Production Inputs	17.0	37.6	6.8
Manufactured Components	33.0	177.8	15.1

Source: Ng and Yeats (1999).

Trade expansion and the growth in production sharing is by no means restricted to East Asia. Processing trade played an important role in the re-orientation and expansion of trade between Central and Western Europe (Hoekman and Djankov, 1997). It is also important for a number of Latin American and North African countries. Examples include the Dominican Republic (where processing trade accounts for over 80 percent of all exports), El Salvador (49 percent), and Tunisia (67 percent) (WTO, 2000). This is driven in part by autonomous reforms to facilitate trade, including the creation of export processing zones, and in part by preferential tariff treatment by major partner countries. Available data suggest there is a strong positive correlation between above average export growth and the share of processing trade in total exports.

These are just several dimensions of the multi-faceted process of global integration that has been occurring. Cross-border trade and investment flows have been a major engine of the process—'machines' that allow countries to transform one set of goods and services into another set that they value more highly. The increase in trade openness and cross-border investment is beneficial for world welfare. There is a positive relationship between openness and economic growth. In a widely cited article, Sachs and Warner (1995) conclude that open developing countries grew by an average of 3.5 percentage points faster than a comparator group of closed economies. Ben-David (2001) shows how a significant and sustained rise in post-Second World War European export-output ratios (compared to the prewar period) was associated with a sustained increase in the average growth rate. Sustained economic growth is crucial in reducing poverty. East Asia, the developing region that has relied on trade the most intensively as part of its development strategy, has seen a number of countries catch up with the industrialized nations in terms of per capita income and significantly reduce the number of people living in poverty.

However, not all countries have been successful in integrating into the world economy. Nor is openness a sufficient condition for economic growth. Ben-David and Papell (1998) examine the post-Second World War growth path of 74 countries and conclude that 46 experienced a significant slow-down in economic growth rates during the period, even though openness ratios were rising. Relatively few countries have been able to attain and sustain growth rates that were high enough to result in convergence with the per capita income levels of industrialized nations. Indeed, country groups with the largest income gaps in 1960 have not shown any 'catch-up' convergence. Income gaps between the majority of countries appear to be increasing rather than decreasing. Reasons for this are complex, but one common factor that characterizes incidences of convergence is the intensity (depth) of trade integration. Countries that trade intensively with each other tend to exhibit a relatively high incidence of income convergence (Ben-David, 2001). Of course, there is much more to the story than trade and trade policy, even though a liberal trade and investment regime is a crucial element. Very much depends on complementary policies that define the business environment—investment in human capital (education), infrastructure, and the quality of public and private sector governance. Much also depends on fundamental endowments such as location. Small land-locked countries surrounded by other low-income countries will inherently face much greater challenges than countries that are in close proximity to large industrialized economies.[2]

Although the term globalization is used incessantly, the world economy still is far from being integrated. As of the turn of the century, only 5-6 percent of the labor force in OECD countries was involved in the production of goods for developing country markets. The OECD share of the capital stock in the developing world did not exceed 11 percent, an amount that constituted less than two percent of the capital stock of the rich nations (World Bank, 1999). Truly global industries such as electronics, aerospace or some consumer good branches coexist with a much larger set of industries that retain a regional or purely national character (Dicken 1998). Moreover, the global economy remains characterized by severe restrictions on the international movement of labor. Even within the high-income country group, labor

---

[2] There is a vigorous academic debate on the relationship between openness and growth. For example, Dani Rodrik, a leading critic of the literature cited earlier, has argued that data and methodological weaknesses do not allow strong conclusions to be drawn (Rodrik, 1997, Rodriguez and Rodrik, 1999). Sceptics agree there is a positive association between openness and growth, but are not convinced the direction of causality is correct–it may also be that growth leads to openness. There is more agreement that a necessary condition for sustained growth is that countries have policies that allow access to technology at world market prices. This includes trade policies that encourage imports of capital equipment and knowledge, as well as establishment of conditions that are conducive to investment.

tends to be less mobile than it was in the nineteenth century.[3] There are few signs that government policies will become significantly more welcoming towards liberalization of the temporary movement of service providers, let alone reduce barriers to labor mobility more generally (Ghosh, 1997). Even abstracting from policy, country-specific business practices and technological factors (such as the need for on-site tailoring of products) continue to favor domestic trade over international transactions. Empirical evidence suggests that international borders have a much more restrictive effect on economic interaction than internal borders separating regions within a country. Among OECD nations the negative impact of international borders is in some cases twenty times higher than for intra-state borders (Helliwell, 1999).

Nevertheless, the process of global integration has progressed rapidly since the 1980s, and can be expected to continue. Science, technology and a growing component of cultural life have become genuinely borderless. Advances in telecommunications and informatics industries and steadily decreasing transportation costs reduce the tyranny of distance. English has become the first second language of the world. Globalization, like any major technological change, gives rise to adjustment costs. The process is exposing serious flaws in national systems of social assistance, environmental protection or tax laws. Interest groups have raised the alarm about negative impacts on the environment, indigenous knowledge, workers rights, national values and local communities. Global integration has cultural and social ramifications as well as economic dimensions, and these must be recognized and managed. On the other hand, there is an enormous opportunity for eliminating poverty, hunger, wars, and economic injustice. Bolstering multilateral cooperation to attenuate negative effects in instances where there are cross-border spillovers and to assist in the realization of the benefits of global integration is a major challenge for governments entering the twenty-first century. International cooperation to maintain open markets is a vital component of any strategy to raise global living standards.

---

[3] As is the case regarding the link between trade openness and growth, there is also a large literature investigating whether the current level of global integration is comparable to that achieved in the pre-World War One period. Space constraints prevent a discussion of this literature. See Held et al. (1999) for an overview of the debate.

1.2. TRADE AND TRADE AGREEMENTS IN HISTORY

Trade has always played an important role in economic development. The type of trade that occurs has evolved over time as technological and institutional innovations led to a decline in transaction costs. Such innovations include 'hard science' inventions such as the sailing ship, the steam engine, development of railroads, aircraft, container shipping, and refrigeration, as well as 'soft' inventions such as the creation of markets, mechanisms to extend credit to traders, and the development of contracts and procedures to enforce them.

International trade and international trade agreements have often gone hand in hand. From a historical perspective the policy stance preferred by economists—unilateral free trade—has been applied relatively rarely, most notably by Great Britain in the second half of the nineteenth century. Abstracting from instances where discriminatory trade policy was imposed by a dominant (colonial) power, the historical record illustrates that trade agreements between sovereign states have frequently been used to overcome barriers to trade. Even in the case of imperial expansion and the pursuit of formal or informal empires by metropolitan powers, trade agreements sometimes were an important instrument. Examples in the nineteenth century were trade treaties negotiated between Britain and Latin American countries such as Brazil and Argentina (Gallagher and Robinson, 1953). Sometimes trade agreements have been a key element in the process of economic integration of independent territories—a noteworthy example was the German customs union (the Zollverein), which was a key building block of what is now the Federal Republic of Germany.

A characteristic of colonial expansion was the application of metropolitan systems of law and protection of property rights to 'associated' territories—indeed, a defining characteristic of an empire is that control extends beyond foreign to domestic policy (Doyle, 1986). This was a fundamental dimension of the Roman Empire and helped create the preconditions for a single, integrated economy. Piracy was suppressed, roads built, and with sea and land substantially secure, commerce spread throughout the Mediterranean. The pottery, bronze, wine and oil of Italy were exchanged for African grain and eastern spices. Economies of scale led to large productive enterprises scattered throughout what was otherwise an overwhelmingly agricultural world (Gibbon, 1776).

The Iberian, Dutch and English empires of the sixteenth century and thereafter were of a different character in that the depth of integration was less. More important were discriminatory trade policies that sought to monopolize trade or to restrict competition. For example, not able to compete with more efficient, Dutch shipping technology and constituting a less attractive market for some colonial products, seventeenth century England imposed trade restrictions on its colonies. The trade of American colonies was often subjected to exclusivity requirements—through a ban on trade with other states or through mandatory use of metropolitan shipping services—and regulated through restrictions on colonial production. Often, regulations prohibited local processing of goods or production of goods that could compete with output produced by the colonial power (Davies, 1997).

Trade relations between European powers and Asian territories initially tended to be less dictated by the former, reflecting more powerful local states. The latter produced goods (such as spices) that were sought after in European markets, forming a natural basis for trade. Often European traders sought to obtain agreement on (or to impose) extra-territorial application of home country law to commercial transactions and the protection of property rights. Local rulers who sought to limit the impact of a foreign presence on their control of society frequently were willing to accept such extra-territoriality. One form this sometimes took was the establishment of so-called treaty ports. Examples were Macao, Nagasaki, and Goa. These served as an air lock between international commercial relations and the control of civil society more generally:

From St. Paul's claim of civis Romanus sum against the subordinate patrimonial kingdom of Herod and the steelyard of the Hanse in London to the immunities of European settlers in Alexandria, Tunis, Constantinople and Shanghai, foreign powers have demanded extraterritorial application of their law over their nationals (both natural and legal persons). The outcome has often been the establishment of a regulated treaty port (Doyle, 1986: 202).

Trade cannot prosper without legal security of property rights and mechanisms to enforce contracts. One lesson from international trade relations between states throughout history is that traders will seek to ensure that such mechanisms are applied. This can be achieved through a variety of means—full-fledged integration into a formal empire being the most far-reaching one; and free trade agreements and treaty ports being less far-reaching solutions.[4]

---

[4] An interesting literature has emerged in the last decade exploring the emergence and maintenance of legal norms in the absence of central authority. A conclusion that emerges from these studies is that the threat of ostracising a member of a club who is reliant on repeated interaction with other members can have a powerful impact as an enforcement device. Government involvement in contract enforcement is not necessarily required. See Benson (1989), Milgrom, North and Weingast (1990), Greif (1993), and Greif, Milgrom and Weingast (1994).

Trade Policy and Trade Agreements

In general, motivations for activist trade policy can be divided into a number of types. First, revenue—governments need income, and taxing trade is often the easiest method of collecting revenue. Taxation of trade for revenue purposes has been a hardy perennial throughout recorded history, and remains important for many developing countries. Of course, those who are subject to the tax have an incentive to lobby for exemptions and invest resources to induce the authorities to lower the tax burden. Taxes imposed by rulers and governments can constitute an important motivation for conquest or the negotiation of tax treaties. Tax policy can have important effects on trade patterns. For example, in the fourth century BC, Rhodes was a key commercial power in the Eastern Mediterranean, controlling the neighboring seas and with a vibrant port. Rhodes charged a two percent tax on the value of cargo carried on all ships entering its harbor, including transit cargo. To divert shipping, Roman traders lobbied for the creation of a free port in Delos. Once established, trade rapidly shifted away from Rhodes, and the port lost most of its harbor tax revenues. This tax competition proved very costly from a social welfare point-of-view: Rhodes used part of its tax proceeds to police the sea-lanes and prevent piracy. Without the revenue, these activities declined, piracy increased significantly, and trade became more costly (Adams, 1993: 83–4).

A second motivation is mercantilist—a belief that imports are bad and exports are good. This belief is generally based on the observation that imports require the transfer of foreign exchange abroad (historically specie—gold or silver), whereas exports bring in foreign exchange. The objective of mercantilist policy is a trade surplus—ensuring that the value of exports exceeds the value of imports. Mercantilism is often driven by nationalism, the perception being that trade surpluses and political power are closely linked. Mercantilist policy therefore tends to favor direct promotion of exports and restrictions on imports through tariffs, quotas, prohibitions, and state monopolies. The policy makes no economic sense. Starting with philosophers and economic thinkers such as David Hume, Adam Smith, John Stuart Mill and David Ricardo, it has been pointed out that imports are desirable and that exports are simply a way to pay for imports. Moreover, a trade surplus will have macroeconomic effects that will act to push the balance of payments into equilibrium.[5] The theory of comparative advantage

---

[5] The fallacy of mercantilist thought regarding the need for a positive balance of trade inspired David Hume to develop his famous 'price-specie flow' mechanism. This illustrated the point

and free trade was developed largely in reaction to mercantilist thought and practice.

Third, trade barriers frequently have been used as instruments for agricultural and industrial development. This was an important factor in the latter part of the nineteenth century, with France, the United States and Germany protecting infant industries behind high tariff walls. After 1870, continental European powers and the United States pursued activist trade policies, including imposition of tariffs, to protect infant industries. French colonies relied heavily on discriminatory trade policies such as tariff walls against the rest of the world, keeping British goods out of these markets. With France, Germany and the United States becoming increasingly industrialized, British trade dominance was eroded and British goods came to be diverted away from traditional export markets, initially the newly industrializing markets, and subsequently rest-of-the-world colonial territories. As a result, Britain also began to pursue preferential trade regimes and became more reliant on its own territories. Eventually this led to the adoption of a system of imperial preferences.

Finally, trade policy is an instrument to redistribute income. By imposing barriers to trade, some segments of society gain at the expense of other groups. Protectionism can constitute good politics. It is a mechanism through which interest groups that support political parties or candidates can be compensated in relatively non-transparent ways. Groups seeking protection will offer political support to the government (or to challengers in elections) as a quid pro quo.

It is often difficult to distinguish between these motivations for restrictive trade policies. Revenue considerations prevail almost universally—even free-trade Britain imposed significant revenue tariffs. The implication of this is that one cannot necessarily determine from the average tariff or the magnitude of tariff revenue collections how high trade barriers are. What matters is the difference in the extent to which domestic and foreign products are taxed. If this difference is small, a country can be characterized as maintaining a liberal trade policy, even if tariffs are imposed. The connection between mercantilism and infant industry protection is very strong— both have strong nationalistic connotations, and both rest on very weak economic foundations (the economics of infant industry protection is discussed further in chapters 5 and 9).

Formal trade agreements generally are concluded among countries seeking to obtain preferential access to markets. They go beyond establishing the

that trade surpluses and associated inflow of specie would drive up prices and result in a loss of export competitiveness.

'rules of the game' in areas such as contract enforcement and the like to address barriers to trade. Trade restrictions have been a perennial feature of international relations throughout history. One of the few exceptions was Great Britain. After the repeal of the Corn Laws (which restricted imports of wheat and other grains) and the conclusion of the Cobden-Chevalier Treaty between Britain and France in 1860 (which greatly reduced tariffs), Britain maintained a free trade stance at home and in the overseas territories it controlled. This free trade policy applied to all sources of supply, not just British goods.[6] Other major powers also liberalized trade. During 1862–7, France concluded a range of commercial treaties with virtually every major trading power in Europe (with the exception of Russia) as well as with the United States. These treaties included a most-favored-nation clause. As in each case the countries involved also negotiated treaties with each other and Great Britain, the trade concessions granted were multilateralized. As of the late 1860s, France was at the center of an impressive network of trade agreements which substantially reduced protectionist trade barriers throughout Europe (Curzon, 1965).

The major exception during this period was the United States, which maintained high tariffs on manufactures to support its industry. Much of this industry was located in the North of the country, which implied that the agricultural sector—concentrated in the South—effectively was obliged to transfer a share of its income to the North as it was forced to pay more for machinery and consumer goods. This is an example of trade diversion that can be associated with the formation of a customs union—see chapter 10 and annex 2. A doubling of average tariffs in 1861 to 47 percent helped set off the civil war: an objective of the South was to escape tariffs through secession from the Union (Adams, 1993: 330).

The nineteenth century was the period during which much of the intellectual debate about free trade emerged. There were two clear camps. Those in favor of free trade included Adam Smith (*The Wealth of Nations*, 1776) and David Ricardo (*On the Principles of Political Economy and Taxation*, 1817). Others argued trade barriers were required to support infant industries. Influential contributions here were Alexander Hamilton's *Report on the Subject of Manufactures* (1791) and Friedrich List's *National System of Political Economy* (1841). The ideas of Smith and Ricardo on the benefits of free trade and the principle of comparative advantage provided the intellectual support for the free trade movement in Europe—both on the European

---

[6] British industry helped enforce this free trade stance. For example, when the British government in India attempted to impose a small revenue tariff in 1853-54, the British textile industry ensured that an equivalent excise tax was levied on Indian textiles (Doyle, 1986, p. 264).

continent and in Britain. Writings by Hamilton and List constituted a source of inspiration for those who favored protection of infant manufacturing industry in the United States and Germany, respectively. As is often the case, there was a time lag between the development of the theories and government action inspired by them. The British free trade movement emerged half a century after the publication of Smith's works. US infant industry protectionism materialized a quarter of a century after the publication of Hamilton's Report.

Despite the rise of infant industry protection in the major powers during the latter part of the nineteenth century, the global economy became significantly more integrated. Global trade expanded much faster than global output. After the First World War, however, countries imposed more restrictive trade policies. To some extent this was in response to the United States, which was unwilling to participate in efforts during the 1920s to reestablish a more open global economy following the disruption to trade that had been caused by the war and war-time policies. As the US economy moved from recession to depression following the 1929 stock market crash, the US Congress adopted the infamous Smoot-Hawley Tariff Act, raising average US tariffs on dutiable imports from 38 to 52 percent. This led US trading partners to impose retaliatory trade restrictions and engage in rounds of competitive devaluation of their currencies. A domino effect resulted, as trade flows were diverted to relatively unprotected markets, forcing down prices, giving rise to protectionist pressures there, and thus leading to higher trade barriers.

At the end of the Second World War, decision-makers were deeply influenced by the lessons of the post First World War period. They perceived the need for establishing mechanisms to avoid both competitive devaluation and the excessive use of trade barriers to guarantee the national market to domestic producers (Gardner, 1969). The negative consequences of the beggar-thy-neighbor policies of the early 1930s were still very vivid in 1945. They inspired the US willingness to pursue the type of international cooperation it had spurned in the 1920s and early 1930s and actively support multilateral liberalization efforts, including efforts to negotiate the International Trade Organization (ITO) and the GATT. In the Anglo-American view, the postwar international economic system was to be constructed in such a way as to remove the economic causes of friction which were believed to have been at the origin of the Second World War. An important element in this vision was the establishment of a stable world economy that would provide all trading nations with nondiscriminatory access to markets, supplies and investment opportunities. There was a strong perception that there was a positive correlation between trade and peace, and, as important, between nondiscrimination and good foreign relations (Bailey, 1932).[7] In the US, the Reciprocal Trade Agreements Act of 1934 had already initiated a shift to a more liberal trade policy stance through the adoption of the unconditional MFN principle, albeit firmly grounded in the principle of reciprocity. This policy was extended after the Second World War and incorporated into the draft charter of the ITO and the GATT.

1.3. FUNCTIONS OF THE MULTILATERAL TRADING SYSTEM

Multilateral cooperation among sovereign nations often occurs through the creation of institutions. Because a central authority is absent in international relations, political scientists have developed the concept of a regime, defined as 'sets of implicit or explicit principles, norms, rules, and decision-making procedures around which expectations converge in a given area of international relations' (Krasner, 1983: 2). The principles and procedures imply obligations, even though these are not enforceable through a hierarchical legal system. Regimes reflect patterns of cooperation over time among members that are based on the existence of shared interests. The multilateral trading system is a good example of a regime. Two viewpoints are helpful in understanding the role of the trading system. The first is to regard it as a mechanism for the exchange of trade policy commitments. The second is to view it as a code of conduct.

The System as a Forum for Exchange

The basis of international cooperation is communication and the exchange of information on national policy objectives and allowing for identification of the potential detrimental impact of policies on foreign economies. This is an important function of any international regime, and is a vital aspect of the multilateral trading system (chapter 2). However, the WTO is more than a forum for communication, it is a forum for the exchange of liberalization commitments. That is, it is a market. Bargaining and negotiation are the main instruments used to reduce barriers to trade and agree to rules of be-

---

[7] The academic literature on the relationship between trade and the probability of war has argued that this may go either way. For example, two countries that are on opposing sides of the globe and do not trade at all are less likely to go to war than two neighbouring states that trade a lot. However, Mansfield (1994) has concluded that, controlling for other factors, there is a robust negative relationship between the volume of trade between country pairs and the probability of a war between them.

havior. MTNs are mechanisms to facilitate the reciprocal exchange of market access commitments.

Whether there is an economic rationale for trade restrictions depends largely on the market power of a country. A small country that cannot influence prices on world markets will generally lose from imposing trade barriers, and therefore has much to gain from multilateral agreement to lower trade barriers. Indeed, such countries should pursue liberalization unilaterally. That other countries also reduce barriers is icing on the cake (see Box 1.2). In contrast, large countries may be able to change the terms of trade—the price of their exports relative to the price of imports—in their favor by restricting trade. However, for the world as a whole the imposition of trade restrictions by one or more countries can only reduce welfare. Large countries thus may find themselves in a so-called Prisoners' Dilemma situation: it is in each country's interest to impose restrictions, but the result of such individually rational behavior is inefficient (see chapter 4). All countries end up in a situation where their welfare is lower than if they applied free trade policies.[8] Both small and large countries therefore have an incentive to cooperate and agree to reduce or abolish trade barriers. Trade and trade liberalization is a positive-sum game.

Box 1.2. Why liberalize trade?

The central concept underlying trade is opportunity cost. Producing (consuming) something comes at the cost of not producing (consuming) something else. An important economic theorem states that there are gains from trade associated with minimizing opportunity costs through the division of labor (specialization). Consider a simple example. Suppose the people of Plains, who are good at raising animals (say cows), must also spend time growing wheat (at which they are less good than in raising cows). Each hour spent growing wheat has a high opportunity cost in terms of cows forgone, but there is no choice but to devote the time required to grow wheat. Suppose the people of Agria are good at farming, but do not have much aptitude for raising cows. Agria will then have a high opportunity cost in terms of time not spent farming. If these two countries/groups of people could trade with each other, they could concentrate on what each one does best. Economists say that they would specialize according to their comparative advantage. This will ensure that total output produced expands in both regions,

---

[8] That is, large countries need to take into account the possibility of retaliation. Another problem is that if tariffs are not set at the optimal level, large countries may easily lose from activist trade policy—even if other countries pursue free trade.

and that each is able to consume more wheat and beef and milk than would be possible without trade.

The decision what to specialize in depends on what one does best compared with the other things that could (or would have to) be done. The people of Plains might be better farmers than those in Agria, in that for every hour invested in farming they get a larger harvest. However, as long as an hour spent by the people in Plains on farming has a higher cost in terms of forgone cows than does an hour spent on farming in Agria, Plains should specialize in cows. What matters is not *absolute*, but *comparative* advantage. International trade provides nations with the opportunity to specialize in production according to their comparative advantage.

This suggests that countries interested in maximizing their wealth should not impose trade barriers. This is certainly the case for small countries that are price-takers on world markets. A practical problem is that there are often political difficulties in liberalizing access to markets, because some people will always lose from liberalization. In principle, such groups can be compensated, as the increase in total output and consumption is always larger than the losses incurred by those who must change the economic activity they are engaged in. Actually compensating the losers is not always easy, however. It is also true that although a country will benefit from liberalizing its trade, it is even better if trading partners do the same. This is one of the primary rationales for engaging in multilateral liberalization efforts and is the raison d'être of the WTO: by making liberalization conditional on greater access to foreign markets, the total gains of liberalization increase and in the process liberalization becomes more feasible politically.

Achieving multilateral trade liberalization is no trivial matter. In all countries there are numerous groups that have different preferences with respect to trade measures. Abstracting from revenue considerations, the structure of protection at any point in time is the result of the interaction between the demands expressed by various groups in society and the supply offered by governments. Attempts to alter this equilibrium and move towards a welfare-increasing reduction in protection will generate opposition by those groups that expect to lose from liberalization. Such losses are usually concentrated in import-competing industries, while the gainers—consumers of the products concerned—tend to be much more diffuse. This gives rise to a political economy problem. Those facing losses have a much greater individual incentive to organize and invest in lobbying against liberalization than those that gain from reform have to lobby for liberalization. Individual gains are relatively small and dispersed among a large number of voters, while losers are more concentrated. This is the main reason why trade restrictions are imposed in the first place.[9] A MTN can solve this problem by confronting those who gain from protection with another lobby that may be equally powerful: the set of firms that benefit from greater access to foreign markets. Similarly, by requiring reciprocal reductions in trade barriers, the prisoners' dilemma that in principle may confront large countries can be overcome, again improving world welfare. Finally, by including many products in the negotiation, losers obtain some automatic compensation through access to cheaper imports.

Trade liberalization helps nations to realize a more efficient utilization of their resources (production capacities). Trade liberalization has two essential effects. First, it brings about a reallocation of resources towards those activities in which the country has comparative advantage. Secondly, trade liberalization expands the consumption opportunities of countries, as more efficient production generates greater income and increased opportunities to buy goods and services from other countries. See annex 2 for an illustration of the standard mechanics of the gains from trade.

A MTN is a market in the sense that countries come together to exchange market access commitments on a reciprocal basis. It is a barter market. In contrast to the markets one finds in city squares, countries do not have access to a medium of exchange: they do not have money with which to buy, and against which to sell, trade policies. Instead they have to exchange apples against oranges: tariff reductions for iron against foreign market access commitments for cloth. This makes the trade policy market less efficient than one where money can be used, and is one of the reasons that MTNs can be a tortuous process.

A Code of Conduct for Trade Policy

One of the results of the market exchange is a code of conduct. The WTO contains a set of specific legal obligations regulating trade policies of member states. These are embodied in the GATT, the GATS, and the agreement on TRIPs. The rules and principles of the WTO constrain the freedom of governments to use specific trade policy instruments. They influence the balance between interest groups seeking protection and those favoring open markets in the domestic political marketplace. Industry associations, labor

---

[9] In the case of developing countries that do not have a well-developed tax administration, taxing trade flows frequently has an important revenue rationale as well. More generally, most people tend to be nationalistic in their thinking about economic matters. Trade policy is by definition a nationalistic policy in that it discriminates against foreign producers.

unions, regional authorities, consumer lobbies and government agencies all interact in determining the policy outcome. The WTO is somewhat analogous to a mast to which governments can tie themselves to escape the siren-like calls of various pressure groups (Roessler, 1985). It is a mechanism through which the political market failure that is inherent in many societies—both industrialized and developing—can be corrected, at least in part, because reneging on liberalization commitments requires compensation of affected trading partners. This increases both the cost and the visibility of adopting inefficient trade policies to placate domestic interest groups. However, much depends on the will of governments to tie themselves to the mast. WTO rules and disciplines—discussed at length in later chapters—embody many holes and loopholes that governments can invoke if they desire to. Much also depends on whether it makes economic sense to tie oneself to the mast. A necessary condition is that abiding by the rules is in the national interest of members. As discussed subsequently, a number of existing WTO rules do not meet this test.

The WTO embodies a rule-oriented approach to multilateral cooperation. This contrasts with what can be characterized as a results-oriented or managed-trade approach—agreements on trade flows, market share or international prices. The WTO establishes a framework for trade. It does not define or specify outcomes. Five principles are of particular importance in understanding both the pre-1994 GATT and the WTO: (1) nondiscrimination; (2) reciprocity; (3) enforceable commitments; (4) transparency; and (5) safety valves.

Nondiscrimination

The principle of nondiscrimination has two components, the MFN rule and the national treatment principle. Both components are embedded in the main WTO rules on goods, services and intellectual property. However, their precise scope and nature differ across these three areas, especially national treatment (see later chapters). The MFN rule requires that a product made in one member country be treated no less favorably than a 'like' (very similar) good that originates in any other country. Thus, if the best treatment granted a trading partner supplying a specific product is a five percent tariff, then this rate must be applied immediately and unconditionally to the imports of this good originating in all WTO members. Because the initial set of contracting parties to the GATT was quite small (only 23 countries), the benchmark for MFN is the best treatment offered to any country, including countries that may not be a member of the GATT. Similar wording applies under the WTO. Disputes can be brought to the WTO alleging not just *de jure* violation of MFN, but also *de facto* violation.[10]

The national treatment rule is the second component of the nondiscrimination principle. It requires that foreign goods—once they have satisfied whatever border measures are applied—be treated no less favorably than like or directly competitive goods produced domestically in terms of internal (indirect) taxation (Article III:2 GATT). That is, goods of foreign origin circulating in the country should be subject to the same taxes and charges that apply to identical goods of domestic origin. A similar obligation applies to nontax policies (regulations) (Article III:4 GATT). In both cases, the obligation is to provide treatment 'no less favorable'. A government is free to discriminate in favor of foreign products (against domestic goods) if it desires, subject, of course, to the MFN rule—all foreign products must be given the same treatment.

MFN applies unconditionally. It cannot be made conditional on considerations of reciprocity. However, exceptions are made for the formation of free trade areas or customs unions and preferential treatment of developing countries. Upon accession of a new member, an existing member may also invoke the WTO's nonapplication clause (Article XIII). These exceptions to MFN are discussed in subsequent chapters. MFN is a basic pillar of the WTO for a number of reasons. The first is economic. Although trade barriers are inefficient instruments (see annex 2), if policy does not discriminate between foreign suppliers, importers and consumers will continue to have an incentive to source from the lowest-cost foreign supplier. The second is to provide smaller countries with a guarantee that larger countries will not exploit their market power by raising tariffs against them in periods when times are bad and domestic industries are clamoring for protection, or alternatively, give specific countries preferential treatment for foreign policy reasons. MFN helps enforce multilateral rules by raising the costs to a country of defecting from the trade regime to which it committed itself in an earlier MTN. If it desires to raise trade barriers it must apply the changed regime to all WTO members. This raises the political cost of backsliding on trade policy because importers will object. Finally, MFN reduces negotiating costs—once a negotiation has been concluded with a country, the results

---

[10] For example, in a recent case (Canada-US Autopact), a WTO dispute settlement panel was asked to consider whether a measure that limits the benefits of an import duty exemption to a certain class of domestic importers without imposing any restrictions regarding the origin of the imported goods constitutes a *de facto* violation of MFN. The panel and the Appellate Body found against Canada, arguing that the extensive intra-firm trade in automotive products between Canada and the US implied that the Canadian duty exemption scheme was likely to benefit imports from the US.

extend to all. This obviates the need for other countries to initiate discussions to obtain similar treatment. Instead, negotiations can be limited to principal suppliers.

National treatment is a general obligation in the GATT, although not in the GATS (see chapter 7). Its role is to ensure that liberalization commitments are not offset through the imposition of domestic taxes and similar measures. By requiring that foreign products be treated no less favorably than competing domestically produced products, foreign suppliers obtain greater certainty regarding the regulatory environment in which they must operate. The national treatment principle has often been invoked in dispute settlement cases brought to the GATT. It is a very wide-ranging rule. The obligation applies whether or not a specific tariff commitment was made, and covers taxes and other policies: all policies must be applied in a nondiscriminatory fashion to like domestic and foreign products. It is also irrelevant whether a policy hurts an exporter. What matters is discrimination.

Reciprocity

Reciprocity is a fundamental element of MTNs, reflecting a desire to limit the scope for free riding that may arise because of the MFN rule, and the desire to obtain 'payment' for trade liberalization in the form of better access to foreign markets. Thus, trade liberalization occurs on a quid pro quo basis. Reciprocity in trade negotiations comes in many guises. It may be diffuse (Keohane, 1984) or specific. If specific, it may be expressed in quantitative or qualitative terms, and may apply to levels or to changes in protection (Winters, 1987a). Although the GATT and the GATS have as underlying goals a broad balance of market-access commitments, MTNs in general and tariff negotiations in particular proceed by agreeing to incremental changes in trade barriers. Convergence in the levels of protection is gradual.

By requiring reciprocity, nations attempt to minimize free riding. In the case of bilateral negotiations, this is done by a suitable choice of products on which concessions are offered and sought; in the case of multilateral across-the-board negotiations, it is done by a suitable choice of products to be exempted from liberalization. Generally, nations are quite successful in minimizing free riding. For example, internalization, defined by Finger (1974, 1979) as the sum of all imports originating in countries with whom a country exchanges concessions as a percentage of total imports of goods on which concessions are made, was about 90 percent for the US in the Dillon (1960–1) and Kennedy (1964–7) Rounds. Allen (1979), focusing explicitly on bilateral bargains made in the Kennedy Round, showed that there was a relationship between the sizes of concessions made on commodity tariffs and the degree of bargaining power a country had on a commodity *vis-à-vis* its major trading partners. Thus, reciprocity is in part a function of the weight a country can bring to bear in a negotiation.

Reciprocity also applies when countries accede to the WTO. Given that new members obtain all the benefits in terms of market access that have resulted from earlier negotiating rounds, existing members invariably demand that potential entrants pay an 'admission fee'. In practice this implies not only that upon joining the WTO a country's trade regime must conform as much as possible with the rules of the GATT, GATS and TRIPs, but that the government will be asked to liberalize access to its market as well. Accession modalities are discussed further in chapter 2.

As noted earlier, a rationale for reciprocity can be found in the political economy literature. Costs of liberalization generally are concentrated in specific industries, which often will be well organized and oppose reductions in protection. Benefits, while in the aggregate usually greater than costs, accrue to a much larger set of agents, who thus do not have a great individual incentive to organize themselves politically. In such a setting, being able to point to reciprocal, sector-specific export gains may help to sell the liberalization politically. By obtaining a reduction in foreign import barriers as a quid pro quo for a reduction in domestic trade restrictions, specific export-oriented domestic interests that will gain from liberalization have an incentive to support it in domestic political markets. A related point is that for a nation to negotiate it is necessary that the gain from doing so be greater than the gain available from unilateral liberalization. By obtaining reciprocal concessions, these gains are ensured (Box 1.3). More generally, reciprocity in trade negotiations can help to offset the externalities that are imposed by countries on each other as they implement trade policies. In effect, by insisting on reciprocity countries may be able to ensure that their terms of trade are not affected detrimentally (Bagwell and Staiger, 1999a).

Box 1.3. Why liberalize on a reciprocal basis?

Hillman and Moser (1995) argue that a useful way to understand the role of reciprocity is to start from the premise that import-competing industries have property rights to their home markets, a right that has been acquired as a result of past lobbying or political support granted to governments. In the same way that protection can be explained as the outcome of a political process where governments seek to maximize political support—taking into account the fact that tariffs are often used for revenue purposes and tend to persist after alternative tax bases are developed—reciprocal liberalization can be explained as the outcome of a political process. In this case the interests of the domestic right-holders (the import-competing industries) are balanced with those of domestic export industries seeking equivalent rights in foreign markets (and lower input costs). If the latter group offers enough political support, erosion of the former group's rights may prove politically rational.

Whatever is offered by one country (the demandeur) in a MTN as a quid pro quo for a demand on an issue, must be of interest to the government asked to alter its policies. Thus, to be effective the offer must help meet the objectives of influential foreign lobbies that will then push for the desired change in policy in their country. Alternatively, offers might be designed to help the government compensate groups that are likely to lose significantly from a reduction in protection. Options here include a gradual reduction in the level of protection and acceptance of safeguard mechanisms (see chapter 9).

Although export interests are the primary players in supporting liberalization in the MTN context, other groups favoring liberalization may also play a role. Examples include consumer or economic-development lobbies (the effect of development aid is frequently offset by protection against developing country exports). To mobilize such groups they must be aware of the detrimental impact of trade policies on their objectives, and these impacts must be large enough to induce them to organize. The provision of information on the effects of protectionist policies is therefore of great importance. Indeed, the need for such information is quite independent of the MTN process, as in many instances a unilateral change in policy would be welfare improving. The main point, however, is that what counts is political support. If consumer and other groups favoring a liberal trade policy do not mobilize and exercise political influence, they generally will be irrelevant.

For reciprocity to work it is important that lobbies favoring open markets do not have other means of getting what they want. Finger (1991) has pointed out that large countries increasingly negotiate increased market access for their exporting firms bilaterally. Such bilateral alternatives weaken the power of reciprocity in the multilateral context, as they reduce the incentives for export interests to support liberalization during MTNs. This is also one of the potential downsides of regional integration.

Enforceable Commitments

Liberalization commitments and agreements to abide by certain rules of the game will have little value if they cannot be enforced. The nondiscrimination principle, embodied in Articles I (MFN) and III (national treatment) of the GATT, plays an important role in ensuring that market access commitments are implemented and maintained. Other GATT Articles play a supporting role, including Article II (on Schedules of Concessions). The tariff commitments made by WTO members in a MTN and upon accession are enumerated in schedules (lists) of concessions. These schedules establish so-called ceiling bindings—the member concerned cannot raise tariffs above bound levels without negotiating compensation with the principal suppliers of the products concerned. The MFN rule then ensures that such compensation—usually reductions in other tariffs—extends to all WTO members, raising the cost of reneging. Once tariff commitments are bound, it is important that other, nontariff, measures that have the effect of nullifying or impairing the value of the tariff concession are not used. Hence the importance of GATT Article XI (prohibiting quantitative restrictions on imports and exports) and the rules on subsidies (see chapter 5).

If a country perceives that actions taken by another government have the effect of nullifying or impairing negotiated market access commitments or the disciplines of the WTO, it may bring this to the attention of the government involved and ask that the policy be changed. If satisfaction is not obtained, it may invoke WTO dispute settlement procedures. These involve the establishment of panels of impartial experts who are charged with determining whether a contested measure violates the WTO. Because the WTO is an inter-governmental agreement, private parties do not have legal standing before the WTO's dispute settlement body. Only governments have the right to bring cases. The existence of dispute settlement procedures precludes the use of unilateral retaliation. For small countries in particular, recourse to a multilateral body is vital, as unilateral actions will be ineffective and thus not be credible. More generally, small countries have a great stake in a rule-based international system, as this constrains the likelihood of being confronted with bilateral pressure from large trading powers to change policies that are not to their liking.

Transparency

Enforcement of commitments requires access to information on the trade regimes that are maintained by members. Numerous mechanisms are therefore incorporated into the agreements administered by the WTO to facilitate communication between WTO members on issues. Numerous specialized committees, working parties, working groups, and Councils meet regularly in Geneva. These interactions allow for the exchange of information and views and permit potential conflicts to be defused in an efficient manner.

WTO members are required to publish their trade regulations, to establish and maintain institutions allowing for the review of administrative decisions affecting trade, to respond to requests for information by other members, and to notify changes in trade policies to the WTO. These internal transparency requirements are supplemented by multilateral surveillance of trade policies by WTO members, facilitated by periodic country-specific reports (Trade Policy Reviews) that are prepared by the secretariat that are discussed by the WTO Council—the so-called Trade Policy Review Mechanism (see chapter 2). This external surveillance also fosters transparency, both for citizens of the countries concerned and for trading partners. It reduces the scope for countries to circumvent their obligations, thereby reducing uncertainty regarding the prevailing policy stance. Transparency is a basic pillar of the WTO. It is a legal obligation, embedded in Article X GATT and Article III GATS.

Transparency has a number of important benefits. It reduces the pressure on the dispute settlement system, as measures can be discussed in the appropriate WTO body. Frequently such discussions can address perceptions by a member that a specific policy violates the WTO—many potential disputes are defused in informal meetings in Geneva. Transparency is also vital in terms of ensuring 'ownership' of the WTO as an institution—if citizens do not know what the

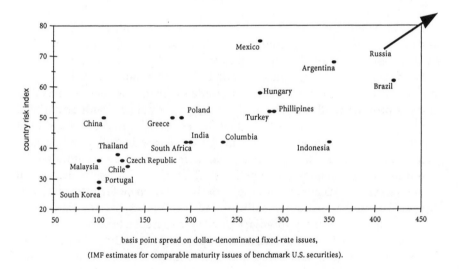

basis point spread on dollar-denominated fixed-rate issues,

(IMF estimates for comparable maturity issues of benchmark U.S. securities).

Source: Francois (1999).

FIG. 1.5   Risk and return in emerging markets, 1994–5

organization does, its legitimacy will be eroded. The Trade Policy Reviews are a unique source of information that can be used by civil society to assess what the implications are of the overall trade policies that are pursued by their government. From an economic perspective, transparency can also help reduce trade-policy related uncertainty. Such uncertainty is associated with lower investment and growth rates and with a shift in resources toward nontradables (Wincoop, 1992; Mendoza, 1997). Countries with policy regimes that are perceived by investors as unstable are generally associated with higher capital costs—investors will demand a risk premium on funds invested in such countries to take into account the probability of losses due to policy reversals. Such premia can be high. Figure 1.5 plots estimates of the basis point spread charged to emerging economies for dollar-denominated fixed rate loans in 1994–5 against country risk indexes compiled by the Economist Intelligence Unit for 1995. Country risk correlates closely with rates of return. The 'safer' a market, the lower the premium. Mechanisms to improve transparency can help lower risk perceptions by reducing uncertainty. WTO membership itself, with associated commitments on trade policies that are subject to binding dispute settlement can also have this effect.

Safety Valves

A final principle embodied in the WTO is that governments should be able to restrict trade in specific circumstances. There are three types of provisions in this connection: articles allowing for the use of trade measures to attain noneconomic objectives, articles aimed at ensuring 'fair competition', and provisions allowing for intervention in trade for economic reasons. The first include provisions allowing for policies to protect public health or national security, and to protect industries that are seriously injured by competition from imports. The underlying idea in the latter case is generally that governments should have the right to step in when competition becomes so vigorous as to injure domestic competitors. Although not explicitly mentioned in the relevant WTO agreement, the underlying rationale for intervention is that such competition causes political and social problems associated with the need for the industry to adjust to changed circumstances. The second type of measures include the right to impose countervailing duties on imports that have been subsidized and antidumping duties on imports that have been dumped—sold at a price that is below that charged in the home market. The objective of 'fair competition' is often in direct conflict with market access, as the instrument used by governments to attain 'fairness' is usually a trade barrier. Such barriers are, however, perfectly legal and permitted as long as they satisfy the criteria laid down in the relevant WTO provisions. Finally, the third type of 'safety valve' allows for actions to be taken if there are serious balance-of-payments difficulties, or if a government desires to support an infant industry.

1.4. FROM GATT TO WTO

GATT was not formally an international organization (that is, a legal entity in its own right), but an inter-governmental treaty. As a result, instead of member states, GATT had contracting parties. This changed with the establishment of the WTO, which is an international organization that administers multilateral agreements pertaining to trade in goods (GATT 1994, as well as numerous issue-specific agreements on antidumping, subsidies, import licensing, and so forth), trade in services (GATS), and trade-related aspects of intellectual property rights (TRIPs). To reflect the fact that the WTO is an organization, in this book we will generally use the term contracting parties to refer to signatories of the old GATT, and members to refer to signatories of the WTO. We also make a distinction between the GATT 1947 (the old GATT) and the GATT 1994 that is embodied in the WTO. The old GATT was both a set of rules and an institution; the new GATT is simply a set of rules that is part of the WTO.

The various treaties overseen by the WTO are between nation states and customs territories, and address government policies. The WTO deals predominantly with the actions of governments, establishing disciplines on trade policy instruments such as tariffs, quotas, subsidies or state trading. Thus, the WTO is a regulator of regulatory actions taken by governments that affect trade and the conditions of competition facing imported products on domestic markets. In this it is no different from the old GATT.

A fundamental perception of the founders of the GATT was that multilateral institutions facilitating cooperation between countries were important not only for economic reasons, but that the resulting increase in interdependence between countries would help to reduce the risk of war (Penrose, 1953; Hirschman, 1969). The expected increase in real incomes following trade liberalization and nondiscriminatory access to markets was expected to reduce the scope for political conflicts. The increase in transparency and the availability of a forum in which to discuss potential or actual trade conflicts was expected to reduce the probability of these spilling over into other domains. The Preamble of the GATT 1947 states that its objectives include raising standards of living, ensuring full employment and a large and steadily growing volume of real income and effective demand, developing the full use of the resources of the world and expanding the production and exchange of goods' (GATT, 1994a, 486). It goes on to say that reciprocal and mutually advantageous arrangements involving a substantial reduction of tariffs and other barriers to trade as well as the elimination of discriminatory treatment in international trade will contribute to the realization of these objectives. Nowhere is any mention made of free trade as an ultimate goal. This continues to be the case under the WTO.

The GATT emerged from the negotiations to create an International Trade Organization (ITO) after the Second World War. The negotiations on the charter of such an organization, although concluded successfully in Havana in 1948, did not lead to the establishment of the ITO because the US Congress was expected to refuse to ratify the agreement. The GATT was negotiated in 1947 between 23 countries—12 developed and 11 developing—before the ITO negotiations were concluded.[11] The countries involved in the 1947 exchange of tariff reductions were anxious that implementation of liberalization not be conditional upon the conclusion of the ITO talks. They therefore created the GATT as an interim agreement. As the ITO never came into being, the GATT was the only concrete result of negotiations.

Although the GATT incorporated the provisions of the commercial policy chapter of the ITO, having been conceived as a temporary trade agreement, it lacked an institutional structure. In the first years of its operation it did not even exist as an entity except once or twice a year when formal meetings of the contracting parties were held (Curzon and Curzon, 1973). Its organizational structure emerged only gradually. While major decisions were taken at the sessions of the CONTRACTING PARTIES,[12] it rapidly became obvious that a standing body was needed. An inter-sessional committee was formed in 1951 to organize voting by airmail or telegraphic ballot on issues relating to import restrictions justified for balance of payments reasons. This committee was replaced in 1960 by a Council of Representatives which was given broader powers and responsibilities for day-to-day management. Throughout the 1947–94 period, the GATT secretariat was formally known as the Interim Commission for the International Trade Organization (ICITO), created during the negotiations on the ITO. It was technically a United Nations (UN) body, as the ITO negotiations occurred under UN auspices. Because the ITO never came into existence, the formal relationship between the GATT (a treaty) and the UN was always tenuous.

Over the more than four decades of its existence, the GATT system expanded to include many more countries. It evolved into a *de facto* world trade organization, but one that was increasingly fragmented as 'side agreements' or codes were negotiated among subsets of countries. Its fairly complex and carefully crafted basic legal text was extended or modified by nu-

---

[11] The founding parties to the GATT were Australia, Belgium, Brazil, Burma, Canada, Ceylon, Chile, China, Cuba, Czechoslovakia, France, India, Lebanon, Luxembourg, Netherlands, New Zealand, Norway, Pakistan, Southern Rhodesia, Syria, South Africa, the United Kingdom and the United States. China, Lebanon and Syria subsequently withdrew.

[12] The term CONTRACTING PARTIES, in capital letters, was used to denote joint actions taken by all signatories to the agreement.

merous supplementary provisions, special arrangements, interpretations, waivers, reports by dispute settlement panels, and Council decisions. As of the early 1990s, a well-oiled GATT machine existed, helping contracting parties manage developments in the trading system, including through surveillance of trade policies and assisting conflict resolution through consultations, negotiations, mediation and dispute settlement.

Some of the major milestones are summarized in Table 1.3. GATT's early years were dominated by accession negotiations, a Review Session in the mid-1950s that led to modifications to the treaty, and the creation of the European Economic Community (EEC) in 1957. In 1962, derogations from the GATT rules in the area of trade in cotton textiles were negotiated. This developed into successive Multifibre Arrangements (MFA-I through MFA-IV; see chapter 6)—a complex system of managed trade that was inconsistent with the basic principles of the GATT. Starting in the mid-1960s, recurring rounds of MTNs gradually expanded the scope of the GATT to a larger number of nontariff policies, and eventually led to the creation of the WTO. Until the Uruguay Round, no progress was made on agriculture and textiles and clothing. The deal that finally allowed these sectors to be subjected to multilateral disciplines included the establishment of rules for trade in services and enforcement of IPRs, as well as the creation of the WTO.

TABLE 1.3 *From GATT to WTO: A chronology*

Date	Event
1947	The GATT is drawn up to record the results of tariff negotiations between 23 countries. The agreement enters into force on January 1, 1948.
1948	GATT provisionally enters into force. Delegations from 56 countries meet in Havana, Cuba, to consider the final draft of the ITO; 53 countries sign the so-called Havana Charter establishing an ITO in March 1948.
1949	Annecy round of tariff negotiations.
1950	China withdraws from GATT. The US Administration abandons efforts to seek Congressional ratification of the ITO.
1951	Torquay round of tariff negotiations. The Inter-sessional committee is established to organize voting by airmail ballot on issues concerning use of trade measures to safeguard the balance of payments. Germany (Federal Republic) accedes to the GATT.
1955	A review session modifies numerous provisions of the GATT. A move to transform GATT into a formal international organization (an Organization for Trade Cooperation—OTC) fails. The US is granted a waiver from GATT disciplines for certain agricultural policies. Japan accedes to the GATT.
1956	Fourth round of MTNs is held in Geneva.
1957	Creation of the European Economic Community.
1960	A council of representatives is created to manage day to day activities. The

Date	Event
	Dillon round is started and is concluded in 1961.
1961	The Short-Term Arrangement permitting quota restrictions on exports of cotton textiles is agreed as an exception to the GATT rules.
1962	The Short-Term becomes the Long Term Arrangement on Cotton Textiles. It is renegotiated in 1967 and extended for three years in 1970 until replaced by the MFA in 1974.
1964	The Kennedy Round begins (concluded in 1967). The United Nations Conference on Trade and Development (UNCTAD) is created to press for trade measures to benefit developing countries.
1965	Part IV (on Trade and Development) is added to the GATT, establishing new guidelines for trade policies of–and towards–developing countries. A Committee on Trade and Development is created to monitor implementation.
1967	Poland becomes the first centrally planed country to accede to the GATT.
1973	The Tokyo Round is initiated (concluded in 1979).
1974	The Agreement Regarding International Trade in Textiles, better known as the Multifibre Arrangement (MFA) enters into force, restricting export growth to six percent per year. It is negotiated in 1977 and 1982 and extended in 1986, 1991, and 1992.
1982	A GATT ministerial meeting—the first in almost a decade—fails to agree on an agenda for a new round. A GATT work program is formulated with a view to establishing an agenda for a new MTN.
1986	Launching of the Uruguay Round in Punta del Este, Uruguay.
1988	A GATT ministerial meeting to review progress in the Uruguay Round is held in Montreal in December. The midterm review is completed only in April 1989.
1990	Canada formally introduces a proposal to create a Multilateral Trade Organization that would cover the GATT, the GATS and other multilateral instruments agreed in the Uruguay Round. A ministerial meeting in Brussels fails to conclude the Uruguay Round.
1993	In June the US Congress grants fast-track authority to the US Administration—under which it cannot propose amendments to the outcome of negotiations—setting a December 15 deadline for talks to be concluded. The Uruguay Round is concluded on December 15 in Geneva.
1994	In Marrakech, on April 15, ministers sign the Final Act establishing the World Trade Organization (WTO) and embodying the results of the Uruguay Round.
1995	The WTO enters into force on January 1. Financial services agreement concluded (US does not sign).
1996	Maritime services talks collapse. Decision to revisit the issue in 2000. The first WTO ministerial conference hosted by Singapore creates working groups on trade and investment, trade and competition policy, transparency in public procurement and agrees to undertake work on trade facilitation.
1997	Forty governments agree to eliminate tariffs on computer and telecom-

Date	Event
	munication products by the year 2000 (the Information Technology Agreement).
	Negotiations on an Agreement on Basic Telecommunications are concluded under GATS auspices, after suspension of talks in 1996.
	A Financial Services Agreement is negotiated that brings on board the US, and expands commitments significantly.
1998	The second WTO ministerial conference commemorating the 50th anniversary of the multilateral trading system takes place on May 18–20 in Geneva.
1999	Appointment of a new Director-General proves contentious and distracts attention from the preparatory process for the 1999 ministerial meeting. Ministerial meeting in Seattle fails to launch a new round.
2000	Negotiations start on the so-called built-in agenda determined at the end of the Uruguay Round—agriculture and services.

There are many similarities between the old GATT and the WTO. The basic principles remain the same. The WTO continues to operate by consensus and continues to be member-driven. However, a number of major changes did occur. Most obviously, the coverage of the WTO is much greater. Moreover, in contrast to the old GATT, the WTO agreement is a 'single undertaking'—all its provisions apply to all members. This implies it is much more important for developing countries than the GATT was. In the dispute settlement area, it became much more difficult to block the formation of panels and the adoption of panel reports (through the adoption of a 'negative consensus' rule: all must oppose a finding). Finally, much greater transparency and surveillance functions were granted to the secretariat through the creation of a Trade Policy Review Mechanism.

1.5. THE CHALLENGE OF GLOBAL COOPERATION

The GATT proved a very successful instrument to induce countries to lower and bind tariffs over time. The idea that a rule-based approach is superior to an outcome- or results-based trading system steadily gained adherents. Whereas many governments in the 1960s and 1970s were engaged in efforts to manage trade—through central planning, barter, or commodity agreements—and actively pursued international agreements that can be characterized as results-oriented, this approach proved unsuccessful. Commodity agreements were difficult to enforce, and the prevalence of central planning and centralized trade was greatly reduced with the dissolution of the CMEA and the USSR.

Recognizing that tariffs were becoming less important as barriers to trade, the agenda of MTNs gradually grew to include various nontariff policies. In part this shift in focus reflected the expansion in use of instruments that circumvented GATT disciplines—voluntary export restraint agreements being an important example (Nogues, Olechowski and Winters, 1986). More recently the focus of attention has turned to domestic regulatory regimes. However, tariffs have not become irrelevant. In OECD countries, tariffs for agricultural production are a multiple of those applied to manufactures, and within manufacturing, there are tariff peaks exceeding 15 percent on many labor-intensive products in which developing countries have a comparative advantage (Table 1.4). Developing countries tend to have barriers against imports of manufactures that are much higher than those prevailing in OECD countries. They also have high rates of protection on imports of many agricultural goods.

Although a significant tariff negotiating agenda still exists, future MTNs will revolve increasingly around nontariff measures (NTMs) and domestic policies that are deemed to have an impact on trade. The interface between trade policy and economic policy more generally defined has become increasingly blurred. Agreeing on the elimination or reduction of NTMs is more difficult than negotiating downward the levels of tariffs. One reason for this is that it is much less obvious that specific NTMs are detrimental to a country's welfare. For example, attitudes towards environmental quality or product safety differ across countries, and this may be reflected in differences in environmental or product standards or in targeted subsidy programs. Economic theory suggests that under certain conditions intervention will be called for (see annex 2). Negotiations on regulatory issues therefore may be zero-sum games (some countries may lose), in contrast to tariff reductions, which are positive sum (all countries gain, even though certain groups in each country will lose unless they are compensated). Another problem, again in contrast to tariffs, is that it can be difficult to agree on what constitutes a NTM. Even if agreement is reached on what types of policies are trade distorting, incrementally reducing their negative impact may not be feasible. For many NTMs, all that may be possible is to agree to apply basic principles of transparency, national treatment, and MFN, and to seek to adopt procedural rules. However, pressures for harmonization of policies have been mounting. Although the GATT traditionally shied away from attempts to agree on common policies, differences in nontrade policies—regarding the environment, labor standards, or antitrust—are increasingly leading to claims that these result in unfair competition and should be countervailed. A major challenge for WTO members going into the next millennium is to deal with these pressures.

TABLE 1.4 *Patterns of protection, 1995 (percent)*

Exporting Region	Importing Region	
	High Income	Developing
Manufactures		
High Income	0.8	10.9
Developing	3.4	12.8
World	1.5	11.5
Agriculture		
High Income	15.9	21.5
Developing	15.1	18.3
World	15.6	20.1

Source: Hertel and Martin (2000).

Experience has amply demonstrated that pressures for protection and in-centives to renege on liberalization commitments will inevitably arise. The Uruguay Round negotiations were a response to the managed trade and new protectionism that had proliferated during the late 1970s and early 1980s. The extensive recourse made by OECD governments to trade-distorting NTMs (antidumping, export restraint agreements, subsidies) was in part driven by exogenous shocks. These included the collapse of the Bretton Woods system of fixed exchange rates, and successive price hikes for crude oil imposed by the OPEC cartel which helped give rise to stagflation (a mix of rising prices, weak output growth and rising unemployment). Matters were compounded by international political developments such as *détente* that reduced the primacy of foreign policy considerations in maintaining coop-eration in trade. As in the inter-war period, trade restrictions formed part of an inappropriate policy response to structural adjustment pressures, which were augmented by the emergence of East Asian countries as competitive suppliers of labor-intensive manufactures. The difference with the inter-war period was that multilateral cooperation did not break down. Although GATT rules were frequently ignored and circumvented, more often than not the letter, if not the spirit, of the rules of the game was honored. The explo-sion of grey area measures, especially VERs, constituted a major challenge to the system, but as discussed at greater length in subsequent chapters, VERs emerged in large part because of GATT disciplines on the use of emergency protection. The launch and successful completion of the Uruguay Round revealed that the major trading nations were willing to maintain multilateral cooperation and strengthen disciplines regarding the use of nontariff meas-ures. The system proved robust during the 1997–8 financial crises—there was no significant increase in protectionism in East Asia or the OECD.

WTO members confront a very different world from that existing in the immediate post-Second World War period. While the US continues to be the dominant economy of the world, it is no longer a public-spirited hegemon willing to tolerate free riding and deviations from multilateral rules by trading partners. Many of the trade disputes and the recourse to NTMs that emerged in the 1980s were in part a reflection of what Bhagwati (1991) has called the diminished giant syndrome of the US. The world economy is much more integrated today than it was in the 1950s. Instead of one dominant economic and political power (the US), there is now a triad (the EU, Japan and the US). None of the three can be relied upon to take up the type of leadership role provided by the US at the end of the Second World War. At the same time, the WTO as an international organization cannot take the lead—it is a weak institution in that it is membership driven, having no power to self-initiate action or to make decisions. At the end of the day what matters is the continued willingness of WTO members to abide by the negotiated rules of the game, and to use the multilateral institution as a mechanism to liberalize trade further and pursue cooperation in areas that give rise to disputes and friction. This requires there to be clear-cut gains for all members—something that is becoming more difficult to achieve as talks confront thorny issues of domestic regulation. However, much still needs to be done on the 'traditional' agenda—the potential gains from further liberalization of trade in goods and services are still very large, for both OECD countries and for developing economies.

1.6. FURTHER READING

John Gallagher and Ronald Robinson, 'The Imperialism of Free Trade', *Economic History Review*, 6 (1953), 1–15 is a classic article on British trade and trade policy during the nineteenth century. Douglas Irwin, 'Multilateral and Bilateral Trade Policies in the World Trading System: An Historical Perspective', in J. De Melo and A. Panagariya (eds.), *New Dimensions in Regional Integration* (London: CEPR, 1993) is an informative and accessible analysis of the historical background to the GATT. *Against the Tide: An Intellectual History of Free Trade* (Princeton: Princeton University Press, 1996), by the same author, is a masterful tour de force that is required reading for anyone with an interest in the case that has been made for and against free trade since prehistoric times. Richard Gardner, *Sterling-Dollar Diplomacy: The Origins and the Prospects of Our International Economic Order* (New York: McGraw-Hill, 1969, 2nd ed.) is an excellent discussion of the motivations and processes underlying the construction of the postwar international economic institutions, including the GATT.

Charles Adams, *For Good and Evil: The Impact of Taxes on the Course of Civilization* (Lanham: Madison Books, 1993) is an entertaining and informative birds-eye view of the role that taxes (including tariffs) have played in the course of recorded history. David Mansfield, *Power, Trade and War* (Princeton: Princeton University Press, 1994) is a careful empirical analysis of the relationship between an open international system, bilateral trade flows and the probability of war.

A good textbook treatment of globalization can be found in Peter Dicken, *Global Shift: Transforming the World Economy* (London, Paul Chapman Publishing Ltd., 1998). Kevin O'Rourke and Jeffrey Williamson, *Globalization and History: The Evolution of a 19th Century Mid-Atlantic Economy* (Cambridge, MIT Press, 1999) analyze the extent of integration that prevailed before World War One.

Jeffrey Sachs and Andrew Warner, 'Economic Reform and the Process of Global Integration', *Brookings Papers on Economic Activity*, 1 (1995), 1–95 is a widely read and influential empirical study that concludes there is an unambiguous positive relationship between openness and economic performance. Dan Ben David, *Free Trade and Economic Growth* (Cambridge, Mass.: MIT Press, forthcoming) is a fascinating exploration of the empirical evidence on the relationship between trade liberalization, economic growth and performance, and income convergence across countries and country groups. Dani Rodrik, *Has Globalization Gone Too Far?* (Washington DC: Institute for International Economics, 1997) provides a rather skeptical view of the benefits of globalization on growth and welfare in the absence of institutions and policies to manage downside risks.

For an appraisal and history of negotiations of the Havana Charter and the General Agreement on Tariffs and Trade see William Brown, *The United States and the Restoration of World Trade* (Washington DC: The Brookings Institution, 1950); and William Diebold, *The End of the ITO* (Princeton: Princeton University Press, 1952). Judith Goldstein, 'Creating the GATT Rules: Politics, Institutions and American Policy', in John Ruggie (ed.), *Multilateralism Matters: The Theory and Praxis of an Institutional Form* (New York: Columbia University Press, 1993), is an insightful analysis of US views and interests in creating the GATT.

There is a large literature on the political economy of trade policy decisions and institutional design issues. An early study of the GATT system that continues to be well worth reading is Gerard Curzon's *Multilateral Trade Diplomacy* (London: Michael Joseph, 1965). I.M. Destler, *American Trade Politics* (Washington DC: Institute for International Economics, 1996), now in its third edition is a classic and regularly updated book on the politics of US trade policy. Arye Hillman, *The Political Economy of Protectionism* (New York: Harwood, 1989) surveys the economic literature. Robert Keohane, 'Reciprocity in International Relations', *International Organization*, 40 (1986), 1–27 discusses the notion of reciprocity from a political science and international relations perspective. L. Alan Winters, 'Reciprocity', in M. Finger and A. Olechowski (eds.), *The Uruguay Round: A Handbook* (Washington DC: The World Bank, 1987) does so from the perspective of an economist. S.H. Bailey, 'The Political Aspect of Discrimination in International Economic Relations', *Economica*, 12 (1932), 96–115 is an often-cited contemporary assessment of the costs of discrimination in trade.

Those interested in the theoretical economic literature on the WTO, reciprocity and nondiscrimination can do no better than consult Kyle Bagwell and Robert Staiger, 'An Economic Theory of GATT', *American Economic Review*, 89 (1999*a*), 215–48. Other recommended theoretical analyses of the GATT include Rod Ludema, 'International Trade Bargaining and the Most-Favored-Nation Clause', *Economics and Politics*, 3, (1991), 1–20.

A clear and accessible introduction to the legal and institutional aspects of the world trading system is presented in John H. Jackson, *The World Trading System: Law and Policy in International Relations* (Cambridge: MIT Press, 1997). John Croome, *Reshaping the World Trading System* (Leiden: Kluwer, 1999) is a detailed negotiating history of the Uruguay Round, written by a GATT insider. The prevalence of NTBs at the beginning of the 1980s is documented and quantified in Julio Nogues, Andrej Olechowski and L. Alan Winters, 'The Extent of Nontariff Barriers to Industrial Countries Exports', *World Bank Economic Review*, 1 (1986), 181–99. Patrick Low, *Trading Free: The GATT and US Trade Policy* (New York: Twentieth Century Fund, 1993) discusses the evolution of US trade policy thinking in the 1980s, the use of contingent protection and VERs, and US attitudes towards the GATT.

Gilbert Winham, 'GATT and the International Trade Regime', *International Journal*, 15 (1990), 786–822, is a leading political scientist's view of the GATT and its role in international relations. Frieder Roessler, 'The Scope, Limits and Function of the GATT Legal System', *The World Economy*, 8 (1985), 287–98 discusses the role of GATT rules as constraints on governments. Alan Deardorff, 'An Economist's Overview of the World Trade Organization', in G. Flake and F. Myeong-Hwa Lowe-Lee (eds.), *The Emerging WTO System and Perspectives From East Asia* (Washington DC: Korea Economic Institute of America, 1996) provides a very insightful and accessible economist's view of the WTO, emphasizing the importance of the institution as a forum for communication.

PART II
THE INSTITUTION

2
The World Trade Organization

The World Trade Organization was established on January 1, 1995. The WTO builds upon the organizational structure of the GATT and its secretariat—to a significant extent it formalizes and extends the structure that had gradually evolved over a period of some 50 years. The Punta del Este Ministerial Declaration launching the Uruguay Round did not call for the creation of a WTO. In principle, it was not necessary to create an international organization to implement the outcome of the negotiations. The Canadian suggestion to establish a Multilateral Trade Organization (MTO) in 1990—subsequently supported by the EU—was therefore something of a surprise. The proposal was motivated by a desire to create a single institutional framework for world trade (Croome, 1999).[1] This would encompass the modified GATT, its sister bodies on services (GATS) and intellectual property (TRIPs), as well as all other agreements and arrangements concluded under the auspices of the Uruguay Round. The US initially opposed the idea, but after negotiations on the substance of the new organization, agreed to the framework that currently exists, including the name change.[2]

At Punta del Este it had been agreed that the negotiations were to be a 'single undertaking'. With the proposal to create the WTO, the concept of a single undertaking was redefined to mean that all GATT contracting parties had to become a WTO member. There was no alternative—remaining a member of GATT 1947 would have no value given that it was an institutional entity that was effectively going to disappear. Developing countries therefore all joined the WTO, something that was not on the agenda at all when negotiations started in 1986. Although the US Congress remained suspicious of any limitations to its powers on trade policy, it also decided to join the new organization. During the ratification debate it became clear that the establishment of the WTO would not do much to change the status quo as far as infringement of its national sovereignty was concerned, as the GATT 1947 was a binding international treaty.

---

[1] For convenience, in this book we use the acronym EU to denote both the European Union and the European Communities. The latter is formally the correct appellation in WTO contexts.

[2] The choice of name was somewhat ironic given the attention that was being given to intellectual property rights, as the acronym WTO was already in use by the World Tourism Organization, a Madrid-based special agency of the UN.

The establishment of the WTO was a significant event. Attempts to put the GATT on a more secure organizational footing had been made periodically since the failure of the US Congress to ratify the ITO. During a 1955 meeting to review the GATT, a number of contracting parties proposed to establish an Organization for Trade Cooperation (OTC). This proposal was much less elaborate than the ITO but it also failed to win the approval of the US Congress (Jackson, 1990). The issue of providing an institutional framework for international trade reappeared again in the UN Economic and Social Council (ECOSOC) in 1963. A group of experts called for the creation of a new UN agency with universal membership and substantial powers in the sphere of international trade (Kostecki, 1979). The idea was that this body would implement recommendations of UNCTAD as well as other relevant policy decisions taken by organs of the UN. The proposal envisaged that the GATT would become the agency's Committee on Tariffs. The proposal did not meet with much interest among the major trading nations. However, the 1964 UN General Assembly resolution establishing UNCTAD provided that it should be concerned with matters relating to the elaboration of a comprehensive trade organization. Nothing concrete came of this—despite lengthy discussions about the need for a New International Economic Order during the 1970s—in large part because of the widely differing philosophies held by industrialized market economies and much of the developing world regarding the appropriate basis for international trade. With the creation of the WTO, an international trade organization emerged that is firmly based on GATT principles—reciprocity and nondiscrimination.

2.1. SCOPE, FUNCTIONS AND STRUCTURE OF THE WTO

The WTO is headed by a Ministerial Conference of all members, meeting at least once every two years. More frequent participation by trade ministers than occurred under the old GATT—where a decade could pass between ministerial meetings—was intended to strengthen the political guidance of the WTO and enhance the prominence and credibility of its rules in domestic political arenas. Past experience of the GATT with ministerial meetings suggests that these can easily be an inefficient use of the time of many ministers from smaller trading nations. This is because in negotiations the controversial issues tend to be solved at the last moment and require agreement between the major players. The latter may take a significant amount of time to strike a deal among each other, thereby marginalizing the potential for participation by ministers of smaller countries. This lesson was brought home again during the Seattle ministerial meeting in late 1999, where many developing country trade ministers essentially came for nothing. Excluded from the main negotiating fora where the major players and a selected subset of smaller countries were trying to hammer out compromises, many ministers spent most of the meeting 'on call'. In the event the meeting failed to launch a new negotiating round (more on this below).

The Marrakech Agreement establishing the WTO charges the organization with providing the common institutional framework for the conduct of trade relations among its members in matters for which agreements and associated legal obligations apply (Article II). Four Annexes to the WTO define the substantive rights and obligations of members. Annex 1 has three parts: Annex 1A entitled Multilateral Agreements on Trade in Goods, contains the GATT 1994 (the GATT 1947 as amended by a large number of Understandings and supplementary Agreements negotiated in the Uruguay Round); Annex 1B, which contains the GATS; and Annex 1C, the Agreement on TRIPs. Annex 2 contains the Understanding on Rules and Procedures Governing the Settlement of Disputes (DSU)—the WTO's common dispute settlement mechanism (the subject of chapter 3 below). Annex 3 contains the Trade Policy Review Mechanism (TPRM), an instrument for surveillance of members' trade policies. Finally, Annex 4—entitled Plurilateral Trade Agreements—consists of Tokyo Round codes that were not multilateralized in the Uruguay Round, and that therefore bind only signatories. Together, Annexes 1–3 embody the Multilateral Trade Agreements. Article II WTO specifies that all the agreements contained in Annexes 1, 2 and 3 are an integral part of the WTO Agreement, and are binding on all members. All of these instruments are discussed further below or in the rest of this book.

The WTO has a number of functions. It is charged with facilitating the implementation and operation of the Multilateral Trade Agreements, providing a forum for negotiations, administering the dispute settlement mechanism, providing multilateral surveillance of trade policies, and cooperating with the World Bank and the IMF to achieve greater coherence in global economic policy-making (Article III WTO). Between meetings of the Ministerial Conference—responsible for carrying out the functions of the WTO—the organization is managed by a General Council at the level of officials. The General Council meets about 12 times a year. On average, some 70 percent of all WTO members take part in Council meetings, usually represented by delegations based in Geneva. The General Council turns itself, as needed, into a body to adjudicate trade disputes (the Dispute Settlement Body—DSB) and to review trade policies of the member countries (the Trade Policy Review Body—TPRB).

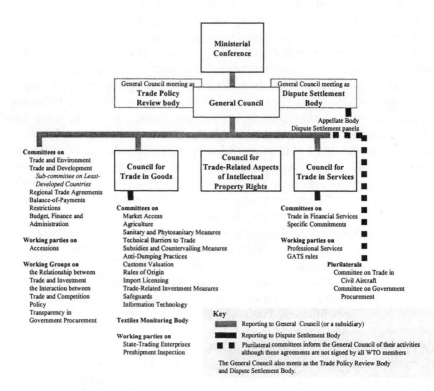

Source: WTO.

FIG. 2.1 The WTO Structure

Three subsidiary councils operate under the general guidance of the General Council (see Figure 2.1): the Council for Trade in Goods; the Council for Trade in Services; and the Council for Trade-Related Aspects of Intellectual Property Rights. Separate committees deal with the interests of developing countries (the Committee on Trade and Development); surveillance of trade restrictions actions taken for balance of payment purposes; surveillance of regional trade agreements; trade-environment linkages; and the WTO's finances and administration. Additional committees or working parties deal with matters covered by the GATT, GATS or TRIPs Agreement. Committees functioning under auspices of the Council on Trade in Goods exist on subsidies, antidumping and countervailing measures, technical barriers to trade (product standards), import licensing, customs valuation, market access, agriculture, sanitary and phytosanitary measures, trade-related investment measures, rules of origin, and safeguards. In addition, working groups have been established to deal with notifications, state-trading enterprises, and to study the relationship between trade and investment, between trade and competition policy and the issue of transparency in government procurement. Similarly, specific committees address matters relating to the GATS or TRIPs. Committees also exist to administer the Plurilateral Agreements—which apply only to those members that sign them (see chapter 11). Given their nature, these are not under the guidance of the General Council but operate within the general framework of the WTO and inform the Council of their activities. All WTO members may participate in all councils, committees, and so forth, except the Appellate Body, dispute settlement panels, the Textiles Monitoring Body, and committees dealing with plurilateral agreements.

Some 40 councils, committees, subcommittees, bodies, and standing groups or working parties functioned under WTO auspices in 2000—more than twice the number under the old GATT. Such bodies are open to all WTO members, but generally only the more important trading nations (less than half of the membership) regularly send representatives to most meetings. Participation reflects a mix of national interests and resource constraints. Least developed countries in particular tend not to be represented at these meetings—often not having a delegation based in Geneva (see chapter 12). All of these fora, plus working parties on accession (averaging close to thirty in the late 1990s), dispute settlement panels, meetings of regional groups, heads of delegations, and numerous *ad hoc* and informal groups add up to 1,200 events a year at or around the WTO headquarters in Geneva. Most WTO business is conducted in English, but many official WTO meetings require French and Spanish interpretation.

The main actors in day-to-day activities are officials affiliated with the delegations of members. The WTO—as was the GATT 1947—is therefore something of a network organization (Blackhurst, 1998). The WTO secretariat is the hub of a very large and dispersed network comprising official representatives of members based in Geneva, civil servants based in capitals, and national business and nongovernmental groups that seek to have their governments push for their interests at the multilateral level. The operation of the WTO depends on the collective input of thousands of civil servants and government officials that deal with trade issues in each member country. Initiatives to launch MTNs and settle disputes—the two highest profile activities of the WTO—are the sole responsibility of WTO members themselves, not the secretariat.

The member-driven nature of the organization puts a considerable strain on the national delegations of members. Many countries have no more than one or two persons dealing with WTO matters; a large minority has no delegations in Geneva at all. Active players in WTO fora tend to have large delegations. In most instances, a member's WTO representative will also cover meetings at UNCTAD, the World Intellectual Property Organization (WIPO), the International Labor Office (ILO), the World Health Organization, the Economic Commission for Europe, and other international organizations located in Geneva.

The WTO secretariat is relatively small—standing at some 500 staff. It's role is to provide members with technical and logistical support, including organizing meetings of governing bodies and preparing background documentation when requested by committees or the Council. It has very little formal power to take initiatives. For example, the Director-General has no authority to initiate dispute settlement proceedings against a member, no matter how blatantly it may have violated WTO rules. The secretariat must abstain from providing interpretations of WTO law or passing judgement on the conformity of a member's policy with the WTO rules. The documents prepared by the WTO secretariat tend to be subjected to close scrutiny by WTO delegations. There is little scope for the WTO Director-General to determine the topics to be put on the WTO agenda. The situation was well described at an informal meeting during the Uruguay Round, where a diplomat addressing the Director-General noted: 'Sir, there is a difference between you and me; I am a Contracting Party and you are a Contracted Party'.

The secretariat plays an important role in reducing transactions costs by distributing information and ensuring transparency by undertaking periodic reviews of members' trade policies. The latter is one of the few areas where the secretariat has been given a mandate to undertake action on its own responsibility. The secretariat also facilitates dispute settlement by supporting the work of panels. Even though WTO secretariat members are not decision-makers, they can have substantial influence as a result of their technical skills, institutional memory and familiarity with the issues. The less knowledgeable and assertive is a chairman of a given working party or committee, the stronger the influence of the secretariat is likely to be. The smaller and less competent a given country's delegation, the more the secretariat's impact is felt. The Director-General, the head of the WTO secretariat, is in some sense the guardian of the collective interest of the member states. The WTO's rules and procedures allow the Director-General to act as a broker—not a decision-maker—in many situations. Historically they have often played an important role in encouraging countries to maintain and strengthen multilateral cooperation in trade (Box 2.1).

The small size of the secretariat is somewhat misleading. As mentioned above, the WTO is a network-based organization. The WTO secretariat and the national delegates in Geneva work in close cooperation with numerous civil servants in their respective capitals. Ministries of trade, foreign affairs, finance, telecommunications, and agriculture, and specialized bodies such as customs authorities, central banks, health and safety standards administrations, environmental protection agencies, national patent and trademark agencies, and so on, all tend to have staff that deal with WTO issues and provide inputs into WTO activities. The total size of the network is impossible to determine, but certainly spans at least 5,000 people. The secretariat's essential function is to keep that network operating smoothly. Once the network nature of the institution is recognized, it becomes clear that the WTO is a much larger entity that the size of the secretariat suggests.

Box 2.1. The Director-General, 1948–2005
A charismatic figure was the first Director-General of the GATT (or Secretary-General as the post was called in the early days of GATT's existence), Sir Eric Wyndham White, who managed the GATT for over 20 years. The survival and functioning of the GATT and its secretariat in the postwar period was to a large extent the result of his creativity and experience (Curzon, 1973). His immediate successor was Professor Olivier Long—a distinguished Swiss diplomat and academic who consolidated many of the GATT's achievements and was the man at the wheel during the Tokyo Round. Long was followed by Ambassador Arthur Dunkel, a Swiss trade official. A skillful mediator, he headed the secretariat during the launching of the Uruguay Round, playing a central role at almost every turning point and crisis that affected the negotiations. Through quiet and tenacious diplomacy he made an important contribution to the final package of the Uruguay Round which was largely based on the so-called Dunkel Draft of 1991. As noted by Rubens Ricupero (1998), Dunkel was not to set foot on the 'Promised Land', and it fell to Peter Sutherland to finalize the last six months of negotiations and usher in the WTO at the 1994 ministerial meeting in Marrakech.

The appointment of Sutherland, a former EU Commissioner, marked a change in the type of person chosen by members to run the secretariat. Whereas the Director-General previously had always been an official, with the creation of the WTO the job has come to be filled by politicians. The higher public profile of the WTO also caused the selection process to become more difficult. In 1995, Peter Sutherland was replaced by Renato Ruggiero. A former Trade Minister of Italy, Ruggiero was a controversial appointment, opposed by the US and many developing countries who preferred a non-European candidate. As a compromise Mr. Ruggiero was given only a four-year mandate, rather than the regular five-year term, and it was understood that his successor would not be a European. Upon his departure in early 1999, drawn-out and fractious consultations among members failed to arrive at a consensus on the selection of his successor. Out of an original field of four candidates, two from developing and two from OECD countries, members split between two candidates, both of whom lobbied hard for the job. In the end, a compromise deal was struck under which it was agreed that each candidate would become Director-General—sequentially. The process was widely regarded as the most contentious and divisive in the history of the GATT/WTO, and a symptom that the governance of the trading system needed to be improved.

The Right Honorable Mike Moore, a former Prime Minister of New Zealand was appointed to head the WTO for a period of three years, starting in September 1999. He is to be succeeded by H.E. Dr. Supachai Panatchpakdi, a former Deputy-Prime Minister of Thailand, who is expected to serve for a three-year period beginning in September 2002. Dr. Panatchpakdi will be the first DG from a developing country. Neither Mr. Moore nor Dr. Supachai is eligible for reappointment as Director-General (*WTO Focus*, no. 41, 1999).

The financial contributions to the budget of the WTO are based on GATT 1947 practice. The WTO's income comes from assessed contributions calculated on the basis of each member's share in the total trade of all WTO members, computed as a three-year average of the most recent trade figures (if this share is less than 0.12 percent, a minimum contribution is assessed). In 1999, the nine largest trading nations contributed approximately two-thirds of total contributions. The EU contribution is assessed separately for each of its member states, and includes intra-EU trade. Voluntary contributions (grants) are provided by industrialized market economies for specific purposes such as technical assistance or training of officials from developing countries. The WTO Appellate Body has a budget that is independent of the WTO's.

2.2. DECISION-MAKING

Most decision-making in the WTO follows GATT practices and is based on bargaining, consultation and consensus. Consensus was the modus operandi of the GATT. Even in cases where GATT rules called for a formal vote—such as on the granting of waivers of GATT obligations to a country (Article XXV GATT)—negotiation and consultations would usually be held to arrive at a consensus text before the formal vote was held (Jackson, 1997). Consensus was facilitated by another GATT tradition—not to allow progress to be frustrated by one party's obstinacy, unless it happened to be one of the major trading powers. Consensus does not mean unanimity. It signifies that no delegation physically present in the Council has a fundamental objection on an issue. Those that are not present—or abstain—do not count. Decision-making by consensus is a useful device to ensure that only decisions on which there is no major opposition—and consequently which have good chances of being implemented—are made. This is important because the WTO has few means of pressing unwilling governments to implement decisions.

Despite the effective lack of veto power, the consensus practice is of value to smaller countries as it enhances their negotiating leverage—especially if they are able to form a coalition—in the informal consultations and bargaining that precede decision-making. It is in this connection that the quality of a country's delegation can be significant in determining its effective influence. Achieving consensus can be a complex process, in part because it may require issue linkages and logrolling. Consensus reinforces conservative tendencies in the system. Proposals for change can be adopted only if unopposed—creating the potential for paralysis. Offsetting this is that consensus can help enhance the legitimacy of decisions that are taken collectively.

Recourse to voting may be made if a consensus cannot be reached. Voting may occur only where provisions allow for this (see Table 2.1). If required, voting is based on the principle of 'one member-one vote'. This distinguishes the WTO from the IMF and other international economic organizations where weighted voting is extensively used. Unanimity is required for amendments relating to general principles such as MFN or national treatment. Interpretation of the provisions of the WTO agreements and decisions on waivers of a member's obligations require approval by a three-quarters majority vote. A two-thirds majority vote is sufficient for amendments relating to issues other than general principles mentioned above. Where not

TABLE 2.1 *Decision-making in the WTO*

Decision-making rule	Type of issue
Unanimity	Amendments concerning general principles such as nondiscrimination
Three-quarters majority	Interpretations of the provisions of the WTO and waivers of WTO disciplines for members
Two-thirds majority	Amendments to the WTO relating to issues other than general principles; accession
Consensus	Where not otherwise specified

otherwise specified and where consensus cannot be reached, a simple majority vote is in principle sufficient. As the issues involved in a majority vote situation will not be central to the functioning of the WTO, this is not likely to lead to conflicts. In all cases, in contrast to the consensus practice, if voting occurs the majority required is relative to all WTO members; not with respect to those members that happen to be present in a particular meeting.

A member is not bound by any amendment that passes a vote if it is opposed to it, and the change is such as to alter its rights and obligations (Article X WTO). The Ministerial Conference may decide to ask a member that does not accept an amendment to withdraw from the WTO, or grant it a waiver. As the major traders must remain part of the WTO for it to retain its value, it is difficult to imagine them being asked to withdraw. Large players therefore cannot be forced to adopt changes they are unwilling to accept voluntarily. It should be noted that the voting rules and mechanisms are somewhat theoretical. In practice voting does not occur. Indeed, WTO members decided in 1995 not to apply provisions allowing for a vote in the case of accessions and requests for waivers, but to continue to proceed on the basis of consensus (WT/L/93). Legislative amendments are also likely to be quite rare, as in practice changes to the various agreements occur as part of broader multilateral rounds.

Some useful criteria to determine a country's influence in the WTO are its share in world trade, its trade dependence or openness (the ratio of exports and imports to GDP) and the absolute size of its market (GDP). A country's trade-policy stance is irrelevant: free traders do not have any more say in the WTO than countries with highly protectionist regimes. The major players are therefore the major trading powers—the EU and the US. The EU, through the Brussels-based Commission of the European Communities, is a major player both because a number of EU member states are among the largest trading nations, and because individual member states no longer have full sovereignty over trade policy: this has been delegated to the Commission.[3] For specific issues, the level of influence is also determined by the importance of the matter for the country. For example, Argentina, a relatively small trading nation, is an important grain exporter and has more influence on decisions concerning international trade in grains than on a topic such as telecommunications. Issues that arise are often product-

---

[3] As EU Member States still have sovereignty over many services and intellectual property issues, a 'code of conduct' has been agreed that allows the Commission to speak on GATS and TRIPs issues. Despite the fact that the EU has a common external trade policy, individual EU members each have a vote in the WTO in cases where recourse is made to voting. The 'payment' for this is that each member pays dues to the WTO based on its total trade, including intra-EU.

specific. What matters then is the country's share of world trade in the product involved, and the importance of the products concerned in total exports of the country. This product-specificity explains much of the bilateral or plurilateral nature of the interactions that take place in the WTO.

Of the top twenty economies in terms of shares in world exports and imports, three are not yet WTO members at the time of writing: China, Russia and Chinese Taipei (Table 2.2). There is a close correlation between the top twenty and who's who in the WTO. While industrialized market economies dominate the list, developing countries are by no means irrelevant. Countries such as Brazil and India have traditionally exerted substantial influence

TABLE 2.2 *Top twenty traders, 1999*

Rank	Exporters	Value	Share	Rank	Importers	Value	Share
1	Extra-EU exports	813.2	20.1	1	United States	944.4	22.3
2	United States	682.5	16.8	2	Extra-EU imports	800.7	18.9
3	Japan	387.9	9.6	3	Japan	280.5	6.6
4	Canada	214.3	5.3	4	Canada	206.2	4.9
5	China	183.8	4.5	5	Hong Kong, China	186.8	4.4
6	Hong Kong, China	174.9	4.3		Retained imports	36.5	0.9
	Re-exports	150.3	3.7	6	China	140.2	3.3
7	Korea, Rep. of	132.3	3.3	7	Mexico	129.0	3.0
8	Mexico	117.5	2.9	8	Taipei, Chinese	104.2	2.5
9	Singapore	109.9	2.7	9	Singapore	101.6	2.4
	Re-exports	46.5	1.1		Retained imports	55.1	1.3
10	Taipei, Chinese	109.9	2.7	10	Korea, Rep. Of	93.3	2.2
11	Switzerland	78.9	1.9	11	Switzerland	80.2	1.9
12	Russian Fed.	73.9	1.8	12	Australia	64.7	1.5
13	Malaysia	73.3	1.8	13	Brazil	61.0	1.4
14	Australia	55.9	1.4	14	Russian Fed.	59.2	1.4
15	Thailand	53.6	1.3	15	Malaysia	58.3	1.4
16	Brazil	51.1	1.3	16	Poland	47.1	1.1
17	Indonesia	48.8	1.2	17	Turkey	45.4	1.1
18	Saudi Arabia	42.3	1.0	18	Thailand	43.0	1.0
19	Norway	39.6	1.0	19	India	42.2	1.0
20	India	32.9	0.8	20	Norway	36.2	0.9

Note: Individual EU members' trade is not reported separately as the EU operates as a bloc in the WTO.
Source: WTO (2000).

both because of their economic size and because they have often acted as spokesmen for other developing countries. Six of the top twenty are middle or low income countries. Small developing economies can be influential as honest brokers between larger players. A case in point was the role played by

Mr. Ali Mchumo, the Tanzanian Ambassador to the WTO, who as chairman of the WTO General Council during 1999, was heavily involved in the difficult process of selecting a new Director-General.

Management of the Secretariat and Daily Operations

Unlike the World Bank or the IMF, the WTO does not have an executive body or board comprising a sub-set of members, some of whom represent a number of countries. Such executive boards facilitate decision-making by concentrating discussions among a smaller but representative group of members. The closest the GATT ever came to such a forum was the Consultative Group of Eighteen (CG18) which was established in 1975. It ceased meeting in 1985, and never substituted for the GATT Council of Representatives (Blackhurst, 1998).

As of late 2000, the WTO General Council had a membership of 141. Achieving consensus among such a large number of countries is not a simple matter. Mechanisms have therefore been developed over time to reduce the number of countries that are active participants in WTO deliberations. The first and most important device is to involve only 'principals', at least initially. To some extent this is a natural process—a country that has no agricultural sector is unlikely to be interested in discussions centering on the reduction of agricultural trade barriers. In general the quad—Canada, the EU, Japan and the US—are part of any group that forms to discuss any topic. They are supplemented by countries that have a principal supplying interest in a product, and the major (potential) importers whose policies are the subject of interest. Finally, a number of countries that have established a reputation as spokespersons tend to be involved in most major meetings. Historically, such countries have included India—a large, poor country that until recently traded very little—Egypt, and the former Yugoslavia. Sub-Saharan African and least developed countries have generally taken a back seat in WTO deliberations.

During the Tokyo and Uruguay Rounds, contentious issues on which deals had to be struck were often thrashed out in the so-called Green room, a conference room adjacent to the Director-General's offices. Green room meetings were part of a consultative process through which the major countries and a representative set of developing countries—a total of twenty or so delegations—tried to hammer out the outlines of acceptable proposals or negotiating agendas. Such meetings generally involved the active participation and input of the Director-General. A convention has since emerged to call such meetings Green room gatherings, no matter where they are held.

Once a deal has emerged, it is submitted to the general WTO membership. Although amendments may be made, these are usually marginal.

The Green room process has great potential to lead to controversial outcomes if countries with strong interests in an issue are excluded or not kept informed and consulted on proposed deals. This became a contentious issue during the Seattle ministerial meeting. Many developing countries that were excluded from critical Green room meetings where attempts were being made to negotiate compromise texts of a draft agenda for a new MTN felt that they were not being kept informed of developments and were not being granted the opportunity to defend their views. Proposals have been made periodically to formalize the Green room process by creating an executive committee to manage the WTO agenda, based on shares in world trade (Schott and Buurman, 1994). To date, no progress in this direction has proven possible in the WTO. Although there was widespread dissatisfaction with the organization of the Seattle meeting, subsequent discussions on 'internal transparency and effective participation of members' revealed that there was no serious interest among most of the membership to explore the merits of creating an executive body.[4]

2.3. TRANSPARENCY: NOTIFICATION AND SURVEILLANCE

Transparency at both the multilateral (WTO) and national level is essential to reduce uncertainty and enforce agreements. Efforts to increase transparency of members' trade policies takes up a good portion of WTO resources. The approach is inspired by what Jagdish Bhagwati has called the Dracula principle: problems may disappear once light is thrown on them (Bhagwati, 1988). The transparency provisions of the WTO relate to both the acts of the WTO itself, and the actions of its members. As far as the WTO itself is concerned, many WTO documents are public.[5] WTO decisions and other major WTO documents are published in a series entitled *Basic Instruments and Selected Documents* (BISD) by the WTO secretariat in Geneva. The secretariat also prepares regular newsletters and publishes ad hoc studies on particular aspects of the multilateral trading system.

---

[4] See WT/GC/M/57, paras. 132-70.

[5] One set of documents that have traditionally not been published are the results of tariff renegotiations (see chapter 9). Moreover, access to the WTO integrated database of members' tariff schedules and other trade measures is restricted to participating governments, impeding access to data by think tanks and NGOs.

Under GATT 1947, smaller trading nations often perceived a lack of transparency concerning agreements reached between the major players in either MTNs or with respect to the settlement of bilateral disputes or trade issues. While bilateral agreements regarding specific trade issues are not necessarily a matter of concern, they may be detrimental to the interests of third parties who are left to determine the potential effects of the deal on their exporters. More important in terms of generating controversy has been the practice of large traders to come to an agreement between themselves and then attempt to present the deal as a fait accompli in a negotiating group or in the General Council. This goes back to the governance and management problem noted earlier. How to keep all members informed and involved in deliberations and still make progress is a major challenge for the WTO. We discuss this issue further in chapter 15.

Turning to transparency of members' trade-related policies, the WTO requires that all trade laws and regulations be published. Article X of the GATT, Article III of the GATS and Article 63 of the TRIPs Agreement all require that relevant laws, regulations, judicial decisions and administrative rulings are made public. There are over 200 notification requirements embodied in the various WTO agreements and mandated by Ministerial and Council decisions. All of these require the existence of appropriate bodies or agencies in members that have the responsibility of satisfying them. For example, WTO members must provide a consolidated notification, including all changes in laws, regulations, policy statements or public notices, to the secretariat each year. So-called enquiry points must be created that have the responsibility for answering questions and providing relevant documents regarding health and product standards and all relevant measures of general application which pertain to or affect the operation of the GATS. The antidumping and subsidies agreements require that national authorities motivate decisions in antidumping and countervailing duty cases.

In February 1995, the Council for Trade in Goods established a Working Group on Notification Obligations and Procedures with the mandate to review the notification obligations and procedures. As a result of recommendations by the group, the notification obligations under GATT 1947 relating to import licensing procedures were eliminated in 1998. To assist members navigate and comply with the many notification obligations the secretariat is required to provide a listing of notification requirements and members' compliance on an ongoing basis and circulate this semiannually to all members.

The WTO also has important surveillance activities. The WTO itself periodically reviews trade policy and foreign trade regimes of members (Box 2.2). The purpose of the Trade Policy Review Mechanism (TPRM) is to contribute to improved adherence by WTO members to the rules and disciplines they have signed on to and achieve greater transparency in, and understanding of, prevailing trade policies and practices (WTO, 1994, Annex IIIA).

Box 2.2. The Trade-Policy Review Mechanism

The WTO's Trade Policy Review Mechanism (TPRM), established during the Uruguay Round, builds upon a 1979 Understanding on Notification, Consultation, Dispute Settlement and Surveillance, under which contracting parties agreed to conduct a regular and systematic review of developments in the trading system. The objective of the TPRM is to examine the impact of trade policies and practices of members on the trading system, and to contribute to improved adherence to WTO rules through greater transparency. The legal compatibility of any particular measure with WTO disciplines is not examined, this being left for members to ascertain.

The TPRM was originally motivated in part by concerns that the only available review of global trade policies at the time was one produced by the US. (Keesing 1998). Although the TPRM suffers from some important limitations—discussed below—it is an important element of the WTO because it fosters transparency and enhances communication, thereby strengthening the multilateral trading system.

Country-specific reviews are conducted on a rotational basis. The frequency of review is a function of a member's share in world trade. The four largest players—the EU, the US, Japan and Canada—are subject to review by the WTO General Council every two years. In principle, the next 16 largest traders are subjected to reviews every four years, and the remaining members are reviewed every six years. A longer periodicity may be established for least-developed countries. The TPR is based on a report prepared by the government concerned and a report by the WTO Trade Policies Review Division. TPRs are supplemented by an annual report by the Director-General that provides an overview of developments in the international trading environment.

By subjecting the largest OECD markets to periodic review, the TPRM shifts the balance of power in the WTO, ever so slightly, in favor of the developing countries, by ensuring that the trade policies of the major traders are subject to regular public peer review (Francois, 1999). Equally important, the TPRM also provides domestic interest groups with information necessary to determine the costs and benefits of national trade policies. A weakness of the TPR process in this connection is that dissemination of reports is limited. At the time of writing, TPRs are only available in hard copy—they cannot be downloaded from the web. Keesing (1998) reports that typical production runs for the English version of a TPR are 900 to 1000 copies, most of which remain in Geneva. Much more could be done to follow up the

Geneva-based TPR process with dissemination and outreach activities in the WTO members that have been reviewed, especially developing countries. A shortcoming of the reports is that they are not analytical in the sense of determining the economic effects of various national policies—how large are the implied transfers, and who benefits and loses from the prevailing policies. This task is left for national stakeholders to undertake (think tanks, policy institutes). To do it they need to be aware of the reports, and have ready access to the data that underlie the reports.

Numerous WTO bodies have transparency and information exchange functions. Many committees that oversee the functioning of specific agreements review the relevant policies of members at intervals varying between three months and two to three years. Matters of interest to developing countries are discussed in the Committee on Trade and Development. Created in 1965 to oversee a new addendum to the GATT—Part IV, dealing with trade and development, which called on high-income nations to give priority to reducing barriers to exports of developing countries—this committee is the general focal point for developing countries to raise trade concerns. As discussed in chapter 12, after the Uruguay Round was completed, this committee devoted much of its time to a discussion of issues related to implementation of the negotiated agreements. It also is responsible for surveillance of regional integration arrangements between developing countries. Multilateral surveillance of trade restrictions for balance of payments purposes takes place in the Committee on Balance of Payments Restrictions. Traditionally a largely ceremonial undertaking, discussions and decisions taken by this committee became significantly tougher after the establishment of the WTO (see chapter 9). The Textiles Monitoring Body (TMB) is responsible for surveillance of all measures taken under the Uruguay Agreement on Textiles and Clothing (ATC), as well as monitoring compliance with the agreed program to liberalize trade in textiles and clothing (chapter 6).

Although it is often argued by NGOs that one of the major failings of the WTO is a lack of transparency of its operations, great progress has been made on this front in comparison to the GATT 1947 situation. The best illustration is the WTO Internet home page, which provides access to much of the documentation that is prepared by and submitted to the WTO—documents that under GATT procedures were 'restricted' and not made available to the public. But more could be done. Much of the data generated by the WTO is not freely available, significantly reducing the transparency role of the WTO. Examples include the WTO's Integrated Database of protection and trade flows and the detailed data underlying the reports of the TPRM, neither of which can be downloaded from the web. Such outputs produced by the secretariat are public goods that should be distributed free of charge. Policies that restrict access to data on trade policies and trade flows are counterproductive, as this impedes the ability of national think tanks and NGOs to build on TPR reports to analyze the effects of the policies that are documented.

It is a truism that to reduce protection, the groups that are negatively affected need to be aware of the costs of such policies. Determining the incidence of the costs and benefits of trade policies—whether WTO legal or not—is not necessarily a task for the WTO secretariat. The WTO is a negotiating forum in which governments attempt to reach agreement on specific issues. Each government pursues its self-interest. Even if no overt attempts are made to influence the outcome of analyses undertaken by the secretariat, WTO members can be expected to contest the results of analysis that is not to their liking, and secretariat staff may have a natural tendency towards self-censorship. Analysis of the data' reported to—and collected by—the WTO secretariat is more suitably done by outside agencies that can feed analyses of the costs and incidence of protection and related regulatory policies into domestic political markets. The clients for the analysis are not governments, but the constituencies in individual countries who are negatively affected by policy (Finger, 1982). To undertake the requisite analysis it is crucial that the data compilation function of the WTO secretariat be maintained and enhanced and that access to all data and information is made publicly available.

2.4. ACCESSION

Membership of the WTO is open to any State or separate customs territory possessing full autonomy in the conduct of its external commercial relations. Accession terms must be agreed between the applicant and the WTO members (Article XII). Accession normally follows a number of stages, negotiations usually being the final substantive phase. Summarizing, the procedure involved is that the government communicates its desire to join the WTO by writing a letter to this effect to the WTO Director-General. In practice, it will usually have requested observer status before this point. The General Council then establishes a working party consisting of interested countries to examine the application. The government seeking accession must then submit a detailed memorandum describing its trade regime. On the basis of this memorandum, members of the working party will discuss and clarify the functioning of the trade regime with the applicant, usually through specific questions that are based upon the memorandum, focusing in particular on its consistency with multilateral rules. WTO inconsistent measures will have to be removed, or be subjected to negotiated special provisions.

A key aspect of this ostensibly multilateral proceeding is its bilateral component. Accession negotiations are held between the acceding government and all members interested in enhancing their access to the markets of the country seeking membership. As part of the accession process, the newcomer negotiates schedules of tariff concessions and specific commitments on trade in services with interested WTO members. Once market access negotiations have been concluded, the report of the working party is forwarded to the General Council. A draft Decision and Protocol of Accession is attached to the report, as is the negotiated tariff schedule. Accession of a new member must be approved by a two-thirds majority of existing members.

Each WTO member has the right to present specific demands to the applicant country, both with respect to tariff and nontariff issues. Not all WTO members make use of this prerogative—most either play no role or confine themselves to passive participation in the accession working party meetings—but all have the opportunity to seek redress for the alleged shortcomings of the applicant country's trade regime. Some thirty countries were involved in the process of WTO accession during the 1995–2000 period. Applicants included important nations such as Russia, China and China Taipei, as well as numerous former USSR republics, other transition economies, and a number of developing countries. All applicants taken together account for about eight percent of global trade in merchandise, five percent of global GDP and 30 percent of global population (Langhammer and Lücke, 1999).[6]

Until the 1990s, the requirement that the applicant's trade regime conform to GATT law was far from a demand that the newcomer be a paragon of liberal trade virtues. New members were required to comply with a limited set of rules. Negotiations tended to be tempered by pragmatism and flexibility. This changed significantly under the WTO—conditions imposed for accession became much more stringent. Aspirant members of the WTO are likely

---

[6] As of October 2000 the following countries were in the accession queue: Algeria, Andorra, Armenia, Azerbaijan, Belarus, Bhutan, Bosnia and Herzegovina, Cambodia, Cape Verde, People's Republic of China, Former Yugoslav Republic of Macedonia, Kazakhstan, Lao People's Democratic Republic, Lebanon, Moldova, Nepal, Russian Federation, Samoa, Saudi Arabia, Seychelles, Sudan, Chinese Taipei, Tonga, Ukraine, Uzbekistan, Vanuatu, Vietnam and Yemen. All have observer status in the WTO. Observer governments that have not yet applied to join WTO include the Holy See (Vatican) and Ethiopia. During 1995-2000, eleven countries joined the WTO: Ecuador, Bulgaria, Mongolia, Panama, Kyrgystan, Latvia, Estonia, Jordan, Georgia, Albania and Oman (in chronological order).

to be requested to bind their whole tariff schedule at, or close to, applied rates. The country seeking accession will usually also have to liberalize access to its markets much more than was the case in the past. Average applied rates significantly higher than 10 percent are unlikely to be accepted. The conditions imposed on applicant countries are often seen by them as excessively burdensome. Progress in expanding WTO membership has consequently been slow—most accessions take several years. Some, such as Algeria, China, Russia and Saudi Arabia lasted substantially longer—at the time of writing China had been negotiating for over 14 years.

There are several reasons why accession is considerably more burdensome than it used to be under the GATT. First, and most obviously, the coverage of the WTO is substantially more far-reaching than the GATT was. Second, a change occurred in the attitude of major trading powers, especially the United States. Before the end of the Cold War and the collapse of the Soviet Union in the late 1980s, the US was willing to tolerate trade policies that were detrimental to its export interests for the sake of foreign policy objectives. In the 1990s, the pursuit of national economic interests became more dominant (VanGrasstek, 1995). Third, the major trading powers increasingly perceived accession to the WTO as a major step in a country's integration into the world economy and as a way of encouraging the acceding government to abandon interventionist economic policies in favor of more open and market-oriented approaches. That perspective is particularly important in accession negotiations of countries such as China and Russia whose potential economic importance is likely to weigh heavily on the system's prospects in the twenty-first century. In a related vein, there appears to be a tendency to exploit incumbent market power and seek commitments from acceding countries that go beyond the letter of the WTO law. For example, a number of transition economies have been asked to make commitments and report progress on privatization of state-owned enterprises—matters on which the WTO is silent.[7]

The bottom line is that a country that desires to enter the WTO is a *demandeur*. It must negotiate with incumbent club members, and more often than not will have little bargaining power. The accession process is asymmetric—the acceding country cannot negotiate additional benefits in excess of those already embodied in existing WTO agreements, whereas the WTO members may—and do—ask for more than the status quo. Indeed, sometimes applicants are asked to do more than incumbent countries have com-

---

[7] As discussed in chapter 5, ownership of firms is not of concern to WTO members. What matters is their behavior. Members may use state-trading enterprises, but such firms may not use their market power to circumvent tariff bindings and related commitments.

mitted themselves to. An example is tariff bindings, where the current rule of thumb appears to be that bindings should be comprehensive and not be higher than double the average import-weighted average applying in OECD countries (some 10 percent). This compares to an average bound rate of incumbent developing countries of 20 percent or so for those commodities that are bound. As discussed further in chapter 5, many tariff lines remain unbound. Other examples are demands for abolition of agricultural subsidies, more comprehensive service sector commitments than were made in the Uruguay Round, and making accession conditional on complete implementation of required reforms (as opposed to allowing a gradual transition path).

2.5. THE WTO AND OTHER INTERNATIONAL ORGANIZATIONS

Although the WTO can justifiably be regarded as a pillar of the international economic order, there are numerous other international organizations that have an important role to play in fostering multilateral cooperation in the area of trade and international exchange more generally. Major examples are the International Monetary Fund (IMF), the International Bank for Reconstruction and Development (IBRD), the various UN bodies such as UNCTAD, UNDP, the UN Economic Commissions, as well as specialized organizations such as the Bank for International Settlements (BIS), WCO, ITU, WIPO, FAO, and the ILO.

The relationship between GATT 1947 and these organizations was largely informal. The only exception was the IMF: Article XV GATT calls for the CONTRACTING PARTIES to cooperate and consult with the IMF on matters relating to foreign exchange reserves, the balance of payments and exchange rate issues. The IMF had a formal role in the Balance-of-Payments Committee, responsible for conducting consultations with countries imposing balance-of-payments restrictions (see chapters 5 and 9). This state of affairs changed with the creation of the WTO. Article III:5 WTO provides that the WTO is to cooperate with the IMF and the World Bank 'to achieve greater coherence in global economic policy making'. Formal agreements were negotiated between the WTO and the Bank and Fund. These aim at strengthening interagency relations through promotion of cooperation and collaboration. The agreements give the WTO secretariat the right to be present at meetings of the Executive Boards of the Bretton Woods institutions, and grant the Bretton Woods institutions observer status at formal WTO meetings. The staff of the three organizations is frequently in touch at the technical level. Periodic joint meetings are held, and technical assistance efforts are coordinated in the context of the so-called integrated framework for least-developed countries (see chapter 12).[8]

Other international bodies that have close links with the WTO include the International Organization for Standardization (ISO), the Brussels-based World Customs Organization (WCO), the World Intellectual Property Organization (WIPO), the Codex Alimentarius Commission (a subsidiary of the UN's Food and Agriculture Organization—FAO), and the International Office of Epizootics. The WTO cooperates with WIPO (through the TRIPs agreement), the ISO (because of the WTO disciplines on product standards), the ITU (telecommunications, e-commerce), and the WCO (which develops rules of origin and classifications of goods).

GATT 1947 and UNCTAD were frequently looked upon as rival organizations, as the two entities have similar areas of interest, but differed greatly in terms of their functions, operations and underlying ideology. They cooperate in a joint venture, the International Trade Center (ITC)—dating back to 1964—which provides export promotion and marketing assistance and related training and consulting services to developing countries. The WTO cooperates more closely with UNCTAD and the ITC than was the case under the old GATT. Technical assistance missions to explain WTO rules and agreements are frequently joint ventures. UNCTAD also provides services that are complementary to the WTO, including activities aimed at strengthening negotiation capacity of developing countries—complemented by research capacity-building efforts of the World Bank and other organizations—and technical assistance in the area of trade facilitation and customs procedures.

2.6. NONGOVERNMENTAL ACTORS AND THE WTO

The WTO is an inter-governmental organization. Only government representatives have legal standing. The private sector and NGOs do not have direct access to WTO meetings and negotiating fora. If such groups have concerns or desires that they would like to see addressed, they must convince their governments to take up the issue. Given that the WTO is a trade organization, it should be no surprise that the interest groups that have historically been listened to most by governments are firms and industry associations. As discussed earlier, the main players on the domestic political front are import-competing and export-oriented industries. In contrast to

---

[8] Chapter 14 briefly discusses the topic of coherence of international policy making.

organizations such as the OECD, where business groups have observer status and participate in some meetings, or the ILO, which has a tripartite governing structure—employer groups, labor unions and governments—the WTO has not allowed nongovernmental entities to participate in its work. Interaction with nongovernmental organizations (NGOs) has been limited to organizations that are directly concerned with issues that are addressed by the WTO. The first formal arrangements for cooperation were concluded with the International Federation of Inspection Agencies (IFIA), in connection with preshipment inspection.

Numerous NGOs, especially those representing environmental lobbies and labor groups have become very active in national and international debates on the WTO. They are particularly interested in enhancing their access to the dispute settlement process and WTO meetings more generally. Their concerns relate in part to transparency of process, and a perception that governments have 'sold out' to multinational business, seeking to conclude agreements that are detrimental to the environment and to workers (Box 2.3). Some would argue that these concerns are totally inappropriate given that the WTO is probably the most democratic international organization extant, in that it operates by consensus and, if voting occurs, it is on the basis of one-member one-vote. Others argue that there are valid concerns relating to the perceived legitimacy of the WTO, and that without action to bring the critics on board and address their worries, the WTO will find it difficult to pursue its mandate—liberalization of trade.

Box 2.3. The International Chamber of Commerce and the WTO
Although the WTO is an intergovernmental agreement, the major 'users' of the trading system are the companies that conduct international business transactions. Does business have privileged access to the WTO? Formally, the answer is no. Thus, the International Chamber of Commerce (ICC), a Paris-based nongovernmental organization linking thousands of companies and business associations around the globe, does not get special treatment relative to other types of NGOs. However, the ICC is an active player in providing a business view on issues its members would like to see addressed by the WTO. The ICC has called for less diverse, complex and opaque rules of origin, modernized and simplified customs procedures and actions to combat extortion and bribery in international business. The ICC favors the establishment of a global WTO framework of rules governing cross-border direct investment, greater disciplines on subsidies (especially in relation to state-owned enterprises) and expanded membership of the WTO plurilateral agreement on government procurement. It has also called for lower customs tariffs, and liberalization of trade in financial services, basic telecommuni-

cations, maritime transport and professional services. The international business community would also welcome more liberal policies towards the cross-border movement of professional, technical and managerial personnel.

The ICC periodically prepares and distributes position papers on such trade policy issues and meets with WTO delegations in Geneva. The Chamber is accredited as a NGO at WTO ministerial meetings and its documents and position papers were posted on the WTO web page during the Seattle ministerial, along with documentation submitted by other NGOs.

Matters such as environment and labor standards, food safety regulation, intellectual property, consumer protection, business ethics and corruption are all issues that concern the citizens of many WTO members. Numerous pressure groups and political organizations in the United States, EU and elsewhere want to include labor and environment into future trade talks and demand that new trade deals contain a 'social clause'. There is an obvious temptation to use the WTO system as an instrument to enforce norms and rules in such nontrade areas. Some of these issues, especially when worded along the lines of 'thou shall adopt my norms' are clearly zero-sum, but many are not.

In principle, encouraging greater participation of single-issue NGOs, the business community and consumer protection groups in debates on the future WTO agenda would be useful to ensure new inflow of ideas and the maintenance of the communication channels with various pressure groups. The challenge of achieving this in a balanced fashion is nontrivial. A distinction needs to be made between enhancing the two-way flow of information, opportunities to observe or voice views at meetings, and giving nongovernmental bodies a seat at the negotiating or decision-making table. The fact that the WTO is an inter-governmental organization in which only governments have standing makes the latter impossible. But it may prove feasible to encourage greater involvement of business organizations and NGOs in the daily operations of the WTO by allowing entities that satisfy certain standards of representativeness to observe meetings of committees and the Council, and to submit briefs to these bodies.

A step in this direction was made by the Appellate Body by deciding to accept amicus briefs by NGOs (see chapter 3 and WTO DS/138). Many WTO members, especially developing countries, object strongly to these decisions, which gave rise to repeated criticisms in the debate in the WTO Dispute Settlement Body on these reports. However, given the negative consensus rule that prevails in the WTO regarding panel and Appellate Body reports, there is little that can be done by members absent a general re-negotiation of the rules in this area.

2.7. CONCLUSION

The WTO grew out of the GATT 1947, which successfully developed and oversaw global trading rules in the period after the Second World War. The creation of the WTO can be seen as the fulfillment of the vision of the participants at the Bretton Woods conference in 1944, albeit half a century later. Although the WTO is very similar to the old GATT in terms of day-to-day operations and general approach, it is less 'diplomatic' and more 'legalistic' than the GATT was. This is perhaps best illustrated by the great expansion in the coverage of its disciplines, the associated increase in dispute settlement cases, and the large number of formal notification requirements. The long accession queue and the intense interest in the operation of the system that can be observed on the part of NGOs, labor unions and business illustrate the importance that is accorded to the institution by civil society. Much of this interest (and concern) is sparked by the WTO's dispute settlement procedures, by the mechanics of the negotiating process that generate the rules of the game, and by the rules of the game themselves. These are the subject of subsequent chapters.

2.8. FURTHER READING

For an influential contemporary discussion of the design of a successor organization to the GATT 1947, see John H. Jackson, *Restructuring the GATT System* (London: Pinter Publishers, 1990). Major players in the Uruguay Round negotiations give their views on the dynamics and process in Jagdish Bhagwati and Mathias Hirsch (eds.), *The Uruguay Round and Beyond: Essays in Honor of Arthur Dunkel* (Ann Arbor: University of Michigan Press, 1998). An informative history of the Uruguay Round negotiations is presented in John Croome, *Reshaping the Trading System* (Deventer: Kluwer, 1999). For an analysis of the WTO as a network oganization see Richard Blackhurst, 'The Capacity of the WTO to Fulfil Its Mandate', in A. Krueger (ed.),*The WTO as an International Organization* (Chicago, University of Chicago Press, 1998). Michael Trebilcock and Robert Howse, *The Regulation of International Trade* (London: Routledge, 1998) is a comprehensive treatment of WTO rules. They also compare WTO disciplines with those that apply in the EU and NAFTA.

Official GATT and WTO documents are periodically published by the secretariat in a series called *Basic Instruments and Selected Documents*. Most documents can be downloaded from the WTO home page, www.wto.org. The WTO publishes an informative bimonthly newsletter called *WTO Focus* that reports on major developments in WTO fora. The WTO web site also offers general information and training material. The WTO Annual Report provides an overview of major developments in trade, trade policy and WTO activities, as well as basic statistics on trade flows and trends. The Trade Policy Reviews published by the WTO secretariat provide a valuable source of information on the trade and related policies maintained by individual WTO members. Many of the TPRs are reviewed each year in a special issue of the journal *The World Economy* entitled 'Global Trade Policy'.

3
Dispute Settlement and Enforcement of Rules

The effective resolution of trade disputes is vital for the smooth functioning of the trading system. The dispute resolution mechanism of the WTO is a unique feature of the institution. Dispute settlement procedures are formal and binding. Most international organizations rely on diplomatic means to resolve disputes. Diplomatic procedures can be uncertain and inconsistent, given that power discrepancies between states often will play a major role in determining the outcome. An effective multilateral dispute resolution procedure is particularly important for small states. Such countries cannot enforce agreements themselves. They also would find it difficult, if not impossible, to oppose the unilateral actions by large traders that would arise in the absence of multilateral dispute settlement mechanisms.

3.1. THE WTO DISPUTE SETTLEMENT PROCEDURES

Dispute settlement under the GATT was based on the consensus principle. This ensured that both parties to a dispute had to agree on the outcome, increasing the likelihood of implementation. It also created opportunities for parties to a dispute to block either the initiation or the completion of the process. This could be achieved through refusal of one of the parties to a dispute to agree to the formation of a panel, delay the appointment of a panel, or refuse to adopt the panel report. In the 1980s and early 1990s, a growing number of fractious trade disputes that could not be resolved gave rise to concerns regarding the effectiveness of dispute settlement procedures. These disputes reflected the intensification of competition resulting from changing patterns of comparative advantage and vaguely worded GATT provisions and differences in their interpretation (subsidies, agriculture). A number of the disputes that were brought to the GATT in the 1980s were essentially attempts by contracting parties to more clearly define GATT provisions—they substituted for negotiations. It is therefore not surprising that they were controversial.

In practice, contracting parties did not employ blocking tactics extensively. The conventional wisdom is that the GATT dispute mechanism worked much better than was generally recognized. Of some 278 complaints considered under general dispute settlement provisions between 1948 and 1994, 110 led to legal rulings by panels, the others being settled before a report was produced. Of the 88 cases where the panel found a violation had occurred, the majority were adopted. Moreover, many of those not adopted did lead to a satisfactory outcome. Hudec (1993) has concluded that overall, over the life of the GATT 1947, the success rate of cases addressed by GATT—that is, disputes settled—was well over 90 percent. After 1980, the rate of nonadoption increased significantly, reflecting the fact that many of the contested issues were in areas where the rules were not clear or that were the subject of ongoing negotiations during the Uruguay Round (Hudec, 2000).

What explains the success of a system that could so easily be blocked? One important reason is self-interest. Losing parties knew that that at some point in the future they would bring cases. If they were to engage in blocking of disputes where the rules are clear, this would greatly reduce the value of ne-gotiated commitments. The GATT (and the WTO) is a repeated game (see chapter 4)—parties know they will interact over an indefinite time horizon. As noted by Hudec (2000), othere factors were that GATT contracting parties 'owned' the agreements and that the disciplines of the GATT generally made good economic sense. In most cases, there were officials and stakeholders in countries losing cases that had an interest in enforcing GATT rules because this ensured that more efficient instruments of trade policy were used.

Disputes usually involve one of the major trading nations as a party. The dispute settlement procedures (DSP) may be initiated whenever a member believes that an action by another member has 'nullified or impaired' a con-cession that was negotiated previously (such as a tariff binding) or breaks a WTO rule and 'impairs the attainment of an objective' of the WTO. As under the GATT 1947, complaints may take three forms (Article XXIII GATT). The first is a violation complaint, which consists of a claim that one or more WTO disciplines or negotiated commitments have been violated. Second, members may argue that although no specific WTO rules are violated, a gov-ernment measure nonetheless nullifies a previously granted concession (Ar-ticle XXIII:1*b*). To bring such a 'nonviolation' complaint the measure must be applied by a government, alter the competitive conditions established in a previous negotiation, and be unexpected (in the sense that it could not have been reasonably anticipated at the time the concessions were negotiated). The third possibility is a so-called situation complaint, under which a mem-ber may argue that 'any other situation' not captured by the violation or nonviolation options has led to nullification or impairment of a negotiated benefit.

Nonviolation cases are potentially important to the functioning of the system as they provide a way for members to raise issues that are not cov-ered by the rules but have adverse effects on a government. Countries such as the US have a tradition of using unilateral trade actions to defend their commercial interests in such cases. Section 301 of the Trade Act of 1974, as amended, allows (and sometimes requires) the US Government to take uni-lateral retaliatory actions against alleged unfair trading practices of partner countries. However, in principle, nonviolation (Article XXIII:*b*) is the WTO instrument to pursue such cases. The use of WTO dispute settlement mechanisms is that its use is mandatory in instances where a dispute concerns matters on which agreements have been concluded. A member may use unilateral instruments to initiate consultations, but if it decides to pursue the case in must first submit the case to the WTO (Article 23.2 DSU). Only if a member does not comply with the rulings of a panel and the WTO authorizes retaliation may instruments such as Section 301 be used to retaliate. Even then, the magnitude of the retaliatory measures that may be imposed must first be determined by the WTO.

Disputes arising under any WTO agreement are dealt with by the Dispute Settlement Body (DSB), which has the authority to establish panels, adopt panel reports, scrutinize implementation of recommendations and authorize retaliatory measures if the losing party to a dispute does not abide by the panel's recommendations. The DSB is essentially the WTO Council—it simply changes name when it considers disputes. The rules of the game are laid out in the Uruguay Round Dispute Settlement Understanding (DSU). The DSU covers all disputes arising under WTO agreements, that is, relating to trade in goods, services and intellectual property. The same procedures are used for settling disputes across all issues—there is a unified dispute-settlement mechanism. However, some of the specific Uruguay Round agreements discussed in chapter 5 contain special dispute settlement provisions. If these procedures differ from the general WTO provisions, the special procedures apply.

Box 3.1. Settlement of disputes

Stage I: Consultations and mediation (Article 4 DSU). Members must initially attempt to solve their disputes through bilateral consultations. The good offices, conciliation or mediation by the WTO Director-General may also be sought, although this is optional. The goal of the consultation stage is to enable the disputing parties to understand the factual situation and the legal claims and hopefully to settle the matter bilaterally.

Stage II: Request for a panel. If parties are not able to secure a solution to their dispute through consultations within 60 days, the establishment of a panel may be requested. The DSB establishes a panel, drafts terms of reference and determines its composition. Drawing on a large roster of potential panelists (who have all been nominated by WTO members), the WTO secretariat suggests the names of three or four potential panelists to the parties to the dispute. Parties have the right to object to a proposed panelist. Panelists serve in their individual capacity, may not be subjected to government instructions, and tend to be members of delegations or retired civil servants knowledgeable in trade matters. They may also include academic scholars. The WTO secretariat provides administrative support and generally prepares the background documentation regarding the facts of the case.

Stage III: The panel at work. The panel usually goes through the following steps: (1) examination of facts and arguments; (2) meetings with the parties and interested third parties; (3) interim review—descriptive and interim reports are sent to the parties, who may request a review meeting with the panel; (4) drafting of conclusions and recommendations; and (5) panel report issued to the parties and circulated to the DSB.

Stage IV: Adoption decision or appeal. The panel report must be adopted by the DSB within 60 days, unless a consensus exists not to adopt, or a party appeals the findings of the panel. Appeals are limited to issues of law or the legal interpretation developed by the panel. An Appellate Body, composed of seven persons who are broadly representative of the WTO's membership, deals with such appeals. In principle, appeal proceedings should not exceed 60 days and must be completed within 90 days. The Appellate Body report is final and is adopted by the DSB.

Stage V: Implementation. If it is impracticable to comply immediately, the offending country is given a 'reasonable period of time' to do so (Article 21.3 DSU). The length of this period can, at the request of the parties, be determined through binding arbitration. If the respondent fails to act within this period, parties are to negotiate compensation pending full implementation (Article 22.2 DSU). If this cannot be agreed, the complainant may request authorization from the DSB to suspend equivalent concessions against the offending country (that is, to retaliate). This authorization is automatic as a consensus is required to refuse it. The magnitude of the retaliation is determined by the DSB, generally on the recommendation of the original panel. Arbitration may be sought on the level of suspension, the procedures and principles of retaliation (Article 22.6).

If there is disagreement whether the respondent has brought its measures into compliance, recourse is to be made to the dispute settlement procedures, that is, the process starts again, using where possible the original panel (Article 21.5). As discussed below, this provision played a prominent role in a number of key cases brought to the WTO after 1995.

Compared to the GATT 1947, dispute settlement under the WTO was strengthened by eliminating the possibility of blocking the establishment of a panel or the adoption of panel reports, introducing time limits for the various stages of panel proceedings, standard terms of reference for panels, creation of an appeals process, improved surveillance of the implementation of panel reports, and automaticity of approval for retaliation in cases of noncompliance with a panel recommendation. Under the WTO, adoption of panel reports can only be blocked by a 'negative consensus', that is, all WTO members must agree that the panel report is fundamentally flawed, a highly improbable event. To counter balance the removal of the blocking option for losing parties, Uruguay Round negotiators created a new standing Appellate Body. This entity can be asked to consider challenges regarding the legal interpretations developed by a panel. Box 3.1 summarizes the various stages involved in settling disputes.

3.2. OPERATION OF THE SYSTEM

Many considered that the strengthening of GATT dispute settlement procedures (DSP) was one of the major results of the Uruguay Round—especially for developing countries. The expectation was that small players would have greater incentives to bring cases (Whalley, 1996; Schott and Buurman, 1994; Croome, 1999). The use of DSP would appear to support the optimistic expectations. Over 160 requests for consultations were brought to the WTO in its first five years of operation; three times more on a per annum basis than under the GATT. Developing countries are more often involved than in the past—over 30 percent of all cases were brought by or against developing countries. Some developing countries successfully contested actions by large players (examples included some of the first cases brought to the WTO: a Costa Rican claim against US restrictions on cotton textiles and a case brought by Venezuela and Brazil contesting US gasoline regulations). Developing countries increasingly also use DSP to contest each other's policies. Disputes between developing countries giving rise to requests for consultations and panels span all regions. Examples have included Brazil—Philippines (desiccated coconut); Guatemala—Mexico (antidumping actions on cement), India—Turkey (textiles), Indonesia—Argentina (safeguards for footwear), and India—South Africa (antidumping duties on pharmaceuticals), Colombia—Nicaragua (import charges), Costa Rica—Trinidad and Tobago (antidumping on spaghetti), and Thailand—Turkey (textiles).[1] However, least developed countries were not involved in DSP at all in the 1995-2000 period (Table 3.1).

---

[1] The WTO home page (www.wto.org) provides a complete listing of all cases and panel reports issued, if any. Some of the cases discussed in this chapter are ongoing. Interested readers may consult the WTO site to see how these cases were resolved.

TABLE 3.1 *Users of Dispute Settlement (April 1994–March 1999)*

Number of disputes as complainant		Number of disputes as respondent	
United States	54	United States	30
EC	43	EC	26
Canada	13	Japan	12
India	8	India	12
Mexico	7	Korea	10
Japan (7) Brazil (6) Thailand (4) New Zealand (4) Honduras (3) Guatemala (3) Switzerland (3) Argentina (2) Hungary (2) Austria (2) Chile (2) Philippines (2) Panama (2) Korea (2)		Canada (9) Brazil (8) Argentina (8) Australia (6) Indonesia (4) Turkey (4) Mexico (3) Chile (3) Ireland (3) Guatemala (2) Slovak Republic (2) Belgium (2) Hungary (2) Greece (2) Pakistan (2) Philippines (2)	
Memo items:			
Quad total	118	Quad total	90
Other OECD	22	Other OECD	27
Developing-Transition	43	Developing-Transition	47
Least Developed	0	Least Developed	0
Grand total	183	Grand total	164

Note: Number of cases in parentheses. Countries that were involved in only one case are not reported. Compilation excludes third parties.
Source: Horn, Nordström and Mavroidis (1999).

The more frequent use of the DSP reflects the great expansion in the coverage of multilateral disciplines and the larger membership of the WTO. Many of the claims that were brought to the WTO in its first five years of operation could not have been brought under GATT as they dealt with sectors where new disciplines were negotiated in the Uruguay Round (agriculture, textiles and clothing or IPRs). More cases by developing countries— often relating to the use of antidumping and safeguards—are also a factor. By far the largest share of cases involve allegations that the principles of non-discrimination have been violated (MFN or national treatment). About half of all cases involve one or both of these rules. Violation of the prohibition on use of QRs follow closely behind (Figure 3.1).

Most observers agree that notwithstanding some significant flaws—discussed below—the DSU works quite well. Most cases are settled bilaterally or are resolved with the losing party implementing the panel or Appellate Body report. The Appellate Body has often corrected aspects of the panel's reasoning—revealing the need for an appeals process—but reversed the findings of the panel relatively infrequently. Of the 31 cases in which panel findings were appealed during 1995–2000, the reasoning and some aspect of the conclusions of the panel were corrected in about half of the cases. Over time, the tendency to reverse panel decision has diminished due to the fact that panels have more jurisprudence at their disposal to base decisions on.

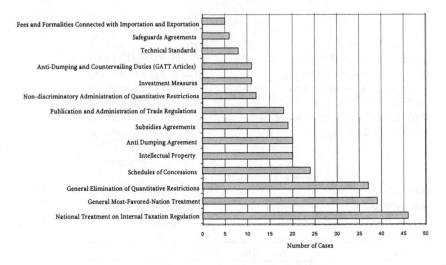

Source: Compiled from the WTO home page. Based on 180 cases, 1995-9.

FIG. 3.1   Major issues in the WTO Dispute Settlement

Major problems that emerged pertained to implementation of DSB rulings and attempts to use the process to address issues where countries have strongly diverging regulatory regimes, especially in the area of public health and safety. Implementation problems were a recurring problem in high-profile cases such as *Bananas*, and revealed a major weakness in the provisions of the DSU. Cases involving regulatory differences also illustrated the existence of implementation-related weaknesses, in particular an excessive reliance on retaliation as the instrument of dealing with situations where a losing party cannot implement the recommendations of the panel because of political constraints. What follows discusses a number of major cases that illustrate the problems that emerged. These involved the EU import regime for bananas, a EU ban on the use of hormones in beef, and a nonviolation dispute between the US and Japan over the Japanese distribution system for film. The latter two cases illustrate the challenge of dealing with domestic regulatory regimes, the topic of chapter 13.

The EU import regime for bananas has long been a bone of contention. In effect, the EU maintains a system that gives preferential access to its market for bananas produced by Africa, Caribbean and Pacific (ACP) countries. As a result Caribbean producers have always had a substantial share of the EU market, to the detriment of Central and South American countries. Preferences for bananas in the EU are long standing. They caused problems between France and Germany during the negotiations leading to the creation of the EEC in 1957—Germany had a free trade regime for bananas and imported from Latin American countries, while France maintained very high barriers to support domestic producers (Messerlin, 2001). These differences led to the imposition of national intra-EU trade barriers, reserving the UK, French and Spanish markets for ex-colonies. The policies were a very inefficient means of assisting ex-colonies—every dollar transferred cost EU consumers $5, of which $3 went to distributors and $1 was wasted (Borrell, 1996).

In 1993, the EU adopted a complex import licensing and distribution system for the EU as a whole, as part of its effort to create a single market. The common market organization that was imposed was based on historical trading relationships, and was designed to continue to provide preferential access for ACP countries (signatories of the Lomé Convention). It involved two tariff quotas (one for traditional ACP suppliers and one for nontraditional ACP and Latin American growers) and four categories of suppliers. Out-of-quota imports were subject to high specific tariffs. Operators traditionally exporting bananas from former British and French Caribbean colonies were granted 30 percent of all import licenses for non-country-specific quotas. These licenses could be used to import ACP bananas or could be sold to firms desiring to import from Latin America. In the latter case, which often occurred, the quota allocation system resulted in a transfer of rents from the (mostly US-based) firms buying the licenses to those granted the quota rights. Borrell (1996) estimated that the new regime was worse than the national ones it replaced: total costs to EU consumers were some $2 billion, while ACP suppliers obtained $150 million—a cost per consumer of over $13 for each dollar transferred.

Latin American producers brought two cases to the GATT contesting the national systems (1992) and the new common EU regime (1993). They won both. The EU concluded a Banana Framework Agreement with four countries (Costa Rica, Colombia, Nicaragua and Venezuela) in 1994 under which they were allocated specific quotas with the understanding that they would not bring a case to the WTO before 2002. In 1996, four Latin American producers left out of this agreement (Ecuador, Guatemala, Honduras, and Mexico), joined by the United States on behalf of US multinational fruit firms, contested the EU import regime in the WTO (see Box 3.2). The EU lost again. Failure to comply with the DSB ruling eventually led to the imposition of retaliatory measures by the US. The US retaliation included a provision allowing for a so-called 'carousel approach' under which a different set of exports from the EU were to be subjected to retaliatory tariffs of up to 100 percent in each six month period. This procedure was designed to maximize the political 'pain' of the retaliation. In this it was successful—as illustrated by lobbying by the UK cashmere wool products industry against the threatened imposition of tariffs on their goods (*Financial Times*, August 26, 2000: 5). In late 2000, US officials indicated that it was unlikely that the US would apply the carousel provision (*Bridges*, November 2000).

Box 3.2. The Bananas Case in the WTO

In 1996, Ecuador, Guatemala. Honduras, Mexico, and the US contested the new EU banana regime at the WTO, claiming it discriminated against their producers and banana marketing companies. The object of attack was not so much the tariff preferences that were granted to ACP countries—for which the EU had obtained a waiver—but the allocation of quotas. The WTO panel report, published in June 1997, found the EU banana import regime in violation of WTO nondiscrimination and market access rules. The dual tariff rate quota regime was found inconsistent with GATT Article XIII (requiring nondiscriminationin allocation of QRs), and the 30 percent allocation of import licenses to traditional sellers of ACP bananas was inconsistent with GATS nondiscrimination rules. On appeal, the Appellate Body endorsed most of the panel's conclusions.

During 1998 the EU revised its regime. It continued to maintain two tariff rate quotas, but assigned import quotas for non-ACP bananas on the basis of historical market shares and abolished the operator categories for allocation of licenses. Consultations regarding the WTO-consistency of the new measures were inconclusive. Just before the January 1999 deadline for implementation, the US sought authorization to retaliate. To this the EU responded that the US should first obtain a panel finding that the new mechanism did not conform to WTO rules something Ecuador then requested. The DSB reconvened the original panel to examine both requests. Concurrently, the US sought authorization from the DSB to retaliate against the EU in the amount of US$520 million, to which the EU responded with a request for arbitration.

Responding to Ecuador, the panel found that the new EU measures were not fully compatible with the WTO. The same panel determined the level of nullification suffered by the US to be equivalent to US$191.4 million. The US subsequently was authorized to raise duties against the EU by that amount. Towards the end of 1999, Ecuador also sought and obtained authorization to retaliate. The Ecuadorian request was a multiple first in the history of the trading system: the first request for retaliation by a developing country, and the first time approval for cross-retaliation was sought. Ecuador argued that its merchandise imports from the EU were too small to allow full retaliation (set at $200 million by the arbitrators) to occur against imports of EU goods.

It obtained authorization to suspend concessions under other agreements, including TRIPs, after having exhausted the possibilities for retaliating against imports of EU consumer goods (the panel concluded that retaliation against imports of intermediates and machinery would be 'ineffective'—that is, too costly for the economy). This use of cross-retaliation was not foreseen by negotiators in the Uruguay Round, who had envisaged the need for cross-retaliation as an instrument to enforce the TRIPs agreement (developing countries not being major exporters of intellectual property intensive goods), not as a vehicle for developing country retaliation.

At the time of writing, Ecuador had not implemented retaliatory actions and negotiations continued. In October 2000 the EU proposed a system of 3 tariff quotas, to be allocated on a first-come-first-served basis, with the adoption of a tariff-only regime by 2006. Latin countries objected to the move away from historical market shares, while the US objected to the tariff quota for ACP bananas.

Source: WTO (www.wto.org), Porges (2000) and Messerlin (2001).

The *Bananas* case illustrated that disagreements between parties on the adequacy of implementing measures have the potential to give rise to a recurring series of panels dealing with essentially the same issue. It also revealed the weakness of the ultimate enforcement threat that is available. Retaliation by Ecuador is unlikely to induce the EU to change its policies—Latin American countries are essentially dependent on the US retaliation. In many cases, however, the US will not be a party to a dispute. And even if it is, the *Bananas* case revealed that US retaliation is not sufficient to bring disputes to closure.

Another interesting case with systemic implications concerned the use of hormones in beef. US beef producers use hormones to accelerate the growth of cattle. Six specific hormones, some or all of which are used in North America, are prohibited in the EU. US producers have used hormones for decades, in quantities that have been deemed safe for human consumption by the US authorities. In April 1996, the US requested the establishment of a panel (Canada followed suit with a case of its own). Both argued that the EU prohibition on the use of hormones restricted exports of meat, and was inconsistent with, among other things, the provisions of the WTO agreement on sanitary and phytosanitary measures (SPS—see chapter 5). A panel found that the EU ban was inconsistent with requirements that members base their sanitary measures on international standards (Article 3.1 of the SPS agreement), have a scientific justification for using national norms (Article 3.3 SPS), use risk assessment procedures that take into account techniques developed by the relevant international organizations (Article 5.1 SPS) and avoid the use of arbitrary or unjustifiable distinctions which result in discrimination or a disguised restriction on international trade (Article 5.5 SPS).

The Appellate Body upheld the panel's finding that the EU import prohibition was inconsistent with Articles 3.3 and 5.1 of the SPS agreement, but reversed the finding that the import prohibition was inconsistent with Articles 3.1 and 5.5. It also reversed the burden of proof in disputes under the SPS agreement, finding that it is up to the complainant to demonstrate that there is no scientific basis for a measure (as opposed to forcing the respondent to demonstrate the scientific basis for its regime). In this case, as in others, the Appellate Body revealed that it is more inclined to allow governments to argue that measures are justified to meet national objectives than panels are.

The time period for implementation was set at 15 months through arbitration. Just before the expiration of this period, the EU informed the DSB that it was unable to comply. Political constraints reflecting a strong lobby in the EU that opposed the use of hormones in meat production made it impossible. In June 1999, the complainants sought authorization from the DSB to retaliate on imports worth US$202 million and C$75 million, respectively. The EU requested arbitration on this, and the original panel subsequently determined the appropriate levels to be US$116.8 million, and C$11.3 million, respectively. The DSB authorized retaliation in these amounts.

The *Hormones* case is an example of the types of disputes that can be expected to become more frequent in the future, that is, cases dealing with differences in regulatory regimes and attitudes towards risk. It is also interesting in that there is widespread agreement that hormones are not a health risk. In that sense the case was an easy one—there is a virtual scientific consensus on the science aspects.[2] Although a case can be made that the EU ban could be justified through invocation of the precautionary principle (under the SPS agreement), the primary reason that hormones are prohibited in the EU has little to do with public safety and much to do with EU agricultural policy. The EU does not desire farmers to use techniques that expand output and increase the cost of the common agricultural policy (Messerlin, 2001). Implementation difficulties and interpretation of agreements pertaining to regulatory regimes are likely to be much more difficult and controversial once cases relating to use of GMOs arrive at the WTO, as there is much less agreement on how to assess the risks.

---

[2] However, in May 2000, the EU notified the WTO that it had obtained evidence that one of the hormones was dangerous for human health.

Nonviolation disputes

Nonviolation disputes are a potentially important avenue for countries to contest WTO legal measures that have serious adverse consequences for their economies. Nonviolation allows such cases to be brought up, and can act as a valuable 'discovery' device. Special provisions on remedies in cases of nonviolation complaints are included in the WTO. Given that by definition the measure that is the subject of complaint is WTO legal, a member cannot be required to change it. The most that can be expected is compensation in another area. Article 26 of the DSU states that:

> where a measure has been found to nullify or impair benefits under, or impede the attainment of objectives, of the relevant covered agreement without violation thereof, there is no obligation to withdraw the measure. However, in such cases, the panel or the Appellate Body shall recommend that the member concerned make a mutually satisfactory adjustment ... compensation may be part of a mutually satisfactory adjustment as final settlement of the dispute.

Under the GATT, nonviolation cases were largely restricted to subsidy-related cases, reflecting the weakness of GATT rules on subsidies. In 1996 the US brought a major case against Japan. This so-called *Kodak-Fuji* case illustrated that government measures, including competition policy actions that are claimed to foster anticompetitive behavior, can in principle be challenged at the WTO—as was originally argued by Hoekman and Mavroidis (1994)—and that nonviolation cases can be used as a transparency device. The panel and the parties generated an immense amount of data and information, much of which helped Japan support its case that there was nothing special about the Japanese film market (Box 3.3).

Another case with a nonviolation dimension that was brought to the WTO concerned asbestos. In December 1996, the French government banned the manufacture and sale of asbestos as a health measure. Canada contested the import ban as a violation of the Agreement on Technical Barriers to Trade (because it was not based on international standards), and a violation of the GATT prohibition on quotas (see chapter 5). Canada also asked the panel to consider the measures under the non-violation provision of the WTO if the panel concluded that no violation had occurred. France (the EU) justified the import ban under Article XX*b* GATT, which allows for import restrictions if necessary to protect human health (see chapter 9), and asked the panel to reject the applicability of non-violation as the measure in question was subject to WTO rules. The panel concluded that there was a violation of Article III GATT in that there was discriminatory treatment of chrysotile fiber products exported by Canada but that this was justified under Article XX GATT. Most relevant for this section, the panel concluded that in principle a non-violation case could be brought under GATT—the panel rejected the EU argument that non-violation cases could only pertain to measures that do not fall under the WTO. But it rejected Canada's non-violation petition, arguing that Canada had not established that it suffered non-violation nullification or impairment of a benefit within the meaning of Article XXIII:1*b*.

Box 3.3. The Kodak-Fuji case and Article XXIII nonviolation disputes

The US has argued for many years that Japanese corporate groups (*Keiretsu*) undermine market access for foreign suppliers by buying predominantly from each other and retaining close vertical linkages between manufacturers, wholesalers and retailers. Kodak, for example, claimed that its access to the Japanese film market was made harder by Fuji's control of film wholesalers. In 1996 the US requested consultations with Japan concerning Japan's laws, regulations and requirements affecting the distribution and sale of imported consumer photographic film and paper. The US claimed that Japanese government measures resulted in less favorable treatment of imported film and paper (a violation of national treatment), were inconsistent with GATT transparency requirements, and nullified and impaired benefits accruing to the US (a nonviolation claim).

A panel was established in October 1996. It found that the US had not demonstrated that the Japanese measures nullified or impaired, either individually or collectively, benefits accruing to the US within the meaning of GATT Article XXIII:1*b*, that the Japanese distribution measures accorded less favorable treatment to imported photographic film and paper, or that Japan had failed to publish administrative rulings of general application in violation of GATT transparency requirements (Article X:1). The panel report was adopted by the DSB on April 22, 1998. It was not appealed.

The panel's decision (over 500 pages long) is very detailed. The panel agreed to treat all the measures attacked by the US (a victory for the US), including decisions of the Japanese competition authorities (the Fair Trade Commission), as possible grounds for complaint. However, the panel noted that the US was only entitled to contest Japanese government measures and not market structures that might have arisen from them. On examining the facts, it concluded that the measures did not reduce market access. Thus, there was no nullification or impairment. The panel did not see anything in Japanese distribution structures that excluded foreigners as a result of public policy, even on a wide interpretation of this term. In particular they concluded that single-brand wholesale distribution is the common market structure—indeed the norm—in major national film markets, including the US.

Kodak had cited a series of government measures including the publication of reports (whose status as government policy measures was open to dispute). The practices complained of included allegations of informal administrative guidance and industrial policy tools that were applied by Japanese firms themselves and served to nullify the opening up of the Japanese film market to outsiders. There were also a number of guidelines on what constituted fair and unfair competition that allegedly deprived Kodak of marketing tools that were of special importance to it as an outsider. Kodak charged that Fuji had a stranglehold on the distribution system that excluded its access to film wholesaling networks, forcing Kodak to sell directly to retailers. A key allegation was therefore the existence of an anticompetitive vertical relationship between Fuji and its primary distributors. Japan replied that Fuji's control of wholesale networks was irrelevant since most of the retailers they served also bought imported film and that Kodak's own distribution system amounted to the creation of a wholesale system of its own.

Source: WTO (www.wto.org) and Holmes (1998).

3.3. SYSTEMIC ISSUES

WTO dispute settlement procedures have a number of characteristics, five of which are worth highlighting: only governments have standing, compensation for damages is customarily not requested or awarded, the ability to enforce rulings is very asymmetric, the costs of the process can be significant, and many cases are settled bilaterally.

Governments as filters

Export industries must petition their governments to bring cases to the WTO—first bilaterally through consultations, then to a panel. Only governments have legal standing to bring cases to the WTO. Thus, export interests must operate through a government filter. If there is a high probability that the government will not be willing to bring the dispute to the WTO, cases may not be brought forward. Governments may not want to bring cases to the WTO for fear of stimulating counter claims (the 'glass house' syndrome). Developing country governments may be unwilling to bring cases if they fear this will have detrimental consequences in nontrade areas (for example, continued aid flows or defense cooperation). It is of course a legitimate function of government to determine priorities and to make the tradeoffs it deems most beneficial for the nation as a whole. Nonetheless, concerns that bringing a case would disturb a country's relationship with a major trading partner to some extent nullifies the rationale for the WTO—the establishment of a rule-based as opposed to a power-based system of trade relations.

One option to address this potential problem is to give exporters direct access to the WTO. Levy and Srinivasan (1996) develop a simple model that explores the possible consequences of such 'privatization', and conclude that this is a bad idea. They show that if a government maximizes national welfare it may have good reasons not to pursue a trade case because the expected national return is negative (due to issue linkage by the partner). Removing a government's discretion to decide whether to prosecute a case can also make it more difficult to make commitments in trade negotiations. The Levy and Srinivasan analysis illustrates the importance of full information—governments must be able to determine as accurately as possible what the cost to the economy is of not prosecuting a case. Domestic consultation and transparency mechanisms are required to ensure that the appropriate trade-offs are made. Their analysis also suggests there is value in seeking to create multilateral mechanisms that reduce the burden on individual countries of identifying and contesting WTO violations.

Remedies

A government found to be in violation of the WTO is generally told to bring its measures into compliance with the rules. How to do this is left to the discretion of the losing party. The most panels can do is to make specific suggestions regarding the way a losing party can bring its measures into conformity if they are requested to do so. The *Bananas* case illustrated that plaintiffs are well advised to request specific suggestions to prevent strategies of 'implementation avoidance' (Hoekman and Mavroidis, 1996). If panels limit themselves to standard recommendations to bring measures into compliance, disagreement between the parties as to the adequacy of the implementing measures taken by the losing party may preclude the complainant from obtaining authorization to take countermeasures. Another panel will first have to rule on the adequacy of the implementing measures. As mentioned above, since there is no obligation to withdraw a measure, in the case of non-violation disputes any satisfactory adjustment must involve cross-compensation of some kind. Nonviolation disputes have been relatively rare, in large part because the remedies on offer cannot address the measure that is being contested.

The standard remedies generally obtained in the WTO context may not provide enough incentives to the private sector to invoke DSP. The length of time it can take for the DSP to run its course is substantial—up to 2½ years if appeals and implementation periods are taken into account (the latter can extend to 15 months). This is a long time for exporters to be subject to a measure that may be a violation of the WTO, especially for countries that do not have a diversified export base. More importantly, standard remedies that require a member to bring its measures into compliance with WTO obligations do not involve any compensation for damages incurred or financial penalties. This further reduces the attractiveness of using the system. If damages or financial compensation could be obtained, the time cost as well as the resource costs associated with DSP (see below) would become much less important.

In principle, there is nothing to prevent countries from seeking compensation—the fact that complainants do not customarily request compensation is rooted in the history of the GATT. Before and during the Uruguay Round, a number of panels recommended that antidumping and countervailing duties collected by contracting parties in cases where GATT rules had been breached should be given back to the importers who had paid them. Such restitution—which is still far from true compensation for damages incurred—was resisted at the time, and most of these panel cases were not adopted. The first ruling, a 1981 case between Finland and New Zealand (transformers), was adopted, and New Zealand issued a refund. In six subsequent cases refunds were not accepted. WTO members have been unwilling to go down the compensation track, perhaps in part due to uncertainty regarding the possible repercussions (such as uncertainty regarding potential liability). Some countries have also argued that their legal systems prohibit compensation. However, historically, developing countries have favored the introduction of rules in the trading system that would allow for claims for monetary damages to be paid to developing countries in instances where illegal measures are imposed against them by industrialized nations. Not surprisingly, GATT contracting parties always rejected this. 'Money damages, said the developed countries, were simply outside the realm of the possible. In effect, they were saying, GATT was never meant to be taken seriously' (Hudec, 2000, p. 7).

In February 2000, a precedent was set by a panel in a case involving illegal export subsidies granted by Australia to a manufacturer of automotive leather. The panel recommended not only that Australia cease applying this measure, but also that the beneficiary of the subsidy be required to reimburse the funds (the case involved A$30 million, or about US$19 million). This was a first for the WTO.[3] The panel report was adopted by the DSB. Interestingly, the plaintiff (the US) had not requested this remedy; it does not support compensation.

---

[3] This had always been possible in principle—what was required was that the panel interpret the relevant language requiring withdrawal of the subsidy as applying as of the date that the subsidy was first applied, rather than as of the date it is found to be illegal. See Hoekman and Mavroidis (1996) for an argument to justify the reasoning of the panel.

Enforcement capacity

Economists often note that there are asymmetric incentives for countries to deviate from the WTO, as the ultimate threat that can be made against a member that does not comply with a panel recommendation is retaliation. Small countries cannot credibly threaten this because raising import barriers will have little impact on the target market while being costly in welfare terms. A possible way out of this dilemma is for small trading nations affected by a dispute to form alliances and retaliate as a group whenever one of the members is affected. More generally, one can conceive of the rules being enforced through retaliation by all WTO members, not just affected members. Both options would reduce the costs to the retaliators, while increasing the cost to the transgressor. However, although multiple parties may bring a joint complaint, only countries with a trade interest may do so. Those not affected cannot participate. Moves to apply the nondiscrimination principle to retaliation—a classic recommendation by economists—have always been resisted by WTO members on the basis that the objective of retaliation is not to punish but to maintain a balance of rights and obligations (the reciprocal bargain) (Hudec, 1987).

Thus, pressure to comply with panel rulings involving small economies is largely moral in nature, although the Ecuador case illustrates the potential that exists under the WTO to expand the threat of retaliation. In practice the system has worked rather well, in that recourse to retaliation has rarely been required to enforce multilateral dispute settlement decisions (Hudec, 1993). This is largely a reflection of the repeated nature of the WTO game and the resulting value that governments attach to maintaining a (reasonably) good reputation. Nonetheless, asymmetry in enforcement ability can affect the incentives to use the system. A basic problem with retaliation is that it involves raising barriers to trade, which is generally detrimental to the interests of the country that does so, and to world welfare more generally. Preferable from an economic perspective would be to encourage use of the provisions in the WTO for renegotiating concessions. This would ensure that the net impact of dispute resolution would lead towards more liberal trade, rather than create mechanisms through which trade barriers are raised, as renegotiation involves compensating members affected by a withdrawal of a concession by reducing other trade barriers. The use of retaliation in the *Bananas* and *Hormones* cases suggests that this is an issue that deserves consideration (Mavroidis, 2000).

Resource costs

Developing countries often note that rich countries such as the US, the EU or Canada—the major players in terms of dispute settlement activity —are well equipped with legal talent, are well briefed by export interests, and have a worldwide network of commercial and diplomatic representation that feeds their systems with relevant data. Developing countries, in contrast, have limited national expertise available and find it difficult to collect the type of information that is required to bring or defend WTO cases. Although to some extent countries can buy legal expertise,[4] scarcity of national administrative resources to identify and prepare cases is a constraint (South Centre, 1999). Developing countries also find it more difficult to supply panelists— the opportunity costs of seconding delegates for panels is much greater than for OECD countries with larger missions in Geneva and more expertise in capitals.

Article 27:2 DSU calls for technical.assistance to be provided to developing countries by the WTO secretariat. The secretariat's ability to satisfy this mandate is very limited. At the time of writing, legal technical assistance services were provided by two outside experts on a part-time basis. The adequacy of the assistance on offer is further reduced by the DSU requirement that such assistance can only be provided *after* a member has decided to submit a dispute to the WTO. Thus, assistance in evaluating whether practices are inconsistent and determining what might be winning cases cannot be given, so that the services of the experts are mostly used when developing countries are respondents. The consensus among developing countries is that the available assistance is inadequate. The ability of developing countries to use the DSU may improve with the creation of an Advisory Centre on WTO Law, one of the few concrete results achieved by the 1999 Seattle ministerial meeting (see chapter 12).

Settlements

An impressive feature of the WTO system is its success in encouraging bilateral settlement of trade conflicts. The presumption underlying the system is that the best way to settle trade disputes is through an out-of-court agree-

---

[4] Until the third *Bananas* case, countries were impeded from bringing nongovernment, private legal counsel before the panel. The Appellate Body decision in this case to allow representation by private lawyers removed this constraint as far as the Appellate Body was concerned. A subsequent panel then decided there were no provisions in the WTO or the DSU that prevented a WTO member from determining the composition of its delegation to panel meetings (Palmeter and Mavroidis, 1999).

ment among the parties concerned. The 60-day consultation period (Box 3.1) is in large part intended for that purpose. Frequently bilateral negotiations and a search for a compromise continue in spite of the initiation of dispute settlement proceedings. Many cases never reach the panel stage, although precise numbers are very hard to come by. The nature of settlements is such that both parties are presumably satisfied with the outcome. Although there is a reporting requirement—parties should notify the secretariat regarding the outcome of settlements (Article 3.6 DSU)—few members do so. The main examples of known settlements are instances where deals are struck after a panel is requested. An illustrative example was a dispute between India and the US over US textile import quotas. The US rescinded the contested quotas before the panel could start its work. There is general dissatisfaction regarding the way Article 3.6 DSU has been implemented. The Trade Policy Review process does little to augment transparency on this front as it generally comes too late and almost never addresses the issue of settlements. A case can be made that retroactive remedies against non-MFN settlements be made possible, or, alternatively, that provisions be created requiring multilateral clearance of settlements before they enter into force (Hoekman and Mavroidis, 2000).

3.4. THE DOMESTIC DIMENSIONS OF ENFORCEMENT

Greater domestic transparency and mechanisms allowing the use of national enforcement mechanisms could do much to increase the relevance of the WTO for the private sector. There are two dimensions of enforcement at the domestic level: generating the information required to defend WTO rights; and creating institutions that reduce the need to rely on WTO-level DSP. The latter is crucial if domestic constituencies are to hold governments accountable for the outcome of international negotiations and to increase the 'ownership' of negotiated commitments.

Upstream Links in the WTO Dispute Settlement Chain

The prevailing type of firm-government-WTO interaction is sketched out in Figure 3.2. A firm has two options in contesting foreign government policies that restrict its ability to contest a market. It can petition the foreign government, either through direct lobbying or through its legal system if a WTO obligation has been violated. Or, it can lobby its own government to take up the issue with the foreign government in question and initiate WTO dispute settlement if a solution is not forthcoming. From the firm's perspective the second route often is not attractive. It must convince its government that the case is worth bringing. This may require considerable resources—a collective action problem must be overcome to bring enough firms in the industry on board. And, if the case is pursued, the outcome (remedy) may not do much to address the concerns of the firm. Thus, many violations are unlikely to be addressed through the WTO.

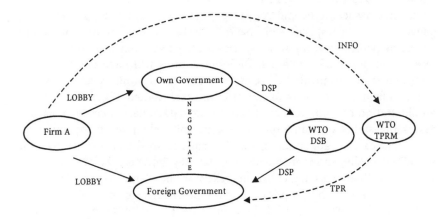

FIG. 3.2 Information Collection and Transmission: The Status Quo

This is not necessarily bad. High entry barriers or thresholds may be beneficial in ensuring that only major cases are brought to the WTO, ones that cannot be resolved through alternative, private mechanisms. It is difficult to make a judgement, however, because the available data on the prevalence and effect of discriminatory policies (whether or not these violate the WTO) are limited. If there are too few cases, an inefficient outcome for individual firms and for the trading system as a whole may result. The problem is similar to that of the production of a public good, where without cooperation underprovision is likely to result. Solutions to the problem require increasing the net benefits to firms of collecting data on potentially WTO-illegal policies. This can be pursued by establishing mechanisms to facilitate private sector cooperation, within and across countries to compile information on potential violations, and by reducing the need to involve governments in the enforcement of WTO commitments. Increasing the reliance on domestic enforcement mechanisms is one avenue through which the latter may be achieved.

Cooperation in Collection and Dissemination of Information

One option to deal with the information problem is for the private sector to cooperate and to create mechanisms through which data on trade (and investment) barriers are collected and analyzed. This could be realized through periodic surveys by an independent entity of multinationals that engage in substantial intra-firm trade, national firms that produce for export, trade associations, and consumer organizations. Such a survey would generate a 'user perspective' on the WTO system, providing information on problems perceived from a managerial perspective. These will often be different from those of regulators. Different entities will have different interests, so it is important that a broad cross-section of industry and consumer interests from a wide range of countries are represented. Figure 3.3 provides an illustration of a possible mechanism. The data collected could be used to assess the status quo on export markets, and help identify potential enforcement cases. Data could also be transmitted to the government and to the WTO. Ideally, an independent 'transparency' body can be envisaged that would coordinate national efforts and assist in the identification of potential WTO violations, lobby for joint actions to be brought to the WTO, and generate publicity. This would help complement the TPRM mechanism by bringing in the private sector more directly into the enforcement process. It would not involve direct access to the WTO, however—national governments would continue to have sole access to WTO DSP.

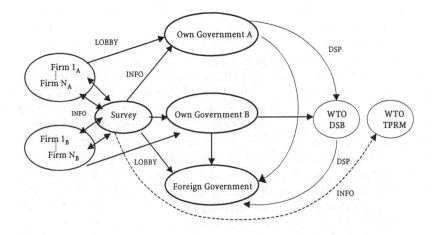

FIG. 3.3   Information Collection: A Survey Model

Although at the margin better information may induce governments to be more proactive, political realities—asymmetric distribution of power, threats of cross-issue linkages—will always be a powerful force constraining governments to assist firms to pursue their WTO rights. This suggests that dispute settlement should be a collective endeavor not only for the reasons emphasized by economists (to increase the credibility of the threat of retaliation), but also to ensure that individual firms or governments do not end up bearing the brunt of a respondent government's displeasure. Clearly, governments cannot be obliged to cooperate, but business and civil society more generally can play a role in lobbying for joint actions to be brought. A global, nongovernmental transparency body can help provide a focal point for such efforts.

Many fora already exist through which businesses cooperate and coordinate their position *vis-à-vis* government policies. The most prominent international body is the International Chamber of Commerce (ICC) located in Paris. The ICC has consultative status in the United Nations system, and is the most visible avenue for international business to express its views on international policy matters (Box 2.3). Other entities include the Business and Industry Advisory Committee, which provides business input into the deliberations of the OECD, and the Alliance for Global Business. In many countries there are similar institutions, as well as numerous industry-specific bodies. Although business associations have become more aware of the potential payoff of investing resources to reduce barriers to trade and investment, they have done relatively little to systematically compile information that would help policymakers identify the key constraints to competition and provide an input into better enforcement of WTO agreements.

Analysis of the information that is compiled must be undertaken if it is to be useful for enforcement purposes. Advisory centers to determine the legality of trade policies could be public-private partnerships, and have a regional dimension by building on the institutions created to implement regional integration agreements (Weston and Delich, 1999). Cooperation across countries can allow economies of scale to be captured and reduce the unit costs of analysis and information processing. Advisory centers geared towards the private sector could also help to give stakeholders a greater incentive to take an interest in the functioning of the multilateral trading system. A recent effort to go down this road is the Advisory Centre on WTO Law (ACWL), an institution established in 2000 to help developing country governments use the WTO dispute settlement system (see chapter 12). However, the ACWL focuses only on the 'downstream' dimension of enforcement, not on the 'upstream' collection of information.

Using National Mechanisms to Enforce National WTO Commitments

WTO rules and commitments are valuable in part because they provide assurances that a given trade policy stance will be maintained. For the potential of instruments such as the TPRM and other transparency devices such as reporting and publication requirements, as well as the DSP, to be fully realized, domestic stakeholders should be able to invoke WTO law and obligations in domestic courts or specialized fora. In many countries this is not the case. Greater access to domestic enforcement mechanism could help enhance the relevance of the WTO. Perhaps the most straightforward way to facilitate domestic enforcement of multilateral obligations is through the creation of 'challenge' mechanisms allowing private parties to contest perceived WTO-inconsistent policies by the government before domestic courts or specialized tribunals. A first step in this direction was made at the WTO level in the (plurilateral) Agreement on Government Procurement (GPA)—see chapter 11. The GPA requires signatories to give private parties access to mechanisms that allow them to contest actions by procuring entities that violate the agreement. In effect, the 'challenge' mechanisms required by the GPA imply that private parties may invoke its provisions before domestic courts (see Hoekman and Mavroidis, 1997). The TRIPs agreement also requires that WTO members have national enforcement mechanisms in place.

3.5. CONCLUSION

The dispute settlement mechanism is one of the unique features of the WTO. Although controversial cases frequently lead to tensions between WTO members, the system has to date worked rather well. The Appellate Body has played more of role than might have been expected, taking a proactive stance with respect to panel reports. The negative consensus rule for nonadoption of panel reports has reduced the scope for overt politicization of the process. Although a number of major disputes generated controversy and attracted a lot of attention in the first five years of the WTO—examples discussed above are the *Bananas, Hormones,* and *Kodak-Fuji* cases—these are the exceptions, not the rule. Most disputes are 'run-of-the-mill' and are resolved smoothly. One problem that emerged in this area is symptomatic of the more general source of conflict that has become more prominent over time: how to address fundamental differences between governments regarding the regulatory regimes they enforce. Differences between societies regarding the amount of risk they are willing to tolerate—for example, the production and consumption of genetically modified organisms (GMOs)—are very difficult to address. Efforts to introduce scientific principles into

WTO rules may not do much to facilitate dispute settlement—this was illustrated in *Hormones*, an issue where there was a virtual scientific consensus.

The incentive for governments to negotiate and abide by international trade agreements depends in part on the effectiveness of enforcement provisions. Enforcement is particularly important for developing countries, as they will rarely be able to exert credible threats against large trading entities that do not abide by the negotiated rules of the game. Domestic enforcement is a vital dimension in enhancing the relevance of multilateral commitments to domestic stakeholders. In most countries, including high-income nations, domestic interests are restricted in their ability to contest actions by national government agencies that violate WTO commitments. Civil society has a strong interest in seeking to maximize the extent to which individuals can invoke international treaty obligations in national legal systems. This will remove a number of layers of uncertainty and complexity associated with bringing cases to the WTO. Strengthening national enforcement mechanisms can help make the WTO a more relevant instrument from an economic development perspective by increasing the 'ownership' of negotiated commitments. It also relaxes the constraint of having to convince one's government to bring a case to the WTO and will reduce the burden of dispute settlement at the WTO level. The easiest way of making WTO commitments enforceable nationally is to expand on the 'challenge' mechanisms that have been introduced in the GPA.

The private sector plays a key role in enforcement. If it does not have an incentive to collect, compile and transmit information on measures that violate the WTO, cases will not be brought. Giving private interests standing in domestic fora via a general challenge procedure could enhance incentives to defend their rights. But private sector participation is also vital in order to ensure that countries can defend their rights at the WTO level. This upstream dimension of enforcement is as important as the efficacy of the downstream panel and Appellate Body process. Providing legal assistance along the lines that have been proposed by a number of WTO members (ACWL, 1999) to developing countries should be beneficial, but remains heavily dependent on firms bringing cases to their governments and getting a receptive hearing. Efforts to outsource some of the enforcement function to an independent 'Special Prosecutor' that is given the mandate to identify and contest WTO violations might help balance the playing field further (Hoekman and Mavroidis, 2000).

Suggestions have been made to increase transparency and strengthen the role of NGOs in DSP by giving them direct access to the WTO. For example, responding to criticism from NGOs, President Clinton proposed that 'hearings by the WTO be open to the public, and all briefs by the parties be made publicly available'. He also suggested that 'the WTO provide the opportunity for stakeholders to convey their views ... to help inform the panels in their deliberations' (Croome, 1998). Greater transparency of WTO processes would be beneficial—although it must be noted that great strides have been made in this regard. The situation under the WTO is an order of magnitude more transparent than was the case under the GATT. However, giving NGOs direct access to WTO DSP is unlikely to improve the process and can be expected to meet vigorous opposition on the part of many WTO members, especially developing countries. While stakeholders should have access to mechanisms that allow them to have a voice in the development of national positions in WTO negotiations and to invoke WTO law at the national level, a good case can be made that this should not extend to direct access to the WTO. In addition to the considerations identified by Levy and Srinivasan (1996) (discussed above), doing so could lead to a situation where NGOs have rights that are stronger than those accorded to WTO members (South Centre, 1999). More fundamentally, it will be very difficult to determine who speaks for (is representative of) global civil society as a whole. Wolf (1999) argues that organizations (NGOs) 'can only represent themselves. If NGOs were indeed representative of the wishes and desires of the electorate, those who embrace their ideas would be in power. Self-evidently, they are not'. Problems of representativeness are obviously compounded at the global (WTO) level.

3.6. FURTHER READING

WTO dispute settlement procedures are discussed in detail by David Palmeter and Petros C. Mavroidis, *Dispute Settlement in the World Trade Organization: Practice and Procedure* (The Hague: Kluwer Law International, 1999). Mitsuo Matsushita, Petros C. Mavroidis, and Thomas Schoenbaum survey the role of the WTO in the broader context of international economic public law in *The WTO Law and Practice* (Oxford: Oxford University Press, 2001). An exhaustive analysis of GATT dispute settlement can be found in Robert Hudec, *Enforcing International Trade Law: The Evolution of the GATT Legal System* (New York: Buttersworth, 1993). Edwin Vermulst, Petros C. Mavroidis and Paul Waer discuss the operation of the WTO appeals process in 'The Functioning of the Appellate Body After Four Years—Towards Rule Integrity', *Journal of World Trade*, 33 (1999): 1–50. An indispensable companion of any analyst of the GATT legal texts is GATT, *Analytical Index* (Geneva: GATT, 1994). WTO cases are published on the Internet by the WTO and can be downloaded from its home page.

Analyses of GATT dispute settlement procedures from an economic and game theoretic perspective can be found in Dan Kovenock and Marie

Thursby, 'GATT Dispute Settlement and Cooperation', in Alan Deardorff and Robert Stern (eds.), *Analytical and Negotiating Issues in the Global Trading System* (Ann Arbor: University of Michigan Press, 1993) and Thomas Hungerford, 'GATT: A Cooperative Equilibrium in a Non-Cooperative Trading Regime?', *Journal of International Economics*, 31 (1991), 357–69. Abram Chayes and Antonia Handler Chayes, *The New Sovereignty: Compliance with International Regulatory Agreements* (Boston: Harvard University Press, 1995) discuss alternative approaches to enforcement of international treaties, arguing that in many, if not most, instances noncompliance with agreements is not deliberate, implying that coercive enforcement through the threat of sanctions (retaliation) is inappropriate.

Jagdish Bhagwati, 'Aggressive Unilateralism: An Overview', in J. Bhagwati and H. Patrick (eds.), *Aggressive Unilateralism: America's Trade policy and the World Trading System.* (New York: Harvester-Wheatsheaf, 1990) and Marco Bronckers, 'Private Participation in the Enforcement of WTO Law: The New EC Trade Barriers Regulation', *Common Market Law Review*, 33 (1996), 299–318 discuss the use of unilateral enforcement mechanisms by the US and EU, respectively.

Robert Hudec, 'The Role of the GATT Secretariat in the Evolution of the WTO Dispute Settlement Procedure', in Jagdish Bhagwati and Mathias Hirsch (eds.), *The Uruguay Round and Beyond: Essays in Honor of Arthur Dunkel* (Ann Arbor: University of Michigan Press, 1998) is a characteristically readable account of the evolution of the role the GATT (and now WTO) secretariat has played in the settlement of disputes. Bernard Hoekman and Petros C. Mavroidis, 'Competition, Competition Policy and the GATT', *The World Economy*, 17 (1994), 121–50 explore the potential usefulness of non-violation dispute settlement as a vehicle to address competition-policy and market-access-related issues.

Advisory Centre on WTO Law, 'Final Proposal Document', 1999 (www.itd.org) and South Centre, 'Issues Regarding the Review of the WTO Dispute Settlement Mechanism', Working Paper no. 1 (February), 1999 discuss developing country concerns and interests with respect to WTO dispute settlement.

4
Negotiating Forum

Negotiation is the driving force of the multilateral trading system. Negotiations are used to agree on rules and procedures, to periodically reduce trade barriers, in instances when new countries want to join the club, and to resolve trade conflicts. The WTO is essentially a permanent negotiating forum in which trade issues may be discussed and agreed upon against the background of the provisions of the various agreements already concluded. Negotiations take place in permanent and ad hoc bodies, and are often informal. Although the WTO is a multilateral institution, it relies very strongly on bilateral and plurilateral interactions among members. Whatever agreements emerge are multilateralized through the MFN rule.

The discussion in this chapter centers on the problems that confront negotiators seeking to obtain agreements, the techniques that are used, and the reasons why MTNs tend to have outcomes that do not maximize national welfare. Although more detailed discussion of the substance of the outcomes of the various MTNs is left for subsequent chapters, it is useful to start with an overview of the major negotiating rounds that have been held since 1948.

4.1. OVERVIEW OF NEGOTIATING ROUNDS

To date, eight rounds of MTNs have been held under GATT auspices. These include Geneva (1947), Annecy (1949), Torquay (1951), another negotiation in Geneva in 1956, the Dillon Round (1960-1), the Kennedy Round (1964-7), the Tokyo Round (1973-9) and most recently the Uruguay Round (1986-94) (Table 4.1). The first five rounds dealt almost exclusively with tariffs. Starting with the Kennedy Round, attention began to shift towards nontariff trade restrictions and to the problem of trade in agricultural products. Although the Kennedy Round dealt only with nontariff measures that were already covered by the GATT, the Tokyo Round addressed policies that were not subject to GATT disciplines (the foremost examples being product standards and government procurement). This trend was continued in the Uruguay Round, which included trade in services, intellectual property, and rules of origin—all matters on which the GATT had very little to say. The rounds get their names from the places at which they were launched or the people who were influential in launching them. With the exception of the early sets of

negotiations held in Annecy (France) and Torquay (United Kingdom), the
actual negotiations occurred in Geneva, where the secretariat is based.

TABLE 4.1 *Trade rounds and selected ministerial meetings, 1947–2000*

Name of round or meeting	Period and number of parties	Subjects and modalities	Outcome
Geneva	1947 23 countries	Tariffs: item-by-item offer-request negotiations	Concessions on 45,000 tariff lines
Annecy	1949 29 countries	Tariffs: item-by-item offer-request negotiations	5,000 tariff concessions; 9 accessions
Torquay	1950–1 32 countries	Tariffs: item-by-item offer-request negotiations	8,700 tariff concessions; 4 accessions
Geneva	1955–6 33 countries	Tariffs: item-by-item offer-request negotiations	Modest reductions
Dillon Round	1960–1 39 countries	Tariffs: item-by-item offer-request negotiations, motivated in part by need to rebalance concessions following creation of the EEC	4,400 concessions exchanged; EEC proposal for a 20 percent linear cut in manufactures tariffs rejected
Kennedy Round	1963–7 74 countries	Tariffs: formula approach (linear cut) and item-by-item talks. Nontariff measures: antidumping, customs valuation	Average tariffs reduced by 35 percent; some 33,000 tariff lines bound; agreements on customs valuation and anti-dumping.
Tokyo Round	1973–9 99 countries	Tariffs: formula approach with exceptions. Nontariff measures: antidumping, customs valuation, subsidies and countervail, government procurement, import licensing, product standards, safeguards, special and differential treatment of developing countries	Average tariffs reduced by one third to six percent for OECD manufactures imports; voluntary codes of conduct agreed for all nontariff issues except safeguards.
Uruguay Round	1986–94 103 countries in 1986 117 as of end-1993	Tariffs: formula approach and item-by-item negotiations. Nontariff measures: all Tokyo issues, plus services, intellectual property, preshipment inspection, rules of origin, trade-related investment measures, dispute settlement, transparency and surveillance of trade policies.	Average tariffs again reduced by one third on average. Agriculture and textiles and clothing subjected to rules; creation of WTO; new agreements on services and TRIPs; majority of Tokyo Round codes extended to all WTO members

Name of round or meeting	Period and number of parties	Subjects and modalities	Outcome
Major ministerial meetings:			
Geneva	1982	Launch of new MTN (sought by US).	Failure to agree on a MTN; establishment of a work program on services.
Brussels	1990	Planned conclusion of the Uruguay Round	Failure to agree on agriculture; in the end negotiations only concluded in December 1993.
Singapore	1996 130 members	Proposals to discuss labor standards, competition and investment policy, procurement and trade facilitation in WTO; elimination of barriers to trade in information technology products; pursue negotiations on basic telecom and financial services.	Information Technology Agreement (ITA). Creation of working groups on competition and investment policy and procurement. Labor standards rejected as a subject for negotiation.
Seattle	1999 135 members	Launch of a new MTN. Major issues included developing country concerns on Uruguay Round implementation, modalities of agricultural liberalization, and competition, investment and labor standards.	Failure to agree on a MTN or on a work program. Members pursue only the 'built-in' agenda inherited from the Uruguay Round.

Note: Other important ministerial meetings include Tokyo (1973), Punta del Este (1986) and Marrakech (1994). The first two launched MTNs, the last concluded the Uruguay Round.

The Early Rounds

The first round of multilateral tariff negotiations was the Geneva round of 1947, which led to the creation of the General Agreement. Some 45,000 tariff concessions covering about half of world trade were exchanged. The 23 countries involved were also participants in the drafting of the Havana Charter (which involved a total of 56 nations), reflecting the fact that originally the GATT was supposed to be embedded in the ITO. Two MTNs were held relatively soon after the creation of the GATT, and largely consisted of accession negotiations. The first took place in Annecy (France) in 1949, at which time nine countries joined the GATT. A second followed in Torquay

(UK) in 1951, with four more countries acceding. This brought GATT membership to a total of 32, as four countries had ceased to participate by 1950. Three of these countries—China, Lebanon and Syria—were original contracting parties, while the fourth—Liberia—had joined during the Annecy negotiation. A third round followed in Geneva during 1955-6, by which time Japan had also acceded, bringing the total number of contracting parties to 33. None of these rounds had as large an impact in terms of reductions in average tariffs as the 1947 meeting did. Indeed, the outcomes were rather minor. For example, the average cut in US tariffs achieved in 1947 was 21.1 percent, whereas cuts in the next three rounds were only 1.9, 3.0, and 3.5 percent, respectively (Baldwin, 1986: 193). By the mid-1950s, the weighted-average tariff of the main industrialized nations had been reduced to some 15 percent.

The Dillon Round (1960-1)

Following the establishment of the EEC in 1957, a series of large-scale tariff negotiations were held under the GATT. As discussed at greater length in chapter 10, WTO rules require that a customs union or free trade area cover substantially all trade and does not result in a higher average level of protection against nonmembers. Nonmember countries that are negatively affected by the formation of a customs union that involves a member country adopting higher tariffs have the right to compensation. Bilateral compensation negotiations with the EEC were supplemented by a round of more general, multilateral tariff negotiations. A total of 34 nations participated. The Dillon Round—named after the US Under-Secretary of State who proposed the talks—yielded relatively modest results, with only 4,400 tariff concessions exchanged. No concessions were granted on agricultural and many other sensitive products, notwithstanding that these were the products where effective tariffs and trade barriers more generally were expected to rise as a result of the formation of the EEC (and more specifically the Common Agricultural Policy).

The Kennedy Round (1963-7)

Named after President Kennedy, some 46 nations participated in the Kennedy Round, although membership of the GATT had reached 74 by the end of the round. A new tariff negotiating method (an across-the-board formula approach) for industrial products was adopted, resulting in an average tariff reduction of 35 percent for trade in such products. Product-by-product negotiations on agricultural trade were less successful. The Kennedy Round was the first MTN to go beyond tariffs and deal with certain nontariff measures (NTMs). It resulted, in particular, in the conclusion of an Antidumping Code (see chapter 9), and an agreement on US customs valuation procedures for certain products (see chapter 5). The Kennedy Round was also the first to include a centrally-planned economy—Poland—which acceded to the GATT at the end of the round, and included efforts that led to the formal inclusion of preferential treatment in favor of the developing countries. This was embodied in a new Part IV of the General Agreement in 1965 (see chapter 12).

The Tokyo Round (1973–9)

Ninety-nine countries, representing nine-tenths of world trade, participated in this MTN, named after the city where the negotiations were launched. Tariffs were reduced on thousands of industrial and agricultural products, and some 33,000 additional tariff lines were bound. The total value of trade affected by tariff commitments was in the range of US$300 billion, measured in 1981 imports. As a result, the average import weighted tariff on manufactured products maintained by industrialized nations declined to about six percent. This represented a reduction of 34 percent (measured in terms of tariff revenue), comparable with the magnitude of tariff reduction achieved in the Kennedy Round. The Tokyo Round also led to the adoption of a range of specific agreements. These included the legalization of preferential tariff and nontariff treatment in favor of developing countries and among developing countries (the so-called Enabling Clause—see chapter 12) and a number of codes dealing with NTMs or specific products. Codes were negotiated on subsidies and countervailing measures, technical barriers to trade (product standards), government procurement, customs valuation, import licensing procedures, antidumping (a revision of a Kennedy Round code), bovine meat, dairy products, and civil aircraft. The use of codes was partly driven by the fact that developing countries objected to expansion of GATT disciplines, implying that the two-thirds majority required to amend the GATT could not be attained. By negotiating a code, like-minded countries were able to cooperate without having all GATT contracting parties on board. At the same time, it was often argued that this weakened the system, as it allowed countries to pick and choose among disciplines that pertained to subjects covered by the GATT (the term 'GATT à la carte' was often used to describe the code approach).

The Uruguay Round (1986–94)

This most recently concluded MTN—named after the country that hosted the ministerial meeting that established its agenda in 1986—continued the trend of widening the negotiating agenda, increasing the number of participating countries, and taking longer to conclude. In addition to policies affecting trade in goods, trade policy measures affecting investment, trade in services, and intellectual property rights were put on the table. The Uruguay Round led to further liberalization of international trade, including not only tariff reductions but also the elimination of tariffs for certain product groups (so-called zero-for-zero agreements), the reintegration of agricultural trade and textiles and clothing into the trading system, and the expansion of GATT disciplines. The GATT 1994 embodies a series of agreements on specific issues—many of them renegotiations of Tokyo Round codes (see chapters 5 and 11). Creation of a new GATT allowed contracting parties to bypass the need to formally amend the GATT 1947, and ensure at the same time that the results of the round were a Single Undertaking that applied to all. The WTO was established to oversee the functioning of the GATT, the GATS, and the Agreement on TRIPs. The average tariff on manufactured products of industrial countries, weighted by the volume of trade in the products concerned, fell from 6.4 percent to 4.0 percent, a cut of almost 40 percent. This compares to a weighted-average duty of 35 percent before the creation of GATT (1947), and around 15 percent at the time of the Dillon Round (the early 1960s).

Major WTO meetings, 1996–9

At the first ministerial meeting of the WTO in Singapore in December 1996, the agenda was intended to center largely on defining a work program for the WTO. In contrast to the stock taking exercises that tended to characterize GATT ministerial meetings, the Singapore ministerial became a negotiating session. High-income countries sought to put government procurement, trade facilitation, competition and investment policy on the WTO agenda, with a minority (led by the US and France) also seeking to introduce the topic of labor standards. During 1996, APEC countries and the EU had been developing an agreement to eliminate trade barriers on information technology products. A proposal to this effect was also put on the table in Singapore. It came as something of a surprise to non-APEC developing countries—some objected to being presented with a precooked deal on essentially a 'take it or leave it' basis—but in the end an Information Technology Agreement (ITA) was concluded among 40 members (see chapter 8).

This is not a Plurilateral Agreement as defined by the WTO but an example of a zero-for-zero agreement under which members agree to abolish tariffs on a set of commodities. Developing countries managed to keep labor standards off the WTO agenda. Members agreed to create working groups to discuss and study the relationship between trade and competition and investment policy disciplines, transparency in government procurement, and trade facilitation.

A number of the Uruguay Round agreements—most notably on agriculture and services—embodied a built-in negotiating agenda, calling for new efforts to reduce trade barriers within five years of the entry into force of the WTO. In the case of both services and agriculture, the outcome of negotiations was largely restricted to the creation of a framework that would allow progressive liberalization in the future. Other agreements contained review provisions. To increase the scope for beneficial tradeoffs across issues and strengthen the trading system, a number of governments (led by the EU) argued that rather than pursue only the built-in agenda, it was preferable to expand the agenda to include merchandise tariffs more generally, as well as new issues. That is, they sought to launch a full-fledged round of negotiations. The Geneva ministerial meeting of 1998 provided the mandate to undertake work to prepare for the launching of a new round at its next meeting, scheduled for the end of November 1999 in Seattle. The Seattle ministerial turned out to be a fiasco and failed to launch a new round. Domestic US politics played a key role, with a Democratic administration confronting a Presidential election unwilling to resist efforts by US labor groups to introduce labor standards into the WTO (Box 4.1). Strong differences on the scope of agricultural liberalization between the EU on the one hand and the US and other agricultural exporters on the other were also important, as was the unwillingness of many developing countries to consider accepting agenda items that were being pushed by several high-income countries—most notably labor standards.

Box 4.1. The WTO and the Streets of Seattle
The protests in the streets of Seattle during the 1999 ministerial meeting involved an improbable alliance of some 30,000 union activists, environmentalists, and religious groups that opposed the process of globalization and were concerned about specific dimensions of the WTO. The protesters ranted against everything from genetically modified crops and child labor to the US embargo on Cuba and the need to protect turtles. A unifying factor was distrust of the WTO system, even though most demonstrators had only a very limited knowledge of what the WTO was about. An important push in the preparation of what some considered as the most important civil dis-

obedience action in the US since the 1960s was given by professional activists of the Direct Action Network. Web sites catalogued the official protesting organizations using encrypted email exchanges among a network of affiliated groups.

The collapse of the Seattle talks was variously blamed on the ineffective and nontransparent decision-making process ill-suited for an organization with such a large membership, the complexity of the issues proposed for consideration, as well as inevitable differences in basic values and culture of the participants. Developing countries strongly refused to discuss any links between trade and labor standards and thought that too little attention was given to their needs. For many of them, the failure of Seattle was a 'blessing in disguise'. For some developed country governments, the street demonstrations were seen as a reflection of the strong links that existed between trade on one hand and the environment, workers' rights and child welfare on the other. Many in the public saw it as a beginning of a new area of 'people over profits', or 'globalization with a human face'. Whatever the perception, Seattle left the WTO bruised and polarized.

The Seattle events were perceived by developing countries as a rich country effort to distort the WTO agenda. In their view, NGOs and other lobby groups based in high-income nations with interests that differed substantially from those of people living in poor nations managed to hijack the meeting. Many saw Seattle as a calculated move to shelter advanced country labor-intensive industries from competition from low-income economies. The Indian mass media noted on a number of occasions that the NGOs agitators in the streets of Seattle were displaying arrogance and disdain for poor countries (Reddy, 2000). As summarized by the trade policy news brief 'World Trade Agenda', the end result was that the 'WTO defeated itself in Seattle as poor preparation combines with bad management, mistrust and US politics' (WTA, 1999).

A major contributing factor was that the meeting was badly prepared and badly managed. Efforts to whittle down proposals into a single negotiating text only started eight weeks before the Seattle meeting. The chairman of the WTO General Council and the Director-General did not manage to get key delegations to bridge enough of their differences. Thus the text that went to Seattle constituted a hodgepodge of issues that no one thought was adequate for a ministerial conference (Odell, 2000a). At Seattle, there was widespread dissatisfaction concerning the role of the chair of the conference (USTR Charlene Barshefsky), who was widely perceived to be pursuing a US agenda as opposed to making good faith efforts to attain consensus on a balanced agenda. Small countries in particular perceived themselves to be left in the cold, not having access to the negotiating fora where potential deals were being thrashed out. In the end, ministers simply ran out of time—they came close to agreeing on a negotiating agenda, but could not extend the conference because the venue had been booked for a convention of optometrists.

Expectations are that a new attempt to launch a round will have to wait until 2001 at the earliest. Although discussions on the built-in agenda (services and agriculture) were launched in 2000, it is unclear whether sector-specific talks—especially on agriculture—have a good chance of being successful (see chapters 6 and 7).

4.2. MULTILATERAL TRADE LIBERALIZATION

As discussed in chapter 1, an important rationale for small economies to engage in reciprocal, multilateral negotiations to liberalize trade (access to markets) is political. It allows governments to offset opposition to liberalization on the part of import-competing industries by creating political support on the part of export interests that obtain greater access to foreign markets. It also allows large countries, that in principle can affect their terms of trade (the prices they get or pay for their exports or imports, respectively) and thus may benefit from trade barriers, to reach higher levels of real income (welfare) by agreeing to mutual disarmament. In the terminology of game theory, large countries are often trapped in an inefficient, noncooperative equilibrium, while small ones may be the hostages of vested interest groups.

MTNs can usefully be viewed and analyzed with the help of game theory and game-theoretic concepts. Game theory is the branch of mathematics that analyzes situations where actions by agents (players) are interdependent. Outcomes depend on how the game (the interaction) is structured (the rules of the game), the information available to the players, and the way that players form expectations about the actions of other players. There are two basic types of games, cooperative and noncooperative. The first type assumes that outcomes of games are efficient in the sense that gains from trade are maximized, and what is at issue is the distribution of the possible gains across players. Cooperative games assume that a binding enforcement mechanism exists and that defection by players from the cooperative solution can be observed by other players. Noncooperative games emerge in settings where there is no central enforcement mechanism and where there is no presumption that outcomes will be Pareto-optimal. A Pareto-optimal situation is one where no party can be made better off without another party being made worse off. The fact that trade policymakers are driven as much by (internal) political as economic concerns affects their choice criteria and thus decision outcomes. From an internal political perspective, a Pareto-optimal outcome is one where no party can be made better off without another party knowing that it is being made worse off (Kostecki, 1983). Information is important, therefore, in ensuring that political and economic notions of optimality do not diverge too much.

MTNs held under WTO auspices can be regarded as efforts to set the rules of the noncooperative international trade game. Countries get together and seek to achieve a consensus regarding the type of game they will play in the future. While MTNs are attempts to coordinate, the outcome of negotiations will rarely be Pareto-optimal. Perhaps the most appropriate way of looking at MTNs is to regard them as institution-setting exercises. Various situations can be identified that may give rise to the creation of institutions. One very well known case is the Prisoners' Dilemma, where players choosing individually rational strategies end up in an equilibrium that is not efficient (Box 4.2).

Box 4.2. The Prisoners' Dilemma in trade policy

The Prisoners' Dilemma is illustrated in the payoff matrix below. The equilibrium outcome of the game has both countries imposing trade restrictions (not cooperating), each obtaining a pay-off of zero. It is inferior to the Pareto-optimal free-trade solution, where each party obtains a pay-off of $P - c > 0$, where P is the benefit of obtaining access to the partner country's market, c are the net costs of opening up its own market, and $P > c$. Such costs consist of political variables, augmented by the possible decline in the terms of trade for certain products.* Noncooperation occurs because it is in each country's interest to impose protection, independent of what the other country does. Whatever policy stance is taken by country B, country A will maximize its pay-off by choosing a protectionist stance, and vice versa for country B. For example, if B chooses free trade, A's pay-off is highest under protection, as $P > P - c$. If B chooses protection, A again will prefer protection, as $-c < 0$. As each country has the same incentive structure, they end up in the noncooperative, inefficient outcome where each earns a pay-off of zero. If the countries cooperated and both implemented free trade, they would each obtain $P - c > 0$. In instances such as these, where individually rational behavior by governments is not efficient, the creation of an institution can help solve the dilemma by fostering cooperation.

	Country B	
Country A	Free trade	Protection
Free trade	$P - c, P - c$	$-c, P$
Protection	$P, - c$	$0, 0$

* *Note*: $P > c > 0$. This specific formulation of the dilemma is drawn from Garrett (1992). Technically, the outcome resulting from noncooperative behavior is often assumed to be a Nash equilibrium, that is, each nation acts to maximize its objectives taking as given the actions of all other nations. The Prisoners' Dilemma is an example of such a situation.

While a convenient illustration, the Prisoners' Dilemma is a very special and narrow game, in that there is only a single outcome that makes both players better off, and there are only two players. For practical situations of trade negotiations, there are usually many possible outcomes that make all countries better off and are Pareto-superior to the status quo. If players interact over time and are able to communicate and make credible commitments, the cooperation problem noted above can be regarded as a subset of a more general class of bargaining situations. In the latter, even if countries at any point in time cannot improve upon their joint welfare, there may exist possibilities to achieve outcomes that are superior to these equilibria if countries are willing and able to trade across issues—that is, expand the agenda. Conversely, there may exist situations where cooperation is not necessary because individually rational strategies lead to a Pareto-optimal outcome. This is the case, for example, in a world where countries cannot affect their terms of trade, markets are perfectly competitive, there are no distortions or rent-seeking interest groups, and governments believe in *laissez faire*. In principle no cooperation problem then exists. The government has no incentive to diverge from free trade. Alternatively—and more realistically—there may exist a dominant country (a hegemon) that enforces cooperation. Conybeare (1987) discusses these and alternative possibilities in greater depth.

In practice, of course, there are rent-seeking groups in each country, governments do not believe in *laissez faire*, and markets are imperfect. In pursuing national objectives, a country may reduce the welfare of other countries by imposing a negative externality on them. An externality arises when a government does not take into account the impact of its actions on other countries—be they good or bad. The economic literature on externalities has focused on two ways to address the problem. One calls for a central authority to impose targeted taxes or subsidies. The other postulates that agents will attempt to bargain their way to a Pareto-optimal situation. The first approach is not very relevant in an international context, as no supranational entity exists that has the power to levy the required taxes (assuming these can be calculated in the first place). At the heart of the second approach lies the so-called Coase theorem (named after Ronald Coase, a Nobel Prize winner in economics): given the existence of enforceable property rights and in the absence of transaction costs, externalities will be bargained away such that a Pareto-optimal outcome results. That is, the market—bargaining—will ensure efficiency. In general, for bargaining over rules of behavior to be possible, it is necessary that players expect to interact with each other over an indefinite time horizon. This creates incentives to cooperate because agreements can be enforced through the threat of retaliation.

The Coase theorem assumes agents have perfect information regarding the economic setting in which they operate and that they can interact costlessly. This includes information on their own and on other parties' utility functions (preferences). In practice these assumptions often will be violated. Thus, usually there can be no certainty that a specific bargaining procedure will lead to an efficient outcome. Bargaining can only solve an externality problem if the external effects are the only cause of market failure, and this is not the case if there exists imperfect information. However, if institutions exist that allow competitive bidding for property rights, an efficient reallocation of such rights may be achieved in a world of incomplete information (Samuelson 1985).

In international affairs, reallocation of, or bidding for, property rights may not appear to be very practical at first glance. Nevertheless, property rights do exist, implicitly defined by rules of sovereignty. That is, nation-states that create externalities implicitly have the right to impose them. The existence of these rights allows negotiations to take place, while the (mutual) negative externalities created by national trade policies are the inducement for countries to pursue them. Because countries interact continuously, agreements are in principle enforceable as long as defectors can be identified and singled out for retaliation. The WTO puts great emphasis on transparency of procedure and mutual surveillance, which facilitates the identification of violators. Subject to certain conditions, affected countries have the right to retaliate if no or inadequate compensation is offered by the nation violating its WTO obligations (see chapter 3).

To a large extent MTNs comprise barter, that is, trades occur in a setting where there is no generally accepted medium of exchange (money). Barter is possible when there are (enforced) property rights, marginal valuations of goods differ, and potential transactors can meet each other. Any introductory textbook of economics will explain that barter is inefficient. Indeed, its inefficiency is one of the historical reasons for the creation of money. However, in international relations there is usually no money and nations are stuck with barter. Three kinds of inefficiencies may arise:

(1) the market (total supply) may not offer any goods a trader is interested in obtaining;
(2) a trader who has something another wants has no interest in what the other has to offer, but is interested in the goods of a third party; and
(3) it may not be possible to equate trader's marginal valuations of goods.

If the first possibility occurs, trade will not be possible and the status quo will be maintained. If the second possibility occurs, trade will only be feasible if a set of potential trades exists such that all members have something that another wants. In this context, economists sometimes speak of barter's need for a double coincidence of wants. Even if this condition is met, trade will only occur if marginal valuations can be (approximately) equated. This is the third potential problem mentioned above. Trade may not take place because goods are indivisible.

All these problems affect MTNs, as these are a marketplace where potential traders meet. To ensure that they do not come for nothing (that is, that there is something to trade), a great deal of care is taken to establish an agenda beforehand. This agenda will have some topics (issues) of interest for all the parties willing to trade. Prior to a MTN, national authorities, industries, and bureaucracies will be engaged in a domestic negotiation to determine interests, priorities, and possible tradeoffs. It is this work by potential participants that leads eventually to the establishment of the agenda of the MTN.

Establishing the agenda of a MTN is a negotiation in itself. Prior to the launching of the Uruguay Round it took a failed ministerial meeting (in 1982) and five years of work in a GATT Senior Officials Group and elsewhere to prepare the agenda that was eventually mostly embodied in the 1986 Punta del Este Declaration. The problem of defining an agenda also dominated the first WTO ministerial conference, held in Singapore in 1996. At that meeting a number of nations pushed for the inclusion of workers' rights (labor standards), environmental norms, foreign investment policies, and competition law as topics to be put on the WTO work program. Many WTO members are vehemently opposed to mixing trade policy discussions with issues of labor standards and in the event it was decided that workers rights was a topic for the ILO, not the WTO. These issues returned to the fore at the second ministerial meeting (held in Geneva in 1998), which were accompanied by street protests and small-scale riots as various NGOs expressed their displeasure over a perceived lack of legitimacy of—and access to—the institution. Both the Singapore and Geneva meetings were not intended to launch MTNs, but were events that could eventually lead to defining a negotiating agenda. As a result, prenegotiation-type maneuvering was very prevalent. The third ministerial meeting, held in Seattle in late 1999, was formally aimed at launching a new MTN. As noted above, it proved impossible to converge on an agenda, and delegates went home frustrated.

For analytical purposes any trade negotiation can be decomposed into four stages: catalyst, prenegotiation, negotiation, and postnegotiation.[1] In the catalyst stage there is a visionary. This could be an interest group or a government. The implied policy vision is the catalyst, defining in broad terms the issues to be negotiated. In the prenegotiation phase, discussions (negotiations) take place on the possible agenda for the formal negotiations. The agenda that is established places constraints on the parameters of the formal negotiation that will follow. In the negotiation stage, formal government-to-government bargaining takes place, with interest-group participation. Subject to the implicit parameters established by the agenda, interests groups lobby negotiators, and preferences for policy packages change. Ultimately, depending on bargaining strategies, tactics, and time constraints, a formal draft of an agreement emerges. The final stage of a MTN is the postnegotiation, implementation stage, which determines how the agreements are embodied in a country's laws and procedures and enforced by its administration, judiciary and legislature. There will frequently be an imperfect correspondence between what was negotiated and what is implemented, making it very important how effective surveillance and dispute-settlement procedures are, and how precisely worded the formal agreement is.

Box 4.3. Lobbying for NAFTA

One of the more impressive lobbying campaigns seen in Washington DC during the 1990s was directed at obtaining Congressional approval of the North American Free Trade Agreement (NAFTA). The Mexican authorities strongly supported the NAFTA deal and adopted a proactive strategy to promote the agreement among the members of the US Congress and the American public at large. The high-level group of lobbyists running the campaign included lawyers, trade policy consultants and communication specialists. The public relations team included former high-ranking US government officials and politicians. To generate public support for NAFTA, a number of public relations firms were retained to develop brochures identifying the advantages of the arrangement, organize a pro-NAFTA publicity campaign, produce a TV-series, monitor and react to media coverage, and assist Mexican officials in organizing lecture tours in support of the NAFTA agreement. Numerous congressional lobbyists worked Capital Hill to ensure Congressional support for NAFTA. Many congressmen and their staff were

---

[1] See Leidy and Hoekman (1993). What follows draws on this paper.

invited to visit Mexico during the campaign. Moreover, a number of large US enterprises, the US Chamber of Commerce and the National Association of Manufacturers grouped together under the umbrella of 'USA-NAFTA' to actively support Congressional ratification.

Issue Linkage

The agenda that is established will determine a set of possible policy packages that could emerge as outcomes or solutions to the negotiation. Not all of the possible packages will be feasible. A necessary condition for the adoption of a package by all participants is that it improves upon the status quo ante or upon whatever is expected to be the status quo if negotiations fail (the so-called threat or no agreement point). Referring to Figure 4.1, the status quo is represented by point x^{SQ}. Assume for simplicity there are two parties to the negotiation, and that the vertical and horizontal axes measure their national welfare (abstracting from lobbying for the moment). All possible outcomes that lie to the left or below the dotted lines radiating out from the threat point are not feasible, as they imply less than the status quo for at least one party. Some policy packages are clearly better for both parties than others. Thus, those packages that form the frontier (x_2 to x_5) dominate all the others for at least one party. The points on the frontier are all Pareto-optimal: if any one of these points is chosen, there are no other packages that make both parties better off. The more possible outcomes there are, the more continuous the frontier will be. In the limit, if what is on the table is perfectly divisible (such as a tariff), the negotiation frontier is a line with an infinite number of Pareto-optimal outcomes. In the more realistic case of a multi-issue negotiation with many nontariff issues, there will be a large number of feasible policy packages, but moving along the frontier will imply discontinuous jumps from one Pareto-optimal point to another. The location of these various policy packages may change over time, as the result of lobbying pressure, learning, and linkage strategies.

The shape of the frontier is not constant. Lobbying pressure affects the effective preferences that ultimately drive negotiations. In the absence of lobbying activity—that is, in the absence of political constraints in a certain area—most governments' notional preferences can be assumed to represent the social welfare. Lobbies, however, will generally inform negotiators of the implied political costs of taking certain positions. Once the government has determined the relative political importance of the groups involved, the options available to satisfy their desires, and the costs of these options, the government's effective preferences may well differ from its notional (unlobbied) preferences. As a result the set of feasible policy packages may shrink.

Trades in a MTN occur both within and across issues. Intra-issue trade is exemplified by tariff negotiations. Countries make bids and offers on the level of specific tariffs, or the average tariff level. In principle, if there are enough issues, cross-issue trade may allow agreement if within-issue trade proves insufficient to generate an improvement on the status quo for all concerned. For example, agreement on a definition of subsidies could be made contingent on agreement that stricter rules be imposed on emergency protection against imports. Linkages play a fundamental role in terms of fostering agreement because they allow side-payments to be made.

In terms of achieving an agreement, issue linkage can play two roles in MTNs (Hoekman, 1989). First, it can be used to achieve reciprocity. That is, it allows a distribution constraint to be met: a balance of benefits and concessions. Linkage is actively used in MTNs to achieve reciprocity. Second, linkage may be used to increase potential gains from trade. In this case linkage is an instrument that allows a more efficient outcome to be attained. As noted earlier, MTNs deal with bargaining problems, that is, the issue is to choose a Pareto-optimal outcome out of a set of many possible such outcomes. Agreement may not occur for procedural reasons, or it may be the case that no better solution exists. Sometimes, this may be the result of not being able to link issues, or of attempting to link the wrong issues. For example, powerful nations may attempt to impose linkages on weaker ones. In this case mutual gain is clearly not the objective. Often, such strategies may be counterproductive, especially if attempted by nations that are open to retaliation.

The problem facing negotiators is generally two-fold: when and what to link. The need for linkage depends on whether there are sufficient mutual gains to be achieved by cooperating within a given issue area, and whether these gains are distributed relatively symmetrically. If gains are too small, or are distributed too asymmetrically, cross-issue linkage quickly becomes necessary. The need to redefine issues and propose linkages explains why MTNs usually require more creativity than distributive ('win-lose') bargaining of the type that arises between a buyer and a seller of a car (Box 4.4).

Box 4.4. Integrative versus Distributive Bargaining and the WTO
The nature of negotiations in the WTO system varies depending on the issues involved and the countries concerned. Negotiation theory makes a useful distinction between distributive bargaining ('win-lose' or zero-sum games) and integrative bargaining ('win-win' games). Parties engaged in distributive bargaining usually determine their respective target points (de-

sired outcomes) and resistance points (the minimal acceptable outcome). The latter determines when to 'walk away' or to reject the offer. For an agreement to occur there must exist a positive settlement range—a set of target points such that the parties can attain a settlement that exceeds the resistance points (Raiffa, 1982). A bargainer must determine an opponent's resistance points through questioning or other tactics. During the negotiation process, participants are likely to modify their perception of how realistic their target points are.

In the context of the WTO, distributive bargaining is not the dominant type of negotiation. Situations in which one party will clearly gain at the expense of the other are rather rare. An example was the negotiation between GATT Contracting Parties and Switzerland that took place in the mid-1990s regarding the conditions of treatment for the secretariat in Geneva, in particular the magnitude of the subsidy that Switzerland would grant to keep the organization in Geneva. There was a competing offer from Germany to host the organization in Bonn, where the move of many government departments to Berlin had led to a large amount of suitable vacant office space and meeting room facilities, which allowed the bargaining to occur.

Non-zero-sum integrative bargaining or 'problem solving' negotiations are by far the most frequent in the multilateral trading system. Integrative bargaining is significantly different from distributive bargaining. Negotiations are a process that aim at resolution of issues, involving cooperation in identifying issues for which an agreement may be feasible, proposing competing solutions, establishing preference orderings over proposals, and a search for a final agreement. Whereas distributive bargaining may call for bluffs and threats, manipulation of information and minimally honest behavior, integrative negotiations require a high level of trust and openness as well as substantial intellectual input. The 'culture' of the WTO negotiations as well as the attitudes and behavior of members differs substantially from that prevailing in the commercial sphere.

The Uruguay Round agreements on TRIPs, agriculture or textiles would have been considerably different—perhaps nonexistent—if no cross-issue linkages had been made. The question of what to link is equivalent to the question of what to trade and can be answered using the basic microeconomic theory of exchange. The necessary conditions for fruitful issue linkage are that marginal valuations of different issues differ across nations, and proposed linkages (trades) result in outcomes that make all parties better off than the status quo ante. For linkage to be feasible, parties must agree on the nature of the set of Pareto-optimal outcomes. The less information parties have about the issues, the fuzzier the Pareto-optimal set will be (Tollison and

Willett, 1979). The same applies if there is disagreement among the parties regarding the effect of alternative proposals. In general, choice of issues will be determined on a political level based on various criteria: nations will attempt to offer concessions on those issues they care least about in return for gains on issues they care most about. How much a government cares about an issue is likely to be as much a function of the strength of different domestic interest groups as of the relative costs and benefits to the nation as a whole. As producer interests tend to be more concentrated on a specific topic than those of consumers—who are affected by all the issues on the table—the former tend to be much better informed than the latter (Downs, 1954). This is one of the factors skewing the outcome of negotiations.

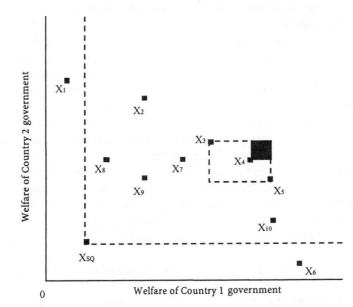

Source: Leidy and Hoekman (1993).

FIG. 4.1. The negotiation space and the set of feasible outcomes

Issue linkages can be thought of as replacing any two possible policy packages with one that represents a weighted average of the elements of the two. Lobbying efforts might be directed toward achieving linkage for several reasons. As noted earlier, linkage can create a region of mutual advantage where previously none existed, or can expand the set of mutually beneficial agreements. Consider, for example, the set of possible policy packages $\{x_1, ..., x_{10}\}$ displayed in Figure 4.1, and assume that the initial placement of these points corresponds to the unlobbied preferences of negotiators. Assume further that x_4 is now the status quo point.

In this case there is no room for agreement without issue linkage. Issue linkage serves to produce a new possible policy package whose value to negotiators, *ceteris paribus*, must fall strictly within the dashed box connecting the linked policy packages. If, for example, proposals x_3 and x_5 were linked, the linked package might fall within the shaded region in Figure 4.1. If so the issue linkage makes agreement possible. While such linkage might be pursued directly by unlobbied governments, interest groups may also pursue issue linkage strategically to move a favored set of policies to the negotiation frontier. Alternatively they might seek to block consideration of unfavored policies. Strong supporters of the status quo might even find it efficient to pursue issue linkages in order to empty the effective negotiation set, that is, let negotiations break down.

Historically, GATT contracting parties tended to constrain themselves to tradeoffs within issue areas, due to their practice of establishing separate negotiating groups for each issue. Attempts to link across issues generally are made at the beginning and at the end of a MTN. In the initial, prenegotiation phase of a MTN, cross-issue tradeoffs occur so as to achieve a balanced negotiating agenda (Winham 1986). It is only in the final stage of a MTN that positions on issues are completely mapped out and the need for linkage in terms of achieving overall agreement becomes clear. Such tradeoffs tend to be made at a high political level under substantial time pressure. The *modus operandi* of the Uruguay Round in this connection was the rule that nothing is agreed upon until everything is agreed upon. Linkage in these cases is focused more on achieving a perceived balance of gains and concessions (reciprocity) than on increasing potential joint gains.

Coalition Formation and the Nondiscrimination Rule

The type of agreement that is likely to emerge from attempts by a group of nations to cooperate will be a function of the number of countries involved, the number of issues, and the extent to which nonparticipants can be excluded from the benefits of an agreement. Intuitively, the feasibility of achieving agreement among a given group of nations in part will be a function of their identity. This, for example, is likely to influence the choice of agenda and may determine the set of feasible issue linkages. Not only the identity of nations, but also the absolute number of participants may be important. Generally, as the number of participants goes up, so will transaction costs. Thus, there will also be a tradeoff between the number and types of players and the possibility of achieving comprehensive agreement. The problem then is determining the optimal choice of issues relative to parties in a negotiation. This by no means trivial problem is made even more difficult once the possibilities for coalition formation are taken into account.

The formation of coalitions or clubs of like-minded countries on an issue is often regarded as a possible way to circumvent free-rider problems and increase negotiating leverage. Limiting the number of parties in a negotiation can also be efficient in terms of generating agreement because of reduced transaction costs. This is not necessarily an argument for excluding nonparticipants from the benefits of an agreement. The primary rationale for exclusion is that it can act as an incentive mechanism to induce participation in the MTN. But the benefits of the WTO have the characteristics of a public good: adding members to the club does not detract from the benefits accruing to existing members. Indeed, the contrary is more likely—implying that efficiency is maximized if all nations are included. Frequently differences in opinion on an issue are deep enough to prohibit consensus from emerging. If it is difficult for those in favor of a proposal to internalize the benefits of implementing it (limit free riding by those not in favor), the MFN rule may lead to a breakdown of the discussions. However, if the benefits resulting from an agreement between a group of like-minded countries are so large that free riding by others is not a constraint, the countries involved may agree to form a club. An important example of such 'privileged groups' (Olson, 1965) were the codes negotiated between a subset of GATT contracting parties during the Tokyo Round. In most instances the signatories applied them on a MFN basis.

Countries that are like-minded on an issue may also form coalitions so as to maximize their joint bargaining power. Among the various types of coalitions that may arise in the context of a MTN, one can distinguish between agenda moving, proposal making, blocking, and negotiating coalitions (Hamilton and Whalley, 1989). The first three of these are the most common in MTNs, as they require only a limited amount of coordination between coalition members because there is no need to arrive at a common position. In the Uruguay Round, the Cairns group—a coalition of 14 agricultural exporters—was an example of a proposal making coalition that became a blocking coalition at the 1990 Brussels ministerial meeting (see chapter 6). Major developing countries often acted as an agenda moving coalition as regards TRIPs, services and TRIMs in the Uruguay Round. African countries provided an example of a blocking coalition during the Seattle ministerial meeting. Being excluded from most green room negotiations, African countries issued a public statement to the effect that they would not adopt the proposed final ministerial declaration. Negotiating coalitions hammer out a common position and thereafter speak with one voice. The major example of such a coalition is the EU. Coalition formation is a relevant strategy for both small and large countries. For the latter the main incentive is likely to be a reduction in transactions costs, and perhaps concern over free riding in certain instances. For small countries the primary attraction is likely to be the potential increase in negotiating power and increased 'visibility'.

As in the case of issue linkage, coalition formation in MTNs can also be used by lobbies in an attempt to shift the location of policy packages in the preference ordering of their governments (Leidy and Hoekman, 1993). Returning to Figure 4.1, consider an interest group in country 2 for whom the policy package x_5 is the worst possible outcome. Assume that country 2 is the EU, country 1 is the US, the lobby is the EU film industry, and x_5 implies far-reaching liberalization that will greatly benefit the US industry. The EU film industry can attempt to remove x_5 from the feasible set in several ways. First, it can lobby for the status quo at home. A small increase in the value of the status quo to its negotiators is sufficient to eliminate x_5 from the effective feasible set. Alternatively, if x_{10} does not contain the offensive provision on film market liberalization, and is thus ranked higher from the EU film lobby's perspective, it could throw its weight behind domestic and foreign groups supporting package x_{10}. If successful, as reflected in a move of x_{10} to the northwest, it may remove x_5 from consideration. Finally, the industry can also attempt to produce a vertical drop in the valuation of x_5 by its government by directly lobbying against it.

4.3. INTEREST GROUPS AND LOBBYING ACTIVITY

The forgoing conceptual discussion of the incentives and effects of interest group lobbying helps to understand why negotiations often end up with agreements that are complex and difficult to comprehend for an outsider. Essentially, all trade negotiations are multi-level, involving both domestic bargaining among interest groups, and negotiations between governments that represent these national interests. In the international relations literature this dimension of international negotiation has been described as a 'two-level' game (Putnam, 1988). In the case of the EU the game is at least three-level, as there are national groups, the EU members states, the European Commission, and the WTO level where the EU seeks to speak with one voice.

Industry associations and large enterprises have a strong interest in taking a proactive stand at both the national and the international level. As firms do not have direct access to the WTO (except through amicus briefs in the case of disputes), they must exercise influence through their governments. Business interests play a major role in the design of trade rules. Often, the details of the disciplines that are negotiated are incomprehensible without an understanding of the forces that brought an issue to the table. Firms also drive the enforcement dimension of the WTO (see Box 4.5). Financial institutions such as American Express, Citibank, and American Insurance Group played a very active role in the Uruguay Round and in the horse trading that occurred during the 1997 negotiations on financial services (chapter 7).

Box 4.5. Interest Groups and the WTO Bananas Case
Lobbying activity played both a major role in the design and evolution of the EU bananas regime (described in the previous chapter), as well as in the disputes that were brought to the GATT and the WTO. Players included:
- Importers of ACP bananas—Three firms (Geest, Fyffes and Jamaica Producers), allied with the Caribbean Banana Exporters Association (CBEA) and its London lobbying office, became the principal beneficiaries of the new (1993) EU regime.
- Producers of Latin American ('dollar') bananas—Dole Foods, Chiquita and Del Monte control 70 percent of global imports and lobbied actively against the proposed 1993 EU regime. Chiquita was the major force behind the USTR's decision to bring the WTO case.
- Importers of dollar bananas—Distributors lobbied and litigated against the 1993 regime in German courts and in the EU.
- Caribbean ACP producers—used the CBEA to lobby in favor of ACP preferences and inclusion of Banana Protocols in the Lomé Convention.
Source: Porges (2000).

The major trading nations recognize lobbying as part of the democratic process and regard it as a useful tool for obtaining information. Hundreds of legislative initiatives are required to manage foreign trade systems, agricultural policies, technical standards, intellectual property regimes and other issues of interest to traders and producers located in WTO members. All such legislation is influenced by interest group lobbying. This applies as much to the EU and other OECD countries as to the US. In the EU, the role of lobbying in shaping trade policy is strongly felt. There are hundreds of European and international federations, as well as hundreds of multinational firms with direct representation in Brussels (de Bony, 1994). Numerous management consulting and public relations firms maintain offices close to the EU Commission and are actively involved in efforts to shape EU trade policy. As of 1998, there were 13,000 professional lobbyists in Brussels, almost one per Commission staff member (World Bank, 2000).

The role of lobbying in the EU can be expected to intensify further given the post-Maastricht emphasis on consultation at every stage in the decision-making process. EU trade policy is the outcome of increasingly complex internal negotiations. In spite of the shift to qualified majority voting that was introduced in the Single European Act, EU members usually aim at consensus. Log rolling among interest groups and decision-making on the basis of the lowest common denominator occur frequently. The laborious process of internal negotiations to arrive at a common stand on issues such as agriculture, intellectual property rights and services liberalization during the Uruguay Round all illustrate the importance for stakeholders of having effective representation in Brussels as well as in their home market.

4.4. RECIPROCITY AND THE MECHANICS OF NEGOTIATIONS

A fundamental concept used in GATT negotiations is reciprocity. Loosely defined, reciprocity is the practice of making an action conditional upon an action by a counterpart. Reciprocity has been a fundamental element in trade liberalization by OECD countries. While there have been exceptions to this pattern (see chapter 1 and Bhagwati and Irwin, 1987), historically mercantilism has reigned. That is, exports were seen as a boon to the economy because they led to an inflow of gold, the hard currency of the times, while imports were bad because they led to an outflow. As mentioned previously, this makes no economic sense—mercantilism is a reflection of what David Henderson (1986) has called 'do-it-yourself-economics'. Over time the rationale for reciprocity changed somewhat, the primary justification becoming one of preventing free riding by countries that continue to maintain high trade barriers. The economic foundations for making trade liberalization conditional upon barrier reductions by trading partners are weak, as the cost of holding back to induce others to follow suit may be very high. Nonetheless, reciprocal trade liberalization was even more prevalent in much of the twentieth century than in the nineteenth. For example, the 1934 US initiative for tariff reduction in the 1930s, following the disastrous tariff wars induced by the passage of the 1930 Smoot-Hawley Act, explicitly required reciprocal concessions (it was called the Reciprocal Trade Agreements Act).[2]

Article XXVIII *bis* of the GATT (entitled Tariff Negotiations) states that:

negotiations on a reciprocal and mutually advantageous basis, directed to the substantial reduction of the general level of tariffs and other charges on imports and exports .... are of great importance to the expansion of international trade. The CONTRACTING PARTIES may therefore sponsor such negotiations from time to

[2] Oye (1992), Low (1993), Rhodes (1993), Bayard and Elliott (1994) and Gilligan (1997) analyze the role of reciprocity in US trade relations.

time. Negotiations under this Article may be carried out on a selective product-by-product basis or by the application of such multilateral procedures as may be accepted by the contracting parties concerned. Such negotiations may be directed towards the reduction of duties, the binding of duties at then existing levels, or undertakings that individual duties or average duties of specified categories of products shall not exceed specified levels. The binding against increase of low duties or of a duty-free treatment, shall, in principle, be recognized as a concession equivalent in value to the reduction of high duties.

Three basic principles therefore apply to tariff negotiations under GATT or WTO auspices:

(1) they are to be on a reciprocal and mutually advantageous basis;
(2) concessions are to be bound; and
(3) they are to be applied on an MFN basis (through Article I of the GATT).

The first two of these principles have tended to apply to developed countries only. Until recently, developing countries have not been required to offer reciprocal concessions or to bind their tariff rates (see chapters 5 and 12).

Reciprocity in the GATT context has been defined in terms of the 1934 Reciprocal Trade Agreements Act mentioned earlier: it implies the exchange of a reduction in the level of protection in one country in return for an equivalent reduction in the level of protection of another country. Reciprocity criteria or formulae used by participants in negotiations may be intra- or inter-issue. An intra-issue criterion provides for the exchange of concessions of an identical nature (tariff concessions against tariff concessions for a given product or group of products). An inter-issue formula provides for the exchange of concessions of a dissimilar nature (such as tariff concessions against removal of quotas). Reciprocity criteria may be product specific—as in so-called item-by-item negotiations—or more general in nature. Examples of the latter are so-called across-the-board trade barrier reductions, which tend to take the form of a formula: a x percent reduction in average tariffs, or a y percent reduction in the dispersion of tariffs. Item-by-item and across-the-board approaches can be applied to tariffs and nontariff measures, although in the latter case quantification tends to be much more difficult. Formula approaches in the case of NTMs tend to take the form of the adoption of general rules, such as transparency and nondiscrimination.

Reciprocity Criteria for Tariffs

GATT contracting parties used a number of criteria to evaluate whether an exchange of tariff concessions is balanced. When considering a reciprocal package or balance of offers, negotiators might be expected to take into account factors such as the effect of reduction in trade barriers on future trade flows, domestic production, employment, and prices. In practice this is generally not the case. The methods used to evaluate offers usually have little relationship, if any, to what economic theory would suggest as reasonable yardsticks. The approaches that have been used are best characterized as providing negotiators with a focal point, that is, something tangible enabling parties to set objectives, evaluate the position of others, assess negotiating progress, and identify acceptable compromises. In the case of GATT talks, the focal point is generally nothing more than a measure that takes into account the relative size of different countries (trade volume) and is simple to calculate using data that are readily available. The last point is important: the choice of focal point used in past negotiations has been driven largely by data availability.

One method is to focus on trade coverage, defined as the reduction in a tariff multiplied by the volume of imports of that product. For example, if imports of a product are US$10 million and the applicable tariff rate is reduced from 50 percent to 35 percent, the trade coverage is 0.15 times 10, or US$1.5 million. A related method that has been used can be referred to as 50 percent equivalents. This also takes into account both the tariff-cut on a good and the value of imports of the good before the cut. A 50 percent equivalent (or one equivalent) signifies that a 50 percent tariff cut took place with respect to US$1 million worth of imports. A tariff cut of 25 percent for a product line in which the value of imports is US$2 million is equal to one equivalent. The general formula is:

$$E = [M \times dT]/50$$

where M is the value of imports and dT is the percentage tariff cut. These methods of assessing reciprocal concessions were often used in the earlier MTNs when trade between two negotiating countries was not bilaterally balanced in a specific product.

Another method is the average cut. Generally, weighted averages rather than simple averages are used in this connection. Suppose that country A imports US$20 million worth of cotton shirts and US$30 million worth of cotton trousers. During trade negotiations it agrees to reduce its tariff on cotton shirts by 5 percent and its tariff on cotton trousers by 10 percent. The weighted-average cut in import tariffs for cotton imports by country A is then:

$$E = (0.05 \times \$20 \text{ million} + 0.1 \times \$30 \text{ million})/(\$20 \text{ million} + \$30 \text{ million}) = 8.$$

The average tariff cut by country *A* in the cotton sector is thus eight percent. Average cuts do not always provide a satisfactory indication of the magnitude of trade liberalization. For example, if a country's tariff is so high as to be prohibitive (no imports come in at all), there will be nothing to weigh the tariff cut by for the product concerned. Use of the formula will then give a biased picture of the extent of tariff cuts. The more restrictive a given import tariff, the less satisfactory is the use of this type of weighted tariff cut average to calculate the value of concessions. Because of such problems, tariff cuts are often also weighted by domestic consumption or production of the products involved, or by the global value of trade in the products.

Reciprocity formulae may be general (across-the-board) or specific (item-by-item). Negotiations conducted on an item-by-item basis rely on a specific reciprocity formula, that is, tariff reduction relating to one product line is exchanged for tariff reduction on another product line. Negotiations conducted on an across-the-board basis rely on a general reciprocity formula. Table 4.2 lists some of the major techniques that have been used in the GATT context.

TABLE 4.2 *Negotiating techniques and formulae*

Technique	Major Characteristics
Item-by-item or bid-offer	Bilateral negotiations based on requests and offers. Main technique used until Kennedy Round; widely used in subsequent rounds and accession talks.
Linear cut in tariffs	Across-the-board negotiating technique involving an identical percentage reduction in barriers across all sectors. Used in Kennedy Round (formula: $T_2 = rT_1$, where T_2 is the reduced tariff, T_1 is the initial tariff, and r is a coefficient ranging between 0 and 1).
Harmonization formula	Aimed at moving the tariff structure of members towards greater uniformity, cutting tariff peaks proportionally more than lower tariffs. In Tokyo Round the so-called Swiss formula was used: $T_2 = RT_1/R + T_1$, where R is a coefficient (set at 14 or 16).
Zero-for-zero negotiations	Complete abolition of tariffs for a sector or group of commodities.

The initial GATT process of negotiations on specific concessions was essentially bilateral. That is, two contracting parties presented each other with request and offer lists, and negotiations centred on achieving a bilaterally balanced exchange of concessions. However, this network of bilateral negotiations subsequently acquires a multilateral dimension because specific tariff concessions once negotiated bilaterally are generalized through the MFN clause. In practice the large players (the US, the EU) negotiate with virtually everyone, whereas smaller players will negotiate primarily with WTO members that are principal suppliers or constitute important markets. The market opening granted by one country is frequently balanced against tariff reductions made by a number of trading partners simultaneously. The rationale underlying this is that a generalization of bilaterally negotiated concessions though MFN may create free rider problems. Any reduction in trade barriers will also benefit other countries that supply the relevant products, and these countries may not have offered reciprocal concessions. The principle of nondiscrimination clashes here with the principle of reciprocity. Under a MFN clause, no conditionality (discrimination) may be introduced once a concession has been granted. However, conditionality (which is the very essence of reciprocity) may be introduced in the negotiating process. Two general techniques have been conceived to deal with the free rider issue. They are the principal supplier rule and the practice of balancing concessions in exchange for so-called initial negotiating rights.

Under the principal supplier rule, requests for concessions on a particular product are normally made by, and only by, the principal (largest) suppliers of a product. This limits free riding, as the concessions granted by an importing country (A) to the principal supplier (B) of a specific product must be balanced by concessions from that principal supplier (B) on products for which A is in turn a principal supplier. The principal supplier mechanism was a long-standing US practice, this being the method used in the negotiation of the network of reciprocal trade agreements starting in the 1930s (Jackson, 1969: 219). The principal supplier rule effectively reinforces the bilateral character of trade negotiations conducted on product-by-product basis. Under an unconditional MFN clause governments have few incentives to grant a trade concession to countries that are not its principal suppliers. Granting a concession to a small supplier implies giving away the concession to the principal supplier, since the latter will benefit from it due to the MFN rule. The principal supplier is the trading nation which benefits the most from a concession and is thus probably prepared to offer more reciprocal trade liberalization than a smaller supplier would be prepared or able to do.

Multilateral product-by-product negotiations based on the principal supplier rule rely on multilateral balancing. Assume that country A is the principal supplier of good 1 to country B, and that B is the principal supplier of good 2 to A. Negotiations are then feasible. Assume further that B imports US$500 million from A, while A imports only US$250 million from B. Although an exchange is certainly possible, because trade flows are unbalanced, B may demand that A reduce its tariff by twice as much as B. If A is unwilling to do this, and the reciprocity rule requires equality in cuts as measured, for example, by tariff revenues, negotiations may break down. Involving another country *C* may allow *A* and *B* to circumvent their problem. If country *C* is the principal supplier of good 3 to *A*, exporting US$500 million, and is also the principal supplier of good 4 to country *B*, with exports of US$250 million, and in turn imports goods worth US$250 and US$500 million, respectively, from *A* and *B*, negotiations are balanced. This is, of course, a stylized example. In practice many goods are involved, and precise balancing is impossible to achieve. The main point is that by involving many countries, more trades are possible under the principal supplier constraint.

While the principal supplier rule reduces the role of smaller supplier countries in multilateral tariff negotiations, it does not eliminate them as players. A factor leading to the involvement of smaller countries is the need for end-game or last-minute balancing. At the end of the bilateral phase of a round, every negotiator knows that his country is not only required to grant the benefits of concessions to other countries but also that it is entitled to the benefits of concessions negotiated between other trading nations. At this stage the negotiators attempt to strike a balance in the global effect of concessions. To achieve that objective they may seek to reshuffle previously made requests and offers. A country that finds out that one of its concessions indirectly benefited another country that refused to grant a reciprocal concession always has the possibility to withdraw the original concession. Thus, the granting of concessions to principal suppliers is often made conditional upon obtaining supplementary balancing concessions from a number of other (smaller) suppliers of the product concerned.

The use of the principal-supplier rule with multilateral balancing reflected an explicit attempt by trading nations to form privileged groups. The aim is that the share of the costs and benefits of a product-specific liberalization that is internalized by club members (principal suppliers) is sufficiently large so that free riding by third parties is no longer a source of concern. The practice of supplementary balancing probably resulted in greater trade liberalization than would have taken place under the strict bilateralism that characterized the pre-GATT trading system. The MFN clause induces requests for concessions from smaller suppliers that would not be players under a conditional MFN approach. The fact that the concession-granting country is able to 'sell' its concession to more than one country allows it to obtain greater compensation than under a system of bilateral bargaining. Greater compensation also implies that more can be offered in terms of market opening (Dam, 1970).

The item-by-item, principal supplier approach was the main technique used in the first five MTNs (up to the Dillon round). Being product-specific, the approach allowed negotiators to be very precise, facilitating an evaluation of the trade effects of concessions. This advantage is offset by the fact that item-by-item, principal supplier negotiations are resource-intensive. They also facilitate the exemption of industries with political clout, are not very effective in reducing barriers where there are no principal suppliers, and can be micromanaged in a way that allows the MFN obligation to be effectively circumvented.

A good example of how a MFN requirement can be circumvented in the context of an exchange of bilaterally negotiated concessions that are formally subject to MFN comes from a 1904 trade agreement between Germany and Switzerland. Germany committed itself to reducing its tariffs on 'large dapple mountain cattle reared at a spot at least 300 meters above sea level and having at least one month grazing each year at a spot at least 800 meters above sea level' (Curzon, 1965: 60). Although this agreement predates the GATT, it has become a classic illustration of the use of creative tariff line definition by trade negotiators to avoid MFN—clearly the provision will not apply to Argentine or Dutch beef! The general approach continued to be used in the GATT context (Finger, 1979). More generally, the extent of liberalization is a function of the level of the tariff classification at which commitments are made. Thus, a commitment to lower tariffs at the four-digit level is much more significant than a commitment at the 8 digit level (because there are many more commodities covered at the more aggregate four-digit level).

Over time, as the number of participants rose, increasing the complexity of item-by-item negotiations while at the same time reducing their utility (as free riding became less of an issue) attempts were made to shift towards an across-the-board approach. The Kennedy Round saw the introduction of a formula approach to tariff reduction. Underlying this shift was not only the expansion of GATT membership, but also the fact that the US Congress approved of the approach (having earlier rejected it as infringing on its sovereignty). EEC concern that its average industrial tariffs were lower than those applying in the United States and Japan also played a role (Jackson, 1969). Across-the-board, formula-based negotiations in GATT have relied on two basic approaches: the linear cutting formula; and a harmonization formula. The linear cutting formula consists in applying the same rate of tariff reduction to all product lines by all participants. It was applied during the Kennedy Round, with developed countries agreeing to reduce their tariffs on industrial products by 50 percent, except for sensitive products. These were put on an exception list, some of which were liberalized on the basis of item-by-item negotiations. As many sensitive items were reduced by a small percentage or totally excluded from the cut, the average tariff reduction in the Kennedy Round was only 35 percent.

The linear approach maximizes the number of tariff lines brought to the bargaining table and leads to the exchange of a greater amount of concessions than negotiations based on a specific reciprocity formula. The formula tends to be preferred by countries with high import tariffs since any equal-percentage tariff cut will leave the high-tariff country with higher tariffs in the end than other nations that started from a lower tariff level. Issues such as tariff escalation, high tariffs and lack of inter- and intra-country uniformity of tariffs may not be satisfactorily addressed under the linear tariff-cutting formula. Negotiators frequently claim that reductions of low tariffs or total elimination of low tariffs are equivalent to substantial cuts of higher tariffs. Low-tariff nations frequently argue that high-tariff nations should reciprocate with higher percentage cuts. Trading nations that maintain import tariffs characterized by a great disparity of tariff rates frequently favor linear tariff cuts, whereas countries with a uniform or flat tariff structure are usually interested in a nonlinear approach that reduces high tariffs more than low tariffs.

Harmonization formulas result in nonlinear cuts in tariffs. There are very many options in this respect. One possibility that was discussed in the Tokyo Round was to cut each tariff by a percentage equal to its initial level. Thus, a 60 percent tariff would be reduced by 60 percent, while a 10 percent tariff would be reduced by 10 percent. The EEC suggested that this approach be repeated four times, with tariffs over 50 percent initially not being reduced below 13 percent. Another proposition made by the US was to employ the formula $X=1.5T_1+50$, where X is the percentage with which tariffs were to be cut. This formula was to apply to all tariffs below 6.67 percent, all others being reduced by 60 percent. This meant that a six percent tariff would fall by $(1.5 \times 6) + 50$, or 59 percent, while a two percent tariff would be cut by 53 percent. This is a clear example of a symbolic harmonization formula, as high tariffs are only subject to a linear cut. From the formulas suggested by the EEC and the US it is clear that the EEC sought more harmonization than the US. Yet another approach, suggested by Switzerland, was to use the formula $T_2 = rT_1/(r + T_1)$. This formula reduced high tariff rates much more than low ones, the ultimate result depending on the value of r that is chosen. In the event the value of r that was chosen by countries ranged between 14 and 16. Thus, a 14 percent tariff would be reduced by 50 percent, tariffs below (above) 14 percent being reduced less (more) than 50 percent.

A general problem affecting across-the-board formula approaches is that agreement must be obtained on which formula to use and on the extent to which exceptions to the use of the rule will be permitted. The larger the scope for exceptions, the less useful it becomes to invest substantial negoti-ating resources in achieving agreement on the use of a general rule. The shift to a general formula approach used in the Kennedy and Tokyo Rounds, while a significant change, did not lead to the demise of item-by-item talks. This was because the formula only applied to products that were not in-cluded in the list of exceptions. These exceptions turned out to be rather significant at the end of the day in both negotiations, as the inclusion of a product on this list by one country tended to lead to the reciprocal addition of products to the list but other countries. In the case of products included in the exception list of the Kennedy and Tokyo Rounds, item-by-item nego-tiations took place. In the Uruguay Round, negotiators did not use a formula approach, instead reverting to item-by-item (sector-by-sector) negotiations.

Whatever approach is used, item-by-item or general, reciprocity of market opening commitments is traditionally measured in terms of incremental rather then absolute trade flows. One dollar of additional market access in one country is exchanged for one dollar of additional market opening in another country. Ernest Preeg, an American negotiator commenting on the Kennedy Round and preceding negotiations, observed that negotiators re-lying on projected trade impact criteria tended to strike a rough balance between the estimated increases in the value of imports and the forecast rise in the value of exports resulting from the tariff concessions (Preeg, 1970).

What is considered *ex ante* advantageous largely depends on the persua-siveness of negotiators. All negotiators will contend that export opportuni-ties gained are greater than import opening conceded, even though logically this cannot be true for all countries at the same time (Curzon and Curzon, 1976). In other words, the bargaining in the GATT forum reflects a balance of perceived advantages at the margin rather than in terms of full equality of market access. Obviously, the complete picture with regard to market access conditions is never absent from negotiators' perspectives. However, it is the balance of incremental reductions that remains in the center of attention when evaluating reciprocity. Jagdish Bhagwati, using a mathematical anal-ogy, has termed this criterion 'first-difference' reciprocity: what effectively is attempted is to equate changes in policy (their 'first derivatives'), not abso-lute levels. Efforts in the 1980s by the US to move from first difference to reciprocity criteria focusing on levels created important tensions in the GATT (Bhagwati, 1991). This was essentially a move back towards the view of reciprocity held by the US in the nineteenth century (Bhagwati and Irwin, 1987).

Tariff concessions in MTNs mean tariff bindings and not necessarily a reduction in applied barriers to market access. A country may liberalize its tariff structure (its applied tariff levels) but as long as it does not bind it at a given level, the liberalization is essentially not considered to be a concession in the GATT context. For example, in the Uruguay Round many developing countries requested recognition of autonomous liberalization that had been undertaken during the 1980s, but had a hard time, in spite of initial general assurances incorporated in ministerial declarations, of getting this accepted by negotiating partners. Similarly, often the applied tariff rate on a product is less than the bound MFN rate contained in a country's GATT schedule. Again, no credit is obtained from applying lower than bound rates. What matters is the level at which tariff rates are bound. As discussed in chapter 1, tariff bindings are fundamental in the GATT context, because it is on the basis of claims that bindings have been violated that a member may initiate dispute settlement procedures.

Welfare impacts are generally not used as measures of reciprocity in the negotiations themselves. Reasons for this include a lack of analytical capacity to undertake the required analysis—especially pre-Kennedy Round—and the difficulty of attaining agreement on the many parameters that must enter into the required calculations. The latter include the respective price and substitution elasticities, data on production, trade and employment, and so forth. However, from a normative point of view policymakers should be concerned with welfare effects of policy, and this is an important role that analysts and think tanks should play. One concept or instrument that is useful for negotiators in this connection is the effective rate of protection.

Effective Protection

Goods traded internationally are rarely wholly produced in one country. In many cases, inputs or parts of the product are imported. The existence of trade in intermediate products makes a great deal of difference for the economic analysis of tariffs and the measurement of their protective effects. A useful distinction in this connection is between the nominal rate of protection (NRP) and the effective rate of protection (ERP). The NRP for a product can be measured as the proportional increase in the producer price of a good relative to free trade (trade undistorted by protection). The ERP differs from the NRP by taking into account the magnitude of protection imposed on the raw materials and intermediate inputs used to produce a good. The ERP is a better measure of the extent to which activities are protected than the NRP because it incorporates information on the structure of production. The higher are the tariffs and NTMs on imported inputs, the lower the ERP will be for goods that use these inputs (Box 4.6).

Box 4.6. Nominal and effective rate of protection
The nominal rate of protection (NRP) can be defined as

$$NRP = (P - P^*)/P^*$$

where P is the domestic tariff inclusive price of a good, and P^* is the free trade price. As the latter cannot be observed in practice, most empirical studies take the world price as a measure of P^*. The effective rate of protection (ERP) can be defined as the proportional increase in value added per unit of a good produced in a country relative to value added under free trade (no protection). The magnitude of the ERP depends not only on the nominal tariff on the final product concerned, but also on the tariffs applied to the inputs used, and the importance of those inputs in the value of the final product. A simple formula for calculating the ERP is

$$ERP = (V - V^*)/V^*$$

where V is the domestic value added per unit of the final good (including the tariffs on that good) and on its inputs, and V^* is valued added under free trade. Value added per unit in turn is defined as the gross value of output minus the cost of inputs used in production: $V = t_f P_f - t_i P_i X$, where t_f and t_i equal one plus the tariff on the final good and inputs, respectively, P_f and P_i are the prices, and X is the amount of input used to produce a unit of the final good. Value added at free trade prices is the same, except that tariffs in this case do not exist (the value of t is one). For example, suppose one ton of steel is worth US$1000 on the world market. To produce it a factory has to buy one ton of iron ore at a world price of US$600. Assume for simplicity that nothing more is needed for steel production. Under these circumstances the value added per ton of steel in our factory will be US$400. If a 20 percent nominal tariff rate is imposed on steel imports and no tariff on iron ore, the effective rate of protection in those circumstances will be

$$(1200 - 600)/400 = 1.5 \text{ or } 50 \text{ percent.}$$

The ERP in this example is more than double the 20 percent NRP on steel. If no tariff is imposed on steel but a nominal tariff of 33 percent is imposed on imports of iron ore, the ERP would be

$$\{1000 - (600+200)\}/400 = 0.5 \text{ or } -50 \text{ percent.}$$

This example illustrates that an NRP of zero does not necessarily imply that trade is undistorted. As another example, assume that cocoa beans account for 95 percent of the production cost of cocoa butter. The imposition of a five percent nominal tariff rate on cocoa butter would then imply an effective rate of protection for the cocoa butter industry of 100 percent.

The WTO focuses only on nominal rates of protection (tariffs). There are no obligations with respect to effective rates. This does not mean that negotiators do not understand the concept. Return to the first example on steel given previously. In this case the incentives for exporters of steel to reduce the 20 percent tariff are greater than is suggested by the nominal rate. The fact that the ERP for most products tends to be higher than the NRP (because governments prefer to protect activities that generate higher value added) explains why tariff negotiations continue to be at the center stage of MTNs, even though the absolute level of tariffs has fallen significantly. An average tariff on highly processed goods of only 10 percent can hide an ERP that is much higher. Interest groups care about the ERP, not the NRP. While lobbying efforts center on influencing nominal rates of protection, much of the political maneuvering that occurs in the domestic trade policy arena is driven by the impact of such protection on the ERP. At the multilateral level, in MTNs the focus of attention is often on the dispersion of tariffs. Attempts to reduce dispersion—the difference between the highest and lowest rates—will have the effect of reducing differences in the ERP for specific goods.

Reciprocity Criteria for Nontariff Measures

Liberalization of NTMs is considerably more complex than tariff talks. There are many kinds of NTMs. Some are imposed to achieve nontrade objectives and only incidentally restrict imports (examples include sanitary controls, labeling requirements, and product standards). There is therefore some difficulty in determining what measures constitute a barrier to trade and which are legitimate instruments of government regulation. As, if not more difficult is applying the concept of reciprocity in negotiations on NTMs. The problem is twofold: the set of potential trades is of a much lower dimension than in the case of tariff negotiations and it is much more difficult to translate the value of proposals into a common denominator (Hoekman, 1993). Because NTM issues are lumpier than tariffs, gains from trade become more difficult to realize, and cross-issue linkages become more important in achieving agreement. The valuation issue is fundamental. In the context of tariff negotiations, it is relatively straightforward to agree how to value requests and offers, although the criteria used have little economic meaning. A metric for NTM negotiations is much more difficult to establish. As discussed in chapter 6, in the agricultural setting attempts have been made to agree on methods that convert various types of government intervention into a producer subsidy equivalent or an aggregate measure of support. In most NTM negotiations the focus is not on principal suppliers or the change in protection, but on specific measures or rules whose implementation is assumed to increase market access, or on easily quantified variables that are not necessarily related to trade. For example, in negotiating an agreement on government procurement (see chapter 11), participants focused on the size of the contracts to be covered and the entities to be included (on the basis of past procurement activity). This allowed a balance to be achieved in terms of the percentage of total procurement to be covered by an agreement.

Many of the issues that have appeared on the agendas of recent MTNs are not easily expressed in terms of a simple quantitative metric. This makes it more difficult for negotiators to determine whether they have achieved reciprocity. This is the case especially when the focus is on agreeing on rules. Often it may not be feasible to make marginal changes in proposed rules without making the rule irrelevant. Instead, deals involve accepting rule x for issue A in return for rule y for issue B, that is, engage in issue linkage. In such a context, it becomes very important to have a clear idea of the implications of alternative rules. This requires substantial analysis of the likely effects on both domestic constituents and on the multilateral trading system. It is not surprising therefore that the approach taken is often one of adopting motherhood principles such as transparency and perhaps nondiscrimination, rather than seeking changes in the substance of regulations.

Rules of Thumb to Assess Welfare Impacts

Assessing the implications of current policies and the likely consequences of changes in policies for economic welfare is an important task for policymakers. At the end of the day the end result of a negotiation should be an increase in national welfare. Although the process will reflect the self-interested behavior of numerous interest groups, so that governments will never end up with an outcome that maximizes welfare, if the gains that accrue to some groups are not sufficient to offset the losses of other groups, agreements will be inefficient. Indeed, they may not be feasible to implement. Officials who are concerned with ensuring that the outcome of negotiations improves the welfare of society, as opposed to the interests of the best organized and powerful interest groups, can use a number of rules of thumb. One such rule is that proposals should reduce the dispersion in effective rates of protection across industries. Another rule of thumb is that across-the-board formulas are preferable to bid-offer approaches to limit incentives for lobbying. In terms of tariff reduction formulas, these two rules would generally suggest that linear reductions (a proportional cut) be avoided. A 'concertina' approach is likely to be better—that is, reduce the highest rates more. The higher is the tariff, the greater the resource allocation costs (these costs rise more than proportionally with the tariff) and the incentives to smuggle and engage in rent-seeking activity.

Another rule of thumb is that 'one size fits all' is likely to be desirable for all countries in only certain circumstances. Thus, it makes sense for basic principles such as national treatment and MFN, but it may not be appropriate in a welfare sense once the subject of negotiation is domestic regulation. In this area rules that center on ensuring transparency and due process are unobjectionable, but efforts to impose uniform substantive disciplines may easily be detrimental to some countries. In the area of regulation it is very important that negotiators have clear instructions and can rely on analysis and expertise in capitals to determine what the impact of a specific rule would be.

4.5. A TYPOLOGY OF KEY ASPECTS OF TRADE NEGOTIATIONS

It is useful to end this chapter with a typology of various aspects of MTNs, drawing upon the discussion in the foregoing sections and relating it to basic concepts used in the contemporary theory of negotiations.

Negotiations are Multi-Issue Barter Exchanges

Barter implies that MTNs involve the exchange of concessions (liberalization commitments). In the process of negotiations participants formulate requests (what they want in terms of liberalization by trading partners) and offers (what they are ready to liberalize themselves). As in any type of market situation, every trader (negotiator) will attempt to get as much as possible in exchange for as little as necessary. Through mutual bargaining negotiators attempt to arrive at a balanced package. The meaning of balanced is likely to differ from case to case, depending on what is being traded. The lack of a fungible medium of exchange requires trade negotiations to have an agenda that allows all the traders to trade something and in so doing improve upon the status quo. Setting the agenda is therefore very important. Actual negotiations are usually preceded by an intensive preparation process during which possible issues are identified, preferences are established, issues are ranked, initial positions are formulated, and a proposal is made with respect to the contents of the negotiating agenda. The process that led to the establishment of the negotiating agenda for the Uruguay Round took five years, starting with the preparation for the 1982 ministerial meeting, during which the US sought but failed to obtain agreement to launch a new MTN. It only ended with the 1986 ministerial meeting in Punta del Este, Uruguay, where agreement was finally reached on the agenda of the Uruguay Round. The efforts to launch a new MTN at the 1999 Seattle ministerial failed largely due to disagreements over what should be included on the agenda.

For any given agenda, there are virtually hundreds of economic, legal and political issues that must be resolved. Each participant, in evaluating possible final outcomes, must carefully consider the tradeoffs it is ready to accept and instruct its delegation accordingly. The main advantage of dealing with a broad range of issues is that it greatly increases the scope for cooperative behavior. When it is possible to determine jointly several negotiating issues, trade officials have an opportunity to considerably enlarge the pie before dividing it. The larger is the range of issues considered, the better the chances are that negotiators will act as cooperative problem solvers.

The lack of a price mechanism in barter trade situations makes it difficult to reveal true preferences, or, conversely, greatly enhances the scope for employing tactics intended to increase a country's potential payoff. Negotiations frequently arrive at an impasse because negotiators are not willing to make sufficient concessions to reach an agreement. Impasses are also part of the negotiating drama. Tensions, threats of deadlock and last minute deals are part of the repertoire of a competent negotiator. When impasses occur, negotiators must attempt to turn to other issues or modify the formulation of issues in search for some alternative terms of possible agreement. Every good negotiating team must maintain a consistent, coordinated position in all areas of negotiations, be able to rank its requests and offers across all issue areas, and be as well informed as possible about the positions of its negotiating partners. This is difficult, of course. In practice MTNs do not result in Pareto-optimal outcomes because offers are often made on a contingent basis to allow obtaining further concessions from its trading partners. Withdrawal of such contingent offers at the end of the day may lead to the unraveling of a carefully constructed, balanced package, and a move away from Pareto-optimality (Baldwin, 1986).

MTNs are Multi-Stage Games

As discussed earlier, a MTN has a number of stages, starting with a country or leader acting as a catalyst, initiating the prenegotiations that lead to the establishment of the agenda, followed by the MTN itself, which is followed in turn by the post-negotiation, implementation stage. The negotiation period, in turn, is in practice usually divided into a number of distinct stages as well. There is generally a learning period, during which participants signal their preferences on the various issues on the agenda, determine the options that exist for forming coalitions of various kinds, and simply engage in fact-finding regarding the various policy options that exist. This is followed by a period of substantive negotiations, with players demanding concessions and responding to the demands of others, thereby mapping out the set of feasible solutions. In this stage, many tentative agreements may be reached, but these are conditional upon the final outcome. The final stage generally starts close to what is perceived to be the deadline for conclusion of substantive talks. In practice, this often has been the date the negotiating authority of the US delegation expires. The fact that the negotiating process evolves in stages may induce negotiating teams to follow a 'nice-guy-bad-guy' approach. Negotiators first adopt an aggressive style when the initial positions are determined. This may involve taking strongly held stances in an adversarial manner. At a later stage in the negotiating process, a new negotiating team replaces the 'bad guy' and pursues a more cooperative tack.

MTNs are Multi-Player Games

MTNs are games with many players. The complexity of multi-party negotiations greatly exceeds those involving only two players. Coalitions may form and each participant must explore what options are available in this connection, and what the implications are of others forming coalitions. Various types of coalitions can be distinguished, ranging from informal and ad hoc, session or issue-specific to formal, multi-issue coalitions. The former tend to be much more prevalent than the latter, as it is generally difficult to agree to negotiate as a bloc. The multi-party nature of MTNs increases the responsibility of negotiators. They are not only engaged in transmitting their country's requests, offers, and negotiating positions, but are also continuously involved in gathering and transmitting information. One of the more important tasks of trade negotiators is to provide feedback on the preferences and interests of negotiating partners, and feel out to what extent negotiating positions are hard or soft. Such information will help their government in strategy formulation, including the pursuit of possible coalitions.

MTNs Take Time and are Repeated

In MTNs, negotiators bargain together over a substantial period of time, and know that they will meet each other repeatedly. The repeated nature of the interaction fosters cooperation by ensuring that if deals made at one point in time are not implemented (or reneged upon), not only will recourse to dispute settlement procedures be feasible, but future deals may be impeded. History matters in repeated games: actions or positions taken will have an effect on negotiating stances of trading partners in future interactions.

Learning will occur, and participants are given an incentive to invest resources in establishing a reputation. Reputation is important in terms of generating trust on the part of negotiating partners that agreements will be implemented, and may also help in exploiting the fact that MTNs have deadlines. As noted earlier, last minute balancing of concessions is a frequent practice in negotiations where initial bargaining takes place essentially on a bilateral basis. The fact that agreements reached on specific issues at intermediate stages of the negotiating process are conditional upon the overall outcome on all the issues increases pressure on negotiators as the deadline for conclusion of the talks is approached. Skilful negotiators prepare for the end-game confrontations of a MTN by explicitly seeking to link issues in a way that makes threats possible and credible.

Governments are not Monolithic

Governments are not monolithic. Participants in MTNs may spend less time negotiating with trading partners than they do internally. There are often large differences within a country on the issues that appear on the agenda—differences among provinces or states, differences between various government departments, as well as differences between consumer, producer and other interest groups. One major actor, the EU, is a composite player. It comprised 12 countries during the Uruguay Round, each of which simultaneously internalized the preferences of relevant domestic interest groups on various topics, and agreed with its 11 partners on the common position to be taken in the MTN on these topics (Basevi, Delbone and Mariotti, 1995).

Both the prenegotiation stage and the period in which the MTN is held will involve substantial interaction between governments and negotiators, and between governments and domestic interests. The extent to which domestic industries (producer associations or even particular major companies) influence both the prenegotiations and the negotiation process varies, depending on the country and issue involved. The influence of trade-policy lobbies is particularly important and transparent in the US, which has institutionalized such interactions through a complex system of general and sector-specific advisory bodies. Because governments are not monolithic, they may at times ask negotiators from other countries to help them in dealing with pressures at home. For example, the US delegation in the Uruguay Round made appeals to its negotiating partners to help it to resist protectionist pressures in America. Diversity of internal preferences is therefore another element that leads to the formation of (implicit) coalitions as well as attempts to link issues.

The Number of Solutions may be Small and Depend on Threat Strategies

The negotiating process is strongly dependent on how important agreement on an issue is for the major players. This depends on the status quo on an issue (or the threat point associated with breakdown of talks). When an agreement is necessary, negotiators may play games, but they know that they finally have to agree. The greater the resources invested (the larger the sunk costs) in a MTN, the lower the probability that they will end up in failure. A corollary of this is that if the probability of failure is high, no negotiations will be initiated. A good example is the 1982 ministerial meeting mentioned earlier, where the US sought to launch a MTN including trade in services and intellectual property on the agenda, something that met with broad-based opposition at the time (Low, 1993). A more recent example was the Seattle ministerial, which failed because members sought to obtain agreement on an agenda that included too many deeply divisive subjects.

Care will generally be taken to only initiate negotiations if there is an agenda that offers the possibility of gains for all concerned. It remains the case that if the status quo on an issue is not that bad from the viewpoint of one or more major trading nations, agreement may not emerge. In such cases the demandeurs on the issue will have to offer enough to substantially improve upon the status quo, something that is not always possible. Thus, in Seattle, EU concerns in the area of agriculture largely reflected the prospective eastward enlargement of the Union. American resistance to discussing antidumping or to consider liberalization of imports of clothing reflected opposition by politically powerful labor unions. Countries may also try to pursue strategies to affect the value of the status quo. Often, what counts is the threat point—the likely outcome of a failure to reach agreement. This may be much worse than the status quo ante. Indeed, the status quo at any point in time will in part be the result of threat strategies. The US has made extensive use of threats before and during MTNs. In the 1980s, for example, it began to pursue preferential trade agreements at least partly to pressure GATT contracting parties to initiate a comprehensive MTN following the failure of the 1982 ministerial to launch a new round. The US also used unilateral trade policy instruments (Section 301, Super 301 and Special 301—see chapter 8) to retaliate (or threaten to do so) against alleged unreasonable ('unfair') trade practices in areas such as IPRs that were not subject to GATT discipline (Bhagwati and Patrick, 1990).

Negotiators may Seek Symbolic Deals

Sometimes trade negotiations appear more similar to negotiations on the adoption of UN resolutions than attempts to agree to binding, specific commitments. Obviously there are many shades between the two extremes of pro-forma talks and substantive negotiations. A prominent example of GATT negotiations that led to a symbolic deal was the adoption of Part IV of the GATT on Trade and Development during the Kennedy Round and the Tokyo Round 'Enabling Clause' calling for special and differential treatment in favor of developing countries (chapter 12). Although these texts are more declarations of intent than firm commitments, they have had an impact on the trading system. The balance of rights and obligations of WTO members frequently extends well beyond legal commitments. Symbolic agreements may become a significant element of that balance. Symbolic deals also have another important function. When an agreement is required for political reasons, but substantive deals are not feasible, a symbolic agreement that incorporates a large zone of ambiguity may still have value for participants. This helps explain why negotiated agreements may be difficult to understand, allow for easy re-imposition of protection, or appear to contain commitments 'made of rubber'.

Perceptions of Equity are more Important than Efficiency

In an investigation of the tariff proposals made during the Tokyo Round, Chan (1985) concluded that the proposal finally chosen (the Swiss proposal—see Table 4.2) is best explained by solution concepts that emphasize fairness considerations. That is, he found that the Swiss proposal distributed the gains from liberalization across players in proportion to the weight (contribution) of each player. Solutions based on efficiency, that is, the maximization of the sum of gains across countries, independent of the distribution, did not work well. Allen (1979) and Baldwin and Clarke (1987) obtained similar results for the Kennedy and Tokyo Rounds, respectively. These findings are intuitive as they reflect the reciprocity approach that underlies MTNs. Thus, outcomes can be expected to reward players proportionately. Brown and Whalley (1980) analyze the efficiency implications of the various formulas that were proposed in the Tokyo Round. They show that countries proposing a particular formula would have gained less in welfare terms from implementing it than they would have gained from implementing the formulas proposed by trading partners. This is because own formulas tended to limit the reduction of barriers in politically-sensitive sectors, where the economic gains from reform are greatest.

4.6. FURTHER READING

Useful background reading on international negotiations is provided by Fred Ikle, *How Nations Negotiate* (New York: Harper and Row, 1964). Howard Raiffa, *The Art and Science of Negotiation* (Cambridge: Harvard University Press, 1983) discusses negotiations and bargaining in general. A practical guide is presented in William Zartman and Maureen Berman, *The Practical Negotiator* (New Haven, Yale University Press, 1982). John Odell, *Negotiating the World Economy* (Cornell University Press, 2000) provides a comprehensive analysis of major economic negotiations conducted by the US since the Second World War. John McMillan, 'A Game-Theoretic View of International Trade Negotiations', in John Whalley (ed.) *Rules, Power and Credibility* (London: University of Western Ontario, 1988) explores the applicability of game theory to MTNs.

Gerard Curzon, *Multilateral Commercial Diplomacy* (London: Michael Joseph, 1965) is a classic reference dealing with the early years of the GATT and its politics and economics. A classic treatise on the Kennedy Round is Ernest Preeg, *Traders and Diplomats: An Analysis of the Kennedy Round under the General Agreement on Tariffs and Trade* (Washington DC: Brookings Institution, 1970). The most comprehensive and interesting account and analysis of the Tokyo Round is offered by Gilbert Winham, *International Trade and the Tokyo Round Negotiations* (Princeton: Princeton University Press, 1986). The prenegotiation dynamics and process of the Uruguay Round is discussed by the same author in 'The Prenegotiation Phase of the Uruguay Round', in Janice Stein (ed.) *Getting to the Table* (London: Johns Hopkins Press, 1989). L. Alan Winters, in The Road to Uruguay, *Economic Journal*, 100 (1990), 1288–303 gives a short review of the issues that were put in the Uruguay Round and their GATT history. Jeffrey Schott and Johanna Buurman, *The Uruguay Round: An Assessment*, (Washington DC: Institute for International Economics, 1994) offer a summary of the outcome of the negotiations. Will Martin and Alan Winters (eds.), *The Uruguay Round and the Developing Countries* (Cambridge: Cambridge University Press, 1996) is a collection of comprehensive papers analyzing the outcome of the Uruguay Round.

Robert Baldwin, 'Toward More Efficient Procedures for Multilateral Trade Negotiations', *Aussenwirtschaft*, 41 (1986), 379–94 offers an accessible review of GATT negotiating techniques and problems. The contributions by Robert Baldwin and Alan Winters in J. M. Finger and A. Olechowski (eds.), *The Uruguay: A Handbook for the Multilateral Trade Negotiations* (Washington DC: The World Bank, 1987) provide succinct treatments of GATT negotiating techniques and principles. Fred Brown and John Whalley assess the welfare implications of the alternative formulas to reduce tariffs that were proposed in the Tokyo Round in 'General Equilibrium Evaluations of Tariff-Cutting Proposals in the Tokyo Round and Comparisons with More Extensive Liberalization of World Trade', *Economic Journal* (December 1980), 838–68.

Robert Tollison and Thomas Willett, 'An Economic Theory of Mutually Advantageous Issue Linkages in International Negotiations', *International Organization*, 33 (1979), 425–49 and James Sebenius, 'Negotiation Arithmetic: Adding and Subtracting Issues and Parties', *International Organization*, 37 (1983), 281–316 discuss the strategy of issue linkage in international negotiations. Mancur Olson, *The Logic of Collective Action: Public Goods and the Theory of Groups* (Cambridge: Harvard University Press, 1965) and Thomas Schelling, *Micromotives and Macrobehaviour* (New York: W.W. Norton, 1978) discuss necessary conditions and incentives for the formation of coalitions or clubs. Giorgio Basevi, F. Delbono and M. Mariotti analyze the complexities for MTNs that involve coalitions, focusing specifically on the EU, in 'Bargaining with a Composite Player: An Application to the Uruguay Round of GATT Negotiations', *Journal of International Comparative Economics* 3 (1995), 161–74.

Jagdish Bhagwati and Hugh Patrick (eds.), *Aggressive Unilateralism: America's 301 Trade Policy and the World Trading System* (Ann Arbor: University of Michigan Press, 1990) is an informative and thoughtful collection of papers exploring the use of Section 301 by the US. Kenneth Oye, *Economic Discrimination and Political Exchange: World Political Economy in the 1930s and 1980s* (Princeton: Princeton University Press, 1992) discusses the role of reciprocal trade bargaining by the US. An excellent account of the Seattle ministerial and the reasons for its failure can be found in *The World Trade Agenda*, no. 16, 1999 (Geneva). John Odell provides a detailed description of the preparatory process leading up to the Seattle ministerial and what went wrong in Seattle in 'The Seattle Impasse and its Implications for the WTO', presented at the conference in honor of Robert Hudec, The Political Economy of International Trade Law (September).

PART III
THE MULTILATERAL TRADE AGREEMENTS

5
Trade in Goods

Governments pursue trade policies for a variety of reasons, including as a means to raise revenue, to protect specific industries (whether infant, senile or other), to shift the terms of trade, to attain certain foreign policy or security goals, or simply to restrict the consumption of specific goods. Whatever the underlying objective, an active trade policy redistributes income by transferring resources to specific industries and the factors of production employed there, usually does so in an inefficient and nontransparent manner, and for precisely that reason tends to be supported by interest groups that lobby for import restrictions.

The GATT essentially regulates the use of trade policies by WTO members. It does not address the basic question whether governments should use domestic or trade policies to achieve particular objectives. That is, the issue of efficiency is not addressed directly. The premise is that inefficient instruments such as trade policy must be accepted, and that the best that can be achieved is to discipline the use of different types of trade policies. Thus, while countries are free to use trade policies, they are generally encouraged to use the least trade-distorting measures. GATT rules are mostly consistent with what economic theory would recommend in many circumstances, but only in the sense of moving governments to use second rather than third best instruments. The objective is to avoid the worst by accepting some bad in government intervention in trade.

Three broad categories of trade policy instruments can be distinguished: measures that affect quantities, restricting the volume or value of transactions; those that affect prices, involving the imposition of a monetary fee (tax) on foreign suppliers; and those that indirectly affect quantities or prices. Virtually any policy or action by a government may have an effect on trade (see Deardorff and Stern, 1998 for a discussion of the many types of policies that have an effect on trade). As noted in chapter 3, this is explicitly recognized in the GATT, in that dispute settlement procedures allow for so-called nonviolation complaints to be brought. Any policy—whether or not it is prohibited under GATT—can be contested if it acts to deny a benefit of the Agreement. This chapter summarizes the main GATT disciplines relating to specific instruments of trade control. For convenience, Box 5.1 lists the major articles of the GATT. Space constraints prohibit discussion of all GATT provisions. Articles dealing with contingent protection (Articles VI,

XII, XVIII and XIX) and exceptions (Articles XX and XXI) are discussed in chapter 9.

Box 5.1. Major GATT Articles

Article	Summary
I	General MFN requirement.
II	Tariff schedules (bindings).
III	National treatment.
V	Freedom of transit of goods.
VI	Allows antidumping and countervailing duties. Superseded by the GATT 1994 Agreement on Antidumping, and the Agreement on Subsidies and Countervailing Measures.
VII	Requires that valuation of goods for customs purposes be based on actual value. Superseded by the GATT 1994 Agreement on the Implementation of Article VII.
VIII	Requires that fees connected with import and export formalities be cost-based.
IX	Reaffirms MFN for labeling requirements and calls for cooperation to prevent abuse of trade names.
X	Obligation to publish trade laws and regulations; complemented by the WTO's Trade Policy Review Mechanism and numerous notification requirements in specific WTO agreements.
XI	Requires the general elimination of quantitative restrictions.
XII	Permits trade restrictions if necessary to safeguard the balance of payments.
XIII	Requires that quotas be administered in a nondiscriminatory manner.
XVI	Established GATT 1947 rules on subsidies. Complemented by the WTO Agreement on Subsidies and Countervailing Measures.
XVII	Requires that state trading enterprises follow MFN.
XVIII	Allows developing countries to restrict trade to promote infant industries and to protect the balance-of-payments (imposing weaker conditionality than Article XII).
XIX	Allows for emergency action to restrict imports of particular products if these cause serious injury to the domestic industry. Complemented by the WTO Agreement on Safeguards.
XX	General exceptions provision—allows trade restrictions if necessary to attain noneconomic objectives (health, safety).

XXI	Allows trade to be restricted if necessary for national security reasons.
XXII	Requires consultations between parties involved in trade disputes.
XXIII	GATT's main dispute settlement provision, providing for violation and nonviolation complaints. Complemented by the WTO Understanding on Rules and Procedures Governing the Settlement of Disputes.
XXIV	Sets out the conditions under which the formation of free trade areas or customs unions is permitted.
XXVIII	Allows for renegotiation of tariff concessions.
XXVIII bis	Calls for periodic MTNs to reduce tariffs.
XXXIII	Allows for accession.
Part IV	Calls for more favorable and differential treatment of developing countries.

5.1. TARIFFS, PARA-TARIFFS AND INDIRECT TAXES

A tariff is a tax levied on products when passing a customs border. Governments levy tariffs on imports and exports, but import tariffs are by far the more important in practice. Customs tariffs may be:

(1) *ad valorem* (a percentage of the value of imported products);
(2) specific (a given amount of money per physical unit, say US$1.5 per litter of wine);
(3) a combination of the two, five percent *ad valorem* plus US$1 per liter of wine).

The GATT does not favor one type of tariff over another.[1] In practice, most tariffs are *ad valorem*. Each may have advantages in specific situations. *Ad valorem* rates are more transparent, and are indexed. If the value of a product increases (because of inflation for example), then tariff revenue will keep pace with price increases. Specific tariffs have the advantage of not requiring customs authorities to determine the value of imports when entering the country, and are by definition not sensitive to changes in the value of goods. The customs tariff is in principle the only instrument of protection allowed under the GATT. The preference for tariffs is consistent with economic theory, in that tariffs are superior to QRs for reasons already mentioned in

---

[1] WTO members may switch from *ad valorem* to specific duties if they desire, as long as this does not result in a violation of a tariff binding.

chapter 1 and discussed further in annex 2. Reasons why tariffs are preferable to QRs include the following:

- Tariffs maintain an automatic link between domestic and foreign prices, ensuring that the most efficient supplier continues to be able to serve the market. This link is cut with quotas.

- It is easy to ensure nondiscrimination between foreign sources of supply using tariffs; under a quota this is much more difficult. Quota allocation is often based on arbitrary decisions of officials.

- Tariffs are transparent. Once established, every trader knows the price of market access for specific products. This is not the case under a quota, where the conditions of market access may depend on timing (for example, under a first-come, first-served allocation scheme), past performance (if quotas are allocated based on historical utilization rates), or corruption (bribery of the officials responsible for licensing).

- Tariffs are also more transparent in that the level of nominal protection under tariff is easily calculated, whereas its estimation is more complex under a quota.

- Tariffs generate revenue for the government, whereas under quotas the tariff equivalent may go to the exporters or to intermediaries, depending on how the quotas are allocated. In most cases, governments do not obtain the created rents—the extra revenue per unit sold that is due to the price-increasing effect of restricting supply is transferred to those who have the quota rights. This is a major incentive for lobbying and rent seeking.

- Tariffs are also more efficient because they reduce lobbying incentives. They benefit the whole industry producing the protected good, reducing the returns for individual firms to lobby for protection. If quotas are an option, traders may seek individual quota allocations that are as large as possible for themselves, inducing further socially wasteful lobbying.

WTO Rules and Coverage

There are two basic rules for tariffs. First, tariffs must be nondiscriminatory (Article I). The main exceptions to the MFN rule are if countries are members of regional integration agreements (chapter 10), provide tariff preferences in favor of developing countries (chapter 12), or confront imports from a nonmember country. Second, members may not raise tariffs above the levels they have bound in their schedules. The tariff concessions made by members upon accession or in periodic MTNs are expressed in the form of tariff bindings inscribed in each member's tariff schedule (GATT Article II). By binding its tariff, a member undertakes not to impose a tariff on a specific product that is higher than the bound rate. A binding may be identical to the currently applied rate; it may comprise a so-called ceiling rate that is higher than the applied rate; or it may consist of a negotiated rate that is lower than the currently applied rate. The last possibility often arises after a MTN has been completed, with the negotiated rate entering into force at a specified future date. A tariff binding establishes a benchmark for the conditions of market access that a country commits itself to. Under GATT rules, any measure taken or supported by a government that has the effect of nullifying or impairing the concession implied by its tariff bindings gives cause for complaint by trading partners. There is no need to show an impact on trade. Thus, the binding not only restricts the possibility of raising tariffs, but also limits the possibility of using measures that have an equivalent effect (however, as discussed in chapter 9, there are various ways around this constraint).

To a significant extent the content of tariff schedules determines the relevance of GATT rules. Formally, the product coverage of the GATT for each member is determined by a positive list approach. Each member includes in its schedule the products (tariff lines) on which it is willing to make tariff commitments. These schedules form an integral part of the GATT. The comprehensiveness of tariff bindings for members has traditionally varied considerably. For most industrialized market economies, the share of bound tariffs in the total number of tariff lines has always been very high for manufactured goods and substantial for agricultural products. Moreover, bindings have tended to be at or near applied rates. The coverage of bindings for most developing countries has traditionally been very low or nonexistent, and usually pertained to ceiling bindings that are significantly higher than applied rates.

Many contracting parties joined GATT 1947 after becoming independent in the 1950s and 1960s. Such former colonies were allowed to accede to GATT without tariff negotiations. Developing countries were also granted special and differential treatment, allowing them not to offer concessions in MTNs. This implied that only nondiscrimination disciplines applied, as countries are free to raise tariffs if there are no ceiling bindings. During the Uruguay Round an attempt was made to expand the coverage of bindings by requiring all WTO members to submit tariff schedules. In contrast to GATT 1947, WTO membership requires a schedule of commitments. Moreover, all WTO members are obliged to bind 100 percent of their agricultural tariff lines—a major change in comparison with GATT 1947, under which agriculture had largely become exempt from disciplines (chapter 6). While there are no rules concerning the product coverage of tariff schedules for nonagricultural goods, developing country participation as measured by the scope of tariff bindings increased substantially during the Uruguay Round. This reflected a realization that greater participation in the multilateral trading system was beneficial, as well as significant unilateral liberalization under-taken by many countries during the 1980s and 1990s.

The coverage of tariff bindings for industrial products pre- and post-Uruguay Round is summarized in Table 5.1. The share of industrial tariff lines bound by developing countries increased from 22 to 72 percent. Most of these bindings relate to 'ceilings' (maximum rates), not applied tariffs. Ceiling rates are much less valuable to traders than if applied rates were in-scribed, but do have some value, as they establish an upper bound on the downside risk confronted by traders and investors (Francois 1999). The dif-ference between the average applied and bound rate is a measure of what has been called the binding overhang. The greater this difference, the deeper the average tariff cut that must be realized in a MTN for the outcome to im-ply actual liberalization. It is often not realized that the focus of MTNs is on tariff bindings, not on applied rates. An implication is that claims that a MTN reduced average tariffs by, say, 30 percent does not necessarily imply that applied tariffs have fallen by that amount.

TABLE 5.1 *Tariff bindings for industrial products*

Country group	Number of lines	Percentage of tariff lines bound	
		Pre-Uruguay	Post-Uruguay
Developed countries	86,968	78	99
Developing countries*	157,805	22	72
Transition economies	18,962	73	98

* Data cover 26 countries accounting for 80 percent of total merchandise trade of all developing country participants in the Uruguay Round.
Source: GATT (1994c).

Economists often ask why developing countries have not bound tariffs at applied rates, especially economies in the process of moving towards mar-ket-determined exchange rates and liberalization of current account trans-actions, or that already have done so. In many cases it simply reflects the mercantilism underlying the GATT (that is, a perception that bindings are negotiating chips). Constituencies in favor of low import barriers may also be unaware of the potential value of binding rates. Finance ministries may be opposed to losing a revenue raising tool. The latter consideration is par-ticularly important for low-income countries that are dependent on taxation of foreign trade for revenue. Finally, countries with overvalued exchange rates and resulting foreign exchange shortages and rationing often have no wish to be subjected to GATT surveillance in instances where measures are required to safeguard the balance of payments (see chapter 9).

In a MTN context, a key issue confronting a country is to determine what the cost-benefit ratio is of binding or not binding at applied rates. One source of benefit is the quid pro quo that may be realized in terms of improved access to foreign markets. This is the benefit that most often appears to be upper most in the minds of policymakers. However, this is arguably not the most important dimension of the tradeoff, especially for small countries with little if any negotiating power. More important is to take into account that binding at or below applied rates can be a powerful tool with which to signal to investors that the government is serious about reducing uncertainty regarding its future trade policy stance. As noted in chapter 1, this can have substantial payoffs in terms of reducing risk premia demanded by investors and stimulating capital inflows.

Other Fees and Charges on Imports

WTO members are constrained regarding the use of fees and specific import taxes that have an effect equivalent to tariffs. Examples include taxes on foreign exchange transactions, internal taxes on imports, service fees affecting importers and special import surcharges. Such para-tariffs as they are sometimes called are often important in developing countries. Data for a sample of forty-one developing countries in the early 1980s indicated that at least one third of revenue from import taxation was generated by para-tariffs. Such measures are frequently subject to arbitrary implementation and are nontransparent (Kostecki and Tymowski, 1985). They are often driven by specific interest groups that have successfully lobbied for earmarked taxes to finance their activities.

In contrast to GATT 1947, the GATT 1994 requires that the nature and level of other duties or charges be listed by tariff line in each WTO member's schedule. Allowance is made for the imposition of fees or other charges, as long as these are commensurate with the cost of services rendered (Article II:2c). Article VIII (on fees and formalities related to trade) requires that all such service fees must 'be limited in amount to the approximate cost of services rendered and shall not represent an indirect protection to domestic products or a taxation of imports or exports for fiscal purposes' (Article VIII:1). Examples of such fees include consular transactions, licensing, statistical services, documentation, certification, inspection, and quarantine, sanitation and fumigation. Article VIII applies irrespective of whether a country has bound its tariffs. The requirement that service fees be cost-based aims to prevent circumvention of tariff bindings.

In a 1988 dispute settlement case brought to GATT concerning the imposition of a uniform *ad valorem* customs user fee by the US it was concluded that such fees must be service-specific (GATT, 1994b, 251). Thus, imposing an average fee equal to the total cost of customs administration divided by the total value of imports was not acceptable. Although the US altered its customs user fee to conform to these findings, other countries continued to maintain *ad valorem* fees that were inconsistent with the GATT. In part this was because service fees in existence on the date of a country's accession to GATT were grandfathered and thus immune from scrutiny. Developing countries also had greater leeway than industrialized countries, as their tariffs often were not bound. As of the mid 1990s, some developing countries continued to maintain customs user fees of five percent *ad valorem* or higher (Zarrouk, 2000).

In principle all grandfathered policies that are inconsistent with the WTO must be abolished. It is likely that over time WTO members will be less tolerant of fees on imports that are not cost-based. The issue arose several times in the WTO. For example, in 1998 the EU contested a Harbor Maintenance Tax maintained by the US as a violation of among others, Articles II and VIII, as well as the Uruguay Round Understanding on the Interpretation of Article II:1b. This Understanding is quite important from a transparency perspective, as it requires members to notify all the duties and charges that apply in connection with importation of goods.

Tariff Escalation

Tariff escalation is closely related to the concept of effective protection (chapter 4). One speaks of tariff escalation if duty rates on raw materials and intermediates are lower than rates on processed commodities that embody the relevant inputs. Tariff escalation has traditionally been a problem for developing countries seeking to process commodities before they are exported. The more escalated is the tariff structure maintained in export markets, the greater the difficulty for such countries to generate value-added at home, as the low tariffs on raw materials (usually duty-free) provide an incentive not to process commodities before they are exported. A group of products where tariff escalation has often been a source of particular concern are natural resource-based products, defined in GATT to include non-ferrous metals and minerals, forestry products and fish and fishery products. As a result of the importance of these products for developing countries a specific negotiating group was established in the Uruguay Round to lower tariff barriers and reduce tariff escalation. Tariff escalation declined as a result of the Uruguay Round in that the absolute difference between tariff levels at various stages of processing fell (GATT, 1994c).

The structure of tariffs maintained by WTO members varies considerably. High tariffs are particularly frequent for agricultural imports in OECD countries, and across all categories in many developing countries. In the EU, about one quarter of post-Uruguay Round imports of manufactured goods is duty free, and some 40 percent are subjected to tariffs below five percent. Tariffs above 25 percent are imposed on a negligible share of imports of manufactures. In the US, duty free imports account for some 80 percent of the total; a tariff rate of more than 10 percent is imposed on less than three percent of imports. Escalation is a feature of almost all tariff structures. The exceptions are the few economies that essentially have a free trade stance (Estonia, Hong Kong), and those that have implemented a uniform tariff, that is, apply the same tariff to imports of all goods (Bolivia, Chile, the Kyrgyz Republic).

There are good economic arguments in favor of applying a low, uniform tariff. These include the fact that such a tariff structure ensures that all activities are treated equally, leaving it to the market to determine what activities are profitable to undertake. Uniformity also has important benefits in terms of incentives for rent seeking, as it sends a signal to firms that there will be no exemptions and that it will not pay to lobby for either higher or lower tariffs. Thus, a uniform rate saves on lobbying costs, and induces less corruption and social waste. Lobbying is unattractive because efforts to increase the tariff will affect virtually the whole economy, and solicit opposition by users of imported inputs. Indeed, a uniform tariff, because it puts pressure on industries that are dependent on imports, creates incentives for lobbying in favor of reducing the average rate. In the case of Chile, which maintained a 11 percent tariff for some years, a decision was made to gradually lower it to 6 percent starting in 1998. Another advantage of a uniform tariff is that it lowers transaction costs—there is no scope to argue about how products should be classified for customs duty calculation purposes. Uniformity also tends to make it easier for the government to monitor the performance of customs agencies—given data on the value of imports it is easy to calculate how much revenue should have been collected. It is often difficult for countries to maintain a uniform tariff in MTNs, especially if these take the form of bid-offer negotiations, as the government cannot participate in such talks. All it can do is to make offers of formula cuts. As a result of this 'constraint'—which is really an advantage from an economic perspective—statements have been made in the WTO Council opposing the use of uniform tariffs. Governments are well advised to resist attempts to convince them not to adopt uniform tariffs (Tarr, 2000).

In addition to deliberate tariff escalation, dispersion in the structure of tariffs often results from duty exemption programs. Exemptions may be granted to enterprises that engage in certain 'favored' activities—a frequent example are foreign investors, which are often granted tax holidays and duty exemption for imported inputs and capital equipment—or to favored individuals and government entities. Such duty exemptions are a costly policy instrument as they can encourage corruption and rent seeking, reduce revenue collected by customs, and distort economic incentives. They may also have negative political economy effects, in that they can greatly reduce the incentives of industries that obtain exemptions to lobby in support of general trade liberalization. An exception to this argument pertains to duty exemptions granted to enterprises that produce for export. Exporting firms must be able to import inputs and components, including machinery, at world prices. Otherwise they will be impeded in their ability to compete on international markets. Many countries have therefore implemented duty drawback or temporary admission schemes as part of their customs procedures. Although such mechanisms are an important tool of export development if they function efficiently, from a political economy viewpoint they also suffer from the problem that they reduce the potential size of the domestic lobby willing to support general import liberalization.

5.2. QUANTITATIVE RESTRICTIONS AND IMPORT LICENSING

GATT rules on quantitative restrictions (QRs) were written when these types of measures were widespread and constituted a major barrier to trade. Despite the fact that GATT rules basically prohibit the use of QRs, they continued to be used by governments to protect domestic import-competing industries. QRs have been particularly prevalent in trade in agricultural products, textiles and clothing, and steel. Over time, the relative importance of QRs as trade restrictions in OECD countries declined substantially. In the Uruguay Round disciplines in this area were strengthened, with the outlawing of VERs, the tariffication of agricultural quotas and the agreement to phase out textile and clothing quotas administered under auspices of the MFA. Notwithstanding the decline in the use of traditional QRs, the GATT provisions banning their use continue to be one of the most frequently invoked bases for dispute settlement. Often these cases concern agriculture or clothing products. But they often also concern measures that have an effect that is equivalent to a quantitative restriction.

The economic case against the use of quotas was summarized earlier. A quota cuts the link between domestic and foreign prices, is generally discriminatory, does not necessarily allow the changing pattern of comparative advantage over time to be reflected in imports, is less transparent, and is more subject to administrative abuse and corruption (see also annex 2). For all these reasons interest groups seeking protection tend to prefer QRs to tariffs. The primary motivation, however, is generally that QRs are less visible to consumers and that the revenue that otherwise would flow to the government is to a large extent captured by those who manage to obtain the quota rights or licenses.

WTO Disciplines

Articles XI–XIV of the GATT provide the legal framework addressing QRs. Article XI prohibits them in principle, except for agricultural commodities if concurrent measures are taken to restrict domestic production (chapter 6). Article XII provides an exception, and allows QRs to be used for balance-of-payments (BOP) reasons. If this is done, Article XIII requires that such quotas in principle apply on a nondiscriminatory basis, while Article XIV allows for a request that the Council waives this requirement. These provisions are complemented by the Agreement of Safeguards, which bans the use of voluntary export restraint agreements (VERs), a specific type of QR (see annex 2).

The basic obligation imposed on members in ArticleXI:1 is to refrain from introducing or maintaining QRs. As noted in earlier chapters, QRs are banned not only because of economic considerations, but also to prevent governments from circumventing tariff bindings. Article XIII requires nondiscrimination if QRs are used. The economic rationale for this is that a global quota is more efficient than selective QRs. Under a global quota traders (importers) are left free to determine from where to source. The direction of trade (sourcing of imports) will then be responsive to changes in prices, quality and transportation costs. However, the inclusion of Article XIII is not driven by efficiency considerations. Instead, it simply reaffirms the MFN principle for QRs. The more country-specific the allocation of the quota rights, the greater the danger of discrimination. Country-specific allocation is usually based on historical market shares. The GATT rationale is that this reduces all exporters' market access rights proportionally.

Despite the general prohibition on QRs, GATT contracting parties continued to use them. Formal QRs were used especially in the agricultural context (industrialized countries) and for BOP purposes (developing countries—see chapters 9 and 12). A very popular form of QR—used increasingly in the 1970s and 1980s—was the VER, which were often negotiated under the threat of antidumping (AD) actions (see chapter 9). Another type of QR are 'undertakings' agreed to by exporters to reduce supply or raise prices in the context of AD investigations. As mentioned earlier, VERs and agricultural QRs were banned in the Uruguay Round. However, tariff quotas have become much more important in agriculture (chapter 6).

Import Licensing

QRs are generally enforced by means of licenses. A separate Agreement on Import Licensing Procedures, which applies to all WTO members, aims to strengthen general GATT obligations in this domain. The agreement resembles closely the code on licensing that was negotiated in the Tokyo Round. It establishes requirements to enhance transparency of licensing systems, including publication requirements, the right of appeal of decisions, and the length of license validity. Licensing can become a source of disputes when the allocation of quota rights is perceived to be biased and violate the GATT nondiscrimination principles. Traditionally, licenses tend to be allocated on the basis of historical market shares, which are one measure of what constitutes nondiscrimination. An alternative would be to auction off the licenses to the highest bidder. The latter approach has the economic advantages of generating revenue for the government and reducing the resource allocation distortions generated by quota systems, but the political disadvantage of eliminating discretion (patronage possibilities) and the opportunity for powerful vested interests to obtain quota rents. The WTO rules on import licensing played a major role in the *Bananas* case discussed earlier, which revolved to a great extent around the procedures used by the EU to allocate import licenses (see chapter 3).

· 5.3. CUSTOMS CLEARANCE–RELATED PROVISIONS

Customs clearance requires the valuation and classification of imports for purposes such as levying tariffs, determining origin, enforcing foreign exchange controls and collecting statistics. Customs procedures may become NTBs if officials incorrectly classify goods or assign goods a value greater than appropriate. An agreement to reduce and bind tariffs would be practically meaningless without a set of rules concerning valuation and classification of imported goods. Arbitrary customs procedures could then be used to ensure that a government (or its officials) collect as much revenue as desired, independent of the formally negotiated tariff schedule. Import-competing industries might also bribe officials to harass importers. To reduce the likelihood that a country's published tariff schedule is not representative of the nominal tariffs that are actually applied, GATT establishes certain rules and principles regarding customs valuation.

Classification

Classification of goods for customs purposes is less troublesome than valuation, as most countries use internationally developed classification systems. The main coding system used for classification purposes during the first forty years of the GATT's existence were the Brussels Tariff Nomenclature (BTN) and the Customs Cooperation Council Nomenclature (CCCN). More recently, countries switched to the Harmonized Commodity Description and Coding System (HS). All these systems were developed by the Customs Cooperation Council in Brussels—now called the World Customs Organization. The HS allows for a greater range of products than its predecessors and permits easier classification of new products. As of the late 1990s, the majority of WTO members were using HS-based systems, either because they are signatories of the HS, or because they apply it on a de facto basis (Box 5.2).

Box 5.2. What is the Harmonized System?

The Harmonized Commodity Description and Coding System (usually referred to as the Harmonized System or HS) provides a legal structure and product typology for the purpose of tariff classification. It comprises 1,241 headings grouped into 96 chapters (in turn subdivided into 21 sections). The system's 5000 subheadings are identified by a six-digit code, each of which is carefully defined and described, with rules to ensure uniform application. The first four digits indicate a product group or family. The fifth and sixth digits designate specific product lines. For instance, 8470.10 is the code for 'electronic calculators capable of operating without an external source of electronic power and pocket size data recording, reproducing and displaying machines with calculating functions' whereas 8470 is the code for electronic calculating machines as a group. The Harmonized System is implemented through an international convention that requires signatories to apply it in a uniform fashion at the six-digit level. Beyond the six-digit level, countries may introduce national idiosyncrasies in their coding systems.

The HS nomenclature was developed under the auspices of the Customs Cooperation Council (now the World Customs Organization or WCO) in Brussels. It is broadly based on an earlier standard, the CCCN, and incorporates certain aspects of the TSUS (the tariff schedule of the United States) and the Canadian tariff nomenclature. The HS came into effect in 1988, and has been revised periodically since then. It is meant to be used not only for

customs purposes, but also for collection of trade statistics and associated transactions (such as transport and insurance). Before the adoption of the HS, countries tended to use the Standard International Trade Classification (SITC) for statistical purposes—developed under UN auspices. This differed substantially from the classifications in use for customs clearance purposes.
Source: See www.wcoomd.org.

The use of the HS by WTO members is important to traders as it reduces uncertainty regarding the treatment of their goods in customs. Knowing how products will be classified allows producers to fine tune their production process and tailor and package their products in a way that minimizes the expected duty burden (Box 5.3). The tariff structure of many countries is idiosyncratic—close substitutes may be subject to widely differing tariffs, providing potential opportunities for producers to arbitrage across classifications.

Although widespread use of the HS has led to a reduction in disputes related to classification, such disputes still occur. An example was a recent case brought by the US against the EU, which had reclassified for tariff purposes certain local area network (LAN) adapter equipment and personal computers with multimedia capability. The US alleged that this had led to a violation of EU tariff bindings (Article II:1 GATT). The panel found against the EU. On appeal, the Appellate Body reversed the panel's conclusion and determined that the EU's tariff treatment of LAN equipment was valid. Although the HS helps to make the customs environment more predictable, it is important to note that WTO members bind their tariffs at the 10 or 12 digit level of disaggregation. At this level, classification is country-specific. As mentioned, the uniform classification only goes down to the six-digit level of disaggregation.

Box 5.3. Product Strategy and Customs Classification
Customs tariffs on agricultural products tend to be substantially higher than on industrial goods. Product classification by customs consequently may have important implications for an exporter's competitive position in a given market. In such cases managers will analyze the differences between product duty rates in order to adjust their product strategy. Three examples:
• The Canadian Dehydrators Association exports alfalfa feed products all over the world. It monitors any modifications in customs rates for particular feed product lines in order to modify its export product mix to minimize import charges. One option that is used is to mix dehydrated alfalfa products with other types of feed (such as grains) in order to benefit from under lower customs rates.

- An East European company exporting food ingredients to Japan used to mix its powder milk with fat and then separate it again in Japan. It did this to pay lower customs duties on 'frozen cheese' rather than the high duties on powder milk and on animal fats that applied when exported separately.
- A US sugar refinery imports 'stuffed molasses', a syrup with a high sugar content, to produce a liquid sugar product for sale to ice-cream and confectionery companies, allowing it to avoid high duties on sugar.
Source: Kostecki (2001) and *Financial Times*, October 20, 2000, p. 10.

Valuation

The provisions on customs valuation contained in the GATT 1947 (Article VII) were not very precise, basically requiring that goods be valued on the basis of their actual value. Before the launch of the Tokyo Round (1973), a number of contracting parties, led by the EEC, felt that certain national valuation practices were restricting international trade. US methods were a major bone of contention, in particular the so-called American Selling Price criterion, which established the value of some imported goods on the basis of the selling price of similar domestically produced goods. Although this clearly violated GATT rules, the US was able to employ this method because it had grandfathered the practice when acceding to GATT. Largely motivated by US practices, in the Tokyo Round a Customs Valuation Code was negotiated which supplemented GATT's valuation provisions and outlawed practices such as the American Selling Price. As was the case with all the codes, participation was voluntary, and most developing countries did not sign the agreement. The US signed the code and reformed its valuation practices to comply with the agreement.

With the creation of the WTO at the end of the Uruguay Round, the Tokyo Round code rules became applicable to all WTO members. Disciplines were also added on preshipment inspection—the practice of requiring the inspection of goods in the country of production before they are shipped—and on rules of origin. The main impact of the Uruguay Round agreement on customs valuation will be on developing countries, as valuation is generally no longer a policy issue in high-income nations. In many developing countries, valuation practices do not conform to the provisions of the agreement, and major efforts are required to bring their systems into compliance.

The agreement on customs valuation (formally the Agreement on Implementation of Article VII of GATT) aims to establish uniform, transparent and fair standards for the valuation of imported goods for customs purposes. The main objective of the agreement is to establish a system which outlaws the use of arbitrary or fictitious customs values and which conforms to commercial realities. In principle, valuation should be based on the transaction or invoice value of the goods—the price actually paid or payable for the goods (subject to adjustments concerning freight and several other charges). This method should be applied when:

(1) there are no special restrictions as to the disposal or use of goods;
(2) the buyer and seller are not related;
(3) no proceeds of the subsequent sales accrue to the exporter; and
(4) the sale or price is not subject to special conditions that cannot be quantified.

The agreement does not prescribe a uniform system regarding shipping, insurance and handling charges. A country may opt for a cost, insurance and freight (c.i.f.), a cost and freight or a free-on-board (f.o.b.) valuation basis. If customs authorities have reasons to believe that the transaction value is inaccurate, they are required to proceed sequentially through five alternative valuation options:

(1) the value of identical goods;
(2) the value of similar goods;
(3) the so-called deductive method;
(4) the computed value method; and
(5) an 'if all else fails' method.[2]

It is only when the customs value cannot be determined under one of these options that the next option in the sequence can be used. However, an importer may request that the computed method be used in preference to the deductive method. In most instances refusal to accept the invoice price will be connected to there being a relationship between buyer and seller. The mere fact of such a relationship is not sufficient grounds for the authorities to reject the invoice price. What matters is that the relationship influences the price. If the value is questioned by customs, the burden of proof is on the importer.

In recognition of fears voiced during the Tokyo Round regarding fraudulent invoicing, especially between related parties, a Protocol to the code gave developing country signatories somewhat greater regulatory flexibility in their customs procedures. Also, technical assistance in implementing code procedures was promised. Despite this, developing country participation in the code remained limited. Fears of reduced tariff revenue as a result of un-

---

[2] The *deductive* value method consists of the unit price at which a significant quantity of imported goods is sold to unrelated persons, subject to deductions for commissions, profit margins, transport and insurance costs. The *computed* method consists of summing the cost or value of materials and other inputs employed in producing the imported goods, and adding an amount for profit and general expenses equal to that applied in sales of similar goods by other producers.

der-invoicing, a wish to maintain discretion in valuing imports, or the administrative burden of implementing code provisions were among the major concerns. In the Uruguay Round, a number of developing countries put forward the view that the need to accept declared values was the main factor prohibiting greater participation in the code. Consequently, they proposed that the agreement be amended to allow more scope for rejecting transactions (invoice) values.

In recognition of developing country implementation concerns, in the Uruguay Round developing countries that were not party to the code were given the right to delay implementing its provisions until January 1, 2000. Application of the computed value method may be delayed for an additional three years, and reservations may be entered in respect of any of the provisions of the agreement if other members consent. Developing countries which valued goods on the basis of officially established minimum values can request a reservation to retain such values on a limited and transitional basis, subject to the terms and conditions required by the other members. Requests for derogations require approval from the WTO Council. An annex to the agreement allows developing countries to request extension of transition periods.

During 1999, in the run-up to the Seattle ministerial meeting, many developing countries requested extension of implementation deadlines. They argued that their customs systems did not yet allow a switch to invoice-based valuation. A problem with using a transactions-based valuation system that puts the burden on customs authorities to query invoice values is that mechanisms and tools must be available for the authorities to determine whether declared values are reasonable. Most OECD countries have sophisticated computer-based systems and risk-assessment techniques that allow them to identify suspect claims, and access to databases that allow them to roughly determine the market value of most commodities that pass the frontier. This is not the case for many developing countries, notwithstanding the technical assistance efforts in this area by organizations such as the WCO, UNCTAD and the IMF. Implementation in developing countries involves much more than a decree that valuation is to conform to the WTO agreement. Customs administrations need to be automated, infrastructure improved, staff trained, and so forth. This generally takes a significant amount of time and requires the investment of substantial resources.

Given that the transition periods negotiated in the Uruguay Round only expired on January 1, 2000, there have been few dispute settlement cases relating to valuation. One of the few disputes was a case brought by the EU in 1996 against Mexico, claiming that Mexico applied c.i.f. value as the basis of customs valuation of imports originating in non-NAFTA countries, and f.o.b. value for imports originating in NAFTA countries. This was argued to raise the valuation basis for imports, although in practice it should not result in discrimination if intra-NAFTA flows are duty-free.[3] Disputes in this area were widely expected in 1999 as transition periods for developing country were expiring. Over 40 developing countries sought extensions of transition periods, and made this an issue at the Seattle ministerial (see chapter 12).

Preshipment Inspection

Trade facilitation is a key requirement for countries seeking to reduce the transactions costs for traders associated with international exchange, and minimizing uncertainty for traders through a reduction in red tape should rank high on the policy agenda of countries desiring to integrate in the world economy. Many countries have therefore pursued alternative mechanisms—on either a transitional or longer-term basis—to facilitate trade while ensuring that revenue and noneconomic objectives are attained. The primary instrument used in this connection is preshipment inspection (discussed below).

As the name suggests, preshipment inspection (PSI) consists of inspection of goods by specialized firms before they are shipped to the country of importation. Governments of importing countries usually decide to engage the services of PSI firms in order to reduce the scope for exporters and importers to engage in either over-invoicing or under-invoicing of imports.[4] Over-invoicing may occur in contexts where there are foreign exchange controls, this being a classic way to transfer capital outside the country. Under-invoicing is usually driven by tax evasion considerations: by under-reporting the value of an imported item, traders may seek to reduce their tax obligation (partially evade applicable tariffs).

Governments use PSI in large part because national customs administrations are not able to undertake the required activities. This may reflect a lack of institutional capacity, or problems related to rent seeking and corruption. Government-mandated PSI should be distinguished from PSI services that are required as part of a contract between buyers and sellers of a product. Most firms that are internationally active in providing inspection services provide preshipment certification and inspection of goods because buyers

---

[3] This case was brought under Article XXIV:5b, that is, the GATT provision dealing with free trade areas, not the valuation agreement.

[4] PSI may have nonrevenue objectives as well. An example would be to ensure that imports meet national (or international) standards of safety or quality. See section 5.6 below.

require it. Such services focus on the specifications and quality of goods, not their value. Government-mandated PSI is predominantly concerned with the determination of the quantity and value of goods imported into their territories. PSI became an issue for GATT in the 1980s because exporters objected to some of the methods used by inspection firms (Low, 1995).

Under the WTO agreement on PSI, countries that use PSI agencies must ensure that such activities are carried out in an objective, transparent and nondiscriminatory manner. Verification of contract prices must be based on a comparison with the price(s) of identical or similar goods offered for export from the same country of exportation around the same time. In doing this, PSI entities are to allow for the terms of the sales contract and generally applicable adjusting factors pertaining to the transaction. The selling price of locally produced goods, the export price of other producers, and the cost of production or arbitrary prices may not be used for price verification purposes.

The PSI agreement requires that WTO members that use PSI establish appeals procedures. Complaints may also be brought to an Independent Entity, established under Article 5 of the PSI agreement. No cases were brought to the entity in the first five years of the WTO, suggesting that no serious problems existed in the implementation of the agreement. In 1996, a working party on PSI was established by the General Council, with a mandate to review the agreement (as provided for under Article 6 of the PSI agreement). The working party consulted with the International Federation of Inspection Agencies (IFIA), the ICC, and a firm of PSI auditors. Overall, the experience with the PSI agreement appears to have been positive. Some 35 WTO members employ the services of PSI companies accredited to the IFIA (Table 5.2).

TABLE 5.2 *Countries using preshipment inspection, April 1999*

Country	Type: Foreign exchange (FX) or revenue (customs)	Number of firms	Split: Geographical/Importers choice
Angola	FX and customs	1	-
Argentina	Customs	6	Importers choice
Bangladesh	Customs (voluntary)	4	Importers choice
Benin	FX and Customs	1	-
Bolivia	Customs	2	Importers choice
Burkina Faso	Customs	1	-
Burundi	FX	1	-
Cambodia	Customs	1	-
Cameroon	Customs	1	-
C. African	Customs	1	-

Country	Type: Foreign exchange (FX) or revenue (customs)	Number of firms	Split: Geographical/Importers choice
Rep. Colombia	Customs	3	Importers choice
Comoros	FX and Customs	1	-
Congo, Dem. Rep.	Customs	1	-
Cote d'Ivoire	Customs	1	-
Ecuador	Customs	4	Importers choice
Ghana	FX and Customs	4	Geographical
Guinea	Customs	1	-
India	Capital goods for export production	3	Importers choice
Iran	Quality and quantity	6	Importers choice
Kenya	Customs	3	Geographical
Liberia	Customs	1	-
Madagascar	FX Customs	1	-
Malawi	CUSTOMS	1	-
Mali	FX and customs	1	-
Mauritania	Customs	1	-
Mexico	Customs	3	Importers choice
Mozambique	FX and Customs	1	
Niger	FX and Customs	1	
Nigeria	FX and Customs	3	Geographical
Paraguay	Customs	2	Importers choice
Peru	Customs	3	Importers choice
Rwanda	FX and Customs	1	-
Senegal	Customs	1	-
Sierra Leone	FX and Customs	1	-
Tanzania	Customs	1	-
Togo	FX and Customs	1	-
Uganda	Customs	1	-
Uzbekistan	FX	1	-

Source: 'Report of the Working party on PSI, G/L/300, March 18, 1999.

Some countries limit inspections to a range of sensitive products, all of which are subject to 100 percent inspections. Others have an across-the-board inspection program subject to 100 percent inspections. The review cited cases of delays in shipments caused by inspectors either being unavailable or failing to arrive for the scheduled inspection. In other cases the inspectors allegedly have little knowledge of the products concerned or lack the necessary language skills. Several developing countries considered that PSI resulted in significant revenue gains for the government (Ghana), prevented the under-valuation of imports (Peru) and reduced fraud and unfair trade practices (Colombia) (*WTO Focus*, no. 20, 1997).

That said, the experience with PSI also demonstrates it is not a panacea. Scandals in Pakistan and a number of African countries where PSI companies were found to have engaged in bribery to obtain contracts, and circumvention of PSI by traders through exploitation of loopholes in the system (for example, minimum value thresholds) reduced confidence in these systems in a number of countries. A lack of ex-post checking of revenues collected against the reports issued by PSI agencies to Ministries of Finance also reduces the usefulness of PSI for countries that use it, especially taking into account that the costs of PSI for governments can be significant. PSI firms frequently charge a fee of up to one percent of the value of goods inspected.[5] The prevailing consensus in the trade and development community is that PSI may be helpful in the short-term but that in the longer-run what is required is serious customs reform and institutional strengthening to allow a government to manage the process itself.

Rules of Origin

A rule of origin is a criterion used by customs authorities to determine the nationality of a product or a producer. Rules of origin are necessary when there is a desire to discriminate between sources of supply. The only multilateral convention dealing with rules of origin is the 1974 International Convention on the Simplification and Harmonization of Customs Procedures (known as the Kyoto Convention), negotiated under auspices of—and administered by—what is now known as the WCO in Brussels. This Convention, which was revised after lengthy negotiations in 1998, provides a short list of products that should be considered to originate in a country because they are wholly produced or obtained there, that is, contain no imported materials. These are largely natural resource-based products extracted or obtained from the territory of the country concerned. Where two or more countries are involved in the production of a product, the Convention states that the origin of the product is the one in which the last substantial transformation took place, that is, the country in which significant manufacturing

---

[5] This practice has given rise to discussions in the PSI Committee concerning the consistency of such fees with Articles II and VIII GATT (discussed above). Proposals have been made that flat fees would be more appropriate.

or processing occurred most recently. Significant or substantial is defined as sufficient to give the product its essential character.

Various criteria can be used to determine if a substantial transformation occurred. These include a change in tariff heading (CTH), the use of specific processing operations which do (or do not) imply substantial transformation, a test based on the value of additional materials embodied in the transformed product, or the amount of value added in the last country where the good was transformed. Under a CTH the value added may be high or low for a given product, so that a value-added criterion may or may not lead to the same result as a CTH test. Different rules of origin may therefore vary widely in their economic effects. If written in ways that make it difficult to satisfy them, rules of origin can be effective protectionist devices. Thus, the setting of rules of origin may be accompanied with rent-seeking activities, as import-competing lobbies have an incentive to either try and to make the rules as restrictive as possible, or to influence the way they are applied. Restrictive rules are particularly a potential problem in the context of the negotiation and implementation of preferential trade agreements (chapter 10). In the application of trade policy that is applied on a MFN basis, the problem is more often vaguely defined criteria that give rise to uncertainty by giving substantial discretion to the import authorities to determine if a particular rule has been met. The more discretion officials have in this area, the greater the incentive to lobby. Such problems are especially prevalent under value-added criteria, as enforcement of such rules requires detailed investigations of the financial accounts of exporting firms. Box 5.4 gives an example of the operation of rules of origin in one of the major nonpreferential trade policy areas where they are important—antidumping.

In contrast to GATT 1947, the WTO includes an agreement on rules of origin. The WTO Agreement on Rules of Origin aims to foster the harmonization of the rules used by members. The agreement calls for a work program to be undertaken by a Technical Committee, in conjunction with the WCO, to develop a classification system regarding the changes in tariff subheadings based on the Harmonized System that constitute a substantial transformation. In cases where the HS nomenclature does not allow substantial transformation to be determined by a CTH test, the Technical Committee is

---

Box 5.4. Origin Rules and Antidumping

One area where the application of rules of origin has become controversial is in the enforcement of antidumping (AD) mechanisms. A European case provides an illustration of how rules of origin can be used to achieve the objectives of a specific lobby. In the mid-1980s, the EU imposed a 20 percent AD duty on 12 Japanese exporters of photocopiers. In 1988, three years after the

AD duty was imposed, a so-called anticircumvention case was brought by the EU industry. It was claimed that the Japanese exporters had circumvented the AD duty by establishing assembly operations inside the EU that imported most of the parts of photocopiers from Japan, adding very little local value. What is relevant here are not the mechanics of AD—discussed in chapter 9—but the role of origin rules. The aim of AD is to protect a domestic industry that is injured by dumping. But, in a world where companies establish alliances with—and equity stakes in—rival enterprises, establishing which firms constitute the domestic industry is not always easy. In the photocopier AD investigation, Canon (Japan) subsidiaries located in the EU were regarded as foreign firms, while a Xerox (US) affiliate was treated as a European firm. Similarly, in the follow-up anticircumvention case, the Canon subsidiaries were investigated to determine how much local (EU) value was added in the production process. What is interesting about this case is not only that the composition of the domestic industry was determined arbitrarily, but that a number of the firms who petitioned Brussels for protection had value added performances that were lower than those of the Japanese firms. These EU firms were basically in the business of importing and distributing photocopiers. They did not produce them. Some even had formal connections with Japanese companies. The AD case was therefore not about dumping, or to protect a national industry, but simply part of a strategy used by individual multinational firms competing for market share. The lack of clearly defined rules of origin introduced one of the elements of discretion that made the strategy attractive to petitioning firms.
Source: Messerlin and Noguchi (1991).

to provide guidance regarding the use of supplementary tests such as value added criteria. Although the harmonization program was to be completed in July 1998, the Technical Committee was unable to meet this deadline due to the complexity of the task it had been given. In late 2000, the WTO Council set a new deadline of end 2000 for completion of the work program. Once the harmonization work program has been completed, rules of origin are to be applied equally to all nonpreferential commercial policy instruments by WTO members—tariffs, import licensing, antidumping and so forth. The Agreement on Rules of Origin also specifies that rules of origin applied to exports or imports should not be more stringent than the rules applied to determine whether or not a good is domestically produced (as is necessary under antidumping, countervailing duty, safeguard and government procurement procedures).

The economic impact of a rule of origin depends on the specific criterion that is used and on the degree of uniformity with which the rule is applied. Rules of origin have been problematical mostly in the context of regional trade agreements and preferential trade regimes for developing countries. However, the harmonized set of WCO rules of origin will not apply to regional agreements. Nor will they apply to GSP schemes. This is not an oversight. Many countries did not want to see constraints imposed on their policy freedom with regard to the implementation of regional integration or the mechanics of trade preferences for developing countries. Rules of origin are a major instrument for 'fine tuning' the effective scope of preferential liberalization at the product level (see chapters 10 and 12).

Towards Rules on Trade Facilitation?

Guidance on good customs practices can be obtained from the WCO, which has developed 'tool-kits' to determine how efficient national practices in this area are, and what could be considered as part of an overall reform strategy. In the 1990s, the WCO negotiated a revision of the 1974 International Convention on the Simplification and Harmonization of Customs Procedures, which had become outdated. For example, there was no recognition of modern techniques of risk assessment, the importance of computerization and electronic data interchange, or the use of ex-post, audit-based systems of control. An updated and completely revamped Kyoto Convention establishing 'international standards and facilitative customs procedures for the twenty-first century' was completed in 1999 (WCO, 1999). Implementing and enforcing the revised Kyoto Convention will require substantial effort and

---

Box 5.5. The Revised Kyoto Convention

The Kyoto Convention comprises a set of principles and detailed annexes that lay out standards and recommended best practices for customs procedures and related administrative practices. Originally drafted in 1973, efforts to revise the Convention to bring it up date to reflect the dramatic changes that occurred in technology and trade practices since the early 1970s were concluded in 1998. The new Convention embodies a comprehensive set of good administrative practices in the area of import and export procedures, transit arrangements, and warehousing. It includes a set of guidelines drawn from best practices in various countries on a variety of customs-related procedures.

A key issue determining the impact of the new convention is whether it will be implemented by WCO members. This will depend in large part on how useful and relevant the guidelines are for customs authorities and the trading community. In contrast to the WTO, the WCO does not have any enforcement mechanisms. This has led representatives of the international express industry (which comprises firms such as DHL and FedEx) to suggest that efforts be made to make implementation of the new Kyoto Convention mandatory for WTO members. Some WTO members have argued that the WTO should not be used to ensure enforcement of an instrument that has been developed by another organization. A counter-argument to this view is that WTO members have already given the WCO the responsibility for developing the rules of origin for nonpreferential trade, as well as responsibility for promoting the WTO Agreement on Customs Valuations (including technical assistance to those countries in transition from the old GATT valuation system). WCO-WTO cooperation in implementing and enforcing the new Kyoto Convention could help encourage a move towards greater harmonization of customs practices among WTO members, which has been argued to constitute a trade facilitation measure that would greatly benefit the international business community (Zarrouk, 2000). However, as argued in chapter 13, it is not clear that uniform rules will necessarily be optimal, given the great differences that exist in initial conditions and the different priorities that confront countries at very different levels of development.

resources. As far as the WTO is concerned, a key issue will be whether the revised Kyoto Convention will be binding on signatories (Box 5.5).

5.4. SUBSIDIES

Subsidies, and measures to counter their impact on trade, frequently gave rise to disputes in the GATT 1947. Subsidization may pertain to import-competing industries or export industries that compete in international markets. If such subsidization distorts trade (expands or reduces trade above or below the free trade level) it may threaten to offset market-opening commitments negotiated in a MTN. From a rule-making perspective, a problem that arises is that subsidies may be a desirable form of government intervention. Tax-subsidy schemes may be required to bring marginal private costs or benefits into alignment with marginal social costs or benefits. The need for this arises when externalities cause social and private costs and benefits to diverge. Usually this implies that private agents are not given an incentive to take into account the costs or benefits of the actions on others in the economy (for an overview of the theory, see Bhagwati, 1971 and the summary in annex 2). Tax-subsidy schemes may be an appropriate means of offsetting externalities or distortions associated with overvalued exchange rates or labor market rigidities if these problems cannot be dealt with directly. They may also be used to redistribute income. Necessary conditions for a more efficient allocation of resources to result from intervention are that the problem has been diagnosed correctly and the policy used is targeted appropriately. In practice, governments are prone to fail as often as markets—especially if account is taken of the incentives of interest groups to lobby for a subsidy or a tax exemption. An advantage that subsidies have from a governance viewpoint is that they are more visible to domestic stakeholders than trade policies—to taxpayers and to the Ministry of Finance. Subsidies can therefore be expected to be subject to greater critical scrutiny than tariffs.

Governments invariably pursue policies that affect the allocation of productive resources and the distribution of income. Such policies may have an impact on the pattern of international trade and investment, and may give rise to frictions and disputes between countries. Many of the measures maintained by governments of a subsidy nature come under the heading of industrial policy. For present purposes industrial policy can be defined to encompass all actions undertaken by governments that have an effect on the structure of production in an economy. This effect may be intended or not, and can be achieved through a variety of policy instruments, of which subsidies are just one. Others include price controls, import restrictions, tax incentives and government procurement policies. All industrial policies are forms of public assistance or taxation of domestic industries. Theoretically, they can be expressed in terms of a direct subsidy equivalent, which may be greater or less than zero, negative subsidy equivalents implying a burden (tax) instead of a benefit. More generally, the appropriate measure is the effective benefit of government assistance to a firm or the economy as a whole. It may well be that other policies maintained by the government outweigh any direct support given to a firm or sector. Such general equilibrium measures of the net or 'effective' support that is implied by policy is rarely considered by governments.

The types of subsidies used by governments to support economic activities include direct payments or grants, tax concessions, soft loans, and government guarantees and equity participation. They may be firm- or industry-specific or generally available. Examples of the latter include regional and activity-specific subsidies (such as the promotion of research and development); subsidies that focus on firms of a particular size (micro or small and medium-sized enterprises); as well as measures aimed at assisting adjustment of industries, protection of the environment, or achievement of cultural objectives. Many subsidies that are sector-specific may have an economy-wide objective. Examples include subsidies to sectors such as health, education, transportation, and communications. Conversely, subsidies that are economy-wide in scope may effectively be industry-specific. An example is the pursuit of an environmental objective whose attainment requires taxes or subsidies that affect primarily specific sectors such as the chemical or the automotive industry. As of the late 1980s, government subsidies to industry (excluding public services and agriculture) in OECD countries averaged about two percent of the value of industrial output (OECD, 1993). Between two-fifths and three-fifths of subsidies went to specific sectors, much of the support going to declining industries such as steel, shipbuilding, and mining. Of the service sectors, available statistics show that rail transport is often highly subsidized, with rates of support varying between 15 percent and 180 percent of total value added produced in this sector. The magnitude of subsidies varies greatly across countries, but a general rule of thumb is that the larger the share of government in GDP, the more prevalent are subsidy programs, both direct financial grants and implicit subsidy schemes that operate through the tax system.

From a rule making perspective a number of issues arise in the subsidies context. One is whether certain types of subsidies should be prohibited and what the criterion should be in determining which measures should be subject to disciplines. Another is whether and how to define rules regarding the countermeasures that governments can take when confronted with foreign subsidies. What should be the criterion for intervening against foreign subsidies? National welfare? The welfare of industries or firms? What is the most effective remedy to respond to foreign subsidy practices? Many of these questions are addressed by the WTO.

WTO Rules

The approach taken in the WTO Agreement on Subsidies and Countervailing Measures (SCM) is to focus on subsidies narrowly defined. Loosely speaking, subsidies are policies that directly impact on the government budget and that affect the production of goods. As discussed in chapter 7, there are no subsidy disciplines for services. Special rules apply to agriculture, where use is made of an Aggregate Measure of Support—see chapter 6. An effort is made in the SCM agreement to distinguish between financial contributions that can be justified on market failure or noneconomic grounds and those that distort the incentive to trade in a major way. The former are unconstrained.

WTO disciplines relating to subsidies have a twofold objective. First, to establish rules to avoid or reduce adverse effects on members, and to prevent the use of subsidies to nullify or impair concessions. Second, to regulate the use of countervailing duties (CVDs) by members seeking to offset the injurious effects of foreign subsidization of products. The GATT 1947 allowed a large measure of subsidy freedom, disciplined primarily by the threat of CVDs. Countervailing duties, discussed in chapter 9, were politically necessary because the substantive disciplines on subsidies were weak. This continues to be the case under the WTO. In this respect, the WTO differs substantially from deep regional integration agreements such as the EU, where strict disciplines are imposed on the use of subsidies and CVDs cannot be used by member states on imports from partner countries. Instead, subsidization is subject to explicit rules and EU competition disciplines. If these are violated, countries can be brought before the European Court of Justice.

The WTO subsidy rules attempt to strike a balance between the need to agree on minimum standards regarding the subsidies that may not be used because they distort trade, and ensuring that measures used by importing countries to offset the effects of foreign subsidy programs are not abused. A key aspect of the WTO rules on subsidies is that certain permitted subsidies are defined to be nonactionable—they cannot be countervailed by members, even if they perceive the subsidies to have a negative impact on their interests. A key criterion in this connection is whether subsidies are specific. Nonspecific subsidies—defined as those where access is general or eligibility is automatic if clearly spelled-out, objective criteria are met—are nonactionable (Article 2 SCM agreement).

Attempts under the auspices of GATT 1947 to deal with the subsidy issue suffered major difficulties. The term subsidy was not defined in the GATT 1947, and agreement on a definition proved elusive. It also proved difficult to determine what types of subsidies distorted trade. These difficulties led to many disputes and panels in the 1970s and 1980s (many of the cases involved agriculture). Progress was made on both fronts during the Uruguay Round. First, agreement was reached on a definition. A subsidy is deemed to exist if there is a financial contribution by a government (or public body). This in turn may involve an actual or potential direct transfer of funds (such as grants, loans, equity infusions, or loan guarantees), forgoing government revenue (tax concessions or credits), or the provision or purchase of products other than general infrastructure. Government funding of a private body to carry out a function which would normally be vested in the government and any form of income or price support is also covered by the definition. In all these cases a benefit must be conferred by the measure to the recipient(s). This definition is embodied in the Subsidies Agreement and applies to nonagricultural products. There are separate disciplines for agricultural production and trade (chapter 6).

Three categories of subsidies are distinguished in the agreement: nonactionable, prohibited and actionable. Nonactionable subsidies are by definition permitted and cannot be contested. They include all nonspecific subsidies—those that do not primarily benefit a specific firm, industry or group of industries. Nonspecificity requires that allocation criteria are neutral, nondiscriminatory, and horizontal (that is, do not distinguish between sectors). Certain specific subsidies are also nonactionable if they satisfy certain criteria. These include R&D subsidies, aid to disadvantaged regions, and subsidies to facilitate the adaptation of plants to new environmental regulations (see Hoekman and Mavroidis, 1996).

Subsidies that are contingent, formally or in effect on export performance or on the use of domestic over imported goods are prohibited (except for least developed countries—see below). An illustrative list of export subsidies, attached to the SCM agreement, mentions the provision of products or services (including transportation) for use in export production on terms more favorable than for domestically consumed goods. It also lists export credits and guarantees or insurance at a cost that is inadequate to cover the long-term operating costs and losses of the insurer (except if a member applies the provisions of the OECD agreement on export credits). A case brought against the US in 1998 made it clear that tax concessions on export income also constitute an export subsidy (see below). A necessary condition is that the government, or an institution under its control, provides the subsidy. All export subsidies are deemed specific, whether targeted or not. If WTO members are found to be using export subsidies by a dispute settlement panel, the remedy will generally be a requirement that the measures be removed within a three-month period.

The third category, actionable subsidies, are measures that are permitted but may, if they create adverse effects on a WTO member, give rise to consultations, invocation of dispute settlement procedures, or the imposition of countervailing duties by an importing country.[6] Adverse effects include injury to a domestic industry, nullification or impairment of tariff concessions, or serious prejudice or threat thereof to the country's interests. Serious prejudice is defined to exist if the total *ad valorem* subsidization of a product exceeds five percent, the subsidies are used to cover operating losses of a firm or industry or debt relief is granted for government-held liabilities. Serious prejudice may arise if the subsidy reduces exports of WTO members, results in significant price undercutting or increases the world market share of the subsidizing country in a primary product. If actionable subsidies have an adverse effect on a member, it may request consultations with the subsidizing member and request a panel if consultations fail to settle the matter within 60 days. WTO members are required to notify their

[6] Countervailing duties are discussed further in chapter 9.

subsidy programs to the WTO secretariat each year, giving information on the type of subsidy, the amounts involved, the policy objective and intended duration as well as statistics allowing their trade effects to be determined. Any member may cross-notify alleged subsidies of other countries that the latter have not notified.

The focus of the WTO disciplines (and dispute settlement) in cases where there is prejudice is on the amount of the assistance given, not on the extent to which a subsidy harms trading partners (competitors). This makes little sense from an economic perspective, although it has the advantage of being straightforward to calculate. Subsidy case law developed under the WTO (discussed in chapter 3) has moved towards more stringent remedies, in that instead of requiring simply the abolition of an illegal measure, panels have started to require repayment of the subsidy by the firms that benefited. This is not necessarily a step in the right direction from an economic perspective, as it ignores the effect of the subsidy. In some cases a subsidy may have no injurious effect, in others, the damage caused may be a multiple of the subsidy.

Developing Countries and WTO Subsidy Disciplines

A number of special provisions for developing and transition economies are included in Article 27 of the subsidies agreement. Members in the process of transformation from a command to a market economy may apply prohibited subsidy programs until 2002. During the same period, subsidy programs involving debt forgiveness are not actionable. Developing country members referred to in an annex (least developed and countries with GNP per capita below US$1,000) are exempted from the prohibition on export subsidies.[7] Once GNP per capita exceeds US$1,000, nonconforming subsidies must be eliminated within eight years. Developing country WTO members not listed in the annex are subjected to a standstill requirement and must phase out their export subsidies over an eight year period, starting from January 1995. The prohibition on subsidies contingent on the use of domestic goods (local content) does not apply to developing countries for a period of five years (8 years for least developed countries), and further extension may be re-

---

[7] Least-developed countries are the 48 nations that are designated as such by the United Nations. The following developing countries will graduate when their GNP per capita has reached US$1,000 per annum (as reported by the World Bank): Bolivia, Cameroon, Congo, Côte d'Ivoire, Dominican Republic, Egypt, Ghana, Guatemala, Guyana, India, Indonesia, Kenya, Morocco, Nicaragua, Nigeria, Pakistan, Philippines, Senegal, Sri Lanka and Zimbabwe. Market exchange rates are used, not purchasing power parities.

quested. If granted, annual consultations with the Subsidies Committee must be held to determine the necessity of maintaining the subsidies. Developing countries that have become competitive in a product—defined as having a global market share 3.25 percent—must phase out any export subsidies over a two-year period.

The traditional difference in subsidy disciplines applying to industrialized and developing countries was narrowed substantially in the Uruguay Round, especially as regards export subsidies, where the prohibition on the use of such instruments was extended to developing countries. Under the GATT, developing countries were free to use export subsidies. There are possible economic rationales for a more lenient stance for developing countries. Subsidies may be beneficial in stimulating economic development if there are externalities to firms operating in export markets. These may arise through the beneficial effects of learning by doing. Marketing experts have argued that quality upgrading and export marketing of nontraditional products by firms has positive spillover effects on other potential exporters in a developing country, potentially justifying an export subsidy. Export subsidies may also be the appropriate instrument to offset an antiexport bias resulting from an overvalued exchange rate or high rates of protection in cases where first-best policies are not available (devaluation or a market determined exchange rate and trade liberalization). Export subsidy programs may also have an important political dimension as they can give credibility to a government's commitment to the maintenance of a policy framework that supports an export-oriented strategy, thus encouraging investment of resources and entrepreneurial energies in the development of foreign markets (Bhagwati, 1988).

Many countries, both developing and developed, pursue export promotion programs. These may involve assistance with penetrating new markets through organization of trade fairs, general advertising campaigns that aim at 'selling' the country and enhancing the visibility of export products, and maintenance of commercial attachés in embassies and consulates. During the 1990s, an increasing number of countries have also implemented so-called matching grant schemes that subsidize a proportion of the cost of improving production facilities, obtaining ISO 9000 certification of management systems, and exploring new export markets. Such schemes could be regarded as export subsidies if the provision of the grant element is made conditional upon exports. However, in principle these types of programs can be designed so that this is not the case.

In most of these cases the rationale for subsidies is the existence of distortions created by market failures or other government policies. However, as is well known, if the source of the problem is policy-induced, the case for a subsidy is very much a second-best one—the appropriate action is to target the source of the problem. More often than not subsidy policies are driven by rent-seeking interest groups, not by a clearly identified market failure. The stricter disciplines that were negotiated in the Uruguay Round are therefore likely to be beneficial. Export subsidies may be optimal from a national perspective, but are distortionary for the world as a whole, can easily be captured by private interests seeking rents, and are difficult to target at a well-defined distortion or market failure.

Summing up, the adoption of a 'green-orange-red-light' approach towards subsidies in the Uruguay Round was important. The approach is both pragmatic and sensible from an economic perspective. Ensuring that subsidies that are not firm- or sector-specific are in principle unconstrained is appropriate as such subsidies are most likely to be used in the pursuit of noneconomic objectives or in efforts to offset market failures. It ensures freedom for governments to use subsidy instruments in cases where there is a rationale for it, and reduces the scope for other countries to second-guess the motivation underlying the use of such instruments. Production subsidies can be the most efficient way to offset externalities, but are more often used to redistribute income. If so, they are likely to distort the operation of markets, but in ways that are very difficult to address. Clearly such subsidies can have detrimental effects on foreign countries, and allowance is therefore made for actions to be taken against their trade effects. But the WTO makes no attempt to get involved in questioning government objectives or to determine whether the policy instrument is necessary or effective or appropriate. The focus is only on the effect of the subsidy. This greatly reduces the scope for disputes, as the focus of attention centers primarily on whether a contested measure is an export subsidy. Export subsidies clearly distort trade and will have direct negative effects on some WTO members.

Subsidy Disputes under the WTO

A number of subsidy-related disputes were brought to the WTO in its first five years. All involved export subsidies. Major cases included disputes between Brazil and Canada regarding export subsidies for aircraft production (Brazilian and Canadian firms are major producers of regional and corporate jets), a case brought by the EU against the US Foreign Sales Corporation (under which US firms can reduce taxes on export income by funneling revenues through offshore tax shelters), and a number of cases by the US alleging that certain provisions of the corporate tax law of a number of European countries constituted de facto export subsidies.

In 1996, Canada brought a complaint against Brazil's export financing program for aircraft (WT/DS46), claiming that subsidies granted under the Brazilian Programa de Financiamento às Exportações to foreign purchasers of Brazil's Embraer aircraft were illegal export subsidies. After consultations and discussions between the two parties, a panel was established in 1998. It found that Brazil's measures were prohibited export subsidies. On appeal, the Appellate Body upheld the findings of the panel, although it reversed the panel on some of its legal interpretations. Upon the initial request for consultations by Canada, Brazil responded by counter-attacking. In March 1997 it contested what it perceived as illegal export subsidies granted to the Canadian civil aircraft industry with a request for consultations, followed by a request for a panel in July 1998. The panel concluded that certain of Canada's measures were inconsistent with the SCM Agreement, but rejected Brazil's claim that the Canadian measures constituted an export subsidy. Canada appealed and lost. The DSB adopted both reports in August 1999. In both cases the complainants perceived that the losing party did not comply with the rulings and requested the DSB to reconvene the original panels to assess implementation.

The panel found that Brazil had not complied. Canada requested authorization to retaliate on C$700 million of imports from Brazil, which sought arbitration. Canada's requested amount reflected its calculation of the value of the subsidy granted to Embraer. Canada noted that the damage to its industry was C$4.7 billion, but that it did not seek to use this as the basis of counter measures. Indeed, both parties agreed that retaliation should be based on the amount of the subsidy, not damage incurred. The arbitrators proceeded on that basis. Brazil argued that C$700 million was a gross overestimate of the effective magnitude of the subsidy, which in its view should be based on the lost sales by Canada (number of aircraft) multiplied by the per unit (illegal) subsidy on each of these sales. The arbitrators rejected this argument. The panel authorized countermeasures equal to C$344 million (WT/DS46/ARB).

These bilateral tit-for-tat actions illustrate a phenomenon that is often hypothesized to exist by observers—governments are leery of bringing subsidy cases because they worry about retaliation. This has been called the 'glass house' effect—if people live in glass houses, they will be concerned about throwing the first stone. As many governments engage in subsidy practices of one kind or another, the glass house effect can be quite strong. As noted earlier, tax systems can involve de facto subsidies. This was illustrated in a case brought by the EU against the US tax treatment of so-called Foreign Sales Corporations (FSC) in late 1997 (WT/DS108). Under the FSC system, any US firm whose exports have at least 50 percent US content can set up a FSC, a shell company that is established in a tax haven. More than 90 percent of FSCs are located in the Virgin Islands, Barbados, and Guam (*Financial Times*, February 25, 2000, p.7). The US firm 'sells' its exports to the FSC, which then 'exports' them, 'subcontracting' the actual transactions involved back to the US company. Up to 65 percent of the FSC's profits are exempt from US tax, reducing the US firm's tax burden by anywhere from 15 to 30 percent (ibid.).

The EU argued that provisions of the US tax code violated the Subsidies Agreement, as they were conditional on exports. In October 1999 a panel found that the FSC scheme was in violation of the WTO. On appeal, the Appellate Body supported the findings of the panel, and rejected arguments by the US that the FSC was permitted under a 1981 understanding that related to a 1976 GATT dispute concerning the forerunner of the FSC, the so-called Domestic International Sales Corporation (DISC) provisions of the pre-1984 US tax code. The DISC allowed US firms to defer taxes on export income. The FSC was adopted in 1984 because the DISC had been found to be inconsistent with GATT subsidy rules. The FSC case was particularly noteworthy because it involved huge sums of money (some US\$3.5 billion in revenue forgone by the US Treasury) and required the US to revise its legislation.

As in the aircraft case, after the EU brought the FSC case, the US retaliated by claiming that EU member states had very similar provisions in their tax codes, and brought cases against Belgium, France, Greece, Ireland, and the Netherlands (it had done the same in the DISC case—see GATT 1994*b*). In each instance the US held that the income tax laws of these countries granted de facto export subsidies. The US claimed that France allowed firms to deduct certain start-up expenses of its foreign operations through a tax-deductible reserve account, Ireland granted certain trading entities special tax rates on income from export sales, Greece gave exporters special annual tax deductions calculated as a percentage of export income, the Netherlands allowed exporters to establish a special fund for export income, and Belgium granted corporations an index-linked income-tax exemption for recruitment of export managers.

Another noteworthy subsidy case concerned a 1998 US complaint regarding Australian subsidies granted to producers and exporters of automotive leather. These involved preferential government loans on noncommercial terms and grants. The panel found that the government loan to the firm was not a subsidy contingent upon export performance, but that the payments under the grant contract were illegal export subsidies, and should be withdrawn within 90 days. The report was adopted in June 1999. In September 1999, Australia informed the DSB that it had implemented the panel recommendations. The US contested this and requested that the original panel be reconvened. The parties reached an agreement that Australia would not raise any procedural objection to the reestablishment of the panel, and that the US would not request authorization to retaliate. This agreement was inspired by what had happened in *Bananas* (see chapter 3). It was also agreed that neither party would appeal the review panel's report. In January 2000, the review panel determined that Australia had failed to withdraw the prohibited subsidies within 90 days, and thus was not in compliance with the recommendations made by the DSB. The panel recommended not only that Australia cease applying this measure, but also that the beneficiary of the subsidy be required to reimburse the funds (the case involved about US$19 million). This was a first in the history of the WTO (although a number of unadopted panel reports had recommended reimbursement of illegal anti-dumping duties under the GATT 1947—see Palmeter and Mavroidis, 1999).

5.5. STATE TRADING ENTERPRISES

From its inception, GATT contracting parties were unconstrained in terms of the ownership of productive assets or the regulation of domestic production. However, it was recognized that enterprises granted exclusive trading rights and privileges could restrict trade and circumvent liberalization commitments. They might do so in a number of ways. First, state-trading enterprises (STEs) could circumvent the MFN principle by discriminating among trading partners in their purchasing and selling decisions. Second, they could limit or expand above the free trade level quantities of imports or exports in contravention of the GATT Article XI prohibition on QRs. Third, they might impose price mark-ups that exceed bound tariff levels. Fourth, they could contravene the national treatment principle by discriminating against imported products in matters affecting, for example, the internal conditions of distribution or sale. Fifth, STEs might engage in nontransparent cross-subsidization activities or benefit from various forms of assistance from governments that distort competition. Finally, STEs might affect competition on export markets if their exclusive privileges allow them to undercut other suppliers.

State trading has been poorly attended to in the history of GATT, in part because it was considered a relatively minor aspect of policy among the original signatories of the GATT. It was also most prevalent in agriculture and services—sectors that remained largely outside the purview of multilateral discipline until the Uruguay Round. GATT provisions establishing rules of behavior for STEs therefore played only a minor role. This situation changed with the introduction of services into the WTO, the prospective accession to the WTO of many economies in transition, and the conclusion of the Agreement on Agriculture. The prominence of state trading as a policy issue consequently increased. State trading also became a higher-profile issue with the emergence of competition policy as a subject of discussion. In effect, state trading is part of a much bigger complex of policy questions to do with the conditions of competition in markets.

The rules of the WTO assume that economic transactions in members are driven by the decisions of enterprises operating in a market environment. Disciplines were included in the GATT on the behavior of STEs in an attempt to ensure that such entities acted in a market-conforming manner. However, the relevant provision of the GATT (Article XVII) gave no clear definition of what constitutes state trading, and a wide range of interpretations of what was meant by state trading was revealed in the notifications that member countries made to the GATT. The Communist authorities of Czechoslovakia submitted a list of their foreign trade organizations engaging in export and import transactions. In the 1970s, Poland and Hungary notified that they did not maintain STEs, while Canada reported as STEs certain of its Crown Corporations (such as the Canadian Wheat Board). These were considerably more independent of the government than private trading firms in a number of other countries (Kostecki, 1982).

There are numerous reasons why governments might be concerned about the existence and behavior of STEs when negotiating commitments to liberalize trade. Most obviously, if an entity is a monopoly, controls essential facilities, or has significant power to affect downstream activities such as distribution, trade policy may be irrelevant in market access terms. Even with zero tariffs, no formal quotas, and full national treatment, STEs may be able to foreclose the market to potential foreign entrants. More generally, a firm with exclusive rights may be able to control the price at which it sources from domestic suppliers and distributes imported goods. If prices paid for inputs are below market clearing levels, the entity will effectively enjoy a subsidy that may reduce market access opportunities for foreign goods. Similarly, the entity may be able to impose high mark-ups on imported goods, thereby reducing domestic demand for foreign products. In all these situations the activities of STEs will have an effect equivalent to a tax (tariff) or subsidy (Lloyd, 1982).

The main GATT provision on STEs is Article XVII, which covers state-owned enterprises, enterprises granted formally or in effect exclusive or special privileges, marketing boards, enterprises controlled by a member, and import monopolies. In the Uruguay Round a working definition of a STE was negotiated (in the GATT 1947 the concept was not defined): 'Governmental and nongovernmental enterprises, including marketing boards, which have been granted exclusive or special rights or privileges, including statutory or constitutional powers, in the exercise of which they influence through their purchases or sales the level or direction of imports or exports'. STEs may therefore be fully privately owned. What matters is not ownership, but exclusivity or special privilege. The right of members to maintain or establish STEs or to offer exclusive privileges is not prejudged. The basic obligation imposed by Article XVII is that members should ensure that STEs not act in a manner inconsistent with the general principle of nondiscrimination (MFN).

Three qualitatively different legal obligations are imposed on STEs, depending on the type of entity involved (Hoekman and Mavroidis, 1994). First, as far as import monopolies are concerned, upon request of trading partners that have a substantial trade in the product concerned, information is to be provided on the import mark-up on the product during a recent representative period, or, if not feasible, the resale price (Article XVII:4b). Second, in their purchases or sales involving either imports or exports, state-owned enterprises, marketing boards and enterprises granted exclusive privileges, such firms are to act in a nondiscriminatory manner (Article XVII:1a). Firms granted exclusive privileges are to make purchases or sales solely in accordance with commercial considerations. Third, governments must ensure that enterprises in their jurisdiction are not prevented from acting in accordance with the nondiscrimination principle (Article XVII:1c).

The margins charged by STEs (their mark-ups) must be scheduled similarly to tariffs (Article II:4). Once bound, mark-ups may not exceed the resulting tariff equivalent. While tariff commitments have been numerous, commitments regarding STEs have been rare. As far as market economies are concerned, in 1952 Italy undertook not to exceed a 15 percent mark-up on wheat and rye imported by the Italian government or its agencies. France made a similar commitment regarding wheat imports by the Office National Interprofessionel des Cereals, and undertook a minimum import commitment with respect to lead, tobacco and cigarettes imported by France's tobacco monopoly from countries other than those of the French Union. Both concessions lapsed with the formation of the EEC.

In the Uruguay Round, negotiators agreed to augment disciplines on—and surveillance of—STEs. The Council for Trade in Goods established a working party on STEs in February 1995. Governments are required to notify all STEs for review by a working party, with the exception of imports intended for consumption by government bodies or STEs themselves. Notifications are to be made independent of whether imports or exports have in fact taken place. Any WTO member that believes another member has not adequately met its notification obligation may raise the matter bilaterally. If not resolved, a counter-notification may be made, for consideration by the working party. The working party was given the task of evaluating the adequacy of notifications and to document the kinds of relationships existing between governments and STEs, and the type of activities STEs engage in. The working party reports annually to the Council for Trade in Goods.

In the pursuit of its mandate, the working party developed a new questionnaire on state trading. A draft Illustrative List of State Trading Relationships and Activities was approved in July 1999 and adopted by the Council for Trade in Goods in October of that year. Most of the work of the working party is transparency-related. Notifications play an important role in this, although it is not clear how comprehensive these are. A total of 58 WTO members notified the existence of STEs as of 1995. For 1998, only 26 members submitted new and full notifications (WTO GL/335).

Unfortunately, little is known about the effect of STEs on trade. Indeed, no comprehensive data is available about the extent of STEs outside of agriculture (Ingco and Ng, 1998). Even if data were available on the prevalence of STEs, information would also be needed on their behavior, as what is of concern is not state trading itself, but the magnitude of the trade distortions that are associated with STEs. The current notification process does not generate these types of data, making it difficult to establish possible focal points for negotiations.

TABLE 5.3 *Share of state-owned enterprises in GDP, 1978–91*
(percent, unweighted averages)

	1978–85	1986–91	1978–91
Developing countries:			
Africa	13.1	12.2	12.9
East Asia	8.8	9.8	9.8
South Asia	6.3	9.7	7.6
Europe and Middle East	30.7	26.5	28.8
Latin America	9.4	10.6	10.2
65 Developing countries	13.0	12.8	12.8
10 Industrial countries	5.6	6.6	6.1

Source: World Bank (1995).

In order to obtain a sense of the potential magnitude of the problem, the extent of public ownership of industry can be used as a proxy. Entities with a majority state-owned equity share accounted for 13 percent of GDP in a sample of 65 developing countries in the late 1980s and early 1990s, as compared to six percent in a group of 10 OECD members (Table 5.3). The role, if any, of these enterprises in trade is unknown. Schmitz (1996) notes that state-owned enterprises in low income countries are much more concentrated in manufacturing activities than is the case for high income nations, suggesting that their role in trade may be much greater than is indicated by their share in national output. In OECD countries, state-owned enterprises are largely found in services. Such entities may have both formal exclusive rights and de facto exclusivity (such as monopoly control of bottleneck or essential facilities in the case of telecommunications).[8]

State-trading and (Former) Centrally Planned Economies

The presumption that WTO members are market economies has required in the past that nonmarket economies make additional commitments upon accession. Given that tariff concessions by centrally planned economies were meaningless or of limited value, GATT contracting parties negotiated global import commitments with Poland and Romania when these countries sought to become members of GATT in 1967 and 1971, respectively. These commitments were included in their protocols of accession. Poland agreed to 'increase the total value of its imports from the territories of contracting parties by not less than seven percent per annum'. GATT contracting parties were permitted to seek 'agreements on Polish targets for imports from the territories of the contracting parties as a whole in the following year'. The Romanian arrangement stated that Romania firmly intended 'to increase its imports from GATT contracting parties as a whole at a rate not smaller than the growth of total Romanian imports provided for in its Five-Year Plan'. This was equivalent to a promise not to decrease the GATT share of imports in the total imports of Romania. Inflation and a depreciation of the US dollar *vis-à-vis* European currencies made these commitments meaningless in the late 1970s, and too burdensome in the 1980s (Kostecki, 1979).

In the case of Hungary, which acceded in 1973, it was concluded that tariff concessions were meaningful, and no voluntary import expansion was negotiated. In all three cases, however, special safeguard provisions were included in the Protocols of Accession allowing for discriminatory actions to be taken against imports from the acceding country. Recent accession negotiations have revealed that economies that are perceived to be less than fully market-based no longer can accede on terms similar to those granted to the East Europeans in the past. This is not beneficial in any event, as a key benefit of WTO membership is MFN, which was not granted to the East Europeans (because of the special safeguard option). During the 1990s, all

---

[8] Article XVII applies only to STEs involved in merchandise trade. Services are the subject of the GATS–see chapter 7.

three East European countries renegotiated their Protocols after the collapse of the CMEA. These renegotiations—as well as accession discussions with economies in transition—revealed that WTO members desire assurances that substantial progress will be achieved towards privatizing enterprises and establishing a market-based regulatory environment. As all three countries are in line to accede to the EU, issues relating to STEs did not become prominent in discussions. However, they have played an important role in accession talks involving other transition economies—see chapters 2 and 12.

Dealing with STEs

There are many types of exclusivity arrangements that could have an effect on trade. They range from total monopoly or monopsony control—under which an entity is granted a monopoly right to import or export—to situations where an entity is obliged to compete with domestic buyers on both the domestic and foreign markets. Governments may allow certain enterprises (STEs) to affect trade flows through the pursuit of regulatory controls that create (or permit) the exercise of market power. They may also pursue policies that have effects analogous to direct subsidies. More generally, any enterprise with a dominant position may exercise its market power and distort competition, independent of any action by government to support its activities. The question therefore arises where the line should be drawn between STEs—however defined—and regulatory policy more generally (Kostecki, 1982). As it stands, Article XVII is worded quite broadly and potentially covers a wide range of activities.

The sources of market access problems arising from state trading include the explicit privileges granted by governments and de facto obstacles arising incidentally from government policies which aim at objectives other than the insulation of privileged suppliers. These impediments to competition can be dealt with in a number of different ways.[9] First, behavioral disciplines could be further developed applying to formal privileges granted to those STEs that governments regard as nonnegotiable and wish to continue to maintain. This behavioral approach can be complemented by efforts to introduce greater economic content into WTO rules by adopting a set of regulatory principles that seek to ensure that STEs will operate in an efficient and least trade-distorting manner. These could be complemented by provisions relating to domestic enforcement mechanisms, perhaps along the lines of the bid-protest or challenge mechanisms discussed in chapter 3. An alternative

---

[9]   What follows draws on Hoekman and Low (1998).

is to pursue negotiations to eliminate state trading. This is the revealed-preferred approach in WTO accession negotiations, where the emphasis is on assuring full trading rights of enterprises and privatization commitments. While straightforward in principle, this approach is inherently limited in the sense that governments will differ regarding the extent to which they are willing to negotiate away their rights to grant exclusive rights and privileges in the pursuit of noneconomic objectives.

The issue of addressing de facto exclusivity is best seen as a more general matter. To the extent that STE-like behavior is facilitated by other government interventions, these should be the focus of attention. Where government policy is not the root of the problem, competition policy questions enter the picture. These, however, should be addressed in the broader context of the current debate on trade and competition. It is important that the 'STE issue' be defined as narrowly as possible in order to ensure that multilateral rules are targeted at those areas that cannot be addressed through the application of general WTO rules and disciplines.

Countertrade and the WTO

Countertrade arrangements involve exporters and importers negotiating reciprocal deliveries in partial or full settlement of specific exchanges. Examples are counter-purchase, offset, buyback, advance purchase and barter (Banks, 1983). Countertrade is a special case of a linked transaction providing for reciprocal buying and selling. This type of reciprocal arrangement may occur in home markets and in international trade. The motivation for counter-trade in the international context includes circumvention of foreign exchange and credit controls, hiding price cuts, satisfying governmentally imposed local content or offset requirements and surmounting barriers to otherwise closed markets (Kostecki, 1987). With the exception of the Government Procurement Agreement (see chapter 11) there is no reference to countertrade in the WTO. Countertrade is a business practice and as such is not of direct concern to GATT. What is of potential concern is if counter-trade regulations adopted by governments imply discrimination or a lack of transparency. But in such cases the relevant provisions of the GATT apply.

5.6. TECHNICAL REGULATIONS AND PRODUCT STANDARDS

Product standards, technical regulations and certification systems are essential to the functioning of modern economies. Standards are usually voluntary, generally being defined by industry or nongovernmental standardization bodies such as the American National Standards Institute, the British Standards Institution, the Deutsches Institut für Normung, and the Association Francaise de Normalisation. Standards have been defined as documents 'established by consensus and approved by a recognized body, that provide, for common and repeated use, rules, guidelines or characteristics for activities or their results, aimed at the achievement of the optimum degree of order in a given context' (ISO Guide, 1991). Technical regulations in contrast are legally binding, and are usually imposed to safeguard public or animal health, or the environment. In most industrialized economies the number of standards greatly exceeds the number of technical regulations. Certification systems comprise the procedures to establish that products or production processes conform to the relevant standard or regulation.

The use of product standards is under the direct control of firms and industries. More often than not standards are market driven, and firms desiring to export to or sell in a market have strong incentives to satisfy prevailing standards, be it to ensure compatibility or to signal that products meet minimum quality norms. In the case of technical product regulations there is no choice. Firms must comply. In the case of both standards and technical regulations, the underlying norms are often determined through a cooperative international process that occurs under the auspices of specialized international bodies. A major player in this field is the International Organization for Standardization (ISO), which is located in Geneva, Switzerland. Whether or not to make norms developed by ISO technical committees mandatory is up to governments.

Technical product regulations are generally intended to be welfare enhancing. This distinguishes this policy tool from many of the other policies that are subject to WTO rules. However, technical regulations and standards (TRS) may have trade-impeding effects as well, which is why they are dealt with in the GATT. The tension that arises if welfare-enhancing policies distort trade flows is becoming increasingly important, and extends beyond the case of product standards. Because standards have been dealt with under the GATT for many years already, WTO disciplines are of interest not only in their own right, but also for what they suggest about the feasibility of dealing with regulation-related topics. Two issues arise in determining whether a legitimate trade concern exists regarding a specific regulation: ascertaining whether it has a discriminatory trade impact, and determining whether this is necessary to achieve the objective of the government.

For an economic rationale for TRS to exist there must be market imperfections. Possibilities include information asymmetries, uncertainty, market power, and externalities in production or consumption. Many standards have the characteristic of a public good in that use by one agent does not reduce other agents' consumption possibilities (Kindleberger, 1983). Frequently, the greater the use made of such standards, the greater the potential gains to users in terms of reduced transaction costs—there are so-called network externalities. Examples include standards of measurement and conventions such as driving on one side of the road. In the public goods case there is a clear-cut case for harmonization, as a common standard is in the interest of all users. Achieving agreement on a specific standard can be difficult, as different groups may have different preferences. Because of free rider problems, government intervention may be required to achieve a common standard. Most standards tend to be impure public goods, in that they benefit a specific, identifiable group (usually an industry and its customers). While government intervention is not necessary, there remains a need for interested parties to cooperate, and to the extent that there are costs to developing a standard, there may be an incentive to free ride.

Although standards may help achieve technical efficiency, they may also allow incumbent firms in an industry to increase their market power. Standards are one of the possible instruments through which a firm or a group of firms can raise their rivals' costs. Assuming there are costs to meet the standard, its existence may reduce the contestability of a market because potential entrants find it less attractive to compete or to enter. The greater are the barriers to entry, the greater will be the profit-enhancing effect of the standard, all other things equal. Thus, standardization may well be employed strategically by firms or groups of firms that aim to create rents (excess profits). If so, the standards-setting activity can be characterized as collusive. In the case of voluntary standards there is no need to lobby governments in order to obtain the rents because the standards are set by industry groups. Government agencies responsible for determining technical regulations can expect to be lobbied by potentially affected parties and may be captured by them.

Because TRS can raise unit costs of production they may inhibit international trade. In general, if TRS differ across countries this will segment markets, even if identical norms are applied in each country to domestic and foreign goods (national treatment applies). Prices for similar goods of uniform quality will then not be equal across countries, as the different standards inhibit arbitrage. Research stimulated by the EU Single Market program in the mid-1980s illustrated how significant such TRS-induced market segmentation can be. A typical example was building tiles where voluntary industry standards differed by EU country. Spain was found to be the lowest cost producer of such tiles, average prices being between 40 to over 100 percent lower than prices charged by producers in other countries such as Germany, France, and the Netherlands (Groupe-Mac, 1988). Such price differences were maintained as the result of a combination of differing standards and government procurement regulations. In France, nonstandard tiles could not be used in public works (about 40 percent of the market), while private firms were hesitant to use nonstandard tiles because insurance companies tended to require that buildings meet industry standards. In Italy, pasta purity laws required that pasta be made of durum wheat, a high quality type of wheat produced in the south of the country. This increased the cost of pasta in comparison to other EU countries, where pasta tended to consist of a mix of wheat qualities. A lack of uniform or mutually recognized standards and regulations may have a significant impact on trade.

WTO Rules

The WTO does not require that members have product standards. Nor does the WTO develop or write standards. The GATT 1994 Agreement on Technical Barriers to Trade (TBT) aims to ensure that mandatory technical regulations, voluntary standards, and testing and certification of products do not constitute unnecessary barriers to trade. There is close relationship between the TBT agreement, the national treatment requirement, and Article XX GATT (which allows for measures to restrict trade if necessary to protect public health or safety—see chapter 9). The link with national treatment (Article III GATT) is that 'like' products produced in foreign countries may be subjected to a variety of conformity assessment requirements that can be construed to be discriminatory but may be necessary to ensure compliance with prevailing regulations. The link with Article XX is that both parts of the GATT deal with measures taken by governments to safeguard public health and safety, among other things. Indeed, the preamble of the TBT agreement repeats language found in Article XX: 'Recognizing that no country should be prevented from taking measures necessary ... for the protection of human ... life or health ... subject to the requirement that they are not applied in a manner which would constitute a means of arbitrary or unjustifiable discrimination between countries where the same conditions prevail or a disguised restriction on international trade ...'. The TBT agreement is complemented by a stand alone agreement dealing with sanitary and phytosanitary measures (discussed in the next section).

The TBT agreement embodies disciplines on the adoption of TRS in member countries, and on conformity assessment, testing and certification procedures. It also has a variety of transparency provisions. The basic rule is that central government bodies do not discriminate (MFN, national treatment) and do not write technical regulations that are more trade-restrictive than necessary to meet legitimate objectives. The latter include national security, the prevention of deceptive practices, the protection of human health or safety, animal or plant life and health, and the environment. Relevant international standards developed by bodies such as the ISO—if they exist—must be used as the basis for technical regulations, except if this would be inappropriate because of climatic, geographical or technological factors. Technical regulations based on product requirements should be worded in terms of performance rather than design or descriptive characteristics. A Code of Good Practice applies regarding the preparation, adoption and application of voluntary standards.

Conformity assessment procedures are also subject to nondiscrimination. Here again, if relevant guides or recommendations issued by international standardizing bodies exist, these are to be used, except if inappropriate for national security reasons or deemed inadequate to safeguard health and safety. In principle, WTO members are to join and use international systems for conformity assessment. The results of conformity assessment procedures undertaken in exporting countries must be accepted if consultations determine these are equivalent to domestic ones. Accreditation on the basis of relevant guides or recommendations issued by international standardizing bodies is to be taken into account as an indication of adequate technical competence of the foreign entity. Members are encouraged to negotiate mutual recognition agreements (MRAs) for conformity assessment procedures, and to apply the MFN and national treatment principles when permitting participation of foreign certification bodies in their conformity assessment procedures.

A third component of standards disciplines is transparency-related, and builds upon the principle of publication of regulations contained in Article X GATT. Each member must establish a national enquiry point to answer questions and provide documents on:
(1) technical regulations adopted or proposed by bodies which have legal power to enforce them;
(2) standards adopted or proposed by central or local government bodies, or by regional standardizing bodies; and
(3) conformity assessment procedures, existing or proposed, applied by enforcing bodies.

Best efforts are to be made to ensure that enquiry points are also able to answer inquiries regarding standards adopted or proposed by nongovernmental standardizing bodies such as industry associations, as well as conformity assessment procedures operated by such bodies. The WTO secretariat is to establish an information system under which national standards bodies or enquiry points transmit to the ISO Information Centre in Geneva

the notifications required under the Code of Good Practice for the preparation, adoption and application of standards.

To date, the agreement has worked smoothly. The committee dealing with
the agreement has held regular meetings, and has completed four triennial
reviews of the agreement—most of which concerned the pre-WTO period
when the agreement was one of the Tokyo Round codes. There have been
few disputes under the agreement. The TBT agreement was invoked in a
1996 case brought by Venezuela and Brazil against US standards for refor-
mulated and conventional gasoline. However, the panel found against the US
on the basis of Articles I and III GATT, not on the basis of the alleged violation of the TBT agreement. Another case that is relevant is *Asbestos*
(WT/DS135/R). As mentioned in chapter 3, this involved an argument by
Canada that a French ban on the manufacture, importation and sale of asbestos violated the TBT agreement because it was not necessary, and was not
based on international standards. The EU argued that the asbestos ban was
not a technical regulation in the sense of the TBT agreement. In considering
these arguments, the panel determined that a measure constitutes a 'technical regulation' if it affects one or more given products, specifies the technical
characteristics of the product(s) which allow them to be marketed in the territory of the member imposing the measure, and is mandatory. The panel
concluded that the general prohibition on marketing asbestos and asbestos-
containing products does not satisfy this definition.

Reducing Transactions Costs: Harmonization and Mutual Recognition

It has been estimated that over 60 percent of US exports are subject to
health, safety, and related standards in their destination markets. Govern-
ment-issued certificates were required for 45 percent of exports to the EU,
private, third-party certification was accepted for 15 percent, and manufacturers self-certification sufficed for the rest (Wilson, 1998). Within the EU,
some 75 percent of the value of intra-EU trade in goods is subject to mandatory technical regulations (European Commission, 1996). Certification in
regulated sectors may involve frequent and redundant sampling of products
and testing for conformity to standards. Some products may be subjected to
100 percent testing—this can effectively block imports if applied only to foreign firms. Duplicative testing and certification requirements have rapidly
become more important as a barrier to international trade. Unter (1998) estimates that redundant testing and conformity assessment procedures faced
by Hewlett Packard increased six-fold between 1990 and 1997.

The GATT rules are helpful for traders in ensuring nondiscrimination and
enhancing transparency of TRS, but clearly more is required if transactions

costs are to be reduced significantly. There are two major policy options: harmonization and mutual recognition. Harmonization may involve unilateral adoption by one country of another's set of rules, or negotiation of a common set of disciplines. Examples abound of unilateral harmonization to the standard of another country. These are often driven by market size disparities: in 1992 Canada adopted US auto emission standards to ensure that its auto makers could realize economies of scale by avoiding separate production lines for the home and US markets. Switzerland adopted the EU TRS regime to ensure that Swiss goods could enter and circulate in the EU on the same basis as EU-produced goods (Messerlin, 1998). Many developing countries use TRS regimes developed in Europe or the US, often by maintaining systems inherited from a colonial past or military occupation. Others have deliberately adopted foreign norms. South Korea imported many German and US product standards in the 1950s as part of a strategy to upgrade the quality of industrial production and foster exports. Unilateral recognition of foreign regulatory regimes can be a complement to adopting the standards of a trading partner or international norms. Thus, foreign certification for certain imports may be accepted as proof of safety. The Underwriters Laboratories (UL) mark is accepted in many countries.

Harmonization to facilitate trade has been pursued most intensively by the EU. The European experience suggests that this is unlikely to be a productive strategy as agreement is very difficult to obtain under a consensus rule. A better approach is mutual recognition, under which countries agree to recognize (accept as equivalent) each others standards and conformity assessment procedures. Mutual recognition agreements (MRAs) are a cooperative mechanism through which the transaction costs associated with conformity assessment systems to establish compliance with standards can be reduced (Box 5.6). MRAs may require some degree of harmonization of either standards or test procedures, especially in areas where mandatory standards or regulations apply, to ensure that the underlying norms satisfy basic minimum standards.

Box 5.6. EU-US Mutual Recognition Agreements

US and EU trade talks on mutual recognition of conformity assessment began in 1992 and aimed at achieving agreement that product test results, inspections, and certifications performed by independent entities would be accepted in both markets. In particular, the EU sought assurance that US testing laboratories and product certification bodies were competent to test for compliance with the essential requirements specified in EU directives. The EU also wanted European firms to be able to test and certify to corresponding US regulatory requirements. The US sought to eliminate the perceived discriminatory effects of the EU's new approach to technical regulations, which mandated product certification by approved European bodies—imposing duplicate testing costs on exporters. The EU's increasingly Community-wide approach to standardization gave US firms an incentive to negotiate MRAs, as these would lower the costs of accessing the EU market as a whole.

Significant differences in European and US testing and certification systems made agreement difficult. The European system relies less on self-declaration of conformity by enterprises than the US system, and more on mandatory third-party testing and certification. Under the EU's global approach to conformity assessment, only recognized testing, certification, and marking institutions are able to issue certification marks. As of end 1997, member states had only certified 600 such bodies to the Commission (out of a total of over 10,000, ranging from large multinationals such as Société Générale de Surveillance (SGS), Inchcape or Bureau Veritas to small in-house testing facilities). Virtually all were European (Messerlin, 1998). Another obstacle concerned the extent to which certification and inspection agencies of one country are willing and legally permitted to devolve authority for testing and inspection to the other country's regulators. It was eventually agreed that the EU would accept that the US Federal Drug Administration (FDA) was an independent agency that could not be overruled.

In June 1997 the US and the EU concluded an MRA that covers conformity requirements in telecommunications equipment, information technology products, medical devices, and pharmaceuticals. The agreement addresses acceptance of test data, laboratory accreditation, and final product certification. As of 2000, certifications performed anywhere by a facility recognized under the MRA in the US or Europe will be accepted, and manufacturers saw their choice of testing laboratories broadened. The agreement also introduced a joint curriculum for training of European and American inspectors.

The MRAs cover over US$40 billion of bilateral trade. The MRA on telecommunications and information technology products alone could save consumers and manufacturers approximately US$1.4 billion, implying that the frictional costs abolished were equivalent to a five percent tax on the goods traded (Wilson, 1998). Although this is a significant cost reduction, the MRAs are regarded as a second-best solution by US industry, which would prefer to rely much more heavily on supplier self-certification instead of third party conformity assessment.

Sources: Wilson (1998), Messerlin (1998), and B. Lionel and G. de Jonquières, 'EU and US agree plan to cut red tape', *The Financial Times*, May 29, 1997.

Mutual recognition proved a powerful tool for increasing competition in the European market. A question for WTO members, and developing countries in particular, is whether mutual recognition is a viable option to pursue in the multilateral context. The process relies heavily on mutual trust in the competence and ability of the institutions responsible for enforcing mandatory standards and a willingness to be flexible in setting minimum standards. Even if developing countries adopt European, American or international (ISO) standards, significant institutional strengthening is likely to be required for partner countries to be willing to accept 'home country supervision'. One result of an unwillingness of OECD countries to recognize developing country standards regimes could be a hollowing out of the MFN principle. An option that might be pursued more vigorously is to put greater reliance on third party conformity assessment of goods and services (Box 5.7). The potential for recognition to reduce transaction costs and increase the real incomes of WTO members can be significant. The EU now requires third-party testing, certification or quality system registration for certain regulated sectors by organizations certified to the Commission by the member states as technically competent. The requirement that these assessments be undertaken by EU-certified bodies raised the costs of testing and certification to non-EU manufacturers in many sectors and was one motivation for EU-US MRA negotiations in the 1990s.

Box 5.7. The SASO International Conformity Certification Program
The Saudi Arabian Standards Organization (SASO) is the sole agency responsible for the preparation, adoption and enforcement of TRS in Saudi Arabia. Mandatory standards are applied equally to both imported and domestically made products to enforce health, safety, and environmental protection, national security, and public morals. SASO has set up the International Conformity Certification Program (ICCP), a pilot conformity assessment procedure that relies on the private sector to inspect shipments for compliance with Saudi standards. The ICCP is a combined conformity assessment, preshipment inspection, and certification scheme to regulate and monitor shipments of selected product categories prior to being shipped to Saudi Arabia. In 1999, the program applied to 66 product categories divided into five groups: food and agriculture, electronics and electrical products, automobile and related products, chemical products, and others. The key element of the program is that each shipment must be determined to be in conformity with SASO standards (or their approved equivalents) before the certificate of conformity (required for every consignment) can be issued. This ensures both exporters and importers of a streamlined customs process

that allows goods to clear faster and to face minimal rejection risk at the
Saudi port of entry.

Test data produced by nationally or internationally accredited laboratories that have been approved by SASO is accepted under the program. At the
conclusion of the SASO-approved laboratory testing, a Conformity Test and
Evaluation Report is issued and submitted to the Regional Licensing Centre
for verification of conformity to SASO requirements. The program closely
follows ISO Guide 28 (General Rules for a Model Third Party Certification
System for products), particularly with regard to products that have
achieved full compliance with Saudi standards. These products qualify for a
Type Approval License that allows imports with a minimum of intervention.
A key aspect of the program is that SASO has contracted a specialized private firm to carry out these activities. This company is in turn assisted by a
network of accredited testing laboratories and inspection bodies around the
round. The SASO experience shows that compliance verification of national
standards might be better and cost-effectively served through private testing
firms and accredited labs.
Source: Messerlin and Zarrouk (2000).

The publication and notification requirements of the TBT Agreement, in
conjunction with the national enquiry points, have an important role to play
in fostering transparency. They help ensure that traders can readily determine the regulatory situation that prevails in markets to which they want to
export. A weakness of the TBT Agreement is that language on voluntary
product standards developed by industry associations is largely of a best-
endeavors nature. This reflects the fact that WTO disciplines focus on government actions—not the private sector. Although the agreement works
smoothly, an important challenge confronting WTO members will be to explore avenues for reducing the transactions costs incurred by traders due to
differences in TRS, and perhaps more important, the excess costs incurred
due to redundant testing and certification requirements. Messerlin and Zarrouk (2000) argue that a top-down approach aiming at eliminating TRS-
related trade conflicts through harmonization or mutual recognition will be
difficult in the WTO context. To date it has only proven possible to a limited
extent in the EU and between a few OECD countries (the US and the EU, New
Zealand and Australia). Extending this model to a group of 141-plus economies will be difficult.

Initiatives using a bottom-up approach to enforcement are likely to be
more fruitful. That is, the emphasis might more productively center on certification activities and an expansion of the role of the private sector in such
activities. In addition to PSI-type models, greater acceptance of the supplier's declaration of conformity could be encouraged (Wilson, 1998).

Moreover, given the importance that is accorded to the role of competent international standards-setting bodies in defining standards, an important issue for WTO members and civil society in member countries is to ensure that the process through which TRS are developed allows for participation by affected stakeholders. To date, the major players in standards-setting bodies have been industry and subsets of the scientific community. Finally, consideration needs to be given to the implications of the burden of proof that is currently imposed on non-members of a MRA that seek to accede. This burden can be quite high and give rise to situations where countries that satisfy technical requirements are nonetheless excluded for political or other reasons. A major policy issue is therefore to ensure that the MFN rule does not get circumvented through the negotiation of MRAs. A necessary condition for this to be the case is that nonmembers have the opportunity to join such agreements.

5.7. SANITARY AND PHYTOSANITARY MEASURES

Sanitary and phytosanitary (SPS) measures are requirements imposed by governments to ensure the safety of products for human or animal consumption, or to protect the environment (plant life). Most governments establish minimum standards that products, plants or animals must meet in order to be allowed to enter their territory. Usually these norms will apply equally to foreign and domestically produced goods, plants or animals. However, as is the case with product standards more generally, differences in norms may act to restrict trade. Such differences became increasingly prominent during the 1980s, with many countries alleging that import-competing industries or lobbies were using SPS measures to restrict trade. SPS measures can very easily be abused, as they can be defined so strictly so as to ensure that no import ever satisfies them. For example, a country with a large sheep industry but no cows may try to prohibit imports of beef to protect sheep farmers by imposing a health-based SPS measure requiring that beef have a fat content that is very costly to attain (say, less than one percent). Alternatively, if it has a beef industry and could consequently be subjected to a claim of violating national treatment, it might impose a very short shelf-life requirement. It could also use a SPS measure to encourage local processing in cases where it has bound its tariffs. Thus, beef for retail sale might be required to have no more than three percent fat, but beef for further processing could have any fat content. Abuses may also occur in the enforcement of SPS measures. Even if a country uses internationally accepted SPS measures for a product, governments will still inspect imports to ascertain whether they satisfy health requirements. Such inspections may be used as a mechanism to reject imports of politically sensitive goods, even if they meet all health and safety requirements (Box 5.8).

Box 5.8. International trade and sanitary and phytosanitary restrictions
Two long running disputes in the 1980s helped motivate negotiators in the Uruguay Round to seek an agreement on SPS measures: Japanese sanitary rules on imports of apples and the EU ban on the use of hormonal substances in livestock and meat products.

Japan formally opened its apple market to foreign competition in 1971. In practice market access continued to be restricted in the decades that followed on the grounds that most imports were not sufficiently protected against pests and plant diseases that could harm Japan's orchards. Apple exporters argued that Japan's phytosanitary regulations were far more stringent than any other country's, and constituted back-door protectionism (GATT Activities, 1987). US trade officials cited Japan's apple import regulations as an unfair-trade barrier and regularly raised the issue in bilateral discussions, driven by Congressional representatives from the state of Washington—a major producer. After years of tension, Japanese authorities finally gave in to the external pressure, declaring that certain US orchards had taken adequate measures to eliminate viruses and moths.

In January 1988, the EU banned the use of hormonal substances in the process of fattening animals intended for slaughter and human consumption. This ban affected US exports of meat to the EU, and caused a trade dispute to develop. The US argued that the ban had no scientific foundation—since the use of hormones by US producers was well within safe margins as determined by a variety of scientific agencies—and therefore constituted an unjustifiable trade barrier. According to the US, the ban—if fully implemented—would reduce exports by US$115 million per year. The dispute was brought to the GATT, with the US choosing to invoke the procedures of the TBT Agreement, this being the only relevant instrument at the time. The EU considered that because the ban was aimed at protecting health and concerned production and processing methods—which were not covered by the TBT agreement—the US did not have a case. The US threatened to increase tariffs on certain European goods if the prohibition on importation and sale of meat treated with hormones was implemented. The EU in turn brought the issue of retaliatory measures by the US before the GATT Council (*GATT Activities*, 1987 and 1988).

These examples illustrate why an agreement on SPS measures was negotiated. Governments expected that the scope for protectionist abuse of food safety and animal or plant health regulations would be considerably reduced as a result of the new agreement. However, as has already been discussed in chapter 3, SPS-related disputes proved to be difficult to resolve. Both the apple and the hormone cases were brought to the WTO.

The WTO Rules

The Agreement on the Application of Sanitary and Phytosanitary Measures was negotiated as part of the Uruguay Round Agreement on Agriculture (discussed in the next chapter). It applies to all SPS measures that may affect international trade. A SPS measure is defined as any measure applied to protect human, animal or plant health from risks arising from the establishment or spread of pests and diseases; from additives or contaminants in foodstuffs; or to prevent other damage from the establishment or spread of pests. SPS measures include all relevant regulations and procedures, including product criteria; processes and production methods; testing, inspection, certification and approval procedures; quarantine treatments; provisions on relevant statistical procedures and risk assessment methods; and packaging and labeling requirements directly related to food safety. As in the case of technical regulations and product standards, there is no requirement that members adopt SPS measures. Nor does the WTO draft SPS norms. The WTO simply establishes disciplines if members implement SPS measures.

The SPS Agreement is *lex specialis* to the TBT Agreement. It stipulates that SPS measures may not unjustifiably discriminate between WTO members, should not be more trade restrictive than required to achieve their objectives, and may not constitute a disguised restriction on international trade. They should be based on international standards, guidelines or recommendations, if these exist, unless it can be proven with scientific evidence that an alternative is preferable. A crucial provision in the agreement requires that SPS measures be based on scientific principles, including an assessment of the risks to human, animal or plant life or health, taking into account risk assessment techniques developed by relevant international organizations. The risk assessment must identify the diseases a member wants to prevent in its territory, the potential biological and economic consequences associated with such diseases, an evaluation of the likelihood of entry, establishment or spread of these diseases, and the associated potential biological and economic consequences.

In the assessment of risks, available scientific evidence must be considered, as well as relevant processes and production methods; inspection, sampling and testing methods, and the prevalence of specific diseases or pests and environmental conditions. In choosing SPS measures that do not pertain to human health, economic factors must be considered as well, including the potential damage in terms of loss of production and cost of control in the event of spread of a pest or disease and the relative cost effectiveness of alternative approaches to limiting risks.

The agreement also embodies a recognition element. WTO members must accept the SPS measures of other members as equivalent—even if they differ from their own—if the exporting country can demonstrate that its SPS measures achieve the desired level of protection. Negotiations to achieve bilateral or multilateral agreements on recognition of the equivalence of specified SPS measures are encouraged. Conformity assessment procedures and fees are to be based on MFN and national treatment, procedures and criteria should be published, confidentiality respected, and an appeals procedure established.

The Committee on Sanitary and Phytosanitary Measures may grant developing countries specified, time-limited exceptions in whole or in part from meeting the requirements of the agreement. Least developed country members may delay application of the provisions of the agreement until mid-2000. Other developing countries were given until mid-1997, subject to certain conditions. The Committee was charged with the development of a procedure to monitor the process of international harmonization and the use of international standards, and the establishment of a list of international standards and guidelines relating to SPS measures that have a major impact on trade. As under the TBT agreement, an enquiry point must exist to provide answers to SPS-related queries from trading partners and to provide relevant documents. If the content of a proposed regulation is not substantially the same as that of an international norm and is likely to have a significant effect on trade, the WTO secretariat must be notified. This must include a description of the regulation's product coverage and a brief indication of the objective and rationale of the proposed regulation.

Two major dispute settlement cases on SPS rules were brought to the WTO in addition to *Hormones* (which is discussed in chapter 3). The first concerned Japanese testing requirements for agricultural products. In a case brought to the WTO in 1997, the US alleged that, for each agricultural product for which Japan required quarantine treatment, Japan prohibited the importation of each variety of that product until the quarantine treatment (fumigation) had been tested for that variety, even though the treatment had proven effective with respect to other varieties of the same product. The products concerned included apples, nectarines, cherries and similar fruit products, as well as walnuts. The US claimed that Japan's measures violated the SPS agreement because they did not have a scientific justification and were more trade restrictive than necessary. The panel agreed with the US on the first count, but not the second. A footnote to the relevant provision (Article 5.6 SPS) specifies that a measure is 'too' restrictive if another SPS measure exists that is reasonably available (taking into account technical and economic feasibility), achieves the desired level of protection, and is significantly less trade restrictive than the measure that is the subject of dispute. The panel found that only the first and last conditions had been demonstrated.

The panel also noted that by not having published the testing requirements for any of the products at issue, Japan had violated the transparency provisions of the SPS Agreement. On appeal, the Appellate Body upheld the panel findings on transparency, absence of sufficient scientific evidence and lack of an appropriate risk assessment (WT/DS76/AB/R). It also upheld the panel finding that the US had not shown that the measures were more trade-restrictive than required to achieve Japan's desired level of protection. This case illustrated that the SPS agreement is a powerful instrument disciplining the use of SPS measures, and that WTO members must ensure that there is a scientific basis for their measures (Article 2.2.) and that such measures are based on an appropriate risk assessment (Article 5.1).

A case brought by Canada in 1997 against an Australian prohibition on the importation of untreated fresh, chilled or frozen salmon further clarified the reach of the SPS agreement. The ban was motivated on the basis of preventing the entry of pests and diseases into Australia. Here again it was concluded that the prohibition was not scientifically justified and was not based on an appropriate risk assessment. The panel also found that the measure violated the 'consistency requirement' of the SPS agreement (Article 5.5), which specifies that in comparable situations the same SPS standards should apply. It concluded that Australia had imposed more stringent norms for adult, wild, ocean-caught Pacific salmon and applied lower standards for whole, frozen herring for use as bait and live ornamental finfish. These arbitrary distinctions were found to result in discrimination or a disguised restriction on international trade. In October 1998, the Appellate Body reversed the panel's finding that the measure was more trade-restrictive than required because the panel had arrived at this conclusion by focusing on Australia's heat-treatment requirement, rather than the SPS measure at issue (the import prohibition). In considering whether the import ban was excessive, the Appellate Body concluded that it was not able to come to a determination given absence of information in the panel report on the relative risks of alternative regulatory options (WT/DS/18/AB/R).

The WTO disciplines on SPS measures are valuable because they establish mechanisms to contest arbitrary and unjustified decisions by Customs, Health, Veterinary or Agricultural authorities to reject goods on the basis of noncompliance with standards. They are process-oriented. No attempt is made in the WTO to agree to the substantive content of SPS measures or to define minimum standards. This is left to specialized bodies such as the FAO. Reference is simply made to the relevant international bodies that address standards-related matters, and countries are encouraged to adopt internationally developed—and therefore consensus-based—standards. This makes it important that all WTO members—including developing countries—have the capacity to participate in the fora that develop SPS norms that affect their industries and consumers. As is the case with TRS more generally, a key need for developing countries in the SPS area is to strengthen standards-related institutions, including risk assessment and management mechanisms, and to develop mechanisms to reduce transaction costs. The private sector can play a role in this connection through preshipment inspection and related certification programs.

WTO members remain free to define their technical regulations, but must notify diverging national standards and are required to motivate them. Nonconforming standards can be challenged, implying that countries such as the US might be forced to abide by the Codex Alimentarius if its regime is successfully challenged in WTO. In the case of SPS measures—where such motivation requires scientific evidence—much depends on how such evidence is evaluated by WTO dispute settlement panels. The *Hormones* case illustrates that even if the science is relatively unambiguous it may be difficult to induce countries to change their SPS regimes (see chapter 3). In many cases the science will not be clear-cut, providing scope for fundamental disagreements. The WTO case law to date suggest that appeals to the 'precautionary principle' may be difficult to sustain (although it should be noted that the EU did not do so in *Hormones*). Insistence by countries that significant leeway be granted to governments on the basis of the 'precautionary principle' may then lead to situations where governments cannot comply with DSB rulings and are forced to accept retaliation. Such outcomes are clearly not beneficial to the trading system.

The precise nature and limits of the disciplines embodied in the SPS agreement is difficult to discern from a reading of its text. There are many fuzzy provisions in the SPS agreement that WTO members must ensure that the rules are clear, make economic sense, and allow governments the freedom to intervene in instances where they perceive a need to do so to attain noneconomic objectives. Trebilcock and Soloway (2000) argue that a case can be made that the Appellate Body's rulings in SPS cases 'are not anchored in a coherent conception of an ideal risk regulation process nor in the appropriate scope and limits of supra-national quasi-judicial review of [SPS] measures. Many aspects of the Appellate Body's decisions involve elaborate exercises in semantic 'shadow boxing' with panel decisions and convoluted parsing of the wording of the SPS agreement'.

5.8. TRADE-RELATED INVESTMENT MEASURES

The value of sales by foreign affiliates of multinational firms now exceeds global exports of goods and services. The observed growth in foreign direct investment (FDI) is a consequence of many changes in the world economy, including the decline in communication and transportation costs, and, importantly, liberalization of FDI regimes in many countries. Perceptions about multinational firms and their effects on host countries have undergone a transformation. Most countries are now quite eager to attract FDI; many offer financial incentives to attract FDI and have concluded bilateral investment treaties (BITs). As of 1999, over 1,600 BITs had been negotiated, compared to some 400 at the beginning of 1990 (UNCTAD, 1999). On the other hand, many countries continue to subject multinationals to performance requirements. For example, multinationals may have to comply with trade-related investment measures (TRIMs) such as local content, export or technology transfer requirements. In fact, it is not unusual to find investment incentives being offered in conjunction with performance requirements and other restrictions on FDI, perhaps to partially offset the negative impact of the latter on the likelihood of investment by multinationals. TRIMs have tended to be concentrated in certain industries, with automotive, chemical, and petrochemical and computer industries leading the list (UNCTAD, 1996). The specific type of policy used often depends on whether FDI is resource-seeking, domestic-market oriented, or export-oriented (Caves, 1996). The schizophrenic nature of the overall policy environment reflects the guarded optimism with which many countries continue to view the entry of multinational firms into their territory.

TRIMs are policies used by governments with a view to forcing foreign investors to meet certain performance standards. TRIMs often involve discrimination against imports by creating incentives (additional to tariffs imposed at the border) to source from domestic producers. The most prevalent TRIMs are local content requirements—a condition that a minimum proportion of inputs used by an investor be of domestic origin. In most circumstances such measures are inefficient. This is because they either act like a tariff on intermediate goods (this is the case for a local content requirement, where manufacturers are forced to use high cost local inputs) or as a QR (this is the case with a so-called trade-balancing requirement, which acts to restrict imports to a certain quantity). A local content requirement, while equivalent to a tariff, is inferior in welfare terms because the government does not collect any tariff revenue.

An economic case for TRIMs requires there to be domestic distortions or externalities from FDI. Absent such market failures, the optimal FDI policy is no policy at all—governments should allow for unfettered market transactions. Thus, under perfect competition, domestic content rules lower welfare by raising the price of domestic inputs: the resulting benefits to input suppliers are outweighed by the costs incurred by final goods producers (Grossman, 1981). As multinational firms typically arise in oligopolistic industries, the presence of imperfect competition in the host economy is an obvious potential rationale for intervention. Analyses of content protection and export performance requirements under conditions of imperfect competition illustrate that the welfare effects of such policies may be positive (Richardson 1993; Rodrik 1987). However, the standard normative prescription applies: more efficient instruments can be identified to address the underlying distortions. For example, in the case of welfare-reducing anticompetitive practices resulting from market power or collusion, vigorous competition policies are called for, while domestic policy distortions such as tariffs should be removed at the source. This approach is implicit in the WTO, which not only aims at progressive liberalization of trade, but also prohibits the use of most TRIMs.

TRIMs were initially one of the more controversial topics on the agenda of the Uruguay Round negotiations. Many developing countries were of the view that attempting to agree to broad-ranging multilateral disciplines on policies affecting investment went far beyond the scope of the GATT, and that the GATT was not necessarily the appropriate forum to address investment-related policies. Certain OECD countries, the US in particular, were of the view that policies distorting investment flows could have a significant impact on trade flows, and should be subject to multilateral trade disciplines. At the start of the Uruguay Round, the US sought to negotiate rules for a long list of TRIMs, including investment-related measures such as remittance policies, ownership limitations, and investment incentives. In the end, the TRIMs agreement that emerged was not very ambitious. It basically prohibits measures that are inconsistent with the GATT national treatment principle (Article III) and the ban on the use of QRs (Article XI). The agreement includes a list of prohibited measures (including local content, trade-balancing, foreign exchange-balancing and domestic sales requirements) and requires that all policies not in conformity with the agreement be notified within 90 days of entry into force of the agreement. All such measures must be eliminated within two, five or seven years, for industrialized, developing and least developed countries, respectively.

The listed prohibited measures were already illegal under the GATT. What the TRIMs agreement essentially does is to reaffirm that GATT rules apply in this area. Although this was a point of view that was long held and defended by most OECD countries, it had been resisted by developing countries. The agreement prohibits both mandatory measures and those 'with which compliance is necessary to obtain an advantage' (such as a tax concession or subsidy). Noteworthy is that export performance requirements were not included in the illustrative list. This is somewhat inconsistent with the GATT's prohibition on the use of export subsidies, as the two instruments are very similar in effect. It was agreed in the Uruguay Round that the agreement was to be reviewed in the year 2000 at which time it might be complemented by provisions on competition and investment policy (Low and Subramanian, 1996). The scope for expanding the Illustrative List of prohibited TRIMs was also to be put on the table at that time. As the five year review deadline coincided with the built-in negotiating mandate on topics such as services and agriculture, TRIMs were expected to be on the negotiating agenda of the 'millennium' round, perhaps wrapped into a more general negotiating group on FDI policies. Following the failure of the Seattle ministerial to launch a round, many developing countries argued in the WTO that the TRIMS agreement was not in their interest and that transition periods should be extended.

Although the TRIMs agreement does not go beyond existing GATT rules, these disciplines are quite powerful. A 1996 case brought by the EU, Japan and the US against provisions of Indonesia's National Car Program may be indicative of the future. Under the contested program, the government granted 'National Car' company status to Indonesian companies that met specified criteria as to ownership of facilities, use of trademarks, and technology. National Car companies were required to meet increasing local content requirements over a three year period; if so, they benefited from exemption from the prevailing luxury tax on sales of cars and exemption from import duties on parts and components. National Cars manufactured in a foreign country that fulfilled the local content requirements were also exempt from import duties and luxury tax. Such imported National Cars were deemed to comply with the 20 percent local content requirement for the end of the first production year if the value of 'counter-purchased' Indonesian parts and components accounted for at least 25 percent of the value of the imported cars (WTO, 1998*b*). The panel found that this program violated the national treatment rule. A major reason Indonesia was targeted was that the policy measures were introduced after the entry into force of the TRIMs agreement. A number of countries apply similar policies but are currently sheltered by the transition period agreed in the Uruguay Round.

In many cases, surveys show that TRIMs require firms to take actions that they would have taken anyway. For example, a policy that requires firms to export is inconsequential if firms were going to export even in the absence of such a requirement. Surveys by the US Department of Commerce for 1977 and 1982 indicated that only six percent of all the overseas affiliates of US firms felt constrained by TRIMs such as local content requirements, although a far greater percentage operated in sectors where TRIMs existed. In other words, TRIMs often failed to bind (UNCTC, 1991). However, the surveys did not take into account that TRIMs may carry efficiency consequences for the world by discouraging FDI in the first place.

The available empirical evidence suggests that local content and related policies are costly to the economy. They often do not achieve the desired backward and forward linkages, encourage inefficient foreign entry, and create potential problems for future liberalization as those who enter the market lobby against a change in regime (Pursell, 1999; Moran, 1998). Governments that are constrained in eliminating costly status quo trade-related policies that aim at industrial development because protected industries are able to prevent their abolition may be assisted by an international agreement to overcome this resistance. Although the economic case against the use of TRIMS by developing countries is strong, rapid elimination of such industrial policies may be politically difficult. In practice, transition periods will be important in phasing out WTO illegal programs, as investment decisions will have been taken in the past on the basis of prevailing policies. One example of a phase-out policy is described in Box 5.9.

Box 5.9. South African TRIMs in the Automotive Sector

South Africa has long had a trade policy designed to support the development of a local car industry. Eight production facilities operated in the country as of the late 1990s, producing 38 models, with an average production run of 37,000 units, a very low amount compared to international best practice. Until the mid 1980s, tariffs on cars were very high, ranging up to 100 percent or more, and car assemblers were subject to requirements and incentives to source locally. Local content requirements aimed to reduce screwdriver assembly operations that would otherwise be profitable because tariffs on parts and components were well below those on cars. Starting in 1989, a decision was taken to increase competition in the sector. A tariff reduction program was designed and announced, and an export incentive scheme was created in order to encourage plants to attain greater scale economies. This involved the granting of (tradable) import credits on the basis of realized export volumes—in effect, net foreign exchange earnings counted towards the minimum (50 percent) local content requirement. In

1995 all local content requirements were abolished and further reductions in tariffs were announced (going beyond the nation's WTO commitments), with an ultimate aim to attain a maximum rate of 40 percent for vehicles and 30 percent for parts in 2002.

The South African phase-out strategy of TRIMs in the car sector sought to balance economic and social policies. The negative impact on the components sector of elimination of local content requirements and the concurrent gradual reduction of tariffs on components was offset in part by the incentive program to encourage exports of automotive products. This increased demand for high quality local output. Although the program distorts incentives—for example, car companies have an incentive to procure high value components in which the country may not have the greatest comparative advantage to maximize import credits—the program led to a significant expansion of automotive exports such as leather seat covers, tires, and exhaust systems, in the process facilitating adjustment to a policy environment without TRIMs.

Source: Black (1999).

5.9. CONCLUSION

Despite the complexities of the various agreements, the GATT is basically a simple agreement. The key disciplines are nondiscrimination (national treatment and MFN), the prohibition on QRs, and a variety of rules that aim to prevent circumvention of the nondiscrimination principle and negotiated market access liberalization (the tariff bindings). The incentive for interest groups—especially import-competing industries—to lobby for protection and government support cannot be regulated away. Such pressures will always arise. Tariff bindings, national treatment, MFN and the ban on QRs establish powerful disciplines regarding the conditions of competition facing foreign products on markets.

Over time, attempts—often successful—have been made to expand disciplines on nontariff measures, thus increasing the scope to bring complaints that market access concessions are being violated. The contestability of markets can be affected by many policies—subsidies, standards, customs procedures, and so forth. Many of these have been addressed in the GATT. The rules often make economic sense in that they encourage transparency and push governments to use more rather than less efficient instruments (tariffs, not quotas). Although the coverage of the GATT expanded steadily over time to encompass almost all trade policies, a few have so far been left untouched. One policy area where GATT imposes no disciplines is with respect to export taxes. This reflects the mercantilist bias of the system. Governments remain free to impose such taxes, despite the fact that export taxes can be equivalent to import duties. As discussed further in chapter 13, if WTO members.initiate discussions on competition policies, export taxes will also have to be put on the table. More generally, where to draw the line between what should be permitted and remain unconstrained and what deserves to be regulated multilaterally is a question that is likely to become increasingly urgent. The TBT and SPS issues discussed in this chapter illustrate that this is not just a question that pertains to the 'new' trade agenda discussed in the following chapters (services, intellectual property, competition, investment, and so forth).

5.10. FURTHER READING

There is no textbook that looks at the economics of all of the policies addressed by the GATT. W. Max Corden, *Trade Policy and Economic Welfare* (Oxford: Oxford University Press, 1997) is a classic text. Another recommended resource on the economics of trade policy is Neil Vousden, *The Economics of Trade Protection* (Cambridge: Cambridge University Press, 1990). Alan Deardorff and Robert Stern, *Measurement of Nontariff Barriers* (Ann Arbor: University of Michigan, 1998) is an excellent discussion of the economic impact of different NTMs and how to measure their impact. The contributions in J.M. Finger and A. Olechowski (eds.) *The Uruguay Round: A Handbook* (Washington DC: The World Bank, 1987) remain a good source of information on GATT rules, practices and history.

The WCO web site, www.wcoomd.org provides information on best practices in customs clearance and the various instruments and tools that have been developed to facilitate trade. For a comprehensive discussion and analysis of government mandated PSI, the best source remains Patrick Low, *Preshipment Inspection Services*, Discussion Paper 278 (Washington DC: The World Bank, 1995). Rules of origin systems are discussed in Edwin Vermulst, Paul Waer and Jacques Bourgeois (eds.), *Rules of Origin in International Trade: A Comparative Study* (Ann Arbor: University of Michigan Press, 1994). Subsidy issues are explored in greater detail by Richard Snape in 'International Regulation of Subsidies', *The World Economy*, 14 (1991), 139–64. Bernard Hoekman and Petros C. Mavroidis, 'Policy Externalities and High-Tech Rivalry', *Leiden Journal of International Law* 9 (1996), 273–318 discuss various subsidy-related aspects of the SCM Agreement.

Michel Kostecki, *State Trading in International Markets* (London: Macmillan, 1982) explores the role of state trading in global trade as of the early 1980s. Approaches towards STEs are discussed in the contributions to Thomas Cottier and Petros C. Mavroidis (eds.), *State Trading in the Twenty-first Century* (Ann Arbor: University of Michigan Press, 1998). The relevance of the legal rules for countertrade is discussed in Frieder Roessler, 'Countertrade and the GATT Legal System', *Journal of World Trade Law*, 19 (1985), 604–14.

John Wilson, *Standards and APEC: An Action Agenda* (Washington DC: Institute for International Economics, 1998) and Alan Sykes, *Product Standards for Internationally Integrated Goods Markets* (Washington DC: Brookings Institution, 1995) are two recommended readings that discuss standards and standardization in the context of trade and trade policy. Michael Trebilcock and Julie Soloway provide a critical assessment of the role of the Appellate Body in SPS dispute settlement cases in 'International Trade Policy and Domestic Food Regulation: The Case for Substantial Deference by the WTO Dispute Settlement Body Under the SPS Agreement', University of Toronto, mimeo. The effect of SPS measures on trade of developing countries is the subject of Spencer Henson, R. Loader, A. Swinbank, M. Bredahl and N. Lux, 'Impact of Sanitary and Phytosanitary Measures on Developing Countries', University of Reading, Centre for Food Research, April 2000. Procedures related to conformity assessment and certification procedures are described in ISO, *Certification and Related Activities*, (Geneva: ISO, 1999).

Theodore Moran, *Foreign Direct Investment and Development* (Washington DC, Institute for International Economics, 1998) surveys the literature and the experience with TRIMs.

6

Sector-Specific Multilateral Trade Agreements

The GATT was conceived as a general agreement that would apply to all merchandise trade. In principle, therefore, GATT rules on nondiscrimination, transparency, tariff bindings and so forth, apply to all sectors. In practice, however, industry-specific pressures for protection in major trading nations created strong incentives for governments to grant 'special' treatment to 'special' sectors. This chapter focuses on two key sectors where pressures for protection proved too strong for the trading system to handle–agriculture and textiles and clothing. Over time these sectors were gradually removed from the reach of many GATT 1947 disciplines. It was only during the Uruguay Round that it proved possible to reintegrate these two sectors into the trading system. Once the Uruguay Round agreements covering these two sectors are fully implemented in 2005, the GATT will indeed be a general agreement. The only exceptions will be the so-called Plurilateral Agreements that bind only signatories. These are discussed in chapter 11 (currently there are only two such agreements, on civil aircraft and government procurement).

This chapter also discusses the Information Technology Agreement (ITA). Although negotiated among a subset of WTO members during 1996, the ITA is applied on a MFN basis. The ITA is noteworthy in that it is sometimes regarded as proof that single sector agreements are feasible in the WTO context, and that it illustrates that it may not be necessary to engage in broader negotiating rounds and cross-issue linkage to achieve liberalization of trade. We argue below that the ITA experience does not support this line of reasoning.

6.1. AGRICULTURE

Poor agrarian economies have a history of taxing agriculture relative to other tradable sectors. As nations become richer, their policy regimes often change from taxing to assisting farmers relative to other producers (Lindert 1991). The post–1950 period saw substantial growth in agricultural protection and insulation in the advanced industrial economies and its spread to newly industrializing economies (Johnson 1973). That tendency accelerated in the 1980s to the point where some protectionist countries went beyond self-sufficiency to generate surpluses. These could only be disposed of with the help of export subsidies. This led to serious budgetary pressures and increasing opposition to the cost of agricultural support policies. It also led traditional agricultural-exporting countries to insist that MTNs focus on reducing agricultural protection.

Historically, agricultural trade policy has tended to be been driven by short run phenomena. Food crises led to export controls, while gluts led to import measures. In terms of relatively recent history, protectionist measures in agriculture of a permanent nature became increasingly prevalent at the end of the nineteenth century. One cause of this was the steady expansion of American production and the resulting fall in world prices. While some nations reacted to the resulting change in incentives by adjusting – for example, the Dutch became more specialized in livestock as the price of feed grains fell – others, including France, Germany, and Austria-Hungary, reacted by protecting existing producers and subsidizing exports if domestic output exceeded consumption. During the inter-war period, agricultural protection and domestic market regulation increased further. After the Second World War, farmers and agricultural ministries in OECD countries exempted agriculture from key GATT disciplines and recurrent MTNs. The US led the way with its request for a waiver in 1955. With the creation of the EEC and its Common Agricultural Policy (CAP) in 1957, European countries also insisted on special treatment for this sector.

The CAP is the preeminent example of how farmers became insulated from foreign competition. It provided for an intervention or support price at which the Community guaranteed to purchase the agricultural output from farmers, and a threshold price (above the internal support price) below which no imports were allowed. In order to isolate the EU market from international competition a variable levy equal to the margin between the threshold price and the lowest representative offer price on world markets was imposed on imports. Moreover, a restitution amounting to the difference between the average world price and the internal EU price was granted to European exporters. The program was extremely costly. Domestic support to agricultural producers averaged more than US$92 billion per year in the EU during 1986–90. However, the EU was not alone. Domestic support in Japan and the US over the same period averaged US$35 and US$24 billion, respectively. In Japan, rice was produced at a cost four times that of competitive producers elsewhere. The same applied to Swiss meat and butter. Budgetary support in the US, the EU and Japan accounted for some 15 percent of government spending; a figure comparable to what was spent on education.

What is Special About Agriculture?

Why do governments intervene in agriculture? And why are the policies that are observed so different across countries? Rationales for intervention include: (1) to stabilize and increase farm incomes; (2) to guarantee food security; (3) to improve the balance of payments; (4) to support the development of other sectors of the economy; and (5) to increase agricultural output (Fitchett, 1987). These reasons are in part noneconomic or driven by special interest politics. The political influence of the agricultural sector is substantial in many countries. Agriculture is mostly food, and food is often very political. President Nyerere of Tanzania used to say that if he needed shoes and apartheid South Africa was the only place where he could get shoes he would not go to South Africa, but if he needed corn and the only place where he could get corn was apartheid South Africa, he would go there. Food shortages can lead to riots, revolutions and wars.

There is a striking difference between the way agriculture is treated in poor and rich countries. In many developing countries, policies tax agriculture and subsidize food consumption of the urban population. In industrialized countries exactly the opposite pattern can be observed: an urban population that is taxed to support farm production and incomes. But in both cases, governments use subsidies, trade barriers, state trading and public purchasing to regulate production and trade (Box 6.1).

Box 6.1 Why poor countries tax, and rich countries subsidize agriculture
It is a stylized fact that average rates of protection for industries tend to decline across countries as capital-labor ratios increase. Thus, industrialized countries with large capital stocks – both physical plant and equipment and human capital – relative to labor are more open to trade than countries with large stocks of labor relative to capital (mostly developing countries) (Rodrik, 1995). However, rich countries tend to be much more protectionist towards agriculture (supporting domestic production and closing-off markets against import competition). In contrast, poor countries tend to promote imports, either explicitly through import subsidies, or implicitly by taxing domestic production. Anderson (1995) argues that this can be explained as follows. In a poor country, food accounts for a large share of total household consumption, whereas in rich countries food accounts for only a small share of expenditure. Moreover, agriculture is the main source of employment in a poor country, while it typically accounts for less than five percent of the labor force in a rich one. In poor countries agriculture is also much less capital intensive than in rich ones. These stylized facts do much to explain the different policy stances that are observed. If agriculture is pro-

tected in a poor nation, the resulting increases in food prices have a large impact on the demand for labor (given the size of the agricultural sector) and thus on economy-wide wages (because labor is mobile). The wage rise will be offset to a greater or lesser extent by the rise in food prices, food being so important in consumption. At the same time the wage increase puts upward pressure on the price of nontradables (services) and has a negative impact on industry by lowering profits. As the gains per farmer of protection are low, and the loss per industrialist is high, the latter will be induced to invest resources to oppose agricultural support policies. Supporting agricultural production in a poor country therefore may not make political sense. The converse applies to rich nations, where agricultural support has much less of an impact on wages (the sector being small), on the prices of nontradables, and on industrial profits.

A simulation model developed by Anderson (1995) that incorporates the basic differences between poor and rich countries reveals that a 10 percent rise in the relative price of manufactures in a poor nation (that is, a tax on agriculture) will reduce farm incomes by only two percent, while raising those of industrialists by 45 percent. In contrast, a 10 percent tax on industry in a rich country (that is, a policy of supporting agriculture) raises incomes of farmers by over 20 percent, while reducing those of industrialists by only three percent. These differences in costs and benefits for different groups in society – in conjunction with the differences in sizes of the various groups – help explain why farmers in rich countries are willing to invest substantial resources to obtain and maintain protection, and why industrialists and urban populations in developing countries are able to benefit at the expense of farmers.

Relative to other sectors of the economy, as of the early 1990s agriculture in many industrialized countries was regulated, subsidized and insulated from market forces to an exceptional degree (Winters, 1987*b*). Production quotas, state purchasing and distribution, subsidies and administered pricing often worked at cross purposes. In the EU, support programs were so effective in stimulating output that they had to be complemented by production quotas and incentives to take land out of production (so-called set asides). Matters were not much better in many developing countries. Marketing boards – monopoly buyers and distributors of food – were often established that set prices for farm products. Farm gate prices were frequently kept low – below world market levels – in a deliberate attempt to lower the cost of subsidizing the prices of basic foodstuffs for the urban population, or in an attempt to tax tradable commodities and generate revenue for the government. The result was often a drop in agricultural output, migration to the cities, and rising imports of food. This pattern was complemented by the effect of OECD countries' food aid, which further reduced the incentive to adopt a more economically rational agricultural policy.

As a consequence of agricultural intervention, countries with no comparative advantage in agriculture not only became major producers but net exporters. Production support policies had to be complemented by export subsidies to allow surpluses to be sold. These in turn led to numerous trade conflicts. As farm surpluses were dumped at subsidized prices in international markets, agricultural trade increasingly became managed trade. During the 1986–90 period, OECD economies annually subsidized exports averaging 48.2 million tons of wheat, 19.5 million tons of coarse grains, 1.8 million tons of sugar, 1.2 million tons of beef, and 1.2 million tons of cheese and butter. Average annual export subsidies in the EU during 1986–90 were more than US$13 billion, with most of the money allocated to exports of bovine meat, wheat and coarse grains, butter and other milk products (GATT, 1994c). The loss of developing country export revenue resulting from agricultural protectionism in the US, the EU and Japan was significant. For sugar and beef alone, it was estimated to be the equivalent of about half of total international development aid (World Bank, 1986). Policies in developing countries tended to make the situation worse for farmers as they often discouraged farm production through a variety of agricultural and nonagricultural policies. The former included state control of inputs and prices, the latter included high import barriers for manufactures and overvalued exchange rates, both of which reduced the incentive to invest in agriculture (Krueger, Schiff and Valdes, 1988).

From GATT 1947 to the WTO

The rules applying to agricultural trade under GATT 1947 were weaker than those for manufactured goods. Many nations have traditionally regarded agriculture as a sector of economic activity that deserves special treatment. This attitude manifested itself during the postwar negotiations on the ITO in US insistence that the ITO not affect its agricultural policies. Although the ITO was never ratified, GATT rules on agriculture were in part written to fit existing US agricultural policies. Disciplines for agriculture differed in two major respects from those on trade in manufactures. First, quotas were allowed for agricultural commodities if concurrent measures were taken to restrict domestic production or used to remove a temporary domestic surplus (Article XI GATT). QRs could also be used to deal with shortages of food or other essential exportables. Second, export subsidies on primary products were permitted, as long as these did not lead to more than an equitable share

of world trade for the subsidizing country. What 'equitable' meant in practice was not clear, however, and differences in interpretation led to a number
of GATT disputes. Over time, more flexibility in the use of QRs and other
NTBs in the agricultural sector was introduced through special waivers
(starting with the US in 1955); in protocols of accession (for example, Switzerland); through limited tariff bindings on agricultural imports (opening
the way for the use of variable levies under the CAP); by allowing residual
grandfathered restrictions on imports of agricultural goods to be maintained; and through a proliferation of various 'grey area measures' such as
VERs and orderly marketing arrangements (OMAs).

By accepting – implicitly or explicitly – the notion that agriculture is
unique, it proved to be virtually impossible to make cross-sectoral linkages
or tradeoffs in MTNs. The establishment of separate negotiating groups for
agriculture, staffed 'by civil servants experienced in the defense of domestic
farm-support policies ... [was] a way of avoiding a trade-off between agriculture and industry' (Josling, 1977: 11). Problems were compounded by the
commodity-specific approach that was usually taken in MTN talks on agriculture. Throughout the 1960s and 1970s, agricultural discussions between
the two major players – the EU and the US – were based on two totally different conceptions. The EU favored the development of a system to manage
world trade so as to facilitate the functioning of the CAP. The US, in contrast,
supported by countries such as Australia, Canada, and New Zealand, sought
significant liberalization, while safeguarding national policies that protected
powerful agricultural interests (such as dairy and sugar producers).

Very little progress was made in the Kennedy and Tokyo Rounds on agriculture. In both MTNs, the basic premise of the EU was that the CAP was
nonnegotiable, and that the focus of discussions should be on stabilizing
world agricultural markets. Thus, the Community proposed that international commodity agreements be negotiated for products such as cereals,
rice, sugar, and dairy. The US in contrast emphasized the need to expand
agricultural trade and to end the special status of agriculture in the GATT. In
the Tokyo Round these incompatible positions deadlocked the negotiations
for a long time. The US refused to allow progress to be made on issues such
as subsidies and standards without seeing some progress made on the agricultural front. This deadlock was broken only after the Carter Administration was inaugurated and Robert Strauss was appointed as Special Trade
Representative (in 1977). President Carter put greater weight on the successful conclusion of the round than his predecessor and was willing to give
in on agriculture. Subsequent bilateral bid-offer negotiations resulted in the
reduction of certain tariffs and an increase in various quotas, but did little to
achieve general US objectives. Two sectoral agreements were negotiated: an

Agreement on Bovine Meat and an International Dairy Arrangement. Neither was far-reaching. The agreement on meat ostensibly was aimed at increasing trade and the stability of the world market. It implied no binding obligations, however, and in practice had little effect, if any. The dairy agreement was more substantive in that it set out minimum prices for major dairy products. However, these prices proved to be unenforceable in practice. A number of disputes occurred regarding circumvention of the minimum prices by certain signatories (especially the EU), which led the United States to withdraw from the agreement in February 1985. Both arrangements were brought into the WTO as Plurilateral Agreements in 1994, but were dissolved in 1999 (chapter 11).

In the early 1980s a constituency emerged in the EU that favored a reduction in agricultural support. Agricultural subsidies were a significant burden for heavily strained government treasuries, and became increasingly difficult to defend as the ideological balance swung towards greater reliance on markets, competition and deregulation. Two successive oil shocks had led to large fiscal deficits, compounding the pressure on government finances. A decision by the US to engage in a subsidy war with the EU in the 1980s – partly driven by a decline in international food prices, which raised opposition to EU export subsidization – also helped to increase the financial pressure. At the same time, agricultural disputes became more intense, and further enhanced the incentive for dealing with agriculture in the GATT.

These factors allowed the ministerial meeting that launched the Uruguay Round to put agriculture on the table in a comprehensive manner for the first time. The Punta del Este negotiating mandate broke new ground in that there was an explicit reference to liberalization, with all policies affecting agricultural trade to be discussed, including domestic and export subsidies. This contrasted with the Kennedy and Tokyo Round ministerial declarations, which emphasized the status of agriculture as a special (unique) sector and were oriented towards the negotiation of commodity-specific agreements. However, as the negotiations commenced, it rapidly became clear that discussions would continue to be dominated by transatlantic ping–pong between the two largest agricultural traders – the EU and the US – which together accounted for about 40 percent of international trade in food. Any agreement required a deal that they could live with. But they were by no means the only players. Other significant actors included the EFTA countries and Japan (with highly protectionist systems and basically in the EU camp) and a group of fourteen traditional agricultural exporters that sought significant liberalization. This coalition was called the Cairns Group and was an ally of the US. It included Argentina, Australia, Brazil, Canada, Chile, Colombia, Fiji, Hungary, Indonesia, Malaysia, New Zealand, the Philippines, Thailand, and Uruguay.

The Cairns Group objective was to gradually attain free trade in agricultural commodities, eliminate production distortions, and ensure that binding undertakings to this effect were made. The US initially sought the complete liberalization of trade in agriculture. It was particularly concerned about export subsidies, and sought their rapid and unconditional elimination. The US also insisted on the need to introduce a clear-cut separation between income support for agricultural producers and policies that affected the level of farm production. Income support could be accepted only if decoupled from production. The EU initially proposed that negotiations first concentrate on emergency measures for certain sectors, including cereals, sugar, and dairy products, to remove structural disequilibria on world markets, followed by liberalization of trade and a reduction of support policies. The EU argued that the goal should not be free trade, but achieving stability and equilibrium in world agricultural markets. It proposed to follow a bid-offer process for specific products along the lines of previous MTNs. It also argued that existing zero (or low) tariff bindings on oilseeds led to severe distortions in the EU market and sought to negotiate a 'rebalancing' of its agricultural protection to make it more uniform. This desire for rebalancing became one of the more contentious issues of the negotiations.[1] Japan supported the idea of a freeze on export subsidy expenditures as a short run step, to be followed by a gradual phase-out, but suggested that domestic subsidies be permitted to maintain a minimum (unspecified) level of self-sufficiency for national security reasons.

Bridging the gap between the EU and the US-Cairns positions proved extremely difficult, not only because of fundamental, substantive differences, but also because of the negotiating strategies that were pursued. Although clearly unacceptable to the EU, for the first two years the US maintained its demand for the total elimination of trade distorting support policies within 10 years. The resulting standoff led to the breakdown of the Montreal midterm review of the round in December 1988. After a four-month period of informal consultations it was agreed that the long run objective in the agricultural area was to be progressive reduction in agricultural support, not

---

[1] In earlier MTNs predating the formation of the European Community, a number of European countries bound tariffs on cotton, soybeans (oil, meal, and seeds), vegetables, and canned fruit at low or zero levels. When these countries joined the EEC, these bindings were incorporated into the common external tariff of the Community. As the CAP led to higher prices of grains, European producers began to import large quantities of soybeans and related products, on which tariff bindings were low. This was a major source of irritation for the EC Commission, which unsuccessfully attempted to close this 'gap in the CAP' in subsequent years.

elimination. This compromise allowed negotiations to continue. In the final phase of the round, discussions remained very contentious, with serious differences of opinion emerging within the EU as well as between the EU and other GATT contracting parties. At the December 1990 ministerial meeting that was supposed to conclude the round, no agreement could be achieved on agriculture, leading to a breakdown of talks on all the issues on the agenda. In effect, the EU refused to accept the compromise text that was proposed by the Chairman of the negotiating group – which would have averaged a cut of about 25 percent in protection levels – as going too far in disciplining export subsidies and the use of specific policies. The proposal would have had significant implications for the CAP – the reform of which was under active discussion at the time. The EU needed to settle its internal debates on agriculture first – in particular to placate the French, who opposed any significant move towards meeting US-Cairns Group demands. Latin American members of the Cairns Group played a major role in opposing any significant weakening of the Chairman's proposed text. Argentina, supported by Brazil, made it clear that they would refuse to accept the proposed deal, and stood ready to scuttle the Uruguay Round over the issue (Ricupero, 1998).

An agreement between the EU and the US was eventually reached–after much brinkmanship–with the so-called Blair House Accord in November 1992. By that time internal CAP reform proposals had been developed by the European Commission, allowing a deal to be struck. The EU obtained agreement that its compensation payment policies – under which farmers were paid to take land out of production – would not be included in the definition of the Aggregate Measure of Support (discussed below). It was also agreed that the AMS would not be product-specific, and that the extent of liberalization would be limited to a cut of about one-sixth over six years, or less than three percent per year (Anderson, 2001). While French farmers in particular continued to oppose the deal, the Commission contained this by arguing that the agreement did not go beyond the internally agreed reform of the CAP.

WTO Rules

The Agreement on Agriculture that emerged from the Uruguay Round has four main parts, dealing with market access, domestic support, export competition, and sanitary and phytosanitary measures (the last item is discussed in chapter 5 above).[2] By the year 2000 existing export subsidies were to be

---

[2]   What follows draws in part on Anderson, Hoekman and Strutt (2000).

reduced by 36 percent in value terms and 21 percent in volume terms from a 1986–90 base, in both cases on a commodity-by-commodity basis. For some commodities only the agreed 21 percent cut in the *volume* of subsidized exports was achieved, because international food prices in the late 1990s were higher than in the late 1980s, so that exportable surpluses could be disposed of with lower subsidy outlays. There is a prohibition on the use of new export subsidies, and remaining (grandfathered) export subsidy levels are bound.

On market access it was agreed that NTBs immediately be converted into tariffs and that industrial countries reduce these tariffs by an average of 36 percent over six years (24 percent for developing countries). All agricultural tariffs are bound. Reflecting the general acceptance of state trading (chapter 5), marketing boards and similar monopolies are only subject to the general prohibition on the use of QRs (Articles XI-XIII GATT). In practice the cut in tariff bindings could be less than one sixth as a *weighted* average, since each tariff item needed to be reduced by only 15 percent of the claimed 1986–8 tariff equivalents (10 percent for developing countries). There was also considerable scope to concentrate tariff reductions in commodity groups with relatively little effect on trade (Josling, 1994).

The tariff bindings that were implemented by WTO members were in many cases far higher than the actual tariff equivalents of NTBs that applied in the 1986–8 base period. The EU, for example, set bindings about 60 percent above the actual tariff equivalents of the CAP in the late 1980s, while the US set bindings about 45 percent higher (Ingco 1996). Many developing countries chose to bind their tariffs on agricultural imports at more than 50 percent and some as high as 150 percent – far above the tariff equivalents of restrictions actually in place in the early 1990s. This 'dirty' tariffication implies that actual tariffs at the beginning of the twenty-first century provide no less protection than did the NTBs of the late 1980s. The so-called 'binding overhang' that resulted is significant. Binding tariffs at such high levels allows countries to set the actual tariff below the ceiling but to vary it so as to stabilize the domestic market, analogous to the earlier EU system of variable import levies and export subsidies. Such 'made to measure' tariffs (Corden, 1974) are often driven by the seasonal calendar—high rates of protection are imposed during periods when locally produced commodities are available. The high bindings implied that the reduction in fluctuations in international food markets that tariffication was expected to deliver would not necessarily be attained (Goldin and Mennsbrugghe 1996).

In recognition of the fact that for some products bound and applied tariffs were set at prohibitive levels, negotiators sought to impose minimum market access commitments. These require that the share of imports in domestic consumption for products subject to prohibitive import restrictions increase to at least five percent by the year 2000 (8 percent in the case of rice in Japan in lieu of tariffication, less in the case of developing countries).[3] The vehicle used to ensure this minimum market access is attained is generally a tariff rate quota (TRQ), under which a certain volume of imports (the quota) enters at a lower tariff, and out-of-quota imports are subject to a much higher tariff. Special safeguard mechanisms are available to protect domestic producers if imports exceed specific trigger quantities or are priced below trigger price levels. There is also scope to minimize the impact of those imports on the domestic market. For example, a country's required rice imports could be of low feed quality or could be reexported as food aid.

The market access rules formally introduce scope for discriminating in the allocation of TRQs between countries. The administration of such quotas tends to legitimize a role for state trading agencies. When such agencies have selling rights on the domestic market in addition to a monopoly on imports of farm products, they can charge excessive mark-ups and thereby distort domestic prices easily and relatively covertly – just as such agencies can hide export subsidies if they are given that monopoly. Elements of quantitative management of both export and import trade in farm products were therefore legitimized under the WTO.

A second major element of the Uruguay Round agreement was a provision that domestic production support to agriculture as measured by an Aggregate Measure of Support (AMS) was to decline by 20 percent by 2000 (again relative to a 1986–8 base period). WTO members were required to calculate and enter their base period AMS in their schedules, as well as the 'final bound commitment level' for the AMS. The AMS includes expenditures on domestic subsidies as well as market price support policies such as administered prices, and therefore captures both border and nonborder policies. In principle it covers all support policies that affect trade. The AMS is aggregated over commodities and programs. Given the goal of reducing the trade-distorting effects of agricultural policies, the AMS excludes instruments that in principle have minimal effects on production and trade. Examples are programs that support agriculture generally and do not involve direct transfers to farmers, income transfers that are de-coupled from production, policies that contribute less than five percent of the value of pro-

---

[3] Countries seeking to delay tariffication were permitted to do so for six years (10 for developing countries) if imports were below three percent of domestic consumption in the 1986–8 base period, no export subsidies were granted and measures to restrict output are implemented. In such cases the minimum market access requirement is higher, increasing from four percent in 1995 to eight percent in 2000.

duction, and direct payments under production-limiting programs based on fixed area and yields and made on 85 percent or less of base period production. EU compensation payments and US deficiency payments – both of which affect production – were also excluded in a separate 'blue box', as part of the Blair House bilateral deal between the US and the EU mentioned above. In contrast to the tariff reduction obligations, which apply at the tariff line, the AMS reduction requirement pertains to the agricultural sector as a whole.[4] Finally, a peace clause was negotiated regarding the use of countervailing duties: members agreed to refrain from new actions for a six-year period.

Developing countries only needed to reduce tariffs, support, and export subsidies by two-thirds of the levels mentioned earlier, and had until 2005 to implement this. They were also exempted from the tariffication requirement for products that are primary staples in traditional diets, as long as imports are at least four percent of consumption by 2005. Only production support that exceeds 10 percent is subject to AMS reduction. Input subsidies for low-income farmers are permitted, as are generally available investment subsidies and export subsidies related to export marketing and internal distribution and transport. It is unclear what the tariff reductions imply in terms of effective liberalization of developing country agricultural markets, as they were not committed to use a particular base year for tariffication. In effect developing countries were granted the freedom to impose tariffs at whatever level they chose to.

What was Achieved?

The data base for the Global Trade Analysis Project (GTAP) at Purdue University incorporates estimates of the effect of such measures as export taxes and subsidies, VERs, and the tariff equivalent of QRs on imports and exports for 1992, as well as how distortions will change with Uruguay Round implementation.[5] By using production for each sector across geographic regions valued at distortion-free prices as weights, it is possible to infer the nominal

---

[4] There is a similarity between the AMS and the 'montant de soutien' concept which was introduced by the EU during the Kennedy Round (see Evans, 1972). The montant de soutien was defined as the difference between the world price of a product and the price received by a domestic producer. In other words, it was the nominal rate of protection taking into account all instruments affecting producer prices. However, in the Kennedy Round the intention was that support measures would be calculated per commodity.

[5] See http://www.agecon.purdue.edu/gtap for details of the GTAP database. The data includes estimates of post-Uruguay Round tariffs and the export tax equivalents for MFA quotas, based on extensive work at the World Bank (see Hertel et al. 1996).

rates of assistance to each sector resulting from these trade policy distortions before and after the Uruguay Round (Table 6.1). The data suggest agricultural protection will fall by about one-fifth or more in advanced and newly industrialized economies but still will be extremely high compared with that for manufacturing. Moreover, agriculture in low- and middle-income economies will remain effectively taxed relative to other sectors because manufacturing assistance will come down by a similar amount.

TABLE 6.1 *Post-Uruguay Round tariffs (and agricultural production and export subsidies)*[b]*, various country groups, 2005 (percent)*

Region	Agriculture	Mining	Textiles	Other
Western Europe	30 (2, 21)	0	11	4
NAFTA	15 (3, 2)	0	18	7
Australia, New Zealand	3 (0, 0)	0	25	9
Japan, Korea	57 (-2, 0)	3	9	4
China, Hong Kong, Taiwan	22 (-5, 0)	1	2	2
Southeast Asia (ASEAN)	19 (-3, -3)	3	15	11
South Asia	19 (0, 0)	8	55	29
North Africa Middle East	24 (-4, 0)	19	38	24
Sub-Saharan Africa	13 (-1, -9)	10	18	9
Central, South America	12 (-1, -1)	6	27	18
Former Soviet Union & Central Europe	8 (0, 0)	1	6	5
Rest of the World	50 (-1, -7)	23	60	28
All OECD economies	*36 (1, 7)*	*1*	*14*	*6*
All developing economies	*20 (-2, -2)*	*6*	*12*	*11*
ALL ECONOMIES	*29 (0, 3)*	*2*	*14*	*8*

[a] Includes 'Former Soviet Union and Central Europe' and 'Rest of the World'.
[b] Production and export subsidy rates for agriculture are shown in parentheses in column 1. It is assumed that agricultural export subsidies in advanced industrial economies will be reduced by 25 percent under the Uruguay Round.
Source: Anderson, Hoekman and Strutt (2000), drawing on the GTAP data base.

In short, implementing the reforms agreed to in the Uruguay Round involved only very modest benefits from liberalization. Agricultural protection and intervention in most high-income countries remains very high relative to the barriers imposed on trade in manufactures. The farm policies of OECD countries (even after the reforms under the Uruguay Round have been taken into account) cause annual welfare losses of some US$40 billion for developing countries (Hertel et al. 2000). This is more than four times the losses that developing countries incur due to OECD import restrictions on textiles and clothing. Given that farmers and rural communities comprise the vast majority of the world's poor, it is important that efforts be maintained to pursue multilaterally agreed reforms that will benefit this group as much as possible. Although urban households with food deficits would incur losses as prices rise, rural producers – where most of the poverty is concentrated – would benefit from the liberalization. The gains for producers would be larger than any consumer losses and would have dynamic multiplier effects for developing economies so that even consumers would benefit in the longer run (Binswanger and Lutz, 2000).

Pursuing the Built-in Agenda

The Agreement on Agriculture calls for new negotiations to be launched in 2000. Pressure to continue liberalization is strong. The shift towards decoupled income support has budgetary implications that is closely scrutinized by finance ministries, and agricultural exporters continue to push for the elimination of trade distorting farm policies. The planned expansion of EU membership (the CAP is not financially sustainable if it is extended to Central European countries) is a factor driving the EU to continue reforming the CAP. There is a lot to be achieved. Average tariffs on agricultural imports are in the 15 to 20 percent range, with peaks for some commodities exceeding 100 percent in many countries, both developing and developed (Table 6.2).

TABLE 6.2 *Import-weighted average tariffs in agriculture, 1995 (%)*

Exporting region	Importing Region	
	High Income	Developing
High Income	15.9	21.5
Developing	15.1	18.3
World	15.6	20.1

Source: Hertel and Martin (2000).

Hertel et al. (2000) estimate that a 40 percent reduction in post-Uruguay Round agricultural tariffs and export subsidies will cause an increase in global real income of about US$60 billion per year. This increases by US$10 billion if domestic support is also reduced by 40 percent, although the uncertainty in the degree to which such producer payments are linked to production decisions makes such analysis difficult. Measured in dollar amounts, developed countries capture the largest gains from liberalization, reflecting the reduction in the cost of agricultural support policies for OECD consumers. However, the percentage real income gains – reported in the first set of bars in Figure 6.1 – are largest in developing regions such as South Asia (other than India) and Southeast Asia (other than Indonesia). Virtually all regions except the net food importing Other Middle East region experience overall gains from these multilateral reductions in agricultural protection. The bulk of these gains derive from efficiency improvements generated in the developing countries themselves (first set of bars in Figure 6.1).

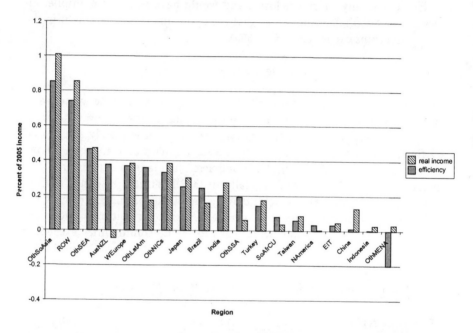

Source: Hertel et al. (2000).

FIG. 6.1 Implications of a 40 percent reduction in agricultural trade barriers

Thus, from an economic perspective, negotiations on market access in developing as well as OECD countries clearly are important.[6] The welfare gains to poor-country farmers from further liberalizing agricultural markets in rich countries are huge. The agenda for negotiations on agricultural trade liberalization is conceptually straightforward and centers on reducing intervention. The simplest approach would be to continue on the path established during the Uruguay Round and seek significant cuts in bound tariffs and export subsidies, and substantial increases in TRQs. This can be achieved through agreement to apply across-the-board formulas to agricultural tariff

---

[6] What follows draws on Hertel, Hoekman and Martin (2000).

bindings and export subsidies, as was done to reduce tariffs on manufactures in the Kennedy and Tokyo Rounds.

Since the Uruguay Round was completed, OECD countries have come to be intensive users of TRQs. As mentioned previously, under a TRQ, there is an out-of-quota tariff that applies to imports above a specified quota quantity. Volumes below the quota limit pay a lower in-quota tariff. Elbheri, Ingco, Hertel and Pearson (1999) provide indicators of the extent to which TRQs are binding access constraints for a number of sensitive agricultural commodities such as sugar, dairy, meats and grains. They conclude that for the US, EU, Canada and Japan, imports exceeded the quota volume in 13 cases out of 16. The allocation of associated quota rents is uneven, with many countries allocating a substantial share of the quota rents to exporters.

Understanding the impact of TRQs is critical to predicting the outcome of attempts to liberalize trade in agricultural products. For example, reducing out-of-quota tariffs will increase imports only if the current demand for imports exceeds the quota amount such that the out-of-quota tariff is operational. If imports are less than the quota level, reductions in out-of-quota tariffs will be ineffective. On the other hand, marginal expansion of the TRQs will be ineffective if imports are greater than the TRQ – the only effect will be to increase the volume of imports on which scarcity rents are earned. If imports are less than the TRQ, expanding the quota will also be ineffective. Only reductions in in-quota-tariffs will stimulate greater imports in this case. Thus, reductions in out-of-quota tariffs may be the most effective instrument for achieving market liberalization in the majority of cases.

Achieving significant cuts in agricultural protection will require substantial efforts to mobilize interest groups and civil society to support liberalization in high-income countries. Expanding the negotiating agenda to include additional issues may help to achieve this (Hoekman and Anderson, 2000). In the Uruguay Round progress was made in designing rules for the application of SPS measures (see chapter 5), one important dimension of the 'new trade agenda', which revolves around domestic regulatory policies. Although multilateral negotiations on such policies can expand the gains from trade and be helpful in the pursuit of domestic regulatory reform, they can also represent a threat to developing country farm exports. Of particular importance in this connection are efforts by high-income countries to enforce national standards and laws extraterritorially. Examples that have already arisen in the WTO context include attempts by governments to impose stricter standards with respect to the inadvertent catching of dolphin and turtles when fishing for tuna and shrimp, respectively. Current WTO rules only allow such 'production process' standards to be applied to imports if it can be shown that the processes targeted have repercussions for the physical characteristics (quality) of the product concerned. An example would be a requirement that shrimp be washed in water of a certain level of purity. But in many cases process standards cannot be justified under this criterion, and this has given rise to disputes (see chapter 13). The potential damage to the global trading system from allowing more general national process standards to be applied to imports is very substantial, as it can eliminate the ability of countries to exploit their comparative advantage.

From an agricultural sector viewpoint, regulatory issues should therefore be considered in future MTNs both for substantive and political economy reasons. The Uruguay Round negotiations on agriculture already focused on some of the relevant issues, notably production subsidies and product standards. Issue areas important for agriculture include the behavior of STEs (for instance, marketing boards), policies towards foreign investment (ownership of land), the efficiency of up- and downstream service suppliers, and the treatment of biotechnology. Agricultural productivity will be determined in part by the existence of structural bottlenecks that reflect policies restricting competition in the provision of key inputs such as credit and of infrastructure services such as transport, storage, and communications (Gulati 1998). Losses of agricultural output due to lack of financial intermediation, poor transportation and storage facilities and substandard communication networks can be significant. For example, an empirical investigation of the determinants of agricultural output in India found that expansion of commercial bank networks and availability of services had a very substantial positive effect on private agricultural investment (Binswanger et al. 1993). A study of the effects of flag discrimination and cargo preference policies maintained by Chile until the late 1970s documented that the result was high costs for shippers and inadequate supply of specialized ships required to transport new products such as fresh fruit and fish to markets. Allowing entry by shifting to the use of taxes on the use of foreign shipping lines and price preferences for domestic suppliers led to substantial diversification of Chilean exporters away from domestic shipping lines, and a decline in average shipping costs (Bennethan et al. 1989). These examples illustrate the importance of further liberalization of trade in services – discussed further in chapter 7.

Accepting to discuss such policy areas can create incentives for groups with interests in the new issues to counter-balance forces favoring agricultural protection. The EU remains a binding constraint – any deal that obliges it to go beyond what can be (has been) agreed internally on CAP reform will always be very difficult to conclude. This was made very clear during the failed ministerial meeting in Seattle, where efforts by the US and the Cairns group to make elimination of export subsidies an objective for negotiations were strongly resisted by the EU. But this is not only an EU issue. Agriculture also remains highly protected in Japan and Korea. Even in the US, a major proponent of multilateral liberalization, a number of agricultural sectors remain highly protected, and pressures to intervene in times of bad harvests are very substantial. Many new trade agenda issues are not agriculture-specific. If efforts are pursued to negotiate disciplines in areas of domestic regulation, a horizontal approach is to be preferred. This implies that rule making efforts be de-linked from the agricultural market access negotiations. Rules should apply across the board with those for agriculture being consistent with (ideally the same as) those currently or prospectively applying to nonfarm sectors.

Net Food Importing Countries

Agricultural liberalization, especially moves towards elimination of export subsidies may increase world prices of food products, and thus have a negative effect on net food importing developing countries. During the Uruguay Round a number of countries expressed concerns regarding the impact of liberalization on food security. Economic research suggests agricultural intervention is not the appropriate policy if the objective is food security. Instead, the key need is to have the foreign exchange (and access to credit) to be able to buy food in times of scarcity. Having the domestic ability to produce food is not required – countries should only specialize in food production if they have a comparative advantage in this activity. As far as adverse terms of trade effects of OECD liberalization are concerned, insofar as these occur they will be offset to some degree by an increase in domestic supply that will be stimulated by higher prices. Current agricultural policies in OECD countries result in large global price swings that are highly detrimental to developing countries. Even if prices of imports rise, complementary reforms at home can make net food importers better off, as they are initially losing welfare by unnecessarily stimulating food imports and the price rise curtails that stimulus (Wang and Winters, 2000). That said, mechanisms are needed to ensure that any price-increasing effects of multilateral reforms do not reduce the real consumption of the poorest in society. Such social safety nets may not exist or function adequately in many countries. As multilateral trade liberalization generally takes a long period of time to be negotiated and implemented, there is in principle ample opportunity for governments to develop or strengthen safety-net programs and complementary policies to maintain real incomes of the poor.

During the Uruguay Round it was noted that institutions such as the IMF and World Bank had instruments available to finance short-term needs should world prices of food increase significantly. Developed country WTO members also committed themselves to continue to provide food aid, as well as technical and financial assistance, to the 48 least-developed and the 18 developing countries that were classified as net food-importers. Specific recommendations were adopted at the 1996 Singapore ministerial meeting regarding negotiations on international food aid commitment levels and related concessionality guidelines. In response, the Food Aid Committee decided in December 1997 to extend the life of the Food Aid Convention through June 1999 and to open the Convention for renegotiation.

6.2. TEXTILES AND CLOTHING

Trade policies towards textiles and clothing imports were gradually exempted from many GATT 1947 disciplines starting in the late 1950s. Being labor-intensive and requiring relatively low technology inputs, the production of textiles and clothing is an activity in which many developing countries have a comparative advantage. Indeed, for a large number of countries this sector is the entry point into the production of manufactures. As domestic industries in high-income nations came under pressure from cheaper imports, initially from Japan, and subsequently from other Asian countries, they successfully lobbied for trade restrictions. Bilateral, discriminatory trade restrictions steadily expanded in terms of product and country coverage, and by the early 1990s a global web of QRs existed. Protectionism was driven by a desire to maintain employment of unskilled or semi-skilled workers. Textile and clothing industries were often regionally concentrated, and accounted for a substantial share of total manufacturing employment in many OECD countries in the 1960s. Trade protection slowed down the adjustment process in OECD countries, but did not stop it. Total employment in the sector declined steadily over time. Trade policy therefore can be seen as attenuating pressure from imports, giving industries more time to adjust (downsize, improve productivity). The policy came at a high economic cost. The price-increasing effect of protection impacted especially hard on lower income groups. For example, estimates for Canada revealed that in relative terms the burden of protection was four times higher for low income consumers than for higher income groups (UNCTAD, 1994).

It was on the occasion of Japan's accession to GATT in 1955, at that time still a developing economy and a major exporter of textiles and clothing, that the concept of market disruption was first extensively discussed in the GATT. The first step towards formalization of a system of managed trade in this sector was the Short-Term Arrangement on Cotton Textiles, introduced during the Dillon Round (1961). This rapidly evolved into a Long-Term Arrangement (1962), which in turn led to four successive Multifibre Arrangements (1974–94) (Table 6.3). The discriminatory character of the MFA was progressively intensified and country and product coverage considerably extended. Initially limited to cotton fabrics, over time wool, man-made fibres, vegetable fibres and silk blends were added. By 1994, MFA-IV had 45 signatories, including 31 developing and Central and Eastern European countries (CEECs) that exported textiles and clothing, and eight importers. Among these, Austria, Canada, the EU, Finland, Norway and the United States applied restrictions, while Japan and Switzerland did not.[7] Exporters were subject to bilaterally agreed quantitative export restrictions or unilaterally imposed import restraints. As textiles and clothing accounted for about 45 percent of total OECD imports from developing countries in the early 1980s, it was the MFA and not MFN that was the cornerstone of the institutional framework for North-South trade.

TABLE 6.3 *A chronology of managed trade in textiles and clothing*

Date	Event
1955	Japan introduces 'voluntary' export restraints (VERs) on cotton textiles shipped to the US. Restraints are continued in 1956.
1956–60	The UK imposes VERs on cotton textiles from Hong Kong, India, and Pakistan.
1961	The US textile and clothing industry makes its support for the 1962 Trade Act and the Kennedy Round conditional on interim restrictions to deal with 'market disruption' caused by surges of imports from low-cost countries. The Short Term Arrangement on Cotton Textiles is negotiated in July 1961.
1962	The Long Term Arrangement regarding International Trade in Cotton Textiles (LTA) imposes a five percent growth limit on imports of cotton products and places an important portion of the North-South trade in textiles under a managed trade regime.
1967	The LTA is extended for three years.
1970	The LTA is extended for another three years.
1973	To gain the support of the textile industry for the 1974 Trade Act (granting negotiating authority to participate in the Tokyo

[7] On the export side, MFA IV covered Argentina, Bangladesh, Brazil, China, Colombia, Costa Rica, Czech Republic, Dominican Republic, Egypt, El Salvador, Fiji, Guatemala, Honduras, Hong Kong, Hungary, India, Indonesia, Jamaica, Kenya, Macao, Malaysia, Mexico, Oman, Pakistan, Panama, Peru, Philippines, Poland, Republic of Korea, Romania, Singapore, Slovakia, Slovenia, Sri Lanka, Thailand, Turkey and Uruguay.

Date	Event
	Round), The US Administration persuades major developing-country garment exporters to accept a Multifibre Arrangement (MFA). The MFA limits the growth of textile and clothing imports to six percent per annum.
1974	A Textile Surveillance Body is created to supervise the implementation of the MFA under the auspices of the GATT textile committee, which is composed of the parties to the arrangement.
1977	An extension is agreed for a five-year period (MFA-II), including a provision for 'jointly agreed reasonable departures' from MFA rules under special circumstances.
1982	MFA-III is negotiated, extending the arrangement for five more years. The 'reasonable departure' clause is dropped.
1985	Developing countries covered by the MFA establish an International Textile and Clothing Bureau to promote the elimination of the arrangement and the return of trade in textiles and clothing to the GATT.
1986	The MFA is extended until 1991 (MFA-IV).
1991	The MFA is extended again until 1994.
1995	The Uruguay Round Agreement on Textiles and Clothing (ATC) sets out the rules for a transition process which is expected to result in 2005 in the full integration of textiles and clothing into the GATT system.
2005	The ATC provides for its own termination on January 1, 2005.

Determining the impact of the MFA is quite complex. Although it has clearly been detrimental to the most efficient suppliers (such as China), to some extent the losses imposed on developing country exporters were reduced because the quotas were generally enforced by the exporters themselves. Insofar as the quota was binding, this implies that rents were being transferred to the exporters that had obtained licenses to export (see annex 2). Estimates of the magnitude of these quota rents are difficult to obtain as few countries auctioned off the quota licenses or established markets in which quota allocations could be traded. A major exception was Hong Kong. Quota prices for constrained items such as dresses, woven parkas, knitted pullovers and cotton sweaters ranged from US$6 to US$40 per dozen in 1996–7 (Spinanger, 1999). Very important was the incentive created by the MFA for geographic diversification of textile and clothing production. For example, as Hong Kong became more constrained, Chinese investors established production facilities in other countries such as Mauritius, which then became significant exporters. A number of developing countries therefore benefited from the quota regime by obtaining a guaranteed market in the US or the EU. Such countries are often higher-cost suppliers than large producers such as India or China, and will be confronted with increasing competition as the MFA is gradually abolished.

Bringing Textiles and Clothing into the Fold

As in the case of agriculture, it was only in the Uruguay Round that textiles and clothing were seriously discussed in a MTN. The reasons were not the same, however. In agriculture, important factors were the financial burden of agricultural support programs and the trade tensions that these programs had caused. In textiles and clothing there was no pressure from OECD Finance Ministries. While consumer organizations in high-income countries undoubtedly did not welcome the cost-increasing effect of the MFA, their voice was barely heard. The main common element was pressure from exporters, in particular those countries that perceived they would do better under a more competitive (less managed) trade regime. An implicit link was established between the demands by the US and the EU to address issues such as services and TRIPs in the Uruguay Round, and the desire of many developing countries to see an improvement in the market access conditions for their manufactured exports, in particular clothing.

Not surprisingly, negotiations were quite difficult. Major areas of disagreement concerned the application of general GATT rules, the modalities of phasing out of the MFA, the duration of the transitional period and its product coverage, and the need for special safeguards. However, these areas were all addressed without the type of brinkmanship that characterized the agricultural negotiations. The ATC stipulates that the MFA will be phased out, and trade in textiles and clothing integrated into GATT over a 10-year period (1995–2004). Integration means GATT rules prohibiting the use of QRs and VERs (see chapter 9) will enter into effect. Products covered by the ATC will be integrated into GATT in four stages. In 1995, at least 16 percent of HS categories under MFA restrictions in 1990 were to be integrated. In 1998 (stage two) another 17 percent of tariff lines were integrated, followed by a further 18 percent in 2002 (stage three). By the end of 2004 the remaining 49 percent are to be integrated.

Implementation by OECD countries in the first five years after the entry into force of the agreement revealed that the hard nuts are to be left for last. Very few textile or clothing categories that are important for developing countries were liberalized in the first stages of the MFA abolition (Spinanger, 1999). The EU and the US carefully chose to liberalize categories where imports were either already unrestricted or were relatively capital intensive. The ATC implementation strategy followed by the US and the EU complies with the letter, if not the spirit of the agreement. It implies that virtually all of the liberalization of the politically sensitive items will be left for the final stage – the end of 2004. Not surprisingly, this has given rise to concerns on the part of developing country exporters regarding the implementation of the agreement. The EU and the US also discriminate in favor of certain developing countries through the instrument of regional integration agreements. These create incentives for so-called outward processing trade and related investments in this sector by providing duty- and quota-free access for products that satisfy rule of origin criteria. These rules often create incentives to use inputs (yarn, cloth) that originate within the region (see also chapter 10).

Supervision of the implementation of the agreement is in the hands of a Textiles Monitoring Body (TMB), which is composed of an independent chairperson and 10 individuals who are broadly representative of the WTO membership, balancing export and import interests. TMB members rotate periodically and are expected to act on a personal basis. The TMB has a conciliatory and semi-judicial role. It examines all measures taken under the ATC, and their conformity with the Agreement's rules and programs for integration and liberalization. Matters on which agreement cannot be reached can be raised under the WTO dispute settlement procedures. As noted in chapter 3, a number of textile-related disputes were brought to the WTO after 1995. Indeed, one of the first cases to be brought by a developing country (Costa Rica) concerned US restrictions on this sector.

Implementation of the ATC will result not only in the abolition of QRs, but also in the demise of the special, bilateral safeguard measures permitted under the agreement. As from the end of 2004, safeguard measures on trade in textiles will have to be compatible with WTO rules – that is, they will have to be nondiscriminatory and conform to the other requirements of the WTO (see chapter 9). Under the ATC, safeguard actions may be discriminatory, are subject to a less stringent injury criterion and do not require compensation of affected exporters.

While the back-loaded nature of ATC implementation raises the possibility that importing countries may not deliver in 2004, the ATC requires that quotas grow substantially over the 10-year transition. This should ensure that import-competing industries are gradually subjected to more competition, and should therefore facilitate the removal of quotas on schedule. Quotas are to grow by 16 percent in stage one, 25 percent in stage two, and 27 percent in stage three. Thus, a six percent permitted growth rate in 1994 will become seven percent per year during 1995–7; 8.7 percent during 1998–2001;

and 11 percent per year during 2002–4. Moreover, although markets for textiles and clothing will also be liberalized through reductions in average tariffs – the trade-weighted tariff average for developed countries is to fall to 12.1 percent down from 15 percent prior to the Uruguay Round – this still implies a level more than double the manufacturing average (Table 6.1).

The demise of the MFA will be a major achievement, not least because the agreement to reintegrate this sector into the GATT reflects a major change in the negotiating strategy of developing countries. They insisted that progress in this area was a quid pro quo for the agreements on IPRs and services. Full realization of free trade was not achieved, of course, and should not be expected any time soon. Tariffs will remain significantly higher than the manufacturing average for most countries, and domestic producers of garments in OECD and emerging market economies can be expected to use antidumping and safeguard actions increasingly in the future. Indeed, the abolition of the MFA – in conjunction with the prohibition on VERs – will put more pressure on antidumping as a safety valve. Given that China's accession protocol embodies far-reaching transitional safeguard clauses that can be expected to be invoked frequently by WTO members, disciplining the use of contingent protection is likely to be one of the main issues confronting the trading system in the post-MFA period. This extends beyond high-income nations, given that middle-income countries such as Mexico and Argentina have started to use antidumping and safeguards against textile imports (see chapter 9).

6.3. THE INFORMATION TECHNOLOGY AGREEMENT

Both the agreements on agriculture and on textiles and clothing are multilateral agreements – they apply to all WTO members. Both are sector-specific and the objective in both cases is to (re)integrate these sectors into the WTO. They differ in that the ATC is a time-bound agreement that expires as of 2005. As mentioned in chapter 4, another type of agreement that may be negotiated under the WTO involves the elimination of barriers for subsets of products. These so-called zero-for-zero agreements became prominent in the Uruguay Round, and continue to be strongly supported by industry groups. A recent example of a zero-for-zero deal that was incorporated into the WTO is the Information Technology Agreement (ITA), concluded in 1997 by 39 countries accounting for 90 percent of world information technology (IT) trade. Participants agreed to eliminate tariffs over a three-year period on almost all IT products on a MFN basis. The major product categories covered by the agreement include computers (including parts and accessories), telecommunication equipment (including modems, pagers and fax machines), semi-conductors, semi-conductor manufacturing equipment, and certain software and scientific instruments. Consumer electronics are excluded. Tariffs were to be cut in four equal installments, with developing country signatories having until 2005 to eliminate tariffs on certain items. Other duties and charges were to be abolished upon the entry into force of the agreement.

The ITA was driven by a coalition of IT firms and industry associations that sought to eliminate barriers to trade in their products and used a variety of international non-WTO mechanisms to build a constituency for liberalization. The ITA was the first liberalization agreement concluded after the Uruguay Round (the agreements on finance and telecoms concluded in 1997 were not stand-alone but continuations of Uruguay Round negotiations that could not be brought to closure during the round). At the time the agreement was concluded some observers noted that such issue-specific, targeted agreements illustrated that the WTO, in contrast to the GATT, could make progress on liberalization without launching a round. It also suggested that 'privileged groups' of the kind discussed in chapter 4 could be constructed, that is, deals involving enough players with an interest on an issue to allow free riding by nonparticipants to be discounted.

A closer look at the ITA negotiating history suggests that there is little reason to believe that it will (or should) be a model for future liberalization initiatives under WTO auspices. Discussions on the coverage of the agreement were contentious, and numerous linkage strategies were employed by participants in efforts to ensure that a 'balance of concessions' would be attained. The IT 'sector' spans many different products, and much of the negotiation involved discussions regarding the coverage of the agreement. The EU insisted that trading partners offer concessions on market access for alcoholic beverages as a condition for signing the ITA. Developing countries attempted to obtain concessions on textiles, although at the end of the day their negotiating leverage proved insufficient.[8] The product coverage of the ITA ended up reflecting primarily the interests of the Quad. It deals only with a subset of the policies affecting trade in the IT products selected.

The ITA is a tariff-only agreement – it proved impossible to address any nontariff policies affecting market access. Consumer electronics – products of greater interest to developing countries as suppliers than to the Quad – also were not included under the ITA. The ITA is therefore a rather unbalanced agreement from a developing country perspective. Elimination of tar-

---

[8] At the time, some were calling the ITA the Information, Textiles and Alcohol Agreement (Fliess and Sauvé, 1998: 62).

iffs on the products included under the ITA will be of benefit to consumers in developing country signatories (including foreign investors), but no quid pro quo was obtained. Standard reciprocity and 'internalization' considerations of the type discussed in earlier chapters were important in the ITA. However, given that any deal would have to be applied on a MFN basis, the US insisted that the ITA signatories must cover at least 90 percent of total production of the IT products included under the agreement.

The ITA was to a large extent the brainchild of major IT companies in the EU and US. These firms and their industry associations – the US Information Technology Industry Council, the European Association of Manufacturers of Business Machines and Information Technology Industry (EUROBIT) and the Japanese Electronic Development Association – were prime movers behind the initiative to eliminate tariffs on their products. They jointly developed recommendations for the February 1995 G-7 ministerial conference on a Global Information Society, proposing that tariffs on the building blocks of the infrastructure of such a society be abolished by 2000. Industry groups continued to push the idea in the context of other fora, especially the Transatlantic Business Dialogue (TABD) and APEC. This constellation of interests was successful at the end of the day in abolishing tariffs on much of their output, but this success came at a cost. It essentially involved taking care of the concerns of a set of large and powerful enterprises in mostly OECD countries. These firms will in the future have less of an incentive to support more general liberalization of their home markets.

6.4. CONCLUSION

If GATT was perceived to lack teeth, it was in part due to the de facto exclusion of trade in agriculture and textiles and clothing from the reach of its disciplines. The agreements reached in the Uruguay Round therefore constituted a significant step forward in the process of reasserting the relevance of the general principles of nondiscrimination and open markets. Without these agreements the WTO would have been much less credible as an organization.

The examples of both agriculture and clothing have much to teach about the political economy of multilateral liberalization and negotiation. The agriculture case illustrates that if domestic lobbies are strong and can mobilize the support of other groups (who may be primarily driven by quite different objectives, including noneconomic reasons), multilateral cooperation can break down. Standard reciprocity does not work in the sense that intrasectoral tradeoffs are not feasible. The domestic interests seeking better access to foreign markets could be and were satisfied through negotiations that were limited to manufactures. The potential gains from trade in policies affecting market access for manufactures were more than large enough to allow significant progress to be made in reducing barriers to trade in manufactures. No linkage was required with agriculture, and US attempts to impose such linkages in recurrent MTNs failed because they were not credible. The cost of total breakdown of a MTN because of lack of agreement on agriculture was simply too great. Progress was made in the late 1980s on agriculture because new interest groups appeared that sought to control agricultural support programs. In the case of the EU, these included finance ministries. The adoption of the Maastricht treaty, which set targets for government deficits and public debt in the run up towards European Monetary Union and the prospect of future enlargement of the EU maintained serious pressure on agricultural expenditure. The emergence of environmental lobbies also played a role. An increasing awareness of the environmental downside of intensive and polluting farming encouraged by existing production support policies helped to undercut support for production-increasing policies. Last but not least, the emergence of the Cairns Group was an important factor. It was less inclined than the US to compromise, as the issue was vital to export interests of the group, and therefore could act as both a proposal making and a blocking coalition.

Although internal political dynamics have played an important role in allowing greater discipline to be imposed on agricultural trade policies, the power of the agricultural lobby remains very strong. Tariff protection remains formidable in many WTO members. Noneconomic considerations continue to play a major role in domestic and international discussions on agriculture. The Agreement on Agriculture states that 'nontrade concerns' must be taken into account in future efforts to liberalize trade in this sector. The preamble to the agreement identifies food security, protection of the environment and ensuring the viability of rural areas as examples of objectives that may be realized through agricultural policies. The 'multifunctionality' of agriculture is frequently used by the EU and other WTO members as a justification for agricultural intervention. A key challenge for the WTO will be to determine where to draw the line regarding the 'legitimacy' of agricultural policies. As argued by Anderson (2001), there is no compelling rationale for permitting the use of trade measures to attain noneconomic objectives. But this is a fight that can be expected to continue for a long time on a different number of fronts. For example, environmental and public safety considerations regarding the use of biotechnology can be expected to become increasingly prominent.

A different story applies in textiles and clothing. Here there were also powerful lobbies in OECD countries that were successful in obtaining protection. But there were no direct budgetary implications that created pressure to abolish such protection. While regressive in income distribution terms, protection of textiles and clothing was not subject to strong opposition from consumer groups, in part because competition was not choked off completely as exporters diversified across developing country locations and firms in the domestic industry improved their productivity or exited. The explanation for the agreement to integrate textiles and clothing into the GATT in this case is more in line with standard reciprocal negotiating dynamics. Developing countries insisted on liberalization as a quid pro quo for agreeing to accept the TRIPs and GATS agreements. This gave the lobbies in the US and the EU who sought disciplines on services policies and stronger enforcement of intellectual property law an incentive to confront the domestic clothing industry. This industry had in any event become smaller, more specialized and itself increasingly engaged in international production. The lower-quality garments industry had declined substantially in size in both the US and the EU in the 1980s, reducing its political clout. Here there is also much less scope to raise 'multi-functionality' concerns and argue that trade policies are required to meet noneconomic objectives. Nonetheless, liberalization will occur slowly. Even after the 10 -year period for phase-out of quotas has passed, textile and clothing tariffs will continue to offer domestic industries levels of protection that greatly exceed those applying to other manufacturing industries. Moreover, import-competing industries are very well aware of the existence of antidumping and safeguard instruments.

6.5. FURTHER READING

T. Warley, 'Western Trade in Agricultural Products', in *International Economic Relations in the Western World 1959–71* (London: Royal Institute of International Affairs, 1976) provides a historical overview of agricultural policies and trade of OECD countries. L. Alan Winters, 'The Political Economy of the Agricultural Policy of Industrialized Countries', *European Review of Agricultural Economics*, 14 (1987), 285–304 discusses the question why farmers have been able to obtain high levels of protection. The same author, in 'The So-called Noneconomic Objectives of Agricultural Support', *OECD Economic Studies*, 13 (1989), 238–66 critically addresses the rationales that have been offered for such policies. Anne Krueger, Maurice Schiff and Alberto Valdes, 'Agricultural Incentives in Developing Countries: Measuring the Effect of Sectoral and Economy-wide Policies', *World Bank Economic*

Review 2(3), 255-72, September 1988 analyze the effects of agricultural and nonagricultural policies on farmer's incentives in developing countries.

Tim Josling, Stefan Tangermann and T. Warley, *Agriculture in the GATT* (London: Macmillan, 1996) provides a comprehensive treatment of forty years of discussions and negotiations on agriculture in the GATT, and includes a summary evaluation of the Uruguay Round Agreement on Agriculture. Richard Higgott and Andrew Cooper, 'Middle Power Leadership and Coalition Building: Australia, the Cairns Group and the Uruguay Round', *International Organization*, 49 (1990), 589–32 discuss the formation and operation of the Cairns group. The post-Uruguay Round agriculture agenda is discussed by Tim Josling, 'Agriculture in the Next WTO Round', in Jeffrey Schott (ed.), *The WTO After Seattle* (Washington DC: Institute for International Economics, 2000) and Kym Anderson, 'Bringing Discipline to Agricultural Policy via the WTO', in Bernard Hoekman and Will Martin (eds.), *Developing Countries and the WTO* (Oxford: Basil Blackwell, 2001).

Carl Hamilton (ed.), *Textiles Trade and the Developing Countries: Eliminating the Multifibre Arrangement in the 1990s* (Washington DC: The World Bank, 1990) contains a set of papers that analyze and describe the workings of the MFA. Irene Trela and John Whalley's contribution to that volume provides quantitative estimates of the economic impact of the MFA. Craig Giesse and Martin Lewin give a detailed review of the history of the MFA in 'The Multifibre Arrangement: Temporary Protection Run Amuck', *Law and Policy in International Business*, 19 (1987), 51–170. Another good source is Vinod Aggarwal, *Liberal Protectionism: The International Politics of Organized Textile Trade* (Berkeley: University of California Press, 1985). Dean Spinanger, 'Faking Liberalization and Finagling Protection: The ATC at its Best', (World Bank, 2000 – downloadable from www.worldbank.org/trade) provides a survey of post Uruguay Round developments in the area of textiles and clothing, including a careful assessment of implementation through the end of 1999.

The negotiating history of the ITA is described in detail in Barbara Fliess and Pierre Sauvé, 'Of Chips, Floppy Disks and Great Timing: Assessing the WTO Information Technology Agreement' (Paris: Institut Français des Relations Internationales, 1998).

7
Trade in Services

Services – which include activities as disparate as transport of goods and people, financial intermediation, communications, distribution, hotels and restaurants, education, health care, construction, and accounting – are vital to the functioning of every economy. Even in the lowest-income countries, services generate more than a third of GDP. In middle-income countries, the share of services generally rises to more than 50 percent of GDP and total employment. Services account for 70 percent or more of economic activity in high-income countries such as the US. Services are essential inputs into the production of all industries and service sector policies therefore can have a major effect on economic performance.

Starting in the 1980s, many countries began to undertake regulatory reforms to increase the contestability of service markets. In part these reforms were driven by changes in technologies that allowed competition to emerge in markets that were traditionally regarded as natural monopolies. Service sector reforms have also been pushed by manufacturing and agricultural interests. In order to benefit from the process of globalization with its attendant 'splintering' or 'fragmentation' of the production chain (see chapter 1), enterprises must have access to efficient service inputs. As nations reduce tariffs and other barriers to trade, effective rates of protection for manufacturing industries may become negative if they continue to be confronted with input prices that are higher than they would be if services markets were contestable. It is therefore not surprising that liberalization and regulatory reform of service markets began to emerge as a high profile policy issue in the 1990s. Nor is it surprising that the multilateral trading system started to focus on policies affecting trade and investment in services, as service suppliers started to recognize the existence of a rapidly growing international market.

The move to consider rules for trade in services started in the early 1980s. The US perceived it had a comparative advantage in services, and sought to link further liberalization of 'old trade' to progress in liberalizing trade in services. The first serious attempt to put services on the GATT agenda was made during the 1982 GATT ministerial meeting. This attempt met with vigorous resistance on the part of many contracting parties and the US failed to establish a consensus to negotiate in this area. However, it did succeed in establishing a GATT work program, with the major countries agreeing to undertake national studies of their services sectors with a view to determining the status quo and the potential implications of applying GATT-type rules to trade in services. This helped to generate a spate of research on an issue that had been virtually ignored by trade economists.

One of the major results of the Uruguay Round was the creation of a General Agreement on Trade in Services (GATS). By establishing rules and disciplines on policies affecting access to service markets, the GATS greatly extended the coverage of the multilateral trading system. This chapter starts with brief overviews of global trade flows in services, the barriers that restrict such trade and the economics of service sector protection and liberalization. This is followed by a summary of the main elements of the GATS and a discussion of the experience obtained in the first five years of the operation of the GATS in expanding the coverage of the agreement. The chapter ends with a brief assessment of the usefulness of the GATS as an instrument for the pursuit of service sector reform and suggestions for further reading.[1]

7.1. CONCEPTUAL AND EMPIRICAL ISSUES

Liberalizing trade in services was long thought to be an oxymoron, as services were believed to be nontradable. Although trade in some services such as transportation has always been significant, technological changes over the past 20 years have made trade in many services more feasible, dramatically increasing the importance of services in international transactions. Trade in services differs from trade in goods because services tend to be intangible and nonstorable (Box 7.1). Proximity between providers and demanders is often required for exchange to be feasible (Bhagwati, 1984, Sampson and Snape, 1985). Certain transactions may occur across borders (via telecommunications media, without there being a need for provider or demander to move), but many require that provider and consumer are in the same place at the same time. This can be achieved through physical movement of consumers to the location of service providers (for example, tourism), or via temporary entry of service providers into the territory of a consumer (for example, consulting). In a statistical sense all the above transactions comprise trade and are registered as such in the balance of payments. They all involve exchanges between the resident of one country and that of another.

Establishment of a commercial presence in a country is another way of contesting the market. Many services are not tradable: cross-border, long-

---

[1] Parts of this chapter draw on Hoekman and Mattoo (2000) and Hoekman and Messerlin (2000).

distance exchange or temporary physical movement of either provider or consumer does not suffice for an exchange to be feasible.

Box 7.1. Services are different

Services have unique characteristics that differentiate them from manufactured products in international trade. The characteristics most frequently noted include:

- Intangibility – services are difficult to touch. To paraphrase the newspaper *The Economist*, services are products you cannot drop on your foot. Consequently, international transactions in services are often difficult to monitor, measure and tax.
- Nonstorability – its is often impossible to store services in inventory. This implies that not only is it more difficult to trade services across space, it is also difficult to trade across time.
- Heterogeneity – services are often nonstandardized and highly tailored to the needs of customers. There is therefore a considerable degree of variation in what is effectively supplied across international borders. The extent of product differentiation is very great.
- Joint production – services are typically produced and consumed at the same time, with customers participating in the production process (in business school parlance, services are often a high-touch industry).

A major question confronting negotiators in the Uruguay Round was whether these differences required a different approach to be taken towards the design of multilateral disciplines for trade in services as compared to goods. Although a good case can be made that in principle the answer is negative, the practical implications of a applying the GATT model to services would have been far-reaching, and WTO members decided to adopt a different approach.

Source: Levitt (1983), Bhagwati (1984).

Firms can then only sell their services in foreign markets by establishing a long-term physical presence. As of the early 1990s, some 50 percent of the global stock of FDI involved services activities. The relative importance of trade in services (as registered in the balance of payments of a country) as opposed to sales of services by affiliates is not known. This is because the latter are not registered in the balance of payments. Once established, foreign firms are considered to be residents of the host country. The best estimates available suggest global cross-border trade in services – through telecom networks and temporary movement of provider or consumer – stood at US$1.3 trillion in 1997 (Table 7.1). If trade is defined to include sales of services by affiliates of multinationals the total rises to US$2.1 trillion.

Trade in Services

TABLE 7.1 *Trade in services by modes of supply, 1997*

Mode of Supply	Category	Value (US$bn)	Cumulative share (%)
Cross border	Commercial services (excl. travel)	890	41.0
Consumer movement	Travel	430	19.8
Commercial presence	Sales by foreign affiliates	820	37.8
Temporary entry	Compensation of employees	30	1.4
Total		2,170	100.0

Source: Karsenty (2000).

Available data on trade in services are very weak compared to those on merchandise. Only a limited number of industrialized countries collect and report statistics on trade in services at a relatively disaggregated level (ten categories or more). Most non-OECD countries only report data on trade in so-called commercial services, broken down into transport (largely freight and passenger transport by sea and air), travel (expenditures by nonresidents – mostly tourists – while staying in a foreign country), and other services. The last category includes items such as brokerage, insurance, communications, leasing and rental of equipment, technical and professional services, income generated by the temporary movement of labor, as well as property income (royalties). Although in aggregate value terms global trade in services is dominated by OECD countries, many developing countries are relatively specialized in exporting services. Small developing countries in particular (defined as those with less than one million people) are highly specialized in exports of services (Table 7.2). In most instances

TABLE 7.2 *Top 15 service traders and countries with highest relative specialization in cross-border service exports, 1997*

Importers:	Share in world	Cumulat. share	Exporters:	Share in world	Cumulat. share			RCA
US	11.1	11	US	16.7	17	Kiribati	71
Japan	9.9	21	UK	7.8	25	Nepal	54
Germany	8.0	29	Japan	7.2	32	Mozambique	53
Italy	5.9	35	Germany	6.6	38	Neth. Antilles	52
France	5.1	40	France	5.9	44	Cape Verde	52
UK	4.8	45	Netherlands	4.8	49	Greece	37
Netherlands	3.7	49	Italy	4.7	54	Egypt	37
Canada	2.7	51	Belgium	3.2	57	Djibouti	36

Importers:	Share in world	Cumulat. share	Exporters:	Share in world	Cumulat. share		RCA
Belgium	2.6	54	Hong Kong	3.0	60	Ethiopia	34
Korea	2.4	56	Singapore	2.7	63	Philippines	32
China	2.2	58	Korea	2.3	65	Vanuatu	30
Spain	2.2.	61	Canada	2.3	67	Latvia	29
Taiwan	1.8	62	Switzer-land	2.0	69	Samoa	28
Malaysia	1.7	64	Spain	1.9	71	Jordan	27
Austria	1.6	66	Austria	1.7	73	Antigua and Barbuda	26

Note: The revealed comparative advantage (RCA) of country i for product j is measured by the item's share in the country's exports relative to its share in world trade. That is, if x_{ij} is the value of country i's exports of j, and X_{ij} is the country's total exports its RCA index equals $(x_{ij}/X_{ij}) \div (X_{iw}/X_{tw})$.

Source: Karsenty (2000).

this reflects the importance of tourism and transportation services. But developing countries have also become large exporters of transactions processing and related back-office services (Jamaica) or information and software development services (India). The potential to exploit recent and emerging technological developments that allow cross-border trade in services and provide firms with incentives to slice up the value chain geographically is enormous (UNCTAD and The World Bank, 1994).

TABLE 7.3 *US Trade in commercial services, 1994 (US$ billion)*

Service Sectors	Receipts by mode		Purchases by mode	
	Exports (BOP)	US Sales (FDI)	Imports (BOP)	Foreign Sales in US (FDI)
Transport	42.9	8.7	40.9	9.6
Communications	2.9	n.a.	6.9	1.1
Insurance	4.9	30.9	13.9	48.7
Computer and data processing services	3.8	16.7	0.4	2.9
Advertising	0.5	n.a.	0.7	3.1
Accounting and management related services	1.8	5.7	0.7	1.6

Source: Chang et al. 1999.

The relative importance of alternative modes of contesting service markets varies across sectors, reflecting the choices of economic agents given the constraints of technological feasibility and policy restrictions. Statistics compiled by the United States, the only country which collects detailed data on sales of foreign affiliates, reveals that transport is the only sector in which cross-border trade is unambiguously more important than commercial presence on both the export and import side (Table 7.3). In telecommunications, the same is true for imports. Commercial presence dominates cross-border sales for other services. Thus, most of the 'action' revolves around FDI. Temporary entry of service providers is of trivial quantitative importance. However, this reflects the stringent barriers that affect this mode of supply – the potential for trade in services through temporary movement of natural persons is enormous (Ghosh, 1997).

7.2. BARRIERS AND POTENTIAL GAINS FROM REFORM

Cross-country data on the magnitude of barriers to trade in services do not exist. Because services are generally intangible and nonstorable, barriers to trade do not take the form of import tariffs. Instead, trade barriers take the form of prohibitions, QRs, and government regulation. QRs may limit the quantity or value of imports of specific products for a given time period, or restrict the number or market share of foreign providers of services that are allowed to establish. Such discriminatory QRs are often complemented by nondiscriminatory measures applying equally to foreign and domestic providers. These may consist of limitations on the number of firms allowed to contest a market, or on the nature of their operations. Frequently, this involves either a monopoly (telecommunications) or an oligopolistic market structure (insurance). Considerations relating to consumer protection, prudential supervision and regulatory oversight often induce governments to require establishment by foreign providers or to reserve activities for government-owned or controlled entities.

Some progress was made after the Uruguay Round to improve data on barriers. Absent a careful and comprehensive sector-by-sector assessment on a country-by-country basis, something that has yet to be done, these efforts have relied on indirect methods. One approach builds on available trade and FDI flow data to construct measures of 'revealed' openness. A first attempt to do this was undertaken by Francois and Hoekman (2000), who used the pattern of bilateral trade to determine what trade 'should' be (using a gravity model regression), and estimated the tariff equivalents that generated the difference between observed and predicted trade flows. Using

Hong Kong and Singapore as 'free trade' benchmarks, the results indicated that average services barriers are often above the applied average tariff on manufactures. Tariff equivalent estimates for some sectors were in the 40 to 60 percent range for a number of countries. Financial data reported by firms listed on stock exchanges can be used to calculate the relative profitability of service activities across countries. Variations in the magnitude of the 'services mark-up' across countries can be suggestive about the prevalence of barriers. Available data reveal that services margins generally range 10 to 15 percentage points above those in manufacturing, and that developing country margins tend to be significantly higher than in industrialized countries.

Attempts have also been made to construct openness indicators for modes of supply, especially FDI, and for specific sectors, using qualitative assessments of the extent to which actual policies raise the costs of entry or operation post-entry. Most of this work has centered on APEC countries. One noteworthy effort was made by the staff of the Australian Productivity Commission, who identify existing policies affecting FDI in APEC nations, assign each a weight, and sum across weights to obtain an overall restrictiveness index. Their results suggest that across APEC countries, communications, financial services and transport were subject to the greatest barriers to FDI, reflecting the existence of ownership limits or an outright ban on foreign ownership. The most restrictive countries include Korea, Indonesia, Thailand and China. Sector-specific openness indicators have been constructed using similar approaches. Indices for financial services in a number of Asian countries constructed by Claessens and Glaessner (1998) suggest that many countries in Asia maintained restrictive policies towards foreign entry. A similar exercise undertaken by Warren (2000) for telecoms suggests that China, Korea and Turkey have the highest restrictions, while the United States, Japan and Australia have among the lowest. Overall, the literature suggests business services, consultancy and distribution are among the least protected sectors. Barriers to competition are higher in transportation, finance, and telecommunications. These are also the basic 'backbone' services that are crucial to the ability of enterprises to compete internationally. Policies towards these sectors appear to be most restrictive in developing countries.[2]

A quantitative assessment of the economic implications of service sector policies requires a general equilibrium approach so as to consider intersectoral relationships. It must also allow for the fact that FDI is a vital mode of

---

[2] Recent compilations of empirical work quantifying barriers to trade in services and their effects include Findlay and Warren (2000) and Stern (2001).

contesting the market. This is a nontrivial challenge for researchers and efforts in this area are still in their infancy. A noteworthy analysis is Dee and Hanslow (2000), who use telecom and financial (banking) services openness indices to estimate the impact of barriers to trade in services on OECD and Asian economies with a computable general equilibrium (CGE) model. They allow not only for entry through FDI, but also distinguish between entry and operating restrictions. According to their estimates, barriers to establishment (entry via FDI) are generally much higher than restrictions on ongoing operations of foreign affiliates. They conclude that the global welfare effect of services liberalization is roughly the same order of magnitude as that associated with full liberalization of barriers to trade in merchandise (agriculture and manufactures). However, the impact of these two liberalization scenarios differs significantly across countries. For economies such as China, Hong Kong, Indonesia the gains from services liberalization are a multiple of the gains associated with goods liberalization, while the converse is true for countries such as New Zealand, Japan, Korea, Singapore, Taiwan, the EU and the United States. China alone would capture two-thirds of the global gain from services liberalization, while the EU and the US would lose. In large part this reflects induced changes in the pattern of FDI stocks and an associated loss in rents to the main providers of FDI. As no information is available on the prevailing level and distribution of rents generated by status quo policies, these results must be taken as suggestive only. However, they illustrate that the benefits of liberalization of trade in services will extend beyond established suppliers, and that the economic channels and implications of liberalization differ from trade in merchandise.

A number of country-specific exercises have also been undertaken which demonstrate the importance of service sector reform. Hoekman and Konan (2000) use a CGE model of Egypt to assess the orders of magnitude that may be involved in eliminating service sector inefficiencies. They conclude that Egyptian GDP might expand by up to four percent of GDP if service sectors become more open to competition. They also note that the greater the extent to which regulatory and administrative practices give rise to resource costs (frictional or transactions costs), the greater the welfare improvement that may result from reform (see annex 2). Chadha (1999) uses a multi-country CGE model that separates out India, and runs simulations making different assumptions regarding prevailing market structures in agriculture, manufacturing and services. He concludes that Indian welfare would expand by 0.7 to 1.4 percent of GDP following a 25 percent global reduction in the assumed level of services protection. Other South Asian countries and Southeast Asian countries are expected to register gains equivalent to three percent of GDP. These numbers are quite large relative to what is usually found using similar types of models to assess the impact of merchandise trade liberalization, and clearly suggest there are potentially great gains associated with regulatory reform in services.

While research on the effects of service sector policies is clearly important and needed, the state of the data on barriers is such that policymakers will have to rely primarily on rules of thumb in determining negotiating priorities. Basic economics suggests that the focus of attention should be on the contestability of markets (artificial entry restrictions) and identifying clusters of activities that are interdependent. There is a growing literature which provides rules of thumb or criteria to identify whether an 'acceptable' level of competition exists in a given service industry. For instance, air routes with less than three operating airlines are unlikely to be under intensive competition, and large gains from regulatory reforms can be expected (Morrison and Whinston, 1997). In the case of multi-modal competition (such as between trains and airlines), price comparisons between similar air routes with and without multi-modal competition can be a good proxy for assessing the capacity of regulatory reforms to deliver the benefits of increased competition. Without undertaking such efforts, appropriate negotiating priorities cannot be determined. In short, benefiting from negotiations requires a large amount of preparatory work, something that many countries devote insufficient attention to. As a result, the process of negotiations is likely to be driven more by well-organized export interests in industrialized countries, as was the case in the Uruguay Round (see below). This is not necessarily bad, but it is unlikely to maximize the potential gains from negotiation.

Two dispute settlement cases brought to the WTO during 1995-2000 dealt in part with the definition of barriers to trade in services. The panels in these cases took a very broad view of the coverage of the GATS. In *Bananas* the complainants argued that the method of distributing import licenses violated the GATS because ACP bananas were largely distributed by EU-based entities. The EU argued that a number of non-EU distributors were allocated quotas for these bananas and that there was therefore no violation of national treatment in distribution. The panel decided to focus not on the nationality of providers, but on the question of allocation of licenses. It recognized that '[t]he operator category rules apply to service suppliers regardless of their nationality, ownership or control' (para. 7.324), but concluded that the allocation scheme nonetheless affected the conditions of competition. Thus, the focus was on outcomes (the 'market share' held by EU firms), and not on discrimination per se. The Canada Autopact panel, brought by the EU and Japan, was asked whether a duty exemption scheme constitutes a measure affecting trade in services. It concluded, based on the *Bananas* panel that no measures can be excluded a priori, and that the exemption scheme therefore affected wholesale trade services. The Appellate Body disagreed stating that this should be determined through an investigation of who supplies wholesale services and how such services are applied (DS139/AB/R, May 31, 2000, para 165).

Political Economy Aspects of Services Liberalization

Depending on local circumstances and political constellations, governments may face more or less opposition to reforms that aim at increasing competition in service markets. Although often supported by the manufacturing sector, which has an interest in having access to a wide array of efficiently produced service inputs, final consumers may oppose liberalization because of concerns about a reduction in the frequency or geographical coverage of services (telecom, transport). Labor unions may be concerned about the potential for large-scale layoffs, and those in society who have benefited from subsidized access to services may resist a change in the status quo that is expected to raise prices or restrict supply.

Thus, governments may be constrained in implementing reforms that would benefit society at large because of the opposition of politically powerful vested interests. International trade agreements offer a potential way for breaking domestic deadlocks by mobilizing groups to support reform. The traditional raison d'être of the GATT is that groups that would benefit from better access to export markets are induced to throw their weight behind import liberalization. Analogous reasoning applies in the services context, with the difference that for many countries, export interests in services are weaker than in manufacturing or agriculture because services are more difficult to trade. In OECD countries, for example, the ratio of exports to output is on average over six times less for services than for goods. In many instances, potentially tradable services are simply not traded at all; the barriers – whether natural or man-made – are prohibitive. As a result, the number and political weight of import-competing sectors may greatly exceed that of export-oriented service sectors interested in obtaining access to foreign markets. If so, there is greater need to mobilize support from exporters of merchandise that require access to competitively priced and high quality service inputs if they are to be able to contest global markets. This in turn puts a high premium on the availability of information and analysis of the economic impact of status quo services policies.

Given that FDI is a significant mode of supplying nontradable services, potential direct investors may have a strong 'export' interest and supply the traditional political economy dynamics that have driven GATT talks. Moreover, opposition by domestic firms to the prospect of increased competition from foreign firms may not be as strong in services as in goods. The gross negative impact on labor employed in services is likely to be lower (given that foreign entrants will often use FDI and employ mostly nationals). The net impact on labor is more likely to be perceived to be positive (as total employment opportunities can be expected to expand). And support for reform by businesses that would benefit from higher quality and lower-prices services is more likely to be stronger. Indeed, those that liberalize first may have a strategic advantage – creating further incentives to pursue domestic reforms. Narrow reciprocity, in the form of 'equivalent' concessions being offered by trading partners, is therefore likely to be less of a priority for countries than was the case for merchandise trade liberalization (Hoekman and Messerlin, 2000).

International agreements can also be helpful in providing focal points for regulatory reform, providing templates for domestic policy measures that are welfare enhancing. An example is supporting the implementation of pro-competitive regulatory regimes. This is particularly important in the case of network-type services (such as financial and telecom services), where there is a need to deal with problems of asymmetric information (moral hazard, adverse selection) or to ensure universal service. One of the beneficial 'didactic' outcomes of the negotiations on financial services (discussed below) was that it helped educate decision-makers on the importance of distinguishing between liberalization and (de-) regulation. Liberalization involves the elimination of discrimination in the treatment of foreign and national services providers and removal of market access barriers – to both cross-border provision and establishment. But this does not restrict the government's ability to enforce regulatory regimes, undertake prudential supervision, conduct monetary policy, or manage external capital flows (Key, 1997).[3] The same applies to other sectors. In all cases, however, the required regulatory capacity must be there, if needed. In principle, multilateral negotiations can help by identifying good regulatory practices and principles that governments should consider adopting, as well as criteria or necessary conditions that must be met before certain reforms should be undertaken.

Another important potential beneficial role multilateral agreements can play is to enhance the credibility of a government's economic policy stance. This can be very important for countries where there is a history of policy

---

[3] In the financial services context, terminological confusion can easily occur. Thus, capital account liberalization—the removal of capital controls and restrictions on the convertibility of the currency—is not the same as financial-services liberalization (allowing foreign firms to operate on domestic markets).

reversal. The WTO offers mechanisms for governments to precommit to a reform path and to lock-in reforms that have already been achieved. However, the credibility impact of WTO commitments depends on the probability that export interests will contest violations of an agreement. As discussed in chapter 3, the credibility payoff for small countries may be limited, as exporters in large nations may have little interest in 'suing' such countries.

Many service activities are highly regulated. The regulatory agencies involved have a vested interest in defending their turf, complicating the needed interagency coordination and cooperation in a negotiating context (Feketekuty, 1988). At the same time, there is frequently a need for appropriate regulation. Regulators may have greater objections to liberalization of cross-border exchange than to FDI, as it is more difficult for them to control industries located in foreign jurisdictions. They may prefer that establishment is required as a mode, as this ensures that they will maintain their control of the activity involved. Whatever their preferences may be, trade negotiators on services must interact and consult with the relevant regulatory authorities, which makes it more complex to engage in negotiations. Such complexity is made worse in the case of federal states where the central government often does not have the authority to make commitments on behalf of lower-level governments.

Another variable that distinguishes services from goods liberalization is that if FDI is the preferred mode of supply, adjustment will be associated with transfers of ownership of industry. Opposition from affected bureaucracies and from groups with noneconomic concerns (such as the impact of 'denationalization' on national culture) may further increase the complexity of liberalization efforts with respect to services. The challenge for policymakers is to enhance foreign competition while ensuring that the need for regulation of service providers in some sectors is satisfied. This requires that the case for liberalization be distinguished from the need for regulation or regulatory reform. Regulation to achieve fiduciary, public health or cultural objectives should be in place and strengthened where necessary, and should apply equally to domestic and foreign providers.

7.3. THE URUGUAY ROUND NEGOTIATIONS

The nonexistence of tariffs as a restraint to trade greatly complicates the life of negotiators seeking to agree to incrementally reduce barriers to services trade. As discussed in chapter 4, negotiators require a focal point – some tangible variable enabling parties to set objectives and assess negotiating progress. In merchandise trade negotiations, the focus is on the value of bilateral trade flows and the associated tariff revenues. Lack of data on trade and the complexities associated with identifying and quantifying barriers to trade makes this approach impossible for services. In the Uruguay Round, rather than focusing on the identification, quantification and reduction of barriers, subjective notions of sectoral reciprocity became the focal point of negotiations. This contrasts with the 'first-difference' approach to reciprocity used in tariff negotiations (Bhagwati, 1988).

Thinking on services evolved considerably over the course of the negotiations. Before and during the 1986 ministerial meeting establishing the agenda of the Uruguay Round, many developing countries defended the view that a MTN should not address services. This position was defended most vigorously by the so-called G-10, which included many of the large and more influential developing countries, including Argentina, Brazil, Egypt, India, Nigeria, and Yugoslavia. While these countries could not block the inclusion of services, they managed to put services on a separate track in an attempt to prevent cross-issue linkages between traditional GATT issues and services.

Early in the negotiations, many developing countries argued that the lack of data on services trade justified excluding service transactions involving establishment by foreign providers from any agreement. In this they were supported by UNCTAD, which proposed that trade in services be defined to occur only when the majority of value added was produced by nonresidents (UNCTAD, 1985). This definition excluded virtually all transactions through FDI, as foreign factors of production that relocate are generally considered to become residents of the host country for economic accounting purposes. Great emphasis was put on the need for governments to be able to impose conditions on inward FDI and support domestic industries. A consequence of this was that a general national treatment obligation of the type found in the GATT was unacceptable.

The US went into the negotiations with the most liberal proposal: MFN was to apply to all signatories and national treatment was to be a binding, general obligation. Trade was to be defined broadly, including FDI (commercial presence). All measures limiting market access were to be put on the table. The EU also entered into the negotiations with the view that trade in services should be defined so as to include all types of transactions required to achieve effective market access. The EU proposed establishing a committee to determine the 'appropriateness' of regulations, with inappropriate measures to become the subject of liberalization negotiations and commitments on a sector-by-sector basis for all participating countries. Any framework agreement for trade in services was to involve only limited obligations of a generally binding nature. National treatment was to be negotiated on a sector-by-sector basis.

Thus, both the EU and major developing countries expressed an early preference for an agreement with relatively soft obligations – the EU arguing that national treatment should only apply to specific sectors, major developing countries opposing even that. Only the US and a number of small open economies – both OECD members and newly industrialized countries like Singapore – were in favor of a 'hard' agreement along GATT lines from the start, with generally binding obligations and universal sectoral coverage. At the end of the day, the EU-developing country preference for a relatively soft framework agreement prevailed. In return for acceptance that trade in services be defined to include all four possible modes of supply and that certain nondiscriminatory measures restricting market access were in principle negotiable, national treatment became a sector-specific commitment. It was also agreed that scheduling of specific commitments would be on both a sector-by-sector and mode-of-supply basis.

Throughout the negotiations lobbies played an important role. The inclusion of services on the Uruguay Round agenda was due in no small part to the efforts of a number of large, mostly American, service companies to get the topic on the table. Leading players in this effort included financial institutions such as American Express and professional services firms such as Arthur Anderson (Heeter, 1997).

7.4. THE GATS

The GATS consists of four main elements:
(1) a set of general concepts, principles and rules that apply to all measures affecting trade in services;
(2) specific commitments that apply only to service sectors and subsectors listed in a member's schedule;
(3) an understanding that periodic negotiations will be undertaken to progressively liberalize trade is services; and
(4) a set of attachments, protocols and annexes that set out sector specific disciplines and Ministerial Decisions that relate to the implementation of the agreement.

The GATS applies to measures imposed by members that affect the consumption of services originating in other members (Article I). The Agreement applies to four modes of supply through which services may be exchanged:

Mode 1: cross-border supply (not requiring the physical movement of supplier or consumer);

Mode 2: movement of the consumer to the country of the supplier;

Mode 3: services sold in the territory of a member by foreign entities that have established a commercial presence; and

Mode 4: provision of services requiring the temporary movement of natural persons.

Trade in services in the GATS context therefore covers both trade in the balance of payments (or national accounts) sense and local sales by foreign affiliates. The Agreement does not apply to services supplied in the exercise of governmental functions. The major provisions of the GATS are summarized in Box 7.2.

Box 7.2. Major provisions of the GATS

Article	Subject matter
I	Definition. Trade in services covers all four modes of supply.
II	MFN obligation. Option to invoke exemptions on a one-time basis.
III	Notification and publication. Obligation to create an enquiry point.
IV	Increasing participation of developing countries. High income countries to take measures to facilitate trade of developing nations.
V	Economic integration. Allows for free trade and similar agreements.
VI	Allows for domestic regulation. Requirements concerning the design and implementation of service sector regulation, including in particular qualification requirements.
VII	Recognition of qualifications, standards and certification of suppliers.
VIII	Monopolies and exclusive suppliers. Requires that such entities abide by MFN and specific commitments (Articles XVI and XVII) and do not abuse their dominant position.
IX	Business practices. Recognition that business practices may restrict trade. Call for consultations between members on request.
XIV	General exceptions. Allows measures to achieve noneconomic objectives.
XVI	Market access. Defines a set of policies that may only be used to restrict market access for a scheduled sector if they are listed in a member's specific commitments.
XVII	National treatment. Applies in a sector if a commitment to that effect is made and no limitations or exceptions are listed in a member's schedule.
XIX	Calls for successive negotiations to expand coverage of specific commitments (Articles XVI and XVII).
XXIX	States that annexes are an integral part of the GATS.

There are annexes allowing for one-time MFN exemptions, addressing the movement of natural persons, excluding air transport services, defining commitments on financial and telecommunications services, and clarifying the potential coverage of maritime transport commitments.

The Basic Rules: Nondiscrimination and Market Access

As in the GATT, the core principle of the GATS is nondiscrimination. Although MFN is a general obligation (Article II), an annex to the GATS allows members to list MFN exemptions upon entry into force of the agreement. Once a member, further exemptions can only be sought by requesting the Ministerial Conference of the WTO for a waiver (which must be approved by three-quarters of the members). MFN exemptions are in principle to last no longer than 10 years and are subject to negotiation in future MTNs, the first of which was to occur within five years of the entry into force of the GATS (Article XIX). The need for an annex on MFN exceptions arose from concerns on the part of some members that an unconditional MFN rule would allow competitors located in countries with relatively restrictive policies to benefit from their sheltered markets while enjoying a free ride in less restrictive export markets. This concern was expressed most vividly in GATS discussions on financial services and telecommunications, prompting industry representatives in relatively open countries to lobby for MFN exemptions as a way to force sectoral reciprocity.

Over 60 WTO members submitted MFN exemptions in 1994, with three sectors in particular being affected: audiovisual services, financial services, and transportation (road, air and maritime). Exemptions in the audiovisual area tend to be justified on the basis of cultural objectives, often aiming at safeguarding preferential coproduction or distribution arrangements with certain countries. Exemptions for financial services were generally driven by reciprocity concerns: countries sought to retain the ability to discriminate against members that do not offer reciprocal access to financial service markets. The goal of many members in this connection was to maintain some leverage *vis-à-vis* the US. Exemptions in the transport area by developing countries often were motivated by the UNCTAD Liner Code – under which they may reserve up to 40 percent of liner shipping routes for national flag vessels.

National treatment (Article XVII GATS) is a so-called specific commitment. It applies only to those services inscribed in a member's schedule, and then only to the extent no qualifications or conditions are listed in the schedule. It is defined as treatment no less favorable than that accorded to like domestic services and service providers. Such treatment may or may not be identical to that applying to domestic firms, in recognition of the fact that identical treatment may actually worsen the conditions of competition for foreign-based firms (for example, a requirement for insurance firms that reserves are held locally). In addition to national treatment, the GATS introduced a second specific commitment: a market access obligation (Article XVI GATS). Six types of market access restrictions are in principle prohibited for sectors a country chooses to schedule. These comprise limitations on the:

(1) number of service suppliers allowed
(2) value of transactions or assets
(3) total quantity of service output
(4) number of natural persons that may be employed
(5) type of legal entity through which a service supplier is permitted to supply a service (for example, branches vs. subsidiaries for banking), and
(6) participation of foreign capital in terms of limits on foreign equity or the absolute value of foreign investment.

While in principle prohibited, if a member desires to maintain one or more of these six measures for a scheduled sector, it may do so as long as it lists them in its schedule. The introduction of a market access commitment in the GATS reflected the fact that the contestability of service markets is frequently restricted by measures that apply to both foreign and domestic entities. The market access article explicitly covers a number of such measures that were felt to be of particular importance. To a degree it is the equivalent of GATT Article XI (which prohibits the use of quotas). In practice, however, the market access obligation overlaps with the national treatment requirement, as prohibited market access-restricting measures may also violate national treatment (Hoekman, 1996).

Other GATS articles address issues such as transparency, domestic regulation, recognition of licenses and certification of service suppliers, exceptions, policies regarding payments and transfers for services, and the behavior of public monopolies. Article III (Transparency) requires all members to establish enquiry points to provide, on request, specific information concerning any laws, regulations, and administrative practices affecting services covered by the Agreement. Article VI (Domestic Regulation) requires that members ensure that qualification requirements, technical standards and licensing procedures are based on objective and transparent criteria, are no more burdensome than necessary to ensure the quality of the services concerned, and do not constitute a restriction on supply in themselves. It requires countries to apply regulations in a 'reasonable, objective and impartial manner' to avoid undermining commitments to market access and national treatment. Moreover, countries must have in place appropriate legal procedures to review administrative decisions affecting trade in services. Article VII (Recognition) promotes the establishment of procedures for (mutual) recognition of licenses, educational diplomas and experience granted by a particular member. It requires members to afford adequate opportunity for other members to negotiate accession to existing bilateral or plurilateral recognition agreements. Article XIV on exceptions is somewhat broader than what is found in the GATT, providing members with the legal cover to take measures to safeguard public morals, order, health, consumer protection and privacy.

Monopoly or oligopoly supply of services is allowed under the GATS, but governments are required to ensure that firms granted exclusive rights by governments do not abuse their market power to nullify any specific commitments relating to activities that fall outside the scope of their exclusive rights. Article IX recognizes that business practices of service suppliers that have not been granted monopoly or exclusive rights may restrain competition and thus trade in services, and requires that members consult with others on request with a view to eliminating such trade-restricting practices. However, no obligations are imposed regarding the scope and enforcement of competition policy rules—Article IX only requires the provision of nonconfidential information. Given the regulatory diversity prevailing across members in the area of competition policy, going beyond an information exchange obligation was not feasible (the issue of multilateral rules for competition law is discussed in chapter 13).

Many GATS disciplines apply only to the extent specific commitments are made. This is a consequence of the 'positive list' approach to scheduling commitments.[4] For example, the balance-of-payments provision (Article XII) applies only for services where specific commitments have been undertaken. It requires that such measures be nondiscriminatory, temporary, and phased out progressively as the invoking member's balance of payments situation improves. As in the GATT context, no recognition is expressed that import

---

[4] In WTO jargon, the coverage of MFN for each GATS member is determined by a so-called negative list—it applies to all services except those listed in the member's annexes on MFN exemptions. The sectoral coverage of national treatment and market access is determined by a positive list—these disciplines only apply to sectors and modes of supply listed in a member's schedule of commitments, and then only insofar as existing measures that violate either of the two provisions are not exempted. The positive list approach to determining the sectoral coverage of specific commitments emerged in large part because many developing countries felt they did not have the administrative resources required to determine all the measures that applied to each sector and decide which they would want to exempt. As many of these countries did not intend to make substantial commitments in any event, they much preferred a positive list approach.

restrictions are second-best instruments to deal with balance-of-payments difficulties. Article XI requires members to refrain from applying restrictions on international transfers and payments for current transactions relating to their specific commitments – it also does not apply generally.

The WTO Dispute Settlement Body is responsible for disputes under GATS. Retaliation from goods to services and vice-versa is possible if this is necessary (so-called cross-retaliation). Thus, if a country finds it needs to retaliate because of noncompliance with a panel recommendation and does not wish to restrict imports of goods, it may retaliate by not complying with some of its service commitments.

The GATS contains no provisions similar to Part IV of the GATT on special and differential treatment for developing countries or accepting the (unilateral) arrangements for tariff preferences that exist for merchandise trade flows (for example, the Generalized System of Preferences). However, Article XIX of the GATS permits developing countries to offer fewer specific commitments than industrialized nations in negotiations, and Article IV calls for special treatment of least developed countries.

The national treatment and market access obligations of the GATS do not extend to government procurement of services or to subsidy policies. The procurement carve-out greatly reduces the coverage of the GATS, as procurement typically represents a significant share of total demand for services such as accounting, consulting engineering, and construction. Dealing with procurement and subsidies proved too complicated and Uruguay Round negotiators left these issues for future deliberations. Article X on industry-specific safeguard actions is also largely a shell, with the Agreement again calling for continued negotiations on this topic. Discussions on all three subjects were held during 1997–2000, with little result. All three topics were on the agenda of the negotiations that were launched to extend the coverage of the GATS in early 2000.

Specific Commitments

As described previously, specific commitments on national treatment and market access apply only to service sectors listed by members, subject to whatever qualifications, conditions and limitations are maintained. As commitments are scheduled by mode of supply as well as by sector, these exceptions may apply either across all modes of supply or for a specific mode. Members also make horizontal commitments that apply to modes of supply, rather than sectors. These are often restrictive in nature. A common example is an 'economic needs test'. Finally, members have the option of making additional commitments by listing actions to be taken that do not fall under national treatment or market access. Table 7.4 illustrates the rather complicated format of schedules of commitments. A consequence of the decisions to distinguish between general and specific obligations, to schedule specific commitments by mode of supply, and to allow for MFN exemptions is that very much depends on the content of the schedules. The GATS is not a particularly transparent or user-friendly instrument.

TABLE 7.4 *Format and example of a schedule of specific commitments*

Commitment type	Mode of supply	Conditions and limitations on market access	Conditions and qualifications on national treatment	Additional Commitments
Horizontal (across all sectors)	1. Cross-border	None	None	
	2. Consumption abroad	Unbound	Unbound	
	3. Commercial presence (FDI)	Maximum foreign equity stake is 49 percent	Unbound for subsidies. Approval required for equity stakes over 25%.	
	4. Temporary entry of natural persons	Unbound except for intracorporate transferees of senior managers.	Unbound except for categories listed in the market access column	
Specific (on a sectoral basis)	1. Cross-border	Commercial presence required	Unbound	
	2. Consumption abroad	None	None	
	3. Commercial presence (FDI)	25% of management to be nationals	Unbound	Establishment of an independent regulator
	4. Temporary entry of natural persons	Unbound, except as indicated in Horizontal Commitments	Unbound, except as indicated in Horizontal Commitments	

Notes: 'None' implies no exceptions are maintained– that is, a bound commitment not to apply any measures that are inconsistent with market access or national treatment. 'Unbound' implies no commitment of any kind has been made.

Virtually all commitments made in the Uruguay Round were of a stand-still nature, that is, a promise not to become more restrictive than already was the case for scheduled sectors. Table 7.5 reports sectoral coverage indicators for national treatment and market access commitments for three groups of countries: high-income countries (HICs) – OECD members, Hong Kong and Singapore; all other countries; and a subset of large developing countries. The latter comprise Argentina, Brazil, Chile, China, Colombia, India, Indonesia, Israel, Malaysia, Pakistan, Philippines, Poland, South Africa, Thailand, and Venezuela. Three indicators are reported. First, a unweighted-average ratio. This is the share of sectors where a commitment of some kind was made. Second, a weighted-average ratio. This adjusts for whether qualifications and exceptions to national treatment and market access were made in each commitment. The weighting scheme used allocates a 0 to unbound commitments, a 1 to commitments not to impose any restrictions, and 0.5 to commitments where restrictions were maintained (see Hoekman 1996 for details). Third, the share of sectors where commitments imply full free trade: that is, no exceptions or qualifications on national treatment or market access are scheduled. The higher the number, the more liberal the country. These ratios are conceptually similar to NTB frequency and coverage indices (Nogues, Olechowski and Winters, 1986).

TABLE 7.5 *Sectoral coverage of specific commitments (%)*

	High-income countries	All other countries	Large developing countries
Market access			
Weighted average	40.6	9.4	17.1
No restrictions	30.5	6.7	10.9
National treatment			
Weighted average	42.4	10.2	18.8
No restrictions	35.3	8.5	14.6
Memo: unweighted average	53.3	15.1	29.6

Source: Hoekman (1996).

HIC members made commitments of some kind for 53.3 percent of all services, as compared to 15.1 percent for developing countries. Commitments made by large developing countries were substantially higher than the developing country average, accounting for 29.6 percent of the total possible. Over one-quarter of developing countries scheduled less than three percent of all services. The weighted average coverage of market access commitments – adjusting for whether exemptions are listed and policies are bound

– for the HIC group is 40.6 percent; that for developing countries 9.4 percent; and that for large developing countries 17.1 percent. Commitments by HIC members implying no restrictions account for 30.5 percent of the total. For developing countries as a whole the figure is 6.7 percent; for the large developing country group the number is 10.9 percent. Numbers for national treatment commitments are very similar. Clearly GATS members were far from attaining free trade in services at the end of the Uruguay Round.

7.5. SECTOR-SPECIFIC NEGOTIATIONS AND AGREEMENTS

In the closing days of the Uruguay Round it became clear that it would be difficult to come to closure on a number of services sectors, including financial services, basic telecommunications, maritime transport, and one important mode of supply: movement of natural persons. (Air transportation was excluded from the ambit of the GATS altogether). Rather than allow a situation to develop where countries would withdraw already tabled commitments in these areas or exempt them from the MFN obligation, it was agreed that negotiations in these sectors were to continue after the establishment of the WTO. Negotiations on financial services, basic telecommunications, natural persons and maritime transport were restarted in the spring of 1994. Those on financial services were to be concluded by July 1995, the others by mid-1996. The negotiations on financial and basic telecom services were eventually concluded successfully. The two others failed.

The Negotiating Group on Movement of Natural Persons was the first to conclude its work in July 1995. Twenty schedules of commitments resulting from the negotiations were annexed to the GATS, which entered into force one year later. These commitments did not go significantly beyond the status quo. The lack of progress on this issue was due in part to the departure of the Indian ambassador in late 1994, who had up to that point pursued an active linkage strategy, making progress on other service negotiations conditional on attaining concessions on the movement of natural persons. Negotiations on maritime transport services proved very difficult. A large number of countries, including the US, maintain cabotage restrictions – a prohibition on the use of nonnational flag vessels to transport cargo within the national jurisdiction. Many developing countries also are signatories to the 1974 UNCTAD Code of Conduct for Liner Conferences which allows a share of up to 40 percent of international liner cargoes to be reserved for national carriers. As no progress could be made to liberalize trade in this sector, the negotiating group suspended talks at the end of June 1996.

Financial Services

Financial services were of great importance to the US, reflecting the strength of the US lobbies that sought improved access to foreign markets. As a result the US was unwilling to accept commitments that it regarded as inadequate. At the very end of the Uruguay Round, it was agreed to extend talks on financial services by 18 months, with a deadline of end June 1995. Although the US invoked MFN exemptions for this sector, it was understood these would not be applied until negotiations were concluded. As the 1995 deadline approached, the US indicated that it considered the offers of Japan and several South-East Asian and Latin American countries to be inadequate and that it would invoke its MFN exemptions. In an effort to salvage as much as possible from the negotiations, the EU then proposed that all other participants maintain their offers through the end of 1997. Negotiations resumed in 1997 and were finally concluded successfully in December of that year – with the US participating (and thus removing its MFN exemptions for this sector). A total of 56 schedules representing 70 members were annexed to the GATS.

Despite the fact that an increasing number of developing countries recognized that a competitive and efficient financial services sector was a condition sine qua non for economic development, and that opening markets to foreign financial firms can strengthen domestic financial systems by creating more competitive and efficient host-country markets, agreement proved elusive. One problem concerned fears of the implications of liberalization for weak domestic financial institutions, and a perceived absence of reciprocity given that many developing countries are importers and not exporters of financial services. Another concern revolved around the implications of GATS rules for management of capital flows and prudential regulation and supervision.

The latter problems were addressed by agreeing that liberalization of capital movements per se is beyond the purview of the GATS, although members are restricted from imposing capital controls that interfere with their specific commitments (except if justified for balance-of-payments reasons). More difficult was where to draw the line as regards the types of regulation that are permitted (policies aimed at increasing the strength and quality of prudential regulation and supervision) and those that should be abolished (policies that act as barriers to trade in financial services) (Key, 1999). An Annex on Financial Services contains a so-called 'prudential carve-out' for domestic regulation of financial services. Included at the insistence of financial regulators, the carve-out allows prudential measures to be imposed to protect consumers of financial services and to ensure the integrity and stability of the financial system.[5]

TABLE 7.6 *Precommitments to future financial services liberalization*

Country	Commitment (1997 Financial Services Agreement)
Egypt	Insurance: relaxation of economic needs test in the year 2000 for life and 2002 for nonlife insurance; foreign equity limit increased from 49 percent to 51 percent as of January 1, 2000 for life and January 1, 2003 for nonlife.
India	Banking: 12 branch licenses per year both for new entrants and existing banks; subject to a 15 percent maximum share of foreign assets in total assets of the banking system.
Indonesia	Insurance and banking: all limitations to be eliminated by the year 2020, subject to a similar commitment by other members.
Philippines	Banking: 10 new licenses for bank branches for the period 1995–2000.
Thailand	Banking: discretionary higher equity participation in banks than bound 25 percent maximum for a period of 10 years, grandfathered thereafter for the absolute amount of equity held.
Bulgaria	Insurance: majority foreign ownership in insurance to be allowed three years after accession
Hungary	Insurance: market access for branches of insurance companies on adoption of required legislation.
Poland	Insurance and banking: as of January 1, 1999, market access through licensed branches of banks and insurance companies to be allowed.
Slovenia	Insurance: limitation on foreign ownership of insurance companies to be abolished with the adoption of required legislation. Banking: branch banking to be permitted, and elements of discretionary licensing removed, after adoption of a new Banking Law.
Brazil	Insurance: commercial presence in work accident insurance, reinsurance and retrocession to be allowed within two years of adoption of legislation. Banking: national treatment for commercial presence for credit card and factoring services within two years of passing required legislation.

Source : Mattoo (2000*b*).

Most commitments made by WTO members were status quo or less than status quo commitments. A few countries used the GATS as a mechanism to precommit to future liberalization (Table 7.6). Of the ten instances noted,

---

[5] It is unclear what the additionality is of the carve-out, as GATS Article VI essentially provides cover for such regulatory intervention as well.

four involve countries that signed far-reaching agreements with the EU to liberalize trade in goods and services. Most of the others represent relatively large markets. Governments of these countries were under substantial pressure to open access to their markets.

Basic Telecommunications

Telecommunications services were split between basic and value-added services during the Uruguay Round. By the end of the round, only commitments had been made for value added services (such as electronic and voice mail or electronic data interchange), and not for basic voice, data transmission, mobile telephony or satellite services. Negotiations on basic telecommunications recommenced in May 1994 with a deadline of April 30, 1996. In the run up to the deadline, negotiations were deadlocked. As in the financial services talks, the US was of the view that offers on the table were inadequate, in part because the required 'critical mass' of membership (to prevent free riding) had not been achieved. In April the US withdrew its offer of open satellite market access and the negotiations collapsed. Other negotiators regarded the US move as serving narrow, domestic political differences (Petrazzini, 1997). In contrast to what happened in the financial services negotiations, the EU or another party to the talks did not take the initiative to extend discussions. Instead, such an initiative was taken by the Director-General of the WTO, who induced the major players to extend the deadline to February 1997. This was accepted, and negotiations were finally concluded successfully in February 1997, with 55 schedules (representing 69 Members) annexed to the GATS. The additional time allowed a number of developing countries to improve their offer – with technical assistance from a group of bilateral donors and multilateral organizations. It also allowed the major players to hammer out difficulties related to differences in prevailing market structures. One such problem concerned international resale of switched telecom services. Because the US is an open competitive market, calls switched through the US by foreign carriers cost relatively little, whereas US carriers were forced to pay much higher fees because many foreign markets were not open. An August 1997 US decision to move to cost-based settlement rates for such payments removed this constraint.

A key feature of the agreement that emerged was a 'Reference Paper' setting out regulatory principles to which signatories may subscribe (by making so-called additional commitments in their schedules, as allowed by Article XVIII GATS). Over 50 members did so. The need for these principles – which draw on elements of the 1996 US Telecommunications Act – arose from a concern that dominant telecom operators might otherwise abuse their market position and restrict competition from new entrants. The reference paper calls for the establishment of an independent regulator for telecoms, the adoption of competitive safeguards, interconnection guarantees (including nondiscrimination), and transparent and nondiscriminatory licensing. The reference paper illustrates both the strengths and the limitations of the multilateral approach. The primary concern of the paper, as of WTO rules in general, is to ensure effective market access. Wider concerns about consumer interests and how they may be affected by monopolistic behavior are not addressed, nor is any focal point provided for regulators regarding the need for and modalities of regulation.

The basic telecommunications agreement is noteworthy in the extent to which countries made commitments to engage in future liberalization. Many developing countries used it as a precommitment device—they bound themselves to introduce competition at precise future dates (Table 7.7). This reflected a recognition that liberalization was in their interest. Ongoing technological developments—the internet, e-commerce—played an important role in the changing attitude towards increasing competition in the telecom sector.

TABLE 7.7 *Selected developing country precommitments in basic telecommunications*

Country	Commitment
Antigua & Barbuda	International voice telephony to be opened to competition as of 2012
Argentina	No restrictions as of November 8, 2000
Bolivia	No restrictions on long distance national and international telecom services as of November 27, 2001
Chile	Limits on competition in national long distance services for a period of four years starting on August 27, 1994
Grenada	Reserved for exclusive supply until 2006, no restrictions thereafter
Jamaica	Reserved for exclusive supply until September 2013, no restrictions thereafter
Trinidad & Tobago	Reserved for exclusive supply until 2010, no restrictions thereafter (no restrictions on fixed satellite services as of 2000)
Venezuela	No restrictions as of November 27, 2000
Cote d'Ivoire	Monopoly until 2005, no restrictions thereafter
Mauritius	Monopoly until 2004, no restrictions thereafter
Morocco	Monopoly until 2001, no restrictions thereafter
Senegal	Abolition of monopoly by January 1, 2007, monopoly to be reviewed in 2003

Country	Commitment
South Africa	Monopoly until December 2003, thereafter duopoly and consideration of more licenses
Tunisia	No restrictions on supply of local calls after 2003
Korea	As of 2001, maximum foreign equity share in facilities-based suppliers to rise from 33% to 49% (in the national supplier—Korea Telecom—from 20% to 33%); foreign ownership of domestic voice resale entities to be allowed in 1999, with maximum equity participation of 49%, to rise to 100% after 2001
Pakistan	Exclusivity on cross border supply of voice telephony to be eliminated by 2004, divestiture of 26% of national monopoly to a strategic investor, to be granted exclusive license for basic telephony for seven years.
Singapore	Competition of facilities-based telecom services to start in April 2000 with up to two additional licenses and periodic subsequent licenses thereafter
Thailand	Additional commitments for voice telephone and other services to be made in 2006, conditional upon the passage and coming into force of new legislation

Source: Adapted from Mattoo (1999).

7.6. ELECTRONIC COMMERCE

The transformation of telecommunication networks, resulting mainly from a marriage of telecommunications with information technology is rapidly driving down transaction costs in international trade. Where once traders had to go to exhibitions, trade fairs, and visit potential clients, buyers and sellers are now increasingly able to use international information and e-commerce networks to interact. Electronic commerce is rapidly changing the face of international trade, reducing the tyranny of distance, eliminating the need for middlemen and greatly impeding the ability of firms to charge significant mark-ups over costs. Estimates of the cost savings that can be realized through business-to-business (B2B) e-commerce procurement are in the 15 to 25 percent range for many industries (Mann, Eckert and Knight, 2000).

From a WTO point of view, e-commerce is a vehicle for international trade in both goods and services. In Canada and Latin America, in 2000, the share of export sales in total revenues was around 80 percent (Mann et al., 2000). E-commerce raises a number of important questions for the WTO. Should e-commerce-specific disciplines be negotiated? What rules should apply to taxation to ensure that it does not become a barrier to trade? Some governments favor strong control and regulation; others opt for a more liberal, hands-off approach. Those in favor of government intervention argue that the Internet can bring their citizens face to face with pornography, gambling, or fraud and note there is no reason why e-commerce should be exempt from taxation or the type of trade controls that apply to mail-order within and across national borders. Liberals argue that the Internet has the potential of transforming the functioning of economies and that government intervention could have potentially serious detrimental consequences by slowing down the growth of networks and the pace of innovation. They also argue that new technologies increasingly offer solutions for Internet users to protect themselves against undesired messages or fraud and that market forces will be more effective than government intervention in ensuring interconnection and contract enforcement.

E-commerce is intimately associated with services. E-commerce involves a mix of telecommunications, information, financial and transportation (express delivery) services. However, the products that are bought and sold may be digitized or tangible goods, or they may be services (access to databases, consulting, advice, and so forth). These products will often be protected through intellectual property rights. International e-commerce is therefore affected by GATT, GATS, and TRIPs. Starting in 1997, WTO members began to wrestle with the question if and how e-commerce should be dealt with in the WTO. Members decided at the 1998 ministerial that electronic delivery of digitized goods and services would be free from customs duties. This commitment was temporary, and one of the questions confronting members is whether to make this exemption permanent. At the 1999 Seattle ministerial, members could only agree that the 1998 moratorium would be extended by another two years.

The net effect of the ban on duties is to act as a subsidy to products that can be digitized, and therefore as a tax on transport services and producers who do not (cannot) use the Internet as a mode of supply. At the margin, both customs and sales tax revenues will also fall (as sales taxes, even if formally applicable, are difficult to collect). There has been a vigorous debate on the merits of extending the ban on imposing duties on e-commerce (note that the ban does not extend to goods ordered over the net – these remain subject to tariffs). Mattoo (2000*a*) argues that much of this debate is confused. If a WTO member has made a commitment in a particular sector to provide national treatment, then all discriminatory taxes (including customs duties by definition) are already prohibited and so the ban adds nothing. Conversely, if a member has not made a national treatment commitment, it remains free to impose discriminatory internal taxes other than customs duties, so again the ban has little value. The appropriate route to ensure liberalization of electronic commerce is to expand the GATS specific commitments.

There are a variety of e-commerce-related issues that the WTO will have to address. Perhaps most important is the classification of products bought and sold. Should e-commerce be treated as a service and be subjected to the GATS rules – the preference of the EU? If so, should e-commerce be regarded as a mode 1 or mode 2 type of transaction? The US has argued that treating all e-commerce transactions as services creates the danger that policy regimes may become more restrictive than the status quo, because many WTO members have not made specific commitments on products that are traded electronically (such as software or database access). Conceptually, however, it is extremely difficult, if not impossible, to define what distinguishes goods from services – the valiant efforts of statisticians to make an unambiguous distinction have never borne fruit (Hill, 1977, 1987). From a practical point of view the EU position may therefore prevail. This then raises a number of other issues, including the mode 1 versus mode 2 classification issue. It arises in part because many WTO members made more liberal commitments under mode 2 for sectors than under mode 1, in large part because many did not perceive any interest in being restrictive on mode 2 – movement of the consumer – and did not associate this mode with e-commerce. However, it has been argued that if a person buys a product from a firm located in a foreign country through e-commerce this is akin to the consumer physically moving to the location of the provider. The only difference is that the 'movement' takes place by interacting with the server of the enterprise. The distinction between modes also has potential implications for enforcement of contracts. Under mode 2, presumably the legal regime of the provider applies in case of a dispute, whereas under mode 1 it may by the buyer's legal system that applies. Determining which jurisdiction applies is something that has not been addressed under the GATS.

Although there are a number of technical issues that must be addressed if the WTO is to be fully supportive of the e-commerce revolution, there does not appear to be a strong case for separate disciplines for e-commerce (an Electronic Commerce Agreement). The issues that arise can be addressed within the existing institutional framework. Most important in this regard is to expand the coverage of specific commitments under the GATS, as these affect both the internet and telecommunications 'backbone' services, the financial services that are critical to allow efficient payment for e-commerce transactions, and the international logistics that are a vital element of delivery of goods that cannot be digitized (distribution services).

7.7. THE CHALLENGE OF EXPANDING THE GATS

Article XIX GATS required members to launch new negotiations on services no later than 2000, and periodically thereafter. As many countries have pursued autonomous reform efforts, one issue is how to fit these into the GATS and use the GATS to push domestic reform efforts forward. Another issue is how to respond to pressure by other countries that desire greater access to the domestic market and what to ask in return. The incentive for countries to schedule both status quo and future (autonomous) reforms depends importantly on the value that is placed on such scheduling by reforming economies themselves and the 'demandeur' countries who seek market access guarantees. Arguments by economists that the WTO can be used as a valuable credibility-bolstering device have proven to be less than compelling to policymakers. In practice, the mercantilist logic of multilateral negotiations is likely to require that industrialized countries improve export market access opportunities for developing countries.

Expanding the coverage of services sectors and modes of supply should be a priority for future negotiations. There is no a priori reason why specific commitments should not cover *all* services and *all* modes of supply. Setting targets for expanded coverage would help provide a focal point for policy makers. Possibilities are the share of sectors that have been scheduled, and the share of commitments that involve a bound promise not to apply any national treatment or market access-violating measures. Both indicators do not require any judgement regarding the importance of actual policies that restrict national treatment or market access, whether or not scheduled. Priority attention should be given to key 'backbone' sectors such as transport, telecoms, and financial services, as well as those clusters that are vital to economic development and participation in the world economy (for example, multi-modal transport and express courier services). Increasing the efficiency of such service sectors will have major payoffs for developing countries in terms of lower prices, higher quality, and greater choice.

From a mercantilist perspective, these backbone services are sectors where enterprises in industrialized countries can be expected to dominate. Traditional negotiating balance imperatives then require that services and modes of supply where developing countries have an export interest also be put on the table. Without reciprocal concessions, developing countries are unlikely to want to bind the status quo or to use the GATS as a precommitment device for planned future reforms. Even though many countries have been undertaking domestic procompetitive reforms in their services sectors, and despite the compelling economic arguments that can be made in favor of using international agreements as a vehicle to make binding commitments to 'lock-in' reforms, negotiating dynamics often impede the use of agreements for this purpose. The situation that arises is similar to what occurred in the Uruguay Round, during which developing countries sought – rather unsuccessfully – to obtain 'negotiating credit' for autonomous liberalization of import barriers that had been implemented prior to and during the negotiations.

Article XIX:3 GATS requires that negotiations to expand the GATS include guidelines or modalities for the treatment of autonomous liberalization that has occurred in the period after the last multilateral round. It is unclear how 'credit' should be defined. Credit that involves granting developing countries the right to 'do less' is unlikely to be in their own interest. It appears more productive to think of credit in terms of the quid pro quo to be put on the table by high income countries and major upper middle income emerging markets in return for a significant increase in bindings by low income and least developed countries. Relevant in this connection is also Article IV:3 GATS, which calls for special treatment of least developed countries. If taken seriously, this should involve an explicit focus on improving access to markets of interest to such countries.

Many potential tradeoffs and linkages within the ambit of the services negotiations can be identified. For example, developing countries have an interest in seeking commitments from OECD countries in the area of national social and medical insurance regimes, to allow patients to undergo treatment abroad. Perhaps the most obvious 'big' area for tradeoffs is liberalization of mode 4 – temporary entry of service providers. Although undoubtedly highly sensitive, it is an area where incremental progress can be made, as a key instrument used to restrict trade through this mode are visa quotas. These can be expanded over time, removing economic needs tests for within-quota visas and adoption of a mode 4-specific safeguard procedure (Hoekman, 2000). It is also an area where opposition within OECD countries is not monolithic – there are many industries that would benefit from a more liberal temporary access regime, and development of coalitions with such industries could help change the status quo.

The current approach to scheduling specific commitments distinguishes between the four modes of supply that define trade (Article I GATS). As a result, national schedules may distort incentives to use the most efficient mode, while also creating uncertainty regarding the rules that prevail in instances where more than one mode is used to service a market. Such uncertainty can also impede dispute settlement. It creates difficulties in predicting how a panel will interpret the schedules, and thus reduces the perceived benefits from initiating dispute settlement procedures. One way to reduce potential inconsistencies in commitments across modes within a specific sector is to require one-to-one mappings between commitments on modes ('nondiscrimination across modes') (Feketekuty, 1998). Such a technological neutrality principle was embodied in the Agreement on Basic Telecommunications. Modal neutrality is an objective worth pursuing because, as is often emphasized in the literature, trade and investment have increasingly become complementary. It is also frequently noted that it will become more difficult to maintain a clear distinction between trade in goods and trade in services, as technology may give producers the choice of delivering their products in tangible or in disembodied (digitized) form. A priori, it would appear that any multilateral disciplines should apply equally to international transactions regardless of the mode of supply.

Some fundamental 'architectural' issues arise here. For example, a case can be made that WTO members should consider developing disciplines that distinguish between trade and investment, with trade in goods or services being subject to a set of common rules, and movement of factors of production being subject to another set of rules. This in effect has been the approach taken in the NAFTA, which includes a separate chapter on investment (in goods or services), which is distinct from the rules relating to cross-border trade (in goods and services). This approach results in much greater consistency and clarity of the applicable rules and disciplines than the current WTO structure. These are longer run questions that must be addressed at some point. For the time being, within the GATS setting, a focus on modal neutrality can be a useful halfway house.

Efforts to attain greater neutrality could be complemented by efforts to expand the ambit of horizontal, procompetitive principles that apply to all sectors. This would help make the GATS both more transparent and more relevant to investors, by allowing negotiating efforts to center more on developing disciplines that make sense from a long-term growth and economic development perspective. As far as network services are concerned a start was made in this direction in the Agreement on Basic Telecommunications' reference paper on regulatory principles in telecoms. Concepts in the reference paper such as 'affecting the terms of participation' and 'essential facilities' could usefully be extended to all network services, even those without any background of monopoly or public ownership.

Care must be taken, however, to avoid attempts at imposing a 'one size fits all' approach to procompetitive regulatory principles, as different service sectors will in general have different requirements and characteristics. Countries will also differ in terms of the weight that is accorded to competition policy compared to direct regulatory oversight by specialized regulatory agencies. Harmonization across countries is unlikely to be first best, and any disciplines, whether sector-specific or horizontal, are best limited to procedural norms that aim at increasing transparency and accountability of regulations and regulators. For example, in multi-jurisdictional situations, central and lower-level governments share responsibility for enforcing regulatory regimes. Quite frequently, the 'action' occurs at the state or provincial level, implying that local regulators must be involved in the development and implementation of procedural rules at the WTO level. Improving communications and dialogue between the trade and regulatory policy communities *within* countries, and between regulators *across* countries are preconditions for achieving progress in this area.

Similar caution should apply to efforts to 'regulate domestic regulation' in sectors where access to a network is not at issue. Adopting a 'necessity test' approach of the type used in the EU – putting the burden of proof on governments to show that a particular regulation that has detrimental effects on foreign providers is necessary to achieve an objective – will be difficult to apply in the WTO. The much weaker integration ambitions that prevail among WTO members and the absence of supranational enforcement can easily lead to disputes regarding what is 'necessary' and put an excessive burden on the dispute settlement system. Attention might more productively focus on expanding the reach of the national treatment and market access principles, abolishing MFN exemptions, and ensuring that MFN applies in the area of standards and mutual recognition.

Outstanding Issues: Subsidies, Procurement and Safeguards

A number of 'outstanding' rule-making issues were left open after the Uruguay Round for further work and discussion: subsidies, procurement and safeguards. The economic case for GATS-specific disciplines in any of these areas is arguably weak. There is nothing services-specific about procurement: any multilateral disciplines should cover goods and services. Of primary importance for foreign firms is to have access to procurement markets, and frequently this can only be achieved if they can establish a commercial presence in a country. If the sectoral coverage of the GATS is expanded and foreign providers are able to access markets, the contestability of procurement markets will be enhanced at the same time (Evenett and Hoekman, 1999).

In the services context any disciplines on subsidies will have to focus primarily on domestic production or operating subsidies – the distinction between export and production subsidies found in the GATT is much harder, if not impossible, to make in practice. It is also much harder to envisage emulation of the main GATT discipline – countervailing duties – increasing the need to agree to substantive rules (harmonization) if members agree to discipline the use of subsidies. Difficulties will immediately arise in distinguishing between what is 'legitimate' and what is not. While there are clearly potential sources of gain for WTO members associated with a set of subsidy disciplines, subsidies will frequently be the most efficient instrument to pursue noneconomic objectives – to ensure universal service, promote regional development, offset income inequalities, and so forth. Cross-subsidies may sometimes be an appropriate second-best instrument for developing country governments (Joskow, 1998; Laffont, 1998).

GATT negotiating history illustrates that agreement on subsidy-related disciplines is difficult to obtain, and that any disciplines may easily be circumvented. Even the EU – which goes much further than the WTO in this area – has encountered recurrent difficulties in enforcing restrictions on the use of state aids. NAFTA does not even try to tackle this issue. Given there is a rationale for subsidies in many contexts and the revealed preference of many governments to use subsidies, it would appear more effective to seek to extend the reach of the national treatment principle to subsidy policies. Given national treatment, there should be less concern about the impact of subsidy policies, allowing the principle of 'subsidy freedom' to prevail. As in the procurement case, what matters most is market access and national treatment.

The economic case for safeguard instruments is also weak. Insofar as governments are under pressure to reimpose protection (discrimination), they already have the opportunity to invoke the renegotiation modalities that are built into the GATS. GATT-type emergency protection is difficult to rationalize in the services context because in many cases it will require taking action against foreign firms that have established a commercial presence (Hoekman, 1993). Why a government would want to do this is unclear, as it can have a major chilling effect on FDI, and will affect negatively the national employees of the targeted foreign-owned firms. If a safeguards measure was to be considered, it would most likely exempt mode 3. But then account must be taken of the fact that this can easily act to induce investment, rather than trade (mode 1), thus distorting incentives (leading away from the modal neutrality objective).

There is, however, one potentially compelling argument for seeking to develop a safeguard instrument. A case could be made that the extremely limited nature of liberalization commitments to date on movement of natural persons (mode 4) is in part due to the nonexistence of safeguard instruments. As this is a mode of supply that is of major interest to developing countries and one on which almost all countries maintain stringent restrictions, one could envisage a safeguard instrument that is limited to mode 4 liberalization commitments. The rationale would be to provide OECD country governments with an insurance mechanism that can be invoked if liberalization has unexpected detrimental impacts on their societies.

Achieving Greater Transparency

It is widely recognized that the 'scheduling technology' used in the GATS does not greatly promote transparency. A fundamental need is to improve the available information on status quo policies. This will facilitate national reform efforts and help identify where the multilateral process can support such efforts. Unfortunately, there is nothing in the GATS or the WTO that encourages and assists countries in generating comprehensive information on applied policies and evaluating the impact of these policies. Some progress was made in the Uruguay Round with the creation of the Trade Policy Review Mechanism, but more can and should be done. Priority should be given to greatly improving statistics and data on trade barriers and entry-cum-operating restrictions in services. Analogous to the role played by the OECD secretariat in compiling information on agricultural policies in the 1980s, international organizations and multinational business should devote the resources required to document the status quo and to put this information in the public domain.

The importance of strengthening capacity to collect and analyze information cannot be over emphasized. A common mistake made by governments involved in regulatory reform is to reduce the ability of agencies to compile the information needed to monitor the impact of reforms. Better information on status quo policies, their effects, and the impact of GATS-based liberalization agreements will assist governments to make policy and provide stakeholders (business, civil society) with the information needed to engage in the domestic policy formation process. One option that deserves serious consideration in this connection is to resurrect an Australian proposal made at the 1996 WTO ministerial meeting to engage in a negative list *reporting* exercise of prevailing policies in services for transparency purposes. This should be accompanied with adequate technical and financial assistance to help developing countries, in particular least developed countries, participate in the transparency exercise.

7.8. CONCLUSION

There is widespread recognition among governments and civil society that pursuit of regulatory reforms in the services area can have large payoffs. In this respect the political context today is quite different from that prevailing in 1986 when the Uruguay Round was launched. Opposition to liberalization certainly exists in many countries, and nations differ on the desirable modalities and speed with which to pursue reforms. There are also valid concerns regarding the need to put in place the appropriate regulatory policies and strengthen regulatory institutions before certain types of liberalization are undertaken. But the thrust of policy in the majority of nations is towards a more market-oriented stance, as is reflected in widespread privatization of utilities, telecom operators, airlines, and so forth. The success of the financial and basic telecom sectoral talks was largely due to the fact that most of the governments involved were convinced of the need to pursue regulatory reforms in these sectors, including liberalization and elimination of entry barriers. This was a precondition for both agreements to materialize – it was clear that the associated regulatory reforms did not go beyond what had already been accomplished or decided in the national (unilateral) context.

A significant expansion of the coverage of national treatment and market access commitments is needed to make the GATS more relevant. The potential scope for tradeoffs in the GATS context is quite large, and there should be no need to rely on cross-issue linkages – although those can certainly be envisaged as well. An obvious linkage strategy *within* services would be a mode 3–mode 4 exchange, with developing countries making bound national treatment and market access commitments on FDI across a wide range of sectors, in return for significant expansion of access to high-income markets through movement of natural persons. Although reform in services has been and will continue to be primarily driven by domestic priorities, the challenge is to make the GATS a more effective device to support domestic reforms. Greater efforts to ensure that developing country service suppliers are granted better access to OECD markets, especially through mode 4, and a willingness to put sectors such as air and maritime transport on the negotiating table would go far towards making the GATS a more relevant instrument.

7.9. FURTHER READING

Geza Feketekuty, *International Trade in Services: An Overview and Blueprint for Negotiations* (Cambridge: Ballinger, 1988) offers an excellent and comprehensive contemporary discussion of issues relating to services trade; why services were put on the agenda; and what the US goals were in the Uruguay Round. See Julian Arkell, 'Lobbying for Market Access for Professional Services', in Michel Kostecki (ed.), *Marketing Strategies for Services* (Oxford:

Pergamon Press, 1994) for an insider's account of lobbying and marketing strategies employed by service sectors in the GATS negotiations and in other fora to enhance access to foreign markets. Various GATS-related topics are discussed in depth in Patrick Messerlin and Karl Sauvant, *The Uruguay Round: Services in the World Economy* (Washington DC: The World Bank, 1990), which also includes a number of country-specific viewpoints. UNCTAD and The World Bank, *Liberalizing International Transactions in Services: A Handbook* (Geneva: United Nations, 1994) provides an integrated treatment of the policy issues that arise in liberalizing services, focusing on all four modes of supply.

John Croome, *Reshaping the World Trading System: A History of the Uruguay Round* (Deventer: Kluwer Law International, 1999) provides a comprehensive discussion of the services negotiations. Jagdish Bhagwati, 'Trade in Services and the Multilateral Trade Negotiations', *World Bank Economic Review* 1 (1987), 549–69 is an excellent contemporary discussion of the issues from a developing country point of view. Bernard Hoekman, 'Assessing the General Agreement on Trade in Services', in Will Martin and L. Alan Winters (eds.), *The Uruguay Round and the Developing Economies* (Cambridge: Cambridge University Press, 1996) offers a detailed analysis of the GATS and the commitments made by WTO members.

Gary Hufbauer and Erika Wada, *Unfinished Business: Telecommunications After the Uruguay Round* (Washington DC: Institute for International Economics, 1997) and Wendy Dobson and Pierre Jacquet, *Financial Services Liberalization in the WTO* (Washington DC: Institute for International Economics, 1998) describe and assess the outcome of the basic telecom and financial services negotiations. Priorities and alternative options to extend the GATS are the subject of papers collected in Pierre Sauvé and Robert Stern (eds.), *GATS 2000: New Directions in Services Trade Liberalization* (Washington DC: Brookings Institution, 2000). Catherine Mann, Sue Eckert and Sarah Knight, *Global Electronic Commerce: A Policy Primer* (Washington DC: Institute for International Economics, 2000) is an accessible book-length treatment of the policy issues that arise in the context of the e-commerce revolution.

8
Protection of Intellectual Property

Multilateral cooperation in the field of intellectual property rights (IPRs) dates back more than a century. The issue has always been of some relevance to the multilateral trading system—for example, dealing with trade in counterfeit goods. However, it was not until the creation of the WTO that enforceable rules regarding ownership rights to intellectual property were embedded in the trading system. As legal systems pertaining to IPRs are an element of domestic regulation, the WTO Agreement on Trade-related Intellectual Property Rights (TRIPs) is a prominent illustration of the trend to extend disciplines on 'behind the border' regulatory regimes.

This chapter provides an overview of the economic rationales for protection of IPRs and the reasons behind moves to adopt multilateral rules in this area. Some of the major conflicts of interest that shaped the TRIPs agreement are summarized, as are the basic elements of the substantive disciplines imposed. The agreement is unique in the WTO context in that it imposes obligations upon governments to adopt a set of substantive rules in an area that traditionally has been regarded to be in the purview of domestic regulation. It is an example of what Tinbergen (1954) has called positive integration. This contrasts with the 'negative' integration found in the GATT, which involves agreements not to use certain policies that directly affect (distort) trade flows—such as export subsidies or quotas—or if used, imposes constraints on when and how trade policies may be applied. The chapter ends with a brief discussion of implementation-related questions, focusing in particular on the options that exist to reduce the potential negative aspects of stronger IPRs on national welfare.

8.1. INTELLECTUAL PROPERTY AND INTERNATIONAL TRADE

Intellectual property can be defined as information that has economic value when put into use in the marketplace (Maskus, 2000). Ownership rights to intellectual assets span those ideas, inventions and creative expression on which there is a public willingness to bestow the status of property (Sherwood, 1990). Examples of legal expressions of IPRs include industrial property, copyrights and so-called neighboring or related rights. Industrial property principally concerns protection of inventions through patents and trademarks. The subject matter of copyright is usually described as literary and artistic works. All these ownership rights are territorial in nature, so that the level and conditions of protection are a function of national laws and enforcement institutions.

The rationale for government protection of IPRs depends considerably on the characteristics of the knowledge that is involved. As a first cut, it can be noted that patents, copyrights and neighboring rights, industrial secrets and industrial designs have one broad commonality: they all fall within the broad category of knowledge goods. They are the result of research and development (R&D)—invention and innovation. In contrast, trademarks and marks of origin are not knowledge goods. Instead, their aim is to allow product differentiation through the creation of brands and to provide information to consumers. Although not knowledge goods, the importance of trademarks and geographic indications of origin in trade—and as potential protectionist devices—is significant (Box 8.1). The issues that arise from an economic perspective are analogous to those that result from the use of technical barriers to trade (see chapter 5). The following discussion therefore focuses primarily on IPRs for industrial property.

Box 8.1. Noix de Coquille de Saint-Jacques and Chimas Whisky

Indications of geographic origin are helpful to both producers and consumers because they reduce information (search) costs. However, national regulations concerning the description or geographic origin of a product may also be used as a protectionist device. A case in point was a 1993 French regulation concerning the description of scallops (a shellfish), which reserved the use of the expression 'noix de coquille de St. Jacques'—under which scallops are sold in France—to shellfish originating in France. As a result, Canadian scallops—which are identical in size, texture and use to French scallops—could not be labeled as coquille de St. Jacques. Canadian exports of scallops to France dropped, as distributors were confronted with the need to relabel the product under another name. This significantly weakened the competitive position of Canadian scallops on the French market. Canada requested a panel on this issue in 1995, alleging that the nondiscrimination provisions of the WTO had been violated. Peru and Chile, two other producers, followed with a similar case. The panels were suspended after the parties came to a settlement.

Indications of geographic origin are particularly contentious for alcoholic beverages. For example, domestic distributors in Chinese Taipei—not a WTO member—have sold spirits labeled 'bourbon', cognac' or 'scotch', there being no legal framework setting rules for claims concerning content, age or origin. Some consumers also found it difficult to differentiate between brand name products and imitations. Thus, 'Chimas Teacher Extra Old Whisky' produced in India was aimed at those who had heard of Chivas or Teachers, two well-known international brands. Such examples are found in many countries, and have been brought to WTO dispute settlement panels. For example, the EU successfully contested the distribution of Chimas Teachers whisky in India. The EU is particularly active in defending trademarks and indications of origin. Efforts to conclude a free trade agreement between South Africa and the EU were stalled for well over a year because of EU insistence that South Africa agree to refrain from labeling exports of alcoholic beverages as grappa or ouzo, even if South Africa is clearly marked as the country of origin. One effect of the TRIPs agreement is that enterprises in developing countries will find it increasingly difficult to use protected names to describe their products.

Knowledge has the characteristics of a public good in that the stock of knowledge does not diminish with consumption: the marginal cost of distributing an additional unit of a knowledge good is zero. Consequently, from a static efficiency perspective the optimal allocation of resources requires that such goods have a zero price. However, this does not take into consideration that inventions have to be produced and that technological innovation can require considerable investment. With a zero price for knowledge goods, investors have no pecuniary incentive to invest in R&D activities. A zero price is therefore socially sub-optimal in a dynamic sense, since it discourages innovation and technological progress. Of course, in practice many types of knowledge cannot be diffused at zero cost. Moreover, investments may need to be made to use and adapt knowledge to fit local circumstances. Thus, creators of many types of inventions are often able to benefit even in the absence of legal IPRs. The empirical evidence suggests that IPRs are needed not so much to promote inventions (many of which would occur anyway) but to provide an incentive to engage in costly R&D activities which turn inventions (pure knowledge) into innovations (products or production processes that can be used in industry). The degree of protection afforded to innovations has an impact on inventor's profits and therefore on investment in R&D.

Patents or copyrights grant an inventor or author a temporary monopoly over the use of the invention or the reproduction of a work and prevent competitors from sharing and using their knowledge without payment. The quasi-rents resulting from the protection enable the owners to recoup their investments and secure their economic interests, thus creating an incentive for the production of knowledge. IPRs also contribute to more rapid public disclosure of inventions, as a necessary condition for the grant of a patent is full disclosure and description of the technology for which protection is being sought. This provides competitors with useful information that can be employed in an effort to invent around the patent—in practice a major source of innovation and technological progress. In the absence of IPRs certain types of industrial inventions and the associated technical information would be kept secret much longer, with detrimental consequences for diffusion.

Governments are generally concerned with establishing an optimal mix between the need for a temporary monopoly to create incentives for innovation and the benefits of free access to knowledge. In formulating their IPR policies they must reconcile static efficiency considerations (which imply that knowledge goods should be free or available at very low cost) with the longer-term objectives of encouraging innovation and technological progress. There is no unique solution to this problem. Whether a given regime is optimal depends on the objectives and circumstances of countries and the economic sectors involved. Conflicts of interest between countries can easily occur. A priori, the case for harmonization of intellectual property regimes is weak—the type of regime that is most appropriate will vary with the level of development of a country.

IPRs became a trade issue for a number of reasons. International trade in goods embodying IPRs has increased substantially in recent decades as the share of manufactures in total merchandise trade has expanded, and within manufactures, the share of 'high-technology' goods has increased. Starting in the 1980s, a number of industrialized country governments increasingly perceived inadequate enforcement of IPRs in importing countries to reduce the competitive advantage of their exporting firms. Although trade in counterfeit goods had been an irritant for the multilateral trading system for a long time, as technologies for duplication became both more advanced and cheaper, trade in goods embodying 'stolen' knowledge became an increasingly contentious issue. Examples of counterfeit include imitations of premium goods such as Rolex watches, Lego toys, and Vuitton handbags, as well as pirate copies of compact discs, software and video films. Resulting disputes were frequently addressed through bilateral channels, with the threat of trade sanctions to induce acquiescence. The US played a prominent role in using unilateral threats of sanctions to deal with perceived IPR infringements in foreign countries. The two main instruments employed were Section 337 of the 1930 US Tariff Act, and Section 301 of the 1974 Trade Act, as amended by the 1988 Omnibus Trade and Competitiveness Act. The former was used against imports into the US, the latter against foreign governments (Box 8.2).

The EU has similar instruments to address foreign trade practices, but has traditionally been much less activist than the US (Bronckers, 1996). In part, the recourse to unilateral 'self-help' instruments by major traders reflected the fact that the International Court of Justice, the main dispute settlement forum in this area prior to the creation of the WTO, requires agreement between the interested parties to submit a case to it. Moreover, many of the countries targeted under instruments such as Special 301 were not signatories of the relevant international conventions in this field, so that recourse to international dispute settlement was simply not available. Of course, these reasons did not justify the use of unilateral, threat-based approaches (see Bhagwati and Patrick, 1990). The appropriate response to the

Box 8.2. Sections 301 and 337 of US Trade Law

Section 301 of the US Trade Act of 1974 gives the President authority to retaliate against foreign trade practices which are deemed to restrict US exports. What such practices were was not spelled out and it was left to the discretion of the President whether to retaliate. A Section 301 action is initiated by private parties (in the US), and initially involves pressure being exerted on the foreign government to adopt different policies. If the response is deemed to be insufficient, attempts to negotiate agreements may be made. If negotiations fail, the US may retaliate by restricting access to its market.

The Omnibus Trade and Competitiveness Act of 1988 introduced changes to 301, rendering it much more threatening for foreign countries. Because Congress perceived the President to be insufficiently vigorous in pursuing foreign unfair trading practices, the 1988 Act called for formal investigations of private complaints. It created a new procedure—'Super 301'—that required the US Trade Representative (USTR) to create an inventory of unfair practices in foreign countries, to select priority targets from that list, set deadlines for removal of the offending measures and to restrict the exports of these countries if the practices concerned were not eliminated. Super 301 was complemented by a new 'Special' 301 provision that pertained to the identification of countries where protection of IPRs was deemed to be inadequate. It is Special 301 that is relevant to this chapter.

Section 337 of the US Tariff Act of 1930 allows for investigations to be initiated to determine whether foreign producers of goods imported into the US are supported by unfair trade practices and are injuring an efficiently operating US industry, act to prevent the establishment of such an industry or are anticompetitive (restrain trade). What these practices are is again not defined precisely, but many of the cases brought against imports under Section 337 have involved claims of infringement of US-held IPRs. The Omnibus Trade and Competitiveness Act of 1988 eliminated the need to demonstrate that the unfair practice had injured a domestic industry if the allegation concerned a violation of IPRs.

problem would be to seek to negotiate a multilateral agreement that would make all parties better off. Eventually this was attempted in the Uruguay Round.

The use of US trade law provisions was challenged under GATT dispute settlement provisions on a number of occasions. In a 1981 case concerning invocation of Section 337 against Canadian exports of certain automotive springs assemblies, the dispute settlement panel found that the application of US law could be justified under GATT Article XX:*d* (General Exceptions— see chapter 9). The panel's findings were endorsed by the GATT Council on the understanding that this did not preclude future examinations of the use of Section 337. A subsequent panel considered an EEC complaint concerning a Section 337 action against exports of aramid fibers by Akzo, a large Dutch multinational. This panel concluded that Section 337 was inconsistent with Article III:4 (national treatment), because it discriminated against imported products alleged to infringe US patents. Another GATT case was initiated by Brazil, after a decision by the US—following a Section 301 investigation—to increase tariffs on a range of Brazilian products in retaliation against perceived inadequate patent protection for pharmaceuticals and fine chemicals in Brazil (see Hudec 1993 for more on these cases).[1]

Business communities in OECD countries maintained that infringements of IPRs constituted a straightforward matter of piracy and theft, and called for multilateral rules and enforcement of IPRs. Many developing countries opposed this strongly, arguing that protection of IPRs was a domestic policy matter, that nonprotection of IPRs on their part had a negligible impact on producers in OECD countries, and that adoption of stronger IPRs would be detrimental to their welfare and development prospects. For example, patent protection was held to be potentially detrimental to food security by raising the costs of inputs (seeds, fertilizers) and to the health of poor segments of the population (which would have to pay more for patent-protected pharmaceutical products). However, opposition was not universal. Some interest groups in developing countries favored stronger IPRs. Examples were industries that depend on inward FDI or licensing for technology, and producers of indigenous and traditional knowledge.

---

[1] In November 1998, sections 301-310 of the US Trade Act of 1974 were the basis of a dispute settlement case in the WTO. The panel concluded these provisions of US trade law were not inconsistent with the GATT because of US undertakings—articulated in the Statement of Administrative Action approved by the US Congress at the time it implemented the Uruguay Round agreements—that it would abide by its obligations under the WTO in the invocation of the law. The DSB adopted the report in January 2000. See www.wto.org.

The eventual acceptance of TRIPs in the Uruguay Round by developing countries reflected a package deal of sorts, comprising a mix of carrots and sticks. The stick was represented by the fear that if they did not agree they would be increasingly vulnerable to unilateral arm-twisting by the US and the EU. Carrots included the (implicit) quid pro quo that was offered by OECD countries in the form of agreeing to the phase-out of the MFA and agreeing to outlaw VERs. A growing perception that IPRs could be beneficial also played a role. Examples included protection of indigenous knowledge and cultural heritage, fostering innovation, and giving domestic industries better access to new technologies.

8.2. INTERNATIONAL CONVENTIONS AND GATT HISTORY

Several international conventions exist which lay down standards for protection of intellectual property. These include the Paris Convention (on patents), the Berne Convention (on copyright) and the Rome Convention (on sound recordings and music) and the Treaty on Intellectual Property in Respect of Integrated Circuits (Table 8.1). These and other conventions are administered by the World Intellectual Property Organization (WIPO), a Geneva-based UN body. Both the Paris and Berne Conventions were first negotiated over a century ago, and have been periodically updated and expanded. The need for international cooperation on IPRs arose over a century ago because IPRs are country-specific, created by national legislation. As creators of innovations must file for an IPR in each jurisdiction where they want protection, they have an incentive to push governments to adopt similar procedures and standards. Little harmonization occurred, however, and

TABLE 8.1 *IPRs: instruments and related international agreements*

Type of IPR	Instruments of Protection	Subject Matter	Main Fields of Application	Major International Agreements
Industrial property	Patents, utility models	New, nonobvious inventions capable of industrial application.	Manufacturing, agriculture	Paris Convention, Patent Cooperation Treaty (PCT), Budapest Treaty, Strasbourg Agreement, TRIPs
	Industrial designs	Ornamental designs	Manufacturing, clothing, automobiles, electronics, etc.	Hague Agreement, Locarno Agreement, TRIPs

Type of IPR	Instruments of Protection	Subject Matter	Main Fields of Application	Major International Agreements
	Trademarks	Signs or symbols to identify goods and services	All industries	Madrid Agreement, Nice Agreement, Vienna Agreement, TRIPs
	Geographical indications	Product names related to a specific region or country	Agricultural products, foodstuffs, etc.	Lisbon Agreement, TRIPs
Literary and artistic property	Copyrights and neighboring rights	Original works of authorship	Printing, entertainment (audio, video, motion pictures), software, broadcasting	Berne Convention, Rome Convention, Geneva Convention, Brussels Convention, WIPO Copyright Treaty 1996, WIPO Performances and Phonograms Treaty, Universal Copyright Convention, TRIPs
Sui generis protection	Plant breeders' rights	New, stable homogenous, distinguishable plant varieties	Agriculture and food industry	Convention on New Varieties of Plants (UPOV), TRIPs
	Database protection	Electronic databases	Information processing industry	European Council directive 96/9/EC
	Integrated circuits	Original layout designs of semiconductors	Microelectronics industry	Washington Treaty, TRIPs
Trade secrets		Secret business information	All industries	TRIPs

Note: All international treaties except TRIPs, the Universal Copyright Convention, and the European Council Directive 96/9/EC are administered by WIPO.
Source: Primo Braga, Fink and Sepulveda (2000).

many international conventions did not go much beyond agreement to apply the national treatment principle.

Most net exporters of knowledge-intensive goods were not fully satisfied with the existing conventions and sought to fill certain gaps through the GATT. For example, the Paris Convention does not stipulate the minimum duration of patents or define what should be patentable. No international agreements existed on proprietary business information (trade secrets). Standards of protection for computer software and sound recordings were deemed to be too weak by the industries concerned. Many countries considered that existing agreements dealt inadequately with counterfeiting and that national laws on trademarks were often too weak or poorly enforced. Finally, producers sought effective multilateral dispute settlement mechanisms to deal with IPR-related issues. Existing conventions did not contain binding, effective procedures in this regard. A major attraction of the GATT was that it had an enforcement mechanism.

GATT 1947 provisions related to IPRs were quite limited. Among the GATT provisions referring specifically to IPRs are those on marks of origin (Article IX)—which require that these not be used to restrict trade—and Articles XII:3 and XVIII:10 which state that a condition for using QRs for BOP purposes is that these not violate IPR legislation. The general exceptions provision of the GATT (Article XX:*d*) states that measures necessary to protect IPRs are not subject to GATT as long as they are nondiscriminatory (see chapter 9). Although GATT rules such as national treatment (Article III), MFN (Article I), transparency (Article X), and nullification and impairment (Article XXIII) applied to actions taken in connection with national enforcement of IPRs, the general relevance of GATT for IPR regulations was limited. In effect, no substantive disciplines applied in this area. Moreover, GATT rules such as national treatment related to products, whereas those of the IPR conventions also concern persons.

IPR-related matters raised in the GATT before the Uruguay Round mainly concerned trade in counterfeit goods, and involved trademark and design infringement, access to and misuse of certification marks, appraisal of the value of IPRs in connection with goods being imported, and use of marks of origin. Informal negotiations on trade in counterfeit goods were held during the Tokyo Round, and led to the tabling of a draft code on the subject by the United States. However, no agreement proved possible on this question (Winham, 1986). The issue was first put formally on the GATT agenda in November 1982, when Ministers asked the Council to determine whether it would be appropriate to take joint action in the GATT framework on trade in counterfeit goods and, if so, what this action should be. In 1985, a Group of Experts established to advise the Council concluded that trade in counterfeit goods was a growing problem that needed multilateral action, but could not agree on whether the GATT was the right forum for this. This question was resolved at the 1986 ministerial meeting at Punta del Este that launched the Uruguay Round.

8.3. THE URUGUAY ROUND NEGOTIATIONS

The negotiation on TRIPs was one of the more difficult of the Uruguay Round, both politically and technically. The issue was relatively new to GATT and involved a North-South confrontation. Industrial countries, led by the US, sought an ambitious and comprehensive agreement on standards for protection of IPRs of all kinds. They argued that negotiations should consider a wide range of IPRs and that enforcement through the dispute settlement system as well as through domestic laws and customs procedures was a necessity. Led by the same countries that opposed comprehensive discussions on services—India, Brazil, Egypt, Argentina and Yugoslavia—developing countries sought to draw a firm distinction between work on trade in counterfeit goods and IPRs more broadly defined. They were willing to cooperate on the former, but opposed the latter. The first order of priority for poor countries was to ensure that unilateral measures to protect IPRs did not cause barriers to legitimate trade. There was a general concern that greater protection of IPRs would strengthen the monopoly power of multinational companies, and detrimentally affect poor populations by raising the price of medicines and food. Given that the duration of patent protection—if granted at all—was generally shorter than in developed countries, this was a valid concern.

The first two years of negotiations were dominated by disagreements over the mandate of the negotiating group. Areas of disagreement included standards of protection, use of unilateral sanctions, the reach of competition law, and the need for—and length of—transitional periods. One of the most difficult questions was how far new rules could go to protect intellectual property. Was it acceptable for GATT contracting parties to draft substantive standards on intellectual property and embody them in an international agreement? Some developing countries, led by India, argued that GATT or its successor organization was not the right place for setting and enforcing IPR standards. They felt that this was a task for WIPO—which already administered some 20 multilateral conventions—and for individual governments themselves. As far as unilateral sanctions were concerned, developing countries wanted industrialized nations to renounce the option of unilateral trade sanctions. They called for a credible commitment to multilateral dispute settlement procedures. This aspect of the negotiations was further complicated by the initial US refusal to change its legislation (Section 337), which a GATT panel had found to be discriminatory in nature (see above). The US linked modifying its laws to conform with the panel recommendations to satisfactory progress in the TRIPs discussions. In the event, at the end of the day the US agreed to comply with the panel's findings, although implementation was problematical (Hudec, 1993).

In contrast to the rest of the Uruguay Round, the TRIPs negotiations were not about freeing trade, but about changing domestic regulatory and legal regimes. In effect, the agenda revolved around getting developing countries to implement existing international IPR conventions (and in a number of areas, to go beyond them). Thus, the TRIPs agenda essentially centered on the adoption of minimum standards for IPRs in the jurisdiction of all countries. The TRIPs talks divided developed countries—the major net exporters of IPRs with norms that would largely meet whatever minimum standards were adopted—from many developing countries—all net importers and many of which did not have legislation. Although the final outcome went beyond existing international conventions in a number of important respects—see below—implying that all countries, including OECD members were obliged to change their IPR regimes to some extent, the major implications were for developing countries.

A good case could be made that the TRIPs talks were zero-sum in the short run, as stronger enforcement of rights in developing countries could result in large transfers from the South to the North (see below). But gains from trade across issues were clearly available, as each group had things to offer that the other wanted. Developing countries wanted to control US trade policy (Section 301), maintain sufficient discretion to safeguard national interests, and minimize the adjustment costs of strengthening IPR protection. OECD countries sought stronger IPR standards, multilaterally agreed, with multilateral enforcement. Incentive structures also differed over the course of the Uruguay Round. Important in this connection is that developing countries were not really a cohesive bloc on the TRIPs issue. Some of the poorer nations that had tightened their domestic protection of IPRs unilaterally so as to attract FDI and technology or as a response to the threat of US action, feared to be undercut by competitors in other developing countries (Mansfield, 1994). Many also increasingly felt that stricter IPR protection was in their interest in the longer run, not only because it was a necessary component of a more general move towards a market economy, but also because of the link between IPRs and FDI and related access to knowledge. But it was the scope for cross-issue tradeoffs that ultimately created the preconditions for a successful conclusion of the negotiations. In exchange for agreeing to

TRIPs, poor nations obtained the prospect of better market access for their textile and clothing exports. Without a TRIPs deal, it is unlikely that the Agreements on Textiles and Clothing and Safeguards could have been concluded.

8.4. WTO RULES ON INTELLECTUAL PROPERTY RIGHTS

The TRIPs agreement is an integral part of the WTO—its provisions apply to all members. It is a far-reaching, complex agreement—with seven major parts and 73 Articles—that covers copyrights and related rights (rights of performers, broadcasters and phonogram producers), layout-designs of integrated circuits, geographical origin indications, trademarks, industrial designs and patents (Box 8.3). The TRIPs Agreement:

(1) establishes minimum substantive standards of protection for the above rights;

(2) prescribes procedures and remedies which should be available in member states to enforce these rights; and

(3) extends basic GATT principles such as transparency and nondiscrimination to IPRs (although allowance is made for the fact that a number of international conventions permit departures from MFN or national treatment in certain circumstances).

Box 8.3. Major provisions of the TRIPs agreement

Article	Subject	Comments
3.	National treatment	Applies to persons
4.	Most favored nation treatment	Reciprocity exemptions for copyright; grandfathering of existing regional and bilateral agreements
6.	Exhaustion	No rule imposed except nondiscrimination
Copyright and related rights		
9.	Observes Berne Convention. Does not require moral rights	
10.	Programs and data compilations protected as literary works	A significant change in global norms
11.	Rental rights	A significant change in global norms
12.	Term of protection	Minimum 50-year term . Clarifies corporate rights
14.	Neighboring rights protection for phonogram producers, performers	
Trademarks and related marks		
15.	Protectable subject matter	Confirms and clarifies Paris Convention

Article	Subject	Comments
16.	Rights conferred	Deters use of confusing marks and speculative registration; strengthens protection of well-known marks
19.	Requirement of use	Clarifies nonuse. Deters use of collateral restrictions to invalidate marks
Article	**Subject**	**Comments**
21.	Licensing and assignment of rights	Prohibits compulsory licensing
22-4.	Geographical indications	Definitions; additional protection for wines and spirits
Industrial designs		
26.	Protection	Minimum term protection: 10 years
Patents		
27.	Subject matter coverage	Patents provided for products and processes in all fields of technology. Biotechnology covered but exceptions allowed for plants and animals developed by traditional methods
28.	Exclusive right for importation	
31.	Other use without authorization of right holder	Severe restrictions on compulsory licenses
		Domestic production can no longer be required; nonexclusive licenses with adequate compensation
33.	Duration of protection	Minimum 20-year patent length from filing date
34.	Burden of proof in process patents	Defendants must prove process differs from patent
Integrated circuits designs		
36.	Scope of protection	Protection extended to articles incorporating infringed design. Significant change in global norms
38.	Term of protection	Minimum 10 years
Protection of undisclosed information		
39.	Trade secrets protected against unfair methods of disclosure	New in many developing countries
Abuse of IPRs		
40.	Control of anticompetitive practices	Wide latitude for competition policy to control competitive abuses, subject to other WTO disciplines
Enforcement of IPRs		
41-61.	Requires civil, criminal enforcement	Costly for developing countries to implement
		No nonviolation cases to be brought for first five years

Transitional arrangements		
65-6.	Transition periods	5 years for developing and transition economies; 11 for LDCs. Only latter can request extension
70.	Pipeline protection for pharmaceuticals	Not required. Provision for maintaining novelty and exclusive marketing rights
Article	**Subject**	**Comments**
Institutional arrangements		
71.	Review and amendment	TRIPs Council to monitor and review agreement on expiration of transitional period

Source: Adapted from Maskus (2000) and WTO (1994).

The agreement builds upon the main international conventions administered by the World Intellectual Property Organization (WIPO). In a number of instances TRIPs established disciplines that go beyond existing international norms. With respect to copyrights, WTO members are required to comply with the substantive provisions of the Berne Convention for the protection of literary and artistic works, except regarding protection of moral rights. Computer software is to be protected as a literary work under the Berne Convention, and copyright is to extend to computerized databases—something that was not part of the Berne Convention. Another significant addition to international rules on copyrights are the provisions on rental rights, giving authors of computer programs and producers of sound recordings the right to authorize or prohibit the commercial rental of their works to the public. A similar exclusive right is also applicable to films. Performers are to be given protection from unauthorized recording and broadcast of live performances (bootlegging). Here again TRIPs goes beyond existing IPR disciplines as the Rome Convention that establishes rights of performers, producers of sound recordings, and broadcasters has few signatories, particularly among developing countries. The TRIPs agreement requires governments to allow recording companies from one country to attack unauthorized reproduction and sale of its products within another country. The protection for producers of sound recordings and performers is to be for at least 50 years, while broadcasting stations are granted a twenty-year period during which use of their programs requires their authorization.

The agreement defines the types of marks eligible for protection as a trademark or service mark. It also specifies the minimum rights that members must grant to mark owners. Marks that have become well known in a particular market enjoy additional protection. For example, owners of foreign marks may not be forced to use their marks in conjunction with local marks. Governments must provide means to prevent the use of any geo-graphical indications that mislead consumers as to the origin of goods and are required to discourage any use that would constitute unfair competition. Trademarks containing a geographical indication that could mislead the public on the true origin of the product are to be refused or invalidated. Geographical indications for wines and spirits are given specific protection. The agreement calls for a multilateral system of registration and notification of geographical indications for wines to be negotiated.

The protection of industrial designs under TRIPs was also strengthened relative to existing international norms. Designs are to be protected for a minimum period of 10 years. Owners of such designs may prevent the im-portation, sale, or production of products bearing a design that is a copy of the protected one.

WTO members must comply with the substantive provisions of the Paris Convention (1967) on patents. At least 20-year patent protection is to be provided for almost all inventions, including both processes and products. The 20-year lower bound implies harmonization toward the standards maintained by industrialized countries (for example, Indian patent length for pharmaceutical production processes was only seven years as of the late 1980s, whereas no patents were provided at all for pharmaceutical products). The permitted exclusions from patentability comprise plants and animals (other than microorganisms), computer programs, as well as biotechnologi-cal processes. However, plant varieties must be given protection, either through patents or a sui generis (special or more specific) system. Inven-tions may be excluded from patentability for reasons of morality, public or-der or because of therapeutic, diagnostic or surgical usefulness. As a general rule, rights conferred in respect of patents for processes must extend to the products directly obtained by the process.

There is substantial flexibility in defining the conditions for awarding patent protection, including recognition of narrow claims, provision of util-ity models and pre-grant opposition procedures. Maskus (2000) notes that such elements of IPR systems helped generate Japanese productivity gains after the Second World War by encouraging local entrepreneurs to pursue process innovations. There are no restrictions on the grounds that may be used to impose compulsory licensing to correct for anti-competitive prac-tices (abuse of IPRs—Article 31 TRIPs). Thus, Brazil retained broad scope for compulsory licensing, including for non-working of rights (Watal, 2000).

The Treaty on Intellectual Property in Respect of Integrated Circuits (1989) provides the basis for the protection of layout designs of integrated circuits. The TRIPs Agreement goes beyond this Treaty by requiring a mini-mum protection period of 10 years and extension of rights to products incorporating infringing layout designs. Trade secrets and know-how of commercial value are protected against acts contrary to honest commercial practices such as breach of confidence. However, the relevant provision of TRIPs (Article 39), does not define what acts are unfair, leaving governments free to allow for reverse engineering (Maskus, 2000). Test data on agricultural or pharmaceutical chemicals submitted to the authorities in order to obtain marketing approval must also be protected against unfair commercial use.

WTO members are obliged to provide procedures and remedies under their domestic law for effective enforcement of IPRs by right-holders (both foreign and national). Such procedures should be fair and equitable, entail reasonable time limits and not be unnecessarily complicated or costly. Requirements on the civil and administrative procedures and remedies include provisions on evidence, injunctions, damages and other remedies. In cases when delay is likely to result in irreparable harm to the right holder, prompt and effective provisional measures must be available. The agreement also deals with measures to be taken at the border by customs authorities against pirated or counterfeit goods.

Article 40 TRIPs recognizes that some licensing practices or conditions pertaining to IPRs may have adverse effects on trade or impede the transfer and dissemination of technology. It allows for members to specify in their legislation practices or conditions that constitute an abuse of IPRs and allow intervention by the government. This provides countries with the opportunity to apply competition legislation if necessary. For example, countries may have a strong interest in applying an international exhaustion rule. This would imply that domestic buyers could purchase patented and branded products wherever they find the most favorable prices. This is fully compatible with the TRIPs agreement, even though the EU and the US are active proponents of a national and regional approach in this area, respectively.

All members had one year following the date of entry into force of the WTO to implement the agreement. Developing countries were entitled to a delay of an additional four years for all provisions of the agreement with the exception of national treatment and MFN. Least-developed countries were granted a twelve-year period to conform (until January 1, 2006), and may request extensions of this period. If a developing country must extend product patent protection to areas of technology that were not protected before TRIPs (for example, pharmaceuticals or agricultural chemicals), it may delay the application of the provisions on product patents to these areas for an additional five years. While it has been claimed that these transition periods are long (especially by the pharmaceutical industry), it should be recalled that the transition periods for the abolition of the MFA is 10 years, and that liberalization under the ATC is heavily back-loaded. While the TRIPs agreement may be too riddled with holes as far as OECD right holders are concerned, a case can be made that developing countries committed themselves to doing more on the IPR front than OECD countries did with regard to traditional issues such as contingent protectionand market access. Indeed, developing countries often point out that many TRIPs disciplines apply with immediate effect, and that this is also true in the area of patents given the requirement to provide for exclusive marketing rights during the transition period (Watal, 2000).

8.5. IMPLEMENTATION CONCERNS AND CHALLENGES

Implementation of the TRIPs agreement will involve substantial adjustments and costs for developing countries. These costs are of two types. First, bringing legislation into conformity and strengthening the domestic institutions that will be charged with enforcing the new laws costs money. Such costs will not be incurred by OECD countries, as they were already largely in compliance with TRIPs standards and had the necessary infrastructure in place. Second, there are economic costs, especially in the short run, insofar as rents are transferred from domestic consumers to foreign holders of IPRs.

Developing countries must revise or adopt new legislation, ensure that judges are trained in the application of IPR law, educate customs and other enforcement authorities so that they understand the new rules, and provide the tools and resources so that they have the capacity to apply them. Efforts must be made to educate the business community and civil society as well. Designing an intellectual property regime that is relevant for the situation and characteristics of a developing country is not straightforward. Simply copying the regime that is in place in an OECD country will not do. The type of intellectual property that needs to be protected varies across countries, as does institutional capacity. Rather than develop a patent office along European or US lines it may be more important to develop mechanisms to protect the fruits of indigenous culture such as music or crafts. How to do this in a cost-effective manner requires research and trial and error experience. At the time the TRIPs agreement was being negotiated, insufficient knowledge existed to allow such concerns to be embodied in the drafting of the agreement.

Finger and Schuler (2000) review World Bank projects in the area of IPRs and conclude that the costs of implementing the TRIPs agreement can be substantial. Required reforms go beyond drafting new legislation, and include enhancing administrative structures (for example, bolstering the capacity to review applications, including investments in computerized information systems and extensive training for staff) and buttressing enforcement. Although developing countries were granted a transition period to implement the agreement, in many cases the time required for upgrading IPR regimes spans a longer period than was granted. Many countries do not have the resources available to undertake the comprehensive reforms and institutional strengthening that is required leaving them open to dispute settlement.

During the first five years of the WTO—when many of the main substantive provisions of the agreement did not yet apply to developing countries—19 TRIPs cases were brought to the WTO (Watal, 2000). These cases mostly involved the Quad. The first WTO dispute settlement case involving the TRIPs Agreement was brought by the US against Japan's copyright regime for the protection of IPRs in sound recordings (the EU brought a similar case subsequently). Other cases brought by the EU included an objection to Section 211 of the 1998 US Omnibus Appropriations Act, alleging it made impermissible the registration or renewal in the US of a trademark if it was previously abandoned by an owner whose business and assets were confiscated under Cuban law. It also brought Section 337 of the Tariff Act of 1930 back to the WTO in January 2000, contending that certain measures continued to violate national treatment.

The US has been the most active user of dispute settlement, with the majority of cases brought against the EU. It complained, *inter alia*, of an alleged lack of protection of trademarks and geographical indications for agricultural products and foodstuffs in the EU, failure to grant copyright and neighboring rights in certain EU member states, nonenforcement of IPRs in Greece (allegations that TV stations in Greece regularly broadcast copyrighted motion pictures and television programs without the authorization of copyright owners), Denmark's alleged failure to make provisional measures available in the context of civil proceedings involving IPRs, and Portugal's term of patent protection under its Industrial Property Act.

The US and the EU also brought cases alleging the absence of an effective system for providing exclusive marketing rights for pharmaceuticals and agricultural chemical products in Argentina and India (a violation of Article 70 TRIPs). Panel and Appellate Body reports issued in 1998 concluded that India had failed to establish a legal basis that adequately preserved novelty and priority in respect of applications for product patents for pharmaceutical and agricultural chemical inventions, and had failed to establish a system for the grant of exclusive marketing rights.

Developing countries have also become more active in safeguarding their interests. For example, in 1998 Thailand asked the US to revoke registration of the 'Jasmati' rice trademark of a US firm. Objections were also raised to the use of variants of the name Basmati for rice, with India taking steps to protect 'Basmati' as a geographical indication. Tea plantations in the region of Darjeeling launched a campaign to protect the 'Darjeeling' brand from foreign imitations. A Belgian watchdog agency was appointed to identify the use of the name 'Darjeeling' in international markets (*International Herald Tribune*, July 6, 1998).

Economic Effects of TRIPs

In addition to direct compliance costs, the TRIPs agreement—once fully implemented—will also give rise to economic costs and benefits. As noted above, IPRs essentially act to create a temporary monopoly for innovators to recoup their investment in inventive activity. As a monopoly, IPR holders can be expected to extract some proportion of consumer surplus by equating

TABLE 8.2 *Estimated static rent transfers from TRIPs implementation (1995, US$ million)*

Country	Outward transfer	Inward transfer	Net transfer
USA	92	5,852	5,760
Germany	599	1,827	1,228
France	0	831	831
Italy	0	277	277
Sweden	13	230	217
Switzerland	474	510	36
Panama	0	0.3	0.3
Australia	177	154	-23
Ireland	71	12	-59
New Zealand	79	8	-71
Israel	125	32	-93
Colombia	132	2	-130
Portugal	138	0	-138
Netherlands	453	314	-139
South Africa	183	15	-168
Greece	197	2	-195
Finland	281	47	-234
Norway	277	25	-252
Denmark	330	77	-253
Austria	358	83	-275
Belgium	470	111	-359

Country	Outward transfer	Inward transfer	Net transfer
India	430	0	-430
South Korea	457	3	-454
Spain	512	31	-481
Mexico	527	1	-526
Japan	1,202	613	-589
UK	1,221	588	-633
Canada	1,125	85	-1,040
Brazil	1,714	7	-1,707

Source: Maskus (2000), updating McCalman (1999).

marginal revenue to marginal cost. This will generate a static deadweight loss for the products that benefit from protection.

The extent to which prices will rise in response to the exercise of stronger market power is a function of several variables (Maskus, 2000). First, market structure before and after IPRs matters crucially. The number of firms (home and foreign) competing with rights holders, the nature of that competition, the ease of market entry and exit, quality differentiation among products, openness to trade, and wholesale and retail distribution mechanisms are all factors that determine the impact of IPRs. Oversimplifying for purposes of discussion, the more competitive the market for a product before the introduction of IPRs, the lower the substitutability of protected for generic products, and the more concentrated the industry producing protected varieties, the greater the impact of IPRs on prices is likely to be. Second, the less elastic is demand, the greater the price increasing effect of enhancing market power through IPRs. Third, the strength of competition policy and the willingness to intervene directly through regulation will determine outcomes. For example, policies towards exhaustion of rights (whether to allow parallel imports) can have a substantial impact. Finally, much depends on the wording of IPR legislation, including the scope of protection, the provisions for reverse engineering as a means of fair competition, and fair-use exemptions in copyright.

In economies that are significant net importers of technologies and knowledge-intensive goods and services, the rents paid by consumers to producers (right-holders) are transferred outside the country. This implies that in an international context, IPRs are not simply a mechanism to redistribute income among different groups in a given society, with an associated static efficiency deadweight loss. They may involve significant transfers across countries. That is, net importers may experience a reduction in national welfare (a terms-of-trade loss) as foreign producers extract rents from domestic consumers.

Maskus and Penubarti (1995, 1997) undertook an empirical examination of this issue and concluded that the strength of national IPR regimes exerted a statistically significant positive effect on imports of manufactures. That is, stronger protection leads to more trade. However, the calculated impacts on actual trade volumes are relatively small. More interesting are investigations that focus on the likely impact of TRIPs on the welfare of economies and the possible magnitude of net transfers across countries. A series of studies have been undertaken that generally conclude that the net transfers from South to North will be positive. A noteworthy attempt to estimate the magnitude of the potential transfers is McCalman (1999). He incorporated information on the volume and price of technology transfers through patents, including the likelihood of local imitation across markets, to estimate the net present value of patents if countries were to enforce TRIPs-type standards of protection. Estimates of the transfers that would arise are reported in Table 8.2. It is clear that the big winner is the US, which obtains an additional transfer (return on IPRs) that exceeds US$5 billion. Other countries that gain include Germany, France, Italy, Sweden and Switzerland. Developing countries such as India, Mexico and Brazil experience significant losses, as do many of the high-income countries included in the sample. As noted by McCalman (1999), the losses due to TRIPs for these developing countries are similar in magnitude to the benefits that CGE studies suggested they would obtain from the market access part of the Uruguay Round. For some, the net static effect is negative—implying a loss from the round. Of course, such calculations must be considered illustrative only, as they pertain only to patents and are dependent on the type of model used for estimation purposes. They do serve to illustrate that in the short run the TRIPs agreement may involve a sizeable transfer to the primary producers of knowledge—the US and the EU.

Policy Implications and Options

Given the negative transfer effect of TRIPs, very much depends on creating the conditions that maximize the potential for beneficial dynamic effects of IPRs, and on obtaining compensation in other areas that is of sufficient value to offset the short run loss. The latter is of course what the Uruguay Round was about. On the former, a variety of policies can be pursued that can reduce the magnitude of the transfer. Examples include taxation of imports of those IPR-intensive goods where foreign producers have significant market (pricing) power, facilitating the absorption and diffusion of know-how, vigorous enforcement of competition law, and direct regulation. The TRIPs agreement allows significant latitude for governments to draft implementing legislation that attenuates the ability of right-holders to abuse their market power.

Regulation of prices is common in many countries, especially of pharmaceuticals. While this can result in firms pricing closer to cost, it can have unintended consequences. If prices are set too low, firms may choose not to sell. Firms will also have an incentive to try to circumvent price regulations by inflating costs. One way they may do this is by setting high transfer prices on imported ingredients (Lanjouw, 1998). Another policy option is an active competition regime that ensures that markets are contestable and that there is vigorous inter- as well as intra-brand competition. One element of such a competition policy could be a liberal parallel import regime that limits the ability of right-holders to segment markets.[2] The economics of this issue are complex. Many experts argue that as long as a producer faces competition from other brands, exclusive distribution arrangements do not matter. But in many developing countries inter-brand competition may be weak because only a few distributors control the market. National exhaustion and legally enforceable exclusive distributor arrangements can then have a detrimental impact on welfare.[3] However, preventing parallel imports can also be beneficial if it results in lower prices than would arise under uniform pricing. The decision whether to adopt international exhaustion is a matter for national authorities to decide independently. Hong Kong's experience illustrates the importance of adopting competition legislation to control 'overshooting' on IPRs. Reportedly, the vigorous enforcement of IPRs has led to the exclusion of gray market, parallel imports and to allegations of abuse of a dominant position, which the Hong Kong government has generally argued to be impossible given its free trade stance. The Director-General of the Department responsible for enforcing IPRs recognized that the absence of a competition law creates problems, but noted that his job was to protect the interests of

[2] Parallel imports involve traders buying goods protected by IPRs in one market and importing them into another market. Such trade does not involve a violation of IPRs of the type that occurs when goods are counterfeited or copied illegally.

[3] An anecdote recounted to the authors is illustrative. Lebanon has an exclusive distribution ('sole agency') law that gives license holders (agents) the right to request Customs to block entry of goods that have not been authorized by the license holder (distributor). On a visit to Germany, a businessman buys a batch of second-hand Siemens-made dentist chairs from a university, which had used them for training purposes. On import into Lebanon, clearance of the shipment was blocked because it had not been authorized by the Siemens agent. The businessman was obliged to pay the agent a large fee and was forced to pay customs duty on the chairs on the basis of the value of new chairs, in effect wiping out his anticipated profit.

rights holders; 'someone else must protect the others' (*Financial Times*, January 8, 1999).

Box 8.4. Kalbe Farma of Indonesia

Kalbe Farma PT is an Indonesian pharmaceutical company located in Jakarta Timur. The firm produces and markets medicaments for therapeutic use. Under the pre-TRIPs Indonesian patent law the firm was able to copy and sell pharmaceutical products that were protected by international patents. Such products were sold by Kalbe Farma in Indonesia and in other developing country markets, including Bangladesh, Malaysia, Myanmar, Nigeria, Sri Lanka and Vietnam. Once the government began drafting legislation to bring its IPR regime into conformity with TRIPs, management reviewed its product development strategy. Kalbe Farma production consisted of drugs that were no longer protected internationally as well as pharmaceuticals which were still under patent protection outside the country, but for which a valid patent had never been filed in Indonesia. The company was free to supply the latter to the Indonesian market, but had to exercise restraint in exporting to markets in which the patent protection was still in force. It also imported a range of products, preparations and ingredients from third party suppliers that were protected. Such imports were expected to become illegal unless acquired from the right holder or a licensee.

Management decided not to wait for the new TRIPs-consistent law to be passed. Kalbe Farma developed a new marketing and partnership strategy involving both foreign companies and Indonesian firms. It focused on securing marketing rights in Indonesia for foreign patented products and to develop and sell generic drugs no longer under patents. The company also initiated negotiations with international pharmaceutical suppliers to acquire licensing rights for a range of products in Indonesia with a view to establish a leadership position in the domestic market. Kalbe Farma also expanded its R&D, recognizing that competition in the pharmaceutical industry was likely to intensify, including through entry of foreign companies attracted by stronger patent protection.

Source: Kostecki (2001).

At the end of the day, it is impossible to generalize regarding the effect of the TRIPs agreement on individual WTO members. The design of the IPR legislation and complementary policies will play an important role. Much depends as well on the impact of IPRs on FDI, on the incentives to innovate, and on the effectiveness of IPR regimes in developing countries in protecting indigenous culture and knowledge. A case study of an Indonesian pharmaceutical firm illustrates some of the factors that will determine how firms respond to TRIPs implementation (Box 8.4).

8.6. CONCLUSION

The GATT and the GATS are similar in that the focus is primarily on market access liberalization, complemented with general rules and principles relating to the application of trade policies. Both agreements aim at reducing discrimination against foreign suppliers of products. However, as noted previously, the GATS created disciplines on certain domestic regulatory regimes that apply equally to domestic and foreign providers. An example is the requirement that an independent regulatory authority be established for the basic telecommunication industry. Similarly, the GATT has also begun to move down this track. An example are the two agreements on product standards, which require WTO members to adopt international standards if these exist and requires a 'defense' where this is not the case. However, the emphasis of multilateral disciplines pertaining to domestic regulatory policies is on procedure and on the overall framework—little substantive harmonization is imposed. Insofar as harmonization disciplines apply—as in the case of standards—the substantive norms are not developed by the WTO but by the competent international bodies, such as FAO. This is not the case with the TRIPs agreement, which establishes minimum, common standards for IPRs that must be satisfied in all WTO members. Although many of these standards were developed under WIPO auspices, TRIPs goes beyond existing conventions in a number of important areas.

The approach taken in the TRIPs agreement is somewhat analogous to a Directive in the EU context: it sets minimum standards, but leaves it to signatories to determine how these requirements will be implemented. Article 1 TRIPs states: 'Members shall be free to determine the appropriate method of implementing the provisions of this Agreement within their own legal system and practice'. Nonetheless, the TRIPs agreement obliges governments to take positive action to protect IPRs in specific ways. GATT and GATS merely impose disciplines on members if they choose to pursue certain policies.

With the TRIPs agreement, US pharmaceutical, entertainment, and information industries, which were largely responsible for getting TRIPs on the agenda, obtained much of what they sought when the negotiations were launched. Their objective was multilaterally agreed minimum standards of IPR protection in all GATT contracting parties, an obligation to enforce such standards, and the creation of an effective multilateral dispute settlement process. It is fair to say that developing countries agreed to substantially more than even an optimist might have predicted in 1986 when the round began.

There are no definitive empirical estimates of the impact of the TRIPs agreement on developing countries (see Maskus, 2000). Although the dynamic effects of the agreement are clearly vital in this regard, the conclusion by Dani Rodrik before the Uruguay Round was finalized continues to hold: 'all evidence and arguments ... point to the conclusion that, to a first-order approximation, TRIPs is a redistributive issue: irrespective of assumptions made with respect to market structure or dynamic response, the impact effect of enhanced IPR protection ... will be a transfer of wealth from [developing country] consumers and firms to foreign, mostly industrial-country firms' (Rodrik, 1994: 449). The estimates of McCalman (1999) cited above suggest that the transfer to OECD countries is not trivial, exceeding US$8 billion (in 1995 dollars). Given that the static welfare gains from the Uruguay Round accruing to developing countries were estimated to be between US$10 and 20 billion (Martin and Winters, 1996), including TRIPs in the equation significantly reduces the net gains from the round (at least in the short run).

The TRIPs agreement was signed because a trade-off was made between IPRs and the rest of the Uruguay Round agenda. The deal to abolish the MFA and reintegrate agriculture into the trading system, the acceptance of a GATS that took a positive list approach to coverage, a stronger dispute settlement mechanism, and the agreement to outlaw VERs are all likely elements in the final equation. While it is not possible to identify specific issue linkages, it is very suggestive that the transition period for the phase-out of the MFA is similar to that for developing countries to fully implement the TRIPs Agreement. There was also recognition that without TRIPs, ratification of the Uruguay Round package by the US Congress was unlikely given the political weight of the US industries supporting stronger IPR disciplines. The regime shift that occurred among many developing countries in the 1980s in attitudes towards inward FDI also played a role. Attracting FDI in certain higher-tech sectors requires enforcement of IPRs. Finally, there is little doubt that the threat of continued unilateral action on the part of the US (but also the EU) played a role.

Although the US and the EU can be expected to enforce the TRIPs agreement vigorously, developments in the late 1990s revealed a willingness, especially with respect to least-developed countries in Africa suffering from the AIDS epidemic, to be show some flexibility in pressuring countries to limit intervention. The US government issued an Executive Order in May 2000 to help make HIV and AIDS-related drugs and medical technologies more affordable and accessible in sub-Saharan African countries. The order prohibits the US government (USTR) from using Section 301 to seek the revocation or revision of IPR policies of beneficiary sub-Saharan African countries that regulate HIV or AIDS pharmaceuticals or medical technologies (for example, by allowing parallel imports or regulating prices) if such policies promote access to HIV and AIDS pharmaceuticals or medical technologies for affected populations. Another necessary condition is that the policies provide adequate and effective IPR protection consistent with the TRIPs agreement. The order does not preclude use of WTO dispute settlement mechanisms. Opposition by US pharmaceutical companies to South African policies became a high-profile issue after the US took South Africa to task for its Medicines Act, which included a provision that allowed for fast track compulsory licensing of medicines and authorization for parallel imports of medicines.[4] At about the same time as the Executive Order was issued, the pharmaceutical industry announced an initiative to reduce prices for antiretroviral drugs for developing countries. G-8 leaders also announced efforts to devote greater resources to accelerate the development and promote the distribution of vaccines for HIV and AIDS, malaria, TB, and other infectious diseases. These developments reflected a recognition of the need to balance enforcement of private rights with public health objectives and priorities. Attaining such a balance is a major challenge confronting OECD countries. An example is how to deliver on the promises made in Articles 66-7 TRIPs to identify measures to encourage the transfer of technology on 'reasonable terms'. Another is to assist developing countries devise mechanisms and build institutions to protect indigenous culture.

8.7. FURTHER READING

For an account of the US multifaceted program in the 1970s to improve the international protection of IPRs and efforts to address the issue in the GATT, see William Walker, 'Private Initiative to Thwart the Trade in Counterfeit Goods', *The World Economy* (March 1981). The role of the United States in bringing the issue of IPRs on the agenda of the Uruguay Round is described in A. Jane Bradley, 'Intellectual Property Rights, Investment, and Trade in Services in the Uruguay Round: Laying the Foundations', *Stanford Journal of International Law*, Spring (1987), 57–98. Carlos Primo Braga, 'Trade Related Intellectual Property Issues: The Uruguay Round Agreement and its Economic Implications', in Will Martin and Alan Winters (eds.), *The Uruguay Round and the Developing Countries* (Cambridge: Cambridge University Press, 1996) provides a comprehensive summary of the TRIPs negotiations and an analysis of the outcome. David Gould and William Gruben, 'The Role of Intellectual Property Rights in Economic Growth', *Journal of Development Economics*, 48 (1996), 323–50 is a useful conceptual and empirical assessment of the relationship between IPRs and economic growth. Keith Maskus,

---

[4] See the web site www.cptech/ip for more details on the history and outcome of the dispute.

Intellectual Property Rights in the Global Economy (Washington DC: Institute for International Economics, 2000) is a highly recommended book-length survey and analysis of the economic implications of the TRIPs agreement. For a summary treatment that focuses on post-Uruguay Round negotiating issues, see 'Intellectual Property Issues for the New Round' by the same author, in J. Schott (ed.), *The WTO After Seattle* (Washington DC: Institute for International Economics, 2000).

Ambassador B.K. Zutshi, India's chief negotiator during the deal-making stages of the Uruguay Round, gives an insiders' view of the TRIPs negotiations from a developing country perspective in 'Bringing TRIPs into the Multilateral Trading System', in J. Bhagwati and M. Hirsch (eds.), *The Uruguay Round and Beyond: Essays in Honour of Arthur Dunkel* (Ann Arbor: University of Michigan Press, 1998). Jayashree Watal, *Intellectual Property Rights in the World Trade Organization: The Way Forward for Developing Countries* (New Delhi: Oxford University Press, 2000) provides a comprehensive legal analysis of the TRIPs agreement, focusing in particular on the options and implications for developing countries. An excellent resource for IPR-related disputes and policy developments is www.cptech.org.

PART IV
HOLES AND LOOPHOLES

9
Safeguards and Exceptions

Virtually all international trade agreements or arrangements contain safeguard provisions and exceptions. Broadly defined, the term 'safeguard protection' refers to a provision in an agreement permitting governments under specified circumstances to withdraw—or cease to apply—their normal obligations in order to protect (safeguard) certain overriding interests. Safeguard provisions are often critical to the existence and operation of trade-liberalizing agreements, as they function as both insurance mechanisms and safety valves. They provide governments with the means to renege on specific liberalization commitments—subject to certain conditions—should the need for this arise (safety valve). Without them governments may refrain from signing an agreement that reduces protection substantially (insurance motive). This chapter focuses primarily on the safeguards and exceptions embodied in the GATT. Those of the GATS are either very similar or still in an embryonic stage.

WTO provisions in this area can be separated into two categories. The first are those that can be used in the event of the occurrence of a predefined set of circumstances which legitimize temporary increases in import barriers. The second constitute permanent exceptions to the general obligations. The first category can be further divided into those dealing with so-called 'unfair' trading practices (such as exports benefiting from actionable subsidies) and those that can be applied without having to demonstrate 'unfairness'. Provisions that allow for the temporary suspension of obligations include:

Antidumping (AD): measures to offset dumping—pricing of exports below what is charged in the home market—that materially injures a domestic industry (Article VI GATT);

Countervailing duties (CVDs): measures to offset the effect of subsidization that materially injures a domestic industry (Article VI GATT);

Balance of payments (BOP): restrictions on imports to safeguard a country's external financial position (Articles XII and XVIII:*b* GATT; Article XII GATS);

Infant industries: governmental assistance for economic development, allowing import restrictions to protect infant industries (Articles XVIII:*a* and XVIII:*c* GATT);

Emergency protection: temporary protection in cases where imports of a product cause or threaten serious injury to domestic producers of directly competitive products (Article XIX GATT);

Special safeguards: provisions embodied in the Agreements on Agriculture and Textiles and Clothing allowing for actions to be taken to restrict trade; and

General waivers: allowing members to ask for permission not to be bound by an obligation (Article IX WTO). In contrast to the other mechanisms, this requires formal approval by the WTO Council.

Provisions allowing for permanent exceptions from the general obligations of the Agreement include:

General exceptions: measures to safeguard public morals, health, laws and natural resources, subject to the requirement that such measures are nondiscriminatory and are not a disguised restriction on trade (Articles XX GATT; XIV GATS);
National security: allowing intervention on national security grounds (Articles XXI GATT; XIV*bis* GATS; 73 TRIPS); and
Renegotiation or modification of schedules: allowing for the withdrawal of concessions (bound tariff reductions or specific commitments) if compensation is offered to affected members (Articles XXVIII GATT; XXI GATS).

Most of these provisions allow for protection of a specific industry. Only three have an economy-wide rationale (balance of payments, general exceptions, national security). All the industry-specific instruments are (imperfect) substitutes for each other, as to a large extent they all address the same issue: protecting domestic firms from foreign competition. In practice the balance of payments provision was also used by developing countries to protect specific industries.

The GATS does not have provisions allowing for contingent or infant industry protection, and an analogue to GATT Article XIX remains to be drafted (see chapter 7). In large part this reflects the difficulty of applying these concepts to trade in services. The GATS does contain provisions allowing for actions to safeguard the balance of payments, for general exceptions and for renegotiation of commitments. These provisions are similar to those of the GATT, except that the language on modification of schedules differs from GATT by calling for mandatory arbitration if no agreement can be reached on compensation.

The goal of the drafters of the GATT was that renegotiation would be the primary mechanism to deal with a need for permanent rebalancing of concessions, and that Article XIX would be used to grant temporary protection to industries finding it too difficult to confront increased import competition. The AD and CVD provisions were included in large part at the behest of the US, Canada and several European nations, which had such statutes on the books, although they were rarely used. During the first 20 years of the GATT renegotiations and Article XIX were the major instruments used (Figure 9.1). Over time, however, industrialized country lobbies increasingly

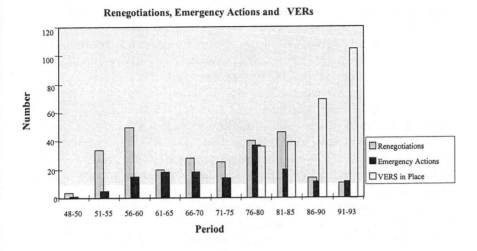

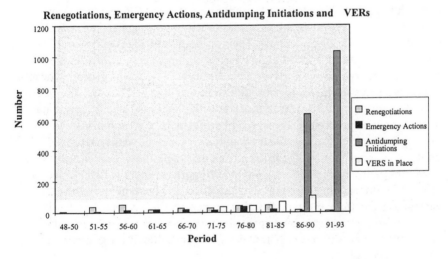

Source : Finger (1999).
FIG. 9.1 Use of safeguard instruments, 1948-93

shifted away from Article XIX actions towards VERs to obtain relief from import competition. VERs became a major instrument of protection in the 1970s as they ensured some compensation for affected exporters and were often directed against countries that did not have initial negotiating rights or principal supplier status (see chapter 4). It was estimated that in the early 1980s, VERs covered some 10 percent of world trade, and that the trade-weighted average tariff equivalent of the VERs was on the order of 15 percent (Kostecki, 1987).

As of the mid-1980s the instrument of choice became AD. Between 1980–6, the EU imposed 213 AD actions, as compared to only 10 Article XIX measures. In the same period, the US imposed five Article XIX measures, as compared to some 195 AD actions (Finger and Olechowski, 1987). The revealed preference for AD and VERs reflected the fact that the conditions that needed to be satisfied to invoke Article XIX protection were relatively stringent. As discussed below, until this was changed in the Uruguay Round, Article XIX actions had to be nondiscriminatory and affected exporters had the right to compensation (or failing adequate compensation, could seek authorization from the GATT Council to retaliate). Governments preferred VERs and AD, as these instruments allowed them to discriminate across exporting countries and did not require compensation.

Developing countries have frequently invoked Article XVIII:*b* of the GATT to justify temporary protection, often because of a desire to use QRs. If developing countries desired to impose tariffs for BOP reasons, they usually would not have to invoke Article XVIII, because most had either not bound their tariffs or had bound them at high ceiling rates. In such cases countries are free to impose higher tariffs without being confronted with a compensation requirement. Over time the use of Article XVIII:*b* by developing countries declined, in part due to efforts by the IMF and the World Bank to induce a shift towards more effective and efficient instruments to deal with BOP problems. Table 9.1 provides a brief summary of the frequency with which various instruments have been invoked. Whatever the political rationale for safeguard instruments, their mere existence may reduce competitive pressure on domestic import-competing firms. They are also all inefficient, in the sense that the costs to consumers are almost invariably larger than the benefits that accrue to the protected industry. In addition, industries can be expected to exploit substitution possibilities across instruments if these exist, making it more difficult for governments to control trade policy.

The various provisions allowing for protection under the GATT can seriously undermine the liberalizing dynamic of the WTO, and limit the usefulness of the WTO to governments that seek protection from protectionist lobbies. Governments (and their advisors) find it very difficult to sell the argument that it makes no economic sense to draft legislation that allows the various WTO provisions to be invoked. Invariably the response will be to point to the US, Canada or the EU—all active users of contingent protection. 'If they use it, why should we refrain' is a frequently heard argument. In

TABLE 9.1 *Frequency of use of safeguard provisions*

Instrument and GATT article	Frequency of use
Periodic—three year—renegotiations at the initiative of the country desiring to raise a bound tariff rate, Articles XXVIII:1 and XXVIII:5.	1955–99: 207 instances[a]
'Special circumstances' renegotiations (requires GATT authorization), Article XXVIII:4.	1948-2000: 64 instances[b]
Waivers under GATT Article XXV.	113 (through March 1994) 40 (through August 2000)
Waivers under Article IX WTO.	
Withdrawal of a concession for infant industry purposes, Article XVIII:*a*.	9 (through July 2000)[b]
Infant industry protection (requiring a release from bindings), Article XVIII:*c*.	9 (through July 2000)[b]
Measures by developing countries for BOP purposes, Article XVIII:*b*.	Used by 24 countries at least once during 1974–86 (total of 3,434 restrictions)
Emergency protection, Article XIX.	1950-94: 150 actions (3.4 per year) 1995-May 2000: 49 cases (9 per year)
Special safeguards under the ATC.	1995-97: 31 requests
Countervailing duties, Article VI.	July 1985-92: 187 actions 1995–2000: 110 measures (including undertakings) as of August 2000
Antidumping duties, Article VI.	July 1985-92: 1148 investigations 1995–June 2000: 1105 measures

[a] Renegotiations were minimal during 1995-2000 as tariffs were modified under rectification procedures or in the context of adopting the Harmonized System.
[b] Zero instances under the WTO through 2000.
Source: Finger (1996, 1999), Finger and Schuknecht (2000), WTO secretariat.

1996 developing countries as a group overtook industrialized countries in terms of the number of antidumping investigations initiated. The trends are therefore worrisome. Some progress was made to strengthen the rules in the Uruguay Round. Much remains to be done. Views on the impact of contingent protection depend significantly on whether these measures are seen as 'facilitating devices', allowing liberalization to proceed, or as mechanisms allowing for backsliding. The debate in this area is analogous to that between optimists and pessimists looking at a glass that is partially filled: an optimist says the glass is half full, the pessimist says it is half empty. Although there is general recognition that contingent protection plays an important political role, the pessimists are concerned that there are excessive opportunities to reimpose protection. Economists also emphasize that some of the instruments that are legal under the WTO make no economic sense (antidumping in particular).

9.1. RENEGOTIATION OF CONCESSIONS

The GATT allows governments to renegotiate tariff concessions and schedules (Article XXVIII). Renegotiation centers on the compensation that must be offered as a quid pro quo for raising a bound rate. Modification of schedules takes three basic forms: 'open season', which may be conducted every three years following a binding; 'special circumstances renegotiations', which may take place when approved by GATT contracting parties; and 'reserved right renegotiations', which may occur anytime during the three year period following a binding if a notification is made by interested governments to that end (Dam, 1970).

Developing countries may follow a simplified procedure to modify or withdraw concessions. In negotiating the compensation required, account is taken of the interests of the country with which the concession was originally negotiated (which has so-called 'initial negotiating rights'—INRs), the interest of the country having a 'principal supplying interest', as well as that of countries having a 'substantial interest'. Principal or substantial supplying interest requires a major or a sizeable share, respectively, in the market concerned, determined on the basis of import statistics for the last three years for which information is available.[1]

Countries having a substantial interest in the concession concerned (the negotiated tariff binding) have consultation rights only, whereas countries that have INRs or are principal suppliers, have negotiation rights. In disputed cases it is up to the Council to determine whether a given country is a principal supplier or whether it has a substantial interest. No such cases arose under GATT 1947. The main objective of the principal supplier rule is to provide for the participation in the negotiations, in addition to the country with the INRs, of countries with a larger share in the trade affected by the

---

[1] Principal supplying interest is determined with reference to the share in the export market; substantial supplying interest is determined in relation to a country's total volume of exports.

concession than the country with INRs might have. This allows a balance to be maintained between the old, previously negotiated situation and new trade patterns that emerge over time. Exceptionally, when the concession to be withdrawn affects trade which constitutes a major part of the total exports of a given country, the country may also enjoy principal supplier status (Article XXVIII:1). The Understanding on the Interpretation of Article XXVIII enhanced the opportunities of affected exporters to participate in tariff renegotiations. The WTO member for which the relative importance of exports of the product on which a tariff is increased is the highest (defined as exports of the product to the market concerned as a proportion of the country's total exports) is considered to have a principal supplying interest if it does not already have so (or an INR) under GATT 1947 procedures. If no agreement is reached on compensation, affected countries may withdraw equivalent concessions

GATS Article XXI is analogous to GATT Article XXVIII, allowing for members to withdraw commitments after a three-year period has elapsed from the time that the commitment entered into force. The intent to modify must be notified to the GATS Council, and gives rise to compensation discussions. If agreement cannot be reached on compensation, the GATS provides for arbitration (no retaliation is allowed until the arbitration process has been completed). If the recommendations resulting from the arbitration are not implemented, affected members that participated in the arbitration may retaliate without needing authorization by the GATS Council. In this respect the GATS goes beyond GATT, which only provides for countries concerned to refer disagreements regarding compensation to the Council for Trade in Goods, who may in turn 'submit their views'.

The mechanisms for—and disciplines on—modification of tariff schedules are important. Before the completion of the Uruguay Round, on average renegotiation of concessions occurred every year with respect to some 100 items, as compared to some 80,000 tariff lines bound. During the 1955–95 period over 30 GATT contracting parties utilized the renegotiation option more than 200 times (Table 9.1). In the first five years of the WTO, renegotiations did not occur due to the fact that adjustments occurred in the context of members adopting and implementing the Harmonized System (see chapter 5).

9.2. WAIVERS

Tariff renegotiations are limited in nature: by definition they only pertain to instances in which a country wants to raise tariffs above previously bound levels. Article XXV:5 GATT allows a member to request a waiver from one or more other obligations. The conditions under which waivers are granted are negotiated. Over 100 waivers were granted in the first 45 years of GATT history (Table 9.1), of which 44 were still in effect in 1994. From a systemic perspective, the waiver option allows for members to obtain an exemption from a specific rule in situations where they might otherwise have been forced to withdraw from the Agreement because of political imperatives at home. Waivers can be good or bad from an economic perspective. For example, a number of waivers were granted under GATT 1947 to countries allowing them to impose surcharges on imports for BOP purposes. Although this is an inferior instrument to deal with a BOP problem, at least it is better than the instrument called for by the relevant GATT provision—that is, QRs.

By far the most famous waiver was one requested by the US in 1955. As noted in chapter 5, QRs are allowed under Article XI of the GATT for agricultural commodities as long as concurrent measures are taken to restrict domestic production or to remove a temporary domestic surplus. Although it was the US that drafted this rule when negotiating the GATT, it proved too stringent for Congress. The latter did not wish to be bound by any international agreement and forced the Administration to ask for a waiver of this obligation in 1955. The waiver was necessary as existing US programs supported domestic industries such as sugar and dairy without incorporating any incentives to reduce output. The root of the problem was Section 22 of the Agricultural Adjustment Act, which states that the Secretary of Agriculture must advise the President if he believes any agricultural commodity is being imported so as to interfere with Department of Agriculture price support programs. Depending on the finding of an investigation into the matter, tariffs or QRs may be imposed. Because Section 22 violated GATT rules, US Administrations were reluctant to apply it. However, Congress had no such inhibitions, and amended Section 22 in 1951 to require the President to carry out its provisions regardless of international agreements, that is, the GATT (Evans, 1972: 72).

Under the WTO, disciplines on waivers were tightened. Article IX WTO allows waivers to be requested for any obligation imposed under a Multilateral Trade Agreement. Waivers under the WTO are time bound—in contrast to the GATT 1947—and are reviewed annually to determine if the exceptional circumstances requiring the waiver continue to exist. Any waiver in effect at the entry into force of the WTO was to expire by January 1997, unless extended by the WTO Ministerial Conference. Some 40 waivers were granted in the first five years of the WTO.

9.3. EMERGENCY PROTECTION AND VERS

Article XIX is GATT's general safeguard clause. It permits governments to impose emergency measures to protect domestic producers seriously injured by imports. The main rationale for the general safeguard clause is to allow some flexibility with respect to tariff commitments, thereby promoting trade liberalization efforts. Article XIX is a safety valve. Designing a safeguard mechanism in such a way that a balance is achieved between making it difficult to open the safety valve and avoiding an explosion of the boiler is not easy. The drafters of the GATT chose to be rather strict in this regard. Necessary conditions for the invocation of Article XIX under GATT 1947 were: (1) the existence of increased imports; which (2) resulted from unforeseen developments; (3) were the consequence of trade liberalization negotiated in a MTN; and (4) caused or threatened serious injury to domestic producers.

Safeguard measures were to be imposed on a nondiscriminatory basis. The interests of affected exporting countries were protected by a requirement that they be compensated. If no agreement was reached in consultations on compensation, an exporting country could be authorized to retaliate (suspend equivalent concessions or other obligations) against the safeguard-taking country. The compensation requirement made Article XIX a substitute for Article XXVIII, the main difference being that the latter allows for a permanent change. Although Article XIX actions were to be temporary in principle, no formal time limits were imposed. As a result some actions taken by contracting parties lasted for many years (Sampson, 1987).

GATT contracting parties took only 150 official safeguard actions during the 1948-94 period. Of these, only twenty involved payment or offer of compensation—mostly in earlier cases—while retaliation occurred in thirteen instances (GATT, 1994*b*). Article XIX was therefore used relatively infrequently. Reasons for this included the requirement that safeguard actions be nondiscriminatory (affect all exporters), a preference for QRs (much more difficult to implement in a nondiscriminatory manner than a tariff), the need to offer compensation, and the fact that in some jurisdictions (such as the US) granting of emergency protection is subject to the discretion of the President, who is required to take into account the impact of taking action on the economy. The relatively stringent conditions for obtaining Article XIX cover for protection reflects the fact that such protection violates earlier tariff commitments. This is not the case under AD. As dumping is defined to be unfair, actions are legitimized as long as it is shown that dumping occurred and that it materially injured domestic industries.

In addition to AD—discussed below—VERs became a favorite safeguard instrument in the 1970s and 1980s. VERs were used to restrain exports of steel and automobiles. While GATT-illegal (GATT, 1994*b*, p. 434)—with the exception of the MFA restraints, which had been sanctioned by the GATT— VERs did not give rise to formal dispute settlement cases. The reason for this was that no one had an incentive to bring cases. Third country exporters, including the principal suppliers with which original tariff concessions on the goods involved had been negotiated, did not oppose VERs restricting their (new) competitors, while affected exporters tended to accept VERs because they allowed them to capture part of the rent that was created. Instead of being confronted with an import tariff, the revenue of which is captured by the levying government, a VER involves a voluntary cut back in volume by exporters. This reduction in supply will raise prices—assuming that other exporters do not take up the slack. Exporters therefore may get more per units sold than they would under an equivalent tariff. Essentially they obtain what would be the quota rents if QRs were to be used (see annex 2). There is a very large literature on VERs that will not be discussed here (see section 9.10). The key point to remember about VERs is that they imply some direct compensation of affected exporters and selectively target exporters. Thus, they partially meet GATT 1947 compensation requirements, while allowing for the circumvention of its nondiscrimination requirement.

By the time of the Uruguay Round, the major objective of 'target' countries was to constrain the use of AD and VERs and reassert the dominance of Article XIX in instances where the need is to slow the growth of imports: the majority of cases. The problem was how to achieve this goal. Two options were available: either to tighten the disciplines on the use of VERs and AD, or to reduce the disincentives to use Article XIX. Both approaches were pursued. Little progress was achieved on the AD front, but VERs were banned and Article XIX made more attractive to import-competing industries. Progress on the latter front was facilitated because importing country governments increasingly recognized that VERs were costly—something that economists did not stop from pointing out in study after study (for example, De Melo and Tarr, 1992).

The Uruguay Round Agreement on Safeguards

A major achievement of the Uruguay Round Agreement on Safeguards is a prohibition of VERs and similar measures on the export or the import side (such as export moderation, export-price or import-price monitoring systems, export or import surveillance, compulsory import cartels and discretionary export or import licensing schemes). Any such measure in effect as of January 1995 was to be brought into conformity with the new rules or phased out by mid-1999. The agreement requires that safeguard measures be taken only if an investigation demonstrates that imports have increased so much as to have caused or threaten serious injury to an import-competing domestic industry. Investigations must include reasonable public notice to all interested parties and public hearings or other mechanisms through which traders and other affected parties can present their views whether a safeguard measure would be in the public interest. Investigating authorities must publish a report setting forth their findings and reasoning. Serious injury is defined as a significant overall impairment in the situation of a domestic industry. In determining injury, the domestic industry is defined as those firms whose collective output constitutes a major share of total domestic output of the product concerned. Factors to determine whether increased imports have caused serious injury include the magnitude of the increase in imports, their change in market share, and changes in the level of sales, production, productivity, capacity utilization, profits, and employment of the domestic industry. The Appellate Body in its case law has made clear all mentioned factors must be examined. A causal link must be established between increased imports and serious injury or threat thereof. When factors other than increased imports are causing injury to the domestic industry at the same time, such injury may not be attributed to increased imports.

Protection must be limited to what is necessary to prevent or remedy serious injury. If a QR is used, it may not reduce imports below the average level of the last three representative years, unless clear justification is given that a different level is necessary to prevent or remedy serious injury. While in principle safeguard actions must be nondiscriminatory, quota rights may be allocated on a selective basis if the Committee on Safeguards accepts that imports from certain members have increased disproportionately in comparison to the total increase in imports, and the measures imposed are equitable to all suppliers of the product. Such 'quota modulation' may be maintained for four years at the most. QRs may be administered by exporters if this is mutually agreed. Thus, although VERs are prohibited, something analogous may be used if implemented as part of a GATT-conform procedure. Safeguard actions based on absolute increases in imports that are consistent with the provisions of the Agreement do not require compensation of affected exporting countries for the first three years. In principle, safeguards should be degressive—the level of protection should decline over time—and not last more than four years. All actions are subject to a sunset clause. The maximum total number of years a safeguard may be applied is eight years. If an action is extended beyond four years, a necessary condition is that the industry is adjusting. If individual market shares of developing countries are less than three percent of total imports, and the aggregate share of such countries less than nine percent of total imports, they are exempt from safeguard actions.

The Agreement on Safeguards brought existing practices that were GATT-inconsistent inside the tent, but subjected their use to multilateral surveillance and rules. Thus, VER-type measures are allowed by the WTO under certain conditions—in contrast to GATT 1947. While this implies a move away from economically preferred policies in an abstract sense, this is an inappropriate benchmark. A better counterfactual for comparison purposes would be continued circumvention of GATT 1947 disciplines, which had become increasingly irrelevant. The ban on VERs is a major achievement. Much will depend, however, on its implementation, which in turn will be a function of the willingness of WTO members to cross-notify VERs and initiate dispute settlement procedures against countries requesting VERs. Past experience suggests that governments may not have a great incentive to do so. Another test is the extent to which quota modulation is applied.

TABLE 9.2 *Safeguard measures (1995–9)*

	1995	1996	1997	1998	1999	Total
OECD countries	2	6	2	2	6	18
Developing countries	0	1	2	10	10	23
Total	2	7	4	12	16	41

Note : OECD member countries include Mexico and Korea). Annual data span November 1 to October 31.
Source : WTO, Safeguards Committee Annual Reports.

The use of safeguards has expanded substantially compared to the pre-Uruguay Round period (Tables 9.1 and 9.2). Much of the increase reflects greater invocation of the instrument by developing countries. India, Korea and Argentina are among the countries that used safeguard actions most frequently in the post-1995 period. The US is the primary user among industrialized countries, also being a leader in the use of quota modulation. This is a worrisome development as it suggests safeguards may be used in an antidumping-like way.

Special safeguard actions have been used under the auspices of the WTO Agreement on Textiles and Clothing (ATC). The ATC contains a special safeguard clause in Article 6, which can be invoked during the implementation period of the ATC (that is, up to 2004) for products being integrated into the WTO. Actions may be taken if imports of a product increase so much as to cause or threaten serious damage to the domestic industry producing like (or directly competitive) products. Damage indicators include standard economic variables such as output, productivity, capacity utilization, inventories, market share, exports, wages, employment, domestic prices, profits and investment (Article 6.3 ATC). Transitional safeguard actions can be applied on a discriminatory basis, in contrast to measures taken under the Agreement on Safeguards. They require demonstration of a sharp and substantial increase in imports, actual or imminent, from the targeted countries. Measures are not to exceed three years duration or until the product is integrated into GATT 1994, whichever comes first. Over 30 actions under the ATC were taken between 1995-7, mostly by the US against developing country textile exporters but also by developing countries against each other (for example, Brazil has been an active user). The measures are reviewed by the Textiles Monitoring Body, and many were rescinded. Two actions led to dispute settlement cases, both involving the US. In both cases, the panels, supported by the Appellate Body, concluded that the US had violated the provisions of the ATC.[2] The panels signaled that the transitional safeguards in ATC were to be regarded as exceptional instruments and that members invoking this provision of the ATC had to be in full compliance with the various criteria laid out in the agreement.

9.4. ANTIDUMPING ACTIONS

Loosely defined, dumping occurs when a firm sells products on an export market for less than what is charged on its home market for the same product. Dumping is also said to occur if the export price of a product is below the cost of production. WTO rules allow action to be taken against dumped imports if dumping causes or threatens material injury to a domestic import-competing industry. This is a weaker standard than the serious injury criterion used in the case of safeguards. AD is an option—there is no requirement to have an AD mechanism. WTO disciplines apply only if the option is invoked. Over 3,000 AD investigations have been initiated by WTO members since the late 1970s, of which over 2,000 occurred in the 1985–99 period. Between 1995 and 1999, during the first five years of the WTO, over 1,000 investigations were initiated (Table 9.3). The main users of AD have traditionally been Australia, Canada, the EU, and the US. Since the creation of the WTO, the use of AD by developing countries has increased dramatically. The top users of AD in 1999 included Argentina, Brazil, India and

---

[2] Costa Rica vs. United States: Restrictions on Imports of Cotton and Man-Made Fibre Underwear, WT/DS24/AB/R (10 February 1997); India vs. United States: Measures Affecting Imports of Shirts and Blouses, WT/DS33/AB/R (25 April 1997).

South Africa. Mexico, an OECD member, became a major user during 1992–95. China is the most frequent target, followed by the US. If expressed in terms of cases per dollar of exports, AD tends to be much more important against developing economies. As of the late 1990s, AD was disproportionally used by developing economies and against developing economies (Finger and Schuknecht, 2000). AD duties tend to be very high when compared to the average tariff applied on manufactures in OECD nations. Duties of 30 to 50 percent are common.

TABLE 9.3 *Antidumping actions (1995–9)*

	1995	1996	1997	1998	1999	Total
OECD countries	114	64	105	136	152	571
Developing countries	46	85	95	97	139	462
Total	160	149	200	233	291	1,033

Note: OECD includes Mexico and Korea).
Source: WTO, Antidumping Committee, Annual Reports.

At the time the GATT was first negotiated, AD was a non-issue. It was included because a number of countries had legislation on the books, but it was rarely used. In 1950, there were only 37 cases, of which 21 taken by South Africa (GATT, 1958, p.14). AD became increasingly controversial during the 1980s as its use expanded. Fifteen AD actions taken by contracting parties were challenged in GATT between 1989–94, of which five led to the creation of panels. In all cases the panel found against the country that had taken the AD action, and in a number of instances recommended that illegal AD duties be removed and reimbursed (Petersmann, 1994). This was very controversial, and led to dispute settlement in this area becoming a major issue in the Uruguay Round. Users sought to circumscribe the power of panels to conclude that specific AD actions violated GATT requirements, or to recommend restitution of duties in cases where AD measures had been imposed in violation of GATT rules.

A Brief Summary of GATT Disciplines

The basic GATT provision dealing with AD is Article VI. Starting in the Kennedy Round, reflecting increasing use of AD, attempts began to be made to further define multilateral disciplines in this area. A code on AD was negotiated in the Kennedy Round. It was opposed by the US Congress, and in practice was only applied insofar as its provisions were consistent with US legislation. In the Tokyo Round, the AD code was renegotiated. This code—which only bound signatories—became the basis of the Uruguay Round agreement on AD (formally entitled the Agreement on Implementation of Article VI).

Dumping is defined in GATT as offering a product for sale in export markets at a price below normal value. Normal value is defined as the price charged by a firm in its home market, in the ordinary course of trade. Trade is considered not to be ordinary if over an extended period of time (normally one year) a substantial quantity of goods is sold at less than average total costs (the sum of fixed and variable costs of production plus selling, general and administrative costs). If sales on its domestic market are too small to allow price comparisons, the highest comparable price charged in third markets is used. Alternatively, the exporting firm's estimated costs of production plus a reasonable amount for profits, administrative, selling and any other expenses may be used to determine normal value (the so-called constructed value). In cases where there is no export price or where it appears to the investigating authorities that the export price is unreliable because of a relationship between the parties to a transaction, the export price may also be constructed. Constructed values should be based on the price at which the imported products are first resold to an independent buyer, or if they are not resold to an independent buyer, 'on such reasonable basis as the authorities may determine'. The comparison of the export price and the normal value must be made at the same level of trade (normally ex-factory) and as close as possible to the same time. Allowance is to be made for differences in factors such as the conditions and terms of sale, the quantities involved, physical characteristics, and differences in relevant costs. In an investigation, exporters must be allowed at least 60 days to adjust their export prices to reflect sustained movements in exchange rates during the period of investigation.

Actions against dumping may only be taken if it can be shown that it has caused or threatens material injury of the domestic import-competing industry. Injury determinations must be based on positive evidence and involve an objective examination of the volume of the dumped imports, their effect on prices in the domestic market, and the impact on domestic producers of like products. A significant increase in dumped imports, either in absolute terms or relative to production or consumption in the importing country, is a necessary condition for finding injury. Significant price undercutting of domestic producers, a significant depressing effect on prices, or the level of the dumping margin are other indicators that may be used. The term significant is not defined. While differences in views as to what is significant might be dealt with through the dispute settlement process, this possibility is limited as panels are constrained in their ability to overrule substantive decisions taken by domestic investigating authorities (see below).

An illustrative list of injury indicators is given in the agreement. These include actual and potential decline in sales, profits, output, market share, productivity, return on investments, or utilization of capacity; factors affecting domestic prices; the magnitude of the margin of dumping; actual and potential negative effects on cash flow, inventories, employment, wages, growth, ability to raise capital or investments. This list is not exhaustive, and no single or combination of factors is decisive. Dumped imports must be found to cause injury because of dumping. The necessary causality must be established on the basis of all relevant evidence before the authorities. Any other known factors that are injuring the domestic industry must be taken into account, and may not be attributed to the dumped imports. Factors that may be relevant include the volume and prices of imports not sold at dumping prices, contraction in demand or changes in the patterns of consumption, trade restrictive practices of—and competition between—the foreign and domestic producers, developments in technology, and the export performance and productivity of the domestic industry.

This very brief summary of the major elements of the AD agreement illustrates that the wording is technical and complex. Many of its articles are only decipherable for lawyers specialized in this particular area of trade law. The wording of the agreement reflects numerous compromises reached in the Tokyo and Uruguay Rounds. It is a combination of elements of the domestic laws and practices of major WTO members and periodic attempts by target countries to limit the protectionist biases inherent in the use of AD in most jurisdictions. These biases have proven difficult to eradicate. The reason for this is simple: AD is fundamentally flawed from an economic perspective and cannot be fixed by tinkering with the methodological arcana of investigations. For all practical purposes, there is nothing wrong with dumping, as it is a normal business practice. The problem is antidumping. As argued by Finger (1993a), the only way to deal with AD is through efforts by negatively affected parties (consumers, users) to alter domestic implementing legislation to allow their interests to be represented in AD cases.

What's Wrong With Dumping?

Dumping is not prohibited by the WTO. All the WTO does is to establish certain rules that apply to governments that seek to offset dumping. Why dumping occurs is not considered relevant under GATT rules. From a normative, economic, perspective this is important, however. A typology of business motivations for dumping is presented in Table 9.4.

TABLE 9.4 *Motivations for dumping*

Type of dumping	Objectives of the exporting firm
Sporadic or random	No deliberate intention to dump
Price discrimination	Maximize profits given differences in demand across markets
Cyclical	Cover at least variable costs and maintain capacity during periods of slack demand
Defensive	Minimize losses due to excess capacity or to deter entry by competitors
Scale economies	Price below cost initially with expectation of re-couping investment outlays (fixed costs) over time as sales expand
Market-creating	To establish a new product as the market leader—revenue, not profit maximization
Head-on	To attack a dominant supplier in an export market
Predatory	To establish a monopoly on an export market

Sporadic dumping may occur without any deliberate intention if the exporting firm has to decide on how much to produce before demand conditions or exchange rates are known. Sporadic dumping may also arise from a lack of experience in pricing a new product. The trading environment facing a firm is usually uncertain, so dumping will often be beyond the control of a firm. For example, unexpected changes in exchange rates may lead a firm to dump even if it had no intention of doing so. However, in most cases dumping reflects a deliberate business strategy followed by exporting companies and constitutes a conscious, premeditated pricing practice aimed at the accomplishment of specific business objectives.

The best known motivation is simple price discrimination between markets. The wording of GATT rules specifically targets this rationale. A firm having some control over prices and operating in two separate markets may find it advantageous to discriminate in its price formation in favor of foreign consumers in order to maximize profits. Price discrimination across markets will occur whenever demand for a product is more elastic in export markets than at home (that is, for any given change in price, foreign consumers change their demand more than domestic customers. Dumping in the sense of spatial price discrimination requires that there are barriers to reimportation of the dumped product into the exporter's home market. Otherwise, price differentials across markets would tend to be eliminated through arbitrage, allowing for transport and transactions costs. As discussed further below, this suggests that the problem with dumping—if any—are the trade barriers that prevent such arbitrage.

As noted above, selling below average total cost can also constitute dumping, and it is not strictly necessary that prices charged in the export market be below those charged at home. Issues of trade policy and differing price elasticities then become irrelevant.[3] The cost-dumping case is important in practice, because many exporters produce exclusively or predominately for export, or sell only specific products for export. Often it may be in a firm's interest to sell below variable or even marginal costs (the cost of producing an extra unit of output) for a while. Although by doing so the firm will make a loss (because its fixed costs are not recovered), this may be necessary in the short run to establish or increase market share, or to enable the firm to move down its learning curve, thus increasing expected long-run profits.

A firm may engage in cyclical dumping to stabilize its production over the business cycle. Dumping arises as the firm reduces prices to cover only average variable costs during periods of slack demand. This can be perfectly rational, insofar as the firm expects better times in the future and perceives the costs of laying off workers and reducing capacity to be higher than continuing production without covering all costs. Indeed, differences in labor markets and employment practices of firms across countries are one factor explaining why firms from some countries are more prone to engage in cyclical dumping than others (Ethier, 1982). If it is very costly for a firm to lay off workers—because of high legislated redundancy payments for example—it will continue to produce more than a firm which confronts a very flexible and less regulated labor market.

Certain forms of dumping have a pronounced strategic dimension. Exporting at prices below production cost may help deter entry by potential competitors into a firm's home market. This can be called defensive dumping (Davies and McGuinness, 1982). A firm may also price exports below total production cost on a longer term basis if such a strategy permits it to realize economies of scale (these exist if unit costs decline as output expands). A firm may need to move down its learning curve as fast as possible. As output increases, production workers tend to become more efficient and unit costs of production fall. Dumping in these cases is part of a strategy to attain an optimal scale of production.

---

[3] The price elasticity of demand for a product is defined as the ratio of the percentage change in the quantity demanded to the percentage change in the price. For example, if prices increase by five percent and the corresponding quantity decreases by more than five percent, demand is price elastic.

A related rationale for dumping arises in cases of new high-technology products (such as video recorders in the 1970s and early 1980s). Here a firm may attempt to discourage domestic firms from engaging in the development of a competing product by establishing a large market share. Products where there is proprietary technology may foster dumping in the early stages of the product cycle. Profitability in such products often depends on consumers choosing a specific standard. In the video case, there were two main competing standards or formats in the 1970s, VHS and Betamax. Both needed to attract enough adherents to form a large enough customer base to recoup investment in R&D. When firms are trying to establish market share quickly, dumping may be part of an effective competitive strategy. A firm may also choose to export at prices that do not cover even marginal cost when, instead of maximizing profit, it prefers to maximize sales. Such 'head-on dumping' may be used as part of an attack on a price leader in a given export market. Head-on dumping was practiced extensively by Japanese semi-conductor and electronics' producers in export markets in the 1980s (Kotler et al., 1987).

The foregoing rationales for dumping are driven by market structures, business cycles, or the characteristics of the products that are produced. Of these deliberate strategies, only one is potentially detrimental to the welfare of the country importing the dumped product: predation. Predation was the original rationale for US AD legislation, passed in 1916. The fear was that a foreign firm (or cartel) could deliberately price products low enough to drive existing domestic firms out of business and establish a monopoly. Once established, the monopolist could more than recoup its losses by exploiting its market power. For predation to work, the monopolist (cartel) must not only eliminate domestic competition, it must also be able to prohibit entry by new competitors. For this to be possible it must either have a global monopoly or it must convince the importing government to impose or tolerate entry restrictions. It is not clear why a government would do this. Not surprisingly, in practice, post-Second World War cases of successful predatory dumping are the exception, not the rule. Research by economists has demonstrated that over 90 percent of all AD investigations would never have been launched if a competition standard—potential threat of injury to competition, as opposed to injury to competitors—had been used as a criterion (Messerlin, 2000). Proponents of AD often have a narrower definition of predation in mind than the economic one described above. The fact that competition from other, outside sources will in most realistic circumstances prevent the formation of a monopoly is considered irrelevant. What matters is the (continued) existence of the domestic industry. But AD will not help in achieving this objective. What is needed is adjustment of the industry, something that AD is unlikely to encourage.

Import-competing firms usually object to underselling, and not to price discrimination or selling below cost. This has been emphasized by de Jong (1968), who noted that popular opinion refers to dumping when foreign producers are able to undersell the domestic supplier in his own market. As described by de Jong, this notion was translated as social dumping in early discussions concerning AD legislation. While this term was not clearly defined, it was apparent that it referred to underselling by foreign firms in the domestic market, made possible by lower labor costs abroad (that is, comparative advantage). In practice, it is underselling that importing-competing firms consider unfair, reflecting their inability or unwillingness to meet the price set by a foreign competitor.

That predation has very little to do with AD as it is practiced is perhaps best illustrated by the United States, which has two antidumping statutes. One, the Antidumping Act of 1916, maintains a predation standard for antidumping, and is very rarely invoked. The other, the Tariff Act of 1930, as amended, has a price and cost-discrimination standard, and is the one usually invoked by import-competing industries. Interestingly, the 1916 Act was the subject of dispute settlement cases in 1998. The cases, brought by the EU and Japan, alleged that the existence of the 1916 Act violated the national treatment rule and WTO disciplines on AD (which stipulate that the remedy to offset dumping is limited to AD duties and undertakings). Japan objected to the provisions of the Act that the importation or sale of imported goods that is found to be unlawful (predatory) may constitute a criminal offence and give rise to claims for damages. The trigger for bringing the case to the WTO was a court action brought under the 1916 Act against affiliates of Japanese companies. These cases are somewhat ironic, in that there is a valid rationale for imposing civil liabilities or criminal penalties in cases where predation is found to exist, as long as the same disciplines apply to domestic firms. A problem in this instance is that US competition authorities may not intervene against pricing practices of firms that are in violation of the 1916 Act, as competition law enforcement has evolved significantly since that statute was passed.

What's Wrong with Antidumping?

AD constitutes straightforward protectionism that is packaged to make it look like something different. By calling dumping unfair, the presumption is that AD is fair and thus a good thing. This is good marketing, but bad economics. From an economic perspective there is nothing wrong with most types of dumping. AD is not about fair play. Its goal is to tilt the rules of the game in favor of import-competing industries (Finger, 1999).

Advocates of AD policies sometimes argue that AD is a justifiable attempt by importing country governments to offset the market access restrictions existing in an exporting firm's home country that underlie the ability of such firms to dump. Such restrictions may consist of import barriers preventing arbitrage, but may also reflect the nonexistence or weak enforcement of competition law by the exporting country. For example, the US has claimed that lax Japanese antitrust enforcement permits Japanese firms to collude, raise prices, and use part of the resulting rents to cross-subsidize (dump) products sold on foreign markets. AD is clearly an inferior instrument to address foreign market closure because it does not deal with the source of the problem—the government policies that artificially segment markets, or allow this to occur. An AD duty may put pressure on affected firms to lobby their government to eliminate such policies—or to abolish private business practices that restrict entry—but does so in a very indirect manner. Once investigations are initiated, any changes in policies or practices cannot have an impact on the finding. In many cases there will not be significant barriers to entry, so there is not much to be done by exporters to improve access to their home markets. Indeed, under current procedures no account is taken of whether price discrimination or selling below cost is the result of market-access restrictions. Building this into the analysis would appear to be a first necessary step.

A key problem with AD is the discretion that often is granted to investigating authorities—or, alternatively, the guidelines under which such authorities are forced to operate by law—to follow procedures that can make the instrument blatantly protectionist. In practice methodologies used to determine whether dumping has occurred and calculate the size of the dumping margin are such that high positive margins can be found in many circumstances. An often-used practice is to calculate dumping margins by using methodologies that raise the normal value and lower the average export price, thereby increasing the dumping margin. Normal values can be biased upward by not including sales in the home market made at prices considered to be below cost, and by excluding sales in the export market that are above the calculated normal value. The latter procedure has been justified on the basis that 'sales at a high price should not be allowed to conceal dumped sales' (Hindley, 1994: 97). In cases where the normal value is constructed on the basis of costs, dumping margins can be inflated through the inclusion of high profit and overhead margins in the calculation of the normal value, but not allowing for this in the calculation of the costs of sales for exports.'

Another problem is that injury criteria may be manipulated by firms. This is potentially of some importance, as the injury test tends to be the main factor constraining the access of import-competing industries to protection (Finger and Murray, 1990). Indicators of injury include trends in market share, employment, profits, capacity, capacity utilization, import penetration, and price underselling (the exporters charging prices below what is charged by the import-competing industry). Many of these variables will not be closely linked to trends in imports, but depend on business cycle influences. While all of these indicators may to some extent be correlated with injury, many can be manipulated by firms, thus creating an incentive for 'indirect rent-seeking' by either feigning that criteria have been met, or by deliberately taking actions that will induce injury as defined in the law (Leidy and Hoekman, 1991). This enhances the threat effect of AD, and may foster so-called cascading of protection.

Under AD, protection follows automatically if the criteria are satisfied. Potential countervailing forces—such as users and consumers—remain outside the administrative process and are effectively neutralized by the law—they do not have legal standing in most jurisdictions. By invoking instruments of contingent protection, an upstream industry that produces an input may significantly injure a downstream industry that uses the input. This increases the probability that downstream firms will seek and gain protection in turn. Indeed, by initiating and winning an AD action, upstream suppliers may be able to manipulate the health of downstream firms to the advantage of both (Hoekman and Leidy, 1992a). As a result, instances of contingent protection may cascade along the chain of production.[4]

This vertical linkage across instances of contingent protection illustrates one way in which AD procedures may facilitate cartelization along the production stream. AD and similar laws may also facilitate tacit or explicit collusion by enforcing existing cartels and substantially reducing price competition in affected markets (Messerlin, 1989, 1990). A credible threat of invocation of unfair-trade laws may provide a means for industries to engage in implicit collusion that could not otherwise be maintained (Leidy, 1994a). AD and similar procedures are initiated by private parties (firms or industry associations). These interested parties are active in pursuing the adoption of more restrictive rules, and employing credible threats of invocation of pro-

---

[4] Research by Feinberg and Kaplan (1992) provides evidence of cascading. In a statistical analysis of all antidumping and countervailing duty cases during the period 1980-86 brought by US producers and users of metals, they found that user industries tended to file for protection after upstream industries, and that the share of all cases accounted for by downstream industries increased significantly over time. Analysis of cases involving producers and users of chemicals led to the same finding.

cedures to negotiate VERs. The expansion of the scope and use of unfair-trade laws has been characterized as reflecting the de facto privatization of trade policy (Messerlin, 1990).

Matters are made worse from a competition and transparency perspective by the practice of negotiating price undertakings with exporters that are subject to AD investigations. Once a preliminary dumping or injury margin has been established, exporters will have some sense of the likely magnitude of the final AD duty that could be imposed. This provides them with an incentive to offer to raise their prices (or cut back supply). Offering such undertakings is explicitly allowed for in the EU's AD legislation (EEC Regulation no. 2423/88), and AD investigations frequently result in undertakings being accepted by the European Commission. The US does not accept undertakings, but in practice similar deals are struck, the difference being that US industry is given (informal) assurances by exporters that they will reduce exports or raise prices. Such agreements often explain why US AD petitions are withdrawn at some point after an investigation has been launched. Undertakings are akin to VERs, and are concluded for the same reasons. Exporters prefer them to the alternative of paying AD duties. With an undertaking they can at least capture some of the rents that are created by reducing supply. The downside of undertakings is similar to the downside of VERs—they are less transparent to domestic users and consumers. Indeed, often it will not be generally known that there are undertakings in place. They may also hide a variety of collusive practices. Undertakings clearly are more detrimental to the national welfare of countries using them than duties are, raising the question why they are used. Possible explanations include transaction costs—it is easier for an administration to rely on industry to carry the burden of monitoring whether a deal is implemented than having customs apply discriminatory tariffs—and foreign policy considerations. By transferring rents abroad, the negative impact on trading partners is reduced.

It is often pointed out that one way to attenuate the negative effects of AD on national welfare is to impose filters that require determining what the likely impact on the economy would be of imposing AD duties. So-called public interest clauses can be introduced that require the authorities to do this. They have not been very effective in practice, in part because the 'public interest' is not defined clearly enough, and in part because those that will be affected negatively are often not consulted. Although losers may be effectively excluded from the process of determining whether to intervene, they do have access to the political system, and may have a strong enough incentive to seek to change the law so that the interests of users are considered. Developments in this direction occurred in the EU and the US during the 1990s. In 1996, the US Congress held hearings on possible modifications to US AD law, pressured to do so by influential industries that relied heavily on imports of components. In the EU, consumer groups have become more vocal and the EU Commission is becoming somewhat more sensitive to the welfare implications of antidumping. For example, in a 1994 case concerning imports of gum rosin, the Commission concluded that 'the negative effects of antidumping measures on the users of gum rosin would be overwhelmingly disproportionate to the benefits arising from antidumping measures in favor of the Community industry'.[5] This finding was motivated by the fact that the EU industry's production capacity was limited, so that imposition of duties would substantially increase the production costs for industries that use gum rosin as an input. Accordingly, the Commission concluded 'that protective measures would not be appropriate and that it would not be in the Community interest to continue the proceeding'. The EU has also become more restrained in taking AD actions against imports from Eastern European nations, many of which are in the process of accession to the EU. The environment in major OECD countries thus may be slowly turning away from the enthusiastic use of AD that characterized the late 1980s and early 1990s (Finger, 1999). However, as noted, developing countries are stepping into the breach.

The Uruguay Round Agreement

The WTO Antidumping Agreement made some progress in disciplining the use of AD. A sunset clause was added. AD duties are to be terminated within five years of imposition, unless a review determines that both dumping and injury caused by dumped imports continues to persist or that removal of the measure would likely lead to the recurrence of dumping and injury. *De minimis* rules were agreed to. Duties may not be imposed if dumping margins are less than two percent, or the level of injury is negligible, or the market share of a firm is less than three percent and cumulatively less than seven percent for all exporters supplying less than three percent. Discretion with respect to methodologies used to determine dumping and injury margins was reduced. In effect, practices such as the biased averaging methodologies described earlier were authorized, but subjected to certain constraints. While these changes made AD somewhat less protectionist, many of the practices that were identified in the 1980s as leading to significant protectionist biases remained untouched.

---

[5] Official Journal, L 41/54, 12 February 1994.

For example, although the agreement calls for an 'average-to-average' comparison of home and export prices in the determination of dumping, authorities may compare a normal value that has been calculated on a weighted average basis with the prices of individual transactions (that is, not take into consideration export sales above normal value), if they 'find a pattern of export prices which differ substantially among different purchasers, regions, or time periods and if an explanation is provided why such differences cannot be taken into account appropriately by the use of a weighted average to weighted average or transaction-to-transaction comparison' (Article 2.4.2). The first condition will usually be met, so much depends on the extent to which explanations are demanded. As no objective criteria have been established—only an explanation is required—this does not appear to be much of a constraint. However, given that before the Uruguay Round, US investigating authorities consistently refused to use average-to-average comparisons, the requirement under the WTO to do so—even though subject to loopholes—was an improvement (Palmeter, 1995).

Procedural biases and methodological abuses are very difficult, if not impossible to regulate away given the definition of dumping. For example, the requirement that AD duties be terminated within five years would appear to be a major improvement from an economic welfare point of view. In practice this may not be a binding constraint, however, as it is conditional upon whether a review investigation finds that dumping and injury continues (or threatens) to persist. Another example pertains to the definition of an interested party in AD cases. This provides users and final consumers of the import a voice during the investigations, but restricts them to providing evidence that is relevant to the determination of dumping, or injury to domestic firms that compete with the imported product. The fact that a duty or undertaking may injure their proper business is not a factor that can be brought forward. The agreement also does not require any consideration of the economy-wide impact of AD duties, the state of competition in the domestic market, let alone an investigation into the market access conditions prevailing in the exporter's home market.

Although the WTO's general dispute settlement mechanism applies, Article 17.6 of the AD Agreement restricts the ability of panels to focus on the substance of a case, as they are required to accept any 'reasonable interpretation' of the facts put before an AD domestic authority. In cases where the Agreement can be interpreted in more than one way, a decision by investigating AD authorities must be accepted if it is based upon one of the permissible interpretations. New information that was not available or used by investigating authorities may not be used by a panel to overturn an AD action (Finger, 1994). In many cases panels will be limited to determining whether the procedural requirements of the Agreement were violated. As noted by Palmeter (1995), a major goal of US user industries in the Uruguay Round was to limit the ability of GATT panels to overturn domestic AD decisions. The standard of review embodied in the Agreement reflects the power of the industries supporting AD. This lobby was strong enough to make this specific issue a deal breaker for the US. It obtained most of what it sought.

Little was done in the Uruguay Round negotiations to discipline AD because the talks were essentially conducted between the users of antidumping measures on the one hand, and the countries that pursued export-oriented development strategies on the other. This meant that the negotiations differed substantially from those in the Tokyo and the Kennedy Rounds, where the negotiating process mainly involved user countries. The user-exporter dichotomy made it difficult to come up with a balanced package deal in the Uruguay Round. Exporting country governments had little to offer in the negotiations. As dumping is a private practice, governments cannot and should not prohibit it. Countries such as Japan, Hong Kong, Korea and Singapore considered that their export trade was detrimentally affected by AD measures, and made many proposals to discipline the use of methodologies that were biased toward finding high dumping and injury margins. In this they had some success, in that practices that were tolerated but not explicitly subject to GATT disciplines became subject to multilateral rules specifying the conditions under which they could be used.

A number of contentious practices could not be resolved in this manner. A good example pertains to so-called anticircumvention measures, which Japan and Korea sought to subject to multilateral rules. Exporting firms may try to circumvent AD actions by establishing assembly plants either in the importing country (where the final product has become subject to AD duties) or in third countries. Anticircumvention became an important issue in AD enforcement as of the late 1980s. In June 1987, the EU adopted legislation allowing measures to be imposed to prevent circumvention of antidumping measures on finished products. Such measures could be applied to products assembled or produced in the EU, using imported materials or parts. In the year following adoption of this Regulation, the EU initiated investigations on electronic typewriters, electronic scales, excavators, and photocopiers. All of these products were assembled or produced by Japanese-related companies in the EU.

Japan challenged the anticircumvention measures before the GATT, arguing that the existence of dumping and injury related to imports of components was not investigated. It also held that the provision contained GATT-inconsistent local content requirements as it stipulated that duties could be imposed if the value of components originating in the country subject to the initial AD duty exceeded the value of all other parts by a specified margin. Finally, Japan noted that the duties were imposed only on manufacturers associated with foreign companies that were already subject to AD duties. Domestic producers were not affected even if they used the same imported components (discrimination). Australia, Hong Kong and Singapore made detailed submissions critical of the EU circumvention regulation. The EU argued that the anticircumvention provision was adopted after experience had shown that the initiation of AD action was frequently followed by the establishment of assembly operations in the EU motivated by a desire to circumvent AD duties. The US supported the EU's objective of combating circumvention of AD duties, it having similar concerns.

The GATT panel that considered the case concluded that the anticircumvention duties on the finished products, being levied on products manufactured within the EU, were not customs duties but internal taxes. Because these were levied on a discriminatory basis, they were inconsistent with national treatment. The EU was requested to bring the application of its anticircumvention mechanism into conformity with GATT obligations. Although Japan won this battle, as adopted panel reports become part of the GATT case law, it did not win the war. No agreement emerged on anticircumvention in the Uruguay Round, as negotiators could not agree on a specific text. The matter was referred back to the Committee on Antidumping Practices.

Numerous disputes have been brought to the WTO regarding the imposition of AD measures. As the agreement's procedural rules are complex and technical, investigating authorities, especially those in developing countries, may find it difficult to jump through all the hoops that are established by the WTO. One can speculate that to some extent the strategy that was pursued in the Uruguay Round was to make it more costly for industry and government agencies to undertake AD actions. Such costs impact disproportionately on developing countries, both as respondents and as users of AD. Space constraints prohibit a detailed discussion of the various dispute settlement cases in the area of AD. Interested readers are referred to the home page of the WTO and the sources mentioned in section 9.10 below.

To recap, dumping is rarely an anticompetitive practice. Predatory pricing is possible, but will not be profitable as long as governments ensure that markets remain contestable. At the same time, AD creates a large number of distortions. The existence of AD induces rent-seeking behavior on the part of import-competing firms, and leads exporting firms to alter production, allocation, and production-location decisions in ways that can easily reduce welfare at home and abroad. The threat effects of AD are important and insufficiently recognized. AD can imply substantial uncertainty regarding the conditions of market access facing exporters and increase the costs of goods for importers. The chilling effect on imports of AD threats can be great. The start of an investigation is a signal to importers to diversify away from targeted suppliers. This signal is strengthened once provisional findings have been issued. These create incentives for the conclusion of agreements with affected exporters. The use of AD to arrive at VER-type undertakings is particularly troublesome. Threat effects can also arise under Article XIX-type safeguard protection, but these will generally be less distorting. Safeguards are more transparent, nondiscriminatory, less arbitrary, and less prone to capture. AD mechanisms are an option allowed under the WTO; they are not required. The best option for governments concerned with equity and efficiency is not to pass AD legislation, and to abolish it if it exists. Safeguards are a much better and more honest instrument to address the problem AD is used for—providing import-competing industries with time to adjust to increased foreign competition (Finger, 1999).

Given that current AD procedures make no attempt to determine whether markets are uncontestable, one way to reduce the protectionist bias that is inherent in the status quo is for governments to put greater effort into determining whether the conditions alleged to give rise to 'unfair trade' actually exist. Suggestions that have been made in this regard include making antidumping conditional on a determination that the exporters' home market is not contestable, and shifting away from an 'injury to competitors' standard towards an 'injury to competition standard' (Hoekman and Mavroidis, 1996; Messerlin, 2000). Greater efforts should also be made to consider the economy-wide effects of taking action by giving users the legal standing to defend their interests. The basic problem is a political economy one: there are powerful vested interests that are in favor of AD. This suggests that a necessary condition for AD reform is greater mobilization of countervailing forces in the domestic political arena. In addition to users, one group that may see its incentives to push for AD reforms increase is the exporter community. The more that developing countries start to use AD against high-income country exporters, the less inclined such firms may be to accept the ongoing geographic spread of this instrument.

9.5. MEASURES TO COUNTERVAIL SUBSIDIZED IMPORTS

Countervailing duty (CVD) or antisubsidy procedures, similar to AD, are allowed under Article VI of the GATT. The objective is again to ensure 'fair competition'. As noted in chapter 5, while the GATT prohibits export subsidies on manufactures, it permits other types of subsidies. However, unless a subsidy is in the 'green box' (the set of permitted and nonactionable measures), governments that consider that their industries are materially injured by imports benefiting from subsidies may impose countervailing measures. A necessary condition is that an investigation determines that imports have been subsidized and have caused material injury to domestic industry. The procedures to be followed in subsidy and injury investigations are described in detail in the Agreement on Subsidies and Countervailing Measures, which in turn is largely based on the Tokyo Round Subsidies Code. As in the case of AD disciplines, the injury test is the key element underlying the agreement's implicit objective of reconciling legitimate national government subsidy policies with the interests of nations affected by those policies. That is, the focus is on dealing with the externality created by foreign government policies.

The US has been the largest user of CVD mechanisms, initiating over 100 investigations since 1985. A substantial number of these CVD cases were not brought to a conclusion, reflecting the introduction of trade-restricting bilateral agreements, as in the cases of many steel products. Other major players such as the EU and Japan have made little use of the CVD mechanism. In part this is because other policies for safeguarding producers' interests are available and easier to implement (AD), and in part because many countries fear that initiation of CVD investigations could lead to retaliatory investigations. As the US does not devote many resources to explicit subsidization of manufacturing, its government has never felt constrained in using CVDs. The use of CVDs has been relatively constant over time. It dipped in the mid-1990s, but picked up noticeably in 1998-9 (Table 9.5).

TABLE 9.5 *Countervailing duties (1992–9)*

	Total, 1992-94	1995	1996	1997	1998	1999	Total, 1995-99
OECD countries	97	10	5	7	18	32	72
Developing countries	40	7	2	2	1	8	20
Total	137	17	7	9	19	40	92

Note: OECD includes Mexico and Korea; annual data spans July 1 to June 30.
Source: WTO, Committee Annual Reports.

One reason for the increase was a more active stance on the part of the EU (which initiated no CVD actions during 1990-95) and New Zealand. The EU, Brazil and South Africa are among the main targets of CVDs. One would have expected a decline in the incidence of CVDs since the Uruguay Round was concluded, given the six-year peace clause contained in the Agriculture Agreement and the greater clarity that was achieved in the Subsidies Agreement regarding what types of subsidies are not countervailable. The US reports that cases initiated during 1988–97 affected only 0.7 percent of total imports, a decline by 50 percent compared to the 1984-94 period, when 1.4 percent of imports were affected (Finger and Schuknecht, 2000). Available data suggest that CVDs are lower than AD duties. In the case of the US, CVDs averaged less than five percent in 80 percent of cases launched between 1995 and 1999.

Political Economy of Countervailing Duties

There are two possible rationales for responding to foreign subsidy policies via import restrictions. The first is to offset the injurious effect of such policies on domestic industries. The second is to induce the foreign government to change its policy. The first rationale has little economic merit, as the imposition of import barriers (CVDs) distorts the decisions of consumers, and will generally reduce the welfare of the country taking action. A subsidy granted to a foreign firm will generally only be one aspect of the industrial policy that is applied by a foreign government. Such governments may also pursue direct and indirect tax policies, engage in investments in infrastructure, and so forth. Given the difficulty of determining the real (general equilibrium) effect of any kind of foreign industrial policy, it will always be very difficult, if not impossible, to determine the appropriate counter action.

The argument that restricting imports of products that have benefited from unfair government assistance can be justified as a means of inhibiting the use of such measures has greater economic merit (Deardorff and Stern, 1987). It may be the case that even though a CVD is welfare reducing in the short run, the threat of CVDs induces foreign governments to refrain from subsidizing. The relevance of this argument depends on whether the cost to the foreign country of a CVD is greater than the benefit it realizes from the subsidy policy. This may not be the case, especially if the policy aims to offset a market failure or is driven by noneconomic considerations. As important, even if the subsidy cannot be justified by market failure or public good considerations, the effectiveness of CVDs depend on the ability of the country imposing them to affect the terms of trade of the country granting the subsidy. Small countries are unlikely to be able to have an impact on the subsidizer's exporters that are large enough to induce them to pressure their governments not to impose the subsidy. A better option is to engage in discussions with the subsidizing country and seek compensation. This is an option that in principle is available under the WTO (see below).

CVDs are superior to AD in that the instrument is better targeted at the source of the perceived externality: foreign government intervention. In contrast to the case of dumping by firms, in the subsidy context it is possible to build a case for 'unfair competition'. However, for most countries countervailing subsidies will rarely make economic sense, unless the subsidy is expected to be temporary. In the case of agricultural subsidization by OECD countries, for example, the policy could be regarded as structural, in that affected producers are well advised to adjust to the situation. Imposition of CVDs is equivalent to throwing good money after bad. After all, the subsidy is equivalent to a transfer from a foreign government to the consumers of the importing country. If a tariff is imposed on these imports, the economy will be worse off than if nothing is done. A CVD may benefit the domestic industry, but is equivalent to a tax on the rest of the economy. Consumers lose the benefit of the foreign subsidy as prices are forced up, and at best the country ends up with an additional deadweight loss. However, this loss is smaller than is the case under a regular tariff, as there is no production distortion (see annex 2).

WTO Disciplines

The GATT history on CVDs revolves around the use made by the US of this instrument, it being the primary user. When the US acceded to GATT, it grandfathered its existing CVD legislation. The negotiation of a Code on Subsidies and Countervailing Measures in the Tokyo Round was driven by a desire by targeted countries to see the US adopt an injury test (which was not required under its law). This attempt was somewhat successful, in that the US signed an agreement that required an injury test. However, in practice, the US made this conditional upon bilateral commitments with respect to subsidy policies. US CVD policies therefore continued to be a source of controversy (Stern and Hoekman, 1987).

In the Uruguay Round the issue of subsidies and CVDs was substantially clarified. The WTO makes a distinction between different types of subsidies, depending on their trade impact and their objective (see chapter 5). Subsidies that have an economy-wide impact and are not specific (education, general infrastructure, basic R&D) or have a noneconomic rationale (regional disparities, income support) are permitted and not subject to the threat of CVDs (nonactionable). For subsidies that are not in this 'green box' and that have adverse effects on trade, WTO members have the choice of initiating CVD investigations or invoking dispute settlement procedures. Both routes may be pursued simultaneously. However, only one remedy may be applied.

As noted in chapter 5, adverse effects include injury to a domestic industry, nullification or impairment of tariff concessions, or serious prejudice or threat thereof to the country's interests. Serious prejudice is deemed to exist if the total *ad valorem* subsidization of a product exceeds five percent, subsidies cover operating losses of an industry or enterprise, or there is forgiveness of government-held debt. Serious prejudice may arise if the subsidy displaces imports of like products on either the subsidizing or third country markets. If actionable subsidies have an adverse effect on a WTO member, it may ask for consultations with the country maintaining the subsidy program. If consultations fail to settle matter within 60 days, the WTO's dispute settlement provisions may be invoked. If a panel deems adverse effects to exist, the subsidy program must be revoked, or the affected country otherwise compensated. If the panel's recommendations are not implemented within six months, the affected country can retaliate by withdrawing equivalent concessions.

Necessary conditions for imposition of CVDs include demonstration of the existence of a subsidy, a finding that a domestic industry producing similar (like) products is materially injured, and a causal link between the subsidization and injury. Injury requires that the volume of subsidized imports has increased, that this has had an impact on price levels or is reflected in price undercutting of domestic firms and that this in turn has had a detrimental effect on the domestic industry. At least 25 percent of the firms in the domestic industry must support the launching of a CVD investigation. Recall that the export subsidy dispute between Brazil and Canada revealed that in the case of an illegal (prohibited) subsidy these rules do not apply. Canada was authorized to retaliate (countervail) up to the amount of the subsidy (as determined by the arbitrators), independently of the injury suffered by the Canadian industry (see chapter 5).

Detailed requirements and deadlines are established regarding the different phases of investigations, including the collection of evidence, the rights of interested parties, the calculation of the extent to which a subsidy benefits the recipient, the determination of injury, possible remedies, and access to judicial review of the CVD decision. As is true for AD, a sunset provision of five years applies, unless a review determines that the abolition of protection would likely lead to the continuation or recurrence of injury. When confronted with CVD investigations, developing countries benefit from *de minimis* thresholds. If the subsidy is less than two percent of the per unit value of products exported, developing countries are exempt from countervail (for LDCs the threshold is three percent). An exemption also applies if the import market share of a developing country is below four percent, and the aggregate share of all such countries is below nine percent of total imports.

As noted previously, CVDs are used much less frequently than AD, and average tariffs imposed are relatively low. Disputes have arisen on the use of subsidies, some of them very high-profile cases—see chapter 3—but these have not extended to the use of CVDs.

9.6. TRADE RESTRICTIONS FOR BALANCE OF PAYMENTS PURPOSES

The GATT permits the imposition of trade restrictions to safeguard a country's external financial position (Articles XII and XVIII:*b*). The inclusion of such provisions reflects the fact that when the GATT was created, a system of fixed exchange rates prevailed (the so-called Bretton Woods system). Fixed exchange rates remove an instrument through which governments can seek to address balance of payments (BOP) disequilibria. If a country with a deficit cannot devalue and if wages are relatively inflexible as well, there is a case for imposing temporary import restrictions. An across-the-board tariff in conjunction with a subsidy to exports is under certain conditions exactly equivalent to a nominal devaluation of the currency (Vousden, 1990).

The BOP provisions of the GATT were widely used by both industrialized and developing countries. The former used Article XII as cover, the latter Article XVIII:*b*. Use of QRs for BOP purposes by developed, mostly European, countries occurred mostly in the 1950s when many currencies were not convertible. In contrast, developing country use of Article XVIII:*b* was fairly constant until the 1990s (Table 9.1). Most developing countries had no need to use Article XIX safeguard actions to protect their industries if needed, as their tariffs were generally not bound or bound at high levels. They did need GATT cover to use QRs, however, and this was the role of Article XVIII—it permits, indeed encourages, the use of QRs for BOP purposes. This was an idiosyncrasy of the GATT 1947, and contradicted the general preference for price-based instruments such as tariffs. In general, an import surcharge would be less distortionary than QRs (see annex 2).

The challenge to OECD negotiators in the Uruguay Round was to close the BOP loophole, which in practice was simply an avenue to legally impose QRs, albeit subject to GATT surveillance. Closing the loophole should have been facilitated by the move away from the fixed exchange rate system that had occurred in the 1970s. The move towards flexible (more easily adjustable) exchange rates reduces the rationale for resorting to trade restrictions to safeguard a country's external financial position. Exchange rate adjustment provides an automatic and effective mechanism for adjustment of current account imbalances if complemented by supporting measures (fiscal and monetary discipline). Experience clearly demonstrates that QRs are not the right instrument to deal with BOP problems. The IMF and World Bank routinely obtain agreements with borrowing governments not to introduce import restrictions for BOP purposes in their adjustment lending to developing countries (Finch and Michalopoulos, 1988).

Most developing countries responded to this line of argument by emphasizing that their foreign exchange shortages did not stem so much from their own policies as from protectionist policies of their trading partners. Although this was a disingenuous argument at best, given that overvalued exchange rates were usually a major cause of foreign exchange shortages and rationing, it was against this background that the issue of BOP escape clauses was considered in the Tokyo Round. A 1979 Declaration on Trade Measures Taken for Balance-of-Payments Purposes reinforced scrutiny over the trade and adjustment policies of industrial countries, but asserted that developing countries should be allowed greater latitude in safeguarding their foreign exchange reserves. During the 1980s, industrialized countries argued increasingly that the clause rendered the participation of developing countries in GATT to a large extent meaningless. This damaged both the trading system (because it undermined adherence to the principles on which the system rests) and developing countries, as the latter had no effective means within the GATT context to counter powerful protectionist interests at home. The measures imposed tended to be permanent, whereas BOP difficulties are mainly of a cyclical nature. The trade restrictions were also often imposed on selected products, rather than being applied across the board as would be necessary for BOP purposes.

WTO Disciplines

In the Uruguay Round, new language on Article XVIII was agreed that reduced the scope to use QRs, and strengthened surveillance of BOP actions. GATT 1947 contracting parties committed themselves to publicly announce time-schedules for the removal of restrictive import measures taken for BOP purposes. They also agreed to give preference to those measures that have the least disruptive effect on trade. Such measures include import surcharges, import deposit requirements or other equivalent trade measures with an impact on the price of imported goods. The use of new QRs for BOP purposes requires a justification why price-based measures cannot arrest the deterioration in the external accounts. Only one type of restrictive import measure may be applied on a product. The emphasis on the use of price-based measures is a significant improvement over the old GATT.

Surcharges or similar measures must be applied on an across-the-board basis. However, exemptions may be made for certain essential products, necessary to meet basic consumption needs or which help improve the BOP situation, such as capital goods or inputs needed for production. A WTO member applying new restrictions or raising the general level of its existing restrictions must consult with the BOP Committee within four months of the adoption of such measures. Each year a member taking BOP actions must provide the WTO secretariat with a consolidated notification providing information at the tariff line level on the type of measures applied, the criteria used for their administration, product coverage and trade flows affected. Countries applying BOP measures must engage in periodic consultations with the BOP Committee. The report prepared for such meetings must include an overview of the BOP situation and the policy measures that have been taken to restore equilibrium, a description of the restrictions that are applied, progress towards removing the restrictions, and a plan for the elimination and progressive relaxation of remaining barriers. The WTO secretariat also prepares a report, using data obtained from the IMF, regarding the macroeconomic situation in the country concerned. The IMF is represented at all BOP Committee meetings.

There is therefore in principle rather close surveillance of BOP actions. Very much depends, however, on the willingness of the BOP Committee to insist that measures are no longer or not justified. Under the GATT 1947 not much could be expected from this Committee (Eglin, 1987). In practice the main source of discipline came from the international capital markets, from international financial institutions and from bilateral pressure by WTO members to stop invoking Article XVIII as cover for trade restrictions. A total of ten developing countries revoked Article XVIII during the 1980s and early 1990s, largely following the adoption of more appropriate macroeconomic policies and unilateral liberalization efforts. Multilateral surveillance exercised by the BOP Committee played only a minimal role a role in this. The GATT dispute settlement system had more teeth. For example, Korea's use of Article XVIII:*b* was challenged in the 1980s by beef exporters, who alleged that Korea no longer had a BOP problem and that restrictions on beef could therefore not be justified by this Article, as claimed by Korea. The panel that dealt with this case found in favor of the petitioners and recommended that Korea be required to eliminate its import restrictions on beef.

Disciplines under the WTO are more binding. The difference between GATT and the WTO was illustrated by a case brought against India in 1997 by the United States. The US claimed that QRs maintained by India—a longstanding user of Article XVIII:*b*—on importation of a large number of products, covering more than 2,700 agricultural and industrial product tariff lines, were inconsistent with GATT Articles XI:1 and XVIII:11 as well as other provisions of the WTO. The panel that considered the allegations found that the measures violated India's WTO obligations and nullified or impaired benefits accruing to the US under the Agreement on Agriculture. The Appellate Body upheld the report, and the panel and Appellate Body reports were adopted in September 1999. Noteworthy is that the Appellate Body rejected India's argument that the panel had no jurisdiction given that the Balance of Payments committee had not pronounced on the matter.

India stated its intention to comply with the recommendations and rulings of the DSB, and drew attention to the panel's suggestion that the reasonable period of time for implementation in this case could exceed 15 months in view of India's status as a developing country. After consultations, the US and India agreed most changes would be made by April 2000, with the remainder to be implemented by April 2001. This case would not have been possible under GATT. It signals the end of decades of invocation by India of Article XVIII as a cover for QRs.

9.7. INFANT INDUSTRY PROTECTION

Article XVIII:*a* GATT allows for the removal of tariff concessions if necessary to establish an industry in a developing country. It does not differ much in substance from Article XXVIII (re-negotiation of tariffs), as compensation negotiations must be initiated. Article XVIII:*c* permits the use of QRs or other nontariff measures by developing countries for infant industry purposes. This provision requires the approval of WTO members, and compensation may also be requested. At the end of the Tokyo Round, the GATT infant industry exception was widened considerably to allow for measures intended to develop, modify or extend production structures more generally, in accordance with a country's economic development priorities. These exceptions have rarely been invoked as a cover for the use of import quotas, probably due to the fact that the BOP loophole embodied in Article XVIII:*b* was preferred. In comparison to the latter, surveillance and approval procedures under the infant industry provisions are more strict, and the possibility of retaliation more likely.

In most circumstances the economic rationale for invocation of Article XVIII:*c* is weak, as a QR in itself will do very little to stimulate the establishment of a competitive industry. Any justification for a government to help in the establishment of an industry must be based on market failure. Even if it is assumed that a government can correctly identify the market failure, a QR will never be an appropriate instrument to offset the source of the distortion. Usually a subsidy of some type will be a less inefficient instrument to promote the establishment of an industry. From an economic viewpoint, the drafters of the GATT were therefore justified in placing relatively stringent conditions on the use of infant industry protection. But, as has been the case with other GATT disciplines as well, the result of this was to induce a shift towards invoking substitute GATT-cover: the BOP route and TRIMs (see chapter 5). Given that a number of countries have used TRIMs for industrial development purposes, as the TRIMs agreement becomes a binding constraint on developing countries, an increase in the invocation of Article XVIII may occur for infant industry purposes. However, enough scope exists to intervene in ways that make more economic sense, through use of subsidies, public investment and the use of safeguard protection if deemed necessary.

9.8. GENERAL EXCEPTIONS

Both the GATT and the GATS contain provisions entitled 'General Exceptions' allowing members to take measures that violate a rule or discipline if necessary to achieve noneconomic objectives (GATT Articles XX; GATS Article XIV). Such objectives include protection of public morals (XX:*a*) and the health and safety of human, plant or animal life (XX:*b*). GATT Article XX also allows controls to prevent imports of goods produced with prison labor (XX:*e*), to conserve natural exhaustible resources (as long as the same measures are applied to domestic production or consumption as well—XX:*g*), to protect cultural heritage (XX:*f*), and to control exports of goods in short supply or subject to public intervention (XX:*i* and *j*). Both GATT and GATS allow for measures needed to secure compliance with laws or regulations that are not inconsistent with multilateral rules (examples mentioned include prevention of deceptive and fraudulent practices, and protection of privacy of individuals). A necessary condition for the invocation of the exception provisions of the WTO is that measures do not result in 'arbitrary or unjustifiable' discrimination between countries, and are not a disguised restriction on international trade. In addition to exceptions that focus on the attainment of noneconomic objectives, all three multilateral trade agreements have a national security exception (GATT Article XXI, GATS Article XIV*bis* and TRIPs Article 73).

The general exceptions articles are purposely worded in rather broad and vague terms. There are no compensation or approval requirements. There is also no notification requirement—it is up to affected parties to raise a measure they perceive to be discriminatory and detrimental to their interests with the member applying them. If that member defends the measure under the exceptions provisions of the WTO, the only recourse is the dispute settlement mechanism. Many panel cases have involved an investigation whether the provisions of Article XX are applicable in specific instances. In many such cases it is the task of the panel to decide if the measure in question is necessary to achieve the government's purported objective. This 'necessity test' is the main discipline on invocation of the exception provisions. For example, in a case concerning a policy imposed in Thailand prohibiting imports of cigarettes, the panel found that this violated Article XI (prohibition on QRs). An argument by the Thai government that the import ban was justified under Article XX as it was necessary to control smoking was rejected, because other instruments were available to restrict imports (so the QR was not necessary). Moreover, and more importantly, the ban was inconsistent with achieving the government's stated goal, as domestic production was unconstrained, thus violating national treatment.

Pressure has increased substantially on WTO members to extend and clarify the limits of the exceptions provisions of the WTO. These pressures are coming from two directions. On one side, various interest groups in OECD countries have sought to induce their governments to invoke the provisions as cover for the imposition of trade barriers motivated by environmental or social concerns. On the other side, exporting countries are concerned that the exceptions articles do not become loopholes importing country governments can use to argue that a particular trade restriction is 'necessary' to achieve a noneconomic objective. Increasing attention is being given by scholars and the trade policy community to alternative approaches that can be considered to ensure that the exceptions articles are not abused. Clearly a critical issue is the application of the criterion whether a measure that discriminates against imported products is necessary to achieve the public policy objective. It has been argued that a useful complement to the 'necessity test' would be to introduce an economic rationality test: is the measure the least cost way of attaining the objective (Mattoo and Subramanian, 1998)? A key question here is who will determine whether measures are necessary, WTO members or the WTO judiciary (panels and the Appellate Body)? These issues are discussed further in chapter 13, as they are among the major challenges confronting the trading system.

National Security

The national security exemptions are particularly ill-suited for dispute settlement, as in such cases panels would have to judge whether trade restrictions are necessary to protect national security. This can obviously be a very sensitive issue, especially as the language of the national security exceptions are particularly vague. Article XXI GATT allows measures to be imposed whenever a government considers this 'necessary for the protection of its essential security interests' both in time of war or 'other emergency in international relations'. Sometimes efforts to invoke a national security rationale are blatantly spurious. When Sweden imposed import quotas on footwear in 1975 it argued that this was motivated by 'national security' concerns because it needed to have a domestic industry to guarantee the country would not be short of army boots in time of war. This argument did not go over well with Sweden's trading partners.

Not surprisingly, GATT was rarely used as an instrument to contest economic sanctions imposed for foreign policy reasons. A US embargo against Nicaragua in 1985 was contested by the Nicaraguan government, but the panel ruled that it did not violate the GATT. It also noted that it was precluded from judging the validity of—or the motivation for—the US action (Jackson, 1997). More recently, a dispute between the EU and the US has tested the limits of the national security exception (Box 9.1).

Box 9.1. National security and the US Helms-Burton Act
The US Cuban Liberty and Democratic Solidarity (LIBERTAD) Act of 1996— more commonly known for the legislators that drafted it, Messrs. Helms and Burton—calls for trade restrictions on goods of Cuban origin, as well as possible refusal of entry visas and work permits for non-US nationals who have (or whose employers have) economic activities in Cuba. Thus, the bill banned visits to the US by directors of foreign firms doing business in Cuba. The EU argued this violated numerous WTO rules, including the basic principles of MFN and national treatment. The US responded that its actions were justified under the national security exceptions of the GATT and the GATS. The EU requested a panel in October 1996. The panel, comprised of three venerable men, including the former GATT Director General Mr. Arthur Dunkel, faced a very difficult task. On the one hand, a whitewash would threaten the credibility of the WTO. On the other hand, the US would have found it virtually impossible to accept an adverse ruling, which would have stirred up large-scale opposition to membership of the WTO. If, as was very probable, the US would have ignored an adverse finding by the panel, it might have encouraged other countries to follow the US example. In the event cooler heads prevailed, and the panel suspended its work at the request of the EU in April 1997 after a bilateral resolution to the conflict was concluded.

9.9. CONCLUSION

Political realities, especially in countries in the process of moving from highly distorted trade regimes to a more neutral policy stance, often dictate that there be mechanisms allowing for the temporary reimposition of protection in instances where competition from imports proves to be too fierce. Safeguard mechanisms are therefore likely to be a precondition for far-reaching liberalization to be politically feasible. Governments need loopholes that permit 'backsliding' for a variety of reasons (Finger, 1996). One that has not been discussed so far is a sympathy motive. Societies tend to have sympathy for groups severely affected by large, exogenous shocks. They support granting assistance to such groups because they too may be affected some day. This insurance motive is complemented by what Corden (1974) has called the conservative social welfare function. Governments tend to oppose large absolute reductions in real incomes of any significant portion of society.

Trade policy is generally an inefficient instrument in that it tends to create more distortions than it solves. Indeed, Deardorff and Stern (1987) have likened trade policy to doing acupuncture with a two-pronged fork; even if one of the prongs finds the right spot, the other prong can only do harm. This applies to protection in response to market disruption as well. Protection is a very costly form of intervention, both in a static sense (as demonstrated by studies of costs per job saved such as Hufbauer and Elliot, 1994 and Messerlin, 2001), and in a dynamic sense (due to the distortions that reduce economic growth). In practical terms, however, given a sociopolitical need to address market disturbance, temporary contingent protection may be the best response in situations where import penetration has increased substantially. The issue then is to design and implement procedures that are effective, equitable, and minimize distortions. The WTO does little in terms of providing guidance to policymakers wishing to rationalize or create an economically sound system to deal with market disruption caused by imports. Allowing for the possibility of emergency protection sends a signal to firms that the government cannot or will not commit itself to a given level of intervention or support. This can negatively influence the performance of particular firms—who may build this insurance into their management decisions. This can in turn give rise to so-called time-inconsistency problems. If a government is pursuing a liberalization program, but firms do not adjust because they expect to be able to obtain protection in the future, it may not be optimal (politically) for the government not to grant such protection (or alternatively, to remove the temporary, emergency protection). The design of the mechanism and the rules and criteria that apply are therefore important. External obligations—such as those applying under the WTO—can help in reducing possible time inconsistency problems, but cannot eliminate them.

In practice the WTO does a bad job by allowing for too many escape valves, some of which make no economic sense. This has given rise to a form of Gresham's law, in that bad provisions (such as AD) have driven out good provisions (safeguards). Countries in the process of developing or reforming their trade laws are well advised not to implement all the options allowed under GATT to impose trade barriers, as it will make it much more difficult to control the trade policy formation process. All that is required is a good safeguards mechanism—AD and BOP actions are best avoided. Countries already caught in the contingent protection morass are well advised to ensure the economic costs of AD are identified and considered. Providing groups that will lose from protection the legal mandate to make the case against intervention is a key requirement for ensuring balance.

Finally, it should be kept in mind that provisions such as Articles XIX and XXVIII GATT (or Article XXI GATS) are only relevant if tariffs have been bound (specific commitments have been made). If this is not the case, countries will have the latitude to simply raise tariffs if the political need for this arises. For the GATT rules to fully bite, tariffs must be bound. For GATS to bind, specific commitments must be made. As discussed in chapters 5 and 7, on both the goods and services front much still remains to be done to achieve full binding of tariffs at applied rates and schedule all service sectors.

9.10. FURTHER READING

Safeguard protection for import-competing industries has been analyzed extensively in the economic literature. Robert Baldwin, 'Assessing the Fair Trade and Safeguards Laws in Terms of Modern Trade and Political Economy Analysis', *The World Economy*, 15 (1992), 185–202 discusses the (political economy) issues and surveys some of the literature. Gary Sampson, 'Safeguards', in J.M. Finger and A. Olechowski (eds.), *The Uruguay Round: A Handbook* (Washington DC: The World Bank, 1987) reviews the history of Article XIX in the GATT through 1986. Alan Deardorff, 'Safeguards Policy and the Conservative Social Welfare Function', in Henryk Kierzkowski (ed.), *Protection and Competition in International Trade* (Oxford: Basil Blackwell, 1987) discusses why governments need safeguard instruments. Brian Hindley, 'GATT Safeguards and Voluntary Export Restraints: What are the Interests of the Developing Countries?' *World Bank Economic Review*, 1 (1987), 689–705 discusses the incentive effects of VERs. A classic paper on VERs is Richard Harris, 'Why Voluntary Export Restraints are "Voluntary"', *Canadian Journal of Economics* 18 (1985), 799–809. Patrick Low, *Trading Free: The*

GATT and US Trade Policy (New York: Twentieth Century Fund, 1993) discusses is some detail the political economy of the US shift towards the use of VERs, as well as the evolution of US trade policy thinking and practice.

Richard Eglin, 'Surveillance of Balance-of-Payments Measures in the GATT', *The World Economy*, 10 (1987), 1–26 reviews the GATT experience with Article XVIII actions and multilateral surveillance. The contributions by Finger, Hindley and L. Alan Winters in *The New World Trading System* (Paris: OECD, 1994) are good summaries of what was agreed on contingent protection in the Uruguay Round. J. Michael Finger, 'Legalized Backsliding: Safeguard Provisions in the GATT', in Will Martin and Alan Winters (eds.), *The Uruguay Round and the Developing Economies* (Cambridge: Cambridge University Press, 1996) is a comprehensive discussion of the various loopholes in the GATT that allow for backsliding. Michael Finger and Ludger Schuknecht, 'Market Access Advances and Retreats: The Uruguay Round and Beyond', in Bernard Hoekman and Will Martin (eds.), *Developing Countries and the WTO* (Oxford: Basil Blackwell, 2000) summarizes the first five years of WTO members' use of safeguards and exceptions.

There is a huge literature on antidumping, both legal and economic. Much of the recent economic work is collected and summarized in Robert Lawrence (ed.), *Brookings Trade Forum* (Washington DC: The Brookings Institution, 1998). J. Michael Finger (ed.), *Antidumping: How it Works and Who Gets Hurt* (Ann Arbor: University of Michigan Press, 1993) is an excellent set of papers identifying why AD makes no economic sense. Patrick Messerlin, 'Antidumping Regulations or Pro-cartel Law? The EC Chemical Cases', *The World Economy*, 13 (1990), 465–92 illustrates on the basis of a particular case how an industry can capture AD procedures to enhance its market power. P.K.M. Tharakan, 'The Political Economy of Price-Undertakings', *European Economic Review* 35 (1991), 1341-59 analyses the use of and motivations for undertakings in EU application of AD. Thomas Prusa addresses the same topic from a US perspective in 'Why Are So Many Antidumping Petitions Withdrawn?', *Journal of International Economics* 33 (1992), 1-20. Patrick Messerlin, 'Antidumping and Safeguards', in Jeffrey Schott (ed.), *The WTO After Seattle* (Washington DC: Institute for International Economics, 2000), and Bernard Hoekman and Petros C. Mavroidis, 'Dumping, Antidumping and Antitrust', *Journal of World Trade* 30 (1996), 27–52 discuss possible reforms that could be considered in the WTO regarding AD. A database on US AD activity for all cases from 1980–95 is available at: http://darkwing.uoregon.edu/~bruceb/adpage.html. This includes Excel spreadsheets, documentation, and links to government agencies involved in AD enforcement, researchers and online working papers. For a comprehensive, insider account of the AD Agreement, see Mark Koulen, 'The

New Antidumping Code Through its Negotiating History', in J. Bourgeois, F. Berrod and E. Fouvier (eds.), *The Uruguay Round Results: A European Lawyer's Perspective* (Brussels: European Interuniversity Press, 1995).

A good source of policy-oriented papers on contingent protection and related issues is *The Journal of World Trade* (Kluwer).

10
Regional Integration

Although a fundamental principle of the WTO is nondiscrimination in the application of trade policy, both the GATT and the GATS make explicit allowance for preferential trade agreements among a subset of members. To avoid abuse of this possibility, both GATT and GATS impose conditions that must be met for an agreement to be permissible and provide for multilateral scrutiny of regional integration agreements (RIAs) between WTO members. This chapter discusses the rationale for RIAs, the rules of the GATT and the GATS, and the challenges that regionalism poses for the multilateral trading system.[1]

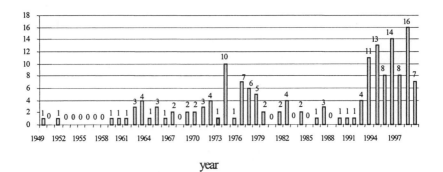

Source: World Bank (2000).

FIG. 10.1 Regional agreements notified to GATT and WTO, 1948–98

Starting in 1948, some 200 regional trade agreements have been notified to the GATT or the WTO. About one-half of all notifications occurred after 1990 (Figure 10.1). Many involve European countries. The EU (itself a RIA) has concluded numerous agreements with neighboring countries, and many non-EU European countries have formed agreements of their own. Major non-European agreements that have been concluded in recent years include the North American Free Trade Agreement (NAFTA)—Canada, Mexico and

---

[1] In revising this chapter from the first edition we have drawn on joint work with Maurice Schiff and L. Alan Winters.

the US—and Mercosur (the Southern Common Market)—Argentina, Brazil, Paraguay, and Uruguay. Virtually all OECD nations are now a member of one or more RIAs—Australia and New Zealand have a long-standing preferential trade relationship, dating back to the 1960s. The long-standing exception is Japan, although that may change. In the late 1990s, Japan announced that it was exploring the creation of a RIA with Korea. Most developing countries are also members of one of more RIAs (World Bank, 2000).

The specifics of each RIA vary greatly from case to case, but they all have one thing in common – the reduction in trade barriers between members and consequent discrimination against trade with other countries. RIAs take many forms, depending on the degree of integration. At their simplest RIAs only remove tariffs from inter-member trade in goods. Many go beyond that to cover NTBs. A few also liberalize services trade and investment. At their deepest, RIAs deal with issues of economic regulation and political cooperation, and represent a step towards nation building.

The economic literature distinguishes between different types of RIAs. In a free trade area (FTA), trade restrictions among member countries are removed, but each country retains its own tariff structure against outsiders. A customs union is a free trade area with common external trade policies. A common market is a customs union that also allows for the free movement of factors of production. Finally, an economic union is a common market that includes some degree of harmonization of national economic policies of member states. In practice, RIAs are often a combination of these ideal types. Many fail to conform to the definitions. For example, contingent protection often remains applicable to intra-bloc trade, implying that internal trade is not truly free.

10.1. MOTIVATIONS FOR REGIONAL ECONOMIC INTEGRATION

In one form or another, RIAs have been around for hundreds of years. There were proposals for a customs union of the provinces of France in 1664. Austria signed FTAs with five neighbors in the course of the eighteenth and nineteenth centuries. Customs unions were precursors to the creation of new states in, for example, Germany (the Zollverein) and Italy. Although nation building objectives have been a major spur to integration historically, there is a strong association between RIAs and the mercantilist instinct to seek access to markets (see chapter 1). Interest in regionalism also has a cyclical component. The 1930s saw great fragmentation of the world trading system as governments struggled with the global depression. 'Solutions' to deal with unilateral protectionism included regional preference schemes and currency blocs. After the Second World War, regional integration contributed to the political reconstruction of Europe through the implementation of the Benelux customs union (1947), the creation of the European Coal and Steel Community (ECSC) in 1952 and the more far-reaching EEC (in 1957).

The creation of the EEC led to a spurt of regionalism between developing countries in 1960s. These were mostly driven by a desire to apply import-substitution industrialization strategies within a larger economic area. The RIAs were generally very protectionist (maintaining high external barriers) and interventionist (many sought to determine administratively which industries to have and where they should be located). They were generally failures (World Bank, 2000). By the late 1970s the ineffectiveness of these RIAs had become evident. None seemed to have contributed strongly to development, some had collapsed and the strains of the debt crisis made many of those that survived largely moribund. In the 1980s a change in attitudes towards international trade and competition occurred. Unilateral liberalization was complemented by a new wave of more open RIAs. The EU played a major role in the resurgence of RIAs by negotiating FTAs with Central and Eastern European and South Mediterranean nations, and expanding its membership. In the Americas, the Canadian-US FTA of 1988 was extended to Mexico in NAFTA in 1994, Mercosur was formed in 1991, and efforts were launched to form a Free Trade Area of the Americas (FTAA). In Asia, ASEAN members extended 25 years of political cooperation to a FTA in 1992. In Africa, a number of initiatives were launched, including the Common Market for Eastern and Southern Africa (COMESA)—which extends as far north as Egypt—and the Southern African Development Community (SADC). In 1998, members of the Arab League renewed their integration efforts by creating a Greater Arab Free Trade Agreement, to be implemented over a 10-year period.

Why Go Regional?

A number of factors lie behind the steady expansion in the number of RIAs. These include the following.

- The demise of central planning. The collapse of Soviet hegemony allowed the countries of Eastern Europe and the Baltic to embrace democracy and market-based economic systems. RIAs with Western European countries were seen as a tool to accelerate and cement the transition to a market economy.
- A shift in the attitude of the US. The US moved from active hostility to enthusiasm towards regionalism in the 1980s, driven in part by an frustration with the slowness of the multilateral process. Also important was

the end of the Cold War, which reduced US willingness to accept preferential liberalization elsewhere in the world while not pursuing this avenue for improving access to major markets itself.

- Domino effects. As major trading partners created trade blocs, so the pressures on others to follow increased as the costs of exclusion seemed to grow—so-called 'domino regionalism' (Baldwin, 1996).
- Globalization. Increased internationalization of markets put pressure on firms, and, through them, governments to seek efficiency through larger markets and improved access to foreign technologies and investment. This led to private sector lobbying for reductions in regulation-related trade costs. These may be perceived to be easier to address in RIAs involving like-minded governments.
- Credibility. Some governments saw RIAs as a mechanism to lock in policy reforms, both economic and noneconomic (for instance, democracy) and to signal such commitments to domestic and foreign investors.
- Politics. RIAs are often driven by foreign policy and national security considerations. Indeed, these often predominate, any economic costs being regarded as the price to achieve the noneconomic objectives. Some problems or issues may be shared by only a limited number of (often neighboring) countries, and can therefore be better resolved on a regional basis rather than multilaterally. Perhaps the most clear-cut example of such a situation is if there is a desire to achieve political integration—the creation of a larger political entity. The German Zollverein is a prominent example; the EU may become another.

As discussed in chapter 1, at any point in time a certain level of market access restrictions emerges as an equilibrium outcome of interactions between different groups in the political market of a country. Assuming for purposes of discussion that unilateral liberalization is not an option, interest groups will have a choice between pursuing regional and multilateral trade agreements. What determines interest group preferences regarding these two options? A RIA by definition involves substantially fewer countries than a MTN. Indeed, many RIAs involve only two countries. This should make them easier to negotiate. The set of possible policy packages that could make all parties better off may well be larger under a RIA, including issues that could not appear on the negotiating agenda of a MTN. Issue linkage or sidepayments therefore may be more feasible as the negotiation set expands, facilitating agreement. RIAs may also involve formal mechanisms to transfer income from one region to another; in the MTN-context this is rarely possible. Many RIAs involve relatively similar countries. The more similar are countries in their endowments and income levels, the likelier it is that intra-industry trade will be significant. This may facilitate regional liberalization (Box 10.1)

Box 10.1. Intra-industry trade and pressures for protection
The magnitude of intra-industry trade is often regarded as an indicator of the extent to which significant adjustment pressures are likely to arise as a result of liberalization. Adjustment costs are likely to be lower if intra-industry trade is high because jobs lost due to customers shifting to more efficient foreign suppliers may to a large extent be offset by the job-enhancing expansion in foreign demand for similar, differentiated goods produced domestically. The political opposition to liberalizing and expanding intra-industry trade tends to be more muted than in instances where trade flows are predominantly of the inter-industry type. In the latter case industries that are less competitive than those abroad will generally be forced to contract substantially. This is not to say that intra-industry trade will not lead to adjustment and thus pressure for protection. Specialized and relatively immobile factors of production injured by import competition can be expected to seek protection. But the injury in this case is more at the firm- than at the industry level. Other firms in the industry will expand. This makes it more difficult to maintain protection, as there will be conflicting interests within industries. The relevance of this for regional integration is that intra-industry trade tends to be high among countries with similar endowments and relatively high per capita income levels—nations that have tended to form RIAs in the post Second World War period. Levels of intra-industry trade between the members of the most successful RIAs—the EU, EFTA, NAFTA and the Australia-New Zealand Closer Economic Relations (CER) agreement—are high, both for trade in goods and trade in services (Globerman, 1992; Edwards and Savastano, 1989; Greenaway, 1987).

Multinational firms may be indifferent between the status quo and a RIA as long as external trade barriers are not raised, and may actively support the RIA if they perceive that the negotiating power of the bloc enhances the probability of obtaining greater access to third markets. Regional liberalization may also be considered to be less uncertain by stakeholders. The more similar are national regulatory regimes, the smaller may be concerns regarding free riding of competitors in potential partner countries. Thus, a preferential agreement to liberalize trade may allow greater internalization of the benefits. The implied reduction in uncertainty with respect to the outcome of liberalization—the distribution of gains and losses—may facilitate its negotiation. The smaller the required changes in regulatory regimes and the greater the confidence that regulations will be enforced in all jurisdictions, the more certainty will exist regarding the conditions of competition that will prevail.

RIAs may also allow more credible commitments to be made. One reason is that the limited number, similarity and proximity of member countries reduces monitoring and implementation costs. Some RIAs have supranational enforcement mechanisms, the EU being the primary example, further reducing uncertainty regarding implementation. Finally, RIAs can be useful instruments through which to experiment with issues that have not yet been addressed in the WTO or to exert pressure on trading partners. Thus, if certain issues cannot be addressed in a MTN, the subset of countries seeking agreement may pursue a RIA in part with a view to inducing other countries to agree to their position. The US decided to negotiate FTAs with trading partners in the 1980s in part because of dissatisfaction with the 1982 refusal of GATT partners to initiate a MTN that covered services trade (Schott, 1989).

Much attention has been devoted to the question whether RIAs are detrimental to world welfare, both in the short run (impact effects) and in the longer run (taking induced growth effects into account). The impact of regional integration on member and nonmember countries will depend on the type of agreement concerned (FTA, customs union, or common market) and on the degree to which intra-regional trade is liberalized. The more extensive internal liberalization is, the greater the resulting increase in competition on regional markets. While this is welfare enhancing for member countries— and presumably the object of economic integration—it may also be associated with greater adjustment pressures for inefficient industries located in member countries. The latter may attempt to shift some of the adjustment burden onto third countries by seeking increases in external barriers. If external barriers are high, trade diversion costs may be significant (see below). Account therefore needs to be taken of the magnitude of implicit discrimination (due to the preferential nature of liberalization) and possible additional explicit discrimination against third countries in the form of greater barriers to imports *ex post*.

Regional integration can be detrimental to members and nonmembers by inducing a shift away from the most efficient supplier of goods or services. To use economic jargon, the formation of a trading bloc can give rise to trade diversion (a shift from an efficient outside supplier to a higher cost regional one, induced by the elimination of tariffs on intra-regional trade— see annex 2). Hirschman (1981), Tumlir (1983) and others have argued that regionalism must involve trade diversion for political reasons, as this is an effective mechanism for compensating lobbies that would oppose more general liberalization. Nonmembers may be harmed through investment diversion as well as trade diversion if enterprises decide to invest inside RIAs and produce locally, rather than export to the RIA. For example, the expected enlargement of the EU to include Hungary, Poland, the Czech Republic and the Baltic States encouraged investment by non-European firms in the automobile, chemical and machine tool sectors. Baldwin, Forslid and Haaland (1996) studied the effect of the announcement of the Single Market in the EU in the late 1980s, and concluded that this had a significant negative impact on inward FDI flows into EFTA countries. FDI only recovered after the EFTA members applied for EU membership or had joined the EEA.

10.2. GATT ARTICLE XXIV: PREFERENTIAL TRADE AGREEMENTS

Article XXIV of the GATT allows FTAs and customs unions if:

(1) trade barriers after integration do not rise on average (Article XXIV:5);
(2) all tariffs and other regulations of commerce are removed on substantially all intra-regional exchanges of goods within a reasonable length of time (Article XXIV:8); and
(3) they are notified to the WTO Council.

The rationale for the first criterion is obvious. If restrictions on imports from nonmember economies are no higher than before, the extent of possible reductions in imports from nonmembers is limited (although clearly not zero—the higher are external barriers, the greater the likely trade diversion). A practical problem faced by the drafters of Article XXIV was that the formation of a customs union by necessity requires changes in the external tariffs of member countries as they adopt a common external tariff. The rule that applies to customs unions is that duties and other barriers to imports from outside the union may not be on the whole higher or more restrictive than those preceding the establishment of the customs union (Article XXIV:5a). The interpretation of this phrase became a source of much disagreement among GATT contracting parties. The rule for FTAs was unambiguous, however. Duties applied by each individual member country may not be raised (Article XXIV:5b).

The second condition is somewhat counterintuitive in that maximum preferential liberalization in itself is likely to be more detrimental to nonmembers than partial liberalization. Requiring it, however, ensures that countries are limited in their ability to violate the MFN obligation selectively. As noted by Finger (1993b), the rationale behind the second condition is a public choice one: it is an attempt to ensure that participants in regional liberalization efforts go all the way. What matters as far as the welfare of nonmembers is concerned is the impact on trade flows and the associated change in prices (see below). This is not recognized in Article XXIV. Even if the two requirements are met, and even if net aggregate imports do not contract, imports of particular products by the region may decline *ex post*, harming producers in the rest of the world.

Determining whether the GATT tests are met is left for the WTO Council to determine. In the past, the Council generally created a working party to establish if the conditions were satisfied. Under the WTO, a Committee of Regional Trade Agreements (CRTA) has taken over this task. The GATT experience in testing FTAs and customs unions against Article XXIV was very discouraging. Various aspects of the rules and their application, including approval by the CONTRACTING PARTIES of regional arrangements before they could be said to have entered into force, proved unsatisfactory. Starting with the examination of the Treaty of Rome establishing the EEC in 1957, almost no examination of agreements notified under Article XXIV led to a unanimous conclusion or specific endorsement that all the legal GATT requirements had been met. As noted by the chairman of the working party on the 1989 Canada-United States Free Trade Agreement, commenting on the inability to reach a consensus, 'Over fifty previous working parties on individual customs unions or free trade areas·have been unable to reach unanimous conclusions on the compatibility of these agreements with the GATT—on the other hand, no such agreement has been explicitly disapproved' (*GATT Focus*, December 1991). As of the late 1980s, only four working parties could agree that a regional agreement satisfied the requirements of Article XXIV (Schott, 1989). It is not much of an exaggeration to say that GATT rules largely were a dead letter, although the consultations that occurred allowed interested nonmembers to express their concerns.

The reasons underlying this impotence were largely political. A conscious political decision was made by contracting parties in the late 1950s not to scrutinize the formation of the EEC. The reason was that it was made clear by the EEC member states that a finding that the Treaty of Rome was inconsistent with Article XXIV would result in their withdrawal from GATT (Snape, 1993). To paraphrase Finger (1993*b*), at the end of the day the GATT blinked. Given that the EEC most likely did not meet all the requirements of Article XXIV, this created a precedent that was often followed subsequently. A result has been that most RIAs notified to GATT embody many holes and loopholes. Indeed, even serious attempts at regional liberalization—and until recently there were not very many of these—did no go much further than the GATT (Hoekman and Leidy, 1993). Although RIAs were tolerated for political reasons, it is also the case that the criteria and language of Article XXIV are ambiguous. Legitimate differences of opinion could exist regarding how to define 'substantially all trade', how to determine whether the external trade policy of a customs union has become more restrictive on average, and what is a reasonable length of time for the transition towards full implementation of a FTA or customs union. Some of these issues were addressed in the Uruguay Round.

The GATT 1994 Understanding on the Interpretation of Article XXIV reaffirms that RIAs should facilitate trade between members and not raise barriers to the trade of nonmembers. In their formation or enlargement, the parties to RIAs should 'to the greatest possible extent avoid creating adverse effects on the trade of other members' (GATT, 1994a, p.31). It was recognized that the effectiveness of the role of the Council for Trade in Goods in reviewing agreements notified under Article XXIV needed to be enhanced. This was to be pursued in part by clarifying the criteria and procedures for the assessment of new or enlarged agreements, and by improving the transparency of all agreements notified to GATT under Article XXIV. Under the WTO, the evaluation of the general incidence of the duties and other regulations of commerce applicable before and after the formation of a customs union is to be based upon 'an overall assessment of weighted average tariff rates and of customs duties collected' by the WTO secretariat. The assessment must be based on import statistics for a previous representative period (to be supplied by the customs union) on a tariff line basis, broken down by WTO member country of origin.

Article XXIV:6 requires WTO members seeking to increase bound tariff rates upon joining a customs union to enter into negotiations—under Article XXVIII (Modification of Schedules, see chapter 9)—on compensatory adjustment. In doing this, reductions in duties on the same tariff line made by other members of the customs union must be taken into account. If such reductions are insufficient compensation, the Understanding requires the customs union to offer to reduce duties on other tariff lines, or to otherwise provide compensation. Where agreement on compensatory adjustment cannot be reached within a reasonable period from the initiation of negotiations, the customs union is free to modify or withdraw the concessions and affected members are free to withdraw substantially equivalent concessions (to retaliate).

The Understanding established a 10-year maximum for the transition period for implementation of an agreement, although allowance is made for exceptional circumstances (to be explained to the Council for Trade in Goods). Working parties are to make appropriate recommendations concerning interim agreements—those with a transitional period—as regards the proposed time period and the measures required to complete the formation of the customs union or FTA. If an interim agreement does not include a plan and schedule, the working party must recommend one. Parties to an agreement may not implement it if they are not prepared to modify it in accordance with the recommendations. Implementation of the recommendations is subject to subsequent review.

Developing countries may, if they wish, invoke provisions of the GATT allowing them to establish agreements that do not meet the conditions of Article XXIV. The 1979 Decision on Differential and More Favorable Treatment of Developing Countries (the so-called Enabling Clause—see chapter 12) essentially removes the 'substantially all' test and allows for preferences between developing countries (that is, the full removal of internal barriers is not required). Mercosur (a customs union) was notified to GATT under this provision, not under Article XXIV.

10.3. GATS ARTICLE V: ECONOMIC INTEGRATION

The GATS is similar to the GATT in allowing for RIAs that liberalize trade in services on a discriminatory basis, subject to conditions and surveillance. The relevant provision, Article V GATS, is entitled Economic Integration, not Free Trade Areas and Customs Unions (as in Article XXIV GATT), reflecting the fact that the GATS covers not only cross-border trade in services but also the three other modes of supply. Analogous to the GATT, Article V GATS imposes three conditions on economic integration agreements. First, such agreements must have substantial sectoral coverage, in terms of the number of sectors, volume of trade affected, and modes of supply. RIAs may not provide for the *a priori* exclusion of any mode of supply. Second, RIAs must provide for the absence or elimination of substantially all measures violating national treatment in sectors where specific commitments were made in the GATS. This must be achieved at the entry into force of the agreement or within a reasonable time frame. Third, RIAs may not result in higher trade barriers against third countries.

The substantial sectoral coverage requirement is weaker than the 'substantially all trade' criterion of Article XXIV. The same conclusion applies regarding the criteria on the magnitude of liberalization required and the external policy stance of the RIA, as the benchmark is not free trade, but the specific commitments made under the GATS by members. As discussed in chapter 7, these are far from implying free trade. Members of the GATS engaged in economic integration efforts intending to withdraw or modify specific market access or national treatment commitments (raise external barriers) must follow the renegotiation procedures set out in Article XXI GATS (Modification of Schedules—see chapter 9). There are a number of loopholes

allowing for the formation of agreements that do not fully comply with multilateral disciplines. For example, Article V:2 of the GATS allows for consideration to be given to the relationship between a particular regional agreement and the wider process of economic integration among member countries. Article V:3 gives developing countries involved in a RIA flexibility regarding the realization of the internal liberalization requirements and allows
them to give more favorable treatment to firms that originate in parties to
the agreement. That is, it allows for discrimination against firms originating
in nonmembers, even if the latter are established within the area. These special and differential treatment type of provisions are unlikely to be very effective in achieving their presumed objective: attracting FDI. More importantly, they weaken the scope of multilateral disciplines, giving governments
(interest groups) an opportunity to pursue agreements that are more detrimental to nonmembers.

10.4. TRADING BLOCS AND THE TRADING SYSTEM

Although Article XXIV is far from perfect from an economic perspective, in
principle it imposes serious discipline, especially after the Uruguay Round
Understanding. A problem has been that consensus cannot be reached on
whether RIAs satisfy the rules, so the Council cannot apply the various provisions that are mentioned in the WTO. Despite the replacement of working
parties by a single Committee on Regional Trade Agreements to review the
WTO compliance of RIAs, as under GATT 1947, agreement in most cases
proved impossible.[2] As under GATT, the reason for this impotence is the
consensus rule. There has also been relatively little use of dispute settlement
procedures to contest the operation or design of RIAs. A rare example was a
1996 case brought by India against Turkey, regarding Turkey's imposition of
QRs on imports of textile and clothing products. These were required because Turkey had entered into a customs union with the EU. The DSB established a panel, which found that Turkey's measures were inconsistent with
Articles XI and XIII GATT. Of interest to this chapter, the panel rejected
Turkey's assertion that its measures were justified by Article XXIV GATT. On
appeal, the Appellate Body upheld the panel's conclusion that Article XXIV
of GATT 1994 did not allow Turkey to adopt, upon the formation of a customs union with other WTO members, QRs that are inconsistent with Articles XI and XIII of GATT 1994 and Article 2.4 of the ATC. However, the Ap-

---

[2] One of the few exceptions was the customs union between the Czech and Slovak Republics—
not surprising given that the two countries were a federation prior to their velvet divorce.

pellate Body also concluded that the legal interpretation of Article XXIV by the panel was erroneous, and determined that a panel should first ascertain whether a RIA complies with Article XXIV before considering other GATT provisions.

Given the impotence of the CRTA, what matters for nonmembers is the effect of RIAs—to what extent do actual RIAs have detrimental effects on the rest of the world? The question has often been posed whether regionalism is a stepping stone or a stumbling block towards multilateral liberalization. There is no consensus on the answer. Indeed, given that regional trading arrangements differ so much and that there is little empirical evidence on their effects, there is no reason to expect a single, simple answer. Some point to the fact that the formation of the EEC and its periodic subsequent expansions contributed to pressures by GATT contracting parties to initiate the MTNs which resulted in significant reductions in the incidence of trade restrictions. It is also often argued that RIAs may facilitate liberalization in areas too complex to be negotiated successfully in the WTO or too difficult to enforce in that setting. Examples include government procurement, antidumping, and investment rules. Once formed, regional arrangements in these areas might provide blueprints for future multilateral liberalization.

Arguments suggesting regionalism may be detrimental to the trading system often revolve around some variant of the optimal tariff argument. As trade blocs expand, so does their market power and, at least in principle, their ability to influence the terms of trade in their favor. If successful, this is detrimental to the rest of the world. Although possibly true in some cases, it is not a well-founded generalization that RIAs will have an incentive to increase their tariffs against the rest of the world. For one thing, there are big differences between FTAs and customs unions. Members of FTAs may have good reasons for lowering tariffs on nonmembers, as this reduces trade diversion (see below).

Whatever the incentives for RIAs to raise external barriers, RIAs impose costs on nonmembers even if they do not raise external levels of protection. Nonmember suppliers become less competitive because they continue to pay tariffs while competing producers from member countries do not. Where there are economies of scale, RIAs may help lower member country firms' costs by expanding their home market. It is impossible to devise a realistic rule that will ensure that the trade policy stance of a RIA will be welfare improving for members *and* the rest of the world (Winters, 1999). What matters is that over time the dynamics move RIAs toward a reduction in the external barriers imposed on nonmembers. This in turn requires careful scrutiny of the incentives that are built into a RIA to achieve this objective. As is the case for trade policy more generally, the most powerful pressures for reform are almost invariably domestic, not external, although external forces can be very useful in supporting domestic constituencies that favor a more liberal trade regime.

Political Economy Considerations

A key factor determining the importance of the effective absence of multilateral disciplines is the extent to which RIAs have detrimental effects on nonmembers. Two aspects are particularly important in this connection: the economic impact on third countries, and the political economy incentives confronting lobbies in RIAs with regard to the level of external protection.

Economists sometimes argue that a necessary condition for preferential liberalization to be deemed multilaterally acceptable is that the volume of imports by member countries from the rest of the world not decline on a product-by-product basis after the implementation of the agreement (McMillan, 1993). The empirical literature suggests that the trade volume test has been met in the past. Although the intensity of intra-regional trade has increased this century, the propensity of regions to trade with the rest of the world, expressed as a percentage of their GDP, has also expanded (Anderson and Norheim, 1993). Global integration—as measured by trade flows and capital flows—does not appear to have been affected negatively by regional integration efforts. There is no strong evidence of significant trade diversion (World Bank, 2000). However, this cannot be said with certainty, as no one knows what would have happened without RIAs. More important, as pointed out by Winters (1997), the 'trade volume test' is a flawed one in that it does not guarantee that nonmembers are not hurt by a RIA.

A more appropriate measure of the impact of a RIA on nonmembers is to focus on what happens to the prices nonmembers get for their exports to RIA members after the agreement is formed. Chang and Winters (1999) show that Brazil's membership of Mercosur was accompanied by a improvement in the external terms of trade. Exporters based in the US, EU, Japan and Korea all saw the relative prices of many of their goods on the Brazilian market fall. There is also some evidence of negative investment effects (Baldwin et al., 1996). These studies suggests that although most of the available trade flow evidence suggests there is not cause for great concern, there is no justification for complacency either.

What matters is not only the economic impact of a particular agreement, but the systemic effects of RIAs. For example, the threat of contingent protection, especially AD, has become an important motivation for third countries to seek to join RIAs as opposed to pursuit of MTNs (Hindley and

Messerlin, 1993). Assessments of RIAs should therefore also consider the incentives for lobbies to seek protection against the rest of the world.

There are various ways through which RIAs may constrain national interest groups and thus foster a more liberal external trade policy (De Melo, Panagariya and Rodrik, 1993). A first can be called the preference-dilution effect: because the region implies a larger political community, each of the politically-important interest groups in member countries will have less influence on the design of common policies. The second is the preference-asymmetry effect: because preferences on specific issues are likely to differ across member countries, the resulting need for compromises may increase the probability of more efficient outcomes. The creation of RIAs may also disrupt the formation of rent-seeking interest groups, as these have to reorganize at the regional level, establishing an institutional structure that allows them to agree on a common position. But, RIAs may also facilitate the adoption of less liberal policies. Consumer interests may be harder to defend in a RIA than at the national level, whereas producer interests are more likely to be strengthened than weakened (Tumlir, 1983). Each national producer group may face less opposition when seeking price-increasing policies, and may indeed find support from other producer groups in other countries that pursue their own interests. The need for striking compromises may then result in a less liberal regulatory regime. Moreover, it may be in the interest of national politicians to let a regional organization satisfy national pressure groups as this is less transparent for domestic voters and can be justified as being necessary to maintain the agreement (Vaubel, 1986).

Much will generally depend on the type of RIA that is involved, FTA, customs union or hub-and-spoke system. The first two types differ from the last in that they imply nondiscrimination between the members of the agreement: any benefit granted to member country B by member country A is also available to member country C. Under a hub-and-spoke system this is not necessarily the case: each country negotiates a separate agreement with the hub country, and perhaps with other spoke partner countries as well. A major difference between a FTA and a customs union or common market is that the latter have a common external trade policy. Whatever the extent of internal liberalization of trade and competition, implementation of a common external trade policy can give rise to an upward bias in the level of external protection over time, especially if import-competing industries pursue instruments of contingent protection such as antidumping actions. The scope for expansion in use and coverage of AD actions in a customs union is amply illustrated by the experience of the EU (Hindley and Messerlin, 1993).

Box 10.2. Pressures for protection: FTAs and customs unions

Under a customs union or common market the potential returns to protection-seeking will be higher than under a FTA: the expected payoff for a unit of lobbying effort increases because the size of the protected market is bigger. Moreover, liberal-minded governments that join a customs union may find it impossible to prevent domestic industries from seeking protection or to block the imposition of protection. For example, it may be the case that certain countries did not use (or make available) contingent protection before joining a customs union. However, once a member country, any domestic firm has access to the central trade policy authority and will be able to petition for AD. Indeed, the welfare gains to liberal countries from joining a customs union that employs contingent protection are reduced, as consumers are faced with higher expected levels of protection without knowing which industries will be affected (Hoekman and Leidy, 1993).

More generally, once a common external trade policy applies, decision-making structures may be biased toward more rather than less protection because of the so-called restaurant bill problem. If a group goes to a restaurant and shares the cost of the bill, each has an incentive to order more expensive dishes than they would if they ate on their own, as to some extent the others are expected to pick up part of the cost. The same is true in the EU (Winters, 1994*b*). The costs of protection are borne by all EU consumers, and are roughly proportional to each country's GDP. Benefits accruing to producers are proportional to the share of each country in total EU production of the good concerned. This establishes an incentive for each government to pursue protection for those products where their share of total EU production exceeds their country's share of EU GDP. Thus, the Netherlands may not like the EU-wide protection for cars sought by France and Italy, but may accept it if other policies are adopted for products in which it is relatively specialized (such as agriculture). Indeed, to the extent that larger countries are able to get the Commission to propose protectionist policies in specific areas, all EU member states have an incentive to ensure that some of their producers also obtain protection.

The external trade policy bias towards protection that may arise under a customs union will be weaker in a FTA. Because there is no common external trade policy, member countries compete in their external trade policies. Industries cannot lobby for area-wide protection. While import-competing firms in member countries may have an incentive to obtain such protection, each industry will have to approach its own government. The required coordination and cooperation may be more difficult to sustain than in a customs union where the centralization of trade policy requires firms to present a common front. In any particular instance, some member country governments will award protection, whereas others will not. If industries in member countries are all competing against third suppliers, protection by one member may benefit industries in other member states. Such free riding can result in less protection than in the absence of the FTA (Deardorff, 1992). This benefit may be offset by other aspects of FTAs. The primary example is the need for rules of origin, which may allow industries to limit the extent of intra-area liberalization and can be detrimental to nonmembers (see Box 10.3 below). Uniform rules could greatly improve matters.

Thus, there may be no net increase in external trade barriers at the formation of a customs union, but there can easily be an upward trend if contingent protection is maintained. In contrast, FTAs have a different dynamic, as members in some sense compete in their external trade policies. Although the political economy of FTAs versus customs unions is complex, on balance, FTAs are likely to be more liberal than customs unions (Box 10.2).

A hub-and-spoke system essentially consists of a set of bilateral trade agreements. Because there is discrimination between members of such a system, less liberalization is likely to result than under a FTA. Moreover, it may be more difficult to reduce the extent of the sectoral exclusions and loopholes over time. Because a hub-and-spoke system involves separate agreements between the hub country and the spoke countries, there is more scope to exclude the sensitive sectors from the coverage of each bilateral agreement (Snape, Adams and Morgan, 1992). Each spoke is likely to have comparative advantage in a somewhat different set of such sectors. In a FTA the scope for exceptions will generally be less because members will have different preferences concerning the extent to which the coverage of the agreement is incomplete. Under a hub-and-spoke system, the potential for maintaining policies that imply an effective reduction in liberalization of internal trade will also be greater. If each country maintains contingent protection options (AD, safeguards) against member countries, powerful import-competing industries in the hub country will have an interest in including wide-ranging safeguard clauses and relatively stringent rules of origin. This was the case in the Association Agreements negotiated between the EU and various CEECs in 1992 (Winters, 1995). By allowing bilateral deals regarding sectoral coverage and the depth of the agreement, vested interests may be created that can prove more difficult to dislodge in future attempts to achieve further liberalization than if the agreement had been applied on a nondiscriminatory basis. As summarized by Bhagwati (1993) such groups may argue that 'the region is our market', and that 'our markets are large enough'.

Box 10.3. Rules of origin in free trade agreements

The extent of intra-regional trade liberalization under a FTA depends on its rules of origin. Upon the formation of a FTA nonmember countries may not only be confronted with trade diversion due to the preferential nature of the abolition of barriers to trade, but also because of an effective increase in protection due to the choice of rules of origin. Assume an intermediate product enters a country free of duty and that this country accedes to a FTA. Industries using this input that export to RIA members may then have an incentive to shift to higher cost regional producers of intermediates in order to satisfy the rules of origin for their product. In effect, the rule of origin is then equivalent to a prohibitive tariff for the original third-country suppliers of components. An additional important factor is whether the rule is cumulative. Suppose a product is imported that has been processed in at least two countries, both of which have preferential status. An origin system is cumulative if the importing country only requires that sufficient processing of the product has occurred in any of the countries to which the preferential agreement applies. That is, it allows the exporting country of the final product to add (cumulate) the value added in other member countries to that added by itself. If the valued added criterion is 40 percent, and 30 percent was added in country 1 and 20 percent in country 2, the product would meet the criterion under a cumulative origin system. Under a noncumulative system of origin 40 percent would have to be added in each country. Noncumulative rules of origin are much more restrictive than rules that allow cumulation.

The more restrictive the rules of origin, the more they will reduce the extent of liberalization implied by the FTA. In an empirical analysis of trade between the EU and individual EFTA countries—each of which in principle had duty-free access to the EU—Herin (1986) found that the costs associated with satisfying the rules of origin imposed by the EU were high enough to induce 25 percent of EFTA exports to enter the EU by paying the relevant MFN tariff. More important for the trading system is the possibility of trade diversion (Krueger, 1992). Article XXIV:5b of the GATT requires that duties and other regulations of commerce applied by members of a FTA are not more restrictive than those applying prior to the formation of the area. The question of whether rules of origin are 'another regulation of commerce' is yet another dimension of GATT rules that is fuzzy and that working parties have not been able to agree on. As argued by the US in connection with the 1972 FTAs between the EEC and EFTA states, the rules of origin would 'result in trade diversion by raising barriers to third countries' exports of intermediate manufactured products and raw materials. This resulted from unnecessarily high requirements for value originating within the area. In certain cases ... the rules disqualify goods with value originating within the area as high as 96 percent. The rules of origin limited non-originating components to just five percent of the value of a finished product of the same tariff heading [for] nearly one-fifth of all industrial tariff headings. In many other cases a 20 percent rule applied' (GATT, 1974:152-53).

Although it would appear that rules of origin are unambiguously detrimental to the welfare of participating countries, this is not the case. Duttagupta and Panagariya (2000) demonstrate that restrictive rules of origin can raise welfare by reducing the magnitude of trade diversion in trade in final goods. However, intuition suggests that in most cases, highly restrictive rules such as the triple transformation or yarn-forward rules used for textile products in NAFTA (products must be made from cloth embodying yarn originating within the region) will be costly to consumers. The obvious solution is to pursue harmonization—to require the use of the non-preferential WCO rules (see chapter 5).

Nonmember Policy Responses

The most obvious reaction of third countries to the formation of a RIA is to seek a reduction in the bloc's external trade barriers. This is the primary role of the WTO. The more external barriers are lowered on a MFN basis, the less the need for multilateral disciplines. Much of the Dillon Round (1960–1; see chapter 4), was devoted to renegotiating a balance of concessions subsequent to the implementation of the EEC's common external tariff (Patterson, 1966). In practice, regional integration (in particular by the EU) has been a recurrent reason for MTNs under GATT auspices. The second component of the Dillon Round was to reduce the level of the common external tariff of the EEC, thereby limiting potential trade diversion effects.

The same type of objectives played a role in the Kennedy and Tokyo Rounds. At the time of the Kennedy Round, the margins of preference for EEC members had increased substantially, as most of the internal elimination of tariffs had been achieved. 'The record leaves no doubt that a compelling factor in the decision of Congress to pass legislation authorizing a 50 percent linear cut in tariffs [in the Kennedy Round—see chapter 4] ... was the belief that the Common Market posed a potentially serious threat to the growth, and perhaps even maintenance of American exports.' (Patterson, 1966: 176). Thus, 'the task of the Kennedy Round ... was to attempt to mitigate [the] disruptive trade effects of European economic integration' (Preeg, 1970: 29). Some success was achieved, as the Kennedy Round reportedly prevented one-third to one-half of the trade diversion that might have occurred from European integration (Preeg, 1970: 220). The first enlargement of the EEC in 1973—to include Denmark, Ireland and the UK—was a factor behind the launching of the Tokyo Round. The CAP also played a role. A major objective of the US was to improve its market access for agricultural products and to curb the EU's use of export subsidies. Links between regional integration and the Uruguay Round included the adoption of the Single European Act (the 1992 program), the implementation of the Canada-US FTA, the negotiations on the NAFTA, and the continuing distortions of world agricultural trade induced by the CAP. The foregoing is not to say that RIAs are good because they give countries an incentive to pursue concurrent MTN-based liberalization. Without the EEC, much more progress might have been made towards multilateral liberalization (Winters, 1994b).

Another policy option is to seek to join existing RIAs. The primary example here is again the EU, which expanded from six to currently 15 member states, with a number of additional accessions likely in the coming years. In North America, Mexico was induced to seek accession to Canada-US FTA, with the result a renegotiated trilateral FTA, the NAFTA. Other Latin American countries have also expressed their interest in joining NAFTA, Chile being the first candidate. To some extent accession may be motivated by market access insurance objectives. The goal is not so much to obtain duty-free access to the regional market, as average MFN tariffs are relatively low for most products, and many potential members tend to be treated preferentially in any event. More important is the elimination of the threat of contingent protection. This may be complemented by a desire to enhance the credibility of recent unilateral liberalization and structural reform efforts. However, particularly important are likely to be the firms in nonmember states that see their competitors get access to an ever larger internal market, allowing them to realize economies of scale and benefit from a reduction in real trade costs. This may well give rise to the 'domino effects' that have been observed in the case of the EU and NAFTA (Baldwin, 1996).

An alternative to accession—which frequently will either not be on offer by member states or not be regarded as desirable by nonmembers—is to seek alternative forms of association with a RIA. Examples of this strategy abound, especially in the European context. The EU has negotiated over two dozen preferential trade agreements with third countries (World Bank, 2000). Recent examples are FTAs with the CEECs, many of which are expected to accede to the EU early in the twenty-first century. The EU also has concluded a range of Cooperation and Association agreements with Mediterranean countries. These agreements illustrate the hub-and-spoke nature of European integration. Instruments of contingent protection generally remain applicable.

The creation of a RIA may also create incentives for third countries to pursue economic integration in turn. This defensive rationale appears to have been important in practice and continues to be so. Regional integration efforts in Africa and Latin America were driven in part by a wish to strengthen their bargaining position *vis-à-vis* major trading partners, reflecting a belief that this would allow them to 'better defend themselves against discriminatory effects of other regional groups' (Patterson 1966: 147). EFTA is an important case in point. EFTA was established in 1960 in reaction to the formation of the EEC. Its membership consisted of European countries that did not want to join the EEC because of concerns relating to the supranational aspects of the EEC and the likely level of the common external tariff (most EFTA countries tended to be relatively liberal). The EFTA reaction to the formation of the EEC was not unique. Japan informally proposed a Pacific Free Trade Area with the US, Canada, Australia and New Zealand in the mid-1960s for the same reason (De Melo and Panagariya, 1993). More recently, Pacific nations agreed to pursue regional free trade under auspices of the Asian-Pacific Economic Cooperation (APEC) agreement. This is an example of so-called 'open regionalism', where RIAs are used as a focal point for concerted liberalization. Essentially this involves the formation of a privileged group (see chapter 4). Free riding problems can be expected to be important in such efforts, and at the time of writing there was a great deal of uncertainty regarding the realization of APEC's goals.

Harmonization is another possible trade policy response of third countries. In general, the larger the region or the more important it is as a trading partner, the greater the incentives for a country to adopt the regulatory standards of the RIA. Third countries will have an interest in adopting identical product standards, and perhaps even similar competition rules and administrative procedures. There will often be a link—implicit or explicit—between harmonization of regulatory regimes and the threat of contingent protection. One factor driving harmonization is to reduce the possibility of being confronted by contingent protection. As RIAs increasingly are instruments for such regulatory harmonization—or for the adoption of mutual recognition procedures—the potential cause for concern on the part of nonmembers is obvious. As discussed in chapter 13, one size fits all is not necessarily optimal.

10.5. CONCLUSION

Participation in a RIA is an option allowed under the WTO. Although subject to conditions contained in Articles XXIV GATT and V GATS, multilateral disciplines are not enforced. On a number of dimensions they are also weak.

An example is the absence of any disciplines with respect to preferential rules of origin in the WTO (Box 10.3). Another is the absence of a requirement that RIAs be open to new members (Bhagwati, 1993). Multilateral surveillance is limited—even if the CRTA were effective, the focus is on WTO tests and not on the economic effects of RIAs. The WTO secretariat has no mandate to monitor the trade value or terms-of-trade effects of RIAs. Developing countries may be able to opt out of WTO disciplines on RIAs altogether by invoking the Enabling Clause, and negotiate preferential tariff reduction agreements for a limited number of products. Such agreements can greatly distort trade flows, generating substantial welfare-reducing trade diversion.

Notwithstanding these caveats, RIAs may embody many good practices and some go far beyond the WTO in terms of liberalizing markets. Thus, in the EU there are no tariffs, no safeguard mechanisms, and full binding of policies. To a large extent the current benchmark for good practice in trade policy is the set of policies and rules that apply to movement of goods, services, labor and capital inside the EU. However, this is certainly not the case as regards EU trade external policies that apply to nonmember countries. The challenge is to pursue multilaterally what the serious RIAs are implementing internally. This has been the trend. Indeed, it appears that developments in RIAs are frequently reflected in analogous developments on the multilateral front. Differences between the RIAs and the multilateral trading system at any point in time have been limited in part because efforts to negotiate RIAs have stimulated concurrent—and largely successful—efforts to achieve further multilateral trade liberalization. Indeed, the multilateral system often leads—GATS and TRIPs are examples (Hoekman and Leidy, 1993).

RIAs represent both a challenge and an opportunity for the multilateral trading system. The opportunity is to use them as experimental laboratories for cooperation on issues that have not (yet) been addressed multilaterally, especially issues where the outcome is applied on a MFN basis. Examples of such issues are discussed in chapter 13. The challenge is to control the discrimination that is inherent in preferential trade agreements. The inability of the Committee on Regional Trade Agreements to come to decisions on whether RIAs satisfy Articles XXIV and V is a problem in this regard. Absent such determinations, transparency—through multilateral surveillance—is important, as this helps mobilize domestic and regional groups who are negatively affected by RIA policies.

Both the GATT and GATS contain provisions relating to transparency and multilateral surveillance. Countries intending to form, join or modify a preferential agreement must notify this, make available relevant information requested by WTO members. Although CRTA efforts to determine the consistency of the agreement with multilateral rules are not effective, they do (or could) generate a lot of information. As in the case of AD, the key need may not be more multilateral disciplines, but greater internal scrutiny by stakeholders in member countries of regional trade policy to ensure that the interests of all groups in society are considered. While multilateral surveillance can be helpful as an objective source of information and analysis, ultimately, domestic transparency requires domestic political will. MTNs can and should play a complementary role. At the end of the day, the more successful the WTO is in reducing external barriers of members through MTNs, the less problematical RIAs will be from a systemic and nonmember perspective. Attempting to impose stricter rules on RIAs, or to use the dispute settlement system, are unlikely to be fruitful strategies.

10.6. FURTHER READING

Classic treatments of the economics of regional integration are Jacob Viner, *The Customs Union Issue* (New York: Carnegie Endowment for World Peace, 1953) and Bela Balassa, *The Theory of Economic Integration* (Homewood: Irwin, 1961). Regional integration and its relationship to the GATT is discussed in depth by the contributors to two conference volumes: Kym Anderson and Richard Blackhurst (eds.), *Regional Integration and the Global Trading System* (London: Harvester-Wheatsheaf, 1993) and Jaime de Melo and Arvind Panagariya (eds.), *New Dimensions in Regional Integration* (Cambridge: Cambridge University Press, 1993). For an excellent historical discussion of the issue of regionalism and preferential liberalization in the GATT context, see Gardner Patterson, *Discrimination in International Trade: The Policy Issues, 1945-1965* (Princeton: Princeton University Press, 1966).

The economics of regional integration are assessed in Jagdish Bhagwati and Arvind Panagariya (eds.), *The Economics of Preferential Trade Agreements* (Washington DC: American Enterprise Institute, 1996). The theoretical literature is surveyed in Richard Baldwin and Anthony Venables, 'International Economic Integration', in Gene Grossman and Kenneth Rogoff (eds.), *Handbook of International Economics, vol.3* (Amsterdam: North Holland, 1997). The relationship between regionalism and multilateralism is the subject of L. Alan Winters, 'Regionalism Versus Multilateralism', in Richard Baldwin, Daniel Cohen, André Sapir and Anthony Venables (eds.), *Market Integration, Regionalism and the Global Economy* (London: Centre for Economic Policy Research, 1998). World Bank, *Trade Blocs* (Washington DC:

The World Bank, 2000), is an assessment of the evidence concerning the impact of RIAs on developing countries and the policy options confronting developing country governments.

11
Plurilateral Agreements

The GATT 1947, a treaty between contracting parties that functioned on the basis of consensus, was very difficult to amend and expand. As discussed in chapters 1 and 2, in an effort to circumvent this problem, in the 1960s and 1970s groups of like-minded countries that sought to agree on more specific rules for policies covered by the GATT negotiated so-called codes of conduct. These codes bound only signatories, and were mostly applied on a MFN basis. Most of the existing codes were mapped into the WTO during the Uruguay Round, and their disciplines became binding upon all WTO members. However, four codes, all concluded during the Tokyo Round, were not converted into multilateral agreements. Instead they were collected in an Annex to the Marrakech Agreement establishing the WTO. The provisions of these so-called plurilateral agreements bind only signatories. As the WTO has no general MFN obligation—nondiscrimination requirements are contained in each of the various multilateral trade agreements—the plurilateral agreements contained in Annex 4 of the WTO are examples of what has been termed conditional MFN agreements. Members are free to discriminate against nonsignatories. New plurilateral agreements can be appended to the WTO on the basis of consensus (Article X:9 WTO).

Of the four agreements included in Annex 4 in 1995, two ceased to apply in September 1987. The International Bovine Meat Agreement and the International Dairy Agreement were terminated after their governing bodies decided that the objectives of the agreements could more effectively be pursued through other WTO bodies, including the Committees on Agriculture and Sanitary and Phytosanitary Measures. As of 2000, only two plurilateral agreements were operational, the Agreement on Government Procurement and the Agreement on Trade in Civil Aircraft. Of the two, the government procurement agreement is by far the more important.

11.1. GOVERNMENT PROCUREMENT

All over the world governments agencies procure goods and services as inputs into the production of public goods and services—education, defense, utilities, infrastructure, health, and so forth. The size of the associated public procurement market is often very large, depending on the economic system of a nation and its GDP. Governments concerned with maximizing the use of

scarce financial resources have developed various procedures and mechanisms to attempt to ensure that public entities procure goods and services
efficiently. A common element in such procedures is to mimic the working
of the market by requiring that public entities seek competitive bids from
potential suppliers of goods and services. Starting in the 1980s, an increasing
number of governments have pursued more far-reaching efforts to enhance
the efficiency of public services by directly subjecting production units to
competitive forces. Examples include privatization of state-owned enterprises, encouraging private entry into sectors traditionally reserved for public entities (such as utilities) and contracting out activities to independent
suppliers.

The cost-minimizing goal underlying competitive bidding requirements
for public entities is frequently complemented by other objectives that may
work against cost minimization. These may include a desire to promote the
development of domestic industry or technology, to support particular types
of firms (such as small and medium-sized enterprises) and to safeguard national security. Often such objectives are pursued through procurement
practices that discriminate against foreign suppliers. Examples of discriminatory policies pursued by governments include outright prohibitions on
foreign sourcing (civil servants must fly national airlines), and formal criteria for foreign sourcing to be permitted (minimum cost or price differentials, satisfaction of offset or local content requirements). Governments may
also favor domestic firms via selective or single tendering procedures under
which no competitive bidding for a contract is initiated, the government
instead directly approaching a specific firm for a bid. Such discriminatory
practices can be very important in terms of restricting access to markets,
given that procurement markets can easily account for 5 percent or more of
GDP in many economies.

If many countries pursue discriminatory procurement practices, the end
result for the world as a whole will be inferior in welfare terms to a cooperative outcome where governments agree to refrain from discrimination. Recognizing this, governments have attempted to negotiate multilateral rules of
the game for public procurement. The Tokyo Round government procurement agreement (GPA) was the reflection of such an effort. Liberalization of
procurement markets has also been pursued in a regional context. Procurement disciplines are prominent in the EU, where member states are prohibited from discriminating against tenders from foreign firms (be they located
in other EU member states or outside Europe). Procurement has also been
an important issue in bilateral trade relations. A number of US laws require
USTR to monitor foreign procurement policies that impact negatively on US

firms, and foreign government procurement figures prominently in USTR's annual Trade Practices report (see the USTR home page).

Discriminatory procurement policies are often considered prima facie evidence of protectionism—governments explicitly favor domestic suppliers of goods and services. However, a price preference policy of 10 percent is not equivalent to a 10 percent tariff. This is because demand by the private sector for imports may not be affected by the preference policy. As long as the government market is only a fraction of total demand for a product—as is often the case—the tariff equivalent will only be a fraction of 10 percent. Indeed, as pointed out by Baldwin and Richardson (1972) in a seminal analysis, if domestic and foreign products are good substitutes and government demand is less than domestic supply, discrimination will have no effect at all. The increased demand by the government for domestic output will be exactly offset by greater private sector imports, so that the policy has no effect on equilibrium prices and production of the domestic industry. This result continues to obtain if there is imperfect competition (oligopoly) as long as goods are perfect substitutes (Miyagiwa, 1991).[1] Imports might actually increase as a result of discriminatory policy if domestic firms are induced to cut back sales to the private sector in an attempt to raise prices. However, if government demand exceeds local production, discrimination will result in domestic prices being bid up, and output of the domestic industry will expand to meet demand. If allowance is made for the fact that in the longer run firms will enter into markets where there are excess profits, over time prices will fall and at the end of the day the discrimination policy may again have no negative implications for welfare.

Other contributions to the literature on procurement note that asymmetric information provides a potential economic rationale for discrimination. McAffee and McMillan (1989) show that if domestic firms have a competitive disadvantage in producing the product (are higher cost producers compared to foreign firms), and only a limited number of firms (foreign and domestic) bid for the contract, a price preference policy may induce foreign firms to lower their bids. If the products procured are intangible (services) or there are problems in monitoring and enforcing contract compliance, discrimination can increase the likelihood of performance. Problems of asymmetric information and contract compliance may give entities a natural preference

---

[1] As noted by Deardorff and Stern (1998), domestic middlemen will always have an incentive to import a good and resell it to the government after processing it enough to qualify as domestic. The same forces therefore apply if goods are imperfect substitutes. Difficulties in determining the origin of products will always reduce the effectiveness of discriminatory policies—such as procurement preferences—that are not enforced by customs officials. The level of tariffs and NTBs applied at the border will be the main constraint on such arbitrage activities.

to choose suppliers located within their jurisdictions as this can reduce monitoring costs. Such proximity incentives will make it more difficult for foreign firms to bid successfully, even in the absence of formal discrimination. The policy issue that then arises concerns the barriers against establishment (FDI) by foreign suppliers.

While there are a variety of situations under which discriminatory procurement will have no effect or may even enhance national welfare by lowering procurement costs, simulation studies suggest that welfare gains are likely to be modest at best. Greater profits of domestic firms or cost savings to public entities will tend to offset by increased prices. As a result, the potential cost savings are reduced (Deltas and Evenett, 1997). Given that in most instances the optimal policy will be difficult to determine and generally will vary depending on the specifics of the situation, in practice favoritism can be expected to be more costly than a policy of nondiscrimination. In many situations the information required to judge if diverging from nondiscrimination is beneficial will not be available. Nondiscrimination has therefore been argued to be a good rule of thumb (Hoekman, 1998). If account is taken of the rent seeking distortions that may be induced by discriminatory policies and the social cost of corruption and bribery, the case for nondiscrimination is substantially strengthened. All of the above arguments regarding the economic pros and cons of discrimination cease to apply if government entities do not maximize social welfare. Nondiscrimination will generally reduce discretion and enhance transparency of the procurement process and thus reduce the scope for rent-seeking. Most important in this connection is transparency and a system of rules to impede corruption. Open and competitive bidding, whether or not there are preferences, is a key instrument in this regard.

The WTO Agreement on Government Procurement

The 1979 Tokyo Round GPA extended basic GATT obligations such as non-discrimination and transparency to the tendering procedures of selected government entities. The GPA was renegotiated twice, most recently during the Uruguay Round. As a result, its coverage was extended substantially. Membership is limited, comprising Canada, the European Communities, the fifteen EU member states, Hong Kong, Israel, Japan, Korea, Norway, Singapore, Switzerland, and the United States.[2] The GPA applies to 'any law,

---

[2] The European Communities refers to the Community's institutions. Formally, there were 25 signatories to the GPA in 1999, as each EU member state has signed the Agreement individually

regulation, procedure, or practice regarding any procurement by entities covered by this Agreement, as specified in Annexes 1-5' (Article I). The concept of procurement covers all contractual options, including purchase, leasing, rental and hire purchase, with or without the option to buy. A so-called positive list is used to determine the reach of the Agreement: it applies *only* to entities listed in an annex. There are three 'entity annexes': Annex 1 lists covered central government entities; Annex 2 lists sub-central government entities; and Annex 3 lists all other entities that procure 'in accordance with the provisions of this Agreement'. Annex 3 is a catch-all category that includes bodies such as utilities. Entities listed in Annex 3 may be partially or totally private. The term entity is nowhere defined in the agreement, reflecting a lack of consensus on what constitutes a public undertaking.

The entities listed in the three annexes are subject to the rules and disciplines of the GPA with respect to their procurement of goods and services if the value of the procurement exceeds certain specified thresholds (see Table 11.1) and the goods or services involved are not exempted from the coverage of the Agreement. As far as goods are concerned, in principle all procurement is covered, unless specified otherwise in an annex. Procurement of services is subject to a positive list: only the procurement by covered entities of services explicitly scheduled in Annexes 4 and 5 are subject to the GPA's rules, and then only insofar as no qualifications or limitations are maintained in the relevant annexes. To give an indication of the orders of magnitude involved in the 1995 extension of the GPA's coverage to sub-central entities and services—the offers made by the US and the EU covered some US$100 billion of purchases (Schott and Buurman, 1994: 74).

The primary obligation imposed by the GPA on covered entities is non-discrimination. This extends not only to imports but also to subsidiaries of locally established foreign firms. The GPA thus goes beyond the GATT, which does not extend national treatment to foreign affiliates. The latter are generally treated as national firms, and governments are free to treat domestic firms worse than foreign ones. Price-preference policies, offsets and similar policies are therefore in principle prohibited. The GPA provides for three tendering methods: open (competitive call for tender), selective, (tendering restricted to prequalified suppliers), and limited (approaching potential suppliers individually). The first two methods are preferred. Entities must publish an invitation to participate for all cases of intended procurement, except for the case of limited tendering, stating the mode of procurement, its nature and quantity, dates of delivery, economic and technical re-

---

in addition to the European Communities. This is because in some dimensions of procurement EU member states retain competence.

quirements, and amounts and terms of payment. Entities must award contracts to the tenderer who 'has been determined to be fully capable of undertaking the contract' and who is either the lowest tender or the tender that is most advantageous in terms of the evaluation criteria set out in the notices or tender documentation.

TABLE 11.1 *GPA Thresholds for coverage of procurement contracts (SDRs)*

Category of procurement	SDRs
Central Government Entities	
Goods	130,000
Services except construction services	130,000
Construction services	5,000,000[1]
Sub-central Government Agencies	
Goods	200,000[2]
Services except construction services	200,000[2]
Construction services	5,000,000[3]
All Other Entities That Procure in Accordance With the Agreement*	
Goods	400,000[4]
Services except construction services	400,000[4]
Construction services	5,000,000[3]

* In general public enterprises or public authorities such as utilities.
[1] Israel: 8.5 million; Japan 4.5 million (with architecture services: 450,000)
[2] US and Canada: 355,000; Israel: 250,000
[3] Israel: 8.5 million; Japan and Korea: 15 million
[4] Canada and Israel: 355,000; Japan: 130,000.
Source: WTO Agreement on Government Procurement.

The nature of procurement is such that most of the time, unless rapid action can be taken, firms will not have an interest in bringing cases contesting violations of the rules of the game. Accordingly, the GPA requires members to establish bid-protest or 'challenge mechanisms'. These must provide for rapid interim measures to correct breaches of the agreement and to preserve commercial opportunities. Such measures may involve suspension and reopening of the procurement process, or compensation for the loss or damages suffered. To facilitate application of WTO dispute settlement procedures, Article XVIII GPA requires each entity, on request, to promptly provide pertinent information concerning the reasons why the supplier's application to qualify was rejected, why an existing qualification was terminated, and to an unsuccessful tenderer, why a bid was not selected. The latter must include pertinent information concerning the characteristics and relative advantages of the tender that was selected as well as the name of the winning tenderer.

A limited number of provisions pertain to developing countries. Although in principle no discrimination is allowed in favor of domestic firms by covered entities, Article V:4 allows developing countries to negotiate 'mutually acceptable exclusions from the rules on national treatment with respect to certain entities, products, or services that are included in their lists of entities'. Such negotiations may also be initiated after signing the agreement (Article V:5). Some scope therefore exists for maintaining a price preference policy. However, the option is limited to certain entities, products or services, and is a function of the relative negotiating power of the country seeking an exception. Article XVI of the GPA allows developing countries, at the time of accession, to negotiate conditions for the use of offsets and domestic content requirements, thus allowing for another form of discrimination against foreign suppliers. Offset requirements may only be used to determine qualification to participate in the procurement process. They may not be used as criteria for awarding contracts. Thus, if a firm offers local content that greatly exceeds the minimum required, this may not be a factor in awarding contracts.

Operation of the GPA

The GPA requires signatories to report annual statistics on procurement by covered entities to the GATT Committee on Government Procurement. Such data reporting was intended to help parties determine how well the Agreement was functioning, in part by providing comparable cross-country information on sourcing practices. Signatories began reporting statistics for the year 1983. Data reported in Hoekman and Mavroidis (1997) for the 1983-92 period—when only central government procurement of goods was covered by the GPA—revealed that the aggregate amount of purchases by such entities was some US$ 62 billion. The largest procurement market, by a substantial margin, opened up under the GPA is that of the United States, which accounted for almost half of this total figure. The data reveal that smaller countries, on average, procured much more on international markets than did large countries. If Canada, the EU, Japan and the US are excluded, about 60 percent of purchases by covered entities exceeding the threshold went to national suppliers (Table 11.2). This compares to more than 90 percent for the large players. EU statistics define 'domestic' as intra-EU sourcing. It is not surprising, therefore, that reported self-sufficiency ratios for the EU-12 are above 90 percent on average. In interpreting these statistics it should be noted that no distinction is made between domestic firms proper and foreign firms that have established a local presence. To the extent that large countries attract a greater amount of FDI, the higher self-sufficiency ratios may be somewhat misleading.

In the EU, Japan and the US, the share of domestic firms in total above threshold procurement by covered entities remained virtually unchanged during 1983-92. For the smaller countries, however, with the exception of Singapore and Switzerland, the share of procurement from national sources declined over time. It is impossible to attribute such changes in sourcing patterns to the GPA—regional developments also played a role, such as the NAFTA in North America and efforts to liberalize EU procurement markets. Unilateral deregulation and privatization policies also must have had an impact. Nonetheless, the finding that smaller GPA members became less nationalistic in their purchasing decisions suggests that practices did become more open. During the same period, the share of contracts that exceeded the threshold tended to increase. In 1983-5, some 39 percent of all procurement by covered entities fell above the threshold. By 1991-2, it had risen to 49 percent (Table 11.2). This can be explained in part by a reduction in the threshold in 1988, from SDR150,000 to SDR130,000. There is an interesting pattern in the procurement data reported by the EU and the US. The former steadily increases the share of contracts exceeding the threshold, and the latter steadily decreases it. As the US had a much larger proportion of procurement above the threshold than the EU in the early 1980s (80 compared to 40 percent, respectively), the two gradually converged. As of the early 1990s, the share of above threshold contracts for both EU and US entities averaged around 60 percent.

TABLE 11.2 *Indicators of GPA performance, 1983–92*
(US$ million and percent)

	Share of Limited Tendering		Share of Procurement Covered Domestically		Share of Procurement Exceeding Threshold	
	1983–5	1990–2	1983–5	1990–2	1983–5	1990–2
Austria	43.2	43.2	51.3	1.5	46.9	43.5
Belgium	10.3	8.6	100.0	100.0	40.0	57.5
Canada	9.7	7.4	92.3	77.4	42.9	46.0
Denmark	4.0	1.4	95.6	79.8	5.8	12.6
Finland	0.3	0.1	95.7	69.1	39.4	18.1
France	33.3	29.6	97.6	97.2	35.1	85.5
Germany	13.3	24.0	97.2	99.1	24.9	61.7
Hong Kong	22.1	28.2	5.8	3.2	67.7	71.2
Ireland	1.8	5.6	100.0	84.8	20.6	29.1

	Share of Limited Tendering		Share of Procurement Covered Domestically		Share of Procurement Exceeding Threshold	
	1983–5	1990–2	1983–5	1990–2	1983–5	1990–2
Israel	5.0	3.3	13.7	25.6	84.0	91.1
Italy	1.0	5.9	99.2	97.8	5.0	60.5
Japan	12.3	21.0	86.1	85.5	37.4	43.7
Luxembourg	39.8	23.9	100.0	97.8	30.9	28.4
Netherlands	16.8	13.5	98.7	86.4	12.1	37.7
Norway	7.1	8.3	48.6	40.4	44.5	58.9
Singapore	0.0	0.0	45.1	67.3	57.9	51.1
Sweden	4.0	4.8	43.7	43.6	27.9	36.9
Switzerland	25.1	27.7	35.7	38.3	43.8	39.8
UK	13.7	6.6	99.4	98.2	29.3	49.0
US	11.5	9.6	86.3	90.4	80.1	66.8
Memo: EU countries	19.0	15.0	98.3	94.9	21.2	54.1

Source: Hoekman (1998), based on WTO secretariat, Annual reports to the Government Procurement Committee, 1984-94.

Under the GPA, open competitive tendering procedures are in principle to be used for all contracts that exceed the relevant threshold. As noted earlier, limited tendering procedures involving an entity negotiating with potential suppliers individually is only allowed under certain conditions and members are required to report data on their use of this method. The issue became important in US-Japan trade relations in the 1980s, following US complaints that the use of limited tendering was excessive (Stern and Hoekman, 1987). The use of limited tendering varies across signatories, from a reported low of zero (Singapore) to a high of over 30 percent on average for France, Italy, Switzerland and Hong Kong. Across all signatories the average share of limited tendering was about 13 percent. By 1992, the EU had caught up with the US in terms of use of limited tendering, both standing at 10 percent. Japan's use of limited tendering rose from around 12 percent during 1983-5 to 21 percent during 1990-2.

The data reported to the GPA Committee are not as useful or informative as they might be. What matters from an economic point of view is primarily the size of government demand for a good or services relative to total domestic supply. As discussed previously, it is especially in cases where the government is a big player relative to domestic supply that there can be significant effects on national welfare and foreign suppliers. Multilateral scrutiny will have potentially the largest payoff if it focuses on such situations.

As the reporting requirements are quite burdensome, an added benefit of a more focused approach to data collection would be a reduction in the costs of surveillance.

Disputes

There have been a number of disputes under the WTO on procurement. All have involved the EU or the US. In 1996, the EU objected to a law of the Commonwealth of Massachusetts that prohibited public authorities in Massachusetts from procuring goods or services from persons who do business with Myanmar. The EU (joined in 1997 by Japan) argued this violated the GPA, as Massachusetts is covered under the US schedule to the GPA. A panel was established, but proceedings were suspended at the request of the complainants, following a bilateral settlement in 1999. In 1997, the EU raised the procurement of a navigation satellite by the Japanese Ministry of Transport, arguing that the technical specifications in the tender were not neutral because they referred explicitly to US specifications. Here also a mutually acceptable solution to the dispute was found (a panel was never established). A third case concerned US allegations that the Korean Airport Construction Authority's practices relating to qualification for bidding as a prime contractor, domestic partnering, and the absence of access to challenge procedures violated the GPA.

There have also been cases involving developing countries that are not members of the GPA. For example, in 1991, two Brazilian firms won an international tender for electric power transformers issued by the Federal Electricity Commission of Mexico. Subsequently, three of the Mexican firms that lost the tender brought an antidumping petition against the Brazilian firms. AD duties ranging from 26 to 35 percent were imposed in September 1993. Brazil requested the Antidumping Committee to conciliate, arguing the AD duty was calculated by comparing prices bid by the different firms for the original tender, and not by comparing prices charged in the home and the export market. This dispute was also resolved bilaterally (Hoekman and Kostecki, 1995).

The Challenge of Expanding Membership

As mentioned above, membership of the GPA is quite limited. Indeed, not all OECD countries have signed it. A major challenge facing WTO members in the coming years is to bring procurement of both goods and services into the WTO. Public procurement markets are too big to be left beyond the reach of the multilateral trading system, and strong pressures can be expected by export interests in the more open countries to improve their access to such markets. The US has made expansion of membership a priority issue, linking this to the broader issue of combating corruption.[3] The history of GATT attempts to deal with this issue suggests that progress will require creativity on the part of negotiators.

One reason low-income countries have been reluctant to accede to the GPA is that they find it difficult to obtain reciprocal concessions from GPA members. Negotiating leverage is a function of the size of the incremental market access that aspiring members can offer, and this tends to be small. Moreover, many developing countries are not players on the international procurement market, implying that the standard mercantilist bargain is not available to move things along. Abstracting from cross-issue linkages such as seeking lower tariffs on labor-intensive export products—as these are difficult to achieve outside a MTN—one option would be to allow the use of price preferences by developing countries. Although more empirical research is required to determine the economic importance of permitting discrimination, price preferences have the advantage of being transparent and less distortive than other types of discriminatory policies that are often pursued (such as bans on participation by foreign bidders or local content and offset requirements). Tariffying such policies through an agreement permitting price preference schemes would also provide a focal point for future multilateral negotiations to reduce discrimination. Such preferences are allowed subject to certain conditions and limits by multilateral development banks. Provisions for their use are also included in the UNCITRAL Model Law on Procurement. Many developing countries have incorporated such preferences into their legislation. Recognition of the potential legitimacy of price preferences may help alter the incentives for accession.

Many of the purchases by government entities comprise services or products where economic forces favor procuring from local suppliers. In such cases, procurement preferences will only be binding if foreign firms cannot contest the market through FDI, or if government entities differentiate across firms on the basis of their nationality. Outright market access restrictions that take the form of a ban on FDI are costly to the economy as a whole, and policy efforts that focus on elimination of such bans are likely to have a greater payoff than attempting to outlaw discrimination.

---

[3] 'This Administration is determined to ... push initiatives to clean up government procurement practices around the world' (*Financial Times*, May 1, 1995, p. 5). In April 1996, largely at the insistence of the US, OECD members agreed not to allow firms to write off bribes against tax obligations (Oxford Analytica, April 18, 1996).

Discrimination is just one, albeit important, dimension of possible multilateral disciplines for government procurement. It is widely believed that there are significant potential gains from disciplines that promote transparent procurement mechanisms, thereby reducing the scope for corruption and rent seeking. A WTO Working Group on Transparency in Government Procurement, established at the 1996 Singapore ministerial, was given the mandate to discuss possible stand-alone rules regarding transparency in procurement. Many developing countries perceive this to be a Trojan horse (a vehicle to start discussing discrimination and extend the coverage of GPA disciplines). However, given that discrimination may be a second-order issue in comparison with corruption, a case can be made that the focus should be on transparency first and foremost.

Negotiating an agreement on transparency in government procurement was to be one of the issues on the agenda of the Seattle ministerial. Such an agreement was strongly supported by GPA members, as well as a number of non-GPA countries such as Australia. Several draft proposals for an agreement were submitted in November 1999, including by the EU, Japan, Australia, and a joint submission by Hungary, Korea, Singapore and the US. These countries sought to conclude an agreement at the ministerial. Many developing countries remained cautious in the run-up to Seattle, emphasizing that much more discussion was needed on the implications of transparency obligations in the procurement area.

11.2. THE CIVIL AIRCRAFT AGREEMENT

The Agreement on Trade in Civil Aircraft aims to reduce both tariffs and NTBs affecting world trade in civil aircraft. It was the only sector-specific agreement covering a manufactured product that was successfully negotiated in the Tokyo Round. It is in part a zero-for-zero tariff agreement, as signatories agree to eliminate import duties on civil aircraft and the bulk of aircraft parts. The agreement also reinforces disciplines on NTMs such as subsidies. Members to the agreement include most leading civil aircraft exporters (the Russian Federation, not a WTO member, is an exception). A Committee on Civil Aircraft oversees the agreement. Its continued existence is to some extent a legacy from the past. The Agreement was originally negotiated because little progress could be made during the Tokyo Round on subsidies. As the WTO Subsidies Agreement applies to civil aircraft—as do all other GATT disciplines—the rationale for a sectoral agreement is unclear.

Disputes regarding trade in civil aircraft have been a recurring element of trade relations between the US and the EU, reflecting the battle for market share fought between Boeing and McDonnell Douglas on the one hand (now merged), and Airbus on the other. The Agreement has done little to reduce the sources of tension between these two dominant players, nor has it been effective in addressing conflicts between smaller aircraft producing nations such as Canada and Brazil. The latter became embroiled in disputes regarding the alleged use of export subsidies in the late 1990s, but the Agreement on Civil Aircraft did not play a role in the various panel cases, which are discussed in chapter 3.[4]

11.3. CONCLUSION

Plurilateral agreements are outliers in the WTO system. Although there are presently only two such agreements, the fact that the WTO offers the flexibility of negotiating such agreements may prove important in the future. One of the benefits of the Tokyo Round 'codes approach' was that it allowed for a 'variable geometry'. The downside of the codes was that they addressed GATT issues and it was not completely clear whether the MFN rule applied to them. There also was no unified dispute settlement system, creating the potential for forum shopping and the development of diverging case law. With the creation of the DSU this problem no longer exists, in principle allowing for greater use of plurilateral agreements. Such agreements are a vehicle for like-minded countries to cooperate in areas not (yet) addressed by the WTO. They allow countries not willing to consider disciplines in a policy area to opt out. Given that it is now clear that the Uruguay Round approach of requiring that all agreements apply to all WTO is problematical for many developing countries, and that issues such as labor standards are unlikely to attract a consensus, the plurilateral option may come to be used more in the future.

11. 4. FURTHER READING

Little has been written on how plurilateral agreements fit into the WTO framework. The trade policy-oriented literature on government procurement and civil aircraft is also relatively sparse. Many of the contributions in Bernard Hoekman and Petros C. Mavroidis (eds.), *Law and Policy in Public Purchasing: The WTO Agreement on Government Procurement* (Ann Arbor:

---

[4] Canada - Measures Affecting the Export of Civilian Aircraft, complaint by Brazil (WT/DS70, WT/DS71); Brazil - Export Financing Programme for Aircraft, complaint by Canada (WT/DS46).

University of Michigan Press, 1997) discuss the genesis, operation and relevance of the GPA to countries at differing levels of development. Contributions also cover the UNICITRAL model law for procurement and procurement regimes of non-GPA members such as India and New Zealand. A classic study of the economics of discrimination in procurement is Robert Baldwin and J. David Richardson, 'Government Purchasing Policies, Other NTBs, and the International Monetary Crisis', in H. English and K. Hay (eds.), *Obstacles to Trade in the Pacific Area.* (Ottawa: Carleton School of International Affairs, 1972). R. Preston McAfee and John McMillan, 'Government Procurement and International Trade', *Journal of International Economics*, 26 (1989), 291-308 make the theoretical case for discrimination in markets characterized by imperfect competition and small numbers of bidders. Albert Breton and Pierre Salmon review the literature and question some of the conventional wisdom regarding the rationales for procurement policies in 'Are Discriminatory Procurement Policies Motivated By Protectionism?', *Kyklos*, 49 (1995), 47-68. The role of the Civil Aircraft Agreement and the rivalry between the EU and US is discussed in Steve McGuire, *Airbus Industrie* (London: McMillan, 1997). For an analysis of the Canada-Brazil aircraft dispute, see *World Trade Agenda*, June 5, 2000, no. 00/11.

PART V
CHALLENGES FOR THE TRADING SYSTEM

12

Integrating Developing Countries and Economies in Transition

For a long time, the GATT was a club that was primarily of relevance to OECD countries. Developing countries did not participate fully. With the creation of the WTO this changed. Developing countries became subject to a large number of new obligations—some newly negotiated in the Uruguay Round, others originally negotiated during earlier rounds among industrialized nations. Although this change greatly expanded the global reach of the organization, the resource costs for developing country governments and societies associated with complying with the new disciplines were often substantial. The Uruguay Round created an implementation 'overhang' that will be with the organization for some time to come. The implementation problems are part of the broader challenge of integrating developing and transition economies into the global trading system. How the members manage the shift from a 'traders club' to a multilateral organization in which 141-plus countries express their views and defend their interests will determine the relevance of the WTO to its poorer members. This chapter briefly reviews the history of developing country involvement in GATT and the experience of the first five years of the WTO, including efforts to negotiate the accession of China and Russia.

12.1. SPECIAL AND DIFFERENTIAL TREATMENT

The terms of developing-country participation in the multilateral trading system have oscillated between reciprocity and disengagement. Three stages can be identified (Table 12.1):

(1) small scale membership of low-income countries in GATT based on a formal parity of obligations, although from the very start developing countries sought special treatment (1947–64);

(2) substantial broadening of developing country membership based on the concept of more favorable and differential treatment (1964–86); and

(4) deepening integration of developing countries into the GATT-WTO system, with a return to reciprocal relationships (post-1986).

The initial premise underlying GATT 1947 was essentially parity of obligations—making no distinction between rich and poor trading nations (Hudec, 1987). In the mid-1950s the concept of giving preferential treatment to developing countries arose, when a large number of colonies approached independence. Two types of preferential treatment can be distinguished. The first consisted of a request for better than MFN access to rich country markets through tariff and other preferences. Such preferences were already in effect, largely reflecting economic relationships built up by France and the UK with their colonies. A second form of preferential treatment consisted of requests for exemptions from GATT rules and mechanisms. Preferences of both types were justified in various ways. One argument was so-called export pessimism. The fear was that if developing countries relied upon exports for growth, their supply of commodities would exceed what could be absorbed by the world. The resulting excess supply and consequent decline in world prices justified trade restrictions by developing countries—in effect, they should impose tariffs to improve their terms of trade (Prebisch, 1952; Bhagwati, 1988). Given their reliance on exports of commodities, export pessimism was complemented by the view that developing countries needed protection to achieve industrialization and economic development, and that a 'new world trade order' was required to break the vicious circle of underdevelopment. Developing countries, it was argued, suffered from foreign exchange shortages requiring protectionist policies to protect their balance of payments. International trade was also seen by some as an instrument of exploitation and self-sufficiency as beneficial. More generally, it was argued that economic development required the pursuit of import substitution policies.

TABLE 12.1 *GATT and developing countries*

Date	Event
1947	Ten what would now be called low-income countries accede to the GATT on essentially the same terms as developed countries. An infant-industry protection clause (Article XVIII) is the main development-specific provision in GATT.
1954–5	Article XVIII is modified to include XVIII:*b* allowing for QRs to be used for BOP purposes whenever foreign-exchange reserves are below what is considered necessary for economic development. This vague test constitutes much weaker discipline than Article XII. It has been invoked extensively (see chapter 9).
1964	Establishment of UNCTAD. A committee for Trade and Development is created in the GATT to address development-related concerns; the International Trade Centre (ITC)—a technical cooperation agency in the area of trade promotion—is charged with assisting developing countries to promote exports.

Date	Event
1965	A new Part IV on Trade and Development is added to the GATT, defining the notion of nonreciprocity for developing countries. However, Part IV contains no legally binding obligations, other than to consult.
1968	The US accepts the Generalized System of Preferences (GSP) – as called for by UNCTAD – under which industrialized countries grant tariff preferences to developing countries on a non-reciprocal basis. Such preferences were voluntary and granted unilaterally. The ITC becomes a joint venture between GATT and UNCTAD.
1971	A GATT waiver is granted authorizing tariff preferences under the GSP. Another waiver is adopted for the Protocol on Trade Negotiations among Developing Countries (Geneva Protocol).
1973-9	More than 70 developing countries participate in the Tokyo Round. The Enabling Clause is adopted. It introduces the concept of 'special and differential treatment' (S&D), makes the 1971 waivers permanent and includes language on graduation. Most developing countries abstain from signing the various Tokyo Round codes.
1986	Developing countries participate in the preparation for a new round. The Punta del Este ministerial declaration launching the Uruguay Round contains numerous references to S&D.
1994	All developing-country GATT contracting parties join the WTO, adopting the results of the Uruguay Round as a Single Undertaking.
1997	The Integrated Framework for Trade-related Assistance for Least Developed Countries is created.
1999	Developing countries are responsible for more than half of all the submissions for the Seattle ministerial meeting.

The institutional expression of this line of thinking was embodied in the creation of UNCTAD in 1964, and the formation of a political bloc of developing countries in the UN called the 'Group of 77' (G-77). One year later, in 1965, developing country demands for special status in the multilateral trading system led to the drafting of a new Part IV of the GATT. This introduced the concept of special and differential (S&D) treatment for developing countries. To a large extent the adoption of Part IV can be seen as a reaction of GATT contracting parties to the creation of UNCTAD. As of that moment,

S&D reigned supreme for the next 20 years. Developing countries were not expected to grant tariff concessions and bind tariffs.[1]

Developing nations successfully invoked the principle of S&D as cover for not engaging in reciprocal reductions of trade barriers. For example, the 1973 ministerial meeting that launched the Tokyo Round stated that the negotiations should secure additional benefits for developing countries in order to achieve a substantial increase in their foreign exchange earnings, diversification of their exports and an acceleration of the rate of growth of their trade. It confirmed that developed nations should not expect reciprocal concessions from developing economies. The inconsistency between these goals and the policy of allowing developing countries to maintain protection and GATT-inconsistent trade regimes was not openly remarked upon. However, during the negotiations, high-income countries repeatedly voiced their dissatisfaction with the reluctance of developing countries to accept and expand GATT disciplines. This found its expression in the negotiation of codes on various issues in which membership was voluntary—see chapters 5 and 11—thus avoiding the veto that was likely by developing countries if an attempt was made to amend the GATT to include new obligations.

One result of the Tokyo Round was a Framework Agreement, which included the so-called 'Enabling Clause'. Officially called Differential and More Favorable Treatment, Reciprocity and Fuller Participation of Developing Countries, it provided for departures from MFN and other GATT rules. The Enabling Clause created a permanent legal basis for the operation of the general system of preferences (GSP) established under UNCTAD auspices. It codified principles, practices and procedures regarding the use of trade measures for BOP purposes (Articles XII and XVIII) and made GATT's Article XIX redundant by giving developing countries flexibility in applying trade measures to meet their 'essential development needs'. It also weakened the reach of Article XXIV on regional integration by eliminating the 'substantially all trade' requirement and the provision banning an increase in the average level of external protection for customs unions. The quid pro quo for the codification of these exemptions was the inclusion of a graduation principle. This was vaguely worded, however, and was more in the nature of a statement of principle.

---

[1] Much depended here on how a country acceded to the GATT. Most developing countries acceded under Article XXVI:5c, under which former colonies could undertake to accept the obligations initially negotiated by the metropolitan government. As these had generally not established separate tariff schedules for their colonies, newly independent states were able to accede without submitting a schedule. Countries that were not ex-colonies were generally required to negotiate accession under Article XXXIII GATT, a tougher proposition that required establishment of a tariff schedule.

The idea that the most successful developing trading nations should begin to move back towards a parity of obligations first appeared in the late 1970s. The basic objective of OECD countries was to progressively integrate into the GATT system developing countries with large markets or substantial trade levels and growth. This strategy was not so much inspired by growing evidence that economic development required liberal trade and pro-market policies—which was being compiled under the leadership of scholars such as Jagdish Bhagwati and Anne Krueger—but because a number of countries had managed to grow sufficiently to become attractive markets. The fact that many such countries often had large positive trade balances with industrialized countries provided an additional incentive to try to impose graduation criteria. A problem in this regard was that no agreement existed on what constituted a developing country. Indeed, the issue was carefully avoided. For example, when Portugal and Israel claimed developing country status in the GATT Balance-of-Payments Committee so as to be able to invoke Article XVIII:*b*, the committee avoided pronouncing itself on the matter. It was left to countries to self-declare their status, usually upon accession to the GATT. Individual contracting parties could also decide for themselves whether to treat a particular trading partner as a developing country. This continues to be the case under the WTO. An exception concerns the group of 48 least-developed countries, where the UN definition is used. In practice, graduation was and is left to bilateral interaction and tends to be limited to obvious candidates. The decision by Korea to cease invocation of Article XVIII to justify trade restrictions (discussed in chapter 9) is an example.

Although the rationale for S&D was based on prevalent theories that import substitution was a necessary element in effective development strategies, it was also the case that GATT's reciprocity dynamic was less effective in a developing economy context. A necessary condition for reciprocity to work is that decision-makers confront lobbies that seek better access to foreign markets. A problem was that potential gainers from such greater access—export industries—often did not exist or were small in developing countries. Moreover, those that might have favored domestic liberalization as a quid pro quo for better access to foreign markets often benefited from preferential (GSP or related) treatment, reducing their incentive to go head-to-head with domestic import-competing industries. Frequently, export industries were also granted exemptions from tariffs on their imported inputs, further reducing incentives to oppose protection. Problems were generally compounded by economic mismanagement that led to high unemployment, inflation and support for noncompetitive industries.

Policymakers in many developing countries were also highly skeptical of the benefits of full participation in the GATT. While the key problem from a development perspective was not GATT and its reliance on reciprocity, but the pursuit of inappropriate economic policies, GATT did little to help convince governments to adopt more liberal trade policies. Only if a country managed through its own efforts to grow, run a trade surplus, and become a potentially attractive export market, were pressures exerted to bring the country into the GATT fold. Finally, global foreign policy considerations also played a role in the acceptance of S&D. Some high-income countries believed that an insistence on reciprocal obligations might help push poor nations to join the Soviet bloc (Kostecki, 1979). A concerted decision by major Third World states not to participate in the GATT would have been contrary to Western interests.

The Value of S&D

The corollary of S&D—free riding—was less beneficial to developing countries than they had expected. One reason was that MTNs were essentially conducted among developed trading nations, who concentrated on their own trade interests. As discussed in chapter 4, the principal supplier rule used in MTNs helps ensure that free riding is minimized (Finger, 1974, 1979). Products of major importance to developing countries such as agriculture or textiles and clothing were either excluded from GATT or granted protectionist treatment on an ad hoc basis. Indeed, as noted in earlier chapters, the fact that developing countries were not playing the GATT game is one explanation for the continued existence of protectionist policies on textiles and clothing, footwear and other 'sensitive' labor-intensive sectors in OECD countries. Once developing country governments started to pursue unilateral liberalization and export-oriented strategies, the existence of high market access barriers in these sectors mobilized export lobbies to support more active participation in the GATT. Moreover, as industrialized country trade barriers were reduced over time through recurring MTNs, the value of tariff preferences was eroded, further reducing the benefits of nonreciprocity. The value of preferences was also diluted because of the uncertainty regarding their applicability over time. Preferences were granted unilaterally, and could be removed unilaterally. The rules determining eligibility to benefit from preference schemes were at the discretion of granting countries. This not only contributed to the uncertainty dimension, but also eroded the value of the preference margin by imposing costs on developing countries (Box 12.1).

Box 12.1. Unilateral preferences are uncertain

To benefit from preferential access, exporters must be able to document that products originate in countries that have been granted preferences. The rules of origin used in the context of GSP schemes are therefore important. An example from the US illustrates how rules of origin may be used to nullify the benefits of preferences. In 1983, the US adopted the Caribbean Basin Initiative, which granted Caribbean countries duty-free access to the US for many products. To determine whether a product was eligible for preferential treatment, a value-added criterion of 35 percent was required. That is, at least 35 percent of the value of the good imported into the US must have been generated in the Caribbean. The preference scheme induced foreign investment in the Caribbean. Among such investors were companies that established operations in Costa Rica and Jamaica to convert surplus European wine into ethanol, which was then exported to the US. This production process met the 35 percent value added test. Two years later, with production and exports doing well, the exporters were hit with a rule change: a US Congressman introduced an amendment to a tax bill raising the value added requirement for ethanol to 70 percent—an impossible requirement to meet for the Caribbean producers. The US industry that had lobbied for this rule change was never threatened by the imports—which never exceeded three percent of US consumption (Bovard, 1991: 22).

12.2. CHANGING ATTITUDES TOWARDS THE TRADING SYSTEM

Developing country stances towards trade policy changed in the early 1980s, reflecting the debt crisis, the demonstration effect of the benefits of the export-oriented policy stance taken by the dynamic economies of South-East Asia, and the collapse of central planning. As national trade policies became more neutral and export industries emerged, interest in the GATT increased. Unilateral changes in national policy stances led to a major shift in both the strategy and the tactics of developing countries in the GATT. They participated actively in the Uruguay Round negotiations, and engaged in reciprocal exchange of concessions. Developing countries had a significant impact on the design of the GATS and the Agreements on Textiles and Clothing and Agriculture, TRIMs, and TRIPs. This influence was already manifest at the 1986 Punta del Este ministerial meeting, where a group of smaller developing and developed economies (the Swiss-Colombian coalition) played a mediating role between the US, the EU, and large developing countries such as Brazil and India. This marked a sea change not just in terms of participation, but also because it became obvious that it was no longer appropriate to regard developing countries as a bloc (assuming this had ever been the case). Instead, countries pursued their self-interest in a much more open way than in the past. This included teaming up with high-income countries if this was appropriate. The Cairns Group—discussed in chapter 6—was a prominent example of a North-South coalition of countries.[2]

In contrast to the Kennedy and Tokyo Rounds, the Uruguay Round was a single undertaking: all agreements were to apply to all members, and all members were to submit schedules of concessions and commitments. Although the single undertaking implied a dramatic change for developing countries, the creation of the WTO does not mean S&D is dead. Ending S&D was not on the Uruguay Round agenda. Indeed, the Punta del Este Ministerial Declaration explicitly stated that

CONTRACTING PARTIES agree that the principle of differential and more favorable treatment embodied in Part IV and other relevant provisions of the General Agreement ... applies to the negotiations ... [D]eveloped countries do not expect reciprocity for commitments made by them in trade negotiations to reduce or remove tariffs and other barriers to trade of developing countries (GATT, 1986: 7).

S&D remains embedded in the WTO. Special provisions for developing and least developed countries can be grouped under five headings: lower level of obligations, more flexible implementation timetables, commitments by developed countries to take into account developing country interests, more favorable treatment for least developed countries, and promises of technical assistance and training. With the exception of the Agreement on Subsidies and Countervailing Measures, no criteria for 'graduation' were agreed to. As mentioned in chapter 5, the SCM agreement has *de minimis* provisions for developing countries and exempts nations with per capita incomes below US$1,000 from CVDs on export subsidies. However, economies that have attained a global market share of 3.5 percent for a product are required to phase out export subsidies. Although BOP rules and procedures were tightened, revocation of Article XVIII remains an issue that is effectively negotiated on an ad hoc basis.

Many of the specific provisions relating to developing countries in WTO agreements have been discussed in earlier chapters. A point to emphasize here is that most of the 97 provisions in WTO agreements calling for S&D treatment of developing countries are 'best endeavor' commitments—they

---

[2] A more recent illustration of the pursuit of self-interest was a December 1998 decision by Brazil to contest the EU's Generalized System of Preferences (GSP). Brazil alleged the GSP to be inconsistent with the Enabling Clause, as well as with the MFN principle, and claimed it led to nullification or impairment of benefits accruing to Brazil. See the WTO dispute settlement home page for details.

are not binding on high-income countries. No dispute settlement cases can be launched by a developing country government on the basis of nondelivery on the promises that were made in the various WTO agreements.[3] The same cannot be said of the commitments that developing countries made— these are binding. In many cases transition periods were negotiated, but implementation of agreements was not made conditional on obtaining adequate financial and technical assistance. In retrospect, this was a mistake (Finger and Schuler, 2000). In the run-up to the Seattle ministerial meeting— which virtually coincided with the five-year mark after which most transition periods were to expire for developing countries (but not LDCs)—it became clear that many countries had not implemented agreements dealing with issues such as customs valuation, standards, and TRIPs.

While it is generally accepted that S&D provisions have had little effect, there is much less agreement on the costs of implementation. Countries such as Egypt and India have proposed that all best endeavors S&D language in WTO agreements be made binding. Finger (2000) has proposed that implementation of agreements that require significant investment in 'bricks and mortar' and training be financed by high-income donor countries. One way to make this linkage formal is to seek agreement that there would be no legal basis for dispute settlement cases if a panel finds that inadequate assistance has been provided for implementation.

12.3. DEVELOPING COUNTRY PARTICIPATION IN THE WTO

With the Uruguay Round integration of developing countries into the multilateral trading system, an important step was taken towards ending the dichotomy that characterized the GATT for several decades. Developing countries play an active role in the WTO. One indication of this was their role in the selection of the Director-General in 1999, which helped result in the agreement to appoint a Thai national in 2002 (see chapter 2). Another indicator of participation is the number of submissions made to WTO bodies. In the run-up to the Seattle ministerial meeting, developing countries submitted close to 100 proposals on topics ranging from traditional market access issues to 'second generation' topics such as competition and investment policy (WTO, 2000). Perhaps the most important indicator is participation in dispute settlement. Developing countries are active users of the system, accounting for a little less than a third of complaints, and increas-

---

[3] The various provisions are identified and discussed in a secretariat document prepared for the Committee on Trade and Development (WT/COMTD/W/66), available on the WTO web site.

ingly use WTO procedures against each other (Box 12.2). However, particularly striking is the growth of cases against developing countries.

Box 12.2. Developing countries and dispute settlement
Developing countries have begun to use multilateral procedures to settle disputes much more than in the past. These go beyond the high-profile cases discussed in chapter 3 (such as *Bananas*). A random selection of cases provides an indication of the types of disputes that have been brought.
- Singapore vs. Malaysia (1994). The first case brought to the WTO. Singapore objected to Malaysian import procedures for plastic resins, alleging discrimination. The case was settled bilaterally in 1995.
- Argentina vs. US (1997). Argentina alleges a restrictive interpretation by the US of the Uruguay Round tariff rate quota for groundnut imports.
- Brazil vs. Peru (1997). Brazil objects to a countervailing duty investigation being carried out by Peru against imports of buses from Brazil.
- Chile vs. US (1997). Chile contests a CVD investigation on imports of salmon, claiming insufficient evidence of injury.
- Colombia vs. US (1997). Colombia argues that US safeguard measure against imports of broom-corn brooms violates the Agreement on Safeguards.
- India, Malaysia, Pakistan and Thailand vs. US (1996). Contest a ban on importation of shrimp and shrimp products by the US under Section 609 of US Public Law 101-162 arguing violation of MFN and use of QRs (see chapter 13).
- Hungary vs. Czech Republic (1998). Hungary objects to a Czech regulation allegedly increasing the import duty on wheat above bound rates on a discriminatory basis.
- Mexico vs. Guatemala (1999). Contests the imposition of definitive AD duties by Guatemala on imports of gray Portland cement, arguing procedures did not conform to WTO requirements.
- Honduras and Colombia vs. Nicaragua (1999). Claim Nicaragua's Law 325 of 1999, which provides for the imposition of charges on goods and services from Honduras and Colombia, violates MFN and tariff concessions.
Source: WTO dispute settlement section of www.wto.org.

Developing countries were defendants in only 8 percent of all the cases brought during the GATT years. This reflected the fact that GATT rules often did not bind. As mentioned, this changed with the establishment of the WTO. The increasing coverage of multilateral disciplines is reflected in WTO dispute settlement statistics: the developing country share in terms of being a defendant rose to 37 percent (Table 12.2). Note that their share of all cases as a complainant remained the same.

TABLE 12.2 *Developing country participation in dispute settlement*

Period	Type of Country	Cases as Complainant	Cases as respondent
GATT, 1948–94	Developed	302 (64.4%)	400 (92.0%)
	Developing	133 (30.6%)	35 (8.0%)
WTO, 1995–2000	Developed	155 (70.8%)	138 (63.0%)
	Developing	64 (29.2%)	81 (37.0%)

Source: Busch and Reinhardt (2000).

Abstracting from dispute settlement, there is enormous variation across countries in terms of their activity in WTO fora. Although countries such as Egypt, Thailand, India and Brazil are very active, many least developed countries are not represented in Geneva at all. A large number of African members essentially do not participate in the WTO. This explains why, with the exception of South Africa, there are no sub-Saharan countries that appear in the list of dispute settlement cases that have been brought to the WTO so far. Although having a resident mission is not a necessary condition for bringing a case to the WTO, not having one impedes the process.[4] The problem extends beyond not having a representative office in Geneva. Even if countries have a delegation at the WTO, the deliberations, consultations and negotiations that are held under its auspices often do not attract much attention in capitals. Representatives are left to operate without instructions and are not integrated into the domestic policy formation process. The result can be an inconsistency between the positions taken by delegations in the WTO and the policies that are actually being pursued by a government towards trade and investment. Often, such discrepancies are compounded by the fact that representation in Geneva is the primary responsibility of the Ministry of Foreign Affairs, whereas domestic economic policy is pursued by the Ministries of Economy, Finance and Planning. As noted by Blackhurst, Lyakurwa and Oyejide (2000), greater integration of sub-Saharan African countries into the global trading system requires building the requisite ca-

---

[4] The converse may also be true—lack of a mission in Geneva may lower the probability of being confronted with a complaint.

pacity to enable them to contribute to shaping and designing the rules of the game. A necessary condition for this is that representatives are kept informed of national policies and objectives and can rely on colleagues in capitals to respond to requests for information and provide instructions (Hoekman and Roy, 2000).[5]

Fifteen of 38 Sub-Saharan African countries had no resident representation in Geneva in 1999. Most of the others had just one or two staffers (including the head of delegation) to follow the dozens of meetings that take place in the WTO each week. Blackhurst, Lyakurwa and Oyejide (2000) argue that a resource-neutral method of increasing capacity to participate in the WTO is to reallocate spending priorities, and shift resources away from diplomatic missions to economic functions. They note that every sub-Saharan country except Mauritius has a larger delegation in either Brussels or New York than in Geneva. Although one can question whether the current allocation of resources is irrational—for example, maintaining trade, development finance and other relationships with the European Commission may well have a higher payoff than participating in the WTO—this is a suggestion that is worth serious consideration. Proposals by the NGO community (for example, Consumers International, a federation of 263 organizations working on consumer rights and protection issues around the world) that participation by developing countries in the WTO should be financed (subsidized) by high-income countries is less compelling. For this to make sense it would need to be determined that the funds involved would not be more effectively used in the developing countries (for projects, infrastructure, and so forth).

A number of international bodies have increased their support for members in dealing with the WTO. The Commonwealth Secretariat expanded its assistance to small member countries engaged in WTO accession, disputes and negotiations. It proposed that the WTO streamline and accelerate accession procedures, establish arrangements to reduce the cost of using dispute procedures, and reduce the minimum budgetary contribution now payable by small states. The Organization for African Unity (OAU) expanded its presence in Geneva in the late 1990s, and assisted member governments to

---

[5] A necessary condition for effective participation is analytical input into the decision-making process. Given the absence of resources in many developing country trade ministries, local expertise in think tanks and academic institutions could be involved more in the process of preparing positions on issues. Encouraging greater interaction between the research community in developing countries and government agencies is an objective of a number of projects supported by the Canadian International Development Research Consortium (IDRC), the UK Department of International Development and international organizations such as the World Bank. See www.worldbank.org/trade.

prepare for Seattle—for example, by organizing a large meeting of member-country trade ministers in Algeria in September 1999. Following Seattle, the African Group at the WTO—which is supported by the OAU office—made a number of proposals to enhance internal efficiency and transparency of the WTO, arguing that the principle of consensus should not be abandoned (see also chapter 14). In the run-up to Seattle, South Africa hosted a workshop for senior advisors to Ministers of Trade in LDCs to prepare for the WTO ministerial meeting. Ministers from the Southern African Development Community (SADC) agreed to common negotiating objectives before the Seattle meeting.[6] These developments illustrate that efforts are being made by African countries to enhance their input and visibility in the WTO. As noted by many observers (see e.g., Blackhurst et al. 2000), part of the solution to participation constraints must involve efforts to cooperate and share the burden of sending representatives to WTO meetings, as well as form coalitions for agenda-setting and perhaps negotiating purposes.

One of the few achievements of the Seattle ministerial was agreement on the part of major traders to support the creation of an Advisory Centre on WTO Law (ACWL). This center, which is to be located in Geneva, is to provide legal assistance to developing country WTO members involved in dispute settlement. The Center's activities are financed in large part by donor countries and cost-sharing by assisted countries (ACWL, 1999). Prior to the Seattle ministerial, major players such as the US and the EU had not indicated a willingness to support (and help fund) an ACWL. Large developing countries such as Argentina, Brazil and India had also been lukewarm. Analogous to the role a public defender plays in domestic legal systems to ensure that all citizens are able to defend themselves, an international mechanism to subsidize the ability of poor nations to bring and defend cases may help to level the dispute settlement playing field to some extent. The statistics on the distribution of cases across developed and developing countries discussed earlier illustrate that the latter are becoming respondents much more frequently than in the past. The ACWL can help the less well-equipped countries deal with disputes. However, for such a mechanism to be most effective, it is important that the 'upstream' part of the DSP chain is strengthened concurrently—see chapter 3.

---

[6] See 'The Challenge of Integrating LDCs into the Multilateral Trading System', WT/GC/W251, July 13, 1999; and SADC Ministers Agreed Negotiating Objectives, WT/L317, October 1, 1999. The secretariat has put together a convenient compilation of all proposals made by members for the Seattle ministerial (JOB(99)4797/Rev.3, November 18, 1999—downloadable from the WTO web site).

12.4. IMPLEMENTATION OF MULTILATERAL AGREEMENTS

A subsidiary body of the WTO General Council, the Committee on Trade and Development is the focal point for trade-related concerns of developing countries. A Sub-committee on Least-Developed Countries focuses on issues of interest to the poorest WTO members. After the Uruguay Round was completed, such concerns centered increasingly on implementation and participation-related issues, in particular the need for technical assistance and the effectiveness of S&D provisions.

Implementation concerns were of three types. One was to ensure that high-income WTO members would deliver on their promises and their commitments to developing countries. A second related to the (in-)ability of developing countries to implement the many Uruguay Round agreements before the various transition periods expired. The third was to question whether the substantive disciplines of some of the WTO agreements were compatible with national development priorities.

Many developing countries were concerned about the way the US and the EU had implemented the first stage of integrating textiles and clothing products into the GATT. As discussed in chapter 6, the first tranches of liberalization essentially excluded any product of significant export interest. The use of transitional safeguards under the ATC by the US also did little to encourage developing countries. As mentioned, two dispute-settlement cases were brought regarding such measures. Although both were won, the signal that was being received was worrisome.

A related issue concerned promises made by high-income countries concerning special and more favorable treatment of developing countries and (implicit and sometimes explicit) offers of assistance. The adequacy of technical assistance has been a recurring concern for developing countries. The 1999 WTO budget provided for only US$470,000 for technical cooperation activities by the secretariat, all of which is used for travel and subsistence expenses of staff, mostly in connection with training seminars and workshops. Most funding for WTO technical cooperation services come in the form of trust funds granted by OECD countries such as the Netherlands and Switzerland. The secretariat has appealed to members to increase its 'regular' budget for technical assistance activities, and is seeking to expand cooperation with specialized organizations such as WIPO, the World Customs Organization, ISO, and the Codex Alimentarius.

At the 1996 Singapore ministerial conference, ministers committed themselves to addressing the problem of increasing marginalization of LDCs in world trade, and to work towards greater coherence in international economic policy making and improved cooperation among agencies in providing technical assistance. Ministers agreed to a Plan of Action for Least Developed Countries (LDCs). It envisaged closer cooperation among the WTO and multilateral agencies assisting LDCs in the area of trade. To implement the plan, an Integrated Framework (IF) on trade-related technical assistance for LDCs was established. The Framework was endorsed in October 1997, at a WTO High Level Meeting for LDCs, where it was decided that six agencies — ITC, IMF, UNCTAD, UNDP, World Bank and WTO — would take joint responsibility for the implementation of the framework for delivering trade-related technical assistance to LDCs (Box 12.3). The IF did little to address the underlying causes of the implementation problems of LDCs. In part this was because it did not address the disconnect between a number of the WTO agreements and the development priorities of low-income countries (Finger and Schuler, 2000; Winters and Wang, 2000), and in part it reflected the lack of adequate funding.

Box 12.3. The integrated framework for technical assistance for LDCs

The primary rationale for the IF was to address the concerns expressed by developing countries regarding inadequacies of the implementation assistance provisions in the Uruguay Round agreements which were of a best-endeavors nature. The WTO itself did not have the budget or the expertise to provide assistance to LDCs on the scale that was needed. Industrialized countries were not willing to transfer the resources required to either the WTO or on a bilateral basis. Nor were they willing to revisit the substantive obligations that had been negotiated in the Uruguay Round with which LDCs were to comply after transition periods had expired. The IF was an attempt to square the circle by shifting the problem to development-oriented agencies that had access to resources. Proponents also argued the IF would help to reduce duplication of effort among the agencies, and generate information on specific needs in trade-related areas.

The IF involved the preparation of 'needs assessments' by LDCs, followed by so-called 'integrated responses' by the six agencies, indicating in which areas they could or were providing assistance. Gaps were to be filled by donor country pledges at 'round tables' that were to be organized for each of the LDCs by the agencies. Needs assessments were produced for 40 LDCs in the two-year period following the 1997 High Level Meeting. The responses indicated little in the way of overlap or lack of coordination among agencies, but did reveal significant demand for additional grant assistance. Only five IF 'round tables' had been held through mid-2000, and in only one case (Uganda) did donors make commitments to provide new (additional) funds. In mid 2000, an independent review of the IF concluded the process had not been effective because needs assessments were not sufficiently embedded in the development plans and strategies of recipient countries, and because inadequate funding had been provided to meet LDC needs.

In response to the review, the six agencies proposed that greater stress be placed on ensuring that trade policy, trade-related technical assistance, and capacity-building needs are articulated in a broader development context to ensure that trade-related assistance needs are assessed alongside a country's other priorities. Insofar as trade concerns were identified as a priority area, it was expected that this would increase the chances that the necessary resources would be made available to LDCs. The agencies also proposed that donor support be sought for the creation of a trust fund dedicated to helping LDCs to develop the necessary analytical and policy framework for mainstreaming trade into national development strategies, for developing programs and projects, and for training and capacity-building.

Source: www.wto.org; Oxford Analytica (2000).

The Uruguay Round and the establishment of the WTO changed the character of the trading system. The GATT was very much a market access oriented institution—its function was to harness the dynamics of reciprocity for the global good. Negotiators could be left to follow mercantilist logic— the end result would be beneficial to all contracting parties. This dynamic worked less well for developing countries, for reasons explained above. For these countries the burden of liberalization rested much more heavily on the shoulders of governments—even if they wanted to, the scope to use the GATT was often limited because exporters had fewer incentives and were less powerful than in OECD countries. The reciprocal, negotiation-driven dynamic also worked much less well for issues that were 'lumpy' and where the terms of the debate revolved around what rules to adopt, not around how much of a marginal change was appropriate. Once discussions center on rules, especially disciplines on domestic policy and regulations, it is more difficult to define intra-issue compromises that make economic sense. Cross issue linkage becomes necessary. Disengagement was not an option during the Uruguay Round—due to the Single Undertaking—so the need was to come up with a balanced package that ensured gains for all players. One can argue whether the package that emerged from the round was a balanced one. Views on this differ widely. CGE studies of the Uruguay Round suggest all regions gained, with the magnitude of the gains depending importantly on the extent to which governments reduced barriers to trade (see Martin and Winters, 1996). Others argue CGE models miss many of the important dimensions of the WTO agreements, especially the rent transfers associated with the TRIPs agreement and the implementation costs generated by the various agreements (Srinivasan, 1998, 2000).

Whatever the conclusion, it is clear that the approach taken towards ensuring and supporting implementation of WTO agreements by developing countries was not an effective one. Limiting recognition of this problem to the setting of uniform transition periods was clearly inadequate. Many would argue that what is needed is greater willingness to allow more flexibility in determining whether all rules should apply to all countries. The case for uniform application of agreements that involve reducing trade barriers—tariffs, NTBs—is very strong. But in other areas requiring minimum levels of institutional capacity—such as customs valuation—a good case can be made that 'one size fits all' is a bad rule (Finger and Hoekman, 1999).

A lesson from post Uruguay Round experience and subsequent thinking is that there is a need to bring trade policy more centrally into the development process and development strategies. This is required at two levels. At the national level, it is necessary in order to ensure that governments have a basis on which to negotiate agreements in an area. They must be able to identify what types of rules will promote development and what type would entail an inappropriate use of scarce resources. At the international level, it is necessary in order to enhance the communication between trade and development assistance bodies in member countries (see also chapter 14). One reason for the implementation assistance problems that were encountered in the late 1990s was that the best-endeavors commitments on assistance that were made by OECD trade negotiators were not 'owned' by counterpart agencies in their governments that controlled the money (development assistance). Progress on both fronts would do much to ensure that future negotiations do not give rise to problems of the type that were created in the Uruguay Round.

In the run-up to the Seattle ministerial, both types of implementation concerns—holding high-income countries to their promises and dealing with the problems of complying with Uruguay Round agreements—were put forward by developing countries as issues to be addressed. Numerous submissions were made, both with respect to old issues and suggestions for topics to be negotiated during the first year of a new round. Many of these proposals were included in the form of bracketed text—an indication there was no agreement on them—in an informal draft negotiating text prepared by the WTO secretariat in late September.[7]

---

[7] A draft circulated to WTO members on October 7, 2000 made virtually no mention of implementation-related proposals, however. This incensed developing countries, who could determine exactly which bits of the draft text had been cut by consulting the newsletter *Inside US Trade*, which published a side-by-side comparison of the October 7 paper and an earlier one that included implementation-related proposals. On October 11, the chair of the General Council released an addendum that consisted essentially of the material that had been excised.

Developing countries sought immediate action to tighten antidumping rules and expand *de minimis* provisions, and relaxation of subsidy rules to allow for export-promoting policies. On SPS and TBT, it was proposed to make technical assistance mandatory and to devise mechanisms to ensure that the views of countries at differing levels of development would be heard in international standards-setting bodies. On clothing, commitments were sought by importing countries to accelerate the elimination of the MFA, and commitments that antidumping would not be applied on goods that were subject to QRs. On TRIMs many countries sought extension of transition periods, an opportunity for governments that had not notified illegal TRIMs to do so and to be granted a transition period to phase them out, and an exemption from the ban on domestic content requirements. On IPRs, the demands included acceptance that the TRIPs agreement does not prevent developing countries from issuing compulsory licenses for drugs listed by the WHO as essential, an extension of transition periods, a prohibition on patenting of plant and animal life, and operationalization of TRIPs provisions for transfer of technology on fair and mutually advantageous terms (*Bridges*, October-November, 1999).

Most of these demands were opposed by the US and many other OECD countries, who did not wish to reopen Uruguay Round agreements. Given the debacle in Seattle, no concrete results emerged from the ministerial meeting. However, it was clear to WTO members that absent progress on implementation concerns it would be very difficult to launch a new round. In the aftermath of Seattle, following the tenth session of the UN Conference on Trade and Development (UNCTAD), the Quad put together a 'confidence-building package'. They proposed a case-by-case consideration of requests for extension of transition periods, improved market access for least-developed countries (but allowing for exceptions, and without mention of antidumping), and a promise 'to undertake to work to devote adequate resources' for technical assistance efforts. All in all, this package was not well received, and did little, if anything, to 'build confidence' that implementation concerns were being taken seriously. The market access offer did not go much beyond the status quo, the technical assistance language was vague, and the case-by-case approach to requests for extension was already largely provided for in the various WTO agreements. Indeed, developing countries had already been seeking, and obtaining, extensions under certain agreements, in particular that on customs valuation.

In May 2000 the WTO General Council adopted a work program to review implementation-related concerns. Given the general unwillingness on the part of OECD countries to reopen Uruguay Round agreements, little resulted from this process. As has been the case in the past, a solution will no doubt emerge over time, and involve a series of (nontransparent) tradeoffs. Many of the concerns of developing countries can only be addressed in the context of a MTN. The implementation agenda and work program is therefore probably best seen as part of a prenegotiation process, somewhat similar to what occurred after the failed 1982 ministerial in the area of services. High-income WTO members recognize that something needs to be done in this area—the trick will be to identify and package the quid pro quo.

12.5. EXPANDING MEMBERSHIP

Implementation is just one dimension of the general challenge of integrating developing countries into the WTO. Another is to expand membership. In December 2000 there were 141 members of the WTO, with another 30 seeking accession. The accession queue comprises developing and transition economies. As noted in chapter 2, the accession process has become quite cumbersome and complicated. A major challenge confronting WTO members is to ensure that membership expansion can be achieved without hollowing out the system.

China

China was a founding member of the GATT but ceased to participate in the late 1940s after it became Communist. China was a participant in—and signatory to—the Uruguay Round, reflecting the fact that negotiations on accession to GATT were initiated during the round. Negotiations were difficult. At the time of writing, negotiations had lasted 14 years. In late 2000, prospects for accession appeared reasonably good, although there were some hesitations on both sides as to whether the terms of the deal were acceptable (*Financial Times*, October 13, 2000). The long drawn-out process had several reasons. First, China is a trade powerhouse. For many countries, China is the major source of cheap labor-intensive imports that are putting severe pressure on domestic industries. As a result, China is often the target of contingent protection. Procedures that are used against Chinese exports do not have to conform to WTO rules. Given the command nature of China's economy, many WTO members were only willing to accept China in the multilateral trading system if it could be shown that China's economy had become sufficiently market-based, with government intervention limited to what tends to be found in most countries. Throughout the 1980s, the economy was still controlled by central or provincial or local state bodies. Representatives of the global business community were of the view that accession should be used as an instrument to open the Chinese market to foreign competition, and as a mechanism for achieving substantial reforms to China's legal and policy regime. Much of the negotiations therefore involved not just market access, but efforts to increase transparency and ensure that a 'level playing field' prevailed on the Chinese market once goods had been imported. Given that China was pursuing reforms throughout the period of negotiations, the regulatory situation was a moving target, also complicating matters.

Second, China sought to be treated as a developing country. The government demanded long transition periods as well as special and differential treatment. There was opposition to significant liberalization at earlier stages of the process, in part in an effort to keep negotiating chips and in part due to a desire to protect inefficient state industries. Negotiators sought to keep tariff bindings significantly above applied rates.

Third, noneconomic considerations played a key role. As with other transition economies, there was a tight linkage between trade and foreign policy stances of OECD countries, especially the United States. The US did not provide China with unconditional MFN status—the Jackson-Vanik amendment to the 1974 Trade Act prohibits the US from granting unconditional MFN status to nonmarket economies that do not allow free emigration. Until China accedes and the US Congress approves 'permanent normal trade relations status', MFN status must be renewed annually by the President, subject to Congressional approval. This was always a tough battle, as MFN was made conditional on China's human rights record and other foreign policy considerations (such as relations with Taiwan). Old-fashioned protectionism also played a role. Democrats with ties to trade unions feared public accusation of job losses resulting from Chinese competition. Republicans, cajoled by conservative religious groups highly critical of China's record of birth controls and religious liberties, were also inclined to be sensitive about supporting MFN. The decision by the US Congress to grant China permanent MFN status in 2000—conditional on accession to the WTO—was therefore a major victory for supporters of the international trading system—particularly given the failure of the US government to obtain 'fast track' negotiating authority. It was also noteworthy in signaling a recognition that the use (or threat) of trade sanctions to pressure China on human rights and other issues was not very effective.

As of early 2001, it was generally acknowledged that negotiations on China's accession had entered their final phase. This reflected far-reaching commitments by China. In principle all enterprises located in China will have the right to trade all goods throughout the customs territory of China (with the exception of those goods that continue to be subject to state trading). A noteworthy feature of the draft protocol is extensive precommitments to liberalization, with many restrictions to be phased out during the 2001-5 period (EU, 2000). These commitments are tempered by transitional periods for elimination of WTO inconsistent polices (QRs, licensing, TRQs). As noted by Michalopoulos (1999), the quid pro quo for this is that China must accept that WTO members have the right to impose measures of contingent protection on the basis of criteria that do not conform to the WTO. The draft protocol of accession contained bracketed text that would allow safeguard actions to be taken on terms that would be much easier to satisfy than those specified in the Agreement on Safeguards. Instead of the 'serious injury' criterion, the looser concept of 'market disruption' would apply, with any actions to be China-specific (i.e. discriminatory). On the AD and CVD side, the draft text put the burden of proof on exporters to demonstrate that 'market economy conditions' prevailed. If authorities decided to the contrary, nonmarket methodologies could be used. It was envisaged that such discriminatory provisions would cease to apply once each WTO member had established that China is a market economy, or within 12 to 15 years after China's accession, which ever came first. Although the final Protocol remains to be negotiated, given that China is one of the main targets of AD actions worldwide and that the nonmarket methodologies employed frequently generate high AD duties, import-competing industries in WTO members can be expected to lobby strongly for the inclusion of provisions along these lines. The textiles and clothing industry is not surprisingly a major player in this debate, starting from the very upstream end of the production chain (Box 12.4).

Bringing China into the WTO will be a major achievement. The treatment of China, in particular with respect to contingent protection, will be an important signal of the extent to which protectionist interests can be controlled in WTO member countries. It seems clear that special safeguards will be included in the Protocol of accession. While this is unfortunate and unnecessary given that the existing provisions in the WTO are wide enough to address import competition, this is in part the quid pro quo for China's insistence that it be granted transitional periods and various loopholes. It should be borne in mind that China has managed to become a major trading nation despite being treated on a discriminatory basis.

Box 12.4. The cotton industry and China's accession

China's imminent accession to the WTO has many ramifications for the global textile and clothing industry. One example concerns international trade in cotton. China is the world's second largest producer, after the United States. Much of the world's trade in cotton is governed by the so-called 'Liverpool rules', established in Liverpool one century ago when this

UK port dominated the trade. The Liverpool Cotton Association (LCA), a body that sets product standards and oversees the trade, would like to see China join the association. The fear of the LCA is that once China is a WTO member and rules restricting trade are abolished, private entrepreneurs will be able to deal directly with foreign buyers. Given that most of China's output has been directed to the local market by the entities currently controlling the distribution of cotton on the Chinese market, and that there is a large stockpile of cotton available in the country, there are concerns that the global market not be flooded with cotton after China has joined the WTO and the liberalization of trading rights has been implemented.
Source: Financial Times, August 17, 2000: 6.

Russia and the Trading System

The relationship between Russia and the GATT has a long history with strong political overtones. The Soviet delegation took active part in the Bretton Woods Conference (1944) preceding the creation of the IMF and the International Bank for Reconstruction and Development (World Bank). Moscow was expected to participate in these two Bretton Woods institutions and in the future arrangements for the multilateral trading system (Mikessell, 1951). At that time the United States favored Soviet participation. The American 'Suggested Charter' that was to provide a basic document for discussions at the London Conference (1946) on the ITO took the monopoly of foreign trade in the Soviet Union for granted and offered technical arrangements to render it more consistent with nondiscrimination.

In the event, the Soviets refused to accept the Bretton Woods agreements, absented themselves from the London and Havana conferences and also stayed away from the Geneva negotiations on the GATT. At the time, Moscow believed that participation in the postwar economic order carried with it a danger that the United States might expand economically and politically into the Soviet sphere of influence. The Soviet expectation of economic crises in the postwar Western world also contributed to the decision to put off economic cooperation. In spite of the *rapprochement* that occurred between certain COMECON countries and the GATT in the 1960s and early 1970s, the USSR continued to remain outside the trading system. Moscow's reluctance was largely motivated by political considerations. The Soviet Union was not a trading power and the GATT—a technical rules-based entity—was not regarded as an appropriate framework for exercising Soviet influence in the trade area. Instead, Moscow pressed for the creation of a comprehensive trade organization under UN auspices, with effective links to UN political organs, and universal membership (Kostecki, 1979).

With the fall of Communism, accession to the GATT and later the WTO began to be perceived as a necessary element of Russia's integration in the world economy. OECD members welcomed and encouraged the change in attitude. At a bilateral US-Russia summit held in Vancouver in April 1993,

---

Box 12.5. Russia and the accession process

Russia applied for accession to the GATT in 1993. A memorandum on the foreign trade regimes was submitted in March 1994. With the establishment of the WTO in 1995, the accession discussions were expanded to include services and IPRs. Numerous working party meetings were held to discuss the foreign trade and related domestic policy regimes, including privatization and tax policies. While there was extensive discussion of many aspects of Russian trade policy over the years—in part driven by recurrent changes in this regime—many issues remained unresolved. These included legislation affecting FDI in services, protection of IPRs, the jurisdiction between federal and local authorities in the area of standards, and issues related to the workings of various RIAs Russia had concluded with neighboring countries (former members of the Soviet Union).

Key decisions Russia had to make included determining the level at which to bind tariffs, the support provided to agriculture and the coverage of specific commitments on services. The government felt that significant levels of protection were necessary during the transition to a market economy to allow restructuring of inefficient state enterprises. Accordingly, the Russian delegation presented initial offers to bind tariffs at rates much higher than those actually applied and proposed to leave a number of tariffs unbound. This strategy was also motivated by tactical considerations. Because applicants cannot typically negotiate improvements in access to markets of WTO members, it was deemed desirable to keep bargaining chips to obtain improved access in future negotiating rounds. As in the case of China, this did not serve to help move talks forward.

The accession process was not pursued vigorously. Political struggles between the executive and the Duma over legislation, frequent changes in governments, the rising influence of economic elites in the energy and service sectors—whose interests might adversely be affected by a liberal service offer—and continued uncertainty regarding the relations between the central government and the regions impeded the process. As in the case of China, a number of concerns prevailing in major OECD countries also made the process more difficult. To some extent the issues were similar, including the reach of state-trading and, for the US, the provisions of the Jackson-Vanik amendment. The latter was important, as on conclusion of the accession negotiations of the Kyrgyz Republic and Mongolia, the US had been forced to invoke the WTO nonapplication clause (Article XVIII). Another difficult question concerned Russia's designation as a nonmarket economy, which had serious implications in terms of the incidence of AD and CVD threats.

Source: Michalopoulos (1999).

US President Clinton supported Russia's accession to the GATT. As in the case of China, progress was slow (Box 12.5).

12.6. CONCLUSION

For a long time, developing countries were effectively second-class members of the multilateral trading system. The insistence on S&D and the refusal to engage in reciprocal negotiations meant that the benefits of GATT membership were substantially diminished. As argued repeatedly throughout this book, the main value of the GATT and the WTO is as an instrument that helps governments maintain a liberal and transparent trade policy, and as a mechanism to open and maintain access to foreign markets. By excluding themselves from the progressive liberalization induced by the dynamics of reciprocity, developing countries greatly reduced the relevance of GATT membership. The end result was that throughout the 1960s and 1970s, levels of protection in developing countries remained much higher than in OECD countries, and that the latter kept higher trade barriers on the goods of primary interest to developing countries. Three decades of experience with the S&D strategy revealed it to be ill advised. The fundamental dynamic of the GATT was and remains reciprocity. Those not willing to play this game found the benefits of free riding to be small. Indeed, from an economic perspective, the strategy was particularly counterproductive, as import substitution proved to be a very costly and ineffective development strategy (Bhagwati, 1988).

External events and the lessons of experience gradually changed the attitude of many countries towards trade policy in the 1980s. The debt crisis induced many nations—especially in Latin America—to change tack, and shift towards a more liberal and neutral policy stance. As important was the demonstration effect of the successful export-based economies of East Asia, and the collapse of Communism in Eastern Europe and the former Soviet Union. The internal political balance of power changed in many developing countries, with export interests becoming more significant. The GATT played a role in this process, but it was a very minor one. The major force was unilateral reform. In contrast to OECD countries, the mercantilist dynamics of trade reform were not important in the liberalization that occurred in most developing countries.

As new centers of economic activity emerged—in Southeast Asia in particular—these countries became subject to increasing pressure to 'graduate'. In the Uruguay Round 'graduation big time' occurred for all developing countries. In return for participating in the WTO—which included signing on to the TRIPs Agreement, the GATS, agreeing to the multilateralization of the Tokyo Round codes, binding of all agricultural tariffs, and a significant increase in binding of industrial tariffs—developing countries helped realize a substantial strengthening of the rule-based multilateral trading system. The quid pro quo they obtained included the abolition of VERs (as part of the Agreement on Safeguards) and the progressive elimination of the MFA. Agriculture was brought back under the GATT, and, although very little actual liberalization was achieved, the framework was created for pursuing this in the future (negotiations were initiated on schedule at the beginning of 2000). As important, developing countries benefit from the increased security of trade relations under the WTO, given the strengthened and unified dispute settlement mechanism. With the inclusion of services and IPRs in the WTO, unilateral threats and actions in these areas can only be taken by industrialized countries after a dispute settlement panel has found a violation and retaliation for noncompliance with panel recommendations has been authorized by the WTO. Finally, membership of the WTO may increase the credibility of domestic economic reforms in developing nations by reducing the uncertainty of trade regimes. This last possibility is of great potential importance, although very much depends on the decisions of governments to exploit the opportunities offered by the WTO by binding tariffs at applied rates, making specific commitments for services, and avoiding the pitfalls of contingent protection.

In the Uruguay Round a grand bargain was negotiated. Clearly many countries gained, both from better market access, and more important, from their own liberalization. The Uruguay Round was a success for developing countries—they obtained much of what they wanted. But not all countries gained. The Uruguay Round left a serious implementation hangover for many least developed countries. In some areas, WTO rules are a 'bridge too soon' for developing nations. Efforts need to be made to move beyond the approach taken in the Uruguay Round to facilitate implementation—uniform transition periods are inadequate. Options in this regard include 'variable geometry'—accepting that some agreements do not have to apply to all countries, leaving it to governments to self-select. The existence of the plurilateral agreement possibility in the WTO provides a vehicle for pursuing this route. In the Uruguay Round, the 'single undertaking rule' and the fact that a new organization was created (the WTO) implied that countries were confronted with a 'take it or leave it' choice. This is unlikely to be replicable.

In future negotiations, greater use of standard principles of cost-benefit analysis would help ensure that the Uruguay Round experience is not repeated. Estimating what the implementation costs for a given country would be before obligations are accepted, and making the provision of financing and technical assistance a condition for initiating a dispute alleging nonimplementation would help assure that the expected payoffs of agreements are positive to all members. Greater efforts are also required to ensure that the agenda of future MTNs embodies items that are of vital interest to developing countries, recognizing that interests will vary across countries. Speaking for many observers in developing countries and in the international development community, the former chief economist of the World Bank called for the next round of MTNs to be more balanced and more equitable (Stiglitz, 2000). Concretely, this would involve an acceptance of considering deep cuts in OECD agricultural protection—given that much of the world's poor are dependent on the rural economy—a willingness to substantially reduce the threat of contingent protection, and the courage to discuss taboo subjects such as the movement of natural persons. Much remains to be achieved by developing countries to further liberalize trade polices and bind tariffs at applied rates. They therefore have substantial negotiating coin with which to push for such an agenda. A necessary condition is that research and analysis is undertaken in countries on what should be pursued.

12.7. FURTHER READING

Much has been written about the role of developing countries in the trading system, and the impact of the free riding strategy that was pursued in the 1960-80 period. Robert Hudec provides an excellent analysis of the issue, as well as a review of the relevant GATT history in *Developing Countries in the GATT Legal System* (London: Trade Policy Research Centre, 1987). An accessible account of the effects of the inward looking, import-substituting development strategies popular in the 1960s and 1970s, as well as the shift towards more outward-looking policies in the 1980s is given by Jagdish Bhagwati in *Protectionism* (Cambridge: MIT Press, 1988). T.N. Srinivasan, *Developing Countries and the Multilateral Trading System: From GATT to the Uruguay Round and the Future* (New York: Harper-Collins, 1998) provides a detailed analysis of the developing country dimensions of multilateral trading rules and the strategies pursued by developing countries in the GATT and the Uruguay Round.

Brian Hindley, 'Different and More Favorable Treatment—and Graduation', in J. M. Finger and A. Olechowski (eds.), *The Uruguay Round: A Hand-*

book for the Multilateral Trade Negotiations (Washington DC: World Bank, 1987) is a short, perceptive review of S&D-related issues written at the start of the Uruguay Round. Rolf Langhammer and André Sapir, *Economic Impact of Generalized Tariff Preferences* (London: Trade Policy Research Centre, 1988) analyze the economic effects of GSP schemes, arguing that these largely benefit those that pursue export-oriented policies—mostly countries that do not need preferences to compete. The contributions in Jagdish Bhagwati and John Ruggie (eds.), *Power, Passions and Purpose: Prospects for North-South Negotiations* (Cambridge: MIT Press, 1984) discuss strategies followed by developing countries regarding international cooperation and global negotiations on economic matters during the 1970s and early 1980s. The contribution by Martin Wolf in that volume ('Two-Edged Sword: Demands of Developing Countries and the Trading System') offers a critical analysis of the impact of developing countries' insistence on nonreciprocity in the GATT.

John Whalley, 'Developing Countries and System Strengthening in the Uruguay Round', in Will Martin and Alan Winters (eds.), *The Uruguay Round and the Developing Economies* (Cambridge: Cambridge University Press, 1996) summarizes developing country negotiating stances and objectives during the Uruguay Round. Rubens Ricupero, the Secretary-General of UNCTAD and a former trade negotiator for Brazil discusses developing country strategies and concerns during the Uruguay Round in 'Integration of Developing Countries into the Multilateral Trading System', in J. Bhagwati and M. Hirsch (eds.), *The Uruguay Round and Beyond: Essays in Honor of Arthur Dunkel* (Ann Arbor: University of Michigan Press, 1998). Gilbert Winham, 'Explanations of Developing Country Behavior in the GATT Uruguay Round Negotiation', *World Competition Law and Economics Review*, 21(3) (1998), 109-34 analyzes the negotiating positions taken by developing countries in the Uruguay Round. J. Michael Finger and Philip Schuler, 'Implementation of Uruguay Round Commitments: The Development Challenge', *The World Economy*, 23 (2000), 511–26, discuss the implementation challenges—including likely resource costs—that confront developing countries as a result of the Uruguay Round, and argue that in a number of areas implementation may make little sense from a development perspective. Michael Finger and L. Alan Winters assess what the WTO can and cannot do for developing countries in 'What Can the WTO Do for Developing Countries', in Anne Krueger (ed.), *The WTO as an International Organization* (Chicago: University of Chicago Press, 1998).

Richard Blackhurst, William Lyakurwa and Ademola Oyejide assess the challenges and opportunities for enhancing the ability of African countries to benefit from the WTO in 'Options for Improving Africa's Participation in the WTO', *The World Economy*, 23 (2000), 491-510. Rolf Langhammer and Mathias Lücke, 'WTO Accession Issues' in Peter Lloyd and Chris Milner (eds.), *The World Economy: Global Trade Policy 1999* (Oxford: Basil Blackwell, 1999) survey the accession experience under the WTO's first years. China's trade regime is analyzed by Zhang Shuguang, Z. Zansheng and W. Zhongxin, *Measuring the Cost of Protection in China* (Washington DC: Institute for International Economics, 1999). Many accession issues are discussed in Frederick Abbott (ed.), *China in the World Trading System* (Dordrecht: Kluwer, 1998). For a detailed discussion of Russia's relations with the GATT and the WTO, see Peter Naray, *Russia and the World Trade Organization* (Basingstoke and New York: Palgrave, 2000).

13
Towards Deeper Integration?
The 'Trade and' Agenda

Starting with the Kennedy Round, MTNs began to focus on domestic regulatory policies and administrative procedures that have an impact on trade. This trend shows no sign of abating. Possible topics for post-Uruguay Round negotiations include subjects such as competition law, labor standards, environmental policy, and FDI regulations. The focus of the GATT was largely limited to the reduction or abolition of discrimination against foreign products or producers. The approach was one of negative or shallow integration: agreement not to do specific things (for example, raise tariffs above bound levels, use indirect taxes to discriminate against foreign products, or use QRs) or to do things in a certain way *if* a government decided to pursue a policy (for example, undertake an injury investigation as part of an AD or CVD action). This approach is more difficult to use to address differences in domestic regulatory regimes. Positive or deep integration may be required: agreement to pursue common policies, to harmonize (Tinbergen, 1954; Lawrence and Litan, 1991). Shallow integration has been (and continues to be) the bedrock of the trading system—it does not require governments to take action, but imposes disciplines if they do. Positive or deep integration in contrast requires governments to pursue common policies.

Deep integration became more prominent on the WTO agenda because the liberalization of traditional trade policy instruments increased the visibility of differences in national regulatory regimes. Calls for deeper integration at the multilateral level range from coordinated application of national policies to the harmonization of regulatory regimes. Such harmonization is sometimes held to be necessary to ensure 'fair trade' or an equality of competitive opportunities for foreign and domestic firms.

This chapter discusses the general issue of dealing with 'behind the border' regulation in the WTO context, and provides an introduction to the main issues that are likely to be prominent on the multilateral negotiating agenda in the coming decade. A key question is to identify the rationale for—and objectives behind—proposals to address a specific issue in the WTO, and determine what type of cooperation is appropriate, if any. In many areas—both old and new—there is still great scope for shallow integration (the elimination of discrimination). In others deeper integration is required in order to realize benefits from cooperation. Independent of the type of cooperation that will generate the greatest gains, it is important to determine whether the WTO is the appropriate forum to address a specific issue. To date, a key criterion for inclusion has been that an issue should be trade-related. This explains why new issues are often discussed in the WTO under the heading of trade and the environment, trade and labor, trade and competition, trade and investment, trade and animal rights, and so forth. A major challenge for the WTO members is to determine where to draw the line: how trade-related should a regulatory issue be to be considered in the WTO?

13.1. CONTESTABILITY OF MARKETS AS A CRITERION

Sovereign states traditionally have pursued limited economic integration in the multilateral context. The approach has been one of reducing barriers to market access, initially border measures such as tariffs and quotas, later domestic policies with a potential trade impact such as subsidies and product standards, and most recently areas where domestic regulatory regimes are directly at issue—such as services or IPRs. The objective has generally been to enhance the contestability of markets for foreign products. Although the Uruguay Round mostly continued to revolve around shallow integration, a number of the agreements that emerged involved deeper integration. Examples are the requirement to value goods on the basis of invoices (transaction values) and the TRIPs agreement. After the Uruguay Round was concluded, the 'Reference Paper' defining minimum standards of regulation for basic telecom providers continued the trend.

RIAs such as the EU suggest that one reason for increasing pressures for deep integration is that this may be a necessary condition for governments to fully commit themselves not to use trade policy anymore—that is, to accept free trade. Another reason is the globalization of production. Firms are centered less and less on purely national markets. Indeed, it has become almost a platitude that what counts for firms are local, regional and global markets, and that these are not necessarily defined by the borders of a nation state. The managerial and technological innovations of the last decades of the twentieth century—such as just-in-time inventory management and the increased tradability of services resulting from declining transport, telecommunications and information technology costs—allow greater specialization and geographic diversification of production. This in turn makes differences in national regulations pertaining to services, FDI, transfer of technology and protection of intangible assets more costly for firms. Enterprises consequently seek to minimize the regulatory constraints to enter, operate in, and exit from markets. Harmonization can be one way to achieve the desired reduction in costs.

Market access has been the raison d'être of the GATT trading system. Should it remain the basic objective of the WTO? The Uruguay Round and subsequent developments suggest many WTO members do not think so. A good case can be made that the focus of the attention of the WTO should extend beyond market access narrowly defined. After all, if there are gains from cooperation on regulatory policies, these should be pursued. However, what should be included and what should be kept off the agenda? We would argue that the criterion should be whether the issue relates to the contestability of markets for goods, services, and factors. If policy areas have a direct bearing on the conditions of competition prevailing on markets, they have a potential place under the WTO.

There are many policies that may affect the contestability of markets for foreign providers. They include traditional trade policies (tariffs, quotas, contingent protection), restrictions on FDI (outright prohibitions or non-national treatment), discriminatory public procurement policies, subsidy practices, and regulatory regimes (including competition law and enforcement, product standards, and policies pertaining to the service sector). A first step for policymakers is to rank-order these issues in terms of impact on the contestability of markets, and in terms of the type of cooperation that is required. The more that can be done through shallow integration, the likelier that agreement is feasible and that the WTO negotiating mechanisms can help. Abstracting from the question of contingent protection, it would appear that the major areas where great progress can still be achieved via the traditional GATT approach of mutual disarmament are tariffs (still very high for agriculture and 'sensitive' industries), government procurement, FDI policies, and regulatory regimes for services. In all these areas what is needed in the first instance is agreement to allow foreign firms to contest domestic markets and for governments to refrain from discrimination—that is, to apply the principles of national treatment and MFN.

Reducing or eliminating discrimination against foreign products and factors is just one part of the equation. Other elements are general regulation of competition and government policies to attain noneconomic objectives. These are also appropriate in principle for inclusion in the WTO insofar as they affect competition on markets. But progress on such issues will inherently be more difficult to achieve. The payoffs of proposals on domestic regulations that apply on a nondiscriminatory basis are less clear, in part because the economics of the issues are often ambiguous. In contrast to trade policy—where there are clear-cut policy recommendations—when it comes to regulation and market structure there are few hard and fast rules of thumb that governments can rely on to ensure that agreements enhance welfare. In part this is because different interests are affected when it comes to regulation, including many issue-specific groups—environmental lobbies, consumer organizations, human rights activists, and so forth. Preferences across societies will differ across countries depending on local circumstances, tastes and conditions.

Many NGOs have objectives that are not related to the market access goal of the WTO. Environmental groups are concerned with improving and safeguarding the environment, both at home and abroad. Other groups are concerned with social standards, or human and animal rights. The aim of these groups is often to export national standards to other countries. In this they may be supported by industries who are worried about their competitiveness *vis-à-vis* firms located in countries that have low environmental or labor standards, or are interested in selling their know-how in meeting standards to foreign enterprises. Such industries may push for import barriers as a way of offsetting the resulting 'unfair competition' or as an instrument to pressure foreign governments to adopt higher standards. Trade policy is rarely an appropriate instrument for attaining environmental or other non-economic objectives. Efficiency considerations require that policy instruments are used that target perceived problems at the source. Trade policy cannot do this (see annex 2). Indeed, in a number of areas it is not even clear that there is scope for gains to be realized from deep integration efforts—the issues are zero-sum.

Figure 13.1 provides a framework for thinking about whether deep integration is called for on an issue, and how useful and feasible efforts in this direction are likely to be in the WTO. Issues are plotted along three dimensions. The horizontal axis depicts the economic forces favoring diversity or uniformity in norms. The vertical axis plots the degree to which there are distributional tensions and differences associated with outcomes. In addition, issues are characterized by how trade-related they are—either strongly, weakly or not at all. In principle the latter should not be in the WTO, unless they are necessary for a globally welfare-improving 'grand bargain'.

Economic forces favoring global norms include uniformity of consumer preferences across nations, economies of scale and scope (including network externalities), or the fact that a particular issue involves a global externality and requires concerted action (for example, ozone depletion). Support for norm diversity, on the other hand, will be stronger the greater are national differences in preferences, willingness to pay for particular standards, consumption patterns, and legal and political institutions. The smaller are the physical spillovers caused by production or consumption in one nation on another, the stronger the case for uniformity.

For example, in principle there is a strong case for the adoption of a common system to classify goods. Classification is strongly trade-related and there are positive externalities from adopting common rules. This also applies to QRs—there is virtual unanimity that this is an economically inferior instrument of protection. A uniform rule—a prohibition—is therefore appropriate. The same applies to rules of origin (ROO)—harmonize—and antidumping (AD)—abolish. At the other end of the spectrum are issues where differences in national preferences, absence of cross-border spillovers, and so forth, call for diversity in rules. Examples are national environmental standards (NES)—which must by necessity reflect local circumstances and preferences or the existence and level of the minimum wage. Many of the issues mapped on the horizontal axis are not unidimensional. For example, in the area of labor market regulation and standards there is a much stronger rationale for uniform rules for core labor standards such as a prohibition on slavery than there is for minimum wage legislation—most

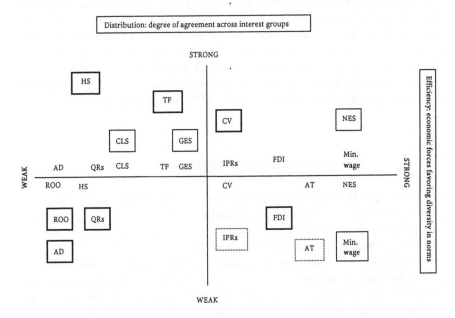

Note: ROO=rules of origin; GES, (NES)=global (national) environmental standards; CV= customs valuation
AT=antitrust; TF=trade facilitation; CP contingent protection CLS=Core Labor standards

Legend: ☐ Strongly trade-related
        ☐ Not trade-related
        ⬚ Weak trade relationship

FIG. 13.1 Diversity versus Uniformity in Rules

will agree that slavery should be outlawed, but such agreement does not exist regarding the need for a legislated minimum wage, let alone the appropriate level.

Although it is relatively straightforward to map issues onto the horizontal axis, whether countries will be able to cooperate—pursue common policies or accept diversity—depends on political forces. A major determinant of outcomes is the extent to which interest groups push or oppose a specific outcome. In the case of the HS classification system, for example, there were no powerful groups that opposed it, although agreeing to the classification took a lot of effort given that customs administrations had different views and concerns. In the case of AD, as discussed in chapter 9, there are vocal and powerful interest groups that oppose introduction of the economically preferable uniform rule—a ban. A good deal of diversity can be expected to continue to prevail. The converse may also arise—a uniform rule is imposed where it may not be optimal (for example, TRIPs).

Some of the issues plotted in Figure 13.1 are not trade-related. Examples are environmental norms and national labor market regulations. As discussed further below, these have little direct bearing on trade, and trade policy is not an effective instrument to enforce whatever norms might be agreed. In some of these instances there is a good case for international harmonization (core labor standards, global environmental spillovers)—but a strong argument can be made that the WTO should not be the forum for such cooperation.

13.2. FOREIGN DIRECT INVESTMENT POLICIES

With the exception of the GATS, there are no disciplines in the WTO regarding policies towards labor or capital movement.[1] GATT disciplines pertain to trade or trade-related policies—they do not extend to the policies used by governments to restrict or attract FDI. GATT also has nothing to say about policies that affect the operations of firms that are established in a member—such as requirements concerning the employment of nationals, limitations on operations inside the country, restrictions on the number or location of plants or branches, and so forth. As long as a policy does not lead to discriminatory treatment of products, a WTO member is free to pursue any policies it pleases with respect to FDI in non-service industries. Some WTO members have argued that there is a need to negotiate multilateral rules for investment policies, such as the right of establishment and national

---

[1] This section draws on Hoekman and Saggi (2000).

treatment for foreign investors. These arguments largely revolve around market access objectives. In many sectors the preferred mode of supplying a market may be through FDI, not exports. If FDI is restricted, foreign firms have an interest in lobbying for rules that guarantee them market access.

More important, trade and investment are becoming increasingly complementary—an ever larger share of global trade is intra-firm, involving exchanges between related enterprises (Hipple, 1990). For example, US Department of Commerce data indicates that two-thirds of US trade involves US multinationals, of which about half is intra-firm (Schatz and Venables, 2000). Much of the FDI that occurs today involves trade. Globalization of production—with firms sourcing from least-cost producers all over the world—makes investment regulations more important to enterprises because such geographic splintering often requires that the firm establish joint ventures or affiliates in various locations to ensure quality, or because technologies are proprietary. At the same time governments seeking to attract FDI may compete with one another—offering subsidies, tax concessions, and so on to investors. Such competition is expensive and inefficient from a world welfare point of view because the total amount of FDI is not influenced by tax incentives—only its location. The end result may be a suboptimal level of taxation of capital relative to other factors of production. Insofar as governments are playing a zero-sum game, they have an incentive to agree to mutual disarmament.

Many countries apply licensing and approval regimes and impose related red tape costs on foreign investors. They may also impose equity ownership restrictions. Such policies may reflect welfare-enhancing attempts to shift foreign profits to the domestic economy or welfare-reducing rent-seeking activities by bureaucrats and their constituents. Sometimes the effect of policies is simply to waste real resources (so-called frictional costs—see Baldwin, 1994 and annex 2). Arguments that have been suggested why WTO members should consider the creation of a multilateral agreement on investment include the following:

- National policies to encourage (subsidize) FDI may impose negative spillovers on other countries leading to an inefficient outcome for the world as a whole. An often mentioned example is tax competition between governments (Moran, 1998).
- An international agreement may serve as a mechanism through which governments can reduce investor uncertainty and reduce risk premia by making irrevocable policy commitments (Francois, 1997, Fernandez and Portes, 1998).
- Given that the GATS covers FDI, it makes no sense not to have similar rules for non-service FDI. General rules are required to ensure that in-

vestment policies do not distort the mode of supply choice of foreign firms (Feketekuty 2000).

• An agreement can be a valuable tool for governments that are hostage to local incumbents that oppose foreign entry by being part of a 'grand bargain'. As FDI and trade are increasingly two sides of the same coin, rules should focus on the full set of policies that affect actors' decisions—both trade and investment-related regulations.

INCENTIVES. From an individual country's perspective, incentives to attract FDI may be justified if there exists, externalities from FDI. For example, developing countries may hope that FDI will generate technological spillovers for local firms, thereby making more efficient use of existing resources. Spillovers may arise by local firms adopting technologies introduced by the multinational through imitation or reverse-engineering, by workers trained by the multinational transferring information to local firms or starting their own firms, and through derived demand by multinationals for local provision of services that can also be used by local firms. There exists a large literature that tries to determine whether or not host countries enjoy 'spillovers' (positive externalities) from FDI (Saggi, 2000) provides a survey). The empirical support for positive spillover effects is mixed, with a number of studies using firm level data concluding that FDI has a negative effect on the performance of domestically owned firms (Aitken and Harrison 1999).

If governments believe that there exists a solid economic case for promoting inward FDI via incentives because of positive externalities, countries may find themselves in a bidding war for FDI. This can be to the detriment of the parties involved if it leads to excessive payment to the investor. The proliferation in the use of incentives to FDI suggests that this is an important possibility, and that there may be a case for international cooperation to ban or discipline the use of fiscal incentives. Clearly a key issue here is whether fiscal incentives are effective. If not, there is no argument for international cooperation on efficiency grounds as the incentives basically end up as transfers to multinationals. On the other hand, it is precisely when such incentives fail to attract FDI that the developing countries have the most to gain from committing to not using them. The evidence on this issue is also far from clear. Many studies conclude that incentives do not play an important role in altering the global distribution of FD. Others conclude that incentives do have an effect on location decisions, especially for export-oriented FDI (Caves (1996) surveys the literature).

Even if incentives affect FDI, the efficiency case against competition for FDI is not clear-cut. Incentives may actually help ensure that FDI goes to those locations where it is most highly valued. Policy may act as an efficient signaling device that improves the allocation of investment across jurisdictions by ensuring that FDI moves to where it has the highest social return. In practice, however, locational competition is generally not driven by information asymmetries. This is the case in particular for efforts by high-income countries to retain or attract FDI that would be more efficiently employed in developing countries. Labor unions and groups representing the interests of local communities may oppose plant closures and efforts by firms to transplant facilities. Similar motivations underlie the use of trade policy instruments such as antidumping by OECD countries. It is important therefore to distinguish between locational incentives employed by developing countries and investment policies used by industrialized nations. The latter are much more likely to be inefficient and focus on attracting industries that otherwise would not have come or would have left. Investment incentives, as well as complementary policies that protect industries that cannot compete and should either exit or relocate (examples are rules of origin in regional agreements and antidumping) are prime candidates for international negotiations (Moran, 1998).

As in the case of subsidies affecting trade, obtaining agreement on what type of incentives should be permitted and what types should be constrained is likely to be difficult. Even if no financial incentives are granted, a country can offer a regulatory environment that may enhance its attractiveness to investors. Some of those regulatory incentives may in turn be considered 'unfair' (for example, low labor or environmental standards). Any type of industrial policy if applied on a national treatment basis may affect the location decision of a firm. As mentioned, the empirical literature on this topic suggests that foreign investors give little weight to fiscal incentives; what matters for them are factors such as the quality of infrastructure, political stability, and labor costs and available skills (Wheeler and Mody, 1992). The pressure on rational governments to engage in investment incentive competitions may therefore be lower than is sometimes assumed. In practice, incentives are likely to be most important—and most expensive—for countries that are attempting to offset policy-induced distortions that reduce their attractiveness for FDI. The solution in these cases is to deal with the distortions—bad infrastructure, political instability, etc.—directly. For these reasons, focusing on extending the fundamental disciplines of the WTO—transparency, national treatment, MFN, and binding of policies—to the investment policy area may be much more productive than focusing on subsidy issues.

CREDIBILITY. It is sometimes argued that a multilateral investment agreement may help countries enhance the perceived credibility of their FDI policies. In order to assess the relevance of the credibility argument for an investment agreement, it is necessary to identify how much of what might be embodied in such an agreement can be pursued and implemented unilaterally. The experience of transition economies re-confirms that economic fundamentals are the crucial determinants of FDI. Some countries that concluded Association Agreements with the EU attracted very little FDI (e.g. Bulgaria) in large part because privatization was not pursued with any vigor, the political environment was uncertain, and the macroeconomic policy such that inflation attained triple digits. The Czech Republic, Hungary and Poland did attract significant FDI inflows, but it is unclear what role the investment provisions of the Association Agreements played. A case can be made that fundamentals drove these inflows, including privatization, re-establishment of private property rights, and geographic proximity to Europe (especially Germany) (Hoekman and Djankov, 1997).

Many countries that are looking for FDI have made use of a variety of existing, non-WTO credibility-enhancing institutions. These include accepting arbitration of disputes under the Convention on the Settlement of Investment Disputes between States and Nationals of Other States, by the International Chamber of Commerce (ICC), or by the UN Committee on International Trade Law (UNCITRAL),[2] depending on the preferences of the investor. Sometimes such commitments are embedded in BITs. Countries that are in the market for credibility can also use existing WTO disciplines to schedule market access opening policies for services (including granting of the right of establishment), and choose to lock in low tariff regimes by binding these under GATT rules. There is still huge scope for developing countries to use the WTO as a credibility enhancing instrument—as noted in chapter 7, the coverage of services commitments is very limited, and tariff bindings for merchandise imports are often significantly higher than applied rates. Although credibility with respect to investment-related policies can certainly be pursued via a multilateral investment agreement, those governments that are convinced they have a need to use external instruments to achieve such objectives could start by exploiting existing instruments much more fully. The same argument applies to RIAs—most do not go very far on the FDI front.

THE ARCHITECTURAL ARGUMENT. The current architecture of the WTO is quite messy: the WTO is an apex institution that embodies three major mul-

---

[2] The International Centre for the Settlement of Investment Disputes (ICSID) operates under the aegis of the World Bank to apply the Convention. The ICC has a Court of Arbitration. UNCITRAL has adopted a set of Arbitration and Conciliation Rules that can be used in the settlement of commercial disputes.

tilateral agreements. Of these, one incorporates FDI as a mode of supply and another protects investments in intellectual property. As is often emphasized, trade and investment have increasingly become complementary. It will become increasingly difficult to maintain a clear distinction between trade in goods and trade in services, as technology may give producers the choice of delivering their products in tangible form or in disembodied form. A priori, it would appear that any multilateral disciplines should apply equally to international transactions regardless of the mode of delivery. This suggests that WTO members should consider developing disciplines that distinguish between trade and investment, with trade in goods or services being subject to a set of common rules, and movement of factors of production being subject to another set of rules. This in effect has been the approach taken in the NAFTA, which includes a separate chapter on investment (in goods or services), which is distinct from the rules relating to cross-border trade (in goods and services). Emulating this approach would result in much greater consistency and clarity of the applicable rules and disciplines.

This is a compelling rationale for discussing FDI-related policies in the WTO. After all, the WTO deals with trade, and there is no reason why this should not extend to trade in capital. Logic suggests that if this path is followed movement of labor should be put on the table as well. Purely from an economic viewpoint, the argument for free movement of labor is no weaker than that for the free movement of capital (Panagariya, 1999). Clearly, countries that play the role of source countries in the movement of capital are likely to play the role of host countries for labor. However, it is unlikely that governments will be prepared to go far down this path anytime soon. The issues involved become considerably more thorny once labor mobility is introduced into the mix, and a complete revamping of the trading system may be required. Account must also be taken of the potential downside— issue linkage can be a two-edged sword. Efforts to expand the agenda to investment may allow groups in society to seek cross-issue linkages in areas such as the environment or labor standards that could be detrimental to the original raison d'être of the WTO: to progressively liberalize international trade.

THE GRAND BARGAIN. The OECD's failure in the late 1990s to negotiate a Multilateral Agreement on Investment (MAI) among supposedly like-minded countries (see Henderson, 1999) suggests that limiting attention to investment policies is a recipe for failure—the agenda needs to be broader to allow tradeoffs and issue linkages. Although a multilateral agreement might prove valuable to developing countries that confront difficulties in removing red tape unilaterally, the negotiation process must allow issues to be brought to the table that are of sufficient interest to domestic constituencies so that they will invest resources to fight for a better investment regime. Foreign pressure for market access may be enough in itself, but generally source country interest groups seeking such access will have to bring something to the table to motivate constituencies in host countries to assist them. More generally, FDI liberalization may be used as a negotiating chip to obtain concessions in other areas. One possibility would be to focus on the broader nexus of policies that affect location decisions by firms, as this could allow tradeoffs between trade and investment policies. There are a large number of issue linkages that would improve global welfare—for example, disciplines on OECD investment incentives for reductions in developing country tariffs.

One should ask what deserves priority. From an economic perspective, the payoff to eliminating entry restrictions facing multinational firms producing nontradables (that is, services) is likely to be greatest, as FDI is the main mode of supply (Hoekman and Saggi, 2000). Similarly, if red tape on inward FDI is motivated in part by the existence of high trade barriers, priority should be given to trade liberalization to facilitate imports. Both can be pursued independently of FDI talks through continued multilateral liberalization of trade in goods and services. The GATS in particular has an important role to play in this connection as it already covers FDI in the sectors where it is most important as an instrument to contest markets—in services industries. The fact that the GATS allows commitments on establishment as a mode of supply weakens the case for making a stand-alone investment agreement in the WTO a negotiating priority. Once substantial further progress has been made to liberalize trade in goods and services on a nondiscriminatory basis, including national treatment and market access through establishment in service activities, it will become much clearer whether the potential benefits of seeking general rules on investment policies are large enough to justify launching a multilateral negotiation in this area.

The 1996 WTO ministerial meeting in Singapore established a working group to examine the relationship between trade and investment policies. This group enhanced the understanding of WTO members regarding the relationship between trade and investment, but did little to span the differences in view regarding the appropriateness of the WTO as an instrument to discipline investment policies. Proponents of multilateral rules included the EU and Japan, supported by a number of other OECD countries and several middle-income developing economies such as Costa Rica and Chile. A large number of developing countries opposed launching investment negotiations, given the uncertainty regarding the likely benefits. Many NGOs—especially environment and development-oriented groups—were also active opponents of negotiating rules in this area. Their concerns were articulated at some length during the attempt by the OECD to establish a Multilateral Agreement on Investment (MAI) in the late 1990s. NGOs opposed the draft MAI text as unbalanced, giving investors too much scope to oppose and circumvent government regulation aimed at social or environmental objectives through provisions on investor-State dispute resolution.[3] While NGO opposition played a role in the demise of the MAI, lack of strong business support was also a major factor. Countries submitted long lists of derogations and exceptions to the general provisions of the proposed MAI, reducing business interest in the negotiation. The MAI illustrated that OECD countries were not ready to agree to disciplines regarding the use of investment incentives, an area of great importance to developing countries.

13.3. COMPETITION LAW

Competition law (antitrust in US parlance) is increasingly attracting the attention of trade policy officials.[4] This is driven by export interests who argue that anticompetitive practices impede their ability to sell goods and services in foreign markets, and by concerns that 'mega mergers' between firms located in different jurisdictions can have anticompetitive effects. National competition law comprises the set of rules and disciplines maintained by governments relating either to agreements between firms that restrict competition or to the abuse of a dominant position (including attempts to create a dominant position through merger). A major objective in most jurisdictions is efficient resource allocation, and thereby the maximization of national welfare, by ensuring that firms do not abuse a dominant position or negotiate competition-restricting agreements that are detrimental to social welfare. The focus of competition laws is on competition, reflecting the belief that this is a powerful force for economic efficiency. However, many laws recognize that specific agreements between firms that may reduce competition can be efficiency enhancing, and make allowance for such agreements. Countries vary in the emphasis that is placed on efficiency—many also include social objectives and 'fairness' considerations in their legislation.

Competition policy has a much broader domain than competition law. It comprises the set of measures and instruments used by governments that determine the conditions of competition that reign on their markets. Anti-

---

[3]   See Kobrin (1998) and Vallianatos (1998) for a discussion of the role of NGOs and their views on investment rules; Henderson (1999) for a comprehensive description and assessment of the MAI story.
[4]   This section draws on joint work with Peter Holmes and Petros C. Mavroidis.

trust or competition law is a component of competition policy. Other components can include actions to privatize state-owned enterprises, deregulate activities, cut firm-specific subsidy programs, and reduce the extent of policies that discriminate against foreign products or producers. A key distinction between competition law and competition policy is that the latter pertains to both private behavior and government policy, whereas antitrust rules pertain only to the behavior of firms.

Many dimensions of competition policy are already on the WTO agenda. Examples include trade policy, subsidies, IPRs and market access in services. The focus of the debate in the WTO is therefore on whether there should be specific rules pertaining to national competition law and its enforcement—one specific element of a nation's competition policy. The WTO is not starting completely from scratch. Three WTO agreements contain provisions on or related to competition law: TRIMs, TRIPs and the GATS. The TRIMs agreement is limited to a call to consider the need for possible disciplines in this area in the future. The TRIPs agreement allows governments to take measures to control anti-competitive practices in contractual licenses that adversely affect trade and may impede the transfer and dissemination of technology. The GATS recognizes that business practices may restrain competition and thus trade in services, but no obligations are imposed on members regarding either the scope or the enforcement of competition law. Members are only obliged, on request, to enter into consultations with a view to eliminating business practices that are claimed to restrict trade in services. The member addressed 'shall accord full and sympathetic consideration to such a request and shall cooperate through the supply of publicly available non-confidential information of relevance to the matter in question' (Article IX). There is no requirement to act, only an obligation to provide information. It is therefore unclear how a restrictive practice is to be eliminated, or what constitutes a restrictive business practice. Indeed, members remain free not to apply competition law to services.

As in the case of the environment or labor standards (see below), a nation's choice regarding the existence substance of its competition laws is currently its own affair. What matters for the WTO is whether such laws—or their absence—have implications for trade. In the case of competition rules the answer is clearly yes. In 1996, the WTO created a working group to investigate the relationship between trade and competition policies. Views on whether competition law disciplines should be incorporated into the multilateral trading system vary widely in both the policy and academic communities. Despite an ever-expanding literature on the subject, the debate remains contentious; there is no emerging consensus regarding whether and how to address competition issues in the WTO. This was reflected in the first report issued by the working group in late 1998, which simply recommended that discussions in the group be continued.

Support for international disciplines on competition law was originally stimulated by US perceptions that international cartels and the absence or non-enforcement of national competition law impeded the ability of US firms to contest markets. The US argued for many years that Japanese corporate groups (Keiretsu) undermined market access for foreign suppliers by buying predominantly from each other and retaining close vertical linkages between manufacturers, wholesalers and retailers. In the 1940s, at the time of the negotiations to establish an ITO, the US supported inclusion of a chapter dealing with restrictive business practices, reflecting its opposition to German cartels and Japanese zaibatsu. In the latter part of the 1990s, the EU was in the forefront, arguing that all WTO members should be required to adopt and enforce competition laws (Janow, 1998). US authorities recognized the need for international cooperation, but were not willing to allow their rules to be subordinated to an international régime. US competition authorities did not want to change their laws in any way or to find themselves fighting market access battles, although US law has begun to provide for this in certain circumstances (Fox, 1997).

Proponents of introducing international competition rules in the WTO have a predominantly market access driven agenda. Non-existent or poorly enforced competition laws are argued to hinder access by allowing domestic firms to foreclose or greatly increase the cost of entry. Other high-income countries argue that the main issue from a WTO perspective is not competition law but the use of traditional instruments of contingent protection such as antidumping to restrict access to markets. This is the position of Japan and other Asian WTO members, most vocally Hong Kong. Smaller countries, especially developing ones, have also been concerned about possible anti-competitive behavior by large (dominant) multinationals. Both the EU and the US are large economic entities, with domestic competition authorities that are well equipped to address anticompetitive behavior that has detrimental consequences for consumers located in their jurisdiction. Developing countries have less capacity to discipline possible anticompetitive abuses by foreign multinational firms on their markets. Perhaps the most obvious example is an export cartel designed to exploit market power on foreign markets. Such cartels benefit home countries if any detrimental effect on home consumers is more than offset by the gains to producers associated with their ability to raise prices on foreign markets. The latter will be to the detriment of foreign welfare if the costs to consumers there outweigh the increase in domestic producer surplus.

This brief introduction illustrates that there is significant variation in the interests of different countries regarding the type of multilateral competition disciplines that might be considered beneficial (acceptable). The main interest of the EU and US is to use competition law disciplines as an export-promoting device and to reduce the scope for conflict in the approval of mergers between large firms; they are less interested in subjecting the behavior of their firms in foreign markets to international disciplines. Market access is also of interest to small countries, but these may be concerned as well with being able to invoke assistance in disciplining anticompetitive behavior of firms located in foreign jurisdictions. Major exporters that are affected by AD want the focus to be on the anticompetitive effect of trade policies, not on competition law per se.

Much of world trade does not occur between independent firms operating on textbook-type perfectly competitive markets. Instead, competition is imperfect in that firms have some power to influence prices on markets, pursue collaborative ventures, or engage in intra-firm trade (see Figure 13.2). Such interactions are by no means an indication that competition is weak, and that there is a need to enforce competition rules. What matters is that markets are contestable. In many of the specific examples mentioned in Figure 13.2, government policy plays a role in reducing the contestability of the market, either through specific actions (such as STEs, allowing international cartels, or discriminatory government procurement) or through more general policy. In principle, there is therefore a good case to be made for focusing on the competitive implications of existing WTO rules.

There are a number of holes in the WTO as far as competition law is concerned. First, purely private business practices restricting access to markets that are not supported by the government cannot be attacked under GATT or GATS. Second, there is no requirement that WTO members have a competition law, let alone that it meet certain minimum standards. Many members have a competition law of some kind, but there are significant differences in norms and their enforcement. Third, the reach of WTO is currently restricted to measures by governments that affect the conditions of competition in their territory. Practices by firms on export markets or tolerance by governments of anti-competitive behavior on export markets by firms headquartered in their territory cannot be addressed. Finally, in a number of areas covered by the WTO—TRIPs being the foremost example—competition law has an important role to play in the implementation of the agreement, but there is no agreement on substantive standards, giving rise to potential for nonviolation disputes.

One problem confronting developing countries is anticompetitive behavior — by foreign governments or firms — that they cannot address.

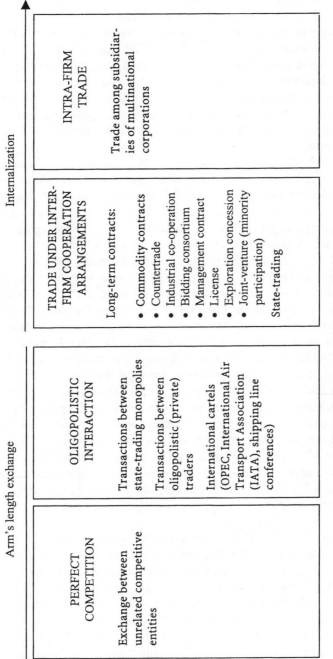

Fig. 13.2 Interaction in international trade

Arm's length exchange ↔ Internalization

PERFECT COMPETITION

Exchange between unrelated competitive entities

OLIGOPOLISTIC INTERACTION

Transactions between state-trading monopolies

Transactions between oligopolistic (private) traders

International cartels (OPEC, International Air Transport Association (IATA), shipping line conferences)

TRADE UNDER INTER-FIRM COOPERATION ARRANGEMENTS

Long-term contracts:

- Commodity contracts
- Countertrade
- Industrial co-operation
- Bidding consortium
- Management contract
- License
- Exploration concession
- Joint-venture (minority participation)

State-trading

INTRA-FIRM TRADE

Trade among subsidiaries of multinational corporations

Examples are export cartels and export taxes. Although export prohibitions or QRs and export subsidies are prohibited (see chapter 5), current GATT rules basically give members the freedom to impose tariffs on exports. They also allow for export monopolies. This implies that members remain substantially free to attempt to raise the relative price of their exports, to the detriment of rest of the world and that efforts to agree to multilateral disciplines regarding the treatment of export cartels in domestic competition law, if successful, will have to be complemented by analogous tightening of the rules regarding the scope for governments to pursue strategic trade policies more generally.

In the 1990s, concerns regarding export behavior were complemented by problems arising in multi-jurisdictional merger cases. Competition authorities want effective leverage over mergers that may have cross border effects, while firms want to minimize the number of agencies they are accountable to. In principle, mergers between firms that will have a very high combined market share in markets where they are not domiciled can be a serious source of concern for a competition authority. Although many global mergers and alliances have been approved without disputes by the major affected jurisdictions, a number of cases in the late 1990s led to tensions. One example was the merger between Boeing and McDonnell Douglas (MDD), where the US and the EU took different views, and only a last minute compromise prevented a serious trade conflict from erupting. The EU was concerned that certain of Boeing's long-term sole-sourcing contractual arrangements with airlines risked permanently excluding Airbus if they were not challenged. Thus, the concern was not only that the merger might result in higher prices for aircraft, but to protect the interests of the only EU competitor of Boeing-MDD (Airbus Industrie). The EU refused to approve the merger unless Boeing agreed not to enforce the sole-sourcing contracts, which in the end it accepted. The contested arrangements were actually unrelated to the merger as they involved Boeing and some of its customers—if they were bad for the EU, they were bad independent of the merger (Mavroidis and Neven, 1998). This raises the question why objections were not raised earlier by the EU (or by MDD in the pre-merger period).

This case illustrated that interests of different jurisdictions can diverge considerably in merger cases. It suggests there may be value to adoption of rules to foster transparency such as harmonization of notification procedures. Less clear is how to address the problem of national authorities making mutually exclusive demands on a merging entity. For an international agreement to have prevented a similar dispute or the eventual negotiated outcome, it would have to impose clear standards for examination and review of mergers. The EU and the US already cooperate on antitrust matters under the auspices of a bilateral agreement that includes so-called positive comity language. This was not sufficient to prevent the dispute. One can question whether international rules could be devised that would be effective in requiring any one jurisdiction to back off in such cases.

How likely is it that countries will use antitrust strategically? Horn and Levinsohn (1996) conclude that this is not very likely, even in areas where it would seem most easily applied—merger policies and export cartels. However, Bond (1997) builds a model that gives rise to strategic behavior by antitrust jurisdictions, and uses this to explain a late nineteenth century 'race to the bottom' in US merger standards (Box 13.1). Whether or not there are serious spillovers associated with merger standards, mergers are often politically sensitive, with national legislatures and governments resisting takeovers by foreign firms. EU decisions to oppose a merger between MCI Worldcom and Sprint, two US-based telecommunications providers, and a joint venture between Time Warner and EMI, led the US Senate antitrust subcommittee to express concerns that EU competition policy enforcement was influenced by a desire to protect EU-based firms (*Washington Post*, October 6, 2000, p. E3). Conversely, there was substantial Congressional hostility to a proposed takeover by Deutsche Telekom of Voicestream Communications in the summer of 2000, on the basis that the German state owned the majority of Deutsche Telekom shares.

Box 13.1. US State-level Regulatory Competition

Technological changes in the late nineteenth and early twentieth century led to a decline in transportation costs (railways, telegraph) and increased competition on many markets in the US. Federal law at the time focused on combating anti-competitive practices of large 'trusts' engaged in inter-state commerce. As the federal statute (the Sherman Act) banned price fixing agreements, this gave firms an incentive to merge. State, not Federal, authorities were responsible for approving mergers and granting corporate charters. This allowed states that were willing to have lax merger standards to pass laws that encouraged firms to merge and incorporate in their states. The most liberal state, New Jersey, managed to attract more than half of all corporations with a capitalization of $10 million or more. By 1902 New Jersey was able to pay off the entire state debt from the tax it imposed on the capital stock of merging firms, and abolish property taxes. Other states tried to follow New Jersey's lead and a 'race to the bottom' ensued. Eventually 42 states adopted laws similar to New Jersey's, although with only limited effect—firms stayed in New Jersey.

The analysis of this episode by Bond (1997) illustrates that incentives to restrict mergers and price-fixing agreements across countries will vary with their endowments and political organization. Differences in the power of interest groups will determine the national antitrust stance. If more weight is put on the profits of merging firms, it is more likely to be permissive; conversely, if consumers are powerful it will be restrictive. If disciplines on antitrust are not harmonized, a race to the bottom can ensue. Centralization of antitrust at a higher level may allow a better cooperative outcome to result.

This analysis can be contrasted with state-level policies aimed at attracting investment. In a recent empirical analysis of the effect of US state policies on the location of manufacturing, Holmes (1998) finds that the share of manufacturing in employment in states with pro-business regulatory environments increases by one third compared to a bordering state without such policies. This result is noteworthy not only in indicating that policies matter, but also in suggesting that differences across states are relatively stable. The measure of policy chosen (whether a state had a law banning requirements that all employees of a firm join a union) has not changed significantly since 1958: in the last two decades only two states passed such laws, while none repealed them. Here there was no race to the bottom. In general, there is little evidence for such 'races' (Vogel, 1995).

The political economy of cooperation on competition law is very different from more traditional trade liberalization. Competition law does not lend itself very easily to incremental changes (the exchange of concessions). Moreover, specific policies that are pursued by governments may be in the national interest. Thus, any agreement to make binding commitments to follow a positive comity rule in mergers (let alone agree on common standards of review) and to prohibit export cartels (or even to agree to provide information) will imply costs for countries that benefit from the exploitation of market power. They can therefore be expected to demand a significant quid pro quo. A problem from a practical perspective is that for the WTO's traditional public choice dynamics (reciprocity) to work, antitrust-related market access barriers affecting a country's exporters must be large enough to offset the gains accruing to industries benefiting from national competition law exemptions. Few major trading countries have competition regimes that significantly restrict access to markets. And those that do can be (and have been) subjected to pressure by large trading partners to change their policies (the application of Section 301 by the US is an example). This suggests that a linkage strategy may well be necessary to make progress in this area.

What about the political economy argument that international competition disciplines might prove helpful to overcome domestic opposition to the implementation of pro-competitive policies? The foundation of the GATT and the WTO is that in the pursuit of a market access agenda, the national welfare is promoted. National antitrust has a very different focus from national trade policy in that the emphasis should be on welfare and the competitive process. This implies that the economic rationale for putting it on the WTO agenda is much weaker than for trade policy—national authorities should already be engaged in combating anti-competitive business practices. The pursuit of a market access agenda may result in outcomes that are detrimental from a welfare point of view (the latter possibility is a major reason some competition authorities are leery of putting antitrust on the WTO agenda). For the WTO dynamic to work, one must start from the presumption that competition law has been or will be captured by domestic producer lobbies, and therefore does not focus on welfare maximization. If so, and this may indeed be the case in some countries, there would be a rationale for pursuing international competition disciplines in the WTO. The problem remains, however, that the WTO process is driven by export interests (market access), not national welfare considerations. There is no assurance that any rules that emerge will be welfare enhancing. Doubts can therefore be expressed regarding the ability of a WTO-based process to play as constructive a role in the area of competition law as it has in the area of trade policy (Hoekman and Holmes, 1999).

Seeking substantive harmonization of antitrust rules is a non-starter. There is too much variance across jurisdictions. Even if similar multilateral rules are adopted, national competition authorities will often weight aspects of a case differently. Optimal policy depends on many national (idiosyncratic) variables. For example, whether a country is better off allowing parallel imports or restricting it depends on the situation—no generalization is possible (Maskus and Chen, 2000). Competition law is an area where 'one size fits all' is inappropriate. Instead, shallow integration would appear a more fruitful approach towards cooperation—including application of the principle of national treatment and increasing the transparency of competition law enforcement. The WTO could play a beneficial role in areas that are most trade-related—such as export cartel exemptions—and increasing the competition scrutiny of the trade policies that are permitted under existing multilateral rules—especially AD. Both will be difficult, but in principle are certainly worth pursuing.

Contingent Protection and Competition Policy

Antidumping policies are sometimes defended as justifiable attempts by importing country governments to offset the market access restrictions existing in an exporting firm's home country that underlie the ability of such firms to dump. Such restrictions may consist of import barriers preventing arbitrage (see annex 2), but may also reflect the non-existence or non-enforcement of competition law by the exporting country. AD may then be defended as a second-best instrument to offset such government-made competitive differences. While not at all a compelling argument (see chapter 9), it provides a rationale to use competition law to discipline AD. Given that the only justification for AD is to deal with predation, the first best option is to replace AD with national competition law enforcement. This is likely to be impossible in the WTO context in the foreseeable future—even though one can argue that the national treatment principle requires that imports be treated the same way as domestic goods, that is, be subject to domestic antitrust (Hoekman and Mavroidis, 1996). A second best option is to apply competition principles to AD enforcement. One possibility is to seek agreement that allegations of dumping are investigated by the antitrust authorities to determine whether the exporting firm or industry engages in anticompetitive practices or benefits from government-created or supported entry barriers in its home market. If a necessary condition for AD action would be a finding that significant barriers to entry exist in the exporter's home market, at least one aspect of the argument would be addressed. A complementary option would be to have the importing country's competition authorities determine whether an AD action would have excessively detrimental effects on competition in the market concerned. Suggestions along the foregoing lines will be opposed by import-competing industries that have come to rely on the threat of AD to reduce competition. But, they are certainly options that could be pursued in a MTN. None of these suggestions involve deep integration.

13.4. TRADE FACILITATION

Reliable, high-speed delivery systems are essential in today's global business environment. Just-in-time supply and effective sub-contracting arrangements depend critically on getting goods and people to where they are needed when they are needed. Border controls and related administrative and documentary requirements can create significant delays in crossing frontiers and may impose significant costs on businesses that are part of integrated global production networks. Such firms do not maintain large (and thus costly) inventories—they rely on obtaining components from partners.

Trade facilitation may be defined as the simplification and harmonization of international procedures affecting trade flows. It focuses in particular on the activities, practices and formalities involved in collecting, presenting, communicating and processing data required for the movement of goods and services across national borders. That means notably import and export procedures, payments, insurance and transportation. The documents required in most export transactions include the commercial invoice, the packing list, a certificate of origin, an insurance certificate, the carrier's declaration (or consignment note), letter of credit or bill of exchange, certification of conformity for product standards, and, in some cases a hazardous cargo certificate. Customs-related transaction costs—not including the opportunity costs of delays—can represent between 2 and 10 percent of a shipment's value (Doran, 1999). This implies that the cost to firms of satisfying customs clearance and related requirements will often exceed the duties paid on their exports. Costs are compounded if there is corruption. Case studies in a number of developing countries and transition economies suggest that unofficial payments may raise the marginal tax rate on imported products by more than 25 percent (Kostecki, 2000). Delays raise costs further. For example, the minimum waiting time for lorries entering Georgia from Turkey in the spring of 1998 was 30 hours (*Financial Times*, March 3, 1998).

Box 13.2. DHL and Customs Procedures

DHL is the world's largest international express carrier, with a 40 percent market share. As of the late 1990s, it maintained over 2,300 service centers around the globe, employing about 50,000 people and delivering over 100 million shipments per year. In addition to transporting documents, it handles parcels and larger shipments. The range of core and supplementary activities comprise order taking, pickup, documentation, real-time tracking of shipments, packaging, transportation and delivery. DHL also provides advice and information to clients and partners. The most important factor causing chinks in DHL's delivery process is customs-related controls and red tape. Getting parcels through the border and ensuring the necessary documentation is in place is an important element of the DHL service chain. DHL's strategic advantage (speed) is directly dependent on the efficiency of customs administration and the skill of DHL staff in developing mechanisms to satisfy customs requirements. The company therefore closely monitors customs administrations around the globe and maintains a high level of in-house customs expertise.

One element allowing rapid delivery is that shipments are often sent before all paperwork has been checked and cleared. In such cases, the DHL customs services staff sort things out after shipment has started. DHL personnel in the field and shippers are contacted 'en route' and informed about customs issues they must deal with urgently. If changes in invoicing are required, these are forwarded to the manager of the customs services unit in the importing country who will take the steps needed to ensure rapid clearance. An Electronic Database Interlink system plays a key role in maintaining continuous communication between local and centralized units, complemented with direct contacts with customs administrations.

Source: Kostecki (2000).

Border controls and associated costs and delays are particularly important for express carrier companies, who generally invest significant resources in dealing with documentary requirements (Box 13.2). E-commerce is playing an important role in this connection by fragmenting containers of goods that could have been cleared on a single entry into dozens of individual shipments that each require separate customs documents and clearance procedures. Given anticipated exponential growth in small shipments to individual consumers and firms, it is no wonder that express couriers are actively promoting trade facilitation (Staples, 1998).

Paper-based and outdated customs procedures are still rife in much of the world. Frequently, the same documentation is required for a small package, a lorry or a ship. Some examples are illustrative. Certified photocopies are often refused in developing countries, although their use is the norm in many high-income countries. Shipments may be delayed because rubber stamps on documents are not pressed hard enough or put in the wrong place. Customs authorities may refuse documents because they are signed in black rather than blue ink (blue being viewed as an indication that a document is original). In a series of case studies undertaken by Kostecki (2001) in Eastern Europe, wine was denied entry because the corks in the bottles were not considered to be in conformity with technical requirements, differences in date indications on the packaging of chocolates in a shipment led to a clearance delay of three weeks, and a British firm had its shipment of cider delayed because customs had no product code for it and refused to label it an 'apple drink'.

International traders have been quicker to apply new information technologies than customs authorities in many countries. Technology now provides traders with the facilities to develop cost effective international systems that employ a 'one stop' data capture facility. The electronic transfer of data between parties involved in trade transactions, including banks, insurers, transport companies, importers and exporters, or forwarders permits the use of comprehensive transaction data files that can also be used for customs and related control purposes (Raven 1997). Technology-driven trading systems render conventional paper-based export and import declarations and traditional customs control points redundant as far as revenue assessment and data capture is concerned. As a result, in OECD countries, customs is increasingly becoming a regulatory and standards-related enforcement body. Access to advanced consignment data enable customs to use profiling techniques to identify high-risk consignments and to concentrate on problem solving rather than on traditional border control.

There is substantial pressure by business that the WTO do something in the area of trade facilitation. Efficient procedures and minimizing redundancy can provide important benefits. Because the costs involved are often frictional, the gains to traders and society can easily exceed those associated with trade liberalization. Red tape does not create rents or revenues as do tariffs or QRs. Instead, it simply generates waste (see annex 2). The costs that are involved cannot be eliminated at the unilateral stroke of a pen. Many of the policies concerned require harmonization of norms if costs are to be reduced. Thus, trade facilitation is one of the subjects on the regulatory trade agenda where deep integration is required if gains are to be maximized. Of course, as noted previously, the WTO has already started down this track. The requirement that valuation of goods for customs purposes should in principle be based on the invoice is an example of deep integration.

Multilateral cooperation between states in trade-related standard setting and regulation predates the creation of the GATT. More than 30 intergovernmental organizations emerged during the 1860-1914 period (Box 13.3). By far the most frequent covered infrastructure: mail (1863), marine signaling (1864), technical railway standards (1883), ocean telegraphy (1897), and aerial navigation (1910). Multilateral institutions allowed a Europe-wide market for industrial goods to emerge. International interconnection norms agreed under auspices of the International Telecommunications Union eliminated the need for telegrams to be printed at each border post, walked across, and retyped. The Radiotelegraph Union aimed to prevent a global radio monopoly by requiring interconnection across different technologies. International railway unions promoted networks by standardizing rolling stock, allowing companies to use each other's rolling stock, and enforcing a single bill of lading—so that a single document could be used for all trans-European shipments. European countries (except for Russia and Spain) adopted the same rail gauge, drove on the left, and aligned signals, brakes, and timetables (Pollard, 1974, pp. 50-51). All this was largely driven by the private sector—business can often achieve cooperation more readily than governments. The uniform bill of lading pre-dates the introduction of the Single Administrative Document used by EU member states for customs clearance by almost a century. The Rail Union of 1890 played a significant role in dismantling protectionism in the late nineteenth century by prohibiting transit duties on goods shipped by rail. The Brussels Tariff Union made the remaining restrictions transparent by publishing lists of tariffs in five languages. Intergovernmental organizations proliferated after World War II with the formation of the UN system. Many of these bodies aim to foster economic growth by developing norms and cooperating to facilitate the expansion of international markets and manage conflicts between jurisdictions. Fora in which governments cooperate in developing standards range from technical requirements for maritime and air transport (International

Maritime Organization, ICAO) to customs procedures (World Customs Organization).

Cooperation continues to be pursued to facilitate trade in numerous bodies, most of which have little to do with the WTO. The Center for Facilitation of Procedures and Practices for Administration, Commerce and Transportation (CEFACT-UN/ECE) is an example. CEFACT evolved from the United Nations Economic Commission for Europe's (UN/ECE) Working Party on the Facilitation of International Trade Procedures. Since 1960, this organization has pursued the harmonization and automation of customs procedures and information requirements, and has issued the internationally recognized UN/ECE Trade Facilitation Recommendations (Staples, 1998). This body also worked extensively on standards for Electronic Data Interchange (EDI), developing the United Nations Electronic Data Interchange for Administration Commerce and Transport (UN/EDIFACT). EDI and EDIFACT facilitate the exchange of trade-related information between parties that typically handle international trade transactions.

Box 13.3. Pre-1914 Trade-Related Inter-Governmental Organizations

Objective:	Organization and date of creation
Infrastructure and related 'software'	International Telegraph Union (1865)
	Universal Postal Union (1874)
	International Railway Congress Association (1884)
	Central Office for International Railway Transport (1890)
	Diplomatic Conference on International Maritime Law (1905)
	Universal Radiotelegraph Union (1906)
	Permanent International Association of Road Congresses (International Automobile Convention) (1909)
Standards	International Bureau of Weights and Measures (1875)
	Metric Union (1877)
	International Bureau of Analytical Chemistry of Human & Animal Food (1912)
Intellectual Property	International Union for the Protection of Industrial Property (1883) (Paris Convention)
	International Union for the Protection of Literary and Artistic Works (1886) (Berne Convention)
Trade	Brussels Tariff Union (International Union for the Publication of Customs Tariffs) (1890)
	Hague Conference on Private International Law (1893)
	International Bureau of Commercial Statistics (1913)

| *Dispute* | Permanent Court of Arbitration (1899) |
| *Settlement* | International Court of Prize (1907; never ratified) |

Source: Adapted from Murphy (1994, pp. 48-49).

NGOs are also very active in trade facilitation. The International Express Carriers Conference (IECC)—sponsored by FedEx, UPS, TNT and DHL; the International Chamber of Shipping; the International Road Transport Union; the International Federation of Freight Forwarders Associations; the International Association of Ports and Harbors; and the International Federation of Customs Brokers Association are some examples. The ICC is also very active, having been instrumental in putting the subject of trade facilitation on the agenda of the 1996 WTO Ministerial Conference in Singapore. WTO ministers agreed to draw on the work of other international organizations on the simplification of trade procedures in order to assess the scope for WTO rules in this area. The ICC encouraged the WTO to work with the WCO to make customs modernization an integral element of WTO customs-related provisions. It also called on WTO members to work with the WCO to provide political support to make the revised Kyoto Convention a binding and enforceable multilateral agreement under the WTO.

As discussed in chapter 5, the revised Kyoto Convention, adopted by the WCO Council in June 1999, is a 'blueprint' for modern and efficient customs procedures. Governing principles of the 1999 Convention are transparency, simplicity and predictability of customs procedures, providing a system to appeal Customs matters, greater use of risk management techniques (including risk assessment and selectivity of controls) and information technologies (including the use of pre-arrival information to drive programs of selectivity), greater reliance on partnerships with national trade communities, and coordinated intervention with other national agencies. The Kyoto convention was negotiated among all the members of WCO, and therefore should have the support of most WTO members. The issue is whether the convention should be made enforceable under the WTO—the same way that many of the provisions of the WIPO conventions on IPRs were made enforceable.

One approach in this area would be to conclude an agreement on trade facilitation based on principles such as nondiscrimination, national treatment, and transparency. This would provide a general legal framework for trade facilitation. More detailed commitments could then be formulated in an annex to the agreement. This might include the various mandatory annexes of the WCO convention. Such an agreement could be plurilateral, but given the nature of the issue—which is clearly intimately related to trade and of relevance to all WTO members—it would appear more appropriate to make this a multilateral agreement.

Developing countries are still struggling to implement the WTO customs valuation agreement, and they have doubts about the value of accepting additional mandatory obligations on trade facilitation given weak institutional structures, lack of modern communications and information systems, inadequately trained staff, and so forth. Developing country governments are also concerned about the prospect of WTO dispute challenges regarding non-attainment of trade facilitation targets and disciplines, if such are negotiated. It is clear that uniform transition periods are not enough to deal with differences in implementation capacities. Even Canada, a developed country with ample resources, took five years to complete implementation of the valuation agreement (Staples, 1998). What is needed is the provision of adequate technical and financial assistance, which should include the involvement of the private sector (multinational business).

Trade facilitation is an area where in principle 'one size fits all' is an appropriate rule, but where it must be recognized that it will take poorer countries much longer to attain the good practices that are enumerated in the Kyoto convention, and that significant technical and financial assistance must be provided. Significant flexibility would need to be built in for WTO members in terms of when and how they satisfy any substantive provisions on facilitation.

One area that could be considered in any trade facilitation agreement is rules of origin.[5] These rules have become extremely cumbersome, especially in the context of preferential trade. NAFTA members' origin audit manual runs to approximately 800 pages long, reflecting the fact that rules of origin have become captive to special interest lobbies. In 1994 the US Customs Service NAFTA Help Desk received over 21,000 inquires from confused importers and exporters regarding rules of origin. Many companies choose to pay the MFN tariff due to NAFTA's complexity. NAFTA value content rules require companies to maintain records that they never kept before, to require information from suppliers that they never needed to give before and to provide certifications about the origin and regional content of goods shipped to customers. Even after the greatest care, companies, their suppliers, and their customers may all have to undergo a long and arduous audit by any one—or more than one—of the three NAFTA governments. NAFTA is not an outlier—similar situations prevail in other FTAs. One solution to the protectionist use (capture) of rules of origin would be to make the non-

---

[5] What follows draws on Staples (1998).

preferential rules of origin that are being developed by the WCO mandatory in new RIAs. Given the impotence of the CRTA—see chapter 10—embedding such a rule in an agreement on trade facilitation might be more effective.

13.5. ENVIRONMENTAL POLICIES

The impact of environmental regulation on trade became the subject of discussions in the GATT in the late 1960s. This was a period when fears arose about the limits to growth and the rapid depletion of global natural resources. Environmental policies began to be pursued with greater vigor in OECD countries, leading to complaints by affected industries that the costs of these regulations reduced their ability to compete on world markets. A Working Group on Environmental Measures and International Trade was established by GATT contracting parties in 1971. However, it never met, as interest in the subject waned following the recurrent oil price shocks and the economic turmoil that followed. In 1991, after a period when environmental issues had again attained a high profile on the international policy agenda, the Working Group was re-activated. In the WTO it was transformed into a Committee on Trade and the Environment, with the mandate to investigate the relationship between environmental and trade policies.

Factors that drove environmental issues on to the agenda included increasing recognition of the existence of cross-border environmental spillovers, perceptions that national environmental policies were inadequate, concerns that trade was bad for the environment, fears that national environmental policy would reduce the competitiveness of domestic firms, and a perception that environmental policies were increasingly being used for protectionist purposes.

CROSS-BORDER SPILLOVERS. Production and consumption activities in one country may have detrimental impacts on other countries. Such negative spillovers or externalities may be physical (air and water pollution, acid rain) or intangible (animal rights, consumption of ivory). In such cases there is a basis for cooperation and negotiation. However, (unilateral) trade policy will not be the appropriate instrument to deal with the externality. Standard economic theory requires that externalities be addressed at their source. This requires that either the production or the consumption activity be curtailed directly by confronting the producer or consumer with the real costs of the activity, or that property rights be assigned that gives owners an incentive to manage and price resources appropriately. For an externality to arise there must be a market failure that results prices of the resources used being too low—marginal private costs of an activity are lower than the true marginal social costs (see annex 2). Trade sanctions cannot offset an environmental externality efficiently, because they affect both consumers and producers of a good, and usually impact on only a part of total production or consumption.

While this is often recognized, trade policy is attractive to environmentalists because it can be used to induce countries to apply environmental policies that are in principle targeted at the source of the problem. The issue here is to determine the appropriate standard of protection and the feasibility of enforcing it. Countries may have very different preferences regarding environmental protection, reflecting differences in the absorptive capacity of their ecosystems, differences in income levels (wealth), and differences in culture. Insofar as there are cross-country spillovers—physical or psychological—the appropriate policies will need to be negotiated. What matters from a trading system point of view is that the choice of environmental policy in cases where there are spillovers is not an issue that is appropriately dealt with in the WTO forum. International agreements on the matter are required, to be negotiated by the competent authorities (not trade officials). Trade policy might be agreed to be the instrument that may be used to enforce internationally agreed obligations. As long as there is consensus on this between WTO members, no legal problem arises. There may well be economic problems, however. The effectiveness of trade sanctions will be limited if the targeted nation does not have the resources to enforce appropriate environmental regulations. In such cases the sanction may make it harder for the country to achieve environmental improvements because the trade barriers reduce income.

'INADEQUATE' NATIONAL POLICIES. The same conclusion with respect to trade policy applies if there are no cross border spillovers. In that case each country must determine for itself what are appropriate environmental policies. The WTO does not impose any constraints on a government regarding pursuit of environmental policies on its territory. If it seeks to prevent the consumption of particular products, it may restrict imports, as long as the ban, tax or product standard is also imposed on domestic goods (recall that GATT Article XX makes allowance for general exceptions—see chapter 9). However, the GATT does prevent the extraterritorial enforcement of national standards. Thus, a WTO member cannot use trade policies to force another member to enforce different (stronger) environmental standards on its territory. Attempts to do so have taken the form of attempts to require foreign firms to use specific production processes. A famous example was a US ban on tuna imports from Mexico, justified by the fact that Mexican fishing boats did not use the dolphin-friendly nets required under US regulations. A GATT panel ruled against the US in this case, greatly enhancing the perception of environmentalists that substantial 'greening of the GATT' was required (Esty, 1994). An important subsequent case (shrimp-turtles) is discussed later in this section. In such instances there is a clear-cut case for compensation if a trading partner seeks to impose standards that are higher and more costly than what is optimal for a country to implement. Using coercive trade sanctions is inappropriate.

TRADE AND THE ENVIRONMENT. A perception that trade is bad for the environment also played a role in bringing environmental issues to the WTO. It has been argued that freeing trade will lead to expansion of production and thus pollution, that liberalization will facilitate relocation of firms to countries with lax regulatory environments, that greater trade implies the need for greater transport, leading to more degradation, and so forth. All of these arguments are weak at best. While trade and liberalization may give rise to such effects, this is negative from a social welfare viewpoint only if appropriate environmental policies are not pursued. If such policies are in place, producers and consumers will take into account the cost to the environment, and this will be reflected in the price of goods and services. As greater trade and specialization subsequent to liberalization will lead to greater wealth, the capacity and willingness of voters to devote more resources to the environment will also increase. Using trade policy to restrict trade so as to reduce environmental degradation is inappropriate. Indeed, often protection will have adverse consequences on the environment. Thus, agricultural support programs have led to the use of production methods that are excessively polluting. Coal subsidies in the EU encourage the use of inputs that are much more detrimental to the environment than imports would be (Anderson, 1992). By restricting imports and subsidizing consumption of local output, consumers are prevented from switching towards less polluting types of energy that originate in other parts of the world—areas where the environmental costs of extraction are often lower as well.

COMPETITIVENESS. Environmental policies may reduce the ability of enterprises located in countries with high standards to compete with those that operate in nations with low standards. This is exactly what the policy aims at. If high standards are what a society wants, then the result should be that the affected activities contract. Restricting imports makes no sense, as it promotes the activities that the environmental policy is attempting to constrain. This, of course, is one reason why domestic industries may seek to 'level the playing field' through trade policy—it is one way to avoiding part of the impact of environmental regulation. More generally, if there is a preference for more environmentally-friendly goods on the part of consumers, there should be a willingness to pay for them.

ENVIRONMENTAL PROTECTIONISM. Environmental policies may unnecessarily (or deliberately) be used to restrict trade. This has been a major concern of many WTO members, and has been an important factor for considering environmental policy in the WTO. Environmental policies have often been of the command and control type rather than more efficient price-based instruments such as taxes. The reason is that such instruments may create rents that can be captured by the industries that are affected by the environmental regulations. Industry then has an incentive to push for inefficient policies in situations where environmental groups are sufficiently powerful to get environmental standards adopted (see annex 2). Environmental policies that are based on regulation rather than taxation may easily have trade restricting effects because the trade equivalent may be a ban on imports. The US tuna-dolphin case noted earlier is a case in point.

The challenge is to determine whether the market-access effect of a domestic measure is necessary to achieve underlying policy objectives. Mechanisms to decide what is legitimate are therefore vital (Box 13.4). There is great danger in acceding to pressure for import barriers that are ostensibly justified on level playing field grounds. The prospect of protection may induce import-competing firms to support environmental groups in their pursuit of regulation. This increases the likelihood of inefficient instruments being chosen, as these generate greater rents. An example of possible process standards is illustrative. Suppose that environmentalists are concerned with excessive killing of turtles by shrimp fishermen and have managed to impose a standard that domestic fishermen must use nets that incorporate effective turtle exclusion devices. The domestic industry may then argue that as a result of this policy they face unfair competition from foreign sources not subject to this regulation. Moreover, environmental groups can be expected to insist that foreign imports of shrimp meet the same standards, not because of any concern for the plight of domestic fishermen, but because of their concern for turtles. A tariff on imports is unlikely to be acceptable to the environmental group. Instead, they are likely to demand a ban on imports. Although there might be a stated willingness on the part of environmentalists to exempt those foreign sources that can prove they do not kill turtles (perhaps because there are no turtles in their waters), in practice this may be very difficult to establish. It involves not only allowing inspection of trawlers, but also providing assurance that no mixing of sources occurs. Even if this can be done by foreign suppliers, establishing the turtle friendliness of their products will take time and be costly, so that the environmental policy will make it more attractive to shift to third markets or to substitute products. Domestic fishermen will not care whether there are turtles in foreign waters. For them what counts is the playing field—domestic regulations raise costs and they would like to be compensated for this. The uniform application of the process standard will both have significant trade-distorting effects and is very likely to increase the level of protection (see annex 2).

As in other areas, greater transparency and more objective analysis of the impact of environmental policies on trade, and vice versa, is required. This is the mandate that was given to the Committee on Trade and the Environment (CTE) at the end of the Uruguay Round. As mentioned above, the CTE was a continuation of a working group that was originally formed in 1971, but had been dormant until 1991. Reviving the group was a reaction by GATT contracting parties to the controversy caused by the tuna-dolphin dispute.

Box 13.4. Economic effects of recycling requirements

A number of US states have passed mandatory recycling laws that require that a minimum percentage of the content of newsprint be recycled material, motivated by a desire to reduce the rate at which old newsprint fills up dumps and landfills. These laws were detrimental to Canadian producers of pulp and newsprint, who use virgin wood (forestry products are a major Canadian export and source of comparative advantage). Some Canadian producers found it prohibitively expensive to import old newsprint to combine with new pulp and paper. The result was 10 percent reduction in their US sales.

Similar types of regulations have been a prominent source of market access disputes in the EU. A 1981 Danish bottle recycling law required that all beer and soft drinks be packaged in reusable containers and that retailers take back all containers sold. Metal containers were banned. Other EU producers contended that the law imposed discriminatory costs on them. Although the law was nondiscriminatory, two-way transportation costs for bottles were prohibitive beyond a distance of 300 kilometers. The EU Commission challenged the law, arguing that less trade-restrictive instruments could attain the government's objectives. However, the European Court of Justice found the disposal and re-use requirements to be legal, and only required that Denmark accept metal containers as long as producers could meet the re-use requirements.

These examples illustrate that although domestic policies can restrict market access, this may be tolerated if it can be justified on the basis of overriding non-economic objectives. But they also illustrate that WTO members need to develop clear rules of the game and establish credible dispute settlement systems to determine when these rules have been violated.

Source: Vogel (1995).

This had caused NGOs to consider the GATT anti-environment, and developing countries to worry that environmental norms were being used to restrict trade. The CTE focused its work primarily on the trade and trade policy aspects of environmental policy, including the trade effects of eco-labeling, provisions in multilateral environmental agreements (MEAs) to use trade sanctions or bans as enforcement or implementation instruments, the environmental effects of agricultural support policies, and trade in domestically prohibited goods. The CTE's report to the first WTO ministerial conference in 1996 report was a disappointment to NGOs, who had lobbied for specific recommendations to make WTO rules more 'environmentally friendly'.

The CTE played a useful role in educating trade officials on international efforts to cooperate on environmental matters—including treaties and conventions. It also played a beneficial role in educating the environmental community regarding the limits of WTO rules. Dialogue between the various communities became more constructive in the second half of the 1990s, and greater transparency played a key role in this process. One illustration of this is the International Centre for Trade and Sustainable Development's newsletter *Bridges*. This newsletter provides a detailed assessment of developments in and outside the WTO that have a bearing on the interface between trade, the environment, and sustainable development, and points readers to WTO secretariat staff that work in relevant areas for information. Another illustration

---

Box 13.5. The Shrimp-Turtles case

Sea turtles are an endangered species that are protected under multilateral environmental agreements. They are often caught by fishermen harvesting shrimp. To reduce the incidence of turtle deaths, the US National Marine Fisheries Service designed a so-called turtle exclusion device (TED) to reduce the likelihood of turtles becoming trapped in the nets of shrimp trawlers. In 1987, the use of such TEDs became mandatory for the US shrimp fishing fleet. Reflecting pressure by US environmental groups concerned with global conservation of sea turtles and the fishing industry—concerned about 'unfair competition'—the US Congress adopted legislation in 1989 (ESA 1973 Section 609) prohibiting the importation of shrimp products from countries that do not use TEDs or similar devices, unless the US certifies them as having US equivalent programs to prevent sea turtle mortality. Initially, the US issued guidelines stipulating that the law would only apply to countries in the Caribbean and the Western Atlantic Ocean where the US was negotiating a regional agreement for the protection of sea turtles. In 1995, the US Court of International Trade ruled that the law should be applied to all imports. In 1997, India, Malaysia, Pakistan and Thailand requested the DSB to establish a panel. The US defended its program under Article XX GATT.

In principle, WTO rules only allow production process standards like the TED to be applied to imports if it can be shown that the processes targeted have repercussions for the physical characteristics (quality) of the product concerned. An example would be a requirement that shrimp be washed in water of a certain level of purity. In many cases process standards cannot be justified under this criterion, requiring countries to invoke Article XX—GATT's exception provision. In the shrimp-turtles case, the relevant provision was Article XXg—which allows for trade-restrictive measures if necessary for the 'conservation of exhaustible natural resources'. The panel

for the 'conservation of exhaustible natural resources'. The panel did not discuss whether and how Section 609 related to the environmental exceptions of Article XX, but focused on the general provision of Article XX stating that measures may not 'constitute ... arbitrary or unjustifiable discrimination' nor be a 'disguised restriction on international trade'. The panel found against the US on this basis. On appeal, the Appellate Body reversed the panel by concluding that Section 609 was aimed at the protection of a natural resource and was therefore covered by (legal under) Article XXg. However, it agreed with the panel that the way Section 609 was applied resulted in arbitrary and unjustifiable discrimination because insufficient efforts had been made to negotiate arrangements to protect sea turtles similar to what had been negotiated with countries in the Western Hemisphere (Latin American countries had been granted 3 years to comply, Asian economies only 4 months). The Appellate Body also criticized the coercive nature of the measure, arguing that it is 'not acceptable in international trade relations for one WTO Member to use an economic embargo to require other Members to adopt essentially the same ... program, ... without taking into consideration different conditions which may occur in the territories of those other Members'.

US environmental groups had feared the panel ruling would lead to renewed political pressure to weaken or repeal the US TED requirements. However, the Appellate Body finding only required that the US find ways to implement Section 609 in a nondiscriminatory manner and make a serious effort to negotiate. Recognizing the political sensitivity of the case, the Appellate Body stressed that 'we have not decided that the ... Members of the WTO cannot adopt effective measures to protect endangered species, such as sea turtles'. Moreover, 'we have not decided that sovereign states should not act together bilaterally, plurilaterally or multilaterally ... to protect endangered species or otherwise protect the environment'. Thus, it emphasized that these types of cases are best addressed through international agreements and negotiation.

Summing up, the Appellate Body decision in the shrimp case signaled that extraterritorial application of national norms can be legal under the WTO (Article XX) and that there is some leeway for countries to use trade policy to enforce norms relating to production process methods (PPMs) that do not have implications for the characteristics of traded products. The fact that the Appellate Body did not explicitly address the PPM issue was attacked by developing countries such as Thailand, who argued that this sent a dangerous signal, potentially opening the door for countries to apply PPM norms in other areas as well (such as labor). However, given that Article XX makes no mention of labor standards, this would not be possible.

Source: WTO (www.wto.org) and Crouse (1999).

was that in the run up to the Seattle ministerial, environmental concerns were prominent in proposals that sought significant reductions in subsidies for fisheries, forestry, and agriculture. Many WTO members regarded this as a rare potential 'win-win' situation where two objectives could be attained with one instrument. Through the work of the CTE, trade and environment issues have been explored at great length. One result has been that there is widespread recognition that trade policy has little if any role to play in the pursuit of environmental objectives, that the WTO does not restrict the use of green policies by members, that MEAs are the appropriate instrument to address global environmental problems, and that carrots, not sticks are called for if a country seeks to induce another to adopt stricter environmental norms. The shrimp-turtles dispute between the US and a number of Asian countries illustrated·these principles (Box 13.5). In many of these cases, a more appropriate approach by concerned NGOs is to push for voluntary labeling or to pursue a consumer boycott. Such approaches allow consumers to make informed choices regarding the products they buy, and create incentives for producers to adopt new technologies and incur the labeling costs by increasing the price of goods that are preferred by concerned segments of the population.

13.6. SOCIAL POLICIES AND LABOR STANDARDS

Discussions relating to workers rights and trade have a long history. Indeed, they predate discussions on IPRs, going back at least 150 years. In the nineteenth century, the question was one of improving working conditions. Trade entered the picture because of concerns expressed by industries that domestic legislation prohibiting child labor or limiting the working week would put them at a competitive disadvantage (Leary, 1996). Recurring international discussions starting in the late nineteenth century led to the creation of the ILO in 1919. The ILO is a unique body, insofar as it is tripartite—bringing together employers, labor unions, and governments. The ILO has passed numerous conventions dealing with various aspects of working conditions. Governments adopt (ratify) these on a voluntary basis.

The ILO has no binding enforcement mechanism, although it does monitor compliance by member states. The constitution of the ILO provided that a member could initiate a complaint that a government was not implementing a convention it had ratified. This could give rise to the establishment of a commission to investigate the case and recommend a remedy, including 'measures of an economic character', that is, sanctions. As noted by Charnovitz (2000), this procedure was never used. As is the case with IPRs, the primary reason proponents are seeking to introduce labor standards into the WTO is because the WTO has a functioning dispute settlement and enforcement system. A complementary factor (as with the environment) is a fear that liberalization of trade and closer integration of the world economy may lead to a race to the bottom, with countries that have high standards being forced to lower them if they want their firms to remain competitive with industrializing countries.

At the insistence of the US and France, labor standards were introduced on the WTO agenda in the final stage of the Uruguay Round. The objective of these countries was to initiate discussions on the introduction of a Social Clause specifying minimum standards in this area, presumably as a precondition for market access. This was not the first attempt to introduce the issue. The US and other OECD countries had made efforts in this area periodically since the 1950s. Although the attempt to establish a committee or working party failed in 1994, calls for linking the benefits of WTO membership, or even membership itself, to the adoption and enforcement of minimum labor standards continued to be heard. Three months after the creation of the WTO, the Director-General of the ILO wrote to the WTO urging that members should be required to ratify ILO conventions on so-called core labor standards, including the prohibition of forced labor and the right for workers to form unions and engage in collective wage bargaining (*Financial Times*, March 9, 1995 p. 9).

Populist calls to reduce differences in labor costs across countries are not at the core of the issue in the WTO context. Labor costs reflect the income and productivity of a country. Insisting that liberalization of trade be made conditional upon convergence in labor costs makes absolutely no sense, and would constitute blatant protectionism. The gains from trade result precisely from differences in costs, which are due to differences in endowments, technological capacities, and output per worker. The focus of attention in the WTO is primarily on so-called core labor standards and basic worker's rights, not the minimum wage. In practice, proponents are seeking the recognition and enforcement of five general rights: banning exploitative use of child workers, eliminating forced labor, preventing discrimination in the workplace, allowing free association of workers, and permitting workers to bargain collectively (Maskus, 1997). Supporters of a social clause in the WTO seek the latitude to impose (multilateral) trade sanctions against countries that do not protect these rights.

Two issues arise. First, is there a link between labor standards and trade—that is, are trade flows distorted because of differences in standards? More specifically, is there a competitiveness issue? Second, are trade sanctions a useful (efficient) tool to enforce core labor standards?

The impact of labor standards on competitiveness of firms depends on the circumstances (Ehrenberg, 1994). It is not necessarily the case that high standards—with respect to social security, for example—will reduce the ability of firms to compete on world markets. If firms can ensure that the incidence of the implicit tax is borne by workers—that is, that the work force pays for the resulting benefits through lower wages—labor costs may be unaffected. Moreover, insofar as the cost-raising effects of worker's rights cannot be fully shifted to workers, the resulting increase in product prices (due to higher costs) will put pressure on the exchange rate (because foreign demand for exports falls as prices increase, all other things equal). The resulting depreciation will lower the standard of living by raising the cost of imports. While the whole economy thus bears the burden of the higher standards, the exchange rate adjustment allows firms to continue to compete on world markets. As in the case of environmental policies, as long as the labor standards in force reflect the desires of voters, the costs of implementation simply reflect the trade-off between monetary and non-monetary wealth that society has made. However, if standards are unilaterally imposed on a country, it is very unlikely that they will reflect the preferences of the population. Imposing a tariff or other trade barriers to offset the cost disadvantage for domestic firms is not necessary to 'level the playing field' and will distort resource allocation. Account should also be taken of the substantial danger that such instruments will be captured by protectionist interests, seeking to limit imports from labor-abundant developing countries. Contrary to what might be expected, however, it is not necessarily the case that labor unions in OECD countries will be the main lobby for protection (Box 13.6).

Box 13.6. Labor Standards and US Labor Unions

One might expect that support for international labor standards by OECD unions and NGOs reflects protectionist interests. However, empirical studies have failed to find compelling evidence suggesting low labor standards have an impact on trade (Rodrik, 1996). If so, they do not affect production and employment, so that protectionism seems an unlikely motivation for pushing labor standards. Krueger (1997) analyzed the determinants of support in the US House of Representatives for the Child Labor Deterrence Act of 1995. Although the proposed law was not passed, it was intended to prohibit imports of goods produced abroad by children under 15 years old, and would subject child labor practices to a review by the US Secretary of Labor. Krueger found (p. 289) that: '...Congressmen from districts with a high concentration of high school dropouts are less likely to cosponsor the Child Labor Deterrence Act' and that higher rates of unionization were not associated with support for the Act. Krueger postulated that an explanation for this result was that unionized workers tend to be more highly skilled, therefore not benefiting directly from a ban on imported goods made with child labor. The implication is that in seeking to strengthen worker rights abroad unions are not pursuing their narrow self-interest. Krueger's results are only suggestive, as legislators may have chosen not to sponsor the legislation even though they were supportive of it (Srinivasan, 1998). Less educated and less skilled individuals tend to vote less and to work in nontradable service industries, therefore possibly carrying less weight in a Congressman's decision whether to be a cosponsor.

Whatever the case may be, much of the concern regarding labor standards in developing countries reflects a genuine concern about the labor situation in low income economies. This concern has been captured in part by import-competing interests (firms), who would like to see competitive pressures reduced. A major problem then is to enhance the understanding of the electorate in OECD countries that linking trade and labor standards is an inappropriate and counterproductive strategy.
Source: Adapted from Stern (2000).

Trade policy is an inefficient tool to enforce labor standards, assuming agreement could be reached on what the relevant standards should be. Trade restrictions will generally have a detrimental effect on the realization of the non-economic objectives that are pursued by pro-labor standards groups. Trade restrictions raise the prices of imports, thus imposing a welfare cost at home, while at the same time worsening the labor situation in the target country. Demand for labor services will fall, and plants will downsize or close. Trade sanctions are akin to a tax on employment of low-skilled workers. Using trade remedies to enforce labor standards would worsen the problems at which they are aimed (by forcing workers in targeted countries into informal or illegal activities). Unemployment will rise, and given the absence or weakness of social safety nets (unemployment insurance), can be expected to have a detrimental impact on poverty. It should come as no surprise, therefore, that developing countries oppose any attempt to link market access to labor standards.

Developing countries in particular are very hesitant to consider even the least controversial norms for fear that this would be the thin end of the wedge. They note that Art. XX:e GATT already contains a provision permitting import restrictions against goods produced by prison labor, that Art. XXI:c GATT allows for UN-mandated sanctions, and that this is all that is required in the WTO. There is considerable international agreement that certain core labor rights should be globally recognized and protected, but this is seen to be the task of the ILO.

Rather than use threats, attainment of core labor standards can be pursued more effectively through instruments that are targeted directly at improving outcomes. For example, efforts could be made to improve the quality of, and access to, primary education for poor children in order to reduce child labor exploitation, via programs to subsidize the purchase of school supplies, provide transportation, and reduce the costs of schooling (Maskus, 1997). It is important to avoid a confrontational approach to this issue and to pursue collaborative solutions that help developing countries improve labor standards. Attempts to force countries to adopt standards that do not reflect national preferences and conditions should be rejected (Bhagwati and Srinivasan, 1996). Gains from trade arise in large part because countries differ, and national social policies are simply one determinant of these differences. They do not constitute barriers to trade, or give rise to 'unfair' trade.

As mentioned, proposals to ensure that basic labor standards would apply in all WTO members made no headway during the Uruguay Round. The issue was put on the agenda of the 1996 Singapore WTO ministerial conference by the US, France and Canada. These countries called for the recognition of such standards and suggested that WTO members work with the ILO to ensure that they are observed. This attempt failed—the Singapore ministerial rejected any attempt to put labor standards on the WTO agenda. No agreement proved possible on even the most minimalist approach that is generally taken towards new issues: the establishment of a working group to investigate the link between trade and labor standards. In the run-up to the 1999 Seattle ministerial the issue was again put forward by the US, which tabled a formal proposal on trade and labor in October 1999. The US called for the creation of a working group on trade and labor to examine the effects of trade on employment, the impact of greater openness on the scope and structure of basic social protections and safety nets in WTO members, the relationship between trade, development and core labor standards, the scope for trade incentives to promote implementation of standards, the magnitude of forced or exploitative child labor engaged in export production, and the impact of derogations from national labor legislation, including in export processing zones, on trade and development.

A statement by US President Clinton during Seattle that he would favor the use of sanctions against violations of trade agreements, including labor provisions, hardened the resolve of developing countries to resist the US proposal (Odell, 2000a). It is clear from the agenda proposed for the working group that the focus of concern is less on labor conditions than the impact of labor regulations (or the lack thereof) on export competition. This emphasis on labor standards in production for export illustrates that developing countries have cause for concern regarding the push to incorporate labor standards in the WTO. After all, there is nothing special about exports. Presumably any concern regarding core labor standards should extend to all production, including production that is not for export. This is another illustration why this is an issue that does not belong in the WTO but needs to be addressed by the ILO.

13.7. DOMESTIC REGULATION

The rhetoric of policy makers and their advisors often suggests that deeper integration is necessary to attain free trade. During the period leading to the creation of the EEC, Jelle Zijlstra, the Dutch Minister of Economic Affairs argued that credible tariff removal required 'common policies on taxes, wages, prices and employment policy' (Milward, 1992, p. 188). Similarly, the Belgian government felt that policy harmonization was required to equalize costs, and that without it a customs union would not be feasible because countries would impose new forms of protectionist policies. The Belgian coal mining industry argued in the late 1940s that a common market could only be accepted if German wage and social security costs were raised to Belgian levels. French officials persistently demanded policy harmonization in the social area—equal pay for both sexes, a uniform working week—as a precondition for trade liberalization (French standards in this area were higher than in other countries).

While governments may seek to agree on common regulatory principles to govern the behavior of public entities or restrict the use of domestic policies, this is best done directly and should not be made a precondition for trade liberalization. A strategy that seeks to link trade policy to regulatory reform in foreign countries will generally be quite costly, given the welfare losses from protection. For small countries, it will also be ineffective. Foreign economic policies are best regarded as part of the environment—they may be detrimental to some groups in society, but this does not offset the gains that can be obtained from trade liberalization. Deep integration based on international standards that is applied on a nondiscriminatory basis to all traders may enhance global welfare. But, the need for deeper integration on most issues, be they old, new or new-new, is limited. Frequently, shallow integration is a more powerful instrument, as it involves competition between regulatory regimes that reflect national circumstances.

WTO rules are aimed at liberalizing trade in products. How goods and services are produced has traditionally been irrelevant under GATT, with the exception of situations listed in Art. XX GATT (such as prison labor). With the WTO this changed: the norms embodied in the TRIPs agreement relate directly to production processes by requiring IPRs to be enforced. The shrimp-turtles case discussed earlier suggests countries may impose process standards for environmental reasons if this can be motivated on global public good grounds. These developments suggest there is a need to determine the extent to which deeper policy integration should be pursued in the WTO. Where to draw the line has become an area of vigorous debate among policy officials, analysts, and civil society.

One option for rule-making on regulatory issues is to become more prescriptive regarding the types of instruments government should use to offset market failure in those instances where society decides the benefits of intervention outweigh the costs. A basic rule of thumb that is suggested by the economic literature is that price-based instruments dominate so-called 'command and control' type of regulation. The latter result in inefficiency for the same reason that quotas are less efficient than tariffs (see annex 2). This suggests that countries should apply regulatory instruments which use the market to encourage flexibility and choice both of products and production techniques: taxes or tradable quotas to deal with environmental externalities, labeling to deal with information asymmetries including risk, and liability insurance to encourage product safety (Rollo and Winters, 2000). However, requiring such economic criteria in the application of regulatory policy as an enforceable WTO rule would involve potentially far-reaching second-guessing of governments by WTO panels. Societies have different tastes, cultures, governmental and legal systems, endowments, and so forth. Regulatory decisions will reflect these different circumstances. Here again one size does not fit all.

If there are cross-border externalities or global public goods, international regulation should be non-discriminatory, restricted in geographical coverage to the scope of the spillovers, and implemented locally, in line with local circumstances and tastes—that is, the regulatory agency should be accountable to the relevant communities (Rollo and Winters, 2000). For the WTO to be the locus of international regulatory efforts, the spillover or market failure that is involved should have a direct bearing on the conditions of competition prevailing on a market.

The discussion in this chapter suggests that there is little scope for the WTO to expand its reach significantly beyond the status quo through deeper integration. The main beneficial role it might play in most areas calling for national regulation is ensuring transparency. Most cross-border spillovers arise in areas in which the WTO has no expertise—they are generally only weakly trade-related, if at all. Allowing for the use of trade sanctions to enforce whatever regulatory norms are adopted will generally be counterproductive in terms of the (noneconomic) objectives that the regulation seeks to attain.

At the national level, the clearest role for the WTO in terms of regulatory regimes concerns those policies that directly affect the ability of foreign providers of goods and services to contest a market. As discussed in chapter 7, nonrecognition of professional certification and qualifications is a major barrier to trade. Similarly, *de facto* discrimination across countries and suppliers due to MRAs for product standards and conformity assessment regimes has a direct effect on trade. These are regulatory areas where deep integration is not necessarily required. Shallow integration—extending the reach of the national treatment and MFN principles, and bolstering the information collection and analysis functions of the WTO, including the TPRM—can do much to reduce the associated cost differentials for traders.

13.8. CONCLUSION

The WTO faces a daunting agenda. A true test of the organization in the coming years will be the extent to which members prove willing and able to increase the contestability of markets by sweeping away policies that imply discrimination against foreign firms and products. Much still needs to be done in the traditional market access domain of the WTO. Services, agriculture and textiles and clothing continue to be heavily protected in many countries. Tariffs on merchandise imports in developing countries are still relatively high. There is also much that needs to be done to control the use of contingent protection, especially antidumping. The new, 'regulatory trade agenda' is by no means necessarily the area where the greatest welfare gains from reform are to be realized. One important reason is that in many of the 'new' areas one size fits all is not the right prescription.

There is substantial scope for governments to accede to pressures from lobbies to impose regulatory policies that have the effect of restricting trade. Such policies are most likely in environment and health-related areas. Many of the more controversial issues that are giving rise to disputes and tensions concern the use of biotechnology, genetically modified organisms (GMOs), patenting of life forms, the use of health and safety standards based on the 'precautionary principle', and the regulation of drugs (pharmaceuticals) and medical service providers. Currently these issues are addressed in a variety of WTO bodies, including the SPS and TBT committees, the Committee on Trade and Environment, the Dispute Settlement Body, and the TRIPs, GATT and GATS Councils. Much of the discussion concerns whether there are (or should be) international standards, and whether specific measures that have a trade-restricting effect are necessary to attain a given regulatory objective. Deep integration in this area will probably prove difficult to achieve. If pursued, the WTO is often not the right forum—other specialized bodies and mechanisms exist that can and should be used, not least because they allow the discussion to extend beyond governments (Box 13.7).

There is substantial scope for further shallow integration of the type that has traditionally been pursued by the WTO. This may include efforts to increase the presumption that governments should use price- and market-based instruments where possible, and avoid the use of direct ('command and control') regulation. This would help reduce the scope for protectionist capture of regulatory regimes. However, moving towards formal multilateral rules that require 'market-friendly intervention' is unlikely to be feasible, nor is it necessarily Pareto optimal given differences in institutional environments and circumstances across countries. A basic element of any approach towards reducing regulatory tensions is greater transparency regarding the rationale for, and analysis of the effect of, intervention. As with antidumping, the focus should be to ensure that domestic groups have access to the information they need to determine the implications of status quo policies, so that they can determine if the benefits of regulatory regimes outweigh the costs.

Box 13.7. GMOs and the Biosafety Protocol

How to treat GMOs is a question of great concern to NGOs and civil society. The financial stakes are huge, as are the economic development and environmental dimensions of the debate. Opposition to trade in products embodying GMOs is mainly driven by fears among consumers and environmental groups that it poses serious risks to public health and bio-diversity. The GMO industry insists that bio-engineered products are safe for consumers and represent no danger to the environment. In the US, producers and industrial users point to the fact that their products have been approved by the US Food and Drug Administration (FDA).

'Traditional' farmers in Europe and in developing countries have also opposed the use of GMOs. EU farmers fear the competitive implications of US dominance in this industry, and the effects of greatly expanded crop yields on prices of their harvests. Developing country farmers are concerned about the potential dependence on bio-engineered seeds and technology, especially given the development of so-called terminator genes in GMO-enhanced seeds, which cannot be replanted.

The GMO issue created serious transatlantic tensions in the late 1990s. Calls for labeling of genetically modified grains by the EU, and general opposition by NGOs and consumers in the EU to the use of GMOs, led to a number of US producers to withdraw from the market through divestitures. GMO producers supported the strict scientific evidence line taken in the WTO SPS agreement, and suggested that labeling should be enough to enable consumers to make their own buying decisions. In the WTO context, the US and Canada proposed the establishment of a working group to review the adequacy of existing rules concerning the use of GMOs. This was opposed by environmental NGOs such as Greenpeace and consumer groups in Europe, who favored an international convention—outside the WTO—that would permit the application of the precautionary principle, and saw this as an attempt to block efforts to negotiate a biosafety agreement by the UN Environment Programme (UNEP).

Here, as in other standards-related areas where there are potentially serious spillovers, international cooperation is the appropriate way forward. In January 2000, a treaty was concluded as an annex to the UN Convention on Biological Diversity. The so-called Biosafety Protocol supported the view of NGOs favoring the precautionary principle by allowing countries to restrict imports of GMOs even if scientific evidence regarding their danger remains uncertain. The Protocol embodies a provision stating that 'it shall not be interpreted as implying an incompatibility with the rights and obligations of a Party under any existing international agreements [i.e., the WTO] applying to the transboundary movements of living modified organisms'. The US (and Canada) accepted this in part because North American consumers had begun to share European concerns about the risks of genetically modified crops. NGOs such as Greenpeace and the Transatlantic Consumers Dialogue played a role in that shift in public opinion, having created an international coalition of organizations that opposed the use of GMOs.

As far as the 'new' issues are concerned that have been discussed in this chapter, investment policies are perhaps the most important in terms of market access and being trade-related. This is an issue area where a classic GATT approach (shallow integration) can work quite well. However, given the enormous agenda that confronts members in liberalizing trade and investment in services, any effort to establish rules on FDI policies in the near future must be part of a grand bargain that significantly improves welfare for all WTO members. Many of the existing investment-related policies that have negative effects on other countries have proven very difficult to address in RIAs and were excluded from the stillborn MAI.

Harmonization of competition laws is both highly unlikely and undesirable. The types of agreements that would be unambiguously welfare improving for the world as a whole imply potentially significant redistribution of resources (profits) across countries, and losses to concentrated interests in OECD countries. Here again potential gains exist, but there will be a need for linkage. In general, investment regimes and competition law are policy areas where many countries need to take actions at the national level, and where there is a great need for technical and financial assistance. Thus, there is certainly a case to be made for cooperation in terms of designing and implementing domestic policies and strengthening national institutions. However, putting these issues on the WTO agenda before substantial national experience has been obtained is putting the cart before the horse.

Although in principle investment policies and competition law 'fit' into the WTO, as both issue areas are trade-related and have an effect on conditions of competition, this is not the case with environmental and labor policies. The latter are subjects where there are certainly potential benefits from global cooperation, but the WTO is not the appropriate forum. This is not to say these subjects are not relevant from a WTO perspective. An important challenge for the future will be to contain the threat of protectionist capture of the environment and labor-standards issues. But reciprocal negotiations on standards in these areas—especially in instances where there are no cross-border spillovers—is clearly inappropriate. In addition to the many reasons discussed in this chapter, it must also be recognized that pursuit of this route would give rise to the possibility that labor and environmental policies become an instrument to retaliate or to seek trade concessions (Roessler, 1998). This would result in the noneconomic objectives that underlie the use of standards in these areas not being realized.

The need for deep integration in most of the 'new' areas is limited at best. Abstracting from a grand bargain, the only example discussed in this chapter where it could have large payoffs is trade facilitation. This is cause for optimism, as the traditional GATT reciprocity dynamics do not work when it comes to deeper integration. Shallow integration remains a powerful source of discipline that can have a significant effect in enhancing the contestability of markets. For example, extending its reach to factor markets would have enormous effects. While this is still a long way in the future, traditional mechanisms such as transparency, exchange of information, surveillance and analysis of the effects of policies can play a major role in helping WTO members adopt more efficient and effective forms of regulation. As argued elsewhere in this book, civil society has a major role to play in this connection. The agenda is to a large extent domestic, implying that domestic actors must determine what are the appropriate policies. Relying on the WTO process to identify 'best practices' is unlikely to be a fruitful strategy.

13.9. FURTHER READING

On the general theme of deep integration and the problems of dealing with domestic policy differences, see Jagdish Bhagwati and Robert Hudec (eds.), *Harmonization and Fair Trade: Prerequisite for Free Trade?* (Cambridge: MIT Press, 1996), G. Burtless et al., *Globaphobia* (Washington DC: Brookings, 1998), and R. Lawrence, A. Bressand and T. Ito, *A Vision for the World Economy* (Washington DC: Brookings, 1996). John Braithwaite and Peter Drahos discuss international efforts to cooperate on regulation in *Global Business Regulation* (Cambridge University Press, 2000).

Rachel McCulloch, 'Investment Policy in the GATT', *The World Economy*, 13 (1990), 541-53, and DeAnne Julius, 'International Direct Investment: Strengthening the Policy Regime', in *Managing the World Economy: Lessons from the First 50 Years After Bretton Woods* (Washington DC: Institute for

International Economics, 1995) discuss the need for—and possible elements of—multilateral rules on investment.). David Henderson, 'The MAI Affair, A Story and Its Lessons' (London, The Royal Institute of International Affairs, 1999) provides a description and critical assessment of the attempt to negotiate a multilateral agreement on investment in the OECD. UNCTAD's annual *World Investment Report* is the standard source of global data on FDI trends.

F.M. Scherer, *Competition Policies for an Integrated World Economy* (Washington DC: Brookings Institution, 1994) provides an introduction to the linkages between competition and trade policies. A. Auquier and R. Caves, 'Monopolistic Export Industries, Trade Taxes, and Optimal Competition Policy', *Economic Journal*, 89 (1979), 559-81 and J. Dreyer, 'Countervailing Foreign Use of Monopoly Power', in R. Amacher, G. Haberler and T. Willett (eds.), *Challenges to a Liberal International Order* (Washington DC: American Enterprise Institute, 1979) analyze many of the questions that arise in dealing with export monopolies and cartels—this is not a new issue. Bernard Hoekman and Petros C. Mavroidis, Competition, Competition Policy, and the GATT, *The World Economy*, 17 (1994), 121-50 analyze the scope to bring competition-related complaints to the GATT, and question the need to give priority to attempting to establish global competition rules in the WTO. Merger-related disputes between the EU and the US are discussed in Simon Evenett, Alexander Lehman and Benn Steil (eds.), *Antitrust Goes Global: What Future for Transatlantic Cooperation?* (Washington DC: Brookings Institution, 2000). Hoekman and Mavroidis discuss various options for introducing competition law criteria and approaches into the enforcement of antidumping law in 'Dumping, Antidumping and Antitrust', *Journal of World Trade*, 30 (1996), 27-52.

A managerial perspective on trade facilitation is presented by Michel Kostecki, *International Marketing and the Trading System* (Geneva: ITC, 2000). The amended Kyoto Convention 'On the Simplification and Harmonization of Customs Procedures' can be downloaded from the World Customs Organization's home page, www.wcoomd.org.

Kym Anderson and Richard Blackhurst (eds.), *The Greening of World Trade Issues* (London: Harvester Wheatsheaf, 1992) collects papers written mostly by trade economists exploring the linkages between trade and the environment. Daniel Esty, *Greening the GATT: Trade, Environment and the Future* (Washington DC: Institute for International Economics, 1994) is a balanced and comprehensive treatment of the issues written more from an environmental perspective.

Ronald Ehrenberg, *Labor Markets and Integrating National Economies* (Washington DC: Brookings Institution, 1994) discusses the economics of labor market regulation and the need for convergence in labor standards in an integrating world economy. Keith Maskus, 'Should Core Labor Standards

Be Imposed Through International Trade Policy?', Policy Research Working Paper 1817, World Bank (www.worldbank.org/trade) surveys and assesses the various arguments that have been made for putting labor standards on the WTO agenda.

Pietro Nivola (ed.), *Comparative Disadvantages? Social Regulations and the Global Economy* (Washington DC: Brookings, 1997) is an in-depth discussion of the tensions that arise between national regulatory regimes and 'competitiveness'. David Vogel, *Trading Up: Consumer and Environmental Regulation in a Global Economy* (Cambridge: Harvard University Press, 1995) is an excellent treatment of the relationship between trade, trade policy and regulatory regimes that discusses a number of cases in depth.

J. David Richardson, 'The WTO and Market-Supportive Regulation: A Way Forward on New Competition, Technological and Labor Issues', *Federal Reserve Bank of St. Louis Review*, July/August 2000, 115-26 argues the WTO must expand its agenda and address regulatory issues. Jim Rollo and Alan Winters, 'Subsidiarity Challenges for the WTO: Environmental and Labor Standards', *The World Economy*, 23 (2000), 561-77 are more skeptical, arguing that there are many reasons for regulation and international cooperation, but that the WTO is often not a good place for doing it, not least because expanding the agenda detracts attention from issues that would unambiguously enhance global welfare.

14
Legitimacy, Coherence and Governance

Trade policy in a pluralistic society is made through a complex process of decision-making involving government, political parties, business interests, trade unions, consumer organizations and other members of civil society. In a changing world, rules and procedures affecting trade age quickly. New technologies and new business needs change lobbying incentives with respect to trade policy, and may alter the need for regulation and associated administrative procedures. Trade rules are therefore subject to continuous pressure for change. This pressure occurs mostly at the national level, but is also reflected at the WTO level. Delegations and the secretariat may be lobbied by interest groups, and are influenced indirectly through research or demonstrations on the streets.

Negotiating power and resources differ dramatically across countries, and across groups within countries. Having a large stake in trade policy, industrial and agricultural interests are often very actively involved in lobbying for or against trade policies at both the domestic and international levels. Small and medium sized enterprises (SMEs) and NGOs of various kinds generally play much less of a role in trade policy debates, although this started to change in the 1990s. One reason for the increased activism was a perception that 'big business' dominated the process, reducing the legitimacy of the trading system. Many developing countries also regard the negotiation outcomes as unbalanced, reducing their sense of 'ownership' of WTO rules and provisions. To a large extent outcomes simply reflect the realities of the international distribution of power and income and the incentives different stakeholders have to lobby for and defend their interests.

An active debate was initiated towards the end of the 1990s on the legitimacy, governance and coherence of the multilateral trading system. This debate was part of a much larger discussion on whether and how to 'manage' the process of globalization. After the Seattle ministerial many NGOs were of the view that the WTO was not inclusive and did not allow them to express their views. Governments countered that the WTO is an inter-governmental organization, and that NGOs have to play by the rules that all interest groups had to play by—that is, use domestic advocacy and consultative processes to get their views reflected in national policies. Of course, a necessary condition for this to be feasible is that such mechanisms exist at the national level. The legitimacy of the WTO is to a large extent dependent on the national processes through which trade policy is formulated and changed, as the WTO is a member-driven organization that operates on the basis of consensus. However, NGOs and other lobbies have clear incentives to exert direct pressure at the 'global' level as well, including at the WTO, in an attempt to complement national efforts to influence global rules of the game.

This chapter discusses the role of industry groups and NGOs in the formulation of trade policies at the national and global level, and the importance of transparency and openness in policy formation to ensure that governments are accountable. Information is a necessary condition for the 'contestability' of policy in national political markets, which in turn is a necessary condition for the 'coherence' of such policies, as well as the legitimacy of whatever multilateral rules are negotiated.

14.1. INDUSTRY AND TRADE POLICY FORMATION

Firms may lobby for policies that shelter them from foreign competition, generate monopoly rights, or exempt them from taxes. The task of policy makers, legislators and civil society is to ensure to the greatest extent possible that such rent-seeking behavior is controlled and filtered through institutions that limit the risk of capture by the powerful. As a general rule, trade policy is the responsibility of the legislative and executive branches. The latter comprise the ensemble of government departments and agencies that are responsible for implementation and often also play a major role in defining and setting policy. The relevant agencies include not only the ministry of trade, but also the ministries of foreign affairs, economy and finance, as well as specialized bodies dealing with agriculture, technical standards, intellectual property, transportation, construction, telecommunications, justice, education, and so forth. The consistency of domestic and external policies is typically a matter that is addressed at the cabinet with the assistance of advisory committees and organizations. Important trade policy decisions frequently require legislative changes and therefore parliamentary approval.

Conflicts are inherent in the process of defining trade policies because almost invariably trade policy involves the redistribution of income across groups in society. Some will gain and others lose from any policy that changes the tax or regulatory regime affecting imports or exports. Tensions (turf fights) between various government departments are likely to occur as well. The required compromise has to be reached though bargaining and decisions by the higher political authorities. For example, the ministry of finance may want to tax foreign trade to generate revenue and oppose liberalization. It may be supported by government departments that confront lobbying for protection by declining industries, but resisted by the ministry of economy, which may seek to use liberalization and tariff exemptions as an instrument of investment and export promotion. The ministry of labor may favor trade barriers to safeguard employment in uncompetitive industries, while the ministry of foreign affairs may favor more open policies as part of a foreign policy strategy. As discussed in chapter 4, interest group preferences can be expected to play an important role in determining the stance taken by sectoral and economic ministries.

Differences in the institutional structure for trade policy-making generally reflect differences in economic and political systems, especially the role of the state in the economy (degree of centralization), the importance of market forces and the strength of private property rights, and the power structure that has emerged over time. To prevent the regulatory capture of sectoral agencies and the policy formation process, there is need for openness—transparency and consultation. Public participation is an efficient mechanism to help decision-makers identify stakeholders and the social benefits and costs of a policy. The objective of consultation mechanisms is to improve both the quality of trade policy and to ensure that it is acceptable to voters or the political support base of the government. Many countries have created a formal structure of general and issue-specific advisory bodies that institutionalize the exchange of information between the business community, other interest groups and the government (Box 14.1). In other nations, business and government rarely meet, or the interaction is limited to a small elite with preferential access.

Box 14.1. Government-Business Interaction in Selected Countries
How governments interact with the private sector varies greatly, depending on political systems and history. For example, in Canada, the advisory system has two principal components: the Team Canada Inc. Advisory Board (TCIAB) and 15 Sectoral Advisory Groups on International Trade (SAGITs). The SAGITs take stands on government proposals and policies concerning specific sectors. TCIAB is concerned with all international trade matters and offers advice on market access, trade and investment promotion and other trade policy matters. Firms are invited to communicate to the Board the major problems confronting them in foreign markets. Information and advice on trade policy and trade promotion activities of interest to government agencies is also solicited, as are proposals to deal with such issues.

In India, the Ministry of Commerce is assisted in trade policy formulation by advisory bodies participating in the Board of Trade. The Indian Institute of Foreign Trade conducts research and training in international trade and also offers inputs into that process. Several sectoral institutes dealing with packaging, diamonds, textiles and chemicals concentrate on industry-specific issues. Statutory commodity boards advise on trade policies for tea, coffee, rubber, spices and tobacco. Industry associations such as the Confederation of Indian Industries, the Federation of India Exporter's Organization, the Federation of Indian Chamber of Commerce, the Associated Chambers of Commerce and academic institutions and think tanks also contribute to policy proposals.

In Morocco, the National Foreign Trade Council, comprising 30 government officials and 36 business representatives, is responsible for preparing advisory opinions on foreign trade issues and new legislative proposals. The private sector of the Dominican Republic is represented in the Commission for the Follow-up of Integration Schemes, the Foreign Trade Commission, the Lomé IV Commission, the National Free Zones Council, and in the national commissions dealing with trade in bananas, coffee and cocoa. The Joint Public-Private Consultative Committee constitutes the main formal government-business forum in Thailand. The Committee, which deals extensively with trade policy issues, is chaired by the Prime Minister and includes several cabinet ministers. The private sector has established the Joint Standing Committee on Commerce, Industry and Banking whose members include influential business groupings: the Board of Trade (a private body comprising business associations), the Thai Chamber of Commerce, the Foreign Trade Chamber of Commerce, and several state enterprises), the Federation of Thai Industries and the Thai Bankers' Association. The Joint Committee is a forum for discussion and coalition building and an important player in the trade policy formation process.

Source: WTO, Trade Policy Reviews, various years.

The formal institutional mechanisms that are found in many countries to encourage public participation in trade policy-making may not reflect the reality of how policy is actually made. What matters is if and how different interests are balanced, and whether all major interest groups have access to the system. The greater the role of the state, the less market oriented the economy, the less business interests are likely to be consulted. As economies open up and political systems become more pluralistic, business interests will have greater incentives and opportunities to express their views. States that emphasize the virtue of enterpreneurship and the allocative role of markets are more prone to accept private business input into trade policy making. These dynamics can be observed in many developing countries. For example, following the autonomous reforms in Latin America in the 1980s, export interests became a factor in trade policy. They played a role in the subsequent push to pursue regional integration. The FTAA initiative, launched in 1994, led to the creation of the Business Network of Hemispheric Integration—with a membership of 400 organizations—as well as the

Americas Business Forum and the APEC Business Advisory Council (Ostry, 2000). Smaller firms frequently perceive that their views are neglected in such bodies, spawning the creation of specialized associations that defend their interests (Box 14.2).

Box 14.2. Philfoodex of the Philippines

Philfoodex is an umbrella organization of mainly small and medium-sized food processing firms in the Philippines. The organization was established in 1986 to defend the interests of food processors. It had more than 180 corporate members in 1999. As the food processing industry developed in the 1980s, smaller firms realized that the Chamber of Food Manufacturers—at the time the major food manufacturers association in the Philippines—was dominated by large sugar producers that had an interest in high prices for sugar. Sugar is important for food conservation and the taste of many food products. The price of sugar is therefore an important factor determining the competitive position of the processing industry.

The trade liberalization approach followed by the Philippines in the 1980s involved reducing tariffs on processed food while maintaining sugar prices above the world market level. As a result, local factories producing sugar-intensive goods such as candies and chocolate had a hard time meeting competition from imports. The industry suffered from negative effective protection (see chapter 4). Starting in the late 1990s, Philfoodex became actively involved in lobbying legislators and government officials for cheaper sugar.

Source: Kostecki (2001).

Corporate Interests at the WTO Level

Numerous industry associations, business coalitions and multinational companies are active in Geneva as well as in national fora. Among the more visible business groups are the European Round Table of Industrialists (Brussels), the Geneva Association (a think-tank of some 80 insurance companies), the World Business Council for Sustainable Development and the US Coalition of Service Industries (CSI) and its counterpart, the European Community Services Group. The Paris-based International Chamber of Commerce (ICC) maintains a permanent representative in Geneva, largely to follow WTO developments. The US National Association of Manufacturers coordinates North American business interests through the 'US Alliance for Trade Expansion' and initiates and supports many US trade liberalization proposals. It played an important role in the TRIPs negotiation. The CSI and British Invisibles—a UK-based association of service firms—were important actors mobilizing support for inclusion of services in the Uruguay Round.

Specialized associations such as the US Dairy Foods Association, the Pork Producers Council, the American Sugar Alliance or the Council of Bars and Law Societies of Europe were also active during the Uruguay Round (Arkell, 1994).

Individual multinational enterprises were also active in the background during the Uruguay Round and continue to have an active interest in the WTO. Global firms such American Express, American International Group, Citibank or Arthur Andersen provided important intellectual inputs and exercised influence during the preparatory phase of the negotiations that led to the conclusion of GATS. They continue to follow WTO developments. The objective of these firms is generally enhanced access to export markets. Certain companies have particularly important stakes in the WTO. Examples are inspection and trade facilitation firms such as Société Générale de Surveillance (SGS), and international express and courier companies such as DHL and Federal Express. SGS maintained a senior position to follow GATT-related matters during the Uruguay Round and assumed a leadership role within the International Federation of Inspection Agencies (IFIA), the body that represents the interests of preshipment inspection firms.

14.2. NGOS AND CIVIL SOCIETY

Industry lobbies clearly play a major role in the formulation of trade policy, both at the national and the international level. That business interests dominate the WTO is not very surprising—after all, business has the largest stake in trade. However, other groups also play a role, especially at the national level. Unions have traditionally been a major political force in many countries, and have had an influence on trade policy. Environmental and human rights groups are also important players, especially in specific cases that directly affect their interests. Business groups are increasingly complemented by (and sometimes face competition and opposition from) NGOs in the trade policy formation process, at the national level, and, more visibly, at the international level.

NGOs are generally non-profit entities with voluntary membership that pursue non-economic objectives. They are a relatively large industry in their own right. According to OECD estimates, NGOs raised $5.5 billion from private donors in 1997. Non-profit groups (mostly NGOs) provided over 8 percent of all jobs in North America and 6 percent in the UK (*The Economist*, January 29, 2000). A common denominator underlying the objectives of many NGOs that are active on the trade front is sustainable development, ensuring that social and ecological objectives are considered in addition to economic ones. In the 1990s, the umbrella concept of sustainable development brought together a large number of diverse groups that pursue environmental, social, human rights, and cultural objectives. These groups are often multinational in nature, linking national organizations in a loose network, increasingly connected to each other through the Internet. In contrast to industry lobbies, many NGOs seek the limelight and are adept at using the media to attract attention to their views. An example was provided at the Seattle ministerial by Greenpeace handing out green condoms to delegates as a way of bringing across their message that in their view what was required was a set of principles to make trade 'safe for the environment'. NGOs are also more inclined to complement activities at the national level with actions that center on global issues and the activities of international organizations.

Declining confidence in political institutions, pressure for decentralization and calls for new forms of direct democracy have been factors leading to NGOs becoming 'mainstream' institutions. Relationships with industry have gradually moved away from the purely adversarial to include partnerships aimed at creating 'win-win' situations between sustainability and efficiency. To the extent that any neat division existed between the corporate and the NGO worlds, by the mid-1990s it was long gone. Governments have also responded to the emergence of NGOs. For example, in the 1990s a Transatlantic Consumer Dialogue (TACD) mechanism was created to allow for NGO input into trade and related policies to complement the Transatlantic Business Dialogue (TABD). Not surprisingly, given the disparity in interests, 'leveling the playing field' is not straightforward. Public Citizen, a US-based NGO, noted that the US Administration did not adopt any TACD recommendations, while accepting numerous TABD proposals (www.citizen.org/pctrade, September 2000).

NGOs and the WTO

Although NGOs have been a noticeable element in the UN system and other international bodies for many years, their influence in MTNs and the GATT was minimal. This changed fundamentally in the Uruguay Round, when environmental groups became concerned that trade liberalization might have detrimental consequences for the environment. It was largely at the behest of NGOs that the Committee on Trade and the Environment was resuscitated in 1991. After the creation of the WTO in 1995, NGOs remained active. In part because of the 'marketing' efforts of WTO secretariat Director-General Ruggiero—who maintained in speech after speech that the WTO was a central player in, and pillar of, the globalization process—NGOs opposing global economic integration began to perceive the WTO as an appropriate target. Groups opposing globalization marched against the organization at the 1998 ministerial meeting in Geneva, and dominated the press coverage of the 1999 Seattle ministerial meeting.

Three broad categories of NGOs can be distinguished in terms of their general approach to the WTO: 'conformers', 'reformers' and 'radicals' (Scholte, O'Brien and Williams, 1999). The 'conformers' endorse the activities and objectives of the WTO system, accept the premise that global integration and a reliance on the market provides the best prospects for economic growth and development, and believe that the WTO as designed is a beneficial instrument. 'Reformers' comprise entities that recognize the value of a multilateral trade system that is based on open markets and non-discrimination, but are concerned that existing procedures or rules result in inefficient outcomes. The reformers want to modify the system. Finally, the 'radicals' seek to abolish the WTO or to substantially reduce its powers and competence.

TABLE 14.1 *Examples of NGOs Active on WTO-related Issues*

Issue	Examples of major NGOs
Labor and human rights	The International Federation of Free Trade Unions (Brussels)
	AFL-CIO (US trade union federation)
	Public Citizen Global Trade Watch (US)
Environment	The World Wildlife Fund (WWF)
	The Sierra Club (US)
	Greenpeace
	Friends of the Earth
Consumer protection	Consumer International
	Transatlantic Consumers Dialogue
	Consumer Unity and Trust Society (CUTS, India)
Economic development	International Center for Trade and Sustainable Development (ICTSD, Geneva)
	Christian Aid
	World Development Movement
	Oxfam
	Third World Network (TWN)
	South Centre (G-77, Geneva)

The vast majority of NGOs are either reformers or radicals. They tend to be active in five areas: labor rights, human rights, environment, consumer protection and economic development. Most NGOs pursue goals that are only marginally trade-related. However, some concentrate on global economic issues and have become active WTO critics. Some of the major NGOs that follow trade are listed in Table 14.1. The largest US trade union federation, the AFL-CIO, is a major player, as is the International Federation of Free Trade Unions (Brussels), which claims to represent 124 million members in 143 countries. Both support the introduction of core labor standards in the WTO.

While most NGOs that are active with respect to international trade are based in high-income countries, the number of Southern NGOs is non-negligible. Many of the more visible and constructive NGOs that focus on the WTO are based in developing countries or are joint ventures between North and South. Among the more prominent, the Third World Network (TWN) is a NGO based in Asia that is generally critical of trade liberalization. The Consumer Unity and Trust Society (CUTS) is a joint venture between African and Asian NGOs that are concerned with consumer protection. The South Centre is an entity created by the G-77 to defend developing country interests in the WTO. The International Center for Trade and Sustainable Development (ICTSD) is based in Geneva. Supported by CUTS and Oxfam, among other bodies, it is the source of an informative newsletter on trade developments in and outside the WTO called *Bridges* (downloadable from www.ictsd.org).

Many of the developing country-centered NGOs focusing on the WTO are of recent vintage. Some were created as a response to the WTO. In contrast, the Northern NGOs that have been active on WTO issues tend to be well-established. NGOs such as the Sierra Club, WWF and Greenpeace have favored the imposition of trade restrictions on products that are deemed to have been manufactured using environmentally damaging production methods, to preserve bio-diversity or forestry stocks, and so forth. Most environmental NGOs tend to be critical of the WTO, reflecting their lack of enthusiasm about globalization. They often argue that WTO-supported liberalization weakens health and environmental standards in the global economy.

Consumer organizations became more active in the world trading system in the 1990s. Their interests include issues related to basic consumer rights (safety, information, choice), as well as the right to an environment that enhances the quality of life. Consumer interests are represented at the international level by networks of consumer organizations such as Consumers International and the Transatlantic Consumers Dialogue. The latter played a major role in mobilizing public opposition to hormone-based meat production. Major development-oriented NGOs include Christian Aid, the World Development Movement and Oxfam. All three have developed positions on a wide range of trade-related issues, including market access and ensuring fair terms of trade for developing countries.

Many of these NGO argue that:

- the WTO is dominated by—and an instrument of—industry lobbyists and multinational corporations, resulting in the neglect of environmental, labor, consumer and sustainable development issues, as well as social cohesion and equity;
- the WTO needs to move to a more participatory approach through the creation of consultation mechanisms and advisory bodies if it is to generate greater trust and mobilize civic engagement and 'ownership'; and
- countervailing power is needed to increase government accountability in trade negotiations and this is best achieved by granting the NGO community direct access to the WTO.

The Marrakech Agreement establishing the WTO explicitly acknowledged the need for a greater involvement of civil society in the trading system. The WTO provides that that the 'General Council may make appropriate arrangements for consultation and cooperation with non-governmental organizations concerned with matters related to those of the WTO' (Article V:2 WTO). Arrangements for consultation and cooperation with NGOs on trade-related issues were put in place in 1996. These arrangements leave consultation with NGOs to the discretion of WTO members, allowing for this on an ad hoc basis.

The premise of WTO members is that democratically elected governments that negotiate trade deals represent their citizens—if they do not, they can and should be voted out of office. If necessary, any deal can then be renegotiated using the mechanisms that have been built into the WTO for that purpose. The primary responsibility for taking into account the different interests of NGOs in trade policy-making is considered to lie at the national level. Efforts to actively engage NGOs directly in the work of the WTO or its meetings are therefore generally rejected by most WTO members. However, NGOs have valid cause for concern if they do not have adequate opportunities to feed their views into the national political and institutional processes through which trade policy positions are formulated. At present, there is little the WTO can do to require members to implement mechanisms that give NGOs access to the policy making process. Some NGOs (such as Consumer International) have therefore proposed that WTO members develop guidelines for national consultation mechanisms and encourage members to adopt and implement them with a view to allowing civil society to participate in national (or regional) trade policy making. Absent a move in this direction, which would be a major step for the WTO, the main role of the institution is to ensure that its operations are transparent and that there is 'full information' so that member governments can be held accountable in domestic political fora.

In democracies, all interested groups have the opportunity to express their views on trade and related policy issues to representatives in the legislature and the government. Given the need to be elected, politicians will be responsive to those interests, as they must mobilize votes come election time. In centralized systems power tends to be more concentrated, and many groups will find it more difficult to express their views and influence the process. Whatever the political system, information is a key ingredient into good policy making and holding governments and legislatures accountable. NGOs and other interest groups can play a valuable role in providing information and collecting data. A major focus of many of the Southern NGOs mentioned above is to provide information, to undertake analysis, and to help build capacity in developing countries to defend their interests.

14.3. GOVERNANCE OF THE WTO

The decision-making mechanics of the WTO were subjected to severe criticism in the run-up and aftermath of the Seattle ministerial meeting. Many low-income developing country WTO members expressed great frustration regarding the difficulty of keeping abreast of developments in the WTO, and objected to being excluded from the consultations and meetings where compromises are struck and deals are made. In early 2000, the WTO Council identified this as a priority issue that should be addressed in order to re-establish confidence in the WTO.

Two proposals have attracted most attention. The first is to move away from consensus and create a decision-making and management structure that relies on an Executive Board or Committee of the type found in the World Bank or IMF. A move in the direction of an executive committee could imply that certain WTO members would speak on behalf of those they were chosen to represent—this is the World Bank or IMF model. An alternative, less ambitious change would be to give the committee the task of hammering out a proposed consensus on issues, which would then need to be ratified by all WTO members (Schott and Watal, 2000). Most developing countries object strongly to the IMF or World Bank model, as they believe that the consensus principle maximizes their ability to safeguard their interests. The Schott-Watal proposal would do this, but has to date not attracted significant support. Rather than pursue major structural reforms, they propose instead that the focus be on procedural improvements to ensure that small group meetings (such as the Green Room) are transparent. This could involve agreeing that consultations be open-ended, that all members are informed that Green Room meetings are being pursued, that all members be given an opportunity to state their views, and that the outcome is reported in a timely fashion to those WTO members not present (Luke, 2000).

The second option, proposed by many of the major NGOs, is to open access to the deliberations of the WTO to civil society representatives. NGOs have noted repeatedly that they can obtain observer status at UN meetings, but are excluded from the WTO. This exclusion pertains not just to sensitive negotiation and dispute settlement sessions, but also to regular committee and Council meetings.

The nature of the process of cooperation makes it difficult, if not impossible, to accommodate private participation in negotiations. The wide range of issues involved and numerous linkages that may be made render the negotiating process complex. Allowing single-issue groups to have a voice in negotiations would preclude many of the needed tradeoffs and bargains. This is a task for governments who have been entrusted with the task of safeguarding the public interest. The required deal-making and posturing cannot be done in the open. Negotiators will not agree to open their backroom bargaining to the continuous scrutiny of groups with vested interests that will immediately publicize all instances where their preferences are not being defended by negotiators. Complete transparency of negotiations will result in deadlock—officials will not be able to make tradeoffs that result in a welfare-enhancing outcome. To put it in Prince Bismarck's words: citizens should not be permitted to observe how laws or sausages are made.

What matters then is accountability *ex post* and access to policymakers *ex ante*. As noted in chapter 4, stakeholders must be able to inform their government representatives of their preferences and interests. Better access at the domestic level should do much to improve the representativeness of positions taken at the WTO by members. Greater transparency at the WTO level can help ensure that governments are held accountable. Decisions by WTO members to derestrict many non-confidential documents more rapidly and to make them accessible to the public through the Internet have done a lot to improve transparency relative to the GATT. The secretariat also has been permitted to play a more active role in interacting with NGOs. Contacts with NGOs have been pursued through ad hoc symposia on WTO-related issues, informal arrangements to receive the information NGOs may wish to make available for consultation by the WTO members, and responding to requests for general information and briefings.

Granting major NGOs with a global reach access to formal, non-negotiating sessions of WTO bodies as observers could help improve transparency. Many of the demands of the NGO community in this regard deserve support. For example, Consumer International has proposed that the WTO introduce accreditation of international NGOs to grant them observer status, following the example of other international organizations, develop criteria for confidentiality to allow automatic derestriction of non-confidential documents, and require the immediate release of draft agendas to facilitate national consultation. The major problem that arises in implementing the proposal to grant observer status is to determine who gets accredited. Given the huge number of meetings that take place every year and the costs of participation, only the largest NGOs are likely to take up the option. One solution to this problem is to require cooperation between NGOs, or to devise a rotation rule. Given the existence of joint ventures such as the ICTSD it would appear relatively straightforward to accredit a small number of NGOs as observers, and require them to provide all interested actors with their reports on WTO meetings.

What about the dispute settlement process? As noted in chapter 3, many NGOs have been eager to obtain access to panels in order to defend environmental and other interests. The Appellate Body has already taken the decision to accept amicus briefs. Going further and allowing observers into the room as observers would require changes in the dispute settlement mechanism—including professionalization of panels. However, as was discussed in chapter 3, there are strong arguments against granting the private sector—be it business or civil society groups—standing to take cases to the WTO.

Greater efforts to ensure transparency do not necessarily have to involve the WTO itself. Another option that might be considered is the creation of an international public interest body that would act as a forum to explore the technical (economic, scientific) and social aspects of specific contentious issues or proposed areas for action at the WTO (Hoekman and Mavroidis, 2000). If this is made independent of the WTO, it could allow for direct access by non-governmental bodies. A transparency body might help shed light and build consensus by identifying whether there are cross-border spillovers, their size, the economic or environmental impact of policies, including their distributional effects within and across countries, and whether alternative instruments exist that could attain governmental or societal objectives (more) efficiently. Such an entity could be used as a discovery mechanism through which greater understanding could be obtained regarding the effects of national policies on various constituencies and stakeholders, both within and across economies. It could play a constructive role by acting as a focal point for exploring the pros and cons of potential multilateral rules in new areas, and a forum to analyze the economic and development impact of specific policy measures that have been taken or are proposed. Such an entity could also be a forum to determine the scientific basis—or lack thereof—of regulatory policies in sensitive areas (biotech, GMOs). Such policies are rapidly becoming a major source of tension and controversy, and developing countries in particular could benefit from a neutral and objective forum in which standards-related policies and issues are analyzed.

In short, a transparency entity could help ensure that the development dimension of current and proposed multilateral rules be considered. As noted by Finger and Schuler (2000), mechanisms to assess the relevance of WTO agreements for the process of economic development are urgently needed. Clearly careful thought needs to be given to the appropriate design and governance of a transparency body. In principle it could be a public-private partnership, including industry associations, think tanks and NGOs among its members, with part of the funding being generated by public institutions. Of great importance is that it have the funding to perform quality work, and be independent of governments and the WTO secretariat. Independence and separation will minimize the extent to which discussions and analysis is influenced by strategic negotiating considerations.

14.4. COHERENCE OF NATIONAL POLICIES

Information mechanisms (transparency) are also required to achieve 'coherence' of national policies. The coherence of policies pursued by international economic organizations was one of the subjects on the agenda of the Uruguay Round negotiating group on the Functioning of the GATT System (FOGS)—Box 14.3. Ensuring coherence with the Bretton Woods institutions (the IMF and the World Bank) is one of five specified functions of the WTO (Article III:5). The rationale for addressing this issue was that macroeconomic or exchange rate policies pursued by WTO members could serve to create pressures for protection and offset trade liberalization.

What coherence means is not defined in the Uruguay Round declaration. A good case can be made that the concept makes little sense, as it focuses on the wrong set of actors. International organizations represent the interests of their owners—member countries. It is up to the governing boards of these organizations to ensure that the mandates that are given to the organizations are 'coherent'. More fundamentally, important problems of 'incoherence' arise primarily at the national level. Given that sovereign governments have the responsibility to design economic, social and other policies to achieve the objectives of the electorate (society), it is up to governments to construct policy packages that do the job. If they do not, they will face the consequences at the next election. Clearly in many cases 'incoherent' national policies will have spillovers in the sense of having offsetting effects on the attainment of a particular objective. Thus, trade barriers that restrict exports of developing countries may help domestic industries, but they work to nullify the development assistance that is provided by the development ministry and NGOs. Incoherence of this type is the natural state of the world, as different groups in society invariably will have different preferences and objectives, and will have different views regarding the policies that should be used in any given situation (Winters, 2000). Such incoherence is another example of the need for information and analysis of policies, and is an issue where NGOs could potentially play a constructive role. In practice, NGOs often ignore the negative implications of trade and industrial policies on the achievement of their objectives.

Box 14.3. The Uruguay Round FOGS negotiation

The launch of the Uruguay Round in 1986 included establishment of a negotiating group on the Functioning of the GATT System (FOGS). The mandate of this group was to strengthen the trading system through better monitoring of trade policies, improving the effectiveness and decision-making of the institution, and increasing GATT's contribution to the coherence of global economic policies. Better surveillance had been strongly endorsed by a group of wise men (the so-called Leutwiler report—see GATT, 1985). At the time there was no analogue to the Article IV consultations of the IMF with its members, the country economic memoranda prepared by the World Bank, or the national economic surveys published by the OECD. A motivation for creating the FOGS group included the very large macroeconomic imbalances that had emerged in the 1980s and the developing country debt crisis. Both generated pressures for protection and in both cases trade barriers impeded the process of adjustment (for example, by limiting the export growth opportunities of highly-indebted countries).

The FOGS group agreed to the creation of the TPRM, but made less progress on the other two issues. The group discussed several areas where trade and macro policies were at odds, but disagreements on the economics were prevalent (for example, the US disagreed with the EU that exchange rate instability had a disruptive effect on trade). In the run-up to the 1988 mid-term ministerial meeting in Montreal it became apparent that little could be done on the broader 'coherence' front. In the end the only coherence-related outcome of the FOGS discussions was the Ministerial Declaration on the Contribution of the WTO to Achieving Greater Coherence in Global Economic Policy Making. This instructed the WTO to 'pursue and develop cooperation' with the Bretton Woods organizations and called on the Director General to

review with the heads of the IMF and the World Bank the implications of WTO's responsibilities for cooperation and the forms such cooperation might take' (GATT 1994*a*, 442). In addition, cooperation with the Bretton Woods institutions was defined as one of the WTO's five explicit functions (Article III:5 WTO).
Source: Croome (1999).

As mentioned, in the WTO, coherence focuses on the World Bank, IMF and WTO. This does not mean that policymakers did not recognize that the coherence problem is a national one. Winters (2000) speculates that trade ministers hoped through the coherence mandate to discipline the activities of other ministers that have a detrimental effect on trade—such as macro-economic policies that lead to real exchange rate appreciation. Another possible explanation is that the trade community (trade ministries) attempted to create a mechanism to induce ministries of finance, development and planning in both OECD and developing countries to allocate resources for the implementation of WTO disciplines—another example of a lack of coherence of national policies (see chapter 12).

Towards Greater National Coherence

Trade policy affects the whole economy: policy decisions should therefore be made in a context that allows not only the interests of all potentially affected actors to be considered, but also the efficacy of the set of policies that are pursued by the government. This will not be done unless an explicit attempt is made to design institutions such that an economy-wide focus is indeed taken. In the legislative context, the coherence of national policies will depend in part on how representatives are elected. If they represent distinct geographic regions, lobbies will seek to influence their representatives, who in turn will seek the support of other representatives. The resulting logrolling can lead not only to highly protectionist outcomes, but also to situations where policies work at cross-purposes.

A fundamental objective of the design of policy institutions should be to limit the extent to which lobbies can capture the policy-making process. Achieving this is difficult, and will depend on the specifics of individual countries. However, some general principles are by now well known. As far as trade policy is concerned, assuming for purposes of discussion that trade taxes are not a necessary revenue-generating instrument, good practices should build upon the recognition that trade policy is an inefficient redistributive instrument. A first requirement then is that the net cost to the economy of a policy is estimated ex ante and monitored ex post, and the incidence of any implicit tax is identified. One way this can be done is by an agency that has a statutory mandate to determine the impact of a trade policy on the economy, both in terms of efficiency (resource cost) and equity (income redistribution).

Such a body should have a pure transparency function: advising the government on the effects and incidence of the trade and investment policy stance that is maintained, as well as the 'coherence' of the trade policy stance with official objectives in other areas—development assistance, for example. Such institutions should have a purely advisory role vis-à-vis the government: the task is to shed light. Institutions of this type have been created in a number of countries (Spriggs, 1991). Many of the proposals for establishment of such bodies have been inspired by the Australian Industries Assistance Commission, currently called the Productivity Commission—for a history, see Rattigan (1986).

14.5. CONCLUSION

A necessary condition for 'ownership' of the WTO by civil society in member countries is that they perceive that multilateral agreements help attain national objectives (and do not work against the attainment of objectives they have a strong interest in). Both business and NGOs have a role to play in attempting to influence policies at home as well as the multilateral rules of the game. A precondition for constructive engagement is a good understanding on the part of NGOs and civil society of what the WTO does and does not do, what it can do, and what it should not do. This requires intellectual honesty and a good faith effort to learn the rules of the system and seek to use efficient policy instruments to pursue objectives.

Legitimacy starts and ends at home. What matters is that society has a say in the process through which policies are negotiated at the WTO by ensuring that there are mechanisms for expressing views to their governments. Such views can be aggregated and expressed directly at WTO meetings, using the media and the Internet as dissemination vehicles. This is an option that NGOs pursued effectively in the late 1990s, attracting global attention for their points of view. But leveraging this attention into policy change requires effective engagement with the national governments that are the members of the WTO, and a willingness to consider the magnitude and incidence of the costs and benefits of alternative policy options that are proposed to attain specific objectives.

A number of the concerns that were expressed by the NGO community regarding the WTO in the late 1990s were valid. Many were not. Compared to most international organizations the WTO does not have a serious 'democratic deficit'. The consensus rule ensures that each member has a voice, and that groups of like-minded countries can block efforts to move in a direction they oppose. Seattle revealed a need to improve the functioning of the WTO, but this does not require major structural changes in the governance of the institution. The WTO plays a valuable role in forcing NGOs to push for more efficient instruments to pursue their noneconomic objectives. The fact that the scope to use trade restrictions as a unilateral instrument to push through specific environmental or social standards is circumscribed is beneficial to world welfare. At the same time NGOs (and business) play a key role in ensuring that civil society perceives the WTO to be of value. Maximizing the two-way flow of information can only be beneficial. This will help identify national and international policy 'coherence' problems and facilitate the accountability of governments. Enhancing access to information on the regular meetings of the WTO, including timely publication of the agenda of meetings, would be beneficial. Greater transparency and objective analysis of issues and proposals is a key input into better policymaking, and NGOs have an important role to play in that regard.

14.6. FURTHER READING

J. Scholte, *et al.*, 'The World Trade Organization and Civil Society', in Brian Hocking and Steven McGuire *Trade Politics: International, Domestic and Regional Perspectives* (London: Routledge, 1999) and D. Esty, 'Non-governmental Organizations at the World Trade Organization: Cooperation, Competition, or Exclusion', *Journal of International Economic Law*, 1 (1998) discuss the WTO's relationship with civil society. S. Charnovitz and J. Wickham, 'Non-governmental Organizations and the Original International Trade Regime', Journal of World Trade, 29 (1995), 111–22 discuss the role of NGOs in the ITO charter. The major NGOs maintain specialized web sites dealing with trade issues. One of the best is the International Centre for Trade and Sustainable Development (www.ictsd.org), which provides links to all the major NGOs, and publishes the informative newsletter *Bridges*.

15
Whither The Trading System?

The GATT was created by governments with a clear vision of the cooperation that was needed to foster economic growth and reconstruction after the Second World War. Although the vision called for an ITO, the GATT managed to fulfil the objectives of the original signatories quite well. It proved a very successful instrument to liberalize trade. The elimination of QRs was locked in under its auspices, and tariffs were reduced very substantially. As of the 1970s, trade barriers in the form of tariffs and QRs had declined significantly in importance, and governments came to be confronted increasingly with the trade-distorting aspects of domestic policies. To use Professor Robert Baldwin's analogy, trade liberalization can be likened to the draining of a swamp: as the water level (average tariff level) falls due to successful pumping efforts, rocks, stumps and all manner of other obstacles (NTBs) emerge (Baldwin, 1970). The GATT 1947 proved very able to drain the swamp. It was much less successful in clearing the drained land (eliminating NTBs), and keeping the water from flooding back (contingent protection). Dealing with the tree stumps and rocks was difficult in part because reciprocal exchange became more difficult. Some of the policies concerned involved zero-sum games. The issue linkages and side-payments required to make progress in establishing multilateral disciplines on regulatory regimes greatly complicated matters.

The Uruguay Round of multilateral trade talks, concluded in 1994 after 8 years of complex and sometimes contentious negotiations, constituted a landmark in the history of the trading system. Agriculture and textiles and clothing, two sectors that for all intents and purposes had been removed from the ambit of the GATT, were brought back into the fold. The system of multilateral rules was extended to include IPRs and services, and, because of the Single Undertaking rule, all countries desiring to become a member of the new WTO were forced to accept a variety of disciplines in areas ranging from customs valuation to subsidies that had largely been developed in the Tokyo Round by industrialized nations.

The Uruguay Round was widely seen to be a major step forward in strengthening the trading system. Simulation models suggested that the welfare gains from liberalization were significant, especially for those countries that had made the most far-reaching market opening commitments. Although it was recognized that certain agreements—most notably TRIPs— were not necessarily in the interest of low income countries and would certainly give rise to short-run costs, it could be (and was) argued that this was more than offset by the inclusion of agriculture, the commitment to phase out the MFA, and the creation of the WTO—an organization with a much stronger dispute settlement mechanism than what had prevailed under GATT.

The WTO confronts a very different economic environment than the GATT did when it was created in 1947. The US hegemony that existed in the 1950s has been eroded. The demise of central planning and the adoption of outward-oriented economic development strategies by many countries in the 1980s led to a reduction in ideological differences and competition. Given that the rule-oriented multilateral trading system was firmly founded on the existence and superiority of a market-based economy, in some sense this constituted a triumph for the GATT. The institution never really played much of a direct role in these developments, however. Integration of international financial markets, unilaterally implemented regulatory changes and technological and managerial innovations fostered what has come to be called the globalization of the world economy. The GATT was a facilitator of this process—having helped to create the necessary preconditions by encouraging OECD countries to reduce trade barriers—but to a large extent governments, especially in developing countries, pursued reforms autonomously. In the process they also addressed issues such as taxation of firms, investment policies, foreign exchange restrictions, the business environment, and so forth. Often actions were taken under pressure from the international capital markets and with the support of multilateral financial and development institutions.

The qualitative change in the nature of cross-border exchange that occurred in the 1990s is important in understanding the challenges facing the WTO. In the 1950s international trade was relatively simple: a product was made in country X and shipped to an importer in country Y. Interactions between producer and buyer were superficial. Trade was of a ship and forget nature (Cooper, 1988). Foreign direct investment was generally a substitute for trade—a way to jump over high tariff walls. This has changed fundamentally. The service intensity of production and consumption increased significantly. It is a commonplace that modern economies have become service economies. Many firms now sell intangibles—processes, performance, information, a life style image—that may or may not be bundled with tangible products. In the current economy, value tends to be closely associated with the performance and utilization of systems composed of material products, services, information of commercial value (trademarks, patents) and client-producer relations. Establishment of a relationship with clients is often crucial, as is ensuring that customers have access to complementary products, services, upgrades, and maintenance. What counts is performance in meeting the customers needs. More often than not this implies custom tailoring of solutions. Strategic partnerships and networking are frequently necessary to provide the solution to a client's problem. Firms increasingly need to enter into ad hoc or more formal relationships with other firms. Production and consumption has become more and more a joint process, requiring inputs and feedback from the customer. Managing the intangible aspects of the production process often requires establishment in a foreign market and access to telecommunications networks and global databases. FDI and trade are more and more complementary, and services account for an ever-increasing share of value added. Perhaps the best illustration of this is the phenomenon of global production sharing discussed in chapter 1.

One implication for the WTO is that the incentive structure of firms regarding the policy stance of governments changes. Firms think global and act local (Levitt, 1983). They have become much more sensitive and averse to regulatory barriers that restrict their ability to interact with clients and suppliers. This in turn has implications for the political economy of the trade policy setting process in many countries. Transnational enterprises with a customer orientation have a greater incentive to form coalitions with export-oriented interests in developing countries to lobby for the opening of local markets and otherwise creating a more competition-friendly environment. Multinationals need to be able to buy from the lowest cost source to stay competitive, while local export interests need to ensure that the regulatory regime allows them to compete for contracts with globally diversified firms. Both have incentives to push for a liberal FDI environment, including divestiture of state-owned enterprises. These changes in incentives help explain the policy developments observed in many countries starting in the 1980s: unilateral liberalization (especially in developing countries), complemented by measures to increase the contestability of service sectors, privatization, regulatory reform, and the expansion of RIAs.

Although WTO members have done much to liberalize access to their markets, much also remains to be done. Perhaps the greatest need pertains to old issues. Barriers to trade in agriculture remain very high in most member countries. Tariffs on manufactures in a number of regions (South Asia, the Middle East, many African economies) also remain high. Tariff peaks remain on labor-intensive sectors in OECD countries. There is still a huge shallow integration agenda in the area of services: the GATS remains far from being a general agreement. The sectoral coverage of specific commitments is limited. Many countries have not guaranteed national treatment or market access for sectors where in practice they pursue policies that satisfy these principles. Powerful protectionist forces still exist in many countries, whether industrialized or developing. The surge in users of antidumping observed in the late 1990s illustrates this clearly. Many governments have so far proved unwilling to lock in or bind currently applied trade regimes. The potential gains from pursuing a traditional market access agenda (liberalization of trade in agriculture, manufactures and services, complemented by further efforts to discipline the use of contingent protection) are still huge.

Multilateral negotiations on non-border policies, administrative procedures and domestic legal regimes have proven to be much more complex than traditional trade policy talks. It is much more difficult, if not impossible, to trade 'concessions'—instead the focus revolves around the identification of specific rules that should be adopted. The disciplines that are proposed by some countries may not be in the interest of others. Given disparities in economic power and resources, to a large extent negotiations on rules can be expected to reflect the agenda of high-income countries (and specific interest groups in these countries). In contrast to traditional trade liberalization, the rules that emerge in a given area may not be consistent with the development priorities of low-income countries. No longer is it the case that 'one size fits all' is necessarily a good rule. With the gradual demise of tariffs and the ever greater prominence of non-tariff, domestic regulatory policies—standards, investment regulations, environmental, social, or competition norms—there is a danger of moving away from positive sum ('win-win') games towards zero sum situations.

The basic rules of the GATT—progressive liberalization of bound tariffs, MFN, national treatment—worked in the interest of all. Any reduction in trade protection achieved by negotiators through the reciprocal exchange of market access 'concessions' was in their own and partner countries interests. Negotiators could safely be delegated the task of negotiating trade barrier reductions. While the outcome was by no means optimal, there was little need for economic policymakers or civil society to be concerned about the potential downside for the economy as a whole of whatever would be negotiated.[1] The basic GATT rules were unambiguously good rules for all members, whether developing or industrialized. The reason was that tariffs do not make much economic sense for small economies and are welfare reducing for the world as a whole. But, this is not the case when it comes to national regulatory regimes. Such regimes (or the lack thereof) may well (and certainly should) be welfare enhancing. Thus, the probability of a potential downside from multilateral negotiations materializes.

---

[1] Of course, interest groups did have reason to monitor outcomes—the point we are making here relates to the national welfare implications of the GATT process.

This is an issue that is particularly important for developing countries. The Uruguay Round marked a change in the attitudes of many developing countries regarding their participation in MTNs. From being largely uninvolved and reactive, many became active participants. However, this did not prevent these countries from being confronted with the large implementation burden associated with the Uruguay Round agreements, although it is not at all clear from a development perspective that the resources required for implementation would not be better used for other purposes (Finger and Schuler, 2000). The Uruguay Round experience illustrated that participation is not enough; it must be informed by analysis of whether proposals are in the national (development) interest. Indeed, the need is for a clear development strategy that maps out what is needed on the trade front, and how, if at all, multilateral agreements and international cooperation can help achieve development objectives. Such a need is especially strong when it comes to 'new' areas that involve either regulatory regimes or require substantial investments and the allocation of scarce human capital.

Greater transparency and information must be an important part of efforts to maintain a liberal trading order. Enhancing the transparency of WTO operations and improving access to and dissemination of WTO databases, reports and information (for example, data underlying national trade policy reviews) would help civil society (think tanks, NGOs) engage in the policy formation process. Much progress has been made in comparison with GATT–1947 in terms of surveillance and collection of basic data on trade policy, but more can and should be done to estimate the magnitude and incidence of costs of protection. It is a truism that to reduce protection and protectionist pressures those that lose (pay) need to be aware of the costs of such policies. The suppliers of, and the clients for, such analysis and information are not necessarily governments, but civil society (think tanks) and the constituencies in individual countries who are affected by policy. In order for the WTO to promote good policy making in member countries, stakeholders must be active in the domestic policy formation process. As argued in chapters 13 and 14, legitimacy and coherence starts and ends at home.

There are a number of other ways to strengthen the constitutional role of the WTO in domestic policy making. One would be for governments to allow domestic firms and consumer organizations to invoke WTO rules and principles in domestic courts. This would help offset the weakness of the dispute settlement mechanism that ultimately depends on the threat of retaliation— a weak threat at best. WTO rules are generally not self-executing (they do not have direct effect) in the domestic legal orders of members. Moving in the direction of direct effect has been resisted by most governments, in part because of an unwillingness to be held accountable, but also because this is an issue that goes far beyond trade policy. A less far-reaching alternative is to create mechanisms to allow private parties to invoke specific agreements before national tribunals through so-called challenge mechanisms. This could do much to increase the domestic sense of 'ownership' of negotiated agreements by stakeholders, and ensure that governments take the negotiating process seriously.

Another avenue to strengthen the trading system is to develop mechanisms to ensure that the burden of implementing agreements is not to the detriment of poorer countries development prospects. Two options can be considered in this connection, beyond a willingness to extend transition periods. The first is to ensure fulfillment of offers of financial and technical assistance by high-income countries. Developing countries have been disappointed by the extent to which such assistance (development aid) was provided after the Uruguay Round. This has contributed to an absence of ownership of many agreements, and a general suspicion of the WTO as an instrument that promotes economic growth and development in all members. Adequate technical and financial assistance can do much to address such suspicions. One constraint has been the absence of a willingness to mobilize the necessary resources. Given that by definition there should be gains from the trades that are reflected in the outcome of MTNs, compensation for implementation costs is certainly available. For example, as discussed in chapter 8, research suggests that the static resource transfers to owners of patents in the US, Germany and France is in the order of US$8 billion. Given that this transfer pertains to knowledge that was generated under a regime where patents were not protected in many developing countries, this is a pure windfall gain. If a share of this gain would be transferred back to the developing world, the implementation burden could be addressed while at the same time pursuing development objectives. There is a large research and capacity-building agenda that needs to be pursued to allow national experience to be built in the various areas high-income countries are interested in addressing in the WTO. In many of these areas national action is in the interest of developing countries, but this must be in place before discussions are launched on multilateral rules, if ever.

A second option is to use the existing opportunities to negotiate plurilateral agreements. Much of the research that has been done on the economics of new issue areas suggests there is a strong case to be made for resisting efforts to steadily expand the ambit of the WTO. In some cases it is clear that the WTO is not the right forum for cooperation. In others it is not clear that there are large gains to be had from cooperation, or that all countries will benefit from signing on to multilateral rules. In the latter cases, plurilateral agreements allow like-minded countries to move ahead in new areas where it is clear that there is no consensus. A major challenge that arises if this path is followed is to minimize discrimination against non-signatories of plurilateral agreements. There is otherwise a serious threat that the trading system gradually will fragment. This is unlikely to be in the interest of developing countries.

The traditional market access agenda that remains to be addressed by the WTO—reducing the level of border barriers, abolishing discriminatory policies—remains quite large. The potential gains from further liberalization and binding of policies affecting trade in goods and services is very substantial. Members are therefore well advised to focus attention on the traditional 'shallow integration' agenda of the GATT/WTO, leaving it to other international bodies and conventions to address non-trade issues that give rise to global spillovers and to assist developing countries pursue development objectives.

That said, the first five years of the WTO revealed a need to improve the functioning of the organization. Even if attention remains largely restricted to a shallow integration agenda, the problems that emerged in the area of dispute settlement, the selection process for senior management (especially the Director General), the limited effectiveness of the Trade Policy Review mechanism, and the efficiency and representativeness of the 'Green Room' process, to name just a few, must be addressed. Many of these issues are relatively minor. Dispute settlement is not. In part the problems that emerged concern matters where the boundary between what is and what is not permitted must be made more precise. Perhaps the most urgent need here concerns health, safety and consumer-related regulation, including for new technologies such as biotech (GMOs, plant varieties, etc.).

ANNEX 1: GATT/WTO MEMBERSHIP, 2000

Albania 2000
Angola 1994
Antigua and Barbuda 1987
Argentina 1967
* Australia 1948
Austria 1951
Bahrain 1993
Bangladesh 1972
Barbados 1967
* Belgium 1948
Belize 1983
Benin 1963
Bolivia 1990
Botswana 1987
* Brazil 1948
Brunei Darussalam 1993
Bulgaria 1996
Burkina Faso 1963
Burundi 1965
Cameroon 1963
* Canada 1948
Central African Rep. 1963
Chad 1963
* Chile 1949
Colombia 1981
Congo 1963
Congo, Dem. Rep. (Zaire) 1971
Costa Rica 1990
Côte d'Ivoire 1963
Croatia 2000
* Cuba 1948
Cyprus 1963
* Czech Republic
(Czechoslovakia) 1993
Denmark 1950
Djibouti 1994
Dominica 1993
Dominican Republic 1950

Ecuador 1996
Egypt 1970
El Salvador 1991
Estonia 1999
European Communities
Fiji 1993
Finland 1950
* France 1948
Gabon 1963
The Gambia 1965
Germany 1951
Ghana 1957
Georgia 2000
Greece 1950
Grenada 1994
Guatemala 1991
Guinea Bissau 1994
Guinea, Rep. of 1994
Guyana 1966
Haiti 1950
Honduras 1994
Hong Kong, China 1986
Hungary 1973
Iceland 1968
* India 1948
Indonesia 1950
Ireland 1967
Israel 1962
Italy 1950
Jamaica 1963
Japan 1955
Jordan 2000
Kenya 1964
Korea, Rep. Of 1967
Kuwait 1963
Kyrgyz Republic 1998
Latvia 1999
Lesotho 1988

Liechtenstein 1994
Lithuania 2000
* Luxembourg 1948
Macau 1991
Madagascar 1963
Malawi 1964
Malaysia 1957
Maldives 1983
Mali 1993
Malta 1964
Mauritania 1963
Mauritius 1970
Mexico 1986
Mongolia 1997
Morocco 1987
Mozambique 1992
* Myanmar (Burma) 1948
Namibia 1992
* Netherlands 1948
* New Zealand 1948
Nicaragua 1950
Niger 1963
Nigeria 1960
* Norway 1948
Oman 2000
* Pakistan 1948
Panama 1997
Papua New Guinea 1994
Paraguay 1992
Peru 1951
Philippines 1979
Poland 1967
Portugal 1962

Qatar 1994
Romania 1971
Rwanda 1966
Saint Kitts and Nevis 1994
Saint Lucia 1993
Saint Vincent and the Grenadines 1993
Senegal 1963
Sierra Leone 1961
Singapore 1973
* Slovak Republic (Czechoslovakia) 1993
Slovenia 1994
Solomon Islands 1994
* South Africa 1948
Spain 1963
* Sri Lanka (Ceylon) 1948
Suriname 1978
Swaziland 1993
Sweden 1950
Switzerland 1966
Tanzania 1961
Thailand 1961
Togo 1964
Trinidad and Tobago 1962
Tunisia 1990
Turkey 1951
Uganda 1962
United Arab Emirates 1994
* United Kingdom 1948
* United States 1948
Uruguay 1953
Venezuela 1990
Zambia 1982
* Zimbabwe (Southern Rhodesia) 1948

Notes: Asterisks indicate founding members of the GATT. Three founding members subsequently withdrew and are not listed: China, Lebanon and Syria. Names in parentheses indicate the country names in 1947. Dates after country names are year of accession to GATT or WTO. During 1995-2000 the following countries joined the WTO: Ecuador, Bulgaria, Mongolia, Panama, Kyrgyz Republic, Latvia, Estonia, Jordan, Georgia, Albania, Oman, Croatia and Lithuania (in chronological order).

ANNEX 2: ECONOMIC EFFECTS OF TRADE POLICY—BASIC CONCEPTS

1. Why Trade?

A simple framework for understanding the gains from trade is laid out in Figure 1. This represents the economy of a country X that can produce two types of products, computers (C) and apples (A) in various combinations or proportions. If it specializes completely in one of these two products, it can produce either P worth of computers or P_1 of apples. More realistically, it will produce some combination. If the country X uses all of its productive resources efficiently, the production possibilities are represented by the curve PP_1. All points above and to the right of PP_1 represent combinations of quantities of computers and apples that are beyond the reach of the country's productive capacity. Points to the left of the PP_1 curve involve either unused capacity or the use of inefficient production techniques.

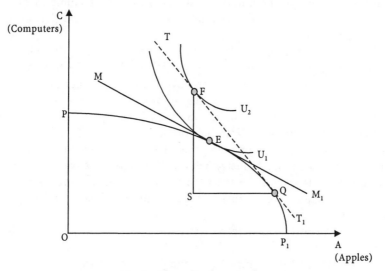

Fig. 1. The gains from trade

The production-possibility curve PP_1 represents the supply side of the economy. Consumer preferences (demand) determine the specific combination of computers and apples that will be produced. A useful device to characterize consumer preferences is the community indifference curve, represented by U_1 and U_2 in Fig. 1. Consumption of C and A yields satisfaction or utility to consumers. Each social indifference curve represents bundles of C and A that generate the same level of utility. Bundles located on a higher indifference curve (U_2) yield greater utility (welfare) than those located on a lower curve (U_1). Indifference curves bend in toward the origin because as consumption of computers falls, more and more apples must be consumed to maintain the same level of satisfaction. There is a diminishing marginal rate of substitution between products—consumers prefer combinations of products to extremes: gin and tonic is better than only gin or only tonic.

With no international trade (that is, in autarchy) and assuming that markets are competitive, the economy will be in equilibrium at point E. At this point the highest possible indifference curve (level of welfare) is attained, given available resources. Point E is the point of tangency between the production possibility curve (PP_1) and the highest community indifference curve (U_1). Thus, at E the slopes of the two curves are equal. In technical terms, at E the marginal rate of transformation in production (which reflects the amount of resources that must be released from production of apples to produce an additional computer) is equal to the community's marginal rate of substitution (the rate at which the representative consumer is willing to substitute apples for computers in consumption). This common ratio determines the price of computers relative to apples (say, two tons of apples for one computer).

If account is taken of the opportunity to engage in trade, the country can achieve a higher level of welfare by specializing in production. What the country specializes in will depend on how relative prices at home (opportunity costs) compare to those prevailing in foreign markets. Assume the relative price for apples is higher in the world market. Producers in X will find it profitable to shift resources from the computer to the apple industry. This is represented by the move along the production-possibility curve from E to Q. Output expands in the industry with a comparative advantage (apples), pulling resources away from the industry which has a comparative disadvantage (computers) (see chapter 1 for a definition of the term comparative advantage).

The shift in resources involved (structural adjustment) is driven by the difference in domestic and world relative prices. As resources move into the industry in which the country has a comparative advantage, marginal opportunity costs increase in that industry (this is because as production of a good increases it generally becomes harder to find factors of production that are as efficient as those already in use, or it may be that each industry uses capital and labor in different proportions). The shift in resources will stop when the domestic cost ratio becomes equal to the world exchange ratio (TT_1

in Fig. 1). As in the autarchy case, equilibrium requires the marginal rate of transformation in production to equal the marginal rate of substitution in consumption. Moreover, both of these must equal the world relative price (or terms of trade). In Fig. 1, this is the case if X produces at point Q and consumes at point F. Trade allows the country to attain a higher level of welfare: U_2 represents a level of utility that was not attainable in autarchy.

Although the country gains from trade, the concept of a community in-difference curve hides the fact that some segments of society may lose from the shift to trade. Workers and owners of computer companies will incur costs as demand for their output falls. What the theorems on the gains from international trade imply is that the gains to those who benefit are larger than the losses incurred by those who lose. That is, the *net* benefits are positive. In principle, those who gain have enough to compensate the losers and still come out ahead. In practice, compensation mechanisms or social safety nets may not exist, or they may be inadequate. This helps explain the resistance that often arises against liberalization of trade. There are also structural adjustment costs. This takes time to work through and is associated with social and psychological, as well as economic costs. Workers may have to be retrained and must find alternative employment.

2. Import Tariffs

What follows illustrates the effects of an import tariff on a single commodity in a small country. A 'small' country is one whose supply and demand decisions do not influence international prices. Fig. 2 shows the country's domestic supply (S) and demand (D) curves for a particular commodity. Since the importing country is small, it faces a horizontal international supply curve S_I, that is, the world price P_w for its imports is constant—no matter how large imports are, there is no effect on the world price. At that price the country's consumption is OQ_4, production is OQ_1 and imports make up the difference equal Q_1Q_4.

Assume that the country M imposes an *ad valorem* tariff of 20%. As a result, the domestic price increases by 20% (to P_t) and imports fall by $Q_1Q_2 + Q_3Q_4$. The higher domestic price induces consumers to buy less ($Q_3 Q_4$) and domestic producers to produce more (Q_1Q_2).

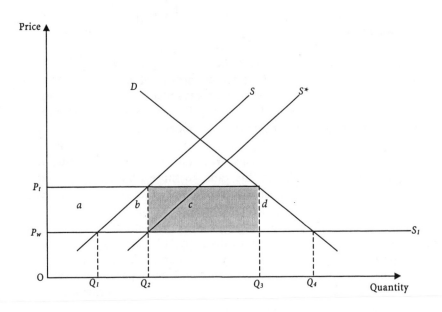

Fig. 2. Effect of trade policy in a small economy

The area under the domestic demand curve in Fig. 2 measures the total welfare that the consumers obtain from consumption of the commodity considered. Since consumers pay an amount equal to the price times the quantity consumed, the triangular area under the demand curve and above the horizontal line at the going price level represents 'consumer surplus'—the difference between the value in use and the price paid.

An import tariff reduces the consumer surplus by the quadrilateral area $a+b+c+d$. However, domestic producers gain area a and the government collects tariff revenue equal to the shaded rectangle c (which equals the tariff times the quantity of imports). From the national point of view, therefore, areas c and a are not losses. They represent the transfers that are induced by the tariff, resources being transferred from consumers to government and producers. The increase in producer surplus (area a) constitutes rents.

The net welfare loss resulting from the import tariff is represented in Fig. 2 by the areas b and d. Area d can be thought of as the loss incurred by consumers from losing the opportunity to consume the additional quantity of the commodity at the pre-tariff price p_w. Area b represents the loss resulting from the fact that domestic production expands beyond the optimal level—the extra output is produced at a cost higher than the world price. Areas b and d represent the net losses to society from imposing an import tariff. These are called 'deadweight' losses—they represent pure waste. If demand and supply are approximately straight lines in the relevant range, then the deadweight loss is equal to the decline in imports times one-half the tariff.

3. Quantitative Restrictions

The foregoing setup is also useful to analyse the impact of quantitative restrictions (QRs). In the case of a QR, the line segment Q_2Q_3 represents the total quantity of imports allowed into the country (the quota). As in the case of a tariff, area *a* represents the increase in domestic producer surplus (rents for domestic producers) and *b+d* are deadweight losses. There are two major differences, however. First, an important shortcoming of a quota is its rigidity. If, for example, technological progress results in a fall in world prices (the world price line or supply curve shifts downward), the only effect is to increase rents. In the case of a tariff this does not occur. Second, area *c* no longer equals tariff revenue. Under a quota, the increase in the domestic price generated by the QR creates so-called 'quota rents.' These rents go to whoever owns the quota rights. If importers get the quota rights, they receive the windfall profit. In the case of a VER, the rents go to the exporters. If the government auctions the quota to the highest bidder, it will capture the rents. The magnitude of the rents that accrue to right holders depends in part on the extent to which lobbying expenses are incurred in obtaining import or export licenses. It is quite possible that competition for licenses results in significant dissipation of rents. Magee, Brock and Young (1989) analyze the determinants of lobbying expenditures and conclude that in general only a fraction of the rents available will be spent on lobbying.

4. Rent-seeking

One of the negative effects of trade controls is that it gives rise to so-called rent-seeking behavior. Rent-seeking (or directly unproductive profit-seeking (DUP) activities—Bhagwati, 1982) involves resources being diverted from productive activity and towards efforts to obtain special benefits such as monopoly status, import licenses, or bureaucratic preferences that generate economic rents (Tullock, 1967, Krueger, 1974). Substantial resources may be devoted to lobbying to obtain quota and similar rights. Profit-oriented firms will use resources in lobbying for monopoly (protection), up to the point where an extra dollar invested in lobbying equals the expected value of the resulting trade protection. Numerous players may enter the rent-seeking market, but only some will be successful. The resources invested in rent seeking generally constitute economic waste and may give rise to 'political corruption' (Tullock, 1988). 'Rent avoidance' activities, that is, actions by other groups in society to oppose rent seeking, increase waste further—such counter-lobbying would not take place in the absence of rent seeking. Incentives to seek and oppose rents are distributed unequally across society. Concentrated interests, such as producers or large firms, have stronger individual incentives to organize and lobby than more dispersed consumers or taxpayers who tend to be much more marginally affected and are concerned by a large number of issues (Downs, 1954).

The analysis of 'rent seeking' changed perceptions of the cost of protection. Traditionally economists considered only the deadweight costs of the distortions introduced by trade restrictions. The realization that the actual social cost of protection may be much greater provides an additional argument against protectionism. As is always the case when it comes to so-called 'second-best' situations (Bhagwati, 1971), one cannot say with certitude that rent-seeking will always be welfare-reducing, nor is it possible to determine to what extent competition for rents will dissipate them. As was pointed out by Bhagwati and Srinivasan (1980), if lobbying resources are pulled away from activities that are characterized by distortions (market failures leading to prices not reflecting true opportunity costs) lobbying may actually increase welfare.

5. Subsidies

Domestic production may expand as a result of a subsidy, in the process reducing imports by lowering the cost (price) of domestic output. The effect of subsidy can also be analyzed in the framework of Fig. 2. Assume away tariffs or QRs. The effect of a subsidy (a monetary payment per unit of production) to domestic producers is to shift the domestic supply curve down vertically from S to S^*. For any level of output, average and marginal production costs are reduced by the amount of the subsidy. Domestic production expands from $0Q_1$ to $0Q_2$ and imports fall. However, the domestic price remains equal to the world price and total domestic consumption remains unchanged. Imports are reduced by less than under a tariff or quota, and national welfare consequently falls less because there is no consumer deadweight loss.[1] The total amount of subsidy (the transfer payment from gov-

---

[1] Note that the converse of this is that offsetting a subsidy on imported goods through a coun-

ernment to producers) is measured in Fig. 2 by area $a+b$. Area a is a pure governmental transfer, whereas area b involves the same inefficiency in resources use as in the case of a tariff or quota and constitutes therefore a deadweight loss.

Although subsidies are a less inefficient means of protection of domestic industry than border measures, they tend to be unpopular for political reasons. Domestic producers prefer quotas or tariffs to an equivalent subsidy because the latter are more visible, perceived as public handouts and are therefore less secure, being subject to periodic approval by the budgetary authorities.

6. Regional Integration: Trade Creation and Trade Diversion

Preferential trading arrangements such as free trade areas, customs unions, or common markets imply a partial movement towards free trade and therefore greater economic efficiency. Whether a particular regional (discriminatory) trading arrangement raises or lowers welfare depends on a number of factors, in particular the relative magnitude of trade creation and trade diversion.

Assume country N trades with two partners B and G. Domestic demand and supply curves are represented by D_N and S_N respectively. Assume all three countries produce steel, and that G is a lower cost supplier than B. Let country N impose a non-discriminatory *ad valorem* tariff on imports of steel. This is shown in Fig. 3 as the vertical distance between S_G and S_{G+T}. As G's steel is cheaper than B's, N imports only from G, total imports being Q_2Q_3 and domestic producers selling $0Q_2$. Assume now that N and B create a customs union. The tariff continues to apply to imports from G, but not to imports from country B. The elimination of tariffs on B makes the S_B the relevant supply function for domestic consumption. Country G loses all its export sales. As B is a higher cost supplier, the resulting efficiency loss equals the rectangle e (the cost difference between G and B times the quantity of steel which is diverted). Since the domestic price of steel declines in N from P_n to P_b, consumption expands from $0Q_3$ to $0Q_4$, production declines from $0Q_2$ to $0Q_1$ and imports increase from Q_2Q_3 to Q_1Q_4. The net welfare gain for N is equal to areas b and d minus area e (the loss in producer surplus—area a—is 'transferred' to consumers, as is the loss in tariff revenue that used to

tervailing duty—see chapter 9—is less distortionary than the imposition of regular tariff. The CVD will impose a deadweight consumption loss—by raising domestic prices above the world price—but does not create a production distortion.

be collected—area *c*) Whether welfare in *N* increases or declines as a result of the customs union depends therefore on whether areas *b+d* (efficiency gains) are greater than area *e* (a welfare loss as this is a part of the initial

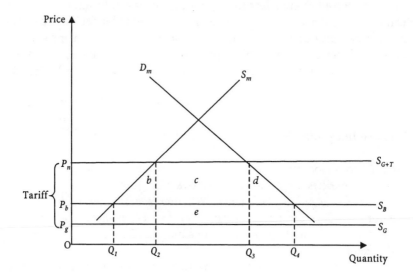

FIG. 3. Regional integration

tariff revenue loss that is not offset). Steel producers see output fall as consumers switch to cheaper steel from *B*. This is trade creation, and improves welfare. However, *N* no longer imports from the most efficient supplier and this creates an efficiency loss, equal to area *e*. There is trade diversion. Steel producers in *B* are happy because they gain export markets. However, country *G* loses the export market to *B* and is therefore negatively affected in market *N* (but may not lose if they shift supplies to the rest of the world). Moreover, *N* may also be a net loser if trade diversion is greater than trade creation.

7. Real Trade Costs

Assume country *N* imposes a variety of duplicative inspection requirements on imports that do not add any social value. For example, customs may require that importers provide data that is not relevant for duty calculation purposes. Goods may be subject to conformity assessment procedures at the border that are equivalent to those undertaken at the point of production or shipment. Such redundant 'processing' requirements raise the costs of trading. Assume the cost per unit of imports of such requirements is equivalent to the tariff depicted in Fig. 3. The result is then that imports equal Q_2Q_3. Assume further that the government decides to remove the requirement for country B, say because of a mutual recognition agreement. Domestic prices fall, domestic producer surplus falls, and consumer surplus increases by area $a+b+c+d$. The net gain for the country is $b+c+d$. This is much larger than what arises if a tariff were to be removed because there is no tariff revenue to be lost—the policies that are removed generated pure social waste. In general, the rectangles that represent revenues, rents or frictional costs are larger than the triangles that reflect efficiency losses. While tariff revenues or quota rents imply transfers across different groups—and thus do not contribute to welfare improvements when policies are changed—when wasteful (frictional) policies are removed, society gains the associated rectangles. This explains why estimates of the welfare gains from eliminating frictional costs are much higher than the gains from abolishing tariffs.

8. Dumping (Price Discrimination) and Profit Maximization

Dumping occurs when a firm sells a good in an export market at a price below that charged in the home market. Assume for simplicity that the firm is a monopolist and that initially there is no trade. The firm will produce Q_1 and sell this at price P_1 in the home market (Fig. 4). This strategy is dictated by profit maximization, which requires that the firm equates its marginal revenue *(MR)* with marginal cost *(MC)*.

Now suppose that the firm has the option to export. The world price is P_2—the firm is too small to affect world prices. Assume further that the domestic and the international markets are segmented—there are tariffs or other barriers to trade which prevent any of the firm's exports from coming back into the domestic market. Being able to sell on the world market alters the firm's marginal revenue curve. In effect, the firm confronts two marginal revenue curves. Up to quantity $0Q_1$ marginal revenue (MR) at home exceeds that on the world market—thereafter MR from selling in the world market is higher. In this new situation the firm will reduce its domestic supply to $0Q_3$ (the point at which MR at home equals MR abroad), in the process raising the domestic price to P_3 (technically, the reason for this is that marginal costs rise as output expands). Given that profit maximization requires that marginal revenue equal marginal costs, the firm will export quantity Q_3Q_2 at the international price P_2. The option of exporting at (the lower) international price increases the firm's profits by an amount equivalent to areas $a+b$ in Fig. 4, the difference between *MR* and *MC* for the exported quantity. The differences in elasticities in demand in the two markets induce the firm to implement a price discrimination strategy: it engages in dumping.

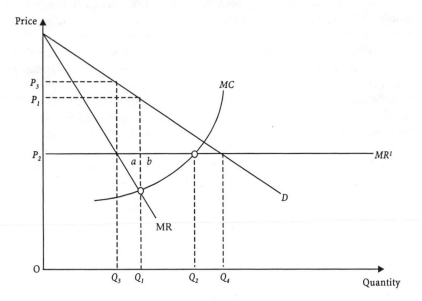

FIG. 4.   Dumping: price discrimination across markets

Is dumping bad from a welfare point of view? Clearly it has no impact on the welfare of foreign consumers or firms—our exporting firm simply prices to market: the world price is given and remains unaffected. However, domestic consumers lose (as the price goes up in the home market).

9. Trade Liberalization as a Pro-competitive Device

The situation in Fig. 4 is one where home prices are significantly above world prices. It is assumed that the economy is small—world prices are taken as given. If the country were to liberalize, the monopolist would confront import competition, with goods priced at P_2. The monopoly would immediately become unsustainable and the firm would be forced to price output at P_2 as well, increasing national welfare. Free trade would result in the domestic firm selling $0Q_2$ into the domestic market (all it's output), and the country importing an additional quantity Q_2Q_4 from the rest of the world. Insofar as dumping is facilitated by the existence of barriers to trade that protect the dumper's home market, the appropriate policy response is not for the importing country to impose antidumping duties, but for the home country to eliminate the barriers to arbitrage that prevent traders from re-exporting the product into the home market. As mentioned in chapter 9, in practice there is no effort in the antidumping context to determine whether there are barriers to arbitrage. Of course, there may be other factors that allow the exporting firm(s) to exercise market power on the home market. If so, there is cause for the application of domestic competition law to determine whether there are anti-competitive practices that are detrimental to national welfare.

9. Dealing with Domestic Market Failure and Externalities[2]

Markets may fail to allocate resources efficiently for a number of reasons. There may be information asymmetries, property rights may not exist, or there are may be externalities. In presence of distortions, intervention by the government may be called for. As distortions seldom directly involve trade, the general conclusion that emerges from the literature is that trade policy should not be used as an instrument to offset distortions. These should be corrected with domestic policies.

Using Taxes to Correct for Externalities

As in previous examples, assume perfect competition. In the absence of externalities, the supply curve, S, measures (vertically) both the marginal private cost (MPC) and the marginal social cost (MSC) of producing a good (Fig. 5). The market equilibrium at quantity Q_e equates the quantities supplied and demanded. The effect of a negative externality (producers do not take into account the impact of their actions on other groups in society) is to make MSC exceed MPC by the amount of the externality, E. Thus, Q_e does not equate the marginal benefit and marginal social cost of producing the good.

[2] What follows draws on Alan Deardorff, 'Lecture Notes on the Economics of Government Intervention', World Bank Institute, 1998. See www.worldbank.org/trade.

Domestic Market

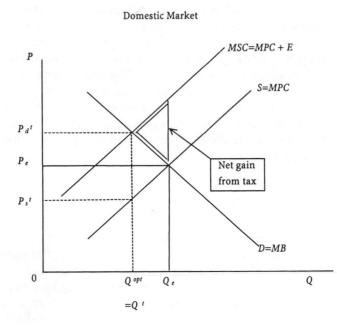

FIG. 5. Domestic market failure: the tax case

This means that this output is not optimal. From a social point of view there is too much production. Because of the negative externality, the optimum is where $MSC=MB$, at the intersection of the demand curve with the MSC curve (which lies a distance E above the supply curve). A tax equal to E will reduce output to the optimal level. The welfare benefit of the reduced externality is equal to E times one-half the drop in output. In the figure, this is the triangle of 'net gain from tax' that is shown. Note that the incidence of the tax is shared between producers and consumers. Producers see the price they receive fall, while consumers see the price they pay increase.

Regulatory Responses to Externalities

A regulation that limits output to Q^{opt} accomplishes the same purpose as a tax in dealing with a domestic externality, and has the same positive effect on national welfare (Fig. 6). However, the amount that the government would have collected in tax revenue goes instead to the producers as increased profits, or rent, from the regulation (their costs go down, while their price goes up). While the tax hurts producers and will be resisted by them if instead of a tax the government uses a regulation, this will be less detrimental to producers and therefore be welcomed by them. Both hurt consumers equally.

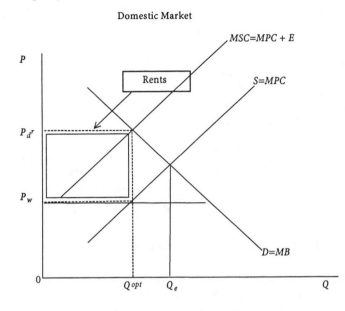

Fig. 6. Using regulation to address a domestic market failure

Allowing for trade

The foregoing assumed there was no trade. If we now allow for trade in the product concerned and consider again a small open economy that cannot affect the terms of trade but is confronted with an externality, the optimum output after imposition of the appropriate tax or regulation is determined by the world price P_w. Domestic output is Q^{opt}, which is less than Q_e. However, by fixing the price to demanders, trade causes producers to bear the whole cost of the tax—the incidence of the tax cannot be shifted in part to consumers. Conversely, if a regulation is used, domestic producers will lose the rents they used to capture. They can be expected to blame this 'loss' on trade, perceiving it as unfair, and they may lobby for some sort of protection, such as a tariff equal to the tax. This is likely to be motivated on the basis of some version of 'leveling the playing field'.

Domestic Market

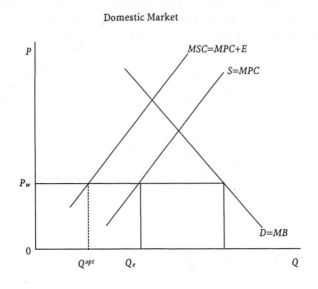

FIG. 7. Offsetting domestic externalities in a small trading economy

This framework is directly relevant to the debates and conflicts that arise in the WTO context regarding the use of regulations requiring (or prohibiting) the use of specific production or processing techniques. These impose additional costs on producers, shifting the supply curve up. The cost of attaining the optimal level of output is borne completely by domestic producers, who then have an incentive to lobby to have imports subject to the same processing requirement to 'level the playing field'. If foreign production generates the same negative externality for the domestic country as domestic production, then this is appropriate. However, if, more realistically, foreign production generates no domestic externality, there is no justification for any burden being imposed on imports. Suppose foreign production occurs in a location where pollution is more readily dissipated, per capita incomes are too low to allow abatement technologies to be used, there is less risk aversion, or there is no concern regarding local environmental spillovers (see chapter 13). In all such cases, a requirement that imports also be processed identically to domestic production (use a particular technology, etc.), simply adds to their cost without generating any social benefit in either the domestic or the foreign country.

Domestic Market

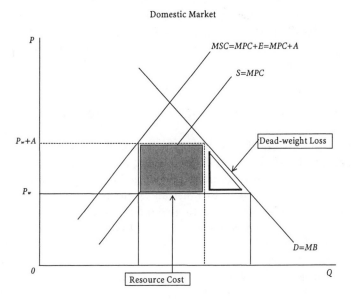

FIG. 8. Leveling the playing field

The processing requirement on imports is akin to a tariff or quota in that it increases production costs and shifts the foreign supply curve up by the amount A, raising the price of imports from the world market to P_w+A (Fig. 8). In the new equilibrium domestic output rises and becomes the same as it was without any policy at all, while consumption and imports are both reduced. Domestic producers are indifferent, since their cost and price have both risen by the same amount. Domestic consumers are worse off as their surplus has declined. Part of that loss is payment for the elimination of the externality, which is a benefit and therefore cancels out. But the rest – the shaded areas in Fig. 8, are net losses for the country and the world. The triangle is the usual deadweight loss of raising the price to consumers above the true marginal cost. The rectangle is an additional social cost, in that real resources are wasted on processing imports that did not need it. These costs constitute pure waste. They do not generate rents or revenues for either interest groups or the state.

Although there is a clear case to use tariffs rather than regulation to 'level the playing field', as this at least generates revenue for the government, a tariff will again negate the benefit from the tax in reducing the externality, as it will result in domestic output expanding beyond the socially optimal level. It will also cause a deadweight loss by raising prices to demanders. In both cases, whatever instrument is used, if there are no externalities in the foreign market, intervention to raise the price of imports is counter-productive. The reduction in domestic output following the imposition of the environment policy is appropriate—there is no justification for imposing the same costs on foreign production.

10. The Inefficiency of a Trade Ban to Address Cross-Border Spillovers[3]

The foregoing discussion of externalities assumed the market failure was domestic and could therefore be addressed by the government. Cross-border spillovers are more difficult to address in a simple framework. However, an analogue to Fig. 5 can be used to illustrate a situation where exporting countries do not consume and importing countries do not produce a commodity whose production gives rise to international spillovers. Assume Fig. 9 maps African supply and East Asian demand for ivory. The externality E reflects the negative impact on the utility of conservationists in other parts of the world that is caused by the slaughter of elephants—that is, the value they put on reducing this slaughter from $0Q_e$ to $0Q_t$.[4] Production (and trade) equal to $0Q_e$ induces a loss for the conservationists equal to the triangle ecj. If they can impose a complete ban on ivory trade, conservationists increase their welfare by this amount, at the cost of total producer and consumer surplus forgone equal to area ace. The latter is clearly much greater than the former, so that the ban is inefficient. In practice, conservationists will not compensate the losers—so that the ban implies a large implicit transfer.

A more efficient solution would be to reduce trade through a tax that equates the global marginal benefit of restricting output to the global marginal cost. Such a tax would reduce welfare in Africa and East Asia, but this would be offset to a large extent by tax revenue (equal to $bdfh$). As is always the case, the tax generates two 'loss triangles' for producers and consumers, but these are offset by equivalent gains for conservationists (reflecting the reduction in the externality). In fact, as conservationists gain area $cdbj$, global welfare increases by bcj (the net gain from the tax). Equity requires that conservationists compensate losers, in particular poor African producers—so that the tax revenue and the value of area bcj should be transferred to these countries. If this is done, conservationists are forced to pay for what they want to achieve, and African producers can be more than compensated

---

[3]   This example is drawn from Anderson (1992, pp. 40ff).
[4]   The supply curves in Figure 9 are not parallel because we assume that the externality (and the associated tax) is proportional to output produced.

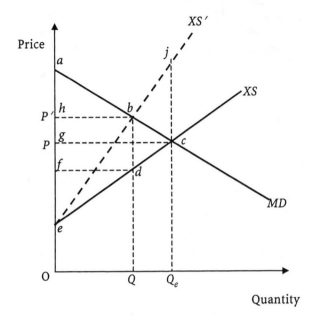

Fig. 9: Using taxes and trade bans to offset global externalities

for their loss. The problem of generating such outcomes in practice is that those who benefit from the alleviation of global externalities are rarely willing to pay. Thus, the needed transfers do not occur, even if tax instruments are employed (which generally is not the case).

Further Reading

An excellent discussion of the economics of non-tariff policies can be found in Alan Deardorff and Robert Stern, *Measurement of Non-Tariff Barriers* (Ann Arbor: University of Michigan Press, 1998). Alan Deardorff's home page on the internet provides a very useful glossary of trade policy terms, including definitions of the many types of policy instruments that are used to restrict or expand trade—see www.econ.lsa.umich.edu/~alandear. The economics of the interaction between environmental and trade policies are discussed in some detail in the contributions to Kym Anderson and Richard Blackhurst (eds.), *The Greening of World Trade Issues* (Hempstead: Harvester Wheatsheaf, 1992). A comprehensive analysis of the political economy of the choice between taxes and regulation to offset externalities and the implications for trade policy and pressures for protection can be found in Michael Leidy and Bernard Hoekman, 'Pollution Abatement, Interest Groups and Contingent Trade Policies', in R. Congleton (ed.), *The Political Economy of Environmental Protection: Analysis and Evidence* (Ann Arbor: University of Michigan Press, 1996).

REFERENCES

ABARE (1999), *Reforming Agricultural Trade Policies*, Research Report no. 99-12 (Canberra: Australia).

Abbott, F. (ed.) (1998), *China in the World Trading System* (Dordrecht: Kluwer).

ACC (1997), *Making Trade Talks Work*, Tokyo, Bridgestone Toranomon Building, 5F, 3-25-2 Toranomon, Minato-ku (Tokyo: The American Chamber of Commerce).

Acheson, K. and Christopher (1999), *Much Ado about Culture: North American Trade Disputes* (Ann Arbor: University of Michigan).

Adams, C. (1993), *For Good and Evil: The Impact of Taxes on the Course of Civilization* (Lanham: Madison Books).

Advisory Centre on WTO Law (1999), 'Final Proposal Document' (www.itd.org).

Aggarwal, V. (1985), *Liberal Protectionism: The International Politics of the Organized Textile Trade* (Berkeley: University of California Press).

Aitken, B. and Harrison, A. (1999), 'Do Domestic Firms Benefit from Direct Foreign Investment?', *American Economic Review*, 89 (3): 605–18.

Allen, D. (1979), 'Tariff Games', in S. Brams, A. Schotter, and G. Schwoediauer (eds.), *Applied Game Theory* (Wuerzburg: Physica-Verlag).

Anderson, K. (1992), 'Effects on the Environment and Welfare of Liberalizing World Trade: The Cases of Coal and Food', in K. Anderson and R. Blackhurst (eds.), *The Greening of World Trade Issues* (London: Harvester-Wheatsheaf).

——— (1995), 'Lobbying Incentives and the Pattern of Protection in Rich and Poor Countries', *Economic Development and Cultural Change*, 43: 401–23 (January).

——— (2001), 'Bringing Discipline to Agricultural Policy via the WTO', in B. Hoekman and W. Martin (eds.), *Developing Countries and the WTO* (Oxford: Basil Blackwell).

——— and Blackhurst. R. (eds.) (1993), *The Greening of World Trade Issues* (London: Harvester-Wheatsheaf).

——— and Norheim, H. (1993), 'History, Geography and Regional Integration', in K. Anderson and R. Blackhurst (eds.), *Regional Integration and the Global Trading System* (London: Harvester-Wheatsheaf).

——— Hoekman, B., and Strutt, A. (2000), 'Agriculture and the WTO: Next Steps', (Washington DC: The World Bank (www.worldbank.org/trade)).

——— Francois, J., Hertel, T., Hoekman, B., and Martin, W. (2000), 'Potential Gains from Trade Reform in the New Millennium', paper presented at the

Third Annual Conference on Global Economic Analysis, Monash University.

Arkell, J. (1994), 'Lobbying for Market Access for Professional Services: Accounting, Architecture, Engineering, and Legal Services', in M. Kostecki (ed.), *Marketing Strategy for Services* (Oxford: Pergamon Press).

Auquier, A. and Caves, R. (1979), 'Monopolistic Export Industries, Trade Taxes, and Optimal Competition Policy', *Economic Journal*, 89: 559-81.

Bagwell, K. and Staiger, R. (1990), 'A Theory of Managed Trade', *American Economic Review*, 80: 779-95.

—————— (1999a), 'An Economic Theory of GATT', *American Economic Review*, 89: 215-48.

—————— (1999b), 'Domestic Policies, National Sovereignty and International Economic Institutions', NBER Working Paper 7293 (August).

—————— (2000), 'GATT Think', mimeo (September).

Bailey, S.H. (1932), 'The Political Aspect of Discrimination in International Economic Relations', *Economica*, 12: 96-115.

Balassa, B. (1961), *The Theory of Economic Integration* (Homewood: Irwin).

Baldwin, R. E. (1994), *Towards an Integrated Europe* (London: CEPR).

—————— (1995), 'A Domino Theory of Regionalism', in R. E. Baldwin, P. Haaparanta, and J. Kiander (eds.), *Expanding Membership in the European Union* (Cambridge, Mass.: Cambridge University Press).

—————— and Venables, A. (1997), 'International Economic Integration', in G. Grossman, and K. Rogoff (eds.), *Handbook of International Economics, iii* (Amsterdam: North Holland).

Baldwin, R. (1970), *Non-Tariff Distortions in International Trade* (Washington DC: Brookings Institution).

—————— (1986), 'Toward More Efficient Procedures for Multilateral Trade Negotiations', *Aussenwirtschaft*, 41: 379-94.

—————— (1992), 'Assessing the Fair Trade and Safeguards Laws in Terms of Modern Trade and Political Economy Analysis', *The World Economy*, 15: 185-202.

—————— and Clarke, R. (1987), 'Game Modeling the Tokyo Round of Tariff Negotiations', *Journal of Policy Modeling*, 9: 257-84.

—————— and Richardson, J. D. (1972), 'Government Purchasing Policies, Other NTBs, and the International Monetary Crisis', in H. English, and K. Hay (eds.), *Obstacles to Trade in the Pacific Area* (Ottawa: Carleton School of International Affairs).

—————— and Winters, A. in J. M. Finger, and A. Olechowski (eds.) (1987), *The Uruguay: A Handbook for the Multilateral Trade Negotiations* (Washington DC: The World Bank).

Banks, G. (1983), 'The Economics and Politics of Counter-trade', *The World Economy*, 6: 159–82.

Basevi, G., Delbono, F., and Mariotti, M. (1995), 'Bargaining with a Composite Player: An Application to the Uruguay Round of GATT Negotiations', *Journal of International Comparative Economics*, 3: 161–74.

Ben-David, D. (2001), *Free Trade and Economic Growth*. (Cambridge, Mass.: MIT Press, forthcoming).

—— and Pappell, D. (1998), 'Slowdowns and Meltdowns: Post-war Growth Evidence from 74 Countries', *Review of Economics and Statistics*, 80: 561–71.

Benson, B. (1989), 'The Spontaneous Evolution of Commercial Law', *Southern Economic Journal*, 55: 644–61.

Bhagwati, J. (1971), 'The Generalized Theory of Distortions and Welfare', in J. Bhagwati *et al.* (eds.), *Trade, Balance of Payments and Growth* (Amsterdam: North Holland).

—— (1977), 'Market Disruption, Export Market Disruption, Compensation, and GATT Reform', in J. Bhagwati (ed.), *The New International Economic Order: The North-South Debate* (Cambridge, Mass.: MIT Press).

—— (1982), 'Directly Unproductive, Profit-seeking (DUP) Activities', *Journal of Political Economy*, 90: 988–1002.

—— (1984), 'Splintering and Disembodiment of Services and Developing Nations, *The World Economy*, 7: 133–44.

—— (1987), 'Trade in Services and the Multilateral Trade Negotiations', *World Bank Economic Review*, 1: 549–69.

—— (1988), *Protectionism* (Cambridge, Mass.: MIT Press).

—— (1991), *The World Trading System at Risk* (Princeton, NJ: Princeton University Press).

—— (1993), 'Regionalism and Multilateralism: An Overview', in J. De Melo, and A. Panagariya (eds.), *New Dimensions in Regional Integration* (Cambridge, Mass.: Cambridge University Press).

—— (1994), 'Fair Trade, Reciprocity and Harmonization: The New Challenge to the Theory and Policy of Free Trade', in A. Deardorff, and R. Stern (eds.), *Analytical and Negotiating Issues in the Global Trading System*. (Ann Arbor: University of Michigan Press).

—— (1998), *A Stream of Windows: Unsettling Reflections on Trade, Immigration and Democracy* (Cambridge, Mass.: MIT Press).

—— (1999), 'An Economic Perspective on the Dispute Settlement Mechanism', in J. Bhagwati (ed.), *The Next Trade Negotiating Round: Examining the Agenda for Seattle* (New York: Columbia University).

Bhagwati, J., and Hudec, R. (eds.) (1996), *Harmonization and Fair Trade: Prerequisite for Free Trade?* (Cambridge, Mass.: MIT Press).

—— and Irwin, D. (1987), 'The Return of the Reciprocitarians: US Trade Policy Today', *The World Economy*, 10: 109–30.

—— and Panagariya, A. (1996), *The Economics of Preferential Trade Agreements* (Washington DC: American Enterprise Institute).

—— and Patrick, H. (eds.) (1990), *Aggressive Unilateralism: America's 301 Trade Policy and the World Trading System* (Ann Arbor: University of Michigan Press).

—— and Srinivasan, T.N. (1969), 'Optimal Intervention to Achieve Non-Economic Objectives', *Review of Economic Studies*, 36: 27–38.

—— —— (1980), 'Revenue Seeking: A Generalization of the Theory of Tariffs', *Journal of Political Economy*, 88: 1069–87.

—— —— (1996), 'Trade and the Environment: Does Environmental Diversity Detract From the Case for Free Trade?', in J. Bhagwati, and R. Hudec (eds.), *Harmonization and Fair Trade: Prerequisite for Free Trade?* (Cambridge, Mass.: MIT Press).

—— Krishna, P. and Panagariya, A. (eds.) (1999), *Trading blocs : Alternative Approaches to Analyzing Preferential Trade Agreements.* (Cambridge, Mass.: MIT Press).

Blackhurst, R. (1998), The Capacity of the WTO to Fulfil Its Mandate', in A. Krueger (ed.), *The WTO as an International Organization* (Chicago: University of Chicago Press).

—— Lyakurwa, B. and Oyejide, A. (2000), 'Options for Improving Africa's Participation in the WTO', *The World Economy*, 23: 491–510.

Bond, E. (1997), 'Competition Policy in Customs Unions: Theory and an Example from U.S. History' (Pennsylvania: Penn State University, mimeo.)

Bony, E. (1994), 'Lobbying the EU: the Search for Ground Rules', *European Trends* (London: The Economist Intelligence Unit, 3rd Quarter), 73–9.

Bora, B. (2001), (ed.), 'Research Issues on Foreign Direct Investment' (Routledge, London).

—— Lloyd, P. J. and Pangestu, M. (2000), 'Industrial Policy and the WTO', *The World Economy*, 23: 543–60.

Bordo, M. D., Eichengreen, B. and Irwin, D. A. (1999), 'Is Globalization Today Really Different Than Globalization a Hundred Years Ago?' NBER Working Paper 7195 (Cambridge, Mass.: June).

Borell, B. (1997), 'Policy-making in the EU: The Bananarama Story, the WTO and Policy Transparency', *Australian Journal of Agricultural and Resource Economics*, 41: 263–76, June.

Bovard, J. (1991), *The Fair Trade Fraud* (New York: St. Martin's Press).

Bradley, A. J. (1987), 'Intellectual Property Rights, Investment, and Trade in Services in the Uruguay Round: Laying the Foundations', *Stanford Journal of International Law*, Spring: 57–98.

Braga, C. P. (1996), 'Trade-Related Intellectual Property Issues', in W. Martin, and L. A. Winters (eds.), *The Uruguay Round and the Developing Economies* (Cambridge, Mass.: Cambridge University Press).

——— Fink, C. and Sepulveda, C. (2000), *Intellectual Property Rights and Economic Development*, World Bank Discussion Paper no. 412.

Braithwaite, J. and Drahos, P. (2000), *Global Business Regulation* (Cambridge, Mass.: Cambridge University Press).

Breed K. (1998), 'Civil Society and Global Governance: Globalization and the Transformation of Politics' in A. Bernard, H. Helmich, and P. Lehning (eds.), *Civil Society and International Development* (Paris: OECD).

Breton, A. and Salmon, P. (1995), 'Are Discriminatory Procurement Policies Motivated By Protectionism?', *Kyklos*, 49: 47–68.

Bronckers, M. (1996), 'Private Participation in the Enforcement of WTO Law: The New EC Trade Barriers Regulation', *Common Market Law Review*, 33: 299–318.

——— (1998), 'The Exhaustion of Patent Rights Under WTO Law', *Journal of World Trade*, 32(5): 137–59.

Brown, D. and Stern, R. (1999), 'Measurement and Modeling of the Economic Effects of Trade and Investment Barriers in Services' (mimeo).

Brown, F. and Whalley, J. (1980), 'General Equilibrium Evaluations of Tariff-Cutting Proposals in the Uruguay Round', *Economic Journal*, December: 838–66.

Brown, W. (1950), *The United States and the Restoration of World Trade* (Washington DC: The Brookings Institution).

Burtless, G. R. Lawrence, R. Litan, and R. Shapiro (1998), *Globaphobia: Confronting Fears About Open Trade* (Washington DC: Brookings Institution).

Busch, M. (2000), 'Democracy, Consultation and the Paneling of Disputes Under GATT', *Journal of Conflict Resolution*, 44: 425–46.

——— and Reinhardt, E. (2000), 'Testing International Trade Law: Empirical Studies of GATT/WTO Dispute Settlement', presented at the Conference in honor of R. Hudec, The Political Economy of International Trade Law (University of Minnesota, September).

Caves, R. E. (1987), 'Industrial Policy and Trade Policy: The Connections', in H. Kierzkowski (ed.), *Protection and Competition in International Trade* (London: Basil Blackwell).

——— (1996), *Multinational Enterprise and Economic Analysis* (Cambridge, Mass.: Cambridge University Press).

Chadha, R. (1999), 'GATS and Developing Countries: A Case Study of India' (New Delhi: National Center for Advanced Economic Research, mimeo).

Chan, K. (1985), 'The International Negotiation Game: Some Evidence from the Tokyo Round', *Review of Economics and Statistics*, 67: 56–64.

Chang, P. *et al.* (1999), GATS, 'The Modes of Supply and Statistics on Trade in Services, Journal of World Trade', 33/3: 93–115 (June).

Charnovitz, S. (2000), 'Should the Teeth Be Pulled? A Preliminary Assessment of WTO Sanctions', presented at the Conference in honor of R. Hudec, The Political Economy of International Trade Law (University of Minnesota, September).

—— and Wickham, J. (1995), 'Non-governmental Organizations and the Original International Trade Regime' *Journal of World Trade*, 29/5: 111–22.

Chayes, A. and Handler-Chayes, A. (1995), *The New Sovereignty: Compliance with International Regulatory Agreements* (Boston: Harvard University Press).

Claessens, S. and Glaessner, T. (1998), 'Internationalization of Financial Services in Asia' (Washington DC: The World Bank, mimeo).

Commission of the European Commission (1996), 'Economic Evaluation of the Internal Market', *European Economy*, Reports and Studies no. 4.

—— (2000), 'The Sino-EU Agreement on China's Accession to the WTO', www.europa.eu.int/comm/trade.

Commonwealth Secretariat and The World Bank (1999), 'Making Small States less Vulnerable: Supporting Development during Globalization', Report by the Joint Task Force on Small States (mimeo).

Conybeare, J. (1987), *Trade Wars* (Princeton, NJ: Princeton University Press).

Cooper, R. (1988), 'Comment', in Leslie Castle and Christopher Findlay (eds.), *Pacific Trade in Services* (London: Allen and Unwin).

Corden, W. M. (1997), *Trade Policy and Economic Welfare* (Oxford: Clarendon Press).

Cottier, T. and Mavroidis, P. C. (eds.) (1998), *State Trading in the Twenty-first Century* (Ann Arbor: University of Michigan Press).

Croome, J. (1998), 'Trade Negotiations in the WTO: The Present Outlook', www.worldbank.org/trade (Washington DC: The World Bank, mimeo).

—— (1999), *Reshaping the World Trading System: A History of the Uruguay Round* (The Hague: Kluwer Law International).

Crouse, D. (1999) 'Guest Editorial: The WTO Shrimp/Turtle Case', Marine Turtle Newsletter 83: 1–3 (www.seaturtle.org).

Curzon, G. (1965), *Multilateral Commercial Diplomacy* (London: Michael Joseph).

—— and Curzon, V. (1973), 'GATT: Traders' Club', in R. Cox, and H. Jacobson (eds.), *The Anatomy of Influence: Decision Making in International Organizations* (New Haven: Yale University Press).

—————— and Curzon, V. (1976), 'The Management of Trade Relations in the GATT', *International Economic Relations of the Western World, 1959–71* (London: Random House).

Dam, K. (1970), *The GATT: Law and International Economic Organization.* (Chicago: University of Chicago Press).

Davey, W. (1999), 'Improving WTO Dispute Settlement', in J. Bhagwati (ed.), *The Next Trade Negotiating Round: Examining the Agenda for Seattle.* (New York: Columbia University).

Davidow, J. (1981), 'The Seeking of a World Competition Code: Quixotic Quest?', in O. Schachter and R. Hellawell (eds.), *Competition in International Business: Law and Policy in Restrictive Practices* (New York: Columbia University Press).

Davies, N. (1997), *Europe : A History* (London: Random House).

Davies, S. and McGuiness, A. (1982), 'Dumping at Less than Marginal Cost', *Journal of International Economics*, 12: 169–82.

De Jong, H. (1968), 'The Significance of Dumping in International Trade', *Journal of World Trade Law*, 2: 162–88.

De Melo, J. and Tarr, D. (1992), 'A General Equilibrium Analysis of US Foreign Trade Policy' (Cambridge, Mass.: MIT Press).

—————— Panagariya, A., and Rodrik, D. (1992), 'Regional Integration: An Analytical and Empirical Overview', in J. De Melo, and A. Panagariya (eds.), *New Dimensions in Regional Integration* (Cambridge, Mass.: Cambridge University Press).

Deardorff, A. (1987), 'Safeguards Policy and the Conservative Social Welfare Function', in H. Kierzkowski (ed.), *Protection and Competition in International Trade.* (Oxford: Basil Blackwell).

—————— (1994), 'Third-Country Effects of a Discriminatory Tariff', *The World Economy*, 17: 75–86 (January).

—————— (1996), 'An Economist's Overview of the World Trade Organization, in G. Flake, and F. Myeong-Hwa Lowe-Lee (eds.), *The Emerging WTO System and Perspectives From East Asia* (Washington DC: Korea Economic Institute of America).

—————— and Stern, R. (1987), 'Current Issues in Trade Policy: An Overview', in Robert Stern (ed.), *US Trade Polices in a Changing World Economy* (Cambridge, Mass.: MIT Press).

—————— —————— (1998), *Measurement of Non-Tariff Barriers.* (Ann Arbor: University of Michigan Press).

Dee, P. and Hanslow, K. (2000), 'Multilateral Liberalization of Services Trade,' Staff Research Paper (Canberra: Productivity Commission, March).

Deltas, G. and Evenett, S. (1997), 'Quantitative Estimates of the Effects of Preference Policies', in B. Hoekman, and P. Mavroidis (eds.), *Law and Policy in Public Purchasing: The WTO Agreement on Government Procurement* (Ann Arbor: University of Michigan Press).

Destler, I. M. (1996), *American Trade Politics* (Washington DC: Institute for International Economics).

Dicken, P. (1998), *Global Shift: Transforming the World Economy* (London: Paul Chapman).

Diebold, W. (1952), *The End of the ITO* (Princeton, NJ: Princeton University Press).

Dixit, A. (1984) 'International Trade Policies for Oligopolistic Industries', *Economic Journal*, 94: 1–16.

—— (1988), 'Anti-dumping and Countervailing Duties under Oligopoly', *European Economic Review*, 32: 55–68.

Dobson, W. and Jacquet, P. (1998), *Financial Services Liberalization in the WTO* (Washington DC: Institute for International Economics).

Doran, M. (1999), 'The Simpler Trade Procedures Board,' quoted by *World Trade Agenda*, Geneva, December.

Downs, A. (1954), *An Economic Theory of Democracy* (New York: Harper & Row).

Doyle, M. (1986), *Empires* (Ithaca, NY: Cornell University Press).

Dreyer, J. (1979), 'Countervailing Foreign Use of Monopoly Power', in R. Amacher, G. Haberler, and T. Willett (eds.), *Challenges to a Liberal International Order* (Washington DC: American Enterprise Institute).

Edwards, S. and Savastano, M. (1989), 'Latin America's Intra-regional Trade: Evolution and Future', in D. Greenaway, *et al.* (eds.), *Economic Aspects of Regional Trading Arrangements* (New York: New York University Press).

Eglin, R. (1987), 'Surveillance of Balance-of-Payments Measures in the GATT', *The World Economy*, 10: 1–26.

Ehrenberg, R. (1994), *Labor Markets and Integrating National Economies* (Washington DC: Brookings Institution).

Elbheri, A., Ingco, M., Hertel, T. W., and Pearson, K. (1999), 'Agriculture and WTO 2000: Quantitative Assessment of Multilateral Liberalization of Agricultural Policies', Paper presented at the Conference on Agriculture and the New Trade Agenda in the WTO 2000 Negotiations, WTO, Geneva, October 1–2, 1999.

Espinosa, C. (2000), 'The WTO Banana Dispute: Do Ecuador's Sanctions Against the EC Make Sense?', *Bridges* (May).

Esty, C. (1998), 'Non-governmental Organizations at the World Trade Organization: Cooperation, Competition or Exclusion', *Journal of International Economic Law*, 1: 1 (March).

Esty, D. (1994), *Greening the GATT: Trade, Environment and the Future* (Washington DC: Institute for International Economics).

Ethier, W. (1982), 'Dumping', *Journal of Political Economy*, 90: 487–506.

Evans, J. W. (1972), *The Kennedy Round in American Trade Policy* (Cambridge, Mass.: Harvard University Press).

Evenett, S. and Hoekman, B. (2000), 'Government Procurement of Services and Multilateral Disciplines,' in P. Sauvé, and R. M. Stern (eds.), *GATS 2000 – New Directions in Services Trade Liberalization* (Washington DC: Brookings Institution).

—— Lehman, A. and Steil, B. (eds.) (2000), *Antitrust Goes Global: What Future for Transatlantic Cooperation?* (Washington DC: Brookings Institution).

Feinberg, R. and Kaplan, S. (1993), 'Fishing Downstream: The Political Economy of Effective Protection', *Canadian Journal of Economics*, 26: 150–8.

Feketekuty, G. (1988), *International Trade in Services: An Overview and Blueprint for Negotiations.* (Cambridge, Mass.: Ballinger Publications).

—— (1992), 'The New Trade Agenda', Occasional Paper no. 40 (Washington DC: Group of Thirty).

—— (1998), 'Setting the Agenda for Services 2000: The Next Round of Negotiations on Trade in Services', in J. Schott (ed.), *Launching New Global Trade Talks: An Action Agenda* (Washington DC: Institute for International Economics).

—— (2000), 'Assessing the WTO General Agreement on Trade in Services and Improving the GATS Architecture' in P. Sauvé, and R. M. Stern (eds.), *Services 2000: New Directions in Services Trade Liberalization* (Washington DC: Brookings Institution).

Fernandez, R. and Portes, J. (1998), 'Returns to Regionalism: An Analysis of the Nontraditional Gains from Regional Trade Agreements', *World Bank Economic Review*, 12: 197–220.

Finch, D. and Michalopoulos, C. (1988), 'Development, Trade, and International Organizations', in A. Krueger (ed.), *Development with Trade: LDCs and the International Economy* (San Francisco: Institute for Contemporary Studies).

Findlay, C. and Warren, T. (eds.) (2000), *Impediments to Trade in Services: Measurement and Policy Implications* (Routledge: Sydney).

Finger, J. M. (1974), 'Tariff Concessions and the Exports of Developing Countries', *Economic Journal*, 335: 566–75.

—— (1979), 'Trade Liberalization: A Public Choice Perspective', in R. Amacher, G. Haberler, and T. Willett (eds.), *Challenges to a Liberal International Economic Order.* (Washington DC: American Enterprise Institute).

P 128

Finger, J.M. (1981), 'Policy Research', *Journal of Political Economy*, 89: 1270–1.

—— (1982), 'Incorporating the Gains from Trade into Policy', *World Economy*, 5: 367–77.

—— (1991), 'The GATT as International Discipline Over Trade Restrictions: A Public Choice Approach', in R. Vaubel, and T. Willett (eds.), *The Political Economy of International Organizations: A Public Choice Approach* (Boulder, Colo.: Westview Press).

—— (ed.) (1993*a*), *Antidumping: How it Works and Who Gets Hurt* (Ann Arbor: University of Michigan Press).

—— (1993*b*), 'GATT's Influence on Regional Agreements', in J. De Melo, and A. Panagariya (eds.), *New Dimensions in Regional Integration* (Cambridge, Mass.: Cambridge University Press).

—— (1994), 'Subsidies and Countervailing Measures and Anti-Dumping Agreements', in *The New World Trading System: Readings*. (Paris: OECD).

—— (1996), 'Legalized Backsliding: Safeguard Provisions in the GATT', in W. Martin, and A. Winters (eds.), *The Uruguay Round and the Developing Economies* (Cambridge, Mass.: Cambridge University Press).

—— (1998), 'GATT Experience With Safeguards: Making Economic and Political Sense of the Possibilities that the GATT Allows to Restrict Imports', Development Research Group, Policy Research Working Paper no. 2000 (Washington DC: The World Bank).

—— (2000), 'Implementation of Uruguay Round Commitments: The Development Challenge' (with Philip Schuler), *The World Economy*, 23(4): 511–25 (Boston: Blackwell Publishers).

—— and Hoekman, B. (1999), 'Developing Countries and a New Trade Round: Lessons From Recent Research' (Washington DC: The World Bank, mimeo).

—— and Olechowski, A. (eds.) (1987), *The Uruguay Round: A Handbook for the Multilateral Trade Negotiations* (Washington DC: The World Bank).

—— and Murray, T. (1990), 'Policing Unfair Imports: The United States Example', *Journal of World Trade*, 24: 39–55.

—— and Schuknecht, L. (2001), 'Market Access Advances and Retreats: The Uruguay Round and Beyond', in B. Hoekman, and W. Martin (eds.), *Developing Countries and the WTO* (Oxford: Basil Blackwell).

—— and Schuler, P. (2000), 'Implementation of Uruguay Round Commitments: The Development Challenge', *The World Economy*, 23: 511–26.

—— and Winters, L. A. (1998), 'What Can the WTO Do for Developing Countries', in A. Krueger (ed.), *The WTO as an International Organization* (Chicago: University of Chicago Press).

Finger, J.M., Hall, K. and Nelson, D. (1982), 'The Political Economy of Administered Protection', *American Economic Review*, 72: 452–66.

Fitchett, D. (1987), 'Agriculture', in J. M. Finger and A. Olechowski (eds.), *The Uruguay Round: A Handbook on the Multilateral Trade Negotiations* (Washington DC: The World Bank).

Fliess, B. and Sauvé, P. (1998), 'Of Chips, Floppy Disks and Great Timing: Assessing the WTO Information Technology Agreement' (Paris: Institut Français des Relations Internationales).

Fox, E. (1998), 'International Antitrust: Against Minimum Rules; For Cosmopolitan Principles', *The Antitrust Bulletin*, 43: 5–20.

Francois, J. (1997), 'External Bindings and the Credibility of Reform', in A. Galal, and B. Hoekman (eds.), *Regional Partners in Global Markets* (London: Centre for Economic Policy Research).

—— (1999), 'Maximizing the Benefits of the Trade Policy Review Mechanism for Developing Countries' (www.worldbank.org/trade), mimeo.

—— and Hoekman, B. (2000), 'Market Access in the Services Sectors', mimeo.

—— and Martin, W. (1998), 'Commercial Policy Uncertainty, the Expected Cost of Protection, and Market Access', Discussion Paper (Rotterdam: Tinbergen Institute, Erasmus University, May).

—— and Wooton, I. (1999), 'Trade in International Transport Services: The Role of Competition' (Rotterdam: Erasmus University, mimeo).

Frankel, J. A. and Romer, D. (1999), 'Does Trade Cause Growth?', *American Economic Review*, 89: 379–99.

Gallagher, J. and Robinson, R. (1953), 'The Imperialism of Free Trade', *Economic History Review*, 6: 1–15.

Gardner, R. (1969), *Sterling-Dollar Diplomacy: The Origins and the Prospects of Our International Economic Order, 2nd edn.* (New York: McGraw-Hill).

Garrett, G. (1992), 'International Cooperation and Institutional Choice: The European Community's Internal Market', *International Organization*, 46: 543–60.

—— (1998), 'Global Markets and National Politics: Collision Course or Virtuous Circle?', *International Organization* (Autumn), 787–824.

GATT (1974), *Basic Instruments and Selected Documents* (Geneva: GATT).

—— (1985), *Trade Policies for a Better Future* (Leutwiler Report) (Geneva: GATT).

—— (1986), *The Text of the General Agreement* (Geneva: GATT).

GATT (1994a), *The Results of the Uruguay Round of Multilateral Trade Negotiations: The Legal Texts* (Geneva: GATT).

—— (1994b), *Analytical Index* (Geneva: GATT).

—— (1994c), 'The Results of the Uruguay Round: Market Access for Goods and Services' (Geneva: GATT).

Ghosh, B. (1996), *Gains from Global Linkages* (New York: St. Martin's Press, and International Organization for Migration).

Gibbon, E. (1776), *The Decline and Fall of the Roman Empire,* 1977 edn. (Harmondsworth: Penguin Books).

Giesse, C. and Lewin, M. (1987), 'The Multifibre Arrangement: Temporary Protection Run Amuck', *Law and Policy in International Business,* 19: 51–170.

Gilligan, M. (1997), *Empowering Exporters: Reciprocity, Delegation and Collective Action in American Trade Policy* (Ann Arbor: University of Michigan Press).

Globerman, S. (1992), 'North American Trade Liberalization and Intra-Industry Trade', *Weltwirtschaftliches Archiv,* 128: 487–97.

Goldstein, J. (1993), *Ideas, Interests, and American Trade Policy* (Ithaca, NY: Cornell University Press).

—— (1996) 'International Law and Domestic Institutions: Reconciling North American "Unfair" Trade Laws', *International Organization,* 50: 541–65.

—— (1998), 'International Institutions and Domestic Politics: GATT, WTO and the Liberalization of International Trade', in A. Krueger (ed.), *The WTO as an International Organization* (Chicago: University of Chicago Press).

Goode, W. (1997), *Dictionary of Trade Policy Terms* (Adelaide: Centre for International Economic Studies, University of Adelaide).

Gould, D. and Gruben, W. (1996), 'The Role of Intellectual Property Rights in Economic Growth', *Journal of Development Economics,* 48: 323–50

Graham, E. M. and Richardson, J. D. (1997), *Competition Policies for the Global Economy* (Washington DC: Institute for International Economics).

Greenaway, D. (1987), 'Intra-Industry Trade, Intra-Firm Trade and European Integration: Evidence, Gains and Policy Analysis', *Journal of Common Market Studies,* 26: 153–72.

Greif, A. (1993), 'Contract Enforceability and Economic Institutions in Early Trade: The Maghribi Traders Coalition', *American Economic Review,* 83: 857–82.

—— Milgrom, P. and Weingast, B. (1994), 'Coordination, Commitment and Enforcement: The Case of the Merchant Guild', *Journal of Political Economy,* 101: 745–76.

Grossman, G. (1981), 'The Theory of Domestic Content Protection and Content Preference', *The Quarterly Journal of Economics*, 96: 583–603.

—— and Helpman, E. (1994), 'Protection for Sale', *American Economic Review*, 84: 833–50.

—— —— (1995), 'Trade Wars and Trade Talks', *Journal of Political Economy*, 103: 675-708.

Groupe MAC (1988), *Technical Barriers in the EC: An Illustration by Six Industries*, Research on the Costs of Non-Europe, vol. 6 (Brussels: Commission of the European Communities).

Hadenius, A. and Uggla, F. (1998), 'Shaping Civil Society', in B. Helmich, and P. Lehning (eds.), *Civil Society and International Development* (Paris: OECD).

Hamilton, C. (ed.) (1990), *Textiles Trade and the Developing Countries: Eliminating the Multifibre Arrangement in the 1990s* (Washington DC: The World Bank).

—— and Whalley, J. (1989), 'Coalitions in the Uruguay Round', *Weltwirtschaftliches Archiv*, 125: 547–62.

Harris, R. (1985), 'Why Voluntary Export Restraints are "Voluntary",' *Canadian Journal of Economics*, 18: 799–809.

Hathaway, D. E. and Ingco, M. D. (1996), 'Agricultural Liberalization and the Uruguay Round', in W. Martin, and L. A. Winters (eds.), *The Uruguay Round and the Developing Economies*, (Cambridge, Mass.: Cambridge University Press).

Heeter, C. (1997), 'Lobbying for Trade Liberalization in Professional Services: The Case of Andersen Worldwide', University of Neuchâtel, mimeo.

Held, D., McGrew, A., Goldblatt, D. and Perraton, J. (1999), *Global Transformations: Politics, Economics and Culture* (Stanford: Stanford University Press).

Helliwell, J. (1998), *How Much Do National Borders Matter?* (Washington DC: The Brookings Institution).

Henderson, D. (1986), *Innocence and Design: The Influence of Economic Ideas on Policy* (New York: Basil Blackwell).

—— (1999), *The MAI Affair, A Story and Its Lessons* (London: The Royal Institute of International Affairs).

Herin, J. (1986), 'Rules of Origin and Differences between Tariff Levels in EFTA and in the EC', Occasional Paper no. 13 (Geneva: EFTA).

Hertel, T. and Martin, W. (2000), 'Liberalizing Agriculture and Manufactures in a Millennium Round: Implications for Developing Countries', *The World Economy*, 23: 455–70.

———— Anderson, K., Francois, J., Hoekman, B., and Martin, W. (2001), *World Trade Liberalization for the New Millennium: An Empirical Study* (London: Centre for Economic Policy).

Higgott, R. and Cooper, A. (1990), 'Middle Power Leadership and Coalition Building: Australia, the Cairns Group and the Uruguay Round', *International Organization*, 49: 589-32.

Hilf, M. and Petersmann, U. (eds.) (1993), *National Constitutions and International Economic Law* (Deventer: Kluwer).

Hillman, A. (1989), *The Political Economy of Protectionism* (New York: Harwood Academic Publishers).

———— and Moser, P. (1995), 'Trade Liberalization as Politically Optimal Exchange of Market Access', in M. Canzoneri, W. Ethier, and V. Grilli (eds.), *The New Transatlantic Economy* (New York: Cambridge University Press).

Hindley, B. (1987), 'GATT Safeguards and Voluntary Export Restraints: What are the Interests of the Developing Countries?', *World Bank Economic Review*, 1: 689-705

———— (1987), 'Different and more favorable treatment — and graduation', in J. M. Finger, and A. Olechowski (eds.), *The Uruguay Round: A Handbook for the Multilateral Trade Negotiations* (Washington DC: The World Bank).

———— (1988), 'Dumping and the Far East Trade of the European Community', *The World Economy*, 11: 445-63.

———— (1994), 'Safeguards, VERs and Anti-Dumping Action', in OECD, *The New World Trading System: Readings* (Paris: OECD).

———— and Messerlin, P. (1992), 'Guarantees of Market Access and Regionalism', in K. Anderson, and R. Blackhurst (eds.), *Regionalism and the Global Trading System* (London: Harvester-Wheatsheaf).

Hipple, F. S. (1990), 'The Measurement of International Trade Related to Multinational Companies', *American Economic Review*, 80: 1263-70.

Hirschman, A. (1969), *National Power and the Structure of Foreign Trade* (Berkeley: University of California Press).

———— (1981), 'Three Uses of Political Economy in Analyzing European Integration', ch. 12 of *Essays in Trespassing* (London: Cambridge University Press).

Hirst, P. and Thompson, G. (1999), *Globalisation in Question* (London: Polity Press).

Hocking, B. (1999), 'Trade Politics: Environments, Agenda and Processes', in B. Hocking, and S. McGuire (eds.), *Trade Politics* (London and New York: Routledge), 1-19.

Hoekman, B. (1989), 'Determining the Need for Issue-Linkages in Multilateral Trade Negotiations', *International Organization*, 43: 693–714.

—— (1993), 'Multilateral Trade Negotiations and Coordination of Commercial Policies', in R. Stern (ed.), *The Multilateral Trading System: Analysis and Options for Change* (Ann Arbor: University of Michigan Press).

—— (1995), *Trade Laws and Institutions: Good Practices and the World Trade Organization* (Washington DC: The World Bank).

—— (1996), 'Assessing the Uruguay Round Agreement on Services', in W. Martin, and L. A. Winters (eds.), *The Uruguay Round and the Developing Economies* (Cambridge, Mass.: Cambridge University Press).

—— (2000), 'Towards a More Balanced and Comprehensive Services Agreement', in J. Schott (ed.), *The WTO After Seattle* (Washington DC: Institute for International Economics).

—— and Anderson, K. (2000), 'Developing Country Agriculture and the New Trade Agenda', *Economic Development and Cultural Change*, 49: 171-80.

—— and Braga, C. P. (1997), 'Protection and Trade in Services: A Survey', *Open Economies Review*, 8: 285–308.

—— and Djankov, S. (1997), 'Determinants of Export Structure of Countries in Central and Eastern Europe', *World Bank Economic Review* 11: 471–90.

—— and Holmes, P. (1999), 'Competition Policy, Developing Countries and the WTO', *The World Economy*, 22: 875–93.

—— and Konan, D. (2000), 'Rents, Red Tape and Regionalism: Economic Effects of Deeper Integration', in B. Hoekman, and J. Zarrouk (eds.), *Catching Up with the Competition: Trade Opportunities and Challenges for Arab Countries* (Ann Arbor: University of Michigan Press).

—— and Kostecki, M. (1995), *The Political Economy of the World Trading System: From GATT to WTO* (Oxford: Oxford University Press).

Hoekman, B. and Leidy, M. (1990), 'Policy Responses to Shifting Comparative Advantage: Designing a System of Emergency Protection', *Kyklos*, 43: 25–51.

—— —— (1992), Cascading Contingent Protection', *European Economic Review*, 36: 883–92.

—— —— (1993), 'Holes and Loopholes in Integration Agreements: History and Prospects', in K. Anderson, and R. Blackhurst (eds.), *Regional Integration and the Global Trading System* (London: Harvester-Wheatsheaf).

—————— and Mattoo, A. (2000), 'Services, Economic Development and the Next Round of Negotiations on Services', *Journal of International Development*, 12: 283–96.

—————— and Mavroidis, P. C. (1994), 'Competition, Competition Policy and the GATT', *The World Economy*, 17: 121–50.

—————— —————— (1996a), 'Dumping, Antidumping and Antitrust', *Journal of World Trade*, 30: 27–52.

—————— —————— (1996b), 'Policy Externalities and High-Tech Rivalry: Competition and Multilateral Cooperation Beyond the WTO', *Leiden Journal of International Law*, 9: 273–318.

—————— —————— (eds.) (1997), *Law and Policy in Public Purchasing: The WTO Agreement on Government Procurement* (Ann Arbor: University of Michigan Press).

—————— —————— (2000), 'WTO Dispute Settlement, Transparency and Surveillance', *The World Economy*, 23: 527–42.

—————— and Messerlin, P. (2000), 'Liberalizing Trade in Services: Reciprocal Negotiations and Regulatory Reform', in P. Sauvé, and R. Stern (eds.), *Services 2000: New Directions in Services Trade Liberalization* (Washington DC: Brookings Institution).

—————— and Roy, J. (2000), 'Benefiting from WTO Membership and Accession', in B. Hoekman, and J. Zarrouk (eds.), *Catching Up with the Competition: Trade Opportunities and Challenges for Arab Countries* (Ann Arbor: University of Michigan Press).

—————— and Saggi, K. (2000), 'Assessing the Case for WTO Disciplines on Investment-Related Policies', *Journal of Economic Integration*, 15: 588–610.

Holmes, T. (1998), 'The Effect of State Policies on the Location of Manufacturing: Evidence from State Borders', *Journal of Political Economy*, 106: 667–705.

Horn, H. and Levinsohn, J. (1996), 'Merger Policy and Trade Liberalization', NBER Working Paper no. 6077.

—————— and Mavroidis, P. C. (1999), 'Remedies in the WTO Dispute Settlement System and Developing Country Interests', (The World Bank: World Bank Institute) (www.worldbank.org/trade).

—————— —————— and Nordström, H. (1999) 'Is the Use of the WTO Dispute Settlement System Biased?, CEPR Discussion Paper 2340 (December).

Hudec, R. (1987), *GATT and the Developing Countries* (Aldershot: Gower, for the Trade Policy Research Centre).

—————— (1987), *Developing Countries in the GATT Legal System* (London: Trade Policy Research Centre).

Hudec, R. (1990), 'Thinking About the New Section 301: Beyond Good and Evil', in J. Bhagwati, and R. Hudec (eds.), *Aggressive Unilateralism* (Ann Arbor: University of Michigan Press).

—— (1993), *Enforcing International Trade Law: The Evolution of the Modern GATT Legal System* (New York: Butterworth).

—— (1998), 'The Role of the GATT Secretariat in the Evolution of the WTO Dispute Settlement Procedure', in J. Bhagwati, and M. Hirsch (eds.), *The Uruguay Round and Beyond: Essays in Honor of Arthur Dunkel* (Ann Arbor: University of Michigan Press).

—— (1999a), 'The New WTO Dispute Settlement Procedure: The First Three Years', *Minnesota Journal of Global Trade*, 8 (Winter): 1–53.

—— (1999b), 'The Agenda for Reform of the Dispute Settlement Procedure', in J. Bhagwati (ed.), *The Next Trade Negotiating Round: Examining the Agenda for Seattle* (New York: Columbia University).

—— (2000), 'The Adequacy of WTO Dispute Settlement Remedies for Developing Country Complainants' (Washington DC: The World Bank, mimeo).

Hufbauer, G. and Elliott, K. A. (1994), *Measuring the Costs of Protection in the Unites States* (Washington DC: Institute for International Economics).

—— and Wada, E. (1997), *Unfinished Business: Telecommunications After the Uruguay Round* (Washington DC: Institute for International Economics).

—— Elliott, K. A., and Schott, J. (2001), *Economic Sanctions Reconsidered*, 3rd edn. (Washington DC: Institute for International Economics).

Hungerford, T. (1991), 'GATT: A Cooperative Equilibrium in a Non-Cooperative Trading Regime?', *Journal of International Economics*, 31: 357–69.

Ikle, F. (1994), *How Nations Negotiate* (New York: Harper and Row).

Ingco, M. D. (1996), 'Tariffication in the Uruguay Round: How Much Liberalization?' *The World Economy* 19(4): 425–47.

—— and Ng, F. (1998), 'Distortionary Effects of State Trading in Agriculture', Policy Research Working Paper no. 1915 (Washington DC: The World Bank).

International Intellectual Property Association (1998), *Parallel Import Protection in 107 Selected Countries* (http://www.iipa.com).

International Trade Centre (1996), *Business Guide to the Uruguay Round* (Geneva: ITC and Commonwealth Secretariat).

Irwin, D. (1993), 'Multilateral and Bilateral Trade Policies in the World Trading System: A Historical Perspective', in J. De Melo, and A. Panagariya (eds.), *New Dimensions in Regional Integration* (London: CEPR).

Irwin, D. (1996), *Against the Tide: An Intellectual History of Free Trade* (Princeton, NJ: Princeton University Press).

Jackson, J. H. (1969), *World Trade and the Law of GATT* (Indianapolis: Bobbs-Merrill).

—— (1990), *Restructuring the GATT System* (London: Pinter Publishers).

—— (1997), *The World Trading System: Law and Policy of International Economic Relations* (Cambridge, Mass.: MIT Press).

—— (1998), 'The Uruguay Round Results and National Sovereignty', in J. Bhagwati and M. Hirsch (eds.), *The Uruguay Round and Beyond: Essays in Honor of Arthur Dunkel* (Ann Arbor: University of Michigan Press).

—— (1999), 'Dispute Settlement and the WTO: Emerging Problems', in J. Bhagwati (ed.), *The Next Trade Negotiating Round: Examining the Agenda for Seattle* (New York: Columbia University).

—— Davey, W. and Sykes, A. (1995), *Legal Problems of International Economic Relations: Cases, Materials and Text* (West Publishing Company).

Jacquemin, A. (1994), 'Goals and Means of European Antitrust Policy After 1992', in H. Demsetz, and A. Jacquemin (eds.), *Antitrust Economics: New Challenges for Competition Policy* (Lund: Lund University Press).

Janow, M. (1998), 'Unilateral and Bilateral Approaches to Competition Policy Drawing on Trade Experience', in R. Lawrence (ed.), *Brookings Trade Forum, 1998* (Washington DC: Brookings Institution).

Jara, A. (1993), 'Bargaining Strategies of Developing Countries in the Uruguay Round', in D. Tussie, and D. Glover (eds.), *The Developing Countries in World Trade: Policies and Bargaining Strategies* (Boulder and London: Rienner; Ottawa: International Development Research Centre).

Josling, T. (1977), *Agriculture in the Tokyo Round Negotiations,* Thames Essay no. 10. (Ashford: Headly Brothers for the Trade Policy Research Centre).

—— (1994), 'Agriculture and Natural Resources', in S. Collins, and B. Bosworth (eds.), *The New GATT* (Washington DC: Brookings Institution).

—— (2000), 'Agriculture in the Next WTO Round', in J. Schott (ed.), *The WTO After Seattle* (Washington DC: Institute for International Economics).

—— Tangermann, S. and Warley, T. (1996), *Agriculture in the GATT* (London: Macmillan).

Julius, D. (1995), 'International Direct Investment: Strengthening the Policy Regime', in *Managing the World Economy: Lessons from the First 50 Years After Bretton Woods* (Washington DC: Institute for International Economics).

Karsenty, G. (2000), 'Just How Big Are the Stakes?', in P. Sauvé, and R. Stern (eds.), *Services 2000: New Directions in Services Trade Liberalization* (Washington DC: Brookings Institution).

Keesing, D. (1998), 'Improving Trade Policy Reviews in the World Trade Organization', Policy Analyses in International Economics 52 (Washington DC: Institute for International Economics) (April).

Kemp, M. and Wan, H. (1976), 'An Elementary Proposition Concerning the Formation of Customs Unions', *Journal of International Economics*, 6: 95-7.

Keohane, R. (1984), *After Hegemony* (Princeton, NJ: Princeton University Press).

—— (1986), 'Reciprocity in International Relations', *International Organization*, 40: 1-27.

Key, S. (1997), 'Financial Services in the Uruguay Round and the WTO', Occasional Paper no. 54 (Washington DC: Group of Thirty).

—— (2000), 'GATS 2000: Issues for Financial Services Negotiations', (Draft for AEI, mimeo).

Kindleberger, C. (1983), 'Standards as Public, Collective and Private Goods', *Kyklos*, 36: 377–96.

Kobrin, S. (1998), 'The MAI and the Clash of Globalizations', *Foreign Policy* 112: 97–109.

Könz, P. (ed.) (2000), 'Trade, Environment and Sustainable Development: Views from Sub-Saharan Africa and Latin America', Geneva: LCTSD.

Kostecki, M. (1979), *East-West Trade and the GATT System* (London: Macmillan Press for the Trade Policy Research Centre).

—— (1982), *State Trading in International Markets* (New York: St. Martin's Press).

—— (1983), 'Trade Control Measures and Decision Making', *Economia Internazionale*, 36: 1–20.

—— (1987), 'Export Restraint Agreements and Trade Liberalization', *World Economy*, 10: 425–53.

—— (1991), 'Marketing Strategies Between Dumping and Anti-Dumping Action', *European Journal of Marketing*, 25: 7–19.

—— (2000), 'DHL Worldwide Express: Providing Just-in-time Services Across Customs Borders in Central and Eastern Europe', in Y. Aharoni, and L. Nachum (eds.), *The Globalization of Services: Some Implications for Theory and Practice* (London and New York, Routledge).

—— (2001), *International Marketing and the Trading System* (Geneva: ITC).

Kostecki, M., and Tymowski, M.J. (1985), 'Customs Duties versus Other Import Charges in the Developing Countries', *Journal of World Trade Law*, 19: 269–86.

Kotler, P., Fahey, L., and Jatusripitak, S. (1987), *La Concurrence Total* (Paris: Les Editions d' Organisations).

Koulen, M. (1995), 'The New Antidumping Code Through its Negotiating History', in J. Bourgeois, F. Berrod, and E. Fouvier (eds.), *The Uruguay Round Results: A European Lawyer's Perspective* (Brussels: European Interuniversity Press).

Kovenock, D. and Thursby, M. (1992), 'GATT, Dispute Settlement and Cooperation', *Economics and Politics*, 4: 151–70.

Krasner, S. (1983), 'Structural Causes and Regime Consequences: Regimes as Intervening Variables', in S. Krasner (ed.), *International Regimes* (Ithaca, NY: Cornell University Press).

Krueger, A. (1974), 'The Political Economy of the Rent-Seeking Society', *American Economic Review*, 64: 291–303.

—— (1992), 'Free Trade Agreements as Protectionist Devices: Rules of Origin' (Duke University, mimeo).

—— (1997), 'International Labor Standards and Trade', in *Annual Bank Conference on Development Economics* (Washington DC: The World Bank).

—— Schiff, M., and Valdes, A. (1988), 'Agricultural Incentives in Developing Countries: Measuring the Effects of Sectoral and Economy-Wide Policies', *World Bank Economic Review*, 2(3): 255–71.

Langhammer, R. (1999), 'The WTO and the Millennium Round: Between Standstill and Leapfrog', Kiel Discussion Paper no. 352 (August).

—— and Lücke, M. (1999), 'WTO Accession Issues' in P. Lloyd, and C. Milner (eds.) (1999), *The World Economy: Global Trade Policy 1999* (Oxford: Basil Blackwell).

—— and Sapir, A. (1987), *Economic Impact of Generalized Tariff Preferences* (Brookfield, Vt.: Gower Publishing Co.).

Lanjouw, J. (1998), 'The Introduction of Pharmaceutical Product Patents in India: "Heartless Exploitation of the Poor and Suffering"?', NBER Working Paper no. 6366.

Lawrence, R. and Litan, R. (1991), 'The World Trading System After the Uruguay Round', *Boston University International Law Journal*, 8: 247–76.

—— and Weinstein, D. (1999), 'Trade and Growth: Import-Led or Export-Led? Evidence from Japan and Korea', NBER Working Paper no. 7264 (July).

—————— Bressand, A., and Ito, T. (1996), *A Vision for the World Economy: Openness, Diversity, and Cohesion* (Washington DC: Brookings Institution).

Leary, V. (1996), 'Worker's Rights and International Trade: The Social Clause', in J. Bhagwati and R. Hudec (eds.), *Harmonization and Fair Trade: Prerequisite for Free Trade?* (Cambridge, Mass.: MIT Press).

Leidy, M. (1994*a*), 'Trade Policy and Indirect Rent-Seeking: A Synthesis of Recent Work', *Economics and Politics*, 6: 97–118.

—————— (1994*b*), 'Quid Pro Quo Restraint and Spurious Injury: Subsidies and the Prospect of CVDs', in A. Deardorff, and R. Stern (eds.), *Analytical and Negotiating Issues in the Global Trading System* (Ann Arbor: University of Michigan Press).

—————— and Hoekman, B. (1991), 'Spurious Injury as Indirect Rent Seeking: Free Trade Under the Prospect of Protection', *Economics and Politics*, 3: 111–37.

—————— —————— (1993), 'What to Expect from Regional and Multilateral Trade Negotiations: A Public Choice Perspective', in K. Anderson, and R. Blackhurst (eds.), *Regional Integration and the Global Trading System* (New York: Harvester-Wheatsheaf).

Levinsohn, J. (1996), 'Competition Policy and International Trade', in J. Bhagwati, and R. E. Hudec (eds.), *Fair Trade and Harmonization: Prerequisites for Free Trade? i: Economic Analysis* (Cambridge, Mass.: MIT Press).

Levitt, T. (1983), 'The Globalization of Markets', *Harvard Business Review*, May-June: 92–102.

Levy, P. and Srinivasan, T.N. (1996), 'Regionalism and the (Dis)advantage of Dispute Settlement Access', *American Economic Review*, May: 93–8.

List, F. (1841), *The National System of Political Economy*, 1928 translation (London: Longmans).

Low, P. (1993), *Trading Free: The GATT and US Trade Policy* (New York: Twentieth Century Fund).

—————— (1995), *Pre-shipment Inspection Services* (Washington DC: The World Bank).

—————— and Subramanian, A. (1996), 'TRIMs in the Uruguay Round: An Unfinished Business?', in W. Martin, and L. A. Winters (eds.) *The Uruguay Round and the Developing Economies* (Cambridge, Mass.: Cambridge University Press).

Ludema, R. (1991), 'International Trade Bargaining and the Most-Favored-Nation Clause', *Economics and Politics*, 3: 1–20.

Luke, D., (2000), 'African Countries and the Seattle Ministerial Meeting: A Personal Reflection', *Journal of World Trade Law*.

Magee, S., Brock, W. and Young, L. (1989), *Black Hole Tariffs and Endogenous Policy Theory* (Cambridge, Mass.: Cambridge University Press).

Mann, C., Eckert, S. and Knight, S. (2000), *Global Electronic Commerce: A Policy Primer* (Washington DC: Institute for International Economics).

Mansfield, D. (1994*a*), *Power, Trade and War* (Princeton, NJ: Princeton University Press).

—— (1994*b*) 'Intellectual Property Protection, Foreign Direct Investment, and Technology Transfer', IFC Discussion Paper no. 19 (Washington DC: The World Bank).

Maskus, K. (1997), 'Should Core Labor Standards Be Imposed Through International Trade Policy?', Policy Research Working Paper no. 1817 (Washington DC: The World Bank).

—— (1999), 'Regulatory Standards in the WTO: Comparing Intellectual Property Rights with Competition Policy, Environmental Protection and Core Labor Standards' (mimeo).

—— (2000), *Intellectual Property Rights in the Global Economy*. (Washington DC: Institute for International Economics).

—— and Chen, Y. (2000), Vertical Price Control and Parallel Imports: Theory and Evidence, Policy Research Working Paper no. 2461 (Washington DC: The World Bank).

—— and Penubarti, M. (1997), 'Patents and International Trade: An Empirical Study', in K. Maskus, P. Hooper, E. Leamer, and J. D. Richardson (eds.), *Quiet Pioneering: Robert M. Stern and His International Economic Legacy* (Ann Arbor: University of Michigan Press).

—— —— (1995), 'How Trade-related are Intellectual Property Rights?' *Journal of International Economics* 39: 227–48.

Mastel, G. (1999), 'Time to Move towards Establishing a WTO-plus', *The Journal of Commerce*, 17: 12.

Matsushita, M., Mavroidis, P. C., and Schoenbaum, T. (2001), *The WTO Law and Practice* (Oxford: Oxford University Press).

Mattoo, A. (1999), 'Developing Countries in the New Round of GATS Negotiations: From a Defensive to a Pro-Active Role' (Washington DC: The World Bank, mimeo).

—— (2000*a*), 'Developing Countries in the New Round of GATS Negotiations: Towards a Proactive Role', *The World Economy*, 23(4): 471–90.

—— (2000*b*), 'Financial Services and the WTO', *The World Economy*, 23(3): 351-86.

—— and Subramanian, A. (1998), 'Regulatory Autonomy and Multilateral Disciplines', *Journal of International Economic Law*, 1: 303–22.

Mavroidis, P. C. (1992) 'Surveillance Schemes: The GATT's New Trade Policy Review Mechanism', *Michigan Journal of International Law*, 13: 374–414.

Mavroidis, P. C. (2000), 'Remedies in the WTO: Between a Rock and a Hard Place', *European Journal of International Law* (forthcoming).

—— and Neven, D. (1998), 'Some Reflections on Extraterritoriality in International Economic Law' (mimeo).

McAfee, R. P. and McMillan, J. (1989), 'Government Procurement and International Trade', *Journal of International Economics*, 26: 291–308.

McCalman, P. (1999), 'Reaping What You Sow: An Empirical Analysis of International Patent Harmonization', Working Paper in Economics and Econometrics, 374 (Canberra: Australian National University).

McCulloch, R. (1990), 'Investment Policy in the GATT', *The World Economy*, 13: 541–53.

McGuire, S. (1997), *Airbus Industrie* (London: Macmillan).

McKeown, T. J. (1983), 'Hegemonic Stability Theory and 19th Century Tariff Levels in Europe', *International Organization*, 37: 73–91.

McMillan, J. (1988), 'A Game-Theoretic View of International Trade Negotiations', in J. Whalley (ed.), *Rules Power and Credibility* (London: University of Western Ontario).

—— (1993), 'Does Regional Integration Foster Open Trade? Economic Theory and GATT's Article XXIV', in K. Anderson, and R. Blackhurst (eds.), *Regional Integration and the Global Trading System* (London: Harvester-Wheatsheaf).

Messerlin, P. (1981), 'The Political Economy of Protection: The Bureaucratic Case', *Weltwirtschaftliches Archiv*, 117: 469–96.

—— (1989). 'The EC Antidumping Regulations: A First Economic Appraisal, 1980-85', *Weltwirtschaftliches Archiv*, 125: 563–87.

—— (1990), 'Antidumping Regulations or Pro-cartel Law? The EC Chemical Cases', *The World Economy*, 13: 465–92.

—— (1997), 'Competition Policy and Anti-dumping Reform', in J. Schott (ed.), *The World Trading System: Challenges Ahead* (Washington DC: Institute for International Economics).

—— (2000), 'Antidumping and Safeguards', in J. Schott (ed.), *The WTO After Seattle* (Washington DC: Institute for International Economics).

—— (2001), *Measuring the Costs of Protection in Europe* (Washington DC: Institute for International Economics).

—— and Noguchi, Y. (1991), 'The EC Antidumping and Anticircumvention Regulations: A Costly Exercise in Futility' (Paris: Institut d'Etudes Politiques, mimeo).

—— and Sauvant, K. (eds.) (1990), *The Uruguay Round: Services in the World Economy* (Washington DC: The World Bank).

—— and Zarrouk, J. (2000), 'Trade Facilitation: Technical Regulations and Customs Procedures', *The World Economy*, 23: 577–94.

Michalopoulos, C. (1999), 'The Integration of Transition Economies into the World Trading System' (Washington DC: The World Bank, mimeo).

—— (1999), 'The Developing Countries in the WTO', *World Economy*, 22: 117–43.

Mikesell, R.F. (1951), 'Negotiating at Bretton Woods, 1944', in R. Dennett, and J. Jonson (eds.), *Negotiating with the Russians* (Boston: Princeton University Press).

Milgrom, P. D. N. and Weingast, B. (1990), 'The Role of Institutions in the Revival of Trade: The Law Merchant, Private Judges, and the Champagne Fairs', *Economics and Politics*, 2: 1–23.

Mill, J. S. (1848), *Principles of Political Economy, With Some of Their Applications to Social Philosophy*, W. J. Ashley (ed.) (1961) (New York: Kelley).

Milner, H. V. (1997), *Interests, Institutions, and Information: Domestic Politics and International Relations.* (Princeton, NJ: Princeton University Press).

—— and Yoffie, D. B. (1989), 'Between Free Trade and Protectionism: Strategic Trade Policy and a Theory of Corporate Trade Demands', *International Organization* 43: 239–72.

Milward, A. (1992), *The European Rescue of the Nation State* (Berkeley: University of California Press).

Mitchell, W. (1969), *An Essay on the Early History of the Law Merchant* (New York: Burt Franklin Press).

Moloney, K. (1997), 'Government and Lobbying Activities', in P. Kitchen, (ed.), *Public Relations: Principles and Practice* (London, International Thomson Business Press).

Moran, T. (1998), *Foreign Direct Investment and Development* (Washington DC: Institute for International Economics).

Murphy, C. (1994), *International Organization and Industrial Change: Global Governance Since 1850* (New York: Oxford University Press).

Mutti, J. and Yeung, B. (1997), 'Section 337 and the Protection of Intellectual Property in the US: The Impact on R&D Spending', in K. Maskus *et al.* (eds.), *Quiet Pioneering: Robert M. Stern and His International Economic Legacy* (Ann Arbor, MI: University of Michigan Press).

Naray, P. (2000), *Russia and the World Trade Organization* (Basingstoke and New York: Palgrave).

Nivola, P. (ed.) (1997), *Comparative Disadvantages: Social Regulations and the Global Economy* (Washington DC: Brookings Institution).

Nogues, J. J. (1993), 'Social Costs and Benefits of Introducing Patent Protection for Pharmaceutical Drugs in Developing Countries', *The Developing Economies* 31: 24–53.

Nogues, J. J. (1998), 'The Linkages of the World Bank with the GATT/WTO', in A. Krueger (ed.), *The WTO as an International Organization* (Chicago: University of Chicago Press).

—— Olechowski, A. and Winters, L. A. (1986), 'Extent of Nontariff Barriers to Industrial Countries' Imports', *World Bank Economic Review*, 1: 181–99.

North, D. (1990), *Institutions, Institutional Change and Economic Performance* (Cambridge, Mass.: Cambridge University Press).

O'Rourke, K. and Williamson, J. (1999), *Globalization and History: The Evolution of a 19th Century Mid-Atlantic Economy* (Cambridge, Mass.: MIT Press).

Odell, J. S. (1990), 'Understanding International Trade Policies: An Emerging Synthesis', *World Politics* 43: 139–67.

—— (2000*a*), 'The Seattle Impasse and its Implications for the WTO', presented at the Conference in honor of R. Hudec, The Political Economy of International Trade Law (University of Minnesota, September).

—— (2000*b*), *Negotiating the World Economy* (Ithaca, NY: Cornell University Press).

OECD (1993), 'Industrial Policy in OECD Countries', *Annual Review 1992*, (Paris: OECD).

—— (1996), *Trade, Employment, and Labor Standards: A Study of Core Workers' Rights and International Trade* (Paris: OECD).

Olson, M. (1965), *The Logic of Collective Action: Public Goods and the Theory of Groups* (Cambridge, Mass.: Harvard University Press).

Ostry, S. (2000), 'The Uruguay Round North-South Bargain: Implications for Future Negotiations', presented at the Conference in honor of R. Hudec, The Political Economy of International Trade Law: Essays in honor of Robert E. Hudec (manuscript).

Oxford Analytica (2000), 'WTO/Technical Assistance', October 18.

Oye, K. (1992), *Economic Discrimination and Political Exchange: World Political Economy in the 1930s and 1980s* (Princeton, NJ: Princeton University Press).

Paarlberg, R. L. (1997), 'Agricultural Policy Reform and the Uruguay Round: Synergistic Linkage in a Two-Level Game?', *International Organization* 51: 413–44.

Paemen, H., and Bensch, A. (1995), *From the GATT to the WTO: The European Community in the Uruguay Round* (Leuven: Leuven University Press).

Palmeter, D. and Mavroidis, P. C. (1999), *Dispute Settlement in the World Trade Organization: Practice and Procedure* (The Hague: Kluwer Law International).

Palmeter, N. D. (1987), 'Rules of Origin or Rules of Restriction: A Commentary on a New Form of Protectionism', *Fordham International Law Journal*, 11: 1–50.

———— (1995), 'United States Implementation of the Uruguay Round Antidumping Code, *Journal of World Trade*, 29, no. 3 (Werner Pub.).

Patterson, G. (1966), *Discrimination in International Trade: The Policy Issues, 1945-1965* (Princeton, NJ: Princeton University Press).

Pelkmans, J. (1990), 'Regulation and the Single Market: An Economic Perspective', in H. Siebert (ed.), *The Completion of the Internal Market* (Tubingen: J.C.B. Mohr).

Penrose, E. (1953), *Economic Planning for the Peace* (Princeton, NJ: Princeton University Press).

Peters, G. (1995), *The Politics of Bureaucracy* (London: Longman Publishers).

Petersmann, E. U. (1997), *The GATT/WTO Dispute Settlement System* (Kluwer: Deventer).

———— (1994), 'The Dispute Settlement System of the World Trade Organization and the Evolution of the GATT Dispute Settlement System Since 1948', *Common Market Law Review*, 31: 1157–1244.

———— (1998), 'How to Constitutionalize International Law and Foreign Policy for the Benefit of Civil Society', *Michigan Journal of International Law*, 20: 1–30.

Pollard, S. (1974), *European Economic Integration, 1815-1970* (London: Thames and Hudson).

Porges, A. (2000), 'The Banana War: Whose Market Access?' (Washington DC: The World Bank, mimeo).

Prebisch, R. (1952), 'The Economic Development of Latin America and Its Principal Problems', *Economic Bulletin for Latin America*, 7: 1–22.

Preeg, E. (1970), *Traders and Diplomats* (Washington DC: Brookings Institution).

Prusa, T. (1992), 'Why Are So Many Antidumping Petitions Withdrawn?', *Journal of International Economics*, 33: 1–20.

Putnam, R. D. (1988), 'Diplomacy and Domestic Politics: The Logic of Two-Level Games', *International Organization*, 42: 427–60.

Raiffa, H. (1983), *The Art and Science of Negotiation* (Cambridge, Mass.: Harvard University Press).

Rattigan, A. (1986), *Industry Assistance: The Inside Story* (Melbourne: Melbourne University Press).

Rayan, M. P. (1998), *Knowledge Diplomacy: Global Competition and the Politics of Intellectual Property* (Washington, DC: Brookings Institution).

Reddy, R. (2000), 'The Meaning of Seattle', *The Hindu*, downloadable on www.indiaserver.com.

Rege, V. (1999), 'Developing Country Participation in Negotiations Leading to the Adoption of WTO Agreement on Customs Evaluation', *World Competition*, 22/1 (March).

Ricardo, D. (1817), *The Principles of Political Economy and Taxation* (Cambridge, Mass.: Cambridge University Press, 1981 reprint).

Richardson, J. D. (2000), 'The WTO and Market-Supportive Regulation: A Way Forward on New Competition, Technological, and Labor Issues', *Federal Reserve of St. Louis Quarterly Review*, 82/4 (July/August).

Richardson, M. (1993), 'Endogenous Protection and Trade Diversion', *Journal of International Economics*, 34: 309-24.

Ricupero, R. (1998), 'Integration of Developing Countries into the Multilateral Trading System', J. Bhagwati, and A. Hirsch (eds.), *The Uruguay Round and Beyond: Essays in Honor of Arthur Dunkel* (Ann Arbor: University of Michigan Press).

Rodriguez, F. and Rodrik, D. (1999), 'Trade Policy and Economic Growth: A Skeptic's Guide to the Evidence', NBER Working Paper no. 7081 (April).

Rodrik, D. (1987), 'The Economics of Export-Performance Requirements', *Quarterly Journal of Economics* 102: 633-50.

—— (1994), 'Comments on Maskus and Eby-Konan', in A. Deardorff, and R. Stern (eds.), *Analytical and Negotiating Issues in the Global Trading System* (Ann Arbor: University of Michigan Press).

—— (1995), 'The Political Economy of Trade Policy', in G. Grossman, and K. Rogoff (eds.), *Handbook of International Economics, iii* (Amsterdam: North Holland).

—— (1997), *Has Globalization Gone Too Far?* (Washington DC: Institute for International Economics).

—— (1999), *Making Openness Work: The New Global Economy and the Developing Countries* (Washington DC: Overseas Development Council).

Roessler, F. (1985), 'The Scope, Limits and Function of the GATT Legal System', *The World Economy*, 8: 289-98.

—— (1985), 'Countertrade and the GATT Legal System', *Journal of World Trade Law*, 19: 604-14.

—— (1998), 'Domestic Policy Objectives and the Multilateral Trade Order', in Krueger, A. (ed.), *The WTO as an International Organization* (Chicago: University of Chicago Press).

Rollo, J. and Winters, L. A. (2000), 'Subsidiarity and Governance Challenges for the WTO: The Examples of Environmental and Labour Standards', *The World Economy* (April).

Sachs, J. and Warner, A. (1995), 'Economic Reform and the Process of Global Integration', *Brooking papers on Economic Activity*, 1: 1-95.

Saggi, K. (2000), 'Trade, Foreign Direct Investment, and International Technology Transfer: A Survey', Policy Research Working Paper no. 2349, (Washington DC: World Bank) (May).

Sampson, G. (1987), 'Safeguards' in J. M. Finger, and A. Olechowski (eds.), *The Uruguay Round: A Handbook for the Multilateral Trade Negotiations* (Washington DC: The World Bank).

Sampson, G. and Snape, R. (1985), 'Identifying the Issues in Trade in Services', *The World Economy*, 8: 171–81.

Samuelson, W. (1985), 'A Comment on the Coase Theorem', in Alvin Roth (ed.), *Game Theoretic Models of Bargaining* (Cambridge, Mass.: Cambridge University Press).

Schelling, T. (1978), *Micromotives and Macrobehaviour* (New York: W.W. Norton)

Scherer, F. M. (1994), *Competition Policies for an Integrated World Economy* (Washington DC: Brookings Institution).

Scholte, J., A. O'Brien, R., and Williams, M. (1999), 'The World Trade Organization and Civil Society', in B. Hocking, and S. McGuire (eds.), *Trade Politics* (London and New York: Routledge).

Schott, J. (ed.) (1989), *Free Trade Areas and US Trade Policy* (Washington D.C: Institute for International Economics).

—— (ed.) (2000), *The WTO After Seattle* (Washington DC: Institute for International Economics).

—— and Buurman, J. (1994), *The Uruguay Round: An Assessment* (Washington DC: Institute for International Economics).

—— and Watal, J. (2000), 'Decision-making in the WTO', International Economic Policy Brief 00-2 (Washington DC: Institute for International Economics).

Schultz, J. (1999), 'Balancing the Relationship between Trade and the Environment in the WTO: Is this the End of the Sea Turtle?', *Asia Pacific Journal of Environmental Law*, 4: 37–60.

Sebenius, J. K. (1983), 'Negotiation Arithmetic: Adding and Subtracting Issues and Parties', *International Organization*, 37: 281–316.

—— (1996), 'Sequencing to Build Coalitions: With Whom Should I Talk First?', in R. Zeckhauser *et al.* (eds.), *Wise Choices: Decisions, Games and Negotiations* (Boston: Harvard Business School Press).

Schatz, H., and Venables, A. (2000), 'The Geography of International Investment', Policy Research Paper 2338 (Washington DC: World Bank).

Sherwood, R. (1990), *Intellectual Property and Economic Development* (Boulder, Colo.: Westview Press).

Shin, H. J. (1998), 'Possible Instances of Predatory Pricing in Recent US Anti-dumping Cases', *Brookings Trade Forum, 1998* (Washington DC: Brookings Institution).

Shuguang, Z., Yansheng, Z., and Zhongxin, W. (1998), *Measuring the Costs of Protection in China* (Washington DC: Institute for International Economics).

Skud, T. (1996), 'Customs Regimes as Barriers to Trade', *Law and Policy in International Business,* 27/4: 969–79.

Smith, M. (1996), 'Accession to the WTO: Key Strategic Issues', in J. Schott (ed.), *The World Trading System: Challenges Ahead* (Washington DC: Institute for International Economics).

Snape, R. (1987), 'The Importance of Frontier Barriers', in Henryk Kierzkowski (ed.), *Protection and Competition in International Trade* (London: Basil Blackwell).

—— (1991), 'International Regulation of Subsidies', *The World Economy,* 14: 139–64.

—— (1993), 'History and Economics of GATT's Article XXIV', in K. Anderson, and R. Blackhurst (eds.), *Regional Integration and the Global Trading System* (London: Harvester-Wheatsheaf).

—— Adams, J. and Morgan, D. (1993), *Regional Trading Arrangements: Implications and Options for Australia* (Canberra: Australian Government Publishing Service).

South Centre (1999), 'Issues Regarding the Review of the WTO Dispute Settlement Mechanism', Working Paper no. 1 (February).

Spinanger, D. (2000), 'Faking Liberalization and Finagling Protection: The ATC at its Best' (Washington DC: The World Bank) (www.worldbank.org/trade).

Spriggs, J. (1991), 'Towards an International Transparency Institution: Australian Style', *The World Economy,* 14: 165–80.

Srinivasan, T.N. (1998), *Developing Countries and the Multilateral Trading System: From GATT to the Uruguay Round and Beyond'* (New York: Harper Collins).

—— (2000), 'Commentary', *Federal Reserve Bank of St. Louis Review,* 82/4 (July/August), 25–30.

—— and Bhagwati, J. (1999), 'Outward-Orientation and Development: Are Revisionists Right?', Center Discussion Paper no. 806 (Yale University).

Staiger, R. (1995), 'International Rules and Institutions for Trade Policy', in G. Grossman, and K. Rogoff (eds.), *Handbook of International Economics,* vol. III (Amsterdam: Elsevier).

Staiger, R. and Wolak, F. (1992), 'The Effect of Domestic Antidumping Law in the Presence of Foreign Monopoly', *Journal of International Economics* 32: 265-87

Stern, R.M. (2000), 'Labor Standards and Trade', in Marco Bronckers and Reinhard Quick (eds.), *World Trade Law: Essays in Honor of John Jackson* (The Hague: Kluwer Law International).

——— (2001), 'Services in the International Economy' (Ann Arbor: University of Michigan Press).

——— and Hoekman, B. (1987), 'The Codes Approach', In J. M. Finger, and A. Olechowski (eds.), *The Uruguay Round: A Handbook for the Multilateral Trade Negotiations* (Washington DC: The World Bank).

Stiglitz, J. (2000), 'Two Principles for the Next Round, or, How to Bring Developing Countries in from the Cold', *The World Economy*, 23: 437-54.

Sykes, A. (1995), *Product Standards for Internationally Integrated Goods Markets* (Washington DC: Brookings Institution).

Tharakan, P.K.M. (1991), 'The Political Economy of Price-Undertakings', *European Economic Review*, 35: 1341-59.

Tinbergen, J. (1954), *International Economic Integration* (Amsterdam: Elsevier).

Tollison, R and Willett, T. (1979), 'An Economic Theory of Mutually Advantageous Issue Linkages in International Negotiations', *International Organization*, 33: 425-49.

Trebilcock, M. and Howse, R. (1998), *The Regulation of International Trade* (London: Routledge).

——— and Soloway, J. (2000), 'International Trade Policy and Domestic Food Regulation: The Case for Substantial Deference by the WTO Dispute Settlement Body Under the SPS Agreement', Paper presented at the Conference in honor of R. Hudec, The Political Economy of International Trade Law (University of Minnesota: September).

Tullock, G. (1967), 'The Welfare Costs of Tariffs, Monopolies and Theft', *Western Economic Journal*, 5: 224-32.

——— (1988), 'Rent Seeking', in J. Eatwell, M. Milgate, and P. Newman (eds.), *The New Palgrave: A Dictionary of Economics*, 4: 147-9 (London: Macmillan).

Tumlir, J. (1979), 'The New Protectionism, Cartels, and the International Order', in R. Amacher, G. Haberler and T. Williett (eds.), *Challenges to a Liberal International Order* (Washington DC: American Enterprise Institute).

——— (1983), 'Strong and Weak Elements in the Concept of European Integration', in F. Machlup, G. Fels, and H. Müller-Groeling (eds.), *Reflections on a Troubled World Economy* (London: Macmillan).

Tumlir, J. (1985), *Protectionism: Trade Policy in Democratic Societies* (Washington DC: American Enterprise Institute).

Tussie, D. (1993), 'Bargaining at a Crossroads: Argentina', in D. Tussie, and D. Glover (eds.), *The Developing Countries in World Trade: Policies and Bargaining Strategies* (Bolder, Colo.: Lynne Rienner).

UNCTAD (1985), 'Services and the Development Process', TD/B/1008/Rev. 1. (Geneva: United Nations).

—— (1994), *The Outcome of the Uruguay Round: Supporting Papers to the Trade and Development Report, 1994* (Geneva: United Nations).

—— (1996), *The TRIPs Agreement and Developing Countries* (Geneva: UNCTAD).

—— (1997), *World Investment Report: Transnational Corporations, Market Structure, and Competition Policy* (New York: United Nations).

—— (1999), *World Investment Report 1999* (New York and Geneva: United Nations).

—— and The World Bank (1994), *Liberalizing International Transactions in Services: A Handbook* (Geneva: United Nations).

Unter, B. (1998), 'Maximizing Custom Benefits: A Global Model for Regulatory Reform', Paper presented at the US-China Standards, Testing and Certification Workshop, Washington DC, February 17-18.

Vallianatos, M. *et al.* (1998), *License to Loot: The MAI and How to Stop It* (Washington DC: Friends of the Earth).

VanGrasstek, C. (1995), 'Statutes and Policies Relevant to the Participation of the United States of America in the Negotiations for the Accession of Belarus to the World trade Organization' (Geneva: UNCTAD, mimeo).

Vaubel, R. (1986), 'A Public Choice Approach to International Organization', *Public Choice*, 51: 39-57.

Vermulst, E., Waer, P., and Bourgeois. J. (eds.) (1994), *Rules of Origin in International Trade: A Comparative Study* (Ann Arbor: University of Michigan Press).

—— Mavroidis, P. C. and Waer, P. (1999), 'The Functioning of the Appellate Body After Four Years: Towards Rule Integrity', *Journal of World Trade*, 33/2: 1-50.

Viner, J. (1953), *The Customs Union Issue* (New York: Carnegie Endowment for World Peace).

Vogel, D. (1995), *Trading Up: Consumer and Environmental Regulation in a Global Economy* (Cambridge, Mass.: Harvard University Press).

Vousden, N. (1990), *The Economics of Trade Protection* (Cambridge, Mass.: Cambridge University Press).

Walker, W. (1981), 'Private Initiative to Thwart the Trade in Counterfeit Goods', *The World Economy* (March).

Wang, Z. K. and Winters, L. A. (2000), 'Putting "Humpty" Together Again: Including Developing Countries in a Consensus for the WTO', Discussion Paper no. 2297 (London: Centre for Economic Policy Research) (April).

Warley, T. (1976), 'Western Trade in Agricultural Products', in *International Economic Relations in the Western World 1959–71* (London: Royal Institute of International Affairs).

Warren, T. (2000), 'The Application of the Frequency Approach to Trade in Telecommunications Services', in C. Findlay and T. Warren (eds.), *Impediments to Trade in Services: Measurement and Policy Implications* (Sydney: Routledge).

——— and Findlay, C. (2000), 'How Significant are the Barriers? Measuring Impediments to Trade in Services', in P. Sauvé, and R. Stern (eds.), *Services 2000: New Directions in Services Trade Liberalization* (Washington DC: Brookings Institution.

Watal, J. (2000), *Intellectual Property Rights in the World Trade Organization: The Way Forward for Developing Countries* (New Delhi: Oxford University Press, India, and London: Kluwer Law International).

WCO (1996), *International Convention on the Harmonized Commodity Description and Coding System* (Brussels: WCO).

——— (1999), *International Convention on the Simplification and Harmonization of Customs Procedures (Amended)* (Brussels: WCO).

Weston, A. and Delich, V. (1999), 'Settling Trade Disputes After the Uruguay Round: Options for the Western Hemisphere', Latin American Trade Network Discussion Paper (June) (downloadable from 'other WTO 2000 links' on www. worldbank.org/trade).

Whalley, J. (1988), *The Uruguay Round and Beyond* (London: Macmillan).

——— (1996), 'Developing Countries and System Strengthening in the Uruguay Round', in W. Martin, and L. A. Winters (eds.), *The Uruguay Round and the Developing Countries* (Cambridge, Mass.: Cambridge University Press).

Wheeler, D. and Mody, A. (1992), 'International Investment Location Decisions: The Case of US Firms', *Journal of International Economics*, 33: 57–76.

Wilcox, C. (1949), *A Charter for World Trade* (New York: Macmillan).

Wilson, J. D. (1996), 'Capital Mobility and Environmental Standards: Is There a Theoretical Race to the Bottom?' in J. Bhagwati, and R. Hudec (eds.), *Fair Trade and Harmonization: Prerequisites for Free Trade?* (Cambridge, Mass.: MIT Press).

Wilson, J. S. (1998), *Standards and APEC: An Action Agenda* (Washington DC: Institute for International Economics).

Wilson, J. S. (1999), 'Product Standards and International Trade' (Washington DC: The World Bank, mimeo).

Winham, G.R. (1979), 'The Mediation of Multilateral Negotiations', *Journal of World Trade Law*, 13: 193–208.

—— (1980), 'Robert Strauss, the MTN, and the Control of Faction', *Journal of World Trade Law*, 14: 377–97.

—— (1986), *International Trade and the Tokyo Round Negotiation* (Princeton NJ: Princeton University Press).

—— (1989), 'The Pre-Negotiation Phase of the Uruguay Round', in J. Stein (ed.), *Getting to the Table: The Process of International Pre-negotiation* (Baltimore: Johns Hopkins).

—— (1990), 'GATT and the International Trade Regime', *International Journal*, 15: 786–822.

—— (1998), 'The World Trade Organisation: Institution-Building in the Multilateral Trade System', *The World Economy*, 21: 349–68.

Winters, L. A. (1987*a*), 'Reciprocity', in J. M. Finger and A. Olechowski (eds.), *The Uruguay Round: A Handbook for the Multilateral Trade Negotiations* (Washington DC: The World Bank).

—— (1987*b*), 'The Political Economy of the Agricultural Policy of Industrialized Countries', *European Review of Agricultural Economics*, 14: 285–304.

—— (1989), 'The So-called Noneconomic Objectives of Agricultural Support', *OECD Economic Studies*, 13: 238–66.

—— (1990), 'The Road to Uruguay', *Economic Journal*, 100: 1288–1303.

—— (1994*a*), 'Subsidies', in *The New World Trading System: Readings* (Paris: OECD).

—— (1994*b*), 'The EC and World Protectionism: Dimensions of the Political Economy', Discussion Paper no. 897 (London: Centre for Economic Policy Research) (February).

—— (ed.) (1995), *Foundations of an Open Economy: Trade Laws and Institutions for Eastern Europe* (London: Centre for Economic Policy Research).

—— (1997), 'Regionalism and the Rest of the World: The Irrelevance of the Kemp-Wan Theorem', *Oxford Economic Papers*, 49: 228–34 (April).

—— (1998), 'Regionalism versus Multilateralism', in R. Baldwin, *et al.* (eds.), *Market Integration, Regionalism and the Global Economy* (London: CEPR).

—— (2000), 'Coherence with no "here": WTO Co-operation with the World Bank and the IMF' (University of Sussex, mimeo).

Wolf, M. (1984), 'Two-Edged Sword: Demands of Developing Countries and the Trading System', in J. Bhagwati, and G. Ruggie (eds.), *Power, Passions and Purpose: Prospects for North-South Negotiations* (Cambridge, Mass.: MIT Press).

—————— (1999), 'Uncivil Society', *Financial Times,* September 1, 12.

World Bank (1986), *World Development Report* (Washington DC: The World Bank).

—————— (1995), *Global Economic Prospects and the Developing Economies* (Washington DC: The World Bank).

—————— (1997), *World Development Report: The State in a Changing World* (Oxford: Oxford University Press).

—————— (2000), *Trade Blocs* (Oxford: Oxford University Press for the World Bank).

World Trade Agenda (1999), Advance Briefing on Issues, Negotiations and Disputes Affecting Global Trade, No. 99/16 (Geneva).

WTO (2000), 'Developing Countries Exports in 1999 Expanded by 8.5%— About Twice as Fast as the Global Average', Press Release 175 (April).

Yang, Y. (1994), 'The Impact of Phasing Out the MFA on World Clothing and Textile Markets', *Journal of Development Studies,* 30: 892–915.

Zartman, W. and Berman, M. (1982), *The Practical Negotiator* (New Haven: Yale University Press).

Zutshi, B.K. (1998), 'Bringing TRIPs into the Multilateral Trading System', in J. Bhagwati, and M. Hirsch (eds.), *The Uruguay Round and Beyond: Essays in Honor of Arthur Dunkel* (Ann Arbor: University of Michigan Press).

INDEX